RockABi

A forty-year journey

By Billy Poore

Edited by Jon Eiche

ISBN 0-7935-9142-2

HAL•LEONARD® CORPORATION

7777 W. BLUEMOUND RD. P.O. BOX 13819 MILWAUKEE, WI 53213

Visit Hal Leonard Online at
www.halleonard.com

This book is dedicated to "my true love," Pepper, who for the last thirty years took the rockabilly ride with me. Thanks, girl, for goin' along with every wild and crazy idea I'd dream up.

It's also dedicated to the memory of one of the best friends I ever had, Danny Gatton. Without him, this book would not be.

Contents

Acknowledgments

First and foremost, I'd like to thank all the great rockabilly artists, who I owe a huge debt, not only for all their music throughout the years, but also for giving me their time and even allowing me the privilege of becoming close friends with many of them and their families. I only wish those of you who have passed on could finally see my completed work.

Others I'd like to thank for their help and encouragement over the weeks, months, and years are: Margie Coffy at Ferndale Oldies, Anna Mae Zangla, Tex Rubinowitz, Bill Bryant, Tony Sturiale, Charlie and Rosemary Feathers, Jonathan Strong, Lewis and Mary Lou Klug, Becky Hobbs, Laurence Beall, Janis Martin, LesLee Anderson, Vernon and Brenda Taylor, the late Carl Perkins, James Intveld, Jay Orr, Charles McCardell, Scott Isler, Bobby Jones, Darren Spears, Bob and Martí Brom, Betty George, Mark Opsasnick, Seiichi Kamiya, Maxine Rowland, Julia Healy, David Loeher of the James Dean Museum, Baxter Buck, Sam Phillips, Jerry Phillips, Jimmy Day, Art Wray, Jerry Clayworth, Linda Cole, Timmie and Julie Norton, Ronnie Mack, John Budritus, Sam Mathis, Dennis and Howard DeWhitt, Mark Bristol at *Blue Suede News,* Trevor Cajiao at *Now Dig This,* Jimmy Denson, Barbara Lesko, Webster's Body Shop, KatyK at Ranch Dressing, David Lee at The Tractor, Jimmy Barnett & Max, Larry Collins, Rocky Burnette, Vince Habel, The B&H Drive In, Tim Warnock, Jo Ann Campbell, Troy Seals, Stacy (Poore) Evans, Bob Timmers at the Internet Rockabilly Hall of Fame, David Lorrison, Jimmie Deuson, and Billy Evans. An immense amount of credit belongs to Danny Gatton, who first pushed for this book to be written and made me believe that I was the one to write it; it's especially hard that he didn't live to see it completed. A very special thanks also goes out to Greg and Pat Williams for having to read this ol' boy's handwriting and put everything into the computer. Last, but not least, thanks to the Hal Leonard Corporation for being the first major publisher to get behind a comprehensive book on this subject.

As always, I thank the good Lord above for watching over me for the past fifty-four years and putting me back on the right track after all the times I jumped.

I sincerely apologize to anyone I may have left out.

Billy Poore has published Rockabilly Revue *magazine since 1989 and also has a record distribution company where many of the artists' recordings he has written about in this book can be found. He can be reached at: Billy Poore, c/o Stacy Evans, P.O. Box 366, Linden, TN 37096. Also, visit Billy Poore on the Internet at*

http://rbillygal@netease.net

Foreword

by Danny Gatton

[Ed. note: The late Danny Gatton dictated this foreword in September 1994, a scant few weeks before his death.]

Probably the first rockabilly record that ever made a real impact on me was "Mystery Train," by Elvis. You know, I really didn't care about the singer as much as I did the guitar players. Chuck Berry records I just loved. I can vividly remember hearing "Maybellene" for the very first time. A friend of mine's father had a 78 of that. I liked Carl Perkins a lot — "Blue Suede Shoes" and all. But the thing that really stands out in my mind is the Elvis stuff and the Gene Vincent stuff.

You see, I never had all these guys' albums. All I ever had were a few singles here and there, whatever my sister would bring home. But, you know, I loved it all. Still do.

Rockabilly deserves to have the same respect in music history as blues, jazz, bluegrass, and other great forms of music, but it's never been given that respect, especially here in the country it was born in. I really don't understand why, to tell the truth, 'cause there's so much garbage out there nowadays. I mean, I'd sure much rather hear some good rockabilly records now than what's on the radio anymore. Even the bad rockabilly records were good to me. I like raw stuff. I like those Moose Club bands.

Danny Gatton (left) and Billy Poore, in Danny's favorite place: his garage, surrounded by his vintage cars.

I'm sure glad to hear that there are lots of young rockabilly bands playing today; maybe there's some hope left after all. And I like that most of them have that fifties look and dress, 'cause I was thrilled years ago when the look to have was the leather jackets and the ducktails thing. It went with all the cool hot rods I was into. That's really always where I was comin' from. I liked guys that wore sharkskin suits and pointy-toe shoes and guys with big pomps and all that.

I love the stories Billy has written in his *Rockabilly Revue* magazine, and without a doubt I've never met anyone who knows as much about rockabilly as he does. It's been like a religion with him. His whole life has been dedicated to it. I know since the fifties he's gone out and seen and met every one of his heroes, like Elvis, Gene Vincent, and all the rest. Nobody could write a book on it like he could, 'cause he's got an honest blue-collar style of writing and he calls it like he sees it. So I set him up with this deal with Hal Leonard and introduced him to the people, because I felt he deserved it. He's worked very, very hard and stuck with it, and I know he'll write a good book, because, like I said, it's been a religion with him, and he's got it down to a science.

How This Trip Began and the Changes I've Seen

At its birth in the 1950s, rockabilly was poor, strugglin' southern boys with $10 guitars and stars in their eyes combining what they heard on hillbilly radio stations with what they heard on the black rhythm & blues radio stations with what they heard colored folks singin' in the cotton fields and then throwin' in a gut-wrenchin' gospel feel they got when they went to church and heard their fire-and-brimstone preachers screamin' and shoutin' about salvation. Today it's different. Steel guitars and pianos have been added, and today's young rockabilly singers and bands come from middle- and even upper-class families living in New York City, Chicago, Hollywood, London, Paris, Yokohama, and hundreds of other places. But then and now, they all have one thing in common: their striving to reach out, with all the yelps and screams of passion, and get the same feel, spirit, and vibrant energy.

I guess unknowingly I started writing this book forty years ago. It was during the Thanksgiving holidays of 1954, when I was ten years old and my parents took me to Bristol, Tennessee, to visit all our relatives. I was born in Bristol, but when I was three years old my family moved to Washington, D.C., where my father had found a good job as an auto mechanic for the municipal government and my mother got on as a secretary. We always went back to Bristol two to three times a year, as my dad had sixteen brothers and sisters and I had tons of cousins.

Probably my favorite cousin between 1952 and 1957 was Brenda, my Aunt Lucille's daughter. Brenda was the same age I was and we both loved hillbilly music. I'd bring my latest 78s and 45s with me and she had her latest ones and we'd spend the whole time I was there playin' 'em over and over again. On this particular Thanksgiving visit in '54, Brenda played me two new records by a new singer named Elvis Presley. I thought that was a real funny name back then; I was used to normal names like Hank, Lefty, or Tex. I didn't know that funny name and those two yellow-label records with that rooster crowin' on 'em would change not only my life forever but the whole world of music, too. I had her play those four songs, "That's All Right, Mama," "Blue Moon of Kentucky," "Good Rockin' Tonight," and "I Don't Care If the Sun Don't Shine," till they were forever embedded in my head. My father gave me some money, and Brenda and I walked to the only record store in Bristol at the time to try to buy 'em, but they were sold out of both of 'em. That about broke my heart. Brenda didn't even know what this guy looked like then, but she said the local country radio station was playin' both records at the time.

There is no doubt in my mind that Elvis Presley, along with Scotty Moore on guitar and Bill Black on bass, and Sam Phillips at the controls, was the first ever to put out on record what we now call rockabilly. Others have laid claim to doin' it, but it was Elvis who had the first rockabilly records out for all the world to hear.

It was the summer of 1955 when the local country station for Washington, D.C., played Elvis for the first time. The station was WARL and the DJ was Don Owens. Elvis's record "Baby, Let's Play House" was gettin' airplay, as it had made the Top 10 of the *Billboard* country charts. Not long after that, "I Forgot to Remember to Forget" would reach the #1 spot.

I don't know exactly who coined the word "rockabilly," but I do know I heard Don Owens using it on the radio as early as late 1955. Washington, D.C., was a hotbed for hillbilly music in the mid fifties, and I remember Elvis coming up to appear on the local TV show hosted by Jimmy Dean (of "Big Bad John" fame) in the late spring of 1955. Elvis returned to the Jimmy Dean show on

March 23, 1956, and at that time also appeared on the Wilson Line boat cruise, on the S.S. Mt. Vernon. On this occasion, Elvis had Scotty Moore, Bill Black, and drummer D.J. Fontana with him to perform.

Between January and March 1956 Elvis gave six performances on Tommy and Jimmy Dorsey's TV show, and he blew my mind. My family had taken me out to the Capitol Arena barn dances to see a lot of big-name hillbilly acts, but I never seen nothin' that set a fire inside of me till I saw this wild Hillbilly Cat with the black shirt, white tie, wild eyes, and cool hair with the longest sideburns I'd ever seen. Mom wasn't worried; I'd grow out of it, like the Davy Crockett phase of '55. Ha! When I went out trick-or-treatin' on Halloween, 1956, I was Elvis, burnt-cork sideburns and all. There were some heated arguments when daddy took me for my bi-weekly visits we always made to Tony Puglisi's Barber Shop.

That year I started keeping a journal on all the artists and bands I saw and met. (I continue to do so, and I'm glad I did, 'cause time has a way of making your memory fade.) By that time rockabilly had exploded like a volcano into mainstream pop music. Artists like Carl Perkins, Gene

Me at Christmas, 1954, wearing my first motorcycle jacket and cap; I had seen Marlon Brando in the movie The Wild One *earlier in the year.*

Vincent, and Eddie Cochran were all zoomin' up the national charts. And in a short two years since Elvis had come out with "That's All Right, Mama," which was simply two guitars and a slappin' doghouse bass, the sound had already begun to change and become more hard-hittin'. Drums had been added, and backup vocals were also starting to be used.

There've been many changes in rockabilly over the past forty years, and the roster of artists has grown long. This book is my attempt to draw the big picture for you. I'll concentrate mainly on those artists who had the major hits, but I won't neglect the ones who made records with a strong impact but whose influence wasn't realized until later. In the process, I hope to show why rockabilly music and its artists will never be considered oldies or nostalgia, like acts such as The Platters, The Coasters, The Drifters, Bobby Rydell, Frankie Avalon, etc. It's the music that The Beatles, Tom Petty, Simon and Garfunkel, Dolly Parton, Gordon Lightfoot, Cyndi Lauper, Bruce Springsteen, and most of today's top recording artists all played when they first started out. It's never gone away and it never will.

The Fifties: Birth and Heyday

In the Beginning There Was Only
the Memphis Sun and the Hillbilly Cat

'm not going to give you a whole history of Sun Records, as you can easily find that in other books, magazines, and the liner notes on numerous reissue albums. I will say when Sam Phillips opened the doors of his Memphis Recording Service in 1950 he was in the business to record weddings, funerals, church socials, and other such events. Sam's slogan in the beginning was "We record anything, anywhere, anytime." He always had a passion for blues and the black artists who sang it on Beale Street in Memphis. By 1951 he was recording these artists and licensing his masters to Chess Records in Chicago. By the spring of 1952, Sam had officially formed Sun Records and started releasing blues records by artists like Joe Hill Louis, Rufus Thomas, The Prisonaires, Little Junior Parker and His Blue Flames, Doctor Ross, Little Milton, Billy "The Kid" Emerson, James Cotton, and many others. For more than two years he released only black artists such as the ones mentioned, totaling twenty-seven records through May 1954.

I had the opportunity to talk with Sam at his studio in 1990. Here's the account he gave me of those days: "Memphis was a tough, racist town in the early fifties. No one under fifty could even begin to realize today what I went through recording black artists back then. The city council tried to shut me down and run me out of town, and when I went into the restaurant next door to the studio after recording these artists all night till daybreak, I'd sit down to order breakfast and the waitress and other locals would walk over and sniff me to see if I'd 'gotten all the stench off' me from 'the niggers' I'd been in there with all night. I was workin' day and night to support my wife, kids, and an invalid aunt at that time, and most of the white folks in this town didn't want me there. It was a different time, man."

Elvis

Poor local white boys who lived in the housing projects started showing up at Sun Records as early as 1952, if only to record personal acetate records just to see what they sounded like. By now it's a well-documented fact that Elvis Presley was one of these boys. It's also a fact that in 1953 Elvis was a shy, introverted mama's boy in a town full of bullies. I've never bought the now-famous myth that in the summer of 1953 Elvis went into Sun Records to record "My Happiness" on acetate as a birthday present for his mother, as his mother's birthday had passed several months earlier. It probably took a lot of guts for this skinny, sensitive eighteen-year-old to fork over his four dollars and sing and play guitar on that song. He knew he had to do it, 'cause he wanted Sam Phillips to take notice. Elvis came in one other time between late 1953 and early 1954 and recorded another acetate that he once again paid for in the hopes that Sam Phillips would take enough interest in him to give him a tryout for Sun Records.

Marion Keisker, Sam's secretary in those days, told me in 1988 what I had always heard: that she recorded both those acetates on Elvis about a year before Sam decided to record and produce him. Marion told me Sam was out of town on both occasions and that she had recorded Elvis on tape because she heard something in his voice she liked and thought Sam might be interested in hearing this boy. She said both times Elvis was polite, very respectful, and nervous. She claimed she played the tapes for Sam, but at the time he wasn't interested. She also remembers seeing Elvis hanging around the studio on a number of occasions before Sam did become interested.

Well, all of what Marion told me is a sore subject with Sam Phillips, and the argument he gave me is a good one. Sam said, "I got no idea how that got in that lady's mind. I don't wanna say nothin' bad about the dead [Marion Keisker passed away on December 29, 1989], but she started tellin' that story on to that fella who wrote that first book on Elvis [*Elvis: A Biography,* by Jerry Hopkins (New York: Simon and Schuster, 1971)]. It's just not so, and I'll tell you why. When Elvis first walked in to cut his record in '53, I was indeed present. I had a Presto 6-N lathe, which was hooked up to a Presto turntable. The needles used on those turntables cost $6. That was a lot of money in those days. Marion or nobody at that time ever touched my machines. I was in debt, trying to support my family, and trying to collect money owed to me. Like I've often said, those were some tough times, when every penny counted, and nobody was allowed to touch that equipment but me. Marion was a fine lady, and I don't know why she went and made up a story like that." I've seen Sam Phillips do a television interview where he came off a braggart and said some really off-the-wall things about Elvis and other artists he had at Sun. But when he answered my questions he wasn't tootin' his own horn at all. He seemed relaxed, clearheaded, straightforward, and extremely honest in what he told me. I've been around the block a whole lot with crazy, wild, eccentric people who were involved in rockabilly music and consider myself a real good judge at when somebody's not tellin' me the truth or not tellin' me the whole story. But when Sam Phillips looked me in the eye and told me he was the one that cut Elvis's first acetate, I had no reason whatsoever to doubt it.

It wasn't until April or May 1954 that Sam Phillips told Marion Keisker to call Elvis to come down to the studio to try out a song he felt might be right for him. As the story goes, Elvis must have flown down there, as he was through the door hardly before Marion had hung the phone up. No one'll ever know what Elvis was thinkin' when he raced down to that studio, but you can bet it was along the lines of this could be his only shot at gettin' himself and his family out of the poor, sometimes ugly environment they were living in. Sam Phillips said the song he wanted Elvis to sing was a ballad called "Without You." Sam had brought guitar player Scotty Moore and bass player Bill Black into the studio to back Elvis up on the song. Scotty and Bill were both members of a popular hillbilly band in Memphis called Doug Poindexter and The Starlight Wranglers. Sam was about to release their only Sun record, "No One Cares for Me No More" b/w "My Kind of Carryin' On." On that spring day in 1954, Sam told Scotty and Bill to work on "Without You" and some others, and when they felt they had somethin', he'd cut 'em. From all accounts that first session took place on July 5, 1954.

I've been told Elvis, Scotty, and Bill worked together practicing a number of different songs on a half dozen or so different occasions within that ten- to twelve-week period since they'd first met. Bill told me some ten years later, "When that first session was cut with Elvis, I couldn't understand why Sam was doin' this. Elvis wasn't nothin' special then. He was a lousy guitar player, not that good of a singer, and only liked to sing pop-type ballads. He made fun of the black blues then, but that's what really made him hit it big-time. The boy did what he was told then. He learned quick to be sure to do and say the right thing to the right people. He's sure come a long way since those days. But we all have." That quote was taken from my notes of over thirty years ago, and I can remember hearin' a little resentment in Bill's voice. Scotty Moore shared the same type of unflattering sentiments towards Elvis when I spoke with him in 1979. From what I've been told, the reasons behind Scotty and Bill's feelings towards Elvis was because of the manner they were discharged in late 1957. By this time Colonel Tom Parker had full control over all of Elvis's business affairs. They were hurt as Elvis never intervened in their dispute with the Colonel.

But back on the night of July 5 and into the early morning hours of July 6, 1954, rockabilly music history was made as Elvis, Scotty, and Bill came in and showed Sam Phillips what they'd come up with. From what's been said and written before, they went through quite a number of songs, like "Without Love," "Harbor Lights," "I Love You Because," and others. Sam let the tape machines run on some of these, but he was unimpressed. The group took a break for some coffee and sodas. Then shortly thereafter, according to Scotty Moore, "Elvis grabbed his guitar, started bangin' on it, singin', jumpin' all around and just started actin' like a crazy fool. Bill picked up his bass and joined Elvis and he started actin' like a fool, too, and I just started playin' along with 'em. Sam had the control room door open and heard all this. He stopped what he was doin' and stuck his head out the door and said, 'What in God's name are y'all doin'?' We said, 'We don't know, just foolin' around.' Sam said, 'Well, back it up, man, and start over and do it all again.' The song we were doin' was 'That's All Right, Mama.' Elvis musta been hearin' Arthur Crudups's version on the black stations and jumped the song into high gear and had fun with it." When Sam got the take he liked the most, he put in just the right amount of tape-delay echo — the "slap-back" sound that he and Sun later became famous for. For forty years now, artists and bands have tried to get that same Sun slap-back sound on their records, but I ain't heard one yet that's ever done it.

During this same session Elvis cut the Bill Monroe classic "Blue Moon of Kentucky" and put some fire into that one also. After numerous takes on that one, Sam decided on one, and he felt he had the two sides he wanted to release on a 45 on Elvis. Scotty and Bill may not have thought Elvis was anything special, but Sam Phillips definitely knew he had something so different that it just might shake the music business up. He was excited enough on these two tunes that he had 'em released within two weeks after they were recorded.

Shortly after the records were cut, Sam took several acetates down to the three most important DJs in Memphis: Sleepy-Eyed John Lepley at WHHM, Bob Neal at WMPS, and Dewey Phillips (no relation to Sam) at WHBQ. All three DJs played the record, but Dewey Phillips by all accounts played it the most. Dewey played both sides so much that first night that when the phone lines finally let up he called Elvis's house and told his father Vernon he wanted Elvis over at the radio station for a live on-the-air interview. His father went over to a local movie theater where Elvis was at and got him down to the station for his first interview.

Scotty Moore was a believer in Elvis now, as within a week after that interview he signed Elvis to his first management contract. This first record was gettin' a really good response at the three major stations in Memphis for the next couple weeks, and then Sam Phillips got Elvis what he needed: he got him on the lineup of the Slim Whitman package show in Memphis. That was Elvis's first live show on a major scale. On the night of July 30, 1954, Elvis was looking out at the largest audience he had ever faced, and when he sang the rockin', up-tempo numbers, his legs started shakin', and Shirley Richardson, who was there and still lives in Memphis, told me the young girls in the audience started screamin'. She said there was an excitement with those teenage girls, including herself, that she had never before seen. I believe those shakin' and wigglin' legs on that first show came out of sheer fright and nervousness more than anything. When you think back on it, it's incredible that within a three-and-a-half-week period Elvis had unknowingly recorded the first rockabilly record, had it released to good response, and created the rockabilly style with those nervous, shaky legs of his.

During August and September 1954, Scotty Moore booked a number of local gigs in and around Memphis for Elvis while Sam Phillips was trying to break Elvis's new record outside of Memphis, where it had already hit #1 on the local charts. Sam Phillips definitely believed he had somethin' in Elvis, and he wasn't givin' up or gettin' sidetracked on other artists he had. In early September 1954 Sam had Elvis go back into the studio with Scotty and Bill and cut his next record, "Good Rockin' Tonight" b/w "I Don't Care If the Sun Don't Shine." It was released on September 22.

Sam had gotten Elvis a one-time shot performing the song "Blue Moon of Kentucky" at Nashville's Grand Ole Opry on October 2, 1954. From all accounts, when Elvis performed his rockin' version of the Bill Monroe country hit that night, the audience gave him a lukewarm response, to say the least, and Opry manager Jim Denny was outraged at Elvis's performance. Legend has it Denny said, "He should go back to Memphis and keep drivin' that truck, 'cause he don't have no future in music." It wouldn't be long, though, before Elvis and others would find out Jim Denny didn't know what he was talkin' about.

In 1954, the biggest radio show in country music other than the Grand Ole Opry was "The Louisiana Hayride," broadcast live in front of a sold-out audience every Saturday night on KWKH radio out of Shreveport, Louisiana. Horace Logan booked all the talent for the show; he was the man responsible for giving Hank Williams a second chance in 1952 after the Grand Ole Opry kicked him out of their show (and town) because of his drinking habits. After Elvis's failure on the Opry, Sam Phillips immediately called Logan and sent him Elvis's first record. Logan decided to give Elvis a guest shot on the Hayride a couple weeks after his Opry show. Elvis performed "That's All Right, Mama" and "Blue Moon of Kentucky" and went over real well with the audience. When Frank Page, the announcer, asked him after his first song how he came up with his unusual style of singin' and performing, Elvis shyly answered, "Well, we just stumbled upon it." Elvis was invited back for another guest shot, and after that one Horace Logan signed him to a one-year contract to become a regular each Saturday night. That contract was signed the first week of November 1954. Other regular members at that time included Jim Reeves, Johnny Horton, Slim Whitman, and Red Sovine. Elvis was still only nineteen years old, and in four short months since that first recording he was on his way up.

Right after Elvis signed the contract with the Hayride, Bob Neal became his manager, taking over Scotty Moore's contract. Neal was able to get Elvis, Scotty, and

Bill regular bookings all over the South and Southwest, as the Louisiana Hayride could be heard throughout Tennessee, Texas, Louisiana, Alabama, Mississippi, Missouri, and Arkansas. Elvis quit his job driving a truck for the Crown Electric Company at that time, and Scotty and Bill also quit Doug Poindexter's Starlight Wranglers. D.J. Fontana, who Elvis had met at the Hayride, played drums with Elvis, Scotty, and Bill on all their live shows during the early months of 1955, though he never recorded at Sun with Elvis.

Elvis's first record, "That's All Right, Mama," sold between 25,000 and 30,000 copies by November of '54. It made an impact on Marty Robbins, who recorded it around that time trying to get the same feel Elvis had, but it didn't come close, although Marty's version did make the Top 10 of the country charts in early 1955.

Elvis's second record, "Good Rockin' Tonight" (which I consider to be the greatest rockabilly record of all time) b/w "I Don't Care If the Sun Don't Shine," had been released in late September 1954 and was getting good airplay, but it sold a little less than the first one — somewhere around 25,000 copies. Elvis, Scotty, and Bill went back in the studio in early December 1954 and recorded two more songs, "Milk Cow Blues Boogie" and "You're a Heartbreaker." Sam released these two on Elvis's twentieth birthday, January 8, 1955. At the time of its release and during the next several months, this record sold less than either one of the first two — somewhere around 20,000 copies. This was puzzlin' for Sam at the time, as by early '55 Elvis was playin' dates all over the South and Southwest in about a dozen different states, doin' between twenty and twenty-five shows a month. Plus he was travelin' back to Shreveport every Saturday night for the radio shows. He was gettin' great response most of the time. Especially from the teenage girls. Elvis was even headlining some package shows Bob Neal had booked as early as February 1955, but even with all this, the two latest records had slipped a little in sales.

Bob Neal knew Colonel Parker, and sometime in February 1955 Parker started booking Elvis on a few shows with artists he had under management contracts. Parker had managed Eddie Arnold and was currently managing Hank Snow. Elvis performed as an opening act for Snow during the late winter and spring of 1955. Sam Phillips put Elvis back in the studio the first week of February 1955 and recorded "Baby, Let's Play House," which he decided to release as the A side of Elvis's fourth

record. He used "I'm Left, Your Right, She's Gone," a song Elvis had recorded the previous December, for the B side of the record. The record was released on April 25, 1955. This was the record that really busted Elvis out as a phenomenon, at least all throughout the South. In June 1955 it was in the Top 10 of the *Billboard* country charts.

It was in June 1955 that teenage Texan singers like Buddy Holly, Bob Luman, and Mac Davis saw Elvis perform during a swing of gigs through the Lone Star State. They all decided this new rockabilly style of music that was settin' the girls crazy was what they wanted to do from then on. Also, in early June, Colonel Parker signed an agreement with Bob Neal that he would book and represent Elvis in all phases of the entertainment business, but that Neal would continue on as his manager. From this point on it's safe to say Colonel Parker was starting to have a big influence on Elvis. Throughout the summer and early fall of 1955 the shows continued and the audiences got bigger and bigger.

Elvis, Scotty, and Bill went into the Sun studio the second week of July and recorded "I Forgot to Remember to Forget" and "Mystery Train," which were released on August 1, 1955, and as it turned out would be Elvis's final record for Sun. It was also his biggest and best-selling record for the label. "I Forgot to Remember to Forget" hit #1 on the *Billboard* country charts. (Although most Elvis fans today believe "Heartbreak Hotel" was his first #1 hit in *Billboard,* "I Forgot to Remember to Forget" actually reached the #1 spot on the country charts two weeks before. And even though the B side, "Mystery Train," became more popular in the seventies, as Elvis would do it in his live performances, it only reached #11 on the country charts at the time it was released.) Elvis, who was known as "The Hillbilly Cat" by this time, could no longer be held down to a small label like Sun.

I'm not gonna go into many more details other than to say that by the fall of 1955, Sam Phillips was forced to sell Elvis's contract. He was close to bankruptcy, from what he told me, as he had paid for and shipped tens of thousands of records for which he had either not been paid or had been paid only partially so he would ship more. These were all for Presley's last two records. His brother Judd Phillips had been breathin' down his neck for money he owed him, and he had numerous other creditors, including Chess Records. Sam'll tell you today, if he hadn't sold Elvis's contract when he did, he'd have gone outta business. He had been gettin' quite a number of offers from major labels such as Columbia, MGM, Atlantic, and others during the summer of 1955, but Sam had set his price. It was $40,000; $5,000 had to go to Elvis for back royalties Sam owed to him, and the remaining $35,000 would go to Sam. By mid November 1955, Steve Sholes at RCA Victor and Colonel Parker worked out a deal with RCA, Hill & Range Publishing Company, and others and raised the money to purchase Elvis's contract from Sun. Elvis was now signed exclusively to RCA Victor, and Colonel Parker took over full control as his manager from Bob Neal. This ended what many consider to be the most exciting recording period of Elvis's life.

I know some readers may think I've given Elvis too much space in a book on rockabilly music, but he was the one who started it all. No doubt Scotty Moore was an excellent guitar player and Bill Black was an exciting and entertaining slap bass player. But without Elvis and his unusual vocal ability with jump-type songs, Scotty and Bill were no more than sidemen in a popular country outfit in Memphis in 1954. Sure, they both worked hard and helped create the musical background behind Elvis, and then Sam Phillips put that special Sun sound on the recordings, but the fact remains, Sam wasn't puttin' out instrumentals. You can think what you want, but it was Elvis who was the one who stumbled onto what became the first rockabilly record. It was Elvis that Sam Phillips signed, and if Scotty and Bill had refused to work with him, Sam would have found two other musicians who would have; Memphis was full of 'em at that time. And if Elvis hadn't walked into that little Sun studio, do you think we would have ever heard of Buddy Holly, Gene Vincent, Carl Perkins, Eddie Cochran, Jerry Lee Lewis, Roy Orbison, or even The Beatles? John Lennon said it best: "Before Elvis there was nothin'."

Carl Perkins

When Elvis left Sun, Sam Phillips was puttin' his money on Carl Perkins. Carl was born in Tiptonville, Tennessee, but was livin' in Jackson, Tennessee, workin' at the Colonial Bakery in the summer and early fall of 1954 when he heard Elvis's first record and the attention it was getting. Jackson's only about seventy-five miles from Memphis. Carl and his two brothers Jay and Clayton had a little country band and were performing at most of the juke joints in and around Jackson on the weekends. Carl's wife Valda heard "Blue Moon of Kentucky" by Elvis

and told Carl that it sounded like some of the hillbilly music he and his brothers had been doin'. Carl soon found out that this record was on the Sun label in Memphis, and it wasn't long before he showed up there.

According to what Carl told me in 1978, when he and his brothers showed up at Sun in the early fall of '54 Marion Keisker wasn't impressed, told them to leave, and said Sam Phillips wouldn't be back that day. But outside they ran into Sam, and Carl told him he had been singin' Elvis's kind of music before he'd ever put the record out. Some years later Sam told Carl he felt sorry for him and the only reason he gave him an audition in October 1954 was 'cause Carl had a look on his face like he might-a fell over dead if he hadn't.

Carl and the band did that audition, and Carl's song "Turn Around" moved Sam. Sam would later say he felt Carl was the best pure honky-tonk singer he had heard up till that time. He heard a soulfulness in Carl's voice that no others had, and that's what made him stand out from the rest. Sam also liked the idea that Carl wrote most of the songs he sang. He felt Carl could rock a little, but he wanted to push him directly in the country market. After several sessions Sam got the takes on two songs by Carl that he wanted to release on a subsidiary label of Sun he had formed called Flip Records. This label would have all country artists on it. (Sam later had to dissolve it because of legal problems, as there was another Flip Records label in California.) Carl's record "Turn Around" b/w "Movie Magg" came out in February 1955, but with little promotion, it sold poorly at the time.

After the release of this first record, Carl and his band started playin' more dates. He recorded his next record, "Let the Jukebox Keep on Playing" b/w "Gone, Gone, Gone," in July 1955. It was released in August, at the same time as Elvis's final record on Sun. "Let the Jukebox Keep on Playing" was pure Hank Williams cryin'-in-your-beer heartbreakin' country soul. (I still love it!) "Gone, Gone, Gone" was stone-hot cookin' rockabilly at its best. With Bob Neal bookin' Carl now and "Gone, Gone, Gone" in the same jump style Elvis was doin', Carl and his band were doin' a whole lotta shows in mid and late '55. But once more the record sales were not all that good, mainly 'cause Sam was concentratin' most of his effort pushin' Elvis, who was his hottest artist.

Carl stayed out on the road all over the South and Southwest doin' package shows with other Sun Records artists, such as Johnny Cash (who had come to Sun in late '54 and had his first release, "Cry, Cry, Cry," in June '55), Charlie Feathers, and others that were booked by Bob Neal. According to Carl, it was sometime during the fall of 1955, while Carl and Cash were touring together, that Johnny told Carl when he was in a restaurant waitin' in line for his supper that he heard this guy say, "Watch out, man, don't step on my blue suede shoes." Johnny told Carl he thought he ought to try and write a song about it. A short time later, when Carl was playin' at a show in Jackson, he said he saw this couple on the dance floor, and the boy seemed to be tryin' to keep his girl away from the new blue suede shoes he was wearin'. Carl said he went home that night and the line Johnny Cash gave him and what he'd remembered seein' on the dance floor made him grab a brown paper potato sack and write out all the words to "Blue Suede Shoes." Sometime in early December 1955 Carl played the song for Sam Phillips. Sam set up a session for Carl about a week before Christmas. Carl had four songs he had written and a few word changes in "Blue Suede Shoes." Sam decided the two songs he wanted to release on Carl were "Blue Suede Shoes" and "Honey Don't."

Johnny Cash had his second release out on Sun by this time, and Sam saw Cash as bein' a consistent seller in the country market. But RCA still hadn't released Elvis's first new record on their label, so the new rockabilly style of music hadn't caught on yet outside the South and Southwest, and Sam wasn't completely positive that it was gonna be the next big thing all over the country. He did go ahead and release "Blue Suede Shoes" the first week of January 1956, and because of the great reaction in Memphis, by the third week of January Sam told his pressing plants he wanted a large quantity on this one; he had a hunch it was gonna be a big seller. How right he was. By mid February, "Blue Suede Shoes" was #1 on all Memphis charts. On March 3 it was the first Sun record ever to make it onto the *Billboard* Hot 100 pop charts — the very same week Elvis's first release for RCA, "Heartbreak Hotel," made its debut. On March 10, 1956, Carl Perkins became the first country singer ever to have a record make it onto the *Billboard* rhythm & blues charts. In April it peaked out at #3 on the R&B charts, #1 on the country charts, and #2 on the pop charts — Elvis's "Heartbreak Hotel" was all that kept it out of going to the top spot there. By mid March 1956, Sam Phillips was shipping out over 20,000 copies a day. "Blue Suede Shoes" went on to become the first million-seller for Sun Records.

Carl went back in the studio in mid March and recorded four more songs for a follow-up record. But tragedy struck on March 21, 1956. On his way to what would have been his first national TV appearance, on "The Perry Como Show," Carl was involved in a bad car wreck. His manager, Dick Stuart, fell asleep at the wheel of the car that Carl and his band were in and crashed into an oncoming truck near Dover, Delaware. The driver of the truck was killed. Carl and his brothers Jay and Clayton suffered severe injuries. His drummer, W.S. Holland, was the only one not taken to the hospital. Carl was in the hospital and off the road for several months recuperating from a broken shoulder, head injuries, and lacerations all over his body.

Carl Perkins's rockabilly career was killed for the most part in that car wreck. When Sam Phillips released Carl's next record in May 1956, "Boppin' the Blues" b/w "All Mama's Children," it only reached #70 on the *Billboard* pop charts and died after four weeks. "Your True Love" made it to #67 in April 1957, but that would about do it. At the end of 1957 Carl did make an appearance, along with fellow Sun Records artist Jerry Lee Lewis, in the film *Jamboree*. The song he sang, "Glad All Over," was recorded at his final session in late fall of that year. Carl then left Sun and in January 1958 signed with Columbia, where he never found the artistic or commercial success he'd previously had. He continued to stay on the road doin' solid rockabilly throughout the rest of the fifties.

Carl and the rockabilly music he did while at Sun Records in the 1950s have had a huge impact all over the world with the artists who came along later, as well as the new young generations of fans who would later discover him. Carl wrote almost every song he recorded while at Sun, and this was at a time when rockabilly, rock 'n' roll, pop, and even country artists were not doin' so. He's known primarily for singin' and writin' "Blue Suede Shoes," but he wrote so many other classic rockabilly tunes that it would take quite a few years of diggin' through the Sun vaults to appreciate how good his writing really was.

The Beatles recognized it when they recorded four of his compositions at the height of the British Invasion, including "Matchbox," "Everybody's Trying to Be My Baby," and "Honey Don't." Carl was also one of the best rockabilly guitarists in the music's history. His licks were solid and hot on rockers like "All Mama's

Children," "Gone, Gone, Gone," "Put Your Cat Clothes On," "Right String Baby (But the Wrong Yo-Yo)," and too many more to mention. Carl's place in 1950s pure rockabilly music as one of the music's best vocalists, writers, performers, and guitarists will always be secure. His songs have stood the test of time and will continue to do so for generations to come. But after he left Sun Records and went with Columbia Records in 1958, his artistic output slipped, and as the sixties came in and he moved on to other labels such as Decca, Carl went back to what perfectly suited him: country music. He could do good country with a beat, though, which he proved in early 1967 with his Top 30 country chart hit "Country Boy's Dream." He was a regular member of the Johnny Cash touring show by this time, where he stayed till the mid seventies. Carl has flip-flopped between rockabilly and country ever since. No matter which, he was able to please his audiences. But it'll always be his Sun recordings that will remain treasured by rockabilly fans around the world.

Carl had consistent success since the mid sixties in country music with his songwriting and continued to stay in good spirits, even though he battled throat cancer the last several years of his life. He passed away from a stroke at age sixty-five on January 19, 1998, but right up to the end he still had the same enthusiasm for rockabilly music as always.

Stickin' with Rockabilly

By the summer of 1956, after the success of "Blue Suede Shoes," Sun Records and Sam Phillips really got on a rockabilly roller coaster. Sam was no longer havin' trouble payin' his bills — thanks to Johnny Cash, whose song "I Walk the Line" zoomed to #1 on the country charts, reached #17 on the pop charts, and went on to sell a million copies by the end of the year — so he was concentratin' on cashin' in on the teenage explosion that wanted rockabilly music. Elvis had become the biggest sensation the entertainment business had ever seen by the end of 1956, having no fewer that ten songs on the pop Hot 100 by November, with three in the Top 10. Plus he had his first movie released during the Thanksgiving holidays, and he was causin' riots in almost every town and city he played. By this time Sam Phillips knew this music was gonna be around a while. Between April and December 1956, Sam tested out a lot of rockabilly boys, tryin' to figure out which ones would click in the teenage market around the country. Some rockabilly artists and songs that Sun released during that period that didn't

make it and had to wait more than two decades to be appreciated were "Rock 'n' Roll Ruby" and "Ubangi Stomp" by Warren Smith, "Slow Down" by Jack Earls, "Trouble Bound" and "Rock with Me, Baby" by Billy Lee Riley, "Red Headed Woman" and "We Wanna Boogie" by Sonny Burgess, "I Need a Man" by Barbara Pittman, "Where'd You Stay Last Night" and "Come On, Little Mama" by Ray Harris, and "Crazy Arms" by Jerry Lee Lewis. Some of these great records sold well in certain regional markets back then, but all failed to hit the mainstream pop charts. Only Roy Orbison's record "Ooby Dooby" made the *Billboard* pop charts — from June to August 1956. It only reached #59 there, but it was enough to keep Sam stayin' with his Sun sound of rockabilly.

All in all, 1956 had been a great year for Sam Phillips and Sun Records. Sam had made enough money to wisely invest in the Holiday Inn hotel chain, which started in Memphis and would soon expand throughout the country and later the world. He would also buy radio stations in various states within the next few years. As 1957 started out, rockabilly music was still the strongest thing on the national music scene; all the major labels had signed rockabilly artists to their rosters. Sam knew he was the creator of this phenomenon, and he was going to continue to capitalize on it.

Sam released six records in late January 1957. Carl Perkins's "Your True Love" b/w "Matchbox" was the only one to hit the *Billboard* Hot 100, and it peaked at only #67; it fared better on the country charts. Sonny Burgess and Roy Orbison had records among this batch, and they sold pretty well. By this time there were young fans like me all over the U.S., at least in the major cities, who were buying almost every record that Sun released. I was hearin' 'em on either the rock 'n' roll radio stations or the country stations all around the Washington, D.C., area. Even those records by Sonny Burgess, Warren Smith, Roy Orbison, Billy Riley, and others got played, and the local record stores would keep 'em in stock.

Billy Lee Riley

The hottest release to come out of Sun's first bunch in '57 had to be "Flying Saucer Rock 'n' Roll" by Billy Riley and His Little Green Men. I know in the spring of 1957 it was gettin' heavy airplay in D.C. and made some local charts. Years later, when I was working as road manager for a tour Billy did, he told me the story behind this song and his near-miss with stardom. He had gone to New York City in the spring of '57 and played on one of Alan Freed's famous rock 'n' roll shows at the Paramount

Theater in Brooklyn. Billy said Freed was so knocked out by his new song and his act that he would soon call Sam Phillips and help make sure Riley would become the next big star on Sun Records. Riley was on cloud nine when he returned to Memphis and told Sam Phillips the great news. According to Riley, before Freed called Sam, Sam called Freed and told him he had another artist, not Billy Riley, that he wanted to be Sun's next big star. That artist was Jerry Lee Lewis.

Lewis had been brought to Sam's attention by Jack Clement, who Sam hired to engineer some of the sessions at Sun startin' in the spring of 1956. Jack had recorded a demo session on Jerry Lee in November 1956 while Sam was out of town, and he played it for him when he got back. (Sam told me he liked what he heard in Lewis, 'cause he could feel his soul comin' through those keys on the piano.) Sam got Jack in and recorded Jerry Lee's first record in December 1956, but it didn't fare that well in sales. Sam said he knew Jerry Lee was unusual and different and he could pound a piano like no white man he had seen; he thought maybe gettin' away from the country boys playin' rockabilly with guitars might just turn into somethin' big. So throughout January and February 1957, Sam had Jerry Lee cut dozens of songs on several sessions at Sun. The two songs Sam liked the most were "Whole Lotta Shakin' Goin' On" and "It'll Be Me." He released 'em in mid May. This was evidently around the same time Billy Riley was in New York doin' Alan Freed's big show.

Riley claims that "Flying Saucer Rock 'n' Roll" was becoming big in a lot of local markets; after the Freed show, he says, Sam got orders for thousands of records from distributors, but refused to send 'em out 'cause he was preparing to put this big push into "Whole Lotta Shakin' Goin' On." He said Sam had 20,000 copies of his record just sittin' there that he refused to send to distributors 'cause he didn't want any attention drawn away from Jerry Lee's record.

As the story goes, Riley barged into the Sun studio drunk as all get-out and started bustin' up the studio and pourin' liquor over the tape machines and other equipment. Sam wasn't there, but somebody at the studio called him up and told him to get over to the studio fast if he wanted anything left of it. When Sam got there he talked to Riley all night and convinced him that he had something else in mind for him, and what it was would make him a full-fledged top star. I've heard when Riley

left he was satisfied and felt his time would come, though it never did.

I can understand Riley's frustrations on the one hand. Here was Jerry Lee Lewis, who was just the backup piano player on Riley's song "Flying Saucer Rock 'n' Roll" when they cut it back in December 1956, and within a period of four or five months he had stolen not only the stardom Riley felt he deserved, but he had also taken Little Green Men band members Roland Janes and James Van Eaton as his new band. On the other hand, I can also understand Sam Phillips's predicament, from what he told me on how he had to do things back then. Sam said, "I wasn't RCA, MGM, or Columbia, man. They could promote dozens of artists at the same time. I could only go full steam on one artist at a time. I had tough choices to make. Some guys like Riley, who was a talented cat, man, had to get left behind if I had a hot record out on somebody like Jerry Lee, 'cause I wasn't like the big New York labels. I had to take the one artist I felt at the time could really go all the way to the top. And that cat back then was Lewis."

Billy Riley hung in there with Sam Phillips at Sun through the end of the fifties. Sam put out three more records on him through 1959, the best being Billy's explosive version of the blues tune "Red Hot." It's a killer song the way Riley ripped it up. That was released in the fall of 1957. It sold around 35,000 copies, but by this time it was too late for Riley. Jerry Lee Lewis was on fire and in the *Billboard* pop Top 10, with record sales toppin' the million mark. After "Whole Lotta Shakin' Goin' On" made its debut on the pop charts on June 24, 1957, it stayed on those charts for an incredible twenty-nine weeks, into the next year. The only other record Sun had at this time that made the pop charts was Warren Smith's song "So Long, I'm Gone," which hit a high of #72 after its debut on June 10 and dropped off after only two weeks. This song was a real good mid-tempo rockabilly number and deserved better.

Jerry Lee Lewis

Up until the summer of 1957, all of the Sun Records artists (at least the rockabilly ones) were playin' all their shows out on the hillbilly circuit. As far as national TV exposure, there was only Red Foley's "Ozark Jubilee." I remember seein' Carl Perkins, Johnny Cash, and Warren Smith on that one, but that was about it. Of course, they all did a lot of local TV guest shots in each city (mostly in the South), as those kinds of shows were popular at that time. But Sam told me it was his brother Jud, who by this point had gotten back involved with him now that Sun was going strong, who was responsible for getting Jerry Lee a guest spot on "The Steve Allen Show" in New York, which was broadcast live on Sunday night, July 28, 1957. Jerry Lee's thumpin' piano and devil-like wild eyes while he was shoutin' out the lyrics of "Whole Lotta Shakin'," along with jumpin' up at the end of the song and knockin' the piano stool across the stage, were all the teenagers across America needed to see. They had witnessed the wildest, newest young madman they could go for who was unafraid to test the adult-controlled establishment. Not since Elvis's appearances on Milton Berle and Ed Sullivan's TV shows had anything been seen like this. Elvis's live shows, and now his movies, like *Loving You,* were all still takin' the bulk of the heat and bein' blamed for the demoralization of teenagers and creation of juvenile delinquency, but now Jerry Lee had made a clear statement he was ready to jump into that fire, and all those teenagers all over the country loved every minute of it.

Forgettin' to Remember to Forget

It was the first weekend after Labor Day, 1957. That was the first big live rock 'n' roll show I ever attended. Until then nobody in the family would take me to see a show of this kind, because TV news was reporting the music at those shows was causin' riots and makin' teenagers go crazy. My Aunt Julie took me to this one, against my mother's better judgment.

The show was held at the Carter Barron Amphitheater in Washington, D.C. — it seated around 8,000 people, and it was full to capacity. The first half of the show consisted of The Mello-Kings, Paul Anka, Larry Williams, and Clyde McPhatter. (I've still got the program book.) They got a good response from the half white, half black crowd — no riots yet.

After intermission and several more acts performed, all the lights went out and the whole place erupted into shrieks and screams. When the stage lights went up, there was who I was waitin' to see at the piano in all his splendor, shoutin' out, "When you hear somebody knockin' on your door, when you see somethin' crawlin' all 'cross your floor, baby, it'll be me, and I'll be lookin' for you." The whole crowd was on its feet stompin', dancin', and just goin' nuts, and it seemed like the crazier they got, the more Jerry Lee cranked the heat up on his songs.

I had sure never seen nothin' like this. Both white and black kids were dancin' in the aisles. My aunt said somethin' about we ought to leave 'cause we might be killed, but I pretended I didn't hear her. The D.C. cops in front of the stage really had to earn their money, 'cause kids were tryin' to get onto the stage while Jerry was poundin' away on the keys, and he seemed to be teasin' 'em with his winks and grins to "Come on Baby, It's Party Time."

By the end of his last song, "Whole Lotta Shakin' Goin' On," he was on his feet, with the audience completely screamin' insane, chantin' for more. It seemed he was supposed to leave the stage, but instead he started back into "Whole Lotta Shakin'." The piano stool was ten feet away, where he'd kicked it earlier; he went and got it and came back, smashed it into the piano keys, and screamed the final words of the song into the mike as the rest of his band played it to the end. I remember him sayin', "That's rock 'n' roll, baby. The show's over now. Y'all can go home." Then he disappeared like a shot off the side of the stage.

That audience was still in a frenzy a good three or four minutes later, chantin' for more Jerry Lee, when Chuck Berry came out to finish the night. It took him well into his first song to win 'em over.

On the ride home I know I didn't hear a word my aunt was saying, 'cause I was thinkin', "Wow! If Jerry Lee Lewis was that wild live, I'd sure like to see Elvis live," 'cause the police in some cities were filming his shows and wanted to lock him up 'cause his shows were causin' riots. I next remember seein' Jerry Lee on "American Bandstand" in November 1957, and the following month I saw both him and Carl Perkins in the movie *Jamboree,* but both performances of his new record "Great Balls of Fire" were real tame compared to that show I'd seen him do. I knew you had to see this cat live to realize how great a showman he was.

Before the TV appearance, "Whole Lotta Shakin' " was strong on the charts, but it was peakin' out in the Top 30. Afterwards sales zoomed, and within a month it reached the Top 10. In August 1957 Jerry Lee was signed up to sing a song in the movie *Jamboree*. This would be his follow-up to "Whole Lotta Shakin'." It was the recently recorded, soon-to-be signature song "Great Balls of Fire." When this song debuted on the *Billboard* pop charts on November 25, 1957, it didn't take but six weeks to peak out at #2, and it stayed there for four straight weeks. ("At The Hop" by Danny and The Juniors kept it out of the top slot.) By this time Sun Records and Jerry Lee Lewis had another million-seller. Jerry Lee's management was takin' bookings on him for the rest of 1958.

"Great Balls of Fire" had a twenty-one-week ride on the *Billboard* pop charts, from late November 1957 till mid April 1958. But because Jerry Lee was gonna be out on Alan Freed's road shows and other tours — including going to Europe and other foreign countries — through '58, Sam Phillips put him back in the studio a couple more times in mid and late January 1958 to do a bunch of songs so he could choose one for a follow-up record. He decided on "Breathless" b/w "Down the Line," which he released in February 1958. It entered the *Billboard* pop charts on March 3, 1958, and eventually stayed there for fifteen weeks, peaking out at #7.

Dick Clark now had a national TV show on Saturday nights as well as his Monday-through-Friday "American Bandstand." Jerry Lee performed "Breathless" on Saturday night, March 8, 1958, and I remember Dick Clark tellin' all the kids to send in five Beechnut gum wrappers (Beechnut sponsored the show) and twenty-five cents and they'd get an autographed copy of the record in the mail. I didn't send for one — I already had my copy — but I'm sure that little promotional scheme helped "Breathless" move up the charts a little faster.

After the Dick Clark show, Jerry Lee was headed out on a seven-week tour with Alan Freed, from late March till mid May 1958; but before he left he had to film the title song for the movie *High School Confidential*. He had first tried out the song during a session at Sun in January, but Sam wasn't satisfied with the takes on it, so in early April, right as the Freed tour started, Jerry Lee came back to Memphis and got a take Sam liked.

After that Alan Freed tour ended in mid May 1958, Sun Records' major rock 'n' roll star faced a major disas-

ter. Nobody in the public at large knew that Jerry Lee had married his thirteen-year-old cousin Myra Gale Brown, who was the daughter of his drummer J.W. Brown, over in Mississippi back on December 12, 1957. Jerry, Myra, and his sister Frankie touched down on May 23, 1958, in London, England, for the start of what was supposed to be a thirty-seven-day tour there. After he'd given a couple performances, the British press, who were following him everywhere (and Jerry loved it) said his new wife looked young and asked Jerry how old she was. Without any reservations Jerry said, "She's fourteen; she just looks young for her age." He was stretchin' the truth by a couple months — she was still only thirteen at the time. It was found out she was his wife because he had to show her papers to the immigration authorities when they came into the country. Well, all hell broke loose. The British press in 1958 didn't like rock 'n' roll any better than the American press. By his third or fourth show, Jerry and his young bride were front-page news in all the British papers, with headlines like "Baby Snatcher" and "Bigamist" (it was discovered that Jerry hadn't bothered to divorce either of his first two wives before Myra). He was bein' booed and called names at his concerts. His final two shows lasted twenty-seven and twenty minutes, respectively. The rest of his tour was canceled, and he flew back to the U.S.; he was back in Memphis by May 28, after less than a week in England.

The U.S. press came down on Jerry when he returned as much as the British had. The adult establishment needed somethin' like this to finish off real rock 'n' roll. They had Elvis safely tucked away in the Army by June 1958, and even though he'd remain in the news and his records and movies would constantly be out there on him, those wild live shows were gone for good. Jerry Lee was the perfect target for a full-out attack on this animalistic music: a low-life southerner who was taking over the minds of all of the teenagers around the country — especially the sweet young thirteen- and fourteen-year-old girls from good families. You would have had to have lived through this period and watched it at the time to get the full impact of what they did to Jerry Lee's career in a matter of a month or two.

Parents were calling radio stations to tell 'em to stop playin' his records, and a whole lot of 'em got scared and did so. Sam Phillips shipped "High School Confidential" (b/w "Fools Like Me") out to all the DJs as soon as he heard the goin's-on in England, and it debuted on the *Billboard* pop charts on June 2, a little over a week after the news broke. This scorchin', rockin' tune was just as good as any of his previous three million-sellers, and to boot it coincided with the release of the major motion picture with the same title, and in the very beginning of the film you saw Jerry Lee and his pumpin' piano up on the big screen knockin' this hard rocker out. That was the best part of this flick on teenage gang activities. The story line and lackluster performances by some of the actors and actresses didn't show much, but The Killer sure showed 'em how to "bop and shake it at the high school hop." It was all too late, though.

Nobody came to Jerry Lee's defense, with the possible exception of Alan Freed, who issued a statement sayin', "What's the fuss about? Southern boys and girls always marry young." Both Freed and Dick Clark (who refused to comment on Lewis) canceled all his future bookings on their tours. The record "High School Confidential" did climb to a high of #21 by the end of June and stayed on the charts throughout the rest of the summer for a total of eleven weeks. This was probably because the movie of the same name was popular at theaters and drive-ins throughout the country during that time. But that's about the only place you saw Jerry Lee Lewis's face. He was off all the big road show tours and was reduced to playin' small dance halls or night clubs where teenagers (who used to buy his records) weren't allowed. His next record, the appropriately titled "Break Up," debuted in *Billboard* on September 15, 1958, and reached a high of only #52, dropping off a short five weeks later.

My theory on remembering all this is that, to put it bluntly, in the conservative fifties, where the only black TV show was "Amos and Andy," which was funny at the time but made all blacks look stupid, the whole lily-white establishment, meaning all forms of media, like newspapers, TV, radio, critics, movies, etc., was all run by mostly bigoted middle-aged, upper-class white people. They were not just trying to squash the black artists like Chuck Berry, Little Richard, and Fats Domino; they were also prejudiced against the likes of Elvis and Jerry Lee Lewis. They were appalled that two white-trash boys from the Deep South were makin' their innocent little fifteen-year-old daughters wet their underthings late at night looking at their pictures on their walls. They needed to crucify and make an example out of Jerry Lee Lewis, to say, "We told you so. We were right about this rock 'n' roll thing."

Lewis never recovered, at least in mainstream pop music. It would take ten years for him to get back to makin' a real good livin', but it was in the country music market (a few records crossed over onto the pop charts). Sam Phillips and Sun Records never really recovered, either. They would continue to chart records on the *Billboard* Hot 100 through the early sixties, but not with the raw, rockabillyish way they had between 1956 and 1958.

Setting Sun

In 1957 Sam Phillips started a subsidiary label of Sun Records called Phillips International Records, and in February 1958 this new label had a rock 'n' roll-type instrumental by Bill Justis, called "Raunchy," reach #2 on the *Billboard* pop charts. This was before the Jerry Lee Lewis scandal. Nothin' Sam Phillips was connected with after that scandal ever came close to reachin' those heights again. In 1959 Carl Mann had a Top 30 hit in *Billboard* with his pop-rock version of "Mona Lisa," and in 1960 Charlie Rich would have another Top 30 hit with "Lonely Weekends." This song was a good, solid piano rocker in the Year of Pop Schlock — like Mark Dinning's "Teen Angel" and Chubby Checker's "The Twist." Both "Mona Lisa" and "Lonely Weekends" came out on the Phillips International label. Probably the best real, true, raw rockabilly record that Sam released on this label was "Love My Baby" by Hayden Thompson. It was a Junior Parker song and was recorded in the fall of 1956. Thompson's vocal treatment on the song was in the same raw style that Elvis had used on Parker's song "Mystery Train" a little over a year earlier. Sam held off on releasing "Love My Baby" until Phillips International was launched in the fall of 1957, probably because Jerry Lee Lewis had gotten so hot. By this time the raw, primitive sound and vocal on this record didn't come up to the standards of the harder rock 'n' roll material out there. I believe if Sam had released it right after Hayden cut it, the record could have seen some decent chart action. Hayden, like Elvis at that time, was a good-lookin' young man with those tough, sultry looks that teenage girls liked.

Anyway, by the summer of 1958 Sam had lost both Carl Perkins and Johnny Cash (who was a consistent big seller in the country market and had crossed over numerous times to the pop Top 40), and his biggest star, Jerry Lee Lewis, had been banished by most radio stations because of the scandal. But the occasional hits on the lower end of the national charts on both Sun and Phillips International Records gave Sam enough enthusiasm to keep pluggin' away into the early and mid sixties. Sam had purchased some property at 639

Madison Avenue in 1958 and moved all his operations into his new building in January 1960. He upgraded all his equipment and made other adjustments to compete in the music business with the advent of the new decade. But the heyday of rockabilly music and Sun Records was gone forever. Songs he recorded between 1954 and 1958 on obscure rockabilly artists such as Charlie Feathers, Jack Earls, Ray Harris, Edwin Bruce, Malcolm Yelvington, Ray Smith, Rudy Grayzell, Narvel Felts, Harold Jenkins (later known as Conway Twitty), Johnny Powers, Vernon Taylor, Maggie Sue Wimberly, Mack Self, Barbara Pittman, Cliff Gleaves, and many others were never hits, and some were never released until two to three decades after bein' recorded, when European labels like Charly Records in England and Bear Family Records in Germany started licensing the material and floodin' the market overseas with them. Most of these were artistic recordings. Today they still have a fresh sound that you can feel when you hear a great artist like Jack Earls sing "Slow Down" or "A Fool for Loving You." On that record he sounds like, if he had died the day after, at least he had lived on the day before to put every emotion in his body into those two songs. That's what counted — especially with Sam Phillips. Blues, rockabilly, or whatever kind of music in those early years, Sam told me he was always listenin' to hear that feel in the music. That's what it was all about.

Sam and his label Sun Records only had one competitor in Memphis in the 1950s. It was Meteor Records, founded in 1952 by Les Bihari and his brother. Between 1955 and 1957 Meteor released some great raw, primitive rockabilly records, the best bein' by artists like Jess Hooper and Junior Thompson. Their biggest-sellin' record was "Tongue Tied Jill" b/w "Get with It" by Charlie Feathers. Narvel Felts remembers this record bein' on just about every jukebox in every town in the South in 1956 and 1957. It got good reviews in a lot of hillbilly and country trade papers and magazines at the time as well. This record brought Charlie Feathers to the attention of the bigger King Records, out of Cincinnati, Ohio, where Charlie went on to record what most rockabilly fans consider his greatest sides.

Meteor Records was recording mostly artists Sam Phillips had rejected. Charlie Feathers was the exception. I've gotten to know Charlie over the past twenty-five years about as well as you can get to know someone, and from bein' around Sam Phillips even the short time I was, I know the one thing both of 'em have in common is stubbornness, especially when it comes to music. Sam

Phillips only released two records on Charlie Feathers on Sun in 1955, and both were country. Sam told me Charlie could have been as big as George Jones in country music, but he just wouldn't listen. Sam saw Charlie as a great hillbilly singer, and that's all he was gonna record on him. Charlie was cuttin' and demo-in' rockabilly songs he had written like "Bottle to the Baby" and "Tongue Tied Jill" at Sun, but he knew Sam was never gonna put 'em out, so when his contract was up with Sun in late '55 he went over across town to Meteor Records, and they seemed glad to put a rockabilly record out on him. Charlie told me when Meteor put his record out Sam came by his house and told him he'd never forgive him for it. I'll leave out the other words Charlie said Sam used.

It took another fifteen years for Charlie Feathers to become recognized as a true artistic genius in rockabilly music. The bulk of the music he made later would prove he made the right move to Meteor Records when he did. All of Meteor's best recordings have been reissued recently on Ace Records, out of England, and they hold up real well all these years later.

But Meteor could not really compete with the man who created the rockabilly sound at Sun Records. Sam Phillips and Sun Records were the beginning of rockabilly. By the seventies and eighties, anyone who made a record for Sun in the late fifties, such as Jerry Lee Lewis, Roy Orbison, and many others, was draped with the rockabilly banner. Even Johnny Cash, who developed his own unique style of what really was country music, is looked upon by some as rockabilly. Which in somewhat of a way is justifiable. Between 1956 and 1958, Johnny had six songs on Sun that crossed over onto the *Billboard* pop charts. Plus he wrote several great rockabilly songs in '55 and '56, including the Warren Smith classic "Rock 'n' Roll Ruby" and Roy Orbison's frantic "You're My Baby." So Johnny Cash definitely deserves high marks in rockabilly music, and not only because he happened to be on Sun Records.

Since 1958 I've either met and talked with, worked with, booked, recorded, or gotten to know and become friends with over 100 artists or musicians who were there and got their start at Sun Records between 1953 and 1965. They all had their stories and versions of what went on while they were there. Some have good memories. Some were glad for the experience. A few are still real bitter and feel they were ripped off big-time. I won't mention any names, but I remember what Sam's son

Jerry told me a few years ago. Jerry said, "My daddy's always had a passion and love for the music like no other person I've ever met. But first and foremost he's always been a businessman. Nobody should ever call him a crook. If they do, they don't know what they're talkin' about, 'cause the fact remains he never twisted anybody's arm to sign his contracts. They signed because they wanted to." So I have to say to those artists that remain bitter, if Sam Phillips had never put your record out on his little yellow label with the rooster on it, then during the seventies and eighties and into the nineties the world would have never heard of you, and you wouldn't have gone over to Europe and other foreign countries for the past two decades and made more money than you ever made in the fifties and early sixties.

I'm not a buddy of Sam Phillips's, and I wasn't there. I just know this little label in Memphis, Tennessee, was the most important record label not only in rockabilly music, but also in rock 'n' roll, country, and even pop music. Let me name some names for you that Sam helped launch into stardom: Elvis Presley, Roy Orbison, Johnny Cash, Conway Twitty, Charlie Rich, Narvel Felts, Ed Bruce, Dickie Lee, Carl Perkins, and last, but not least, The Killer, Jerry Lee Lewis. No other record label in the history of rock 'n' roll, major or independent, can claim this kind of success. The artists I've mentioned didn't have just fleeting success. It lasted, as their music does today. It was all because of one man's determination and dream to create real music — not what we have on the radio and charts today. In Sam's words, "Man, back then I was just tryin' to create and make music I could feel. It had to have that true-blue feel to it. That's all I wanted, man. I wasn't tryin' to make history." Well, Sam, maybe you weren't, but you sure did!

Major Labels and Movies Jump
on Rebellious Youth Music

*E*veryone gives credit to Alan Freed for naming the new music of youth "rock 'n' roll" sometime in 1952. Older black R&B artists have often said the phrase was used to describe their upbeat boogie woogie music before that time, but no one can argue that it was Freed who popularized the term. But who invented or first popularized the name "rockabilly"? I can't honestly say. I will clear up one rumor that's been going around for over a decade, though.

A lot of rockabilly fans have read or heard it was Johnny and Dorsey Burnette who first came up with the term "rockabilly" for the music they were doin', because Johnny's son was named Rocky and Dorsey's son was named Billy. They were born a little over a month apart in May and June 1953. I discussed this rumor with Billy once, who found it quite amusing and kind of ridiculous. He told me that both his father and his uncle were heavy into boxing and were both Golden Gloves champions in Memphis, and his father and uncle named 'em after boxers they admired at the time, like Battlin' Billy Dunn and Rocky Marciano. He said his father (who passed away August 19, 1979) had never mentioned any connection with their first names and rockabilly music to him. I also spoke briefly with Rocky about this, and he said he'd seen his dad and uncle given credit for that before, but he couldn't say that it was a fact. So just let me say, and not to take away from any of the great contributions to rockabilly music that Johnny Burnette and his trio made, that I'll never believe they were the ones who first termed this music rockabilly.

I can't tell you who it was that did, either. I can only tell you the first time I heard it called that. That was in the late fall of 1955, when I heard Don Owens, DJ on the local D.C.-area country station, say, "Because you can't get enough of it, from the calls we're gettin' here at the station, we're gonna give another spin of 'I Forgot to Remember to Forget' by that young new Hillbilly Cat from Memphis, Elvis Presley, who's just been signed to

RCA Records. The boy's movin' uptown with his rockabilly sound, so here it comes one more time, folks." Those were his words, and then the song started. I can't say who might have said it before Don Owens, but that was the first time I'd ever heard the term.

Bill Haley

Well before the word was ever used or Elvis had his first record out on Sun Records, there was a group by the name of Bill Haley and His Comets, which a very small portion of rockabilly fans today (especially in Europe) consider a rockabilly act. With all due respect to this group, they never did a rockabilly song in their entire career, before 1954 or thereafter. They signed with the Essex record label in 1952 and in the summer of 1953 had a record called "Crazy Man Crazy," which reached #15 on the *Billboard* pop charts, and which some people consider the first rock 'n' roll record. That, along with the success of their cover version of Big Joe Turner's R&B hit "Shake, Rattle and Roll" got them signed to the major label Decca Records in 1954, where they continued to chart in the *Billboard* pop Top 30 with hits like "Dim, Dim the Lights," "Mambo Rock," and "Birth of the Boogie." Then in the summer of 1955, Bill Haley and His Comets gave us the first #1 rock 'n' roll record in *Billboard* with "Rock Around the Clock." It stayed #1 for eight weeks straight and was on the charts for a total of twenty-four weeks. It was featured in the major motion picture *Blackboard Jungle*. Of all this there is no doubt, and it's all been well documented in other books. What I'm gettin' at here is by the early fall of 1955, Bill Haley and the six original Comets had reached their peak by doin' the new rock 'n' roll music. Nothing they ever did resembled true rockabilly music in the 1950s. By the late winter of 1956, Haley and his group would never again see the *Billboard* Top 10. Believe me, I'm definitely not trying to take away any of their great achievements in rock 'n' roll in the mid 1950s, but the music this seven-piece outfit did never fit into the category of rockabilly. True rockabilly music between 1954 and 1956 was being done by southern boys. Haley and his group were all from the northern states. I'm only including him in this because there's a few older hard-core fans that I know, whatever reasons I give, I'll never convince them this wasn't a rockabilly group in the 1950s.

Now, for those few fans of Haley, I'll give you some other facts you may not want to hear. Bill Haley could have never kept rock 'n' roll goin'. The reasons are pretty simple. Rock 'n' roll was new, wild, exciting, youthful music for teenagers who wanted to hear something other than the dull, simple melodies of the likes of Eddie Fisher and Perry Como. Bill Haley was already thirty years old when "Rock Around the Clock" hit #1. At that time he also had the misfortune of looking like someone who might work with a teenager's parents in an office and come over for Sunday barbecues. By late '55 and early '56, teenagers in the U.S. were rebelling and hoping to find a wild, no-holds-barred, good lookin', cool, crazy-eyed leader they could follow and relate to. They found one at the movies in James Dean, and it would only take till the spring of '56 for 'em to find one for their music: Elvis Presley. While Bill Haley continued to tour, appear on TV, have minor hit records, and be featured in B movies like *Rock Around the Clock* and *Don't Knock the Rock* during 1956 and 1957, it was Elvis who owned both those years in rockabilly and rock 'n' roll — I should say, in all of mainstream pop music. Without Elvis, the Adult Establishment could have squashed rockabilly and rock 'n' roll music dead in its tracks in 1956, instead of having to wait a few more years when they finally were able to do it.

The Major Labels

Chuck Berry, whose record "Maybellene" crossed over onto the *Billboard* pop charts and reached a high of #5 in the early fall of 1955, was about the only black rock 'n' roller to do that before Elvis hit. If you want to include Fats Domino, he also reached #10 on the same pop charts at that time, but it was Pat Boone's lily-white cover of the same song, "Ain't That a Shame," that really got the airplay, as it zoomed to #1. It would take almost another year for either of these artists, and also Little Richard, to get back into the Top 10, and it was because Elvis single-handedly opened the floodgates for black rock 'n' roll artists to get equal airtime on white-dominated mainstream pop radio stations by the summer of 1956.

If there was ever a true black rockabilly artist in '55 and '56, it had to be Chuck Berry. While Elvis was still on Sun Records in early and mid 1955, he was regularly performing a frantic, wild treatment of "Maybellene" at most of his live shows. Chuck Berry had many other songs, like "Thirty Days" and "Brown-Eyed Handsome Man," that had more of a rockabilly groove to 'em than some later white artists labeled as rockabilly ever were able to muster. In 1957, on the back of Chuck's first album for Chess Records, *After School Session,* he was referred to as a "Rockabilly Troubadour." Chuck's musical and vocal sound was much closer to rockabilly than anything Bill Haley and His Comets ever recorded, and I've heard all their earliest recordings.

All during the period starting in the spring of 1956, when Elvis started exploding with his wild rockabilly style of music in live shows across the U.S., on national TV, and finally on the movie screen, the major and independent record labels were snatchin' up competitors. The other five major record companies — Capitol, Decca, MGM, Columbia, and Mercury — all were looking to sign up wild, crazy, good ole boys from the South to take on Elvis and get their hands on some of the dough RCA was rakin' in.

Capitol Records signed Gene Vincent and His Blue Caps in the spring of '56. I'll cover Gene in depth in the next chapter, as outside of Elvis, he was probably the most important raw rockabilly artist in the fifties. In 1956 he was also the most successful other than Elvis.

In early '56 Decca Records signed two young Texas rockabilly boys. Buddy Holly cut some great songs in Nashville, but it would take him over a year to reach his huge successes on Brunswick and Coral Records. His releases on Decca failed at the time, and it would take over a decade for these songs to gain their well-deserved recognition, first in Europe and later in the U.S. Johnny Carroll's 45 releases for Decca also failed to make the charts. His recordings would also receive high acclaim in years to come.

MGM Records released 45s on Andy Starr like "Rockin' Rollin' Stone," "She's A-Going Jessie," and "Round and Round" throughout 1956. All these songs were terrific examples of primitive, totally uninhibited rockabilly. But it was all to no avail, as they never made the charts or achieved the sales results the company had anticipated. One reason was probably that Andy Starr never toured with the black or white rock 'n' roll artists. He was mainly touring with country acts, and his live shows were limited to the southern and southwestern states. MGM also had been releasing records on Marvin Rainwater, who didn't start out as a rockabilly-style artist, in 1955, but by 1956 some of the records they released on him were headed in that direction. But he, too, failed to make a dent in the *Billboard* pop charts of 1956.

Mercury Records had releases on Eddie Bond and Sleepy La Beef in 1956 that also failed in the pop market.

Columbia Records had a good deal of success in the country field in '56 with Johnny Horton. Johnny had two Top 10 hits on the *Billboard* country charts: the classic rockabilly song "Honky Tonk Man" (which Dwight Yoakam revived exactly thirty years later and had a Top 10 hit on) and "I'm a One Woman Man." Both these songs were solid examples of good early rockabilly.

Independent Labels

Back in the mid and late fifties, besides the six main record labels, there were dozens of independent labels that were able to hold their own against the big boys, and teenagers like I was at that time didn't realize they were independently owned, because they always had lots of different artists out that were hitting the top of the charts. The one that comes to mind right away is Dot Records. Although they were based in the Nashville area, they weren't a country label. Their big artist in '55 and '56 was Pat Boone, but during this same time they had a string of Top 10 hits by pop artists Jim Lowe, Gale Storm, and others. Their lone rockabilly contribution during the summer and fall of 1956 was Sanford Clark's Top 10 song "The Fool."

Other independent labels that were looked upon as majors in '56 were: King Records, out of Cincinnati, who had great rockabilly releases on Charlie Feathers and Mac Curtis that failed to chart nationally; Liberty Records, who signed a young Eddie Cochran; Imperial Records; Specialty Records; Roulette Records; ABC Paramount Records; Gone/End Records; Coral/Brunswick Records; Atlantic/Atco Records; Cameo Records; Okeh Records; Cadence Records; Kapp Records; and way too many more to name. All these labels tried to find that lasting rockabilly artist to compete with Elvis during the two biggest years the music enjoyed — from the spring of 1956 to the spring of 1958 — but it never happened. Elvis would wind up knockin' all the wanna-be's out cold during this entire period. His biggest pop competitor, Pat Boone, never came close.

Let me say a few more words about Elvis, 'cause he was the first and biggest star ever of not only rock 'n' roll, but rockabilly also. A number of older rockabilly fans feel that when Elvis left Sun Records he left rockabilly music behind. Charlie Feathers has often said, "Elvis really died when he left Sun Records." I've never agreed with that. RCA never really captured that "Sun sound" on Elvis, but he recorded "My Baby Left Me" for RCA, and they put it on the B side of "I Want You, I Need You, I Love You," and it reached #31 on the *Billboard* charts, and it holds up almost as well as anything he ever cut for Sun. Right through 1959, when the Frankies, Bobbys, and Fabian — smooth-singin', dreamy, dreary-eyed teenage idols — were ruling the charts, Elvis slammed onto the top of the charts soundin' like he'd lost his mind with the frantic "A Big Hunk o' Love." My point here is if you consider Billy Lee Riley's "Red Hot" rockabilly and don't look on "A Big Hunk o' Love" as rockabilly, you better listen again; something's wrong with your ears.

Country and Pop Artists

Anyway, when Marty Robbins had a hit on the country charts with "That's All Right, Mama" in late 1954 on Columbia Records, after hearin' Elvis's version on Sun, Columbia signed acts like The Collins Kids and Sid King and The Five Strings during 1955. They were both marketed in country then. Sid King's group had virtually no national success. The Collins Kids went on to make some fabulous rockabilly records throughout the fifties and achieved a good degree of success on the "Ranch Party" TV shows in California, but they also failed to chart a record nationally on either the country or the pop charts. Their records were easily found, though, at least where I lived. These kind of acts were safe ones. They weren't the threat to teen morals that Elvis and Gene Vincent were.

Nashville tried jumping on the bandwagon in '56 and '57. They recorded rockabilly songs like "Teenage Boogie" by older, established country stars like Webb Pierce. It came natural for Little Jimmy Dickens, as he had been singin' hillbilly boogie songs like "Rockin' with Red" for several years by this time. They tried this new brand of music on others, such as Bobby Helms, Justin Tubb (Ernest Tubb's son), Del Reeves, LeRoy Van Dyke, Jerry Reed, and even Faron Young (who later said he hated every minute of it). The list goes on and on. Most had very little or no success at all. Dolly Parton stated recently she's not ashamed that her first record, when she was thirteen years old, was a rockabilly song called

"Puppy Love." It's too bad George Jones doesn't feel the same way about his 1955 record "Rock It" on Starday Records (he told me in 1993 he'd like to burn every copy left of it), 'cause it's a case of the Young Possum goin' berserk on scorchin' hot, hard-drivin', screamin' rockabilly.

Another artist of note to have his first release on the Texas-based Starday label was Link Wray. Starday released two rockabilly sides on him in 1956, "Teenage Cutie" and "Got Another Baby," under the name Lucky Wray. Link was on lead guitar, with his younger brother Doug on drums and his older brother Vernon on lead vocals. The band, called The Wray Men, was based in the Washington, D.C., area, but I honestly don't remember hearin' this record on the radio at the time. A year and a half later, every teenager in D.C. knew who Link was when the classic instrumental "Rumble" became a big hit nationally and made #1 locally. Link's guitar style was ahead of its time in the fifties, and we all in the D.C. area took him and his band for granted throughout the sixties and seventies, 'cause he was easily found at a cheap price almost any night in some nearby bar or nightclub.

In the fifties most artists like Gene Vincent, Eddie Cochran, and Jerry Lee Lewis came under the banner of rock 'n' roll, but today they're all considered rockabilly. Between 1955 and 1958 your strictly rock 'n' roll artists were Bill Haley and His Comets, Little Richard, Fats Domino, Danny and The Juniors, Jimmy Rodgers, The Platters, Frankie Lymon and The Teenagers, The Coasters, Little Anthony and The Imperials, The Drifters, Dion and The Belmonts, Lloyd Price, Boyd Bennett and The Rockets, Duane Eddy, Ray Charles, Sal Mineo, Jackie Wilson, Paul Anka, The Champs, Sam Cooke, The Diamonds, Hank Ballard and The Midnighters, and way too many more to mention. Pop artists from before the rockabilly and rock 'n' roll era continued to have hits; it took awhile to get the likes of Perry Como, Teresa Brewer, Doris Day, Mitch Miller, The Four Aces, The McGuire Sisters, Kay Starr, and others out of the Top 10. Some of them would go on selling albums in the adult market, but after 1958 most of them wouldn't see any more big hits. It was now the era of 45 rpm records, which were bought exclusively by teenagers.

As far as strictly rockabilly music goes, it reached its peak by the spring and summer of 1957. It was so hot by the spring of '57 that Columbia Records, out of New York, released a 45 called "Rock-A-Billy" by a pop singer named Guy Mitchell. (If you see this record somewhere for a dime today, don't buy it. It's the worst piece of garbage you'll ever hear. It has absolutely nothing to do with rockabilly music either musically or lyrically.) There was even a paperback book in the late fifties titled *Rockabilly.* Besides the artists I've mentioned, and how the record labels were makin' lots of dough on rockabilly by now, along with the books and novelty songs, that only leaves Hollywood — and you know the movie industry was going to capitalize on it.

At the Movies

I guess movies about the defiant teenage culture started to make a real impact with Marlon Brando's role as Johnny in *The Wild One* in 1954. In 1955 the two big movies in that same vein were *Rebel without a Cause,* featuring the passionate James Dean, and *Blackboard Jungle,* which launched the teenage anthem "Rock Around the Clock." So by 1956, the major motion picture studios — but mostly the independent ones — really started churnin' out what were mainly low-budget films, such as *Hot Rod Girl, Teenage Rebel, Rock Pretty Baby, Rumble on the Docks, Violent Years, Teenage Devil Dolls, One Way Ticket to Hell,* and others. Most of the aforementioned, all from '56, were basically films about juvenile delinquents, and most didn't feature live rock 'n' roll or rockabilly artists. Some had the new music in the background at wild parties. The best movie of 1956, without question, was *The Girl Can't Help It.* This was a movie by a major studio, with a fairly decent plot for its time, plus it had professional, top-notch, real actors (which was a rarity for films of this kind). To top all this off, it was in beautiful wide-screen Technicolor (another rarity). The three main stars of the movie were Tom Ewell, Jayne Mansfield, and Edmond O'Brien. What makes this film special for rockabilly fans is you get to see Gene Vincent and His Wild Blue Caps do their top 10-million-seller "Be-Bop-A-Lula." That was definitely worth the twenty-five-cent admission I had to pay to get in back then. The second treat you get is seein' a seventeen-year-old Eddie Cochran doin' one of his earliest great rockabilly songs, "Twenty Flight Rock." This was a real good rockabilly and rock 'n' roll movie, with other solid performances by Little Richard, Fats Domino, The Platters, and Eddie Fontaine (who some fans today consider to be a rockabilly artist), among others.

Starting in 1956, the man who popularized the phrase rock 'n' roll starred in a series of a half dozen rock 'n' roll music-oriented films. First there was *Rock Around the Clock*, which, along with Alan Freed, starred Bill Haley, and had performances by him and his Comets, along with The Platters and Freddie Bell and The Bellboys. Freed's next starring role, in the 1956 film *Rock, Rock, Rock*, is good viewing for rockabilly fans because of The Johnny Burnette Trio's fantastic performance of their song "Lonesome Train." Chuck Berry, LaVern Baker, The Moonglows, Frankie Lymon and The Teenagers, and The Flamingos also do songs in the film. And I have to mention that Elvis's first movie, *Love Me Tender*, was released during the Thanksgiving holidays of 1956. The movie was a western. The title song was sittin' at #1 at this time, and Elvis had another five songs on the *Billboard* pop charts all at this same time, including the song "Poor Boy," from the movie, plus his great rockabilly rendition of "When My Blue Moon Turns to Gold Again." Even in his first movie, a year after leaving Sun Records, Elvis was still the King Rockabilly Cat!

When 1957 rolled in, teen movies were being cranked out at a rapid pace. Like I said, this was rockabilly music's biggest year, and there was even one movie titled *Rockabilly Baby*. It wasn't very good, to say the least, but it shows that the "magic word" in 1957, even in movies, was "rockabilly." Among the dozens of other movies released that year were *Dino* (which starred Sal Mineo), *Teenage Wolfpack*, *Teenage Doll*, *Motorcycle Gang*, *Reform School Girl*, *The Delinquents*, and *Dragstrip Girl*; the titles give you a pretty good idea of the flavor of these films. Alan Freed starred with various

rock 'n' roll artists in a couple movies that year, *Don't Knock the Rock* and *Mister Rock and Roll*. In these two movies there are no actual rockabilly artists of note. The one movie in '57 that gave you the most rockabilly stars had to be *Jamboree*. It had a pretty weak plot, but full performances by Carl Perkins rockin' on "Glad All Over" and Jerry Lee Lewis beltin' out "Great Balls of Fire" made it well worthwhile. Other rockabilly artists in this film were Charlie Gracie singin' "Cool Baby," Buddy Knox doin' "Hula Love," and Jimmy Bowen performing "Cross Over." These three artists did not do the hot, frantic rockabilly Lewis and Perkins did, but they were considered rockabilly then.

Eddie Cochran appeared briefly singin' a song called "Cotton Picker" in the delinquent film *Untamed Youth* in 1957. This was not one of Cochran's high points, by any means, but it has some historical value.

In '57 there were two terribly acted, low-budget movies that in recent years have become cult classics among rockabilly fans around the world. One is *Carnival Rock*, and Bob Luman's three songs in the film are killer rockabilly. An eighteen-year-old James Burton backs Luman up on lead guitar. Burton later went on to play some solid rockabilly guitar on the early Ricky Nelson songs, then later worked for Elvis during his Vegas years. David Houston also does a good job on a rockabilly number in the film, but it's Luman's perfomances that'll blow you away. It was his greatest rockabilly moment ever captured on film. The second film, *Rock, Baby, Rock It*, is

Forgettin' to Remember to Forget

When I was growin' up with my sister Anna Mae, my mother was the strict one toward us and pop was the fun one. Lookin' back, we both had a happy childhood and loved 'em both, but at the time we didn't think "Mother knows best!" My sister and I both had to have discipline, and my mother was going to see we got it, so she sent us to Catholic school to make sure the nuns gave it to us.

The nuns in school were always right and you didn't question their rightness on anything to my mom, 'cause they were God's servants and God told them what to do. What I couldn't figure out, though, when I was in the sixth grade in 1956, was why God told Sister Irma to slap the daylights out of me for seein' Elvis in the movie *Love Me Tender*. I knew Father Reed told us at church repeatedly at the 9:00 a.m. children's school mass that the *Catholic Standard* newspaper had condemned the movie because of Elvis's immoral, seductive gyrations, and we'd go to hell if we got hit by a car comin' out of the movie house after seein' it. But I figured after I confessed it to him in confession I was in the clear with God and everybody. I didn't know he'd tell Sister Irma!

definitely a must for hard-core rockabilly fans. This was a very low-budget film that was made in the Dallas area. I don't know where they came up with these "actors," who are so bad at bein' serious they're actually downright hilarious, but they're not what's important about this film. The important thing here is Texas-born rockabilly singer Johnny Carroll's performances of several songs, including "Crazy, Crazy Lovin'," "Wild, Wild Women," "Hot Rock," and the title track, which had been licensed to Sun Records in '57. All of the other songs were released on Decca Records in 1956 and '57, but Sun's new subsidiary label, Phillips International, was about to release a new 45 on Carroll soon. Johnny had an acting role in *Rock, Baby, Rock It*, but what makes this film a must-see is that his musical performances are just too wild to be described. He never had a hit and never really made it, but his insane, screamin', shakin', wild abandonment in this movie'll show what adults in 1957 feared the most about what was going wrong with the youth of America. Both *Carnival Rock* and *Rock, Baby, Rock It* have been legally out in select video stores since 1987. A final note on *Rock, Baby, Rock It* is there's lots of other rock 'n' roll and rockabilly performers (but none compare to Carroll), like Roscoe Gordon, The Cell Block Seven, The Five Stars, and others. There's also a performance by The Belew Twins that's hilarious, because when they dance in the middle of a song with two twin girls in the audience, you'd think by the way they're dancing they have this horrible disease in their legs. It has to be seen to be believed.

Elvis's second movie, *Loving You*, was released in the summer of 1957 in full-blown, gorgeous, living color. This remains my favorite Elvis Presley movie. Back then it set the standard for my life. First, because of his looks and dress. He had a greasy pompadour in duck tails with sideburns, drove an open-motored thirties hot rod, wore dungarees (as they were called then) cuffed up two inches, a black shirt, dungaree jacket with the collar turned up in the back and down on the sides, and motorcycle boots. He had that sultry, I-don't-give-a-damn, screw-the-world look on his face. (Throughout the 1960s, when Elvis made all his dumb beach and race car movies, I did the best I could to look like his character Deke Rivers in *Loving You*. In the early eighties, when I finally had a will made, I put in it that when I finally leave this world, I have to be buried in the same garb Elvis wore in that movie, 'cause wherever I'm goin', I want to look like that Rockabilly Cat I saw on

the big screen in 1957.) Second, the music Elvis did in the movie was some of his best rockabilly ever. That cat was downright ferocious on songs like "Mean Woman Blues" and the final song in the movie, "Got a Lot o' Livin' to Do." Six of the seven songs were good rockabilly cuts.

In the fall of '57, Elvis had his third movie released, *Jailhouse Rock*. This one was in black and white, and it was definitely great, with hard-hittin' rockabilly tunes like "Baby I Don't Care," "Treat Me Nice," the title cut, and others, and he had that great, defiant rockabilly attitude he put across in *Loving You*. He was still tourin' across the U.S. and Canada in between movies throughout 1957. *Jailhouse Rock* gives you for the first time in a movie a chance to see how the big-time record labels can easily rip an artist off — that part of the movie is not fictitious. Those things really do happen. Elvis's dance sequence on the song "Jailhouse Rock" (which he choreographed himself) is considered by many as his greatest performance ever captured on film.

In December '57 Elvis got his draft notice and would be under Uncle Sam's control within a few months. He had to wind up filming on his fourth film, *King Creole*, which was released in the late spring of 1958 after his induction into the Army. There were quite a few ballads and one stupid high school song out of the eleven songs in the movie; but there were still a few songs, such as "Trouble," "Dixieland Rock," and the title track, that showed he still ruled the rockabilly roost. But this would be the final time he showed it on the screen until ten years later, when he did what's now called his "'68 Comeback TV Special." We needed a good dose of that in '68, and he had something to prove to himself. But by then, as great as he was, he was thirty-three, not twenty-one, twenty-two, or twenty-three, and those years will always go down as the greatest musical period in his life. Youth is what rockabilly will always be about, and Elvis had it all in the fifties.

Rebellious teenage culture, rock 'n' roll, and rockabilly still rolled along in the movies all during 1958. Some of the teenage films that year were *Young and Wild*, *High School Hellcats*, *Dangerous Youth*, *Juvenile Jungle*, *The Cool and the Crazy*, and *Live Fast, Die Young*. All these were your low-budget films that were geared to the drive-in movie teenagers. Drive-ins were at their peak then. Most of these movies didn't contain live music. One of the ones that did was Alan Freed's *The Big Beat*, with Fats Domino and others.

Sing, Boy, Sing featured Tommy Sands in his first starring role. Sands did a bunch of songs that were supposed to be wild rockabilly, but he just couldn't pull it off. This movie was released over a year after Sands was supposed to be the new big threat on Elvis. The story is, Elvis had been offered the starring role in a live dramatic TV production titled "The Singing Idol" — a play of sorts. Colonel Parker turned it down and suggested Sands for the lead role. (The Colonel had managed Sands between 1952 and 1956.) He got the part, which included singing the song "Teenage Crush." The show got real high ratings; right away Capitol Records released the song, and it shot to a high of #2 in the early spring of 1957. But that was it for Sands. He wasn't a rockabilly, as hard as they tried to manufacture him into one. That song and the ones that followed, for the most part, like "Goin' Steady" and "Ring-A-Ding-A-Ding," were probably the beginning of things to come a couple years later: they were either dreamy, sugar-coated poppy fluff or silly, hokey-soundin' up-tempo numbers. To Tommy Sands's credit, by early 1959 he made a few songs with a good backing band called The Sharks, such as "The Worryin' Kind," "I Ain't Gittin' Rid o' You," and "Is It Ever Gonna Happen," that were all tough soundin' bluesy rockabilly numbers. He had finally found the sound, but by then rockabilly music was almost dead, and it was too late. The release of *Sing, Boy, Sing* was almost too late, too, in the spring of '58, although the title track did reach #24 on the *Billboard* pop charts. *Sing, Boy, Sing* was a movie version of "The Singing Idol"; the TV production brought in all kinds of fan mail for Tommy Sands, so 20th Century-Fox bought the rights to the story and had him repeat his starring role on the silver screen.

Over the summer of 1958, the teenage film *High School Confidential* was a good, hot, cookin' flick for a thirteen-year-old kid like me, if only to see Jerry Lee Lewis's last great fifties hurrah, rockin' out and bangin' on the piano, screamin' out the title track. He was a phenomenal sight to see then, on the back of this flatbed truck. This was some strong rockabilly here. But the best of all the rockabilly movies in '58 had to be the American International flick *Hot Rod Gang*, the reason being the raw, wild, spontaneous performances by Gene Vincent and His Blue Caps on "Dance in the Street," "Baby Blue," "Lovely Loretta," and "Dance to the Bop." Early in 1958, "Dance to the Bop" climbed to #23 on the *Billboard* pop charts. It would be Gene's last chart hit in the U.S., but what a way to go out. And *Hot Rod Gang* was definitely his finest hour on film.

After '58, there really weren't a lot of great rockabilly performances in films here in the U.S. I remember seein' the first British rockabilly-type film, *Rock Around the World*, starring Tommy Steele, in '58. Steele couldn't pull it off, though. Cliff Richard came along in 1959 with another British movie, *Expresso Bongo*. Richard played a rockabilly/rock 'n' roll singer; he wasn't no wild Elvis or Gene Vincent type, but he wasn't too bad. In 1959 and '60, Billy Fury would emerge as the best gutsy rockabilly artist the British would find in those early days. He had a natural feel and spirit for the music, and a couple years later he starred in *Play It Cool*.

In early 1959, Alan Freed gave us his final major film before the Payola Scandal, which ended his career and eventually his life. The film was titled *Go, Johnny, Go*, and even though we had to sit through the wimpy Jimmy Clanton's acting (if you can call it that) and songs, we got to see great rockabilly performances by the likes of Eddie Cochran, Jo Ann Campbell, Ritchie Valens, and Chuck Berry. Jackie Wilson, The Cadillacs, and others also appeared in this film. It still holds up well today. *The Ghost of Dragstrip Hollow*, another 1959 release, also had some good rockabilly-oriented music in it.

In 1958 Conway Twitty had his only #1 hit: "It's Only Make Believe," on MGM. I guess you could consider it an Elvis-sound-alike rockabilly ballad. Conway had auditioned for Sun Records in '56, but failed to get a release, and then moved along to signing a deal with Mercury Records and had a couple releases in 1957. One of those songs, "I Need Your Love," a stone-hard rockin' rockabilly side, was on the *Billboard* pop charts in May of that year. When he was dropped by Mercury about a year later, he signed with MGM and had his biggest hit on "It's Only Make Believe." He had a couple more Top 10 rockabilly songs in 1959, and this led to his appearance in the 1959 teenage film *Platinum High School*, where he sang the title track. He made another one of these films in 1960, called *College Confidential*. I guess he'd graduated by then, huh? Neither one of these films was very good; Conway's performances were the only interesting aspects of them. But by this time, it was about all that there was.

The last thing I'll say here is that Robert Mitchum (a real actor) was at his best in the 1958 movie *Thunder Road*. You may not consider the song "The Ballad of Thunder Road" a rockabilly song, but Robert Mitchum sure drew a lot of rockabilly cats and juvenile delinquents out to buy that record and go to drive-in theaters to see that movie over and over again. I guess it was 'cause he was playin' a tough kind of rockabilly cat in that flick. That movie stayed popular at drive-ins for years, well into the mid sixties. Mitchum never looked or acted better or cooler than he did in *Thunder Road*. When the song "The Ballad of Thunder Road," sung by Robert Mitchum himself, first debuted on *Billboard* on September 8, 1958, it reached a peak of #62 on the *Billboard* pop charts and had an eleven-week run. That film was so popular and stayed around so long that four years later

Capitol Records re-released "The Ballad of Thunder Road," and it made it onto the *Billboard* pop charts once more on February 24, 1962. This go-round, it made it up to #65 and stayed on the charts for ten more straight weeks. Both the song and the film have had such an impact on rockabilly fans over the years that even as recently as 1993 the Nashville-based rockabilly band The Planet Rockers recorded a great updated version of it, and it was released on a 45 in Europe on No Hit Records.

The Biggest Stars and Hit Songs

Long-term success in music is rare. Not many artists or acts last for more than a few years. For every exception like Elvis, Frank Sinatra, or The Rolling Stones, there are dozens like Zager and Evans (remember "In the Year 2525"?), New Kids on the Block, or Joan Jett and The Blackhearts that prove the rule. In this respect rockabilly is no different than mainstream rock or pop; most of the big rockabilly artists of the 1950s had only one or maybe two real big hits and then they vanished into obscurity. But even though rockabilly artists disappeared from the radio and charts in a matter of a few years, their music has always been brought back by the generations that followed. The reason is simple: it's real music. This hasn't happened with Bobby Vee, Paul Anka, Bobby Rydell, Johnny Mathis, The Diamonds, Bobby Vinton, or even Bill Haley. Most started about the same time, but you'll only hear their songs on oldies radio today. By them. I don't believe young artists in the future will ever bring back songs by The Bee Gees, Barry Manilow, Phil Collins, or Madonna. Those were all manufactured. They weren't real. Rockabilly music was. It was unrestrained, spontaneous, frantic music, unleashed on a generation of teenagers that wanted to break away from the restricted, dreary lives they saw their parents leading. This music made you feel like you had total freedom to do and become whatever you wanted back in the mid and late fifties. In this chapter, I'll concentrate on the handful of artists who had the biggest hits.

As I've already spent so much time on Elvis, I'll do the best I can to not repeat myself. The fact is, though, Elvis set the standard. He was the first rockabilly artist, the wildest live performer, the one singled out and blasted by almost every adult then for the destruction of the morals of 1950s youth. He was also the one who had the most hit records. From March 3, 1956, through October 20, 1959 (one and a half years after his induction into the Army), Elvis's songs were only off the *Billboard* pop charts for a mere two weeks (the last week of October and the first week of November, 1958). This happened because RCA Victor was spacing his 45 releases out until his discharge in March 1960. It's incredible to think that, even at the height of the teen-idol pop crap that was being dished out on the radio, on August 10, 1959, Elvis knocked Paul Anka's song "Lonely Boy" out of the #1 slot with his scorchin' rocker "A Big Hunk o' Love." It stayed at #1 for two weeks. Another fact is that from the time Elvis debuted on the *Billboard* country charts on July 16, 1955 (while on Sun Records), with "Baby, Let's Play House," he never missed a week havin' a song on those charts until October 20, 1958 — again, well after his induction into the Army. He was really never considered or accepted as a country artist, but he holds the #15 position in the category of longevity for the song "I Forgot to Remember to Forget," which remained on those country charts for an astonishing thirty-nine weeks, from September 1955 till June 1956, and this was when the *Billboard* country charts only had a Top 15 list. It also needs to be added that Elvis stayed on the *Billboard* R&B charts consistently between 1956 and 1958. Between November 1954 and December 1957, Elvis toured more than any other rockabilly artist, to larger crowds than any other. Between January 1956 and January 1957, he was seen consistently on TV. And finally, between November 1956 and October 1958, his four full-length motion pictures could be seen at theaters and drive-ins across the country at almost any time. During the summer of 1959, Colonel Parker had them all in re-release while Elvis was stationed in Germany. Say what you may about the Colonel, but even though he took 50 percent of Elvis's money, he earned it. He made sure the teenagers wouldn't forget his boy while he was out of their sight, physically at least. When Elvis returned from the Army in March 1960, his greatest period in rockabilly music was forever gone, never to return — but oh, what a ride he gave us all in such a short period.

Gene Vincent

To me, Gene Vincent was always and will always be the next best thing to Elvis in wild, uninhibited rockabilly music. This cat was undeniably, excitingly brilliant. Gene had a much better vocal backup group than Elvis. Elvis's Jordanaires were polished ba-da-ba-dop smooth session singers in Nashville. The Blue Caps, on the other hand, were younger lookin', cool dressed, local boys from the area of Norfolk, Virginia, who screamed with wild, spontaneous frenzy behind Gene's pantin', breathy, stutterin', hiccuppin' lead vocals. They beat the hell out of The Jordanaires in the backup department. In rockabilly history, The Blue Caps should go down as the greatest backup group there ever was. Gene Vincent was always the dominant figure, but between the spring of 1956 and the fall of 1958, nobody could touch his Blue Caps in the backup band department. During that time there were many personnel changes in the group, but whether it was Cliff Gallup or Johnny Meeks on lead guitar, Jack Neal or Bobby Jones on bass, or Dickie Harrell, Juvey Gomez, or Clyde Pennington on drums, it really didn't matter, 'cause the ones that followed all picked up and fell right into the perfect groove of the cats that had been there before them. And aw, man, Gene had two of the wildest cats there ever were in Paul Peek and Tommy "Bubba" Facenda during 1957 and 1958 on handclaps and backing vocals. Today, Vincent fans refer to 'em as the "Clapper Boys." No matter how hard new rockabilly artists may try forever in the future, they'll never be able to top this ragin', roarin' backup group known as The Blue Caps during their two-year heyday with Vincent. In the summer of 1956, adults, parents, city officials, religious leaders, and so on were scared of Elvis for disintegrating the morals of their young people. Well, I can tell ya they should-a been downright terrified of Gene Vincent.

Gene's biggest hit, "Be-Bop-A-Lula," reached a high of #7 on the *Billboard* pop charts in July 1956, and it stayed on the charts for twenty weeks. It reached even higher on the country charts, gettin' up to #5, and stayed on those charts for seventeen weeks. It also was high on the R&B charts, as well as making the Top 20 in England. Gene Vincent was no Elvis copycat. What he was, though, was the first real wild rockabilly competition Elvis was to have this early on.

Gene Vincent and His Blue Caps charted only six 45s in *Billboard* between 1956 and 1958, and only three of these can be regarded as major hits: "Be-Bop-A-Lula" in '56, "Lotta Lovin' " in '57, and "Dance to the Bop" in late '57 and early '58. But next to Elvis, Gene Vincent charted the biggest album by a real rockabilly artist on the *Billboard* Top 40 chart in the 1950s: *Bluejean Bop*. It reached a high of #16. Buddy Holly did have his album *The Buddy Holly Story* reach #11 in late April of 1959, but I believe this would not have happened except that, first, it was a greatest hits package and not an album of new material, and second, it was quickly put out to capitalize on the tragedy of his death in a plane crash on February 3 of that year.

Even though Gene Vincent didn't have the continuous big chart hits, Capitol Records in the U.S. continued to release albums on him — a total of six between 1956 and 1960. They did so because the albums warranted it. They all sold well during a time when teenagers were only buying 45s. (Teenagers didn't really start buying albums until the mid sixties, when The Beatles came in.) Sometimes it takes thirty or forty years for fans, musicians, artists, and the like to really realize the true genius of an artist such as Gene Vincent. In Europe, especially France, they've idolized Gene since the fifties. He continued to have hits in foreign countries through the mid sixties and played to huge audiences.

I recently spoke with Jerry Merritt, who started playing lead guitar for Gene on shows during the spring of '59, about the tour of Japan that I knew Gene had done during July of that year. (Jerry wrote several songs Gene recorded for his last U.S. Capitol Records album, *Crazy Times*, recorded in August 1959, and a couple more songs Gene recorded for Challenge Records in 1966. He remains active in rockabilly music today.) He told me Gene was the first American rock 'n' roll artist to ever play Japan, and they were met at the Tokyo airport by 10,000 screaming fans who wanted to see this great American rocker. He said Capitol Records had set up this tour, which lasted about three weeks. They were backed up by a good Japanese band that knew all Gene's songs. During one five-day period they played to almost 300,000 fans, and by the time the tour ended, over 800,000 wild Japanese rock 'n' roll fans had witnessed the frantic stage power of Gene's performances. They were treated like royalty; in the presidential suite at their hotel, they had to have about twenty policemen in the halls at all times to guard Gene from fans.

All this was happenin' over there while here in Gene's own country the #1 song was Paul Anka's sappy "Lonely Boy" (four weeks runnin'). The writing had been on the wall, though, since early 1958 to plot the death of real rock 'n' roll and rockabilly music. Dick Clark was reaching his peak by this time. His TV show "American Bandstand" was watched by more teenagers than any other show in the country. And starting in the spring of '58, you began to see the likes of Frankie Avalon singing his Top 10 silly songs like "De De Dinah" and "Gingerbread" a lot more than you did Buddy Holly and The Crickets and other true rockabillies. By the time Gene Vincent was bein' mobbed by hundreds of thousands of Japanese rock 'n' roll fans in the summer of '59, the teen idol market dominated the scene in the U.S.

There was no other course for the wildest rockabilly showman to take but to head overseas. Starting from the first week of December 1959 right up until literally a week before he died, Gene Vincent would spend most

Forgettin' to Remember to Forget

Even though, like I said in Chapter 1, I didn't go to an all-out rock 'n' roll show until September 1957, I did see Gene Vincent and His Blue Caps in August 1956, at the Casino Royale, a plush supper club in Washington, D.C. When I read in the paper that they would be playing there, I was eager to see 'em. I had Gene's 45 "Be-Bop-A-Lula" and liked it a lot, and I had seen him and The Blue Caps on the Perry Como TV show about a month earlier. I asked and complained and whined until finally my folks agreed to let good ole Aunt Julie take me.

We got there well before the show started and got a good table. We were about finished eating when all the stage lights went off and an announcer said, "For your musical enjoyment, the Casino Royale is proud to present one of today's top acts of radio, TV, and records, Gene Vincent with his fabulous Blue Caps." The lights went up and Gene roared into "Well, I lead an evil life, so they say, but I'll hide from the devil on Judgement Day" — the beginning of "Race with the Devil." I got goosebumps with excitement. When Gene finished the song, he went right into another about as frantic as the first one. It was "Jump Back, Honey, Jump Back." The drummer and one other guy in The Blue Caps were lettin' out wild screams during the guitar solos. After that song, the audience gave a rousing applause. Gene then went into a ballad, but most of that hour-and-a-half show was blistering rockabilly and rock 'n' roll.

The Blue Caps were crazy and wild, playin' off Gene's movements, and even though he had a brace on his left leg, he rocked and dropped to one knee while turnin' the whole mike stand (and they were heavy back in those days) upside down while he was singin'. Gene did "Be-Bop-A-Lula" midway through the set, and when he got called back at the end of the show for an encore, he did it again. The crowd went wild.

The Blue Caps wore really cool-looking blue suit coats and matching pants. Of course, they all had these fabulous sky-blue caps on their heads. Gene had a shiny white jacket and black slacks. They all had cool black shirts and white ties.

After the show Aunt Julie walked me up to the stage, sweaty-palmed, to get Gene's autograph. He had his coat off by this time. Midway through his show, he had taken off his tie and thrown it out in the audience. When Gene took my guest menu out of my hand to sign it, he said, "What's your name, little fella?" "Ba-Ba-Billy." Gene grinned. "Well, Billy, did you like the show?" "Oh, yeah, I liked it a lot, and I got your record. I play it all the time." Gene really brightened up and said, "Hey, that's great. You're the first one to tell me that in here. We got a new one comin' out soon. I think you'll dig that one too." Then I blurted out, "That was a really neat tie you had on and threw out to that lady that caught it. She was really lucky. I wish I had one like that, 'cause they make me wear real ugly wide maroon ones every day in school, and I hate it." Gene started laughin' and bent over and whispered in my ear, "You know, little cat, I hate ties, too, and you bought my record, so you know what I'm gonna do? I'm gonna give you somethin' real special. You'll like it better than any old chokin' tie." He walked over to the tall guy who had been playin' lead guitar, took the blue cap off his head and winked at him, and came back and plopped it on my head and said, "Now, there you go. You're gonna be the coolest cat on your block." Well, I was on top of the world. My aunt started thanking him and tellin' him what a nice man he was to do that. Gene said, "It was nothin'; thank y'all for comin'. Now cat, you keep listenin' for Gene Vincent, OK?" All I could get out of my mouth was "You betcha." And brother, let me tell you, did I ever.

of his time in England, but also doin' shows in various countries. He did many in France, as well as Germany and elsewhere. From all accounts I've heard from fans that were there, Gene's frantic stage performances drove the thousands of his true believers completely berserk. I've also been told Gene's offstage antics, with the drinkin' problem he had, were so outrageous there's no way to describe them.

They called Gene Vincent "The Black Leather Rebel" during this period in Europe, 'cause that's what he was decked out in from head to toe. In 1956, Elvis may have been the first rockabilly cat who truly defined the word "cool," but as early as 1960 (and probably before) Gene truly defined the word "punk." When the new wave of punk rockers arrived on the scene in the late seventies and early eighties and thought they were doin' something new by trashing and settin' fire to their hotel rooms, shootin' pistols into walls and ceilings, and gettin' arrested for drunken drugged-up brawls they were gettin' into, little did they know it had all been done before, when they were still in diapers.

Some of the best film footage on what Gene Vincent was like live can be found in the 1958 film *Hot Rod Gang*. It's been bootlegged for years, and I still don't think American International Pictures has ever put it on the market legally. It's considered by fans of Vincent and rockabilly as the best example of what to judge as the standard for sheer uninhibited rockabilly music, because of the wild performance not only Gene gave, but The Blue Caps too.

Gene's only other major (or independent, for that matter) U.S. record label deal between 1960 and 1969 was for Challenge Records, which resulted in two 45 singles in 1966 and one in 1967. Capitol Records here in the U.S. had given up releasin' 45s on him around late 1961. These three Challenge 45s do not hold up with the greatest work Gene recorded for Capitol between 1956 and 1959. But I have to say, one of the songs for Challenge, "Ain't That Too Much," was just that. It was downright great vocally, and proved Gene Vincent definitely had not given up on solid rock 'n' roll the way he knew it should be sung. By '66, with the exception of Jerry Lee Lewis, virtually about every other original fifties rockabilly or rock 'n' roll artist had given up or turned to Nashville and country music here in the States. Gene recorded two separate Challenge sessions, in June 1966 and March 1967, in Hollywood, on occasions when he flew back to the U.S. to visit his parents and

children. The twelve songs in all that he recorded during these two sessions were licensed and released in 1967 by the major label London Records in England on a full-length album over there simply titled *Gene Vincent*.

In the fall of 1969 Gene came out with his first U.S. album in nine years, *I'm Back and I'm Proud,* on the Dandelion label.

I saw Gene a second time in April 1970, when he played a small club in Waldorf, Maryland, called The Wigwam. He had gained weight and his hair was gettin' thin, but when he launched into "Be-Bop-A-Lula," he sounded as good as I remembered in '56 or on records. I spent some time talkin' and drinkin' with him between sets and after the show. I told him about our first meeting almost fourteen years earlier. He got a real kick out of it. He told me it was Cliff Gallup's blue cap he'd given me. He also told me about a new song he was gonna record, called "Sunshine," that was gonna put him back on the charts. But it didn't work out that way.

Gene's final album, on the Kama Sutra label, was appropriately titled *The Day the World Turned Blue*. I bought it in early 1971, and as usual, Gene's voice was as good as ever. It wasn't rockabilly, it wasn't country, and most of it couldn't really be considered rock 'n' roll like he did in the fifties. What it was, though, was Gene Vincent, and that's all that mattered to me.

On October 12, 1971, Gene tripped and fell at his parents' home in California, and an ulcer burst, causin' him to vomit up blood. He died at the hospital within an hour. I was driving home when I was switchin' channels on the radio and they were playin' "Be-Bop-A-Lula" on a station that normally didn't play oldies, so I stopped on that channel. When the song ended, the DJ said, "That was a million-seller from 1956 by Gene Vincent, who died earlier today in California at the age of 36." Those words cut me like a knife. Gene looked bad physically when we had spent that night partying only a year and a half earlier, but he released a couple albums since then, and I figured things had been going OK for him. I hadn't read or heard anything to the contrary. When I heard the news of his death, I had no way of knowing his personal life was in a shambles.

As the years went on, people I talked with who knew him well would tell me how self-destructive Gene could be at times. His daughter Melody, from his second marriage, told me she believed, as I did, that he was really a good person at heart, although he had a bad reputation, justifiably so as it turned out, for heavy drinkin' and gettin' into fights, among other things. Joe Brown, who backed Gene up on lead guitar in England, Scotland, and parts of Europe in 1960 and 1961, gave me good insight on Gene's problems and wild behavior. But Gene's personal problems ain't what count. The facts are what matter most, and they can't be denied. Forty years after rockabilly's birth, here we are in the mid 1990s, and when rockabilly music fans in the know between sixteen and sixty the world over picture the consummate, total rockabilly artist and performer, they picture Gene Vincent. For good reason, too.

Compare him to Elvis. When Elvis came into the living rooms of conservative American homes on TV in 1956, though he projected the snarling, sneery, threatening side to America's youth, there was still an underlying polite, innocent, naive charm about him. Not so with Gene; what you saw was what you got, and it was wild to the core. The biggest difference between Elvis and Gene in, say, 1957, was when Elvis looked at the parents' precious fifteen- and sixteen-year-old daughters, he had a sexual look that said, "I'm gonna seduce your daughter." Gene's look, on the other hand, said, "I'm gonna rape your daughter." That's it in a nutshell.

Elvis's rebellious image was relatively short-lived, as he was safely tucked away in the Army within two years, and upon his return in March 1960, Colonel Parker, to keep him on top and makin' millions, made sure he changed with the times. While Elvis was in America in the early sixties in the movies singin' silly songs like "There's No Room to Rhumba in a Sports Car" dressed in a suit and tie, Gene Vincent was live on stage somewhere in England dressed in mean black leathers screamin' out "I'm Gonna Catch Me a Rat" to the hysterical delight and screams of a real live audience.

Elvis's and Gene's 1950s rockabilly and rock 'n' roll music holds up today better than any of the rest. They could both do frantic hard-bitin' rockers, tough-edged bluesy tunes, and Gene could match or even outdo Elvis on smooth ballads. Looking back, Elvis's ballad "Love Me Tender" is actually a really boring song, but Gene's ballad "Important Words" is so soulful and smooth, it makes your heart bleed. Colonel Parker controlled Elvis even in the fifties. Nobody was able to control Gene Vincent. They both had the potential in their great voices to put across whatever they wanted and make you feel it, but Gene Vincent used it more than Elvis.

Where Elvis for the most part would inspire thousands of jump-suited, mostly no-talent look-alikes, Gene inspired The Beatles. Especially John Lennon. In 1961 and '62, The Beatles opened shows and backed Gene up in England and Germany. John Lennon loved Gene Vincent and his music. It's been said he completely idolized him. You can see this on the cover of Lennon's 1975 album titled simply *Rock 'n' Roll*. You see Lennon standing in a sleazy doorway, leaning against the wall dressed in a black motorcycle jacket, white T-shirt, cuffed blue jeans, and black boots, with a dark, glaring look on his face and his hair pomped up and swept back. The first song on side one of that album is "Be-Bop-A-Lula."

Later there were many more besides Lennon and The Beatles who patterned themselves after Gene and recorded many of his songs. Robert Gordon and The Stray Cats are the best-known. Gene's music will be done and redone for generations to come. But it's Gene's dangerous, greasy, violent image that'll keep setting the standards for the youth of the twenty-first century. It'll never go away. It's downright disgraceful that the almighty powers that be who are in control of who's elected to the Rock 'n' Roll Hall of Fame here in America took until 1998 to put Gene Vincent in it. And as recently as 1993, when Jeff Beck put out *Crazy Legs*, a tribute album mostly to Gene's first guitar player Cliff Gallup, with a singer doin' all Gene's songs, his major label wouldn't promote it. That's a fact. But Gene Vincent's music and image will never go away, because kids in generations to come will always find out Gene never sold out to the fickle fads and trends of the music industry like all the others did to try to stay on top. Gene was the only one who continued to sing and record wild rockabilly and rock 'n' roll to the very end. He's been referred to over the years as "The Screamin' End." I wrote an article on him some years ago called "The Tortured Soul of Rock 'n' Roll." Gene was both. He was the ultimate rockabilly, and I'm sure glad we had him as long as we did.

I'll end with this: On Gene's final U.S. major-label album, *The Day the World Turned Blue* (recorded a year before his death), there was one song Gene did called "How I Love Them Old Songs." There was one main line throughout the song, and especially on the fade-out at the end, that Gene sang with extreme conviction. The line is, "The dancin's over, but the music she goes on. Gosh darn my soul, how I love rock 'n' roll." You couldn't-a wailed it better, cat, right up to The Screamin' End.

Buddy Holly

The great state of Texas produced dozens of really great rockabilly artists like Johnny Carroll, Bob Luman, Mac Curtis, and others who all had major recording contracts as early as 1956 and '57. Most of these acts, like others across the country at that time, were trying to follow in the footsteps of Elvis. All the Texas boys had an advantage on the rest of the country, though, because startin' in late 1954 and continuing through all of 1955, Elvis probably spent more time playing shows in the Lone Star State than in any other. Bob Luman told me in 1965 that all the teenage boys in Texas who were playin' the hillbilly music of the day, including himself and Buddy Holly, stopped dead in their tracks when they saw what Elvis was slammin' out on stage. He said they all started doin' Elvis's songs and writin' ones like 'em. He told me that Elvis's fifties songs and style still had an influence on him and probably always would. That's why he kept 'em in his live shows. Bob continued to do so right up to his death in 1978.

The biggest and greatest rockabilly star to come out of Texas in the late 1950s was Buddy Holly, backed by his band The Crickets. He had the hit records — seven of 'em, all between the late summer of 1957 and late summer 1958. Only a year; such a short time when you think back on it. But what an incredible impact those records and other songs Buddy did would have on future generations of artists and fans.

Buddy Holly was as unlikely a rock 'n' roll or rockabilly star in the late fifties as there ever was. Back then you had to be good lookin'. Elvis, Ricky Nelson, Eddie Cochran, Buddy Knox, and others all were good lookin' cats whose pictures those young teenage girls wanted to pin up on the walls of their rooms. Buddy Holly's looks sure didn't fit into this pattern. With those horn-rimmed glasses he looked more like the straight-A school bookworm.

Buddy was born in Lubbock, Texas, on September 7, 1936. In 1954 he teamed up with Bob Montgomery (who later went on to become one of the top producers of country music in Nashville) and started recording demos of mostly songs Montgomery had written. Today they sound like basic simplistic hillbilly-type Texas tunes of their day. None of these songs would give you a clue to the Tex-Mex brand of rockabilly that Buddy would create about two years later.

When he met and saw Elvis perform this new style of what was then called "hillbilly bop" as early as the late

fall of 1954, Buddy's whole direction in music changed. Where Buddy first saw Elvis was in his hometown of Lubbock, Texas, at the Cotton Club. This was the biggest dance hall and showplace in the area for top performers in hillbilly music. In 1992 I met and talked with Sonny Curtis, who played fiddle on those early 1954 demos of Buddy's, and he remembers those days like this: "In the beginning when I joined up with Buddy and Bob, they had a bass player, and sometimes a steel player would sit in, and I was on the fiddle, and all we did was straight country tunes. But then Buddy went out and saw Elvis when he first hit town. Buddy was so taken by him he learned every song Elvis had out at that time. He wanted to drop most of the country stuff and make his whole show rock 'n' roll. At that time they called Elvis the Hillbilly Cat and called what he was doin' hillbilly bop, so Buddy came up with the term western bop for what he was doin'. This was in mid '55 some time, and he was puttin' Chuck Berry and Fats Domino songs in the show as well. Buddy had a whole lot of ambition, and he figured if Elvis could do it, he could. When Elvis first came around and Buddy saw Elvis with just a stand-up bass and no drums, Buddy didn't want no drums. Later on, when Elvis came back with a drummer, Buddy put drums back in his show. Whatever he saw Elvis do, then that's what he did. He sang Elvis's songs just like he did, too. By this time I was just hangin' around at the show with him and the other guys. By the end of '55, Buddy got a solo contract with Decca up here in Nashville, and I was playin' lead guitar then with him, and Buddy and me along with Don Guess on bass and Jerry Allison on drums drove up to Nashville and did a couple sessions. That was in '56, and we were all just excited young kids back then. We didn't fit in with all the big shots in Nashville, but they didn't really know what to make of us or the rock 'n' roll stuff we were playin', so I remember they just let us go on and do what we wanted. RCA had Elvis, and they [Decca] just wanted to have a rock 'n' roll artist and record out on their label. By that time Buddy pretty much knew what he wanted, and he was strong-willed and didn't want to be told how to do his music. Decca released a couple of records on him that failed to make it from those sessions, but it didn't discourage him, 'cause he hooked up with Norman Petty in Clovis, New Mexico, and later showed 'em all he knew how his music should be done. We stayed friends right up till the end."

The two 45s Decca released in 1956 were "Blue Days, Black Nights" b/w "Love Me" and "Modern Don Juan" b/w "You Are My One Desire." I remember hearin' "Blue Days, Black Nights" on WPGC radio in the summer of 1956 in Washington, D.C., and I liked it. The little record store where I was buyin' all my Sun records didn't have it, but they special-ordered me a copy. Back then, though, I don't think Buddy Holly was seen on any of the local TV music shows in our area.

As far as Sonny Curtis goes, one of the songs Buddy recorded in 1956 during those Decca Records sessions in Nashville was "Rock Around with Ollie Vee." Sonny Curtis wrote the song, and it's one of the hottest soundin' rockabilly songs Buddy Holly ever recorded. Hundreds of rockabilly artists and bands around the world have recorded or performed this song now for almost three decades. It wouldn't be released until after Holly's death in 1959, but it was the first of many solid artist compositions for Curtis. Sonny has continued to stay active right up to the present day. After Buddy's death, he along with Joe B. Mauldin on upright bass and Jerry Allison on drums re-formed The Crickets and carried on Buddy's music all throughout the 1960s. Buddy had all his major hits on Brunswick and Coral Records. The group with Sonny Curtis had releases on Brunswick in 1959 and Coral in 1960, including one album on Coral. These records failed to chart here in the U.S., and The Crickets moved on to Liberty Records, where they stayed from 1961 to 1965. Liberty Records released several albums, which also failed to chart, but the 1960s version of The Crickets was extremely popular in Europe. (Buddy Holly with his Crickets had toured in England before his fatal plane crash.) So while the music scene here got into a watered-down version of rock 'n' roll, the 1960s Crickets made the British charts several times, their two biggest hits being "Don't Ever Change," reaching #5 in 1962, and "My Little Girl," makin' it up to #17 in 1963. During the late seventies and early eighties, The Crickets toured with Waylon Jennings (Holly's lead guitarist on his final tour) and have continued to perform at festivals, mostly in Europe.

When Buddy's contract was up with Decca, he continued to play shows in Texas and to work out his musical arrangement ideas with his friend and drummer Jerry Allison, who had been with him for almost two years by this time. The two of them had written and recorded a version of "That'll Be the Day" on the July 1956 Decca Records sessions in Nashville. The Decca people decided not to release the song, but Buddy and Jerry were high on it and were continuing to work on developing it. It finally paid off. Buddy, along with Allison, bass player

Larry Welborn, and friend Niki Sullivan, drove from Lubbock, Texas, over to Clovis, New Mexico, and cut a new version of "That'll Be the Day" at Norman Petty's studios on February 25, 1957. Word had gotten around that Petty had the most advanced studio in the Southwest, and it was only about a hundred-mile drive from Lubbock. Petty was having success with his own instrumental records under the name of The Norman Petty Trio, and two records cut at his studios a few months earlier were just hittin' the *Billboard* charts: Buddy Knox's "Party Doll" and Jimmy Bowen's "I'm Stickin' with You."

The version of "That'll Be the Day" recorded for Decca seven months prior was good, but lacked the punch it needed. When you listen to the two of 'em back to back you can really hear the chemistry between Buddy and Jerry. And that drummin' on that song and all future ones to come out of the Clovis studio really helped immensely to create the Buddy Holly rockabilly sound. On this new version, Buddy wanted backup vocals, and they really worked. By all accounts the song was cut live over and over again till they got the take they were happy with. The other song they cut that day was "I'm Lookin' for Someone to Love," another original song by Buddy. Both sides of this record, which would finally come out on Brunswick Records in late May 1957 after being turned down by both the Roulette and Columbia record labels, were good hard-drivin' rockabilly. Buddy Holly and his Crickets didn't sound like Elvis anymore. They had created the Tex-Mex brand of rockabilly.

Buddy got the title for the song from the 1956 John Wayne movie *The Searchers*, when in a response to something that was said to Wayne in the movie he heard The Duke say in his unmistakable style, "Well, that'll be the day." After its release it took over two and a half months for it to finally debut on the *Billboard* Pop 100 charts, on August 12, 1957. Buddy's Crickets now consisted of Joe B. Mauldin on bass, Jerry Allison on drums, and Niki Sullivan on rhythm guitar. Buddy sang and played lead most of the time. When they weren't playin' shows, they stayed in the studio, recording more new songs while they waited for "That'll Be the Day" to break into the charts. They recorded more than two dozen different songs during this waiting period, and it's good that they did, as when the record finally broke into *Billboard*, Buddy Holly and The Crickets took on a grueling touring schedule that started in New York at the Brooklyn Paramount Theater in August of '57 and would continue through October of '58 with not more than a few days off here and there for recording new material. All the material that was recorded during that two-and-a-half-month wait produced Buddy Holly's biggest hit records.

"That'll Be the Day" went gold, selling well over a million copies, and hit the #1 spot in *Billboard* in December 1957. This record was released under the name The Crickets, on the Brunswick label. It stayed on the charts for twenty-two weeks. Buddy's next release, "Peggy Sue," was in the last week of October 1957. It debuted in *Billboard* on November 11. But this record came out on the Coral record label, under the name of Buddy Holly only, even though The Crickets were the backup group and it was recorded in July 1957. The Coral and Brunswick Record labels were both subsidiaries of Decca Records. On Brunswick, Buddy and his group were promoted as The Crickets, but on Coral he was promoted as Buddy Holly only, even though The Crickets backed Buddy on every session he ever did except for his final one in October 1958.

On December 1, 1957, Buddy Holly and The Crickets appeared on "The Ed Sullivan Show." "That'll Be the Day" was riding at the top of the charts, and now "Peggy Sue" was on the charts and gettin' heavy airplay. It would finally peak out at the #3 position in *Billboard* in early 1958, also staying on the charts for twenty-two weeks.

Brunswick released "Oh Boy" around the same time as "Peggy Sue." It made its debut in *Billboard* on November 25, 1957, reached a high of #10 by early 1958, and stayed on the charts for twenty weeks. "Oh Boy" would be the last Top 10 record Buddy and The Crickets would have. His next release on Brunswick still faired well, though, reaching a high of #17 after its debut in *Billboard* on March 3, 1958, staying on the charts for fourteen weeks. That song was "Maybe Baby." Two and a half months later, on May 26, 1958, the song "Rave On" was released on the Coral label. This one barely reached the Top 40, peaking out at #37 and dropping off the charts after only a ten-week run. This song was a good, solid rocker to boot.

Buddy Holly and The Crickets had stayed on a constant, hectic touring schedule for a full year by the time "Rave On" dropped off the charts the first week of August 1958. During that year, Buddy was also plenty visible on national TV shows such as "The Ed Sullivan Show," the "Arthur Murray Dance Party" show, "American Bandstand," Dick Clark's Saturday night prime-time show, etc., as well as being seen on almost every local "American Bandstand"-type show in the U.S. Every major

city had one. Buddy had to have been on a hundred of these shows and done another hundred or so radio interviews, along with playing over 300 show dates on various package tours, such as Alan Freed's, Irving Feld's, and Dick Clark's Caravan of Stars. So when you ask yourself why were the first two record releases Buddy had out during the first six months of 1958 starting to slip dramatically (and it would get worse) with all this exposure and work, along with both bein' great examples of rockabilly music, there's only really one answer. The conservative establishment in the mid to late fifties figured rock 'n' roll and rockabilly music sung wildly by either white boys from the South and Southwest (such as Buddy Holly) or colored people (such as Chuck Berry and Little Richard) would only be a quick fad that wouldn't last more than a year or so. After more than two and a half years they were worried. By the end of 1957, local and national politicians were all still blastin' away at rock 'n' roll and its artists for being the ruination of America's youth. The religious across the country of all faiths were constantly seen on the news doin' the same thing. But during the first six months of 1958, three major events took place that would cause rockabilly and rock 'n' roll artists like Buddy Holly to lose their Top 10 positions on the charts. The first one was a gift to the establishment: Sometime between late '57 and early '58, one of the most frantic, hard drivin', screamin' rock 'n' rollers on the scene, Little Richard, had suddenly decided to give the rest of his life to serving God and stop doing the devil's music. (He flip-flopped between rock 'n' roll and serving the Lord on several occasions in the sixties and seventies.) The second event of that year of course was Elvis's induction in the army on March 24, 1958, as a regular soldier with a shaved head and no special treatment. The third event was the most devastating to keeping good rockabilly and rock 'n' roll music high on the charts. It was the discovery that Jerry Lee Lewis (then twenty-two years old) had married his thirteen-year-old cousin Myra.

That scandal, in the early summer of 1958, was when rockabilly and rock 'n' roll music really died. Not at all like Don McLean would later put out in his song "American Pie." With the exception of Elvis's recordings, mostly made prior to his induction in the service and released throughout 1959, the wildest, big hit artists in rockabilly and rock 'n' roll would never see another great rockin' time in the *Billboard* Top 10 charts again.

Buddy Holly saw the writing on the wall during the summer of 1958. During that time, Brunswick records released the fourth (and what would be the final) 45 under the name The Crickets during Buddy's lifetime. It was in the same up-tempo rockabilly-ish vein as their past releases. The record, "Think It Over," made it up to #27 after its debut in *Billboard* on July 21, 1958, but quickly dropped off the charts a short eight weeks later. The flip side of the record, "Fool's Paradise," a mid-tempo rocker, was on the chart for one week at #58 on August 4, 1958, the same date that "Early in the Morning" on Coral Records, under the name Buddy Holly, debuted in *Billboard*. This was one heck of a good, solid, kickin' song belted out by Buddy at his rockabilly best. A week earlier, "Early in the Morning" had hit the charts by The Rinky-Dinks on the Atco record label. It had originally been recorded and put out under the group name of The Ding Dongs on the Brunswick label. This was done a few weeks prior, and Brunswick was trying to conceal the identity of the lead singer, who was actually Bobby Darin. Atco quickly found out, put a halt to it, picked up the master, and rushed it out to capitalize on the hot novelty song Darin had zoomin' up the charts then called "Splish Splash." A little confusing, but true. Darin co-wrote the song, but Holly's version by far was much, much superior to The Rinky-Dinks, Ding Dongs, whatever. Darin's version reached #24 and stayed on the charts for ten weeks (of course, "Splish Splash" rose to #3). Buddy's version peaked out at #32 and dropped off after only seven weeks. Your difference here, I believe, lies in Darin being a northern pop rock 'n' roller on the rise, while Buddy was a southwestern, gutsy-soundin' rockabilly singer with a real, true, live feel for this type music. Darin's version (recorded before "Splish Splash") wasn't that bad, but it couldn't come close to Holly's intensity. Holly recorded his version in New York City, though. One of his first sessions outside Clovis, New Mexico.

So by the end of September 1958, when "Early in the Morning" by Buddy fell off the charts, good, raw rockabilly wasn't anywhere to be found in the *Billboard* Top 10, 20, 30, and so on, and solid rock 'n' roll was also fadin'. When Buddy's song fell off those charts, the #1 record in the country was the pop song "It's All in the Game," by Tommy Edwards. That's where music was headin'. Not to say we wouldn't have minor flashes of rockabilly-soundin' songs later in '58 and '59, but they were all mostly in the bottom half of the Top 100.

By the early autumn of 1958, Buddy Holly was makin' the biggest changes in his career and music up to this point. He was permanently moving to New York City. He had just recently married his wife, Maria Elena, and got an apartment in Greenwich Village. From all accounts, Buddy wanted his two longtime friends in The Crickets, Joe B. Mauldin and Jerry Allison, to move there with him, but they were homesick for Texas and declined. After constant touring for a year and a half, Buddy, Joe B., and Jerry were all glad for a break. Another break was Buddy's split with Norman Petty and the contracts Petty held on him. While The Crickets' leaving was friendly, some accounts say the split between Holly and Petty was not that easily worked out. But nonetheless, Buddy's next recording session was under the guidance of Dick Jacobs, who produced the four titles that came out of what would be Buddy's final studio recording session, on October 21, 1958, at the Pythian Temple in New York City. Buddy wanted to make a new start and find a song that would put him back at the top of the charts. Good pop music at this time seemed to be the best direction for him to take. All four songs from that session (which wouldn't be heard until after his tragic death) were far from anything he had recorded in the past. Those songs were "True Love Ways," "Moodreams," "Raining in My Heart," and "It Doesn't Matter Anymore." All four of these songs were pop ballads. Buddy was backed by The Dick Jacobs Orchestra. "True Love Ways," which Holly wrote, is a beautiful pop ballad, sung beautifully with a lot of true meaning you can feel in Buddy's voice.

I may offend some Buddy Holly fans by sayin' this, but it needs to be said: Buddy's always been given credit for being the first rock 'n' roll/rockabilly artist to use strings in his music, but it would be more correct to say Buddy Holly was the first *ex*-rock 'n' roll/rockabilly artist to use strings in his music — which was now pop music. I know in my heart Buddy loved rockabilly and rock 'n' roll, but for all commercial purposes it was dead in the fall of '58 when he recorded these songs. And he knew it better than anybody. Oh, Buddy would go on that fatal winter dance party tour and perform all his rockabilly hits, like "That'll Be the Day," "Peggy Sue," "Oh Boy," and others, 'cause the audiences demanded it; they were all well-known big hits. But if rockabilly had really been doin' OK, he wouldn't have had to go way out in the sticks to Clear Lake, Iowa, to perform in the dead of a winter snowstorm.

Buddy asked Waylon Jennings and Tommy Allsup to go out and back him up on that last tour, which they did. Buddy had met Waylon in Texas when Waylon was a disc jockey. Waylon has stated to me and many others that Buddy was the first one in his life to make him believe in himself as an artist and believe that he could achieve anything he wanted in life. Buddy produced Waylon's first record, in September 1958, in Clovis, New Mexico. A few months later, in December, Buddy, along with Phil Everly, produced as well as played rhythm guitar on two songs by Lou Giordona in New York City. Producing is what I believe Buddy would have done if his new direction in music had failed to succeed. He was an intelligent person with street smarts, very determined, and if he was alive today it's more than likely to believe he would have become one of the all-time top producers, like Jimmy Bowen went on to be in Nashville — Bowen also bein' an ex-rockabilly artist from Texas. But Buddy's

rockabilly music was great; Bowen's never did hold up remotely close to his.

Buddy's last chart record before his death, "Heartbeat," debuted in *Billboard* on December 28, 1958, and only reached #82, dropping off the charts after only four weeks. It had been recorded in Clovis, New Mexico, during the summer of '58, with backing by his now-defunct Crickets. So when his plane crashed and he died, he was off the charts.

A final point I feel I have to make is that for years I've been reading in books, magazines, liner notes, etc. that because Buddy Holly wrote most of his own songs, that

Forgettin' to Remember to Forget

If you've been readin' this book from the beginning, you're probably wondering by now why I haven't given you some kind of personal story on seein' a live show of Buddy Holly and The Crickets or maybe gettin' an autograph from him or meeting him by February 1959. I had opportunities in the summer of 1958, as by that time I was fourteen years old and my mom would let me take the streetcar (and later the bus) down to the old Raleigh Hotel in N.W. Washington, D.C., where "The Milt Grant Show" was broadcast live on Channel 5 TV and teenagers would dance to their favorite records of the day. Grant would usually have two, sometimes three guests who had hit records on either the local or the national charts. During that summer I went down to Grant's show eight times, to get autographs from the likes of Dale Hawkins, Vernon Taylor, Chuck Berry, Joe Bennett and The Sparkletones, Jody Reynolds, Link Wray, Ray Vernon, Terry and The Pirates, and even Tommy Sands. So why then did I only buy and love all of Buddy Holly's music, but never really cared to meet him or see a live show he was on?

The answer is easy for me. To be real honest, like it or not, when I watched Buddy Holly and The Crickets on "Ed Sullivan," "American Bandstand," "Milt Grant," and a few others, though I really dug the music a lot, his appearance and stage presence did nothin' for me. He didn't move around hardly at all while playin' guitar, and if he did, it wasn't in a cool way. Now remember, I was only fourteen and was at my most impressionable age, and in '58 I was into seein' a rockin' act. While Buddy's music was good and had a distinctive, unique sound with Allison's different approach of drummin' on tunes like "Peggy Sue," it lacked the frantic abandonment I had heard earlier in Elvis's songs such as "My Baby Left Me," "Jailhouse Rock," "Hard Headed Woman," etc. Also, I had seen Gene Vincent's menacing, tortured, breathy performances of "Be-Bop-A-Lula" both in the film *The Girl Can't Help It* and on "The Ed Sullivan Show," as well as witnessing his live club act. Plus Gene's performance in the film *Hot Rod Gang*, doin' four wild songs, holds up today as still some of the downright coolest rockabilly performances you'll ever see. Both Elvis's and Gene's and also Jerry Lee Lewis's TV and movie performances, dress, and defiant manners (though polite at times during interviews), were rebellious, and they had a tremendous effect on me as well as many other young teenagers in the late fifties. Buddy's music, appearance, and TV performances just did not come close to those I've just mentioned. Buddy and The Crickets were just nice, polite, conservatively dressed cats from Texas, though they laid down some of the best rockabilly music of the late fifties.

For me and a few of my friends in St. Francis De Sales Catholic School who were finally about to graduate and get cut loose from the old-style nuns who had been hammerin' away at us (I'm talkin' about real physical abuse here) for several years about Elvis bein' the devil's disciple and leading us straight into the fires of hell (I had felt like they were the ones who had put me through real hell!), Elvis and Gene were freein' our souls from '56 to '58. I hope you understand, but Buddy Holly just didn't make me feel that way.

made him more of a true artist than Elvis, 'cause Elvis virtually never wrote a single song. I believe if Buddy was with us today he would agree with me, whether Elvis sang a song by Arthur "Big Boy" Crudup, Little Richard, Chuck Berry, or Hank Snow in the 1950s, if you were a rockabilly fan you knew that song belonged to Elvis no matter who had come out with it before him. Listen now, I'm not an Elvis nut. It's only the music with me today that counts at my age, and when I listen to how Elvis interpreted these other artists' songs, it was pure genius on his part, though he wouldn't have wanted to hear that. But just because he failed to write his 1950s material made him in no way inferior to Buddy Holly as bein' a true artist.

I'd be the last one to pick on Buddy Holly, 'cause when I heard the news on my radio the morning of February 3, 1959, that Buddy Holly, The Big Bopper, and Ritchie Valens had all been killed in a plane crash somewhere near Mason City, Iowa, I was stunned. When I got to school, all the kids were talkin' about it. Nothin' since rock 'n' roll and rockabilly music began had ever happened such as this. This plane crash was certainly the first devastating blow to us kids back then. That whole day I remember that they played all Buddy's hits, as well as the ones by The Big Bopper and Ritchie Valens. Buddy's new record had been on the radio for several weeks, but had failed to reach the *Billboard* charts at the time of the plane crash. That song was "It Doesn't Matter Anymore" (written by Paul Anka). At lunch time outside in the schoolyard I remember a few girls crying, and I was real sad. I had never heard Buddy do a song like this. It was really a beautiful song, as was "Raining in My Heart," the flip side, which the radio stations were also playing. I knew there were violins in it, but it would be years later before I found out there were cellos, violas, and even a harp in it also.

Had Buddy Holly not died on that bitter cold, dark early morning in February '59, I don't know, and nobody for that matter can say, how high the song "It Doesn't Matter Anymore" would have gotten to on the charts, but when it finally did debut in *Billboard*, on February 23, 1959, it made it all the way up to #13 and stayed on the charts till the first week of May. It was Buddy's biggest record in over a year. The B side, "Raining in My Heart," made the charts on March 30 and reached #88, then dropped off after two weeks. In the U.S., Coral Records followed it up with "Peggy Sue Got Married" and then "True Love Ways." Both failed to chart over here. "True

Love Ways" should have been a hit, in my opinion. But America and its always-new, youthful music listeners and buyers have always been known for having a short memory when it comes to great artists. Coral Records kept releasing 45s and LPs right on through the sixties. Guys like me were sure glad, 'cause of what kind of garbage was on the charts and radio during the first half of the decade. Overseas in England and many other countries, they weren't so quick to forget. "It Doesn't Matter Anymore" debuted in the British Top 20 on March 7, 1959, and wound up reaching the #1 spot there and stayin' in the Top 20 until August. Buddy's songs continued to peak out in the Top 10 till the end of 1963, well into when The Beatles were the biggest thing in music all over Europe and ready to conquer America within a few months.

It's the music these artists like Buddy Holly, Elvis, Gene Vincent, and others leave us that really counts the most. If it's great, like most of theirs was, it will inspire generations to come to keep reworking it. Buddy Holly has influenced too many artists and bands from the sixties right up to the present to mention, but here's just a few: His music certainly influenced The Beatles (especially Paul McCartney); even their name was a take-off on The Crickets. The Hollies also took their name because of the influence Buddy had on their music. The Rolling Stones were probably the first band or artist to chart one of his songs, "Not Fade Away," both here in the U.S., at #48, and in England, at #3. This was during the spring of 1964. In the seventies Linda Ronstadt had several big chart hits with Buddy's songs. Fleetwood Mac and Eric Clapton also were heavily influenced, and in the early and mid 1980s there was no denying Marshall Crenshaw's original music was pure Buddy Holly-sounding all the way. The 1978 major motion picture *The Buddy Holly Story*, starring Gary Busey in the title role, garnered Busey an Academy Award nomination for his dynamic, charismatic performance (though he did not win) and was a huge box office smash. This movie drew a lot of criticism from Holly's friends, family, and fans 'cause the facts were so wrong and distorted, but it holds up because of Busey's great performance and renditions of Holly's songs. Buddy's music will always live on and keep being reissued to new generations of fans and artists alike. He'll always be one of the top pioneers in rockabilly music, and it will always be that music that will come back time and time again. It was Buddy Holly's original brand of Texas rockabilly that should always make the Lone Star State proud of its native son.

I've already mentioned Don McLean's 1971 hit "American Pie." I don't mean to take anything away from Buddy Holly's importance as a rockabilly artist when I say that McLean got it wrong — the music had already died before Holly's plane went down. On the other hand, I have to say here there was a tribute song devoted to Buddy Holly that did him justice. The song, "Tribute to Buddy Holly," came out on Holly's old label, Coral Records, by an artist by the name of Mike Berry. Berry was a British rocker. This song didn't make the charts here in the U.S. upon its release in the fall of 1961 (as by now the pop music that was comin' out was mostly pure fluff), but it did get some airplay in the Washington, D.C., area, so I got a hold of a copy of it. It made it up to #18 in England and was a big hit in other European countries. It's the best rockabilly-type tribute to Buddy Holly and his music you'd ever want to hear.

Well, up to now I've covered extensively five of the six artists in rockabilly music between 1954 and 1958 that were the biggest stars and had the biggest hit records during rockabilly's heyday, along with being the most influential to later generations: Elvis, Gene Vincent, Carl Perkins, Jerry Lee Lewis, and Buddy Holly. That only really leaves one more: Eddie Cochran.

Eddie Cochran

Eddie Cochran, like both Carl Perkins and Buddy Holly, wrote or co-wrote the majority of his hits and other songs he recorded. Eddie was the youngest of five children. All the rest of his brothers and sisters were born in Oklahoma City, Oklahoma, where his parents originally came from, and after Eddie became a rockabilly star in the late fifties he always referred to Oklahoma City as his birthplace, as he was so proud of his Okie heritage. But in the early 1930s, when the Great Depression hit the hardest, Eddie's father, Frank, moved his family to Albert Lea, Minnesota (about ninety miles south of Minneapolis) after receiving a job offer there. Eddie was born there on October 3, 1938. He started playing guitar when he was twelve years old. The following year his family moved to California, to a suburb of Los Angeles called Bell Gardens. There he began playing in various musical groups and showing a real talent as a guitarist.

In January 1955, just a few months after starting high school, he dropped out to tour California with Hank Cochran (no relation) and his new hillbilly band. Hank decided to call the group The Cochran Brothers. By May, the band was signed to a one-year contract with Ekko

Records, a little label based in Memphis. They immediately recorded four songs, two which were released shortly thereafter as their first single record — "Mr. Fiddle" b/w "Two Blue Singing Stars," a tribute song to the late country singers Jimmy Rodgers and Hank Williams. In October, Ekko released the other two songs — "Guilty Conscience" and "Your Tomorrow Never Comes." All four of these songs were basic, straight-out hillbilly, and sales were poor.

It was during October 1955 that Eddie Cochran met Jerry Capehart. Capehart was ten years older than Eddie, and he was working at trying to get local musicians to record songs he was writing. For four years, from late '55 to late '59, Capehart co-wrote with Eddie many of the songs he recorded, including his biggest hits, "Summertime Blues" and "C'mon Everybody." He would also act as manager, promoter, booking agent, road manager, etc. for Eddie, as well as being the person responsible for getting him signed to Liberty Records, where Eddie had all his hits.

At the end of 1955, The Cochran Brothers were still under contract to Ekko Records, even after the lackluster sales of their first two records. They wouldn't be free to record under their own name for another label until the spring of 1956. So Capehart used them to back him up on two records that came out on the Cash record label (a subsidiary of Dolphin) in early '56. They were all songs he had written, and both records failed to garner much sales. In anticipation of the end of The Cochran Brothers' contract with Ekko, Capehart put them into the studio in April 1956 to cut a bunch of songs he could shop to other labels. This session was a turning point in both the Cochrans' careers. "Heartbreak Hotel," Elvis's first record for RCA Victor, was climbing into the Top 10 on the *Billboard* pop charts, and Eddie wanted to be part of this new sound. Eddie and Hank Cochran had written a song, called "Pink Peg Slacks," that was different from any of the hillbilly numbers they had done up to then. It was pure raw rockabilly, though very primitive sounding. Another song, "Latch On," had a similar feel to it. Even the ballads recorded at this session were not of the country type The Cochran Brothers had done previously.

They were under contract for one final session for Ekko Records, and that took place right around the end of April '56. Four songs came out of this session, and it was the official end of The Cochran Brothers' recording career, though in recent years it's been written that Hank and Eddie did another session sometime in July. Ekko Records released the third and final record by The Cochran Brothers in June '56, from this April session: "Tired and Sleepy" b/w "Fool's Paradise." "Tired and Sleepy" is a killer rockabilly song all the way. Both Eddie's and Hank's vocals had adapted to the new frantic youth music. But while Eddie (who was still only seventeen years old) was gettin' into this wild-type hillbilly with a hard beat, Hank was not. The record was only out a short time when Hank and Eddie parted ways. Hank went on to write songs for some of the biggest stars in country music. Eddie stayed with Capehart as a solo artist.

During June of '56, Capehart and The Cochran Brothers were mostly on the road. When they weren't, Capehart and Eddie were writing songs together. During this time, Capehart landed both Eddie and Hank Cochran a one-record deal for each of 'em to record rockabilly numbers on the Crest record label, out of Hollywood, California. So a session date was set up in mid July '56, and Eddie recorded "Skinny Jim" b/w "Half Loved." "Skinny Jim" was weakly written, but Eddie's vocal delivery was fairly good on this primitive-soundin' frantic rockabilly song. "Half Loved" proved that no matter how hard Eddie tried, he couldn't handle a real slow ballad at this early age. Hank cut "Let's Coast Awhile" b/w "Drowning All My Sorrows." They were both pretty good attempts on Hank's part at trying to do rockabilly, but he was so uncomfortable with 'em he had Crest put the record out under the name Bo Davis. Both records were released in August 1956, and both died a quick death. After that, Hank was out of the picture for good as far as rockabilly went, and Eddie spent the rest of the summer and well into the fall of 1956 doin' session work for many different artists, mostly country ones (it's been said he would rather play guitar than sing), and writing songs with Jerry Capehart and others.

It was sometime during July 1956, when Eddie and Jerry Capehart were doing background music for a low-budget film, when the producer asked if Eddie could sing. When Eddie told him yes, he asked if Eddie would be interested in appearing in another film a friend of his was directing. Eddie thought at the time he was joking, but told him yeah, that sure he was interested, and for the producer to give him a call. The next day the guy called Eddie and told him to cut an acetate on his song "Twenty Flight Rock," which he did, and on August 14, 1956, Eddie went to the Twentieth Century-Fox studios in Hollywood and they filmed his cameo spot for the movie *The Girl Can't Help It* (see Chapter 2).

On September 8, Liberty Records signed Eddie to a one-year contract. It only made sense. By the summer of 1956 every major label in the U.S. was lookin' for competition for RCA Victor, who by this time had Elvis in the #1 slot with two million-selling singles and a million-selling album. Though Liberty Records had planned to release "Twenty Flight Rock" in December 1956 in conjunction with the release of the film, it was shelved for a full year, as they had decided to put Eddie in the studio in January 1957 and record a version of a song called "Sittin' in the Balcony." This song was out on a small independent label in Durham, North Carolina, called Colonial Records (who later in '57 and '58 put out several good rockabilly records on Crash Craddock), by an artist who then went under the name Johnny Dee, who was actually a young John D. Loudermilk. Dee's version of "Sittin' in the Balcony" was sellin' a lot of copies and receiving heavy airplay in a number of major markets around the U.S. by January '57, and Colonial Records was offering to sell the master to the highest-bidding major label. Liberty lost out to ABC Paramount (who had also purchased "A Rose and a Baby Ruth" by George Hamilton IV — a hokey teen ballad that had a great fast-movin' hillbilly/rockabilly B side called "If You Don't Know [I Ain't-a-Gonna Tell You]"). So when the heads at Liberty Records lost out on picking up "Sittin' in the Balcony" by Johnny Dee, they decided to have Eddie cover the song. (Right before this happened, Eddie made a second appearance in a real low-budget movie called *Untamed Youth*, singing a song called "Cotton Picker." I have to say it was pretty poor.)

Both versions of "Sittin' in the Balcony" were gittin' steady airplay by DJs in February and March 1957. I did like "Sittin' in the Balcony" back then, but it wasn't really a rockabilly record like "Twenty Flight Rock" was. For more than three decades now, Eddie's song "Twenty Flight Rock" has become a rockabilly classic covered by artists and bands on small independent labels as well as top stars like The Rolling Stones and The Stray Cats. But in the spring of 1957 it was the mid-tempo teen-oriented "Sittin' in the Balcony" that turned out to be the first record to put Eddie Cochran on the charts. Johnny Dee's version hit *Billboard* first, on March 16, and Eddie's version came on the following week, on March 23. Eddie did have the stronger version, and while Dee's version only reached #38 and stayed on the charts eleven weeks, Eddie's version made it into the Top 20, peaking out at #18 and remaining on the charts for thirteen weeks.

Eddie was now a full-fledged rockabilly/rock 'n' roll star, and in April '57 he went out on tour on all of the package shows of the day (by now he had a top booking agent in New York) and stayed on 'em practically the whole time throughout the end of the year. The little time he did come off the road he spent in the studio laying guitar tracks down on too many artists to name. Eddie would continue to do this session work right up until he left for his final fatal overseas tour in January 1960. He just loved playing guitar, arranging songs, and helping out with ideas on all kinds of songs.

In 1957, when rockabilly and rock 'n' roll ruled the music business, the package shows were the thing of the day. All the top promoters and biggest DJs in the U.S. had 'em. They played all over the country in the biggest movie houses, opera houses, outdoor stadiums, amphitheaters, and so on. They were all sellouts most of the time also. Each one would have a minimum of eight or nine acts and a maximum of up to fifteen or sixteen. They'd travel around the country on big buses with huge banners advertising their shows. There would always be what I'd call today a house band that would back up all the lesser-known artists or the ones with maybe only one hit under their belt; the headliners on the show would come on at the end and have their own musicians backing them up. The lesser-known acts would usually do anywhere from two to four songs, while the headliners would always do between five and seven songs, sometimes more if the audience demanded it. All of 1957, 1958, and even most of 1959 were definitely the greatest times for these type shows. Your local, lesser-known, up-and-coming artists, and sometimes major stars, could also be seen at various venues like National Guard armories and fire halls, but in the late fifties they didn't play the night club circuit for the most part, because they all appealed to the twelve-to-seventeen age market. Eddie Cochran played on all these package tour shows, as well as makin' the circuit on all the teen dance shows, such as "American Bandstand." During the spring and summer of '57 he was also seen in both films *The Girl Can't Help It* and *Untamed Youth*, which were continually showin' on the drive-in circuit.

Elvis wasn't on any of those package tours I just spoke of, 'cause when he toured he didn't need any supporting acts. But Eddie Cochran did need them, and he built up close friendships. Especially the one with Gene Vincent, whom he first met in April 1957, when the two of them were doing a week-long stint with about eight or nine other acts at a big theater in Philadelphia. The two of them struck up a friendship during that week that would last right to the final day of Eddie's life in April 1960. Today when rockabilly fans think of Gene they automatically think of Eddie and vice versa. On The Stray Cats' final album for EMI America in 1989 there was even a song on it called "(We're Gonna Rock with) Gene and Eddie," written by Brian Setzer. Even today The Stray Cats still perform the song live all around the world, and fans always go wild as they realize the three members of The Stray Cats got more from Gene and Eddie than any other rockabilly artists that ever lived.

Two members of Gene's fifties band The Blue Caps, Bubba Facenda and Dickie Harrell, remember that Eddie turned up on the bill of more shows with Gene than any other rocker in '57 and '58. They both told me wherever they were on the road goin' into a new town for a series of shows, no sooner would they get to the theater's dressing room and turn around and there'd be Eddie again. On one of Gene's final recording sessions with The Blue Caps, during the final week of March 1958 at Capitol Records Studios in Hollywood, Eddie was in town and found out Gene and his gang were cutting new songs for what would become the final album before Gene would split with The Blue Caps in the fall of '58. So Eddie came by four days of that week, sang backup vocals on seven of the songs that were recorded, and according to Bubba Facenda came up with a lot of good ideas on the arrangements of certain songs as well as doin' all the bass vocal parts. It was Eddie's deep bass vocal that started out the classic Vincent song "Git It." Eddie's "Well oh, well oh, wop, whip, whip, whips" are legendary and are really what makes that song exceptional, along with, as always, Gene's sultry vocals. (Dave Edmunds did a fine cover of this song in the seventies.)

Eddie was touring and riding pretty high in the spring of '57 when "Sittin' in the Balcony" began to slip down on the charts. Liberty Records decided to release his second single in May. Eddie had recorded the two sides in March. The A side was another sugar-coated teen mid-tempo tune called "One Kiss." Eddie wasn't a great singer by any means, but he had this gravelly, gutsy vocal ability to put across even sappy songs such as "One Kiss." Eddie and Jerry Capehart wrote the song together, as well as its flip side, "Mean When I'm Mad." I have to mention here that Jerry Capehart was rarely separated from Eddie all during his touring schedules throughout 1957. As far as this new record, it never even made it onto the *Billboard* charts, though the company spared no expense in promotion in the trade papers, as well as putting a full-color picture sleeve on it — the only one Eddie would have on a single during his lifetime. It's a high-dollar sleeve today if you can find it. But all this was to no avail, as the record really didn't break out big in any of the major markets and the DJs didn't pick up on it. I might add that "Mean When I'm Mad" holds up real well. That was the side I thought was best back then. While it too was mid-tempo, Eddie's vocals were tough soundin' and you could hear a cuttin' edge to 'em. It had a bit of a blues feel to it, but musically could have been produced a lot meaner, which the song's lyrics called for. It was the best cut out of the four songs Liberty had released thus far.

Liberty Records wasn't about to give up on Eddie, though, even with the failure of "One Kiss." It's just that they had their own ideas on what they felt the teen market would go for. When the Liberty Records heads found that the DJs were still playing "Sittin' in the Balcony" and that "One Kiss" didn't stand a chance, they put Eddie back in the studio for his third session of 1957. In July, during one of his tour breaks, they had chosen some songs they wanted him to record along with a couple he and Jerry Capehart had written. On this session they wanted enough material for a planned future release of an album on Eddie. They held back one song, titled "Drive-In Show," maybe 'cause they felt it could be as big as or bigger than "Sittin' in the Balcony"; it sort of had the same theme to it. Poor Eddie, they had him singin' these hokey, trite, teen-oriented lyrics such as "I bet my peanuts to a candy bar you'll be cuter than a movie star." "Drive-In Show" did make the *Billboard* pop charts, in September 1957, but only got up to #82 and dropped off after six weeks. Again, on the B side, "Am I Blue," Eddie rocked hard. This is one real hot song, mainly 'cause Eddie hit you in the face with some exciting rockabilly-ish vocals. His voice was in great rockin' form on this cover tune.

Even though "Drive-In Show" only got up to #82, Eddie was constantly in demand for shows and touring. In early October 1957, he did his first shows overseas. He flew to Australia to be on a number of shows in various cities that was headlined by Little Richard and Gene Vincent and The Blue Caps. Another American artist, Alis Lesley (see Chapter 5), was also on the bill. Eddie was backed up by Johnny O'Keefe's band, The Deejays. O'Keefe was Australia's #1 rockabilly/rock 'n' roll artist in the late fifties. Eddie left the tour in mid October and came back to America for a chance to join up with Irving

Feld's "Biggest Show of Stars" of '57, which was headlined by Chuck Berry, Buddy Holly and The Crickets, Fats Domino, Paul Anka, and others. This show crisscrossed the U.S. for the next two months, playing in almost every major city. Eddie would wind up his "Biggest Show of Stars" tour in December '57 and go on to finish out the year playing Alan Freed's annual "Christmas Holiday Spectacular" shows at the Brooklyn Paramount, with a lineup that included Chuck Berry, Jerry Lee Lewis, Buddy Holly and The Crickets, Jo Ann Campbell, The Platters, The Everly Brothers, and a bunch of others. Alan Freed was always the MC. Ask anybody who was there and they'll tell ya these'll always remain the greatest rock 'n' roll shows of all time.

In November 1957, Liberty finally released "Twenty Flight Rock." The B side, "Cradle Baby," had been recorded for Eddie's planned album, which also was released in November. "Cradle Baby" was a solid up-tempo track and great for a B side because of Eddie's energetic vocals once more. Eddie's vocals were raw, riveting, primitive rockabilly, even on his pop-type songs. Unfortunately, Liberty usually backed him up with The Johnny Mann Singers, who most of the time just weren't needed or were so smooth-soundin' they messed up Eddie's vocal and lead guitar work, so help me. The Jordanaires would-a worked better, but if Eddie needed any vocal backup, it should-a been a group like The Blue Caps.

In 1956 I started checking out the *Billboard* charts to see how high up my favorite songs were goin'. I've always been into statistics. Well, when I saw that Eddie Cochran's record "Twenty Flight Rock" never even made it onto the *Billboard* pop charts, it was hard to believe, but I reckon when you think back on it now, one reason could be that Liberty Records could have waited too long to release it. The song was recorded as a demo in the summer of '56, and their planned release date was December '56 or January '57. At that time rockabilly and rock 'n' roll were still in the primitive stages, with some of Elvis's old Sun songs (now re-released on RCA Victor) like "I Don't Care If the Sun Don't Shine" hittin' the pop charts along with "Roll Over Beethoven" by Chuck Berry and "Be-Bop-A-Lula" by Gene Vincent and The Blue Caps. But by November '57, all these artists had a more technically advanced sound high on the charts, like Elvis's "Jailhouse Rock," Chuck Berry's "Rock 'n' Roll Music," and Gene Vincent's "Lotta Lovin'." All these were solid and rockin' — they were just more polished than the songs they had out a year prior. So I guess it was just bad timin' for Eddie's "Twenty Flight Rock," though almost forty years later I hear new bands consistently playin' that one, and they'd never think of singin' "Sittin' in the Balcony."

When Eddie's first album, *Singin' to My Baby*, came out, I was just finally glad to get it (it would turn out to be the only one released during his lifetime). "Twenty Flight Rock" wasn't on it. I remember gettin' it right before Christmas 1957. I wasn't buyin' many albums back then. Forty-fives were the main thing in late '57 for teenagers anyways. This LP had a really cool lookin' cover with Eddie and his classic Gretsch guitar. But the songs on it, though good, were a bit puzzling. I had four of the twelve songs on 45s. Six of the others were either ballads, such as "Have I Told You Lately That I Love You," or teen-type sounds, like "Proud of You." The two best rockin' and rockabilly type songs on the whole album that I didn't have were "Completely Sweet" and "Stockings and Shoes." Little did I know at Christmas 1957 that the best was yet to come with Eddie Cochran's music.

When the new year of 1958 came in, Eddie was still a hot act on the touring circuit, even with the lack of sales on his last couple of singles. His new LP was in the stores and doin' well. But though he played guitar on four or five sessions for artists signed to different labels, Eddie really hadn't recorded any new material for his label Liberty in almost six months. There were some major changes in store. The second week of January 1958, Eddie went into Liberty Custom Recorders Studio in Hollywood to cut a couple new songs. Before this he had done all his recording at Goldstar Studios in Hollywood. He had recorded practically all his recordings at Goldstar for over a year and a half, goin' back to The Cochran Brothers' material. Goldstar was a popular demo-type studio, 'cause their rates were lower than most of the others. Up until his final recording session, he would now do most of his own recording sessions at Liberty Custom Recorders, but would still always go back to Goldstar to play on other artists' recordings plus do demos of his own, including numerous instrumentals, as well as start to get into producing other artists. Another important factor starting in 1958 was that he seemed to gain some control on the choice of material he was recording, and finally it seemed The Johnny Mann Singers were gone from all of his future recordings.

The two songs Eddie recorded at his first session in January '58 were "Jeannie, Jeannie, Jeannie" and "Pretty Girl." "Jeannie, Jeannie, Jeannie" was the A side of his first single of '58, released the last week of January. It was one hard-drivin' rocker. Though Eddie didn't write this song, it was tailor-made for his vocals and lead guitar work. Today it stands out as a classic rockabilly number and is sung and recorded by young rockabilly bands and artists around the world. It remains a favorite of rockabilly fans everywhere. The Stray Cats recorded it on their first album, back in 1981. The B side, "Pocketful of Hearts," had been recorded six months earlier. Not too bad of a mid-tempo song, though. "Jeannie, Jeannie, Jeannie" did scratch the bottom of the *Billboard* pop charts for one week, on March 10, 1958, but that was it.

The next song Liberty tried was called "Teresa." They wanted Eddie to cut it with a female chorus backing him up. He recorded it on March 3, 1958, and it was probably the worst of the sappy teen-oriented material (especially lyrically) that Liberty put out on him. I guess they felt that Eddie, with his good looks, would eventually crack the charts with syrupy fluff like "Teresa" and break into the teen idol market that was by now starting to hit into high gear. As always, Eddie's great-soundin' vocals, with that southern drawl of his, at least make this song listenable. But today when I hear the mushy female backup chorus I feel like saying I'm sorry, Johnny Mann, I'll take your singing group over this. "Teresa" never even made it onto *Billboard* at all. That might have sent a message to the Liberty Records heads that this stuff was never gonna cut it with Eddie Cochran and his original and unique guitar style. The B side of "Teresa" was fantastic. It was the other song he had recorded in early January '58, when he cut "Jeannie, Jeannie, Jeannie." It was called "Pretty Girl," and Eddie had co-written it with Jerry Capehart. Eddie was punchin' out solid rockabilly all the way in its finest form. Excellent vocal and lead guitar work. But hey, it was "Teresa" that Liberty was pushin', and to no avail. "Pretty Girl" was only lucky enough to get heard by Eddie's loyal fans like me who were continuing to buy everything that came out on him back in the late fifties. "Teresa" was probably the biggest bomb and the weakest-selling record Eddie ever had with Liberty Records.

Eddie continued to do personal appearances around the country from March to May 1958, as well as playing on a couple studio dates for other artists and singing backup with Gene Vincent's Blue Caps at the end of March. Jerry Capehart (who was still acting as Eddie's manager and working closely with him) realized as Eddie did that they needed a real big hit record to put him over the top and keep momentum goin' for his personal appearances and TV dance shows. They needed to come up with something really good. It happened that in late April a sixteen-year-old girl named Sharon Sheeley, who was an aspiring songwriter at the time, came by to see Jerry Capehart to play him a new song she had written called "Love Again" that she thought would be perfect for Eddie to record. She had gotten Ricky Nelson to record the very first song she had ever written, "Poor Little Fool," which had just been released as the A side of Nelson's new record She had first been introduced to Eddie by Phil Everly when she was his date backstage at Alan Freed's big Christmas show at the Brooklyn Paramount the previous December. Eddie didn't remember her, but she remembered Eddie. After listening to "Love Again," Capehart felt Eddie should record it, and if Ricky Nelson (who was the #2 top selling artist at this time; only Elvis was in front of him) was recording the girl's songs, there was no reason for Eddie not to take a shot on one of hers. But they'd have to come up with a song for the other side.

Eddie came over to Capehart's on a couple of different nights, where the two of them would sit around and try out some new songs other artists had given them and try to come up with ideas to write a new song between the two of 'em. According to Baker Knight, who had come to L.A. by the early part of 1958 and started hanging around with Eddie and Jerry Capehart in the hopes of gettin' one of his songs recorded or maybe a rockabilly record deal, he was there on the night Eddie and Capehart came up with a new song. It was the song that Eddie Cochran would be forever remembered for. According to Knight, Eddie had been foolin' around with a speeded-up blues-soundin' guitar riff, and Capehart had come up with a couple lines and a title: "Summertime Blues." Knight goes on to say, "I was supposed to help 'em write some on it, but we were all young back then, and as always we'd be partyin' and knockin' back some beers, and we'd get sidetracked 'cause none of us were comin' up with anything worthwhile on 'Summertime Blues,' so I went in the other room and crashed out for a couple hours. When I woke up, I'll be damned if they didn't have the whole song finished. I can still picture Eddie singin' 'there ain't no cure for the summertime blues' in Jerry's living room." Shortly after this, Knight wrote the song "Lonesome Town," which became a Top 10 hit for Ricky Nelson at the end of 1958. In 1959, Ray Peterson recorded Knight's composition "The Wonder of You," which hit big that year and again in 1964 and went on to become a classic song since Elvis Presley's version hit the Top 10 in 1970. Knight had some rockabilly records out on the Kit and Decca record labels in '56 and '57, but today he seems proudest of Eddie Cochran playin' guitar on one of his songs, "Just Relax," which came out on Coral Records in 1959.

Eddie went in the Goldstar Studios (which he still preferred over Liberty Custom Recorders) the first week of May 1958 and cut "Love Again," and the following week went back to Goldstar, this time to cut "Summertime Blues." Capehart and Sharon Sheeley were present at both sessions. After Liberty Records heard it, they decided to release it almost immediately, because "Teresa" had been the biggest bomb of Eddie's career. So a month after "Teresa" had come out they released "Love Again" as the A side and "Summertime Blues" as the B side. No more needs to be said on the ones who choose which side should be pushed. It went out on June 11, 1958. It was pretty common in the late fifties for rock 'n' roll DJs to flip a record over to see if they or the kids listenin' liked the other side better. A good example of this is when Jack Scott's first big hit, "Leroy," started takin' off in late May 1958 and the DJs flipped it over and found "My True Love" on the B side about a month later and started givin' that side all the airplay. Though "Leroy" started out strong, it only rose to #25 on *Billboard*, while "My True Love" got all the way up to #3. In the case of "Love Again" b/w "Summertime Blues" by Eddie, it was hot outside in June of '58, and on the grooves of the B side of "Love Again" the DJs and kids heard flames comin' through on Eddie's blisterin' guitar riffs and gravel-type vocals. "Love Again" never stood a chance. Because of its late release, "Summertime Blues" didn't make its debut onto the *Billboard* pop charts until August 4, but it reached a peak at #8 by late September and stayed on the charts for sixteen weeks. Eddie finally had his first Top 10 hit. (In the summer of 1994, thirty-six years later, Alan Jackson had a #1 hit on the *Billboard* country charts with "Summertime Blues.")

Eddie had established himself at last as a major star by the fall of 1958 with "Summertime Blues." He continued to tour throughout the rest of '58, and in between he was always in the studio, recording his own songs or producing and playing on other artists' recordings. His follow-up record to "Summertime Blues" was another great rockin' song that he and Capehart had written, called "C'mon Everybody." After its debut in *Billboard* on November 24, it rose to a high of only #35, but it stayed on the charts for twelve weeks. Eddie Cochran was hittin' his stride in rockabilly music by early '59, recording some of his finest songs. His guitar and vocal styles were unique and strictly his own. What I was waitin' for at that time was for Liberty to release a second LP on him. That was always the normal thing to do after an artist had a huge hit like "Summertime Blues," but it never happened.

During December 1958, Eddie was one of the stars on a huge package show at the Lowe's State Theater in New York City put together and hosted by Alan Freed. It featured some of the greatest artists in rock 'n' roll and rockabilly at that time, such as Chuck Berry, Jackie Wilson, The Everly Brothers, The Cadillacs, Jo Ann Campbell, The Flamingos, The Crests, Jimmy Clanton, and several others. Eddie, who had just recently turned twenty years old, had Sharon Sheeley with him, who was his steady girlfriend by this time. Alan Freed had a deal with the Hal Roach Studios to do a quick teenage music flick, titled *Go, Johnny, Go*, to be filmed in early January 1959. It would star the rising new teen idol of the day, Jimmy Clanton. Freed wanted Eddie to do a couple of songs in it. Eddie and Capehart had several new ones they had written together that they were planning to record for Eddie's next single release. They were "Teenage Heaven," "My Way" (two of the strongest Eddie Cochran rockabilly songs you'd ever want to hear; George Thorogood had "My Way" on one of his albums in the late seventies), and "I'll Remember." They filmed Eddie singin' "Teenage Heaven" and "I'll Remember," but the latter song got cut and wasn't seen in the film, and as far as I know has been lost forever. "Teenage Heaven" was a really good song, but his performance of it in on screen was downright silly — dressed in a dull sweater and slacks, not playin' his guitar but acting like it was a girl he was dancing with. But I guess they told him how they wanted him to perform it, and that's Hollywood.

Nineteen fifty-nine was tough on real rock 'n' roll and rockabilly performers such as Eddie, Jack Scott, Ronnie Hawkins, Gene Vincent, and others 'cause of all the Fabians and Rydell-type pretty boys, but you'll read about that in Chapter 6. Eddie's new single, "Teenage

Heaven," released in January 1959, only sat in the *Billboard* Top Pop 100 charts for one week, on March 16, 1959, at #99. When Eddie heard the news of the plane crash in Iowa that took the lives of Buddy Holly, Ritchie Valens, and The Big Bopper, it hit him hard. He had done shows with all of 'em, but he and Buddy had become good friends and had some good times together on the road. Two days after the crash, on February 5, 1959, Eddie went into Goldstar Studios and recorded a version of a tribute song called "Three Stars." Eddie's version of the song wouldn't be released until many years after his own death. At the same time, the writer of the song, a disc jockey by the name of Tommy Dee, also recorded it, and the Crest label released it almost immediately; it debuted on the *Billboard* pop charts on March 30, reaching a high of #11 and staying on the charts for twelve weeks. But Eddie's version had much more feeling than Tommy Dee's did. It was a really sad song.

Eddie was still in demand and stayed on the road across the U.S. performing live shows. As usual, when he wasn't performing, he was actively doin' session work, right on through to the end of 1959. One of the artists he played guitar for on a late-1959 session in Hollywood was ex-Sun rockabilly artist Roy Orbison, who was makin' the changeover into pop-teen music with a song called "Sarah Lee."

In April '59, Eddie recorded a great rockabilly number called "Weekend," but it wouldn't be released until after his death. He went back in the studio in June and recorded what would be his next single release, "Somethin' Else," which was Eddie once again beltin' out some of the gutsiest lyrics and layin' down more of the most solid, electrifying rockabilly guitar riffs anyone could ask for. Even the B side, Eddie's mid-tempo version of "The Boll Weevil Song," holds up well. When I first heard it after its release in July 1959, I was lookin' for it in *Billboard*. It was such a good song I was thinkin' then it might not even make it. But it did finally debut in *Billboard* on August 31, and to my pleasant surprise got up to #58 and stayed on the charts for nine weeks. "Somethin' Else" is definitely one of the best roarin' rockers that hit the charts during late 1959. It's a shame it had to be his last chart record.

His next release, "Halleujah, I Love Her So" b/w "Little Angel," released in October '59, never even made it onto the charts, though it did get some good airplay. Eddie was still doin' a lot of tourin', especially throughout the midwestern states, and he was one of the few who hadn't given up on rockabilly and real rock 'n' roll. By the end of 1959, though, Eddie and Jerry Capehart pretty much ended their relationship. They each wanted to make their own decisions concerning their careers. Also, according to Capehart, by the end of 1959 Eddie was pretty much fed up with the pop music scene. When I talked with Eddie's mother, Alice Cochran, on the phone back in 1980, she told me it wasn't that so much as it was all the traveling and shows on the road to promote his records that he was most tired of. She told me she remembered Eddie tellin' her that after he did this three-month tour of England in early 1960, he wasn't goin' on the road any more. He was only gonna do session work and get into the production end of the business.

Before he left on his final tour of Britain in mid January 1960, Eddie went to Goldstar Studios one last time and recorded three more songs, so that Liberty would have new material to release while he was overseas. The last songs he recorded were one he co-wrote with his brother Bob Cochran called "Three Steps to Heaven," a good rockin' cover version of a country song called "Cut Across Shorty," and a song Sharon Sheeley had written called "Cherished Memories." "Three Steps to Heaven" b/w "Cut Across Shorty" would get released here in the

U.S. while Eddie was still on tour in England, but it failed to make the charts here, even after Eddie's death only a month later. The fickle teens here in the U.S. had for the most part forgotten Eddie by then. But the kids in England sure hadn't. They had their own rock 'n' roll and rockabilly idols who had started doin' well over there (in my opinion, the best was Billy Fury), but they were hungering for these American originals like Gene Vincent and Eddie Cochran.

Eddie arrived in England on January 10, 1960. He and Gene Vincent proved to be a one-two punch knockout package all over England, Scotland, and everywhere they went over there. The promoters were ecstatic at the response and sales receipts from all the sold-out shows. It was a grueling tour at a rapid pace, and besides doin' all the concerts there was always the radio DJs of the day that Eddie and Gene had to do interviews with. It must have rejuvenated Eddie's interest in live performing, 'cause before it was finished on April 16, Eddie had agreed to come back within a couple of weeks to rejoin Gene for another ten-week tour, starting on April 27, 1960. Eddie had to be back in California no later than April 17, 'cause he had signed commitments he had to fulfill. Sharon Sheeley, who by hers and most accounts was Eddie's fiance at this time, had flown over to join Eddie on April 4, and she's said in interviews that she

Forgettin' to Remember to Forget

Well, let me tell ya, when I read the news of Eddie's death on the mornin' of April 18, 1960, it completely devastated me. I was sixteen years old at the time, and I couldn't hold back the tears. My mother couldn't understand at all why I was so upset. I can remember her saying to me, "You didn't know this person. He's just a singer." There's no way she could have known what Eddie and his music meant to me. I had never had a parent, brother, sister, or anyone in the immediate family or close to me die and just be gone that quick before this. Eddie Cochran was the first. By this time I was a regular dancer on the Milt Grant TV show, and while I had seen Eddie on it several times since 1957, I figured I'd get the chance to meet him, as he'd have another hit record before too long and hit D.C. and Grant's show to promote it.

One thing his death did for me, though, was I knew from that moment on I was gonna dedicate the rest of my life to his kind of music, hard hittin', in your face, hot cookin' rockabilly and rock 'n' roll. His death caused me to just walk around in a fog for the next several days and try to hold the tears back. I skipped school for the first time the Tuesday afterwards (Easter Monday was a holiday). All I could do was play his records over and over again.

In his song "Teenage Heaven," Eddie sang about what every sixteen-year-old cat like me wanted to hear. His words in that song were all I needed to keep me goin'. The ones like "I want a house with a pool, shorter hours in school, and a room with my own private phone, while Dad picked up all the bills, and yeah man, that's Heaven to me." That pretty much sums it all up.

and Eddie were planning to be married when they got back to California.

If you talk to anyone who was there, they'll tell you that Eddie Cochran and Gene Vincent did some of their greatest rockabilly and rock 'n' roll shows ever over there. It must be true, judging from photos of Eddie on stage in England; these are the only photos of him I've ever seen with him wearin' leather pants. They sure wouldn't-a put up with that in the early spring of 1960 here in the States.

All of it came to a sudden end, though, in the early morning hours of Easter Sunday, April 17, 1960. The driver of the cab that was taking Eddie, along with Sharon Sheeley and Gene Vincent (who was asleep in the back seat), to the airport lost control of the car on a bad curve he was takin' at an estimated seventy miles an hour and it flipped over a number of times and finally crashed into a concrete light post about 150 feet away. Eddie died of head injuries. I've heard that Eddie and Sharon were singing "California Here I Come" on the way to that airport that night. The driver's and Sharon Sheeley's

injuries were minor, and Gene Vincent was only in the hospital a few days recovering from a broken collar bone, but one of the truly great rockabilly and rock 'n' roll artists of all time was gone from sight, out of this world forever. I know Gene Vincent never really recovered from losing his best friend. I don't know which path in music Eddie Cochran would have taken had he lived. It's been written he might have gone into the commercial-soundin' junk that they were shovin' out in 1960, as other former rockabilly stars I admired, like Johnny Burnette, went on to do, with songs like "You're Sixteen."

Liberty Records went on to release a few singles and a couple albums over here after Eddie's death. The title of one of those early-1960s albums couldn't have been more appropriate. It was called "Never to Be Forgotten." And while the Bobbys who were so popular at that time soon would be forgotten, Eddie Cochran and his music never would, to this very day. Eddie's bigger than ever all over the world, and I'm really glad of it, for he was one of the greatest artists in rockabilly history.

Other Artists Still Influential Today

*U*p to this point I feel I've given you the facts, some statistics, and my honest feelings on the six most important artists from rockabilly's brief beginning and heyday between 1954 and 1958, those being Elvis Presley, Gene Vincent, Eddie Cochran, Buddy Holly, Carl Perkins, and Jerry Lee Lewis. They were certainly the ones who had the most hit records in rockabilly music, along with influencing future artists and generations of fans to continue to listen and find out how great their rockabilly music really was during this time period. But there are other artists and acts who also made some great music between 1954 and 1958, who, though they never had a *Billboard* chart hit, have continued to have their music reissued, and who've had a huge impact on performers and fans worldwide over the past twenty-five years.

Johnny Burnette

One of these acts was Johnny Burnette and The Rock 'N Roll Trio. This group consisted of Johnny Burnette on lead vocals and rhythm guitar, his brother Dorsey on upright, slappin' bass, and Paul Burlison on lead guitar. They did three recording sessions for Coral Records between May 7, 1956, and March 22, 1957, where they laid down twenty-five of the hottest, most frantic, killer, pure rockabilly songs that would be sung, done, redone, and re-recorded by future mainstream artists as diverse as The Yardbirds, Aerosmith, The Cramps, Robert Gordon, The Stray Cats, The Rolling Stones, and others.

All three of 'em, Johnny, Dorsey, and Paul, grew up in the tough Lauderdale Courts low-income housing projects in Memphis during the forties and early fifties. In 1948 Elvis Presley and his parents would move there from Tupelo, Mississippi. The only other thing they would have in common with Elvis, though, was all three of these boys were workin' day jobs at Crown Electric Company in Memphis during 1953 and '54, at the same time Elvis worked there.

Johnny, Dorsey, and Paul officially formed their musical trio in the fall of 1953. At first they were just known as The Johnny Burnette Trio. Sometime in 1954 they changed their name over to Johnny Burnett (without the "e") and his Rhythm Rangers.

After Sun Records released "That's All Right, Mama" by Elvis in August 1954, and it started garnering a lot of attention and getting heavy airplay on several radio stations in Memphis and surrounding areas, The Burnette Trio auditioned for Sam Phillips at Sun Records. When I asked Sam about this in 1990, he told me they were good, but he felt their sound was too country, and he was puttin' all his time into Elvis. So when Sun Records passed on Johnny, Dorsey, and Paul, they headed about eighty miles south, down to a little town in Mississippi called Booneville, where they recorded two country songs for a little label there called Von Records.

I'm not trying to take one thing away from Johnny and Dorsey Burnette and Paul Burlison. All I want to do here is set the record straight, because in liner notes for various (mostly foreign) record albums on great artists that came out of Memphis in the early and mid fifties such as Johnny Burnette and his Trio, Charlie Feathers, and others, they'll write that they were singin', writin', and recording rockabilly music before Elvis's first Sun Records. It's all hype to sell their albums. There're no facts to back it up. The facts are they were all country boys singin' country music till they heard Elvis.

So anyway, Johnny Burnett and his Rhythm Rangers released a two-sided country 45 on the Von label with the A side titled "Go Mule Go." This record failed to create much attention, even in the South.

By early October 1955, the three of them were gettin' nowhere in the Memphis area, even after switchin' over to their brand of rockabilly, so they moved to New York City. They got some notice performing on Ted Mack's

"Amateur Hour" TV show, and by April 1956 got signed to Decca records.

The first 45, on Decca's subsidiary Coral, was "Tear It Up" b/w "Your Undecided," released on June 5, 1956. "Tear It Up" today is one of the all-time rockabilly classics. It's been recorded by such diverse artists as rockabilly pioneer Charlie Feathers in the sixties, Rod Stewart in the seventies, The Stray Cats in the eighties, and dozens more. As great as was, it never made the national charts, although it became a big regional hit, especially in the northeast.

Both Buddy Holly and Johnny Carroll cut some great, now classic rockabilly songs for the Decca label during the same period The Johnny Burnette Trio cut theirs. But being as they were promoted out of Decca's Nashville base, neither one got to tour outside of the South and Southwest, and the country DJs didn't give 'em much airplay, while the pop, Top 40 DJs were playing the majors or highly promoted independent-label records coming out of New York City and Los Angeles. It was a real shame with Johnny Carroll's records, because his were as pure and scorchin', hot rockin' as The Burnette Trio's stuff. One more of many examples comin' out of Nashville was an artist by the name of Andy Starr (also known as Frank Starr). He had several solid releases on MGM Records that should have been hits from their hard rockin' sounds, such as "Rockin' Rollin' Stone," "Round and Round," "Old Deacon Jones," and others. But the few big tours he went on were all in the South and on the country music circuit. Holly, Carroll, and Starr all were never able to get exposure on any national TV shows when their records were released.

After "Tear It Up" failed to hit the national charts, Coral Records released "Oh Baby Babe" b/w "Midnight Train." The A side, "Oh Baby Babe," was a direct rip-off, steal, whatever you want to call it, of Elvis's hit "Baby, Let's Play House" from a year earlier. The Burnette record sold poorly and didn't do nearly as well as "Tear It Up" had done.

Johnny and the boys cut their next session in Nashville between July 2 and July 5, at Bradley's Barn studio, with Owen Bradley overseeing the session and being listed as producer. That four-day session has to be considered The Johnny Burnette Trio's finest hour in their rockabilly musical careers. Johnny Burnette's burnin' hot, gut-wrenchin' vocals and screams, which all sounded so natural in his great Memphis drawl, never sounded better on wild rockabilly classics like "Train Kept

A-Rollin'," "Honey Hush," "Lonesome Train (On a Lonesome Track)," "Your Baby Blue Eyes," "Rockabilly Boogie," "Rock Therapy," etc.

The Johnny Burnette Trio continued to gain momentum the rest of the summer and into the early fall of 1956, touring consistently. After "Oh Baby Babe" failed to take off, Coral Records released "Train Kept A-Rollin'" b/w "Honey Hush" on October 5. This record was the band's biggest seller, and hit #1 on the Memphis charts. For good reason, too. Both sides are two of the best examples of what pure, scorchin', unrestrained rockabilly music should sound like.

Back at that time, in pop music, as well as R&B, country, rock 'n' roll, and rockabilly, more than 90 percent of the time you'd buy a record and one side would be fast or at least mid-tempo and the other side would be a ballad. But in the case of "Train Kept A-Rollin'" b/w "Honey Hush," two of the best all-time rockabilly cuts ever were placed on a single record. Johnny Burnette screamed both these sides with every ounce of energy he had in him. What really enhanced both these tracks was Paul Burlison's fuzztone guitar, which, from what Paul told me, was a complete accident at the time. It seems one of the tubes in his amp got knocked loose, and it made the sound distorted. The band and audiences liked it, so Paul would just pull that one tube out a little bit whenever he wanted to get that sound.

Around the same time this new record was released, they filmed a spot for Alan Freed's new rock 'n' roll movie, *Rock, Rock, Rock*. Their performance of "Lonesome Train (On a Lonesome Track)" really made that movie for me.

Their first and only album, *Johnny Burnette and His Rock 'N Roll Trio*, came out at the end of 1956. It never made the charts, nor did the new fourth 45 of theirs, "Lonesome Train (On a Lonesome Track)" b/w "I Just Found Out," but it sure don't take away from the greatness of everything them boys did up to that time.

The songs on the new single were included on the LP, as was those from the previous successful one, "Train Kept A-Rollin'" b/w "Honey Hush," and eight new songs. Not that there was even one bad song on this album, but without a doubt, the standout, killer cuts that drove me insane with delirious excitement back then were "All By Myself," "Rockabilly Boogie," "Your Baby Blue Eyes," and the best rockabilly rendition I ever heard on the "Stick" McGhee R&B classic "Drinkin' Wine,

Spo-Dee-O-Dee, Drinkin' Wine." They were all the head-banger songs of their day, and they sound as good today as they did way back then.

I've heard artists and bands like Harry Fontana and The Lonesome Trains do versions of these songs in the early nineties, and Harry does 'em in a great wild, frantic vocal style. He's real talented. His lead guitarist, Barbara Nadine, copies Paul Burlison's licks real good, but the originals still just can't be duplicated.

Like I said, there wasn't a bad song on the whole album. "Lonesome Tears in My Eyes" doesn't have the bite and edge the aforementioned have, but Johnny's stutterin' vocals carry the song and make it really great. On the song "Sweet Love on My Mind," Dorsey Burnette does the lead vocal and does a really terrific job on turnin' this Wayne Walker country composition into a fast-paced rockabilly song with their unique, strong arrangement to it. Though Dorsey's vocals were always suited better for country music, he did a few great rockabilly numbers after he left The Rock 'N Roll Trio as a solo artist for Imperial in late '58 and '59. I have to add this: rockabilly revivalist Robert Gordon did the best cover version of "Sweet Love on My Mind" on his 1980 album *Bad Boy* for RCA Records. It rivals Burnette's, in my opinion, and RCA musta thought so, cause they made it the first song on side one of the LP.

The only other two songs I haven't mentioned off of this fantastic album are both real good, but back in '56 they were the first songs I'd heard Johnny sing that were not really in his unique vibrant rockabilly vocal style. "Chains of Love" was already an R&B classic by Big Joe Turner. I guess the weakest song on the whole LP had to be the pop-flavored mid-tempo song "I Love You So." It was the most different song I had heard Johnny sing up to this point. I had no idea in early '57 it was a sign of things to come later. While I've grown to enjoy listenin' to this song today, I have to say here that late in 1981, Robert Gordon recorded a great version of "I Love You So" in his own rockabilly arrangement that's pumped it up with good energy and turned it into a solid rockabilly belt-out ballad.

During the first three months of 1957, Johnny Burnette and The Rock 'N Roll Trio had a lot goin' for 'em. They had a full calendar of constant touring all over the country, with a lot of momentum goin' from the new album release, the new 45 release of "Lonesome Train (On a Lonesome Track)" startin' to receive strong airplay, and the movie *Rock, Rock, Rock* bein' seen in theaters and drive-ins around the country. It would seem they were destined to break through on the *Billboard* national charts at any moment. Well, it just didn't happen. "Lonesome Train (On a Lonesome Track)" only became a regional hit in certain cities, as had their previous three records. Their album (as great as a pure rockabilly album could ever be) didn't sell well at all. But remember, it was geared straight at the teenage market, and the relatively new 45s were the main platters that mattered most to them.

Coral scheduled time at Bradley's Barn studio in Nashville for one more attempt at a song that could push 'em into the national charts at last. So on March 22, 1957, Johnny, Dorsey, and Paul went in the studio and recorded four new songs.

They immediately returned to the road and continued on a grueling schedule of live engagements that their booking agency had 'em on for the next six months. Well, one night in June 1957, after a show they had done in Niagara Falls, Johnny and Dorsey got into a really bad fight. So bad that Dorsey quit The Rock 'N Roll Trio and went home to Memphis. Johnny Burnette called Memphis and got ahold of Johnny Black, who was the brother of Elvis's bass player, Bill Black, and played solid stand-up, slappin' rockabilly-styled bass like his older brother. He took Dorsey's place with The Rock 'N Roll Trio on the rest of their dates.

On May 5, a little over a month before Dorsey quit, Coral Records released two of the four new songs The Trio had recorded in March. The two songs were "Eager Beaver Baby" b/w "If You Want It Enough." "Eager Beaver Baby" was done in Johnny's own fabulous stammerin', hiccup rockabilly style, but restrained somewhat in comparison with the previous four 45s. "If You Want It Enough" was pop-flavored right from the start, complete with the "Bop, Bop-Ba-Doo-Ba Dop" vocal chorus all the way through. Even so, it was listenable because Johnny still sang it with as much energized rockabillyish vocals as you could get away with in a song that really called for a smoother style of singing.

On August 20, 1957, The Johnny Burnette Trio had their sixth single out, "Butterfingers" b/w "Touch Me." Even though Johnny and the group had a full tourin' schedule throughout the summer and early fall of '57, this record really got bad results as far as sales went. The songs again were taken from The Trio's final session back in March. "Butterfingers" was nothin' more than a silly pop tune. These types of songs were bein' pushed more by the major labels by the summer of '57. "Touch Me" was better, a mid-tempo, rockabillyish-ballad with haunting, eerie sound. This was pretty much the end officially for Johnny Burnette and his Rock 'N Roll Trio. A month and a half after the release of this record, Johnny decided to disband the group. It was early October 1957, "Butterfingers" failed to chart, and Johnny and Paul Burlison were both burned out from constant touring for a year and a half with no major chart success. They both went home to Memphis.

Dorsey's greatest rockabilly record as a solo artist, "Bertha Lou" b/w "Till the Law Says Stop," came out at the end of 1957 on the Cee-Jam record label, and both sides are dynamite rockabilly all the way. It failed miserably at that time, but hearin' it today, Dorsey proved he could rock with any of 'em. It's worth mentioning here that even though Johnny Burnette and The Rock 'N Roll Trio had disbanded during the fall of '57, Coral Records must have felt they had an impact, as they released a final record by the group on December 5, 1957, "Rockabilly Boogie" b/w "Drinkin' Wine, Spo-Dee-O-Dee," off their album. In 1960 Coral released "Rockabilly Boogie" b/w "If You Want It Enough" with only Johnny Burnette listed as the artist. Since the late seventies, "Rockabilly Boogie" has become rockabilly revivalist Robert Gordon's signature song.

While Dorsey recorded for Imperial during '58 and '59, Johnny moved on to a new label called Freedom Records, which was a subsidiary of Liberty Records. Johnny signed with Freedom in late 1958 and had three 45 releases through the summer of 1959. He was still writing his own songs, and as late as 1959 he was still writin' 'em for the most in the same frantic, primitive rockabilly style he had always done. Not everything was rockabilly musically, but he sang it at least in his own unique rockabilly vocal style.

I was finding Johnny Burnette records at the dime store in 1959, and when I heard the first one on Freedom Records, called "I'm Restless" b/w "Kiss Me," I thought "Kiss Me" was really good. I eventually found a second record by Johnny on the Freedom Label, with one side called "Gumbo" and the flip side called "Me and the Bear." This was in the summer of 1959. I thought "Gumbo" stunk, but "Me and the Bear" knocked me out. In the grooves of that side, Johnny was beltin' out the wildest, most scorchin' rockabilly screamin' lyrics I'd heard him do since the 1956 Rock 'N Roll Trio records. I couldn't figure out how he could turn out and

write such a great song on one side, and on the other side, which he also wrote, there he was singin' pop Caribbean-soundin' junk.

In the summer of 1960, Johnny finally had that big hit he'd been lookin' for. The song was called "Dreamin'." It hit the *Billboard* Top 100 pop charts on July 25 and rose to a high of #11, stayin' on the charts for fifteen weeks. His follow-up record, "You're Sixteen," was even a bigger pop hit. It debuted in *Billboard* on October 31 and rose all the way up to #8, stayin' on the charts fifteen more weeks. Both of these songs were trite, teen, silly, pop-flavored garbage. Johnny Burnette went on to have three more 45s that hit the Top 100 through December 1961. All five songs were on Liberty Records. None of them was written by him. I consider Johnny one of the best rockabilly/rock 'n' roll songwriters of the 1950s. But by the summer of 1960, solid, raw, or even pop-flavored rockabilly had seen its day pass on, with only a few minor bottom-of-the-chart exceptions.

Dorsey Burnette also found chart success. He had signed with Era Records, and his first release, "(There Was a) Tall Oak Tree," debuted on the *Billboard* pop charts on February 1, 1960, reaching a high of #23, and stayed on the charts for fifteen weeks. The song was in a country/folk vein, and folk-type music was becoming really big at this time. His follow-up song, "Hey Little One," reached #48 in the summer of 1960. Dorsey wrote those songs, and they suited him real well. Dorsey always wanted to sing country music, and he had the voice for it. Right up until his untimely death on August 19, 1979, from a heart attack at the age of 46, he was still on the *Billboard* country charts, after having a string of fifteen chart hits between 1972 and 1979.

For the most part of Dorsey's musical career, he did things on his own terms, where Johnny, on the other hand, was more willin' to bend with the trends in music as the years went by. After his pop hits ended and Liberty Records dropped him in 1962, he had releases on the Chancellor label in late '62, then signed with Capitol Records in 1963, where he had several releases in '63 and '64. In '64, at the time of his death, he had a record out on the Magic Lamp label. All the songs were pop-type songs, but he never gave up, right to the end. The end came for Johnny on August 1, 1964, on Clear Lake, out in California. The news report at the time said his death was the result of a boating accident. Johnny was only thirty years old when he died. Even though for the last four years of his life he recorded and released

Forgettin' to Remember to Forget

*I*n the fall of '59, I started my first year of high school and was a regular dancer on Milt Grant's TV show. Johnny Burnette turned up on a Friday afternoon in October, to promote his third release on the Freedom label, "Sweet Baby Doll" b/w "I'll Never Love Again." When he got off the elevator, I walked up to him and told him I had his album and 45s when he was with The Rock 'N Roll Trio, and I asked him if he had time could I talk to him about 'em. I remember him smilin' and sayin', "Sure we can, man. Come on back to the dressing room."

When I started talkin' with Johnny, I told him how great all those Rock 'N Roll Trio records were, and that I still played 'em, 'cause there were only a few real rock 'n' rollers still puttin' out good records. Johnny asked me if I liked Ricky Nelson, and I told him yeah. I added that I liked his and Dorsey's songs that Ricky sang the best, 'cause they were always good rockers. Johnny told me he appreciated me sayin' that, and that Ricky was a good friend of his, and that he loved rockabilly and fast rock 'n' roll songs the best, but his label was more than ever trying to push ballad sides, since "Poor Little Fool" had been his biggest hit ever. Johnny told me, "Man, I love to just let it all out and go wild during my show, but they told me at my label if I'm ever gonna have a big hit, I gotta go with what's happenin' now. I'm just gonna have to find one of those kind of songs soon. Though I do think you'll really dig this new record I got out that I'm doin' on the show today. I got some copies out in the car, and before I leave, I'll get you one."

Johnny lip-synched "Sweet Baby Doll" on the show, and I flipped over it. For late 1959, it was a really great rockabilly song. Of course, once again, it was Johnny's dynamic vocal that made the song so hot soundin'. After the show, I walked with him over to the garage where his car was parked, and he gave me a copy. There was gonna be a record hop that night, and Johnny said he'd be there. He said he'd look for me, and I told him he wouldn't have no trouble findin' me.

I got there about 7:30 p.m. It went from 8:00 p.m. to 11:00 p.m. Milt, as always, was the host. After some local opening acts, prize drawings, and an intermission, finally Johnny Burnette was announced. He opened up with a gritty, knock-out version of Lloyd Price's hit from earlier that year, "Stagger Lee." I was completely unprepared for this song, along with Johnny's rockabilly-styled movements across from one side of the stage to the other. Johnny got that audience, especially the girls, excited and screamin' for more. No, rockabilly and rock 'n' roll hadn't died in the fall of '59 in Hyattsville, Maryland. Johnny Burnette brought it alive, man! He kept dishin' out hot-as-fire real rock 'n' roll, and both the band and everybody else in the National Guard armory went wild for it and loved every minute of it. For over half an hour ('cause the crowd was yellin' for more, so he was the only act on the show that got an encore), Johnny tore it up with frantic stage moves, to the delight of that crowd. He rocked out on songs like "Rip It Up," "Whole Lotta Shakin' Goin' On," "Ready Teddy," "Maybellene," "That'll Be the Day," and his new record, "Sweet Baby Doll." He also did the song he had written for Ricky Nelson, which was still on the charts at that time, called "Just a Little Too Much." The only ballad he did was "It's Only Make Believe."

In the middle of the set, Johnny said to the crowd that he wanted to dedicate the next song to me. Then he broke into a scorchin' version of "Train Kept A-Rollin'" and followed it up with two more songs he'd done with The Rock 'N Roll Trio, "All By Myself" and "Honey Hush." He was rockin' all over the stage, droppin' to his knees, and playin' right up to the screamin' girls up front. It was crazy. I don't think Milt Grant knew how he was gonna get Johnny off without a riot happenin'. His last song was "Great Balls of Fire," and he ran off stage, but now the guys were gettin' rowdy, so Milt had to come out and bring Johnny back for one more, a rockin' version of "Corrine, Corrina."

I was lucky again and got to hang out with Johnny for close to an hour after the show. We exchanged addresses, and he said he'd send me an 8x10 autographed picture when he got back home, but for me to write him and keep in touch. I didn't write until "Dreamin'" hit in 1960, but he sent the photo, along with a handwritten letter thankin' me for my long-time support and sayin' that he'd probably be doin' Milt Grant's TV show again (which he did) and was lookin' forward to seein' me if I was there (which I was). I kept that letter and picture in a safe place at my mother's home in Brentwood, Maryland, even after I got married in 1968. Unfortunately, it's since disappeared.

all pop or pop/country songs, mostly cover hits of the day, he still did 'em well, and in a select number of them I could still hear his great Memphis vocal style comin' through. I went out and searched for his records right up until his death.

Johnny Burnette's Trio recordings and some of his pre-Liberty records hold up with the greatest raw rockabilly records of all time. With me, they're right up there with Elvis's Sun records and Gene Vincent's '56 to '58 recordings. You may turn on what's now called "Classic Radio" and hear Johnny singin' "Dreamin' " and "You're Sixteen," but those songs will only be sung by oldies bands. They're nostalgia. That wasn't the real Johnny Burnette, deep in his soul. Songs like "Train Kept A-Rollin' " and "Tear It Up" were pure creative genius that was always deep in Johnny's heart and soul, and his first and main love. Those are the songs that'll be brought back over and over again, as they have been for more than two decades now.

Additional Artists

In future chapters you'll read at length about such stars of the late fifties as Jack Scott, Conway Twitty, Dale Hawkins, Ricky Nelson, and others, but I'd like to close out this chapter by at least mentioning or listing a number of great rockabilly artists, along with others who were put in the rockabilly category back then. In my opinion, some of these did make rockabilly-styled records, and others only thought they did. None of these artists or groups had Top 10 national records, but most all of 'em had records that hit at some position between 1956 and 1958 on the *Billboard* pop charts. I'll probably leave out a few, but I went out and bought most of these records at the time.

Hayden Thompson was born and raised in Booneville, Mississippi, and he had his first 45 record release on Von Records there (where The Burnette Trio would cut their first sides), "Act Like You Love Me" b/w "I Feel the Blues Coming On." This was probably sometime in early October 1954. Von Records was an offshoot of the Von Theatre in Booneville, which held a Saturday night show on which Hayden was a regular. After his record ran its course in late '54 and early '55 on the little country circuit down around Mississippi and surrounding states, he left his weekly stint at the Von Theatre. By the spring of '56, when rockabilly really broke through, Hayden and his band toured all over the South and Southwest. He was a hot act at that time.

Hayden had done some recording earlier in '56 with Sam Phillips at the controls, but it wasn't until December '56 that Sam got out of Hayden what he was lookin' for, on the Junior Parker blues classic "Love My Baby." It was the same drivin' raw-edged rockabilly feel Elvis had at the beginning. This song remains Hayden's signature song to this very day all around the world to rockabilly fans. But for whatever reasons, Sam held the record back until the fall of '57, when he finally released it on his new Phillips International label. Sam released five records simultaneously, including a good rockabilly song by Texas rocker Johnny Carroll (who came to Sun in June '57 after Decca failed to renew his contract) and the pop/rock-flavored instrumental "Raunchy," by Bill Justis. Phillips International struck gold with "Raunchy," which stayed five months on the *Billboard* pop charts, peaking at #2. Hayden's and Johnny Carroll's records, along with the other two, failed to chart nationally. But "Love My Baby" is more in demand now than it was back in late '57.

Hayden did at least one more recording session at the old Sun studios after this record came out, and he continued to tour down south. By early 1958, he knew he wouldn't get another release on Sun or Phillips International, so he moved to Chicago, where he still lives today. He continued to make a livin' doin what he loved best, playin' music — rockabilly and rock 'n' roll at first, then country. He continued to have 45 record releases on various independent labels, and in 1966 Kapp Records signed him to a contract that resulted in three 45s and an album. Hayden finally got a "real job" in 1976. He thought he'd hung his guitar up for good.

Then, in 1984, he got a call from England to come over and headline some shows there and in Holland. Rockabilly was having a big resurgence both here and in Europe, with young bands and artists like The Stray Cats, The Blasters, Dave Edmunds, Robert Gordon, and Shakin' Stevens all hittin' on the national charts and drawin' large audiences at concerts. The Europeans don't forget anybody and search out everybody who ever made a rockabilly record in the fifties. They started bringin' the original fifties artists over there sometime in the mid to late seventies. The time couldn't have been more right for Hayden Thompson in 1984. He went over there and the crowds went wild for him. Dave Travis, who's an artist in his own right, put a band together and produced Hayden's first rockabilly album, *Booneville Mississippi Flash*, which was released in '85 on Charly

Records, and Hayden's been consistently goin' to dozens of countries around the world ever since. Various European labels have continued to re-release just about everything he recorded in the fifties and sixties.

Joe Bennett and The Sparkletones were a group that consisted of four teenage boys from Spartanburg, South Carolina. They were all between the ages of fourteen and seventeen years old when they recorded a song called "Black Slacks" that would ensure their place in any rockabilly book as one of the best raw, hot-soundin' rockabilly songs that would endure the test of time. Rockabilly bands all over the world still include this song in their live sets, and even today, nearly two decades after Robert Gordon first recorded it, he still has to sing it in live sets, as it's one of his most requested songs. When "Black Slacks" debuted on the *Billboard* pop charts on August 26, 1957, it only reached a high of #17, but it stayed on the charts for nineteen weeks, into the early part of January 1958. Joe Bennett and The Sparkletones' follow-up record, "Penny Loafers and Bobby Socks," debuted in *Billboard* on December 23, 1958, but only made it up to #42 and dropped off the charts after only eight weeks. These two records came out on ABC Paramount Records, and the company released several more 45s by the group in 1958, and a couple of the songs were pretty good rockabilly songs, but those failed to chart. They had releases for the Paris record label in 1959 and 1960, more teen-oriented pop stuff by then, and those also failed to come close to making the national charts. It didn't matter. Those southern teenage boys left their mark in rockabilly history with that one great song "Black Slacks."

There's no way I can end this chapter without tellin' you somethin' about a minor hit artist who made probably what was the most scorchin', screamin', berserk rockabilly 45 to make the charts in the early spring of 1958. I can't think of a wilder vocal rockabilly record on the *Billboard* charts as late as '58 than "Bop-A-Lena," by Ronnie Self, from Tin Town, Missouri. Back then they called Ronnie "Mr. Frantic," and when you hear "Bop-A-Lena" it ain't hard to figure out why. Ronnie was only eighteen years old when "Bop-A-Lena" debuted on the *Billboard* pop charts on March 10, 1958. It only rose to a high of #63 and dropped off the charts after only a seven-week run, but it was enough for me to see him perform it on Milt Grant's TV show, as well as on "American Bandstand." "Bop-A-Lena" was on Columbia Records, on which Ronnie had several other strong

releases and a four-song EP, also in '58 and '59. Ronnie's first record came out in 1957 on ABC Paramount Records, and it's a highly sought-after rockabilly record called "Pretty Bad Blues." Between '59 and '62, Ronnie had four or five releases on Decca Records, and in '63 he had one release on Kapp Records. In late 1959, Ronnie was the writer of Brenda Lee's first pop Top 10 hit, "Sweet Nothin's." He also wrote Brenda's next record, the #1 song "I'm Sorry." It's the song Brenda Lee's most remembered for, and her biggest hit ever. Brenda recorded several other Ronnie Self compositions. Ronnie will always be remembered by rockabilly fans for his own great, crazy, wild, spontaneous rockabilly vocal sounds on songs like "Bop-A-Lena," "Ain't I'm a Dog," and "Pretty Bad Blues." Those songs, along with a few others from Ronnie's rockabilly period from 1957 to 1959, are the ones that hold up so well that they're still being reissued on both vinyl and CDs to this very day. "Mr. Frantic" couldn't have been more on the money with rockabilly firecrackers like those jumpin' tunes.

On January 6, 1958, Jimmy Dee and his group The Offbeats debuted on the *Billboard* pop charts with one hot-sounding rockabilly song, called "Henrietta." The song itself was not a wild, frantic, racing tune, but Jimmy Dee's vocals were screamin', loose, and wild. This made that rockin' song what it is: one gutsy, gritty rockabilly hit song. It was on Dot Records and managed to climb up to a high of #47 and remain on the charts for ten weeks. It got a lot of airplay in D.C., but I can't ever remember seein' Jimmy Dee and The Offbeats on TV back at that time. After a few more releases on Dot Records, Jimmy Dee and The Offbeats went on to have records come out on more than a half dozen small independent labels between 1959 and 1963, but "Henrietta" remains their sole trip to the *Billboard* pop charts with a fantastic rockabilly song.

Dale Wright was lucky enough to make two trips onto the *Billboard* pop charts with rockabilly songs during 1958. His record "She's Neat" debuted in *Billboard* on January 13, 1958, and it stayed on the charts for thirteen weeks, reaching a high of #38. This record was on the Fraternity Records label, out of Cincinnati, Ohio, as was his second chart rockabilly hit, "Please Don't Do It," which debuted in *Billboard* on August 25, 1958, only reaching #77 and droppin' off after only a five-week run. But the last half of 1958, that was normal for any good-soundin' rockabilly song, as it was gettin' harder and harder to get high on the charts with rockabilly tunes that had an edge to 'em. Neither one of Dale Wright's hits had that much of a tough-soundin' edge by any means, but they both still hold up as pretty good rockabilly songs. Most of Dale's other 45s that I bought after that were more teen-oriented songs.

Marvin Rainwater has been referred to in articles, liner notes on albums, and some other books as an American Indian rockabilly singer. Well, there's only a fraction of truth in that entire statement. Marvin was born Marvin Karlton Percy in Wichita, Kansas, on July 2, 1925, and he's one-quarter Cherokee Indian. He only dabbled in rockabilly music from 1956 to 1958, while it was at its peak. Marvin's first love was country music when he got in the business full-time in the early fifties. He also had a crossover pop/country vocal style that MGM Records, the label he signed with in 1955, utilized real well on a lot of his songs. The only rockabilly song that was a major hit for him (which I felt was his best rockabilly-styled song) was "Whole Lotta Woman." On March 31, 1958, this song only reached up to #60 on the *Billboard* pop charts and dropped off after only two weeks, but it hit #15 on the country charts for one week, on April 14, 1958. Marvin made other good rockabilly-oriented records, such as "I Dig You Baby," but they failed to do anything for him. All his records did well in the D.C. area, as he continued to be a popular artist there through 1960.

Eddie Fontaine is considered by some as a rockabilly artist, and on September 22, 1958, he had one lone record debut on the *Billboard* pop charts. The song is called "Nothin' Shakin'," and it got up to #64 and then dropped off the charts after only three weeks. Eddie sang it with a lot of fire and energy, and I consider it a pretty good record. It's in the rockabilly vein, although it's definitely got a northern sound to it, because Eddie was from the North. Eddie just passed away a few years ago. He started out playin' lounge clubs in Las Vegas and continued to do so throughout his life in between his various acting parts in TV and movies. His most famous was during the 1970s, when he played the part of Fonzie's father in the hit series "Happy Days." "Nothin' Shakin'" was on the Argo label. It was Eddie's only rockabilly record.

One real good song that was solid rockabilly all the way was the lively rockin' tune "Love Bug Crawl," by Jimmy Edwards, on Mercury Records. It hit the *Billboard* pop charts on January 20, 1958, and though it only reached #78 and stayed on the charts for a short

three weeks, it's well remembered and loved by a lot of fans to this day.

The Cincinnati-based King Records (which had many hits at that time and many more continuing into the early seventies in the R&B market) were never able to crack the *Billboard* pop charts with a big rockabilly national hit, but, oh boy, did they ever try hard. Between the summer of 1956 and well into 1958, King Records released some of the greatest southern rockabilly music in its wildest, primitive, purest form. Startin' in '56, they signed artists such as Charlie Feathers, Mac Curtis, Hank Mizell, Joe Penny, Bob and Lucille, Bruce Chanell, and a score of others. They probably had the best overall stable of rockabilly artists outside of Sun Records in Memphis. It would take some fifteen to twenty years later for another generation of fans across the ocean in Europe to first bring attention to the artistic greatness of these songs and artists.

I've probably had a closer personal and professional relationship with Charlie Feathers than with any other artist that recorded and released authentic rockabilly records back in the mid to late fifties. Charlie has always downplayed the eight songs he recorded up in Cincinnati, which were released in 1956 and 1957 on four 45 singles on King Records. The fact remains that all over the world, these four records remain the greatest examples of pure, exciting rockabilly music you'll ever hear. Charlie and his band The Musical Warriors were able to get the feel right on every one of those sides. Me or no one else will ever convince Charlie, but the greatest rockabilly songs that ever came out on records by him were songs like "One Hand Loose," "Bottle to the Baby," "Everybody's Lovin' My Baby," and the other five songs King released back then. Those songs have always been his most requested songs at his live shows, both in this country and in Europe.

Sleepy La Beef, like Charlie Feathers, has become another influential first-generation rockabilly artist who has really never strayed too far from the music he loves playin' and singin' best of all, rockabilly music. In the late fifties, he had releases on the Starday label out of Houston, Texas, and the major label Mercury Records, where he came out with my personal favorite rockabilly song by him, called "All the Time." His records in 1957 were under the name Sleepy La Beef, as he's known around the world in rockabilly music today. Sleepy also had earlier, highly sought after, releases on the Picture record label and the Wayside record label under the name Tommy La Beef.

For Sleepy La Beef, Charlie Feathers, Mac Curtis, Narvel Felts, Andy Starr, Hayden Thompson, Johnny Carroll, Ronnie Dawson, and so many other rockabillys who made records in the 1950s, we'd have to wait almost two decades to hear their music released on European import albums, as most of these never met with national success. From 1958 on, I was fortunate enough to find a good number of 'em in discount bins, as I was always searchin' for the great music of the late fifties I had missed, but I found out by the mid seventies that I had missed more than I could believe.

The Great Pretenders

Except for some bigger-name artists who over the past twenty years have been considered as doin' rockabilly music in the late fifties (most of whom I'll mention later), I'm going to list some of the biggest hits by artists who were called rockabilly between '56 and '58, but who, to me, were on the weak, teen-oriented side of rockabilly.

Charlie Gracie and Buddy Knox are two good examples. European record labels that have released Gracie's songs on reissued albums in recent years have labeled him as a rockabilly artist from back in the fifties. Nothin' personal, but sorry, Charlie, not in my book, and not in most rockabilly fans' minds around the world. All the songs Charlie Gracie did, from his #1 hit "Butterfly" in 1957 on out (and I've heard 'em all), such as "Fabulous," "Cool Baby," and others, were simply teen-oriented pop/rock 'n' roll then and now.

Buddy Knox, who had a #1 *Billboard* chart record in 1957 with "Party Doll," and another Top 10 record later that year with "Hula Love," is considered rockabilly by some fans around the world. I have to be honest and say I really never have considered him or any of his early hits rockabilly, although I bought 'em when they came out 'cause they had a bit of a rockabilly sound to 'em, but I've always considered 'em more popabilly. Buddy did have a couple chart records that were fairly good rockabilly songs, though, such as "Somebody Touched Me" in the fall of 1958 and "I Think I'm Gonna Kill Myself" in the spring of 1959 on Roulette Records.

Jimmy Bowen, who formed Buddy Knox's band The Rhythm Orchids in late '56, and who since the mid sixties has gone from top West Coast producer to major record label head in Nashville, had a couple of pretty good rockabilly-flavored songs: "I'm Stickin' with You," which was a big hit and made it to #14 in the spring of

'57, and "Warm Up to Me Baby," which got to #57 in the summer of 1957. Both these records were on the Roulette record label.

On July 9, 1955, the group Boyd Bennett and His Rockets were the first of several artists to chart with a song called "Seventeen," on the Cincinnati-based King Records (which had many hits at that time and many more continuing into the early seventies in the R&B market). Why some writers and historians have continued to even consider this recording a rockabilly song is beyond me. When it came out and today, by every rockabilly fan and major writers and authorities on this song and artist, it's simply looked upon as a good pop song with a bit of rock 'n' roll flavor. Boyd Bennett and His Rockets reached a high of #5 and stayed on the pop charts for seventeen weeks with this song. The Fontaine Sisters' version went higher and lasted longer, but it was just watered-down pop garbage, as were the other cover versions of the time. Boyd Bennett and His Rockets at least had a rock 'n' roll sound on their version. But my moral here is please don't let anybody try to convince you "Seventeen" by Boyd Bennett and His Rockets is even close to being a rockabilly song. It wasn't then and it isn't now. All you gotta do is listen to it.

King Records put out a couple more records on Bennett and his group, and again, no rockabilly sound was found to be heard. The final time on King Records we heard of Boyd Bennett and His Rockets was when King released, of all things, "Blue Suede Shoes" by the group, and it debuted on the *Billboard* pop charts on April 14, 1956. The terrible, wimpy, pop version by Boyd Bennett and His Rockets trying to cover a great southern rockabilly song like this was both disgusting and a disaster. But they did manage to break onto the *Billboard* pop charts. Their version only got up to a high of #63, but it managed to hang on the charts for ten weeks. Anyway, except for a stupid novelty song that came out on Mercury Records by Boyd Bennett called "Boogie Bear" late in 1959, we'd never have to hear from him again.

I'll close this chapter out by tellin' you of three other records from 1958 that were considered rockabilly at that time. All three made the *Billboard* pop charts back then.

The first two records were by a young rockabilly singer and guitarist who had a haunting, unique style on the guitar sound of his first huge hit, "Endless Sleep." The artist's name was Jody Reynolds. He was born in Yuma, Arizona. After "Endless Sleep" debuted in *Billboard* on

May 19, 1958, on the independent Demon Records label, it eventually went to the #5 position, staying on the charts for a seventeen-week run. This song was what I guess you'd call a rockabilly ballad, and it was well ahead of its time. I don't know if it was the first, but it was the first I can recall, of all the teen suicide, tragedy-type songs that became huge hits in the sixties. I'm speakin' of the teary, emotional, sappy ones like "Teen Angel," "Moody River," "Leader of the Pack," "Tell Laura I Love Her," "Patches," "Laurie," "Last Kiss," "Ebony Eyes," and a lot more. "Endless Sleep" not only had a great guitar sound to it, but Jody Reynolds's vocal style had that tough rockabilly edge to it. The B side of "Endless Sleep" was a good, raw-soundin', fast rockabilly tune called "Tight Capris." Not a great song, but it definitely holds up well for a B side. Jody had one other song that hit the *Billboard* pop charts, on August 18, 1958, but it only made it up to #66 and dropped off after only a short five-week run. He played the same haunting guitar sound on it, and it sounded real close to "Endless Sleep," though it didn't have the near-tragedy type lyrics. The song was called "Fire of Love." I really liked the B side better, 'cause it was another fast rockabilly song, called "Daisy Mae." "Endless Sleep" was such a big hit, at least I got to see Jody Reynolds on "American Bandstand" and the Milt Grant show back in '58, and I thought he was pretty cool. After "Fire of Love," I found a couple more records by him on the Demon record label in bargain bins and was glad to get them. They were pretty good rockabilly also.

Most books and magazine articles, along with liner notes on the back of some reissue albums, refer to Ersel Hickey as a rockabilly artist, and that's about as far from the truth as you can get. Everything I've heard by Ersel Hickey (and I've heard more than I should have dared listen to) just sounds like plain weak pop music to me. Ersel Hickey had only one hit on the *Billboard* pop charts, called "Bluebirds over the Mountain," which made it up to #75 after it debuted on April 28, 1958. It dropped off the charts after only six weeks. I'm sure the reason he was considered a rockabilly artist was because of one photography session he did for Epic Records and one photo they used to promote him back in '58, 'cause he had the look, the droopin' pompadour, the cat clothes from head to toe, the stance with his legs spread wide and knees bent, and his guitar stuck out there in his arms like he was one wild rockin' cat. This photograph has been used probably more than any other in rockabilly history to show the ultimate look. I bet postcards and 8x10 photos of Ersel's perfected look have probably sold more copies than all the so-called rockabilly records he ever made all put together.

Hip-Shakin' Honeys of the Golden Era

The main artists who became stars by doin' rockabilly music were all, or at least 98 percent, men. And though there were some fifties chicks who laid down some really great rockabilly sounds, there was no wild, crazy-eyed, frantic girls or women who performed and recorded rockabilly music during its biggest, most dominant period in mainstream music, at least none that were ever able to reach anywhere on the national charts in *Billboard* or *Cash Box*. It's always bothered me when I read magazine articles, liner notes on female albums, or chapters in books that are titled "Wild, Wild Women," or "Wild Rockabilly Gals of the Fifties." To me, when the word "wild" is used in rockabilly or rock 'n' roll in the 1950s, it can only apply to top record-selling artists such as Elvis, Gene Vincent, Chuck Berry, Little Richard, and Jerry Lee Lewis. For a few years, those five great artists scared the daylights out of the older conservative American public, city officials, religious congregations, and leaders all across our country by their outlandish, so-called obscene, live stage performances. The girls and women who sang rockabilly music during the mid and late fifties didn't scare or worry anybody at that time. The kind of live shows Elvis, Chuck Berry, and the rest were doin' back in '56 and '57 not only wouldn't have been tolerated, but also actually wouldn't really have been thought of by girls and women to do. It was a different time. It wouldn't be until 1977 and later that "wild" could maybe be used to describe some of the rockabilly gals who came along from then on.

There're three women that sang rockabilly music in the 1950s that you hear the most about today: Janis Martin, Brenda Lee, and Wanda Jackson. These three women each had at least one *Billboard* pop chart hit between 1956 and 1960 singin' rockabilly music. Now, like most of their male contemporaries, all three of these young ladies who recorded some fantastic examples of rockabilly music all came from country music backgrounds.

Janis Martin

I'll start with Janis Martin, 'cause Janis was the first girl to reach the *Billboard* pop charts, if only for one week, with a rockabilly song. That song was called "Will You Willyum." It debuted on the *Billboard* pop charts on May 5, 1956, at #50, and the following week it was off those charts. Janis Martin had just turned sixteen years old then. She was born on March 27, 1940, in Sutherlin, Virginia. At an early age, Janis showed a big interest in music. Country music was the music where she was at in the late forties. She had mastered the guitar by age six and started singin'. She had a big, powerful, strong voice for a little girl. Between the ages of eight and ten, Janis entered a dozen talent contests in three surrounding states from where she lived and won first place in eleven of them.

When Janis was eleven years old, she became a regular member of the WDVA "Radio Barndance" show in Danville, Virginia. A couple years later, she moved over to "The Old Dominion Country Barndance" radio show, out of Richmond. All during this period, Janis was touring with top country artists all over the southern states. She stayed with the "Old Dominion Banrndance" until right after her first record came out, in the spring of 1956. According to Janis, "My manager was Bert Retine. He was out of Danville, Virginia, where the 'Barndance' was. How I come to gettin' signed with RCA Victor was when Carl Stutz and his songwriting partner Carl Barefoot wrote a song called 'Will You Willyum' in late 1955, just when rock 'n' roll was startin' to take off. These two guys were radio announcers on WDVA, the station that carried the 'Barndance,' and they'd already gotten one big hit under their belts when their song 'Little Things Mean a Lot' became a big pop hit in the early fifties. They had me cut a demo, I guess sometime around Christmas 1955, and they sent it to their publisher in New York. Well, their publisher took the rights to their song and took it over to Steve Sholes at RCA Victor Records, and before January 1956 was over, I was signed up to a contract with RCA, and they had me in the studio in Nashville recording 'Will You Willyum' and one I wrote called 'Drugstore Rock 'n' Roll.' I had a couple o' pretty good years after that, till they cut me loose and I went to raisin' my kids." That was the way Janis put it.

Between January 1956 and July 1958, Janis Martin recorded thirty or so songs in eight recording sessions in Nashville, all produced by Chet Atkins. That also is to the best of Janis's recollection. There's a whole lot more to Janis's story, though. Even though Janis only had a half dozen or so 45 single releases between the spring of 1956 and the fall of 1958, plus one four-song EP in the spring of 1957, she made and left her mark as the first teenage girl to lay down some of the best all-around rockabilly songs you'll ever hear. At sixteen and seventeen years old, Janis had a great voice for the new rockabilly sound in music. All of these songs today are available on the Bear Family Records CD collections, out of Germany. Virtually every song she recorded at RCA can be found on 'em, and when you hear 'em today, even though most weren't even released in the fifties, you'll find that Janis Martin had the voice to belt out the early real rockabilly sound as far as quantity went. Janis's best rockabilly songs were "Drugstore Rock 'n' Roll," "Ooby Dooby," "My Boy Elvis," "Little Bit," and "Bang Bang," which were all released by RCA Victor from '56 to '58. But some of the ones they chose not to release until Bear Family Records came along in 1979 and released 'em were just as good or even better. Others that are now available, such as "Good Love," "Cracker Jack," "Barefoot Baby," and especially "Let's Elope Baby" (which has always been my personal favorite), are some of the best examples of early great female rockabilly music.

Janis Martin had two busy years during 1956 and '57. These were rockabilly music's greatest years, also. Soon after her first 45 release, Janis was promoted by RCA Victor Records as the female Elvis Presley. Elvis not only approved of her using that title and gave his permission for it, but Elvis even went as far as to send Janis his best wishes for a long career, as well as a dozen roses, when she appeared at the RCA Victor Records convention in Miami, Florida, during the spring of 1956 to introduce herself to RCA's music representatives from all around the world. Later on in late '56 and '57, other pop/country or rock 'n' roll-type female artists who sang

various forms of rockabilly music, such as Jean Chapel and Alis Lesley, would also stake claim to the title of "The Female Elvis Presley," but Janis Martin was really the only artist who justly deserved it. In 1956 and 1957, it was no put-down to be known as the female Elvis, as practically every artist, male or female, who was trying to break into mainstream rock 'n' roll was copying Elvis's musical style and movements anyway. (I'm only referring to white artists and performers.)

Janis Martin appeared on "The Tonight Show," "The Ozark Jubilee," and even once on "American Bandstand" before it went coast-to-coast. Janis was voted The Most Promising Female Artist of 1956 at the annual disc jockey convention that year and received a *Billboard* music award plaque for this honor. She toured with the biggest stars in country music during '56 and '57. In late 1956, RCA Records had Janis join and become a regular member of the Jim Reeves show. Janis traveled with Jim Reeves's Big Show of Country Stars exclusively for five or six months. This show toured Army bases in Europe into the early spring of 1957. When this showcase of stars returned to the U.S., Janis was the one artist who was selected to appear on "The Today Show," then hosted by Dave Garroway, to talk about the group's experiences in Europe and to sing her latest record, "My Boy Elvis," which was hot on Top 40 radio in New York then. Janis Martin was only seventeen years old at the time, and the network TV "Today Show" didn't want Jim Reeves or any of the other top, older country stars on their program. They wanted Janis Martin. Why? 'Cause Janis Martin's records, even though they weren't makin' the *Billboard* pop or country charts, were still outselling every top country artist in Nashville in 1956 and '57, when rockabilly and rock 'n' roll was the hottest music goin'. In those days, country music records that hit #1 were lucky if they sold 20,000 or 30,000 records.

Janis told me that everywhere she performed and appeared, the crowds all loved her, and she got a better response most of the time than most of the top country stars. She was havin' the time of her life. But being upstaged by a sixteen- or seventeen-year-old country girl from Danville, Virginia, sure didn't sit well with the likes of a lot of those top country artists back then. Especially when she's appearing on the sacred stage of "The Grand Ole Opry" in Nashville and she kicks her shoes off and dances around singin' "Barefoot Baby." Sure, the audience loved watchin' this young, pretty teenage country girl wail this song out and dance in her bare feet, but the old-timers who ran everything then sure frowned upon this kind of behavior, to put it mildly. They were still having trouble with drums being used in the mother church of country music. That had only been recently, but reluctantly, accepted. So Janis's behavior was disapproved of. My, how far country music has come after all these years.

Here's a true story Janis said I could tell, so I will. According to her, "I was out on tour in '56 with a country package show in the South, and everybody's cars were full, and I was ridin' in Porter Wagoner's car, 'cause he had the most room and was at the top of the country charts and headlining the show. After a couple shows, I messed up as far as Porter was concerned, 'cause in this one town we played, I came on right before him and just went out there and sang and danced all over the stage, and the crowd went wild. When I did my last song and my time was up, I left the stage and Porter came on. Well, through his whole first country song, that audience, which was on the young side that night, just kept yellin', 'Janis, Janis, Janis, we want Janis.' After the show and I went to get in Porter's car, he told me I'd have to find my own way to the next town, and that was that. I had to call my daddy up, and he had to drive over 100 miles to come and get me and take me to the other towns booked on that tour. I was just a young kid, and I knew a lot of 'em down there felt the same way as Porter, but I didn't give a damn what they thought about me, and I just kept goin' out doin' what I loved to do, and that was entertaining people."

Janis told me the only big star in music outside of country artists she performed with was Pat Boone. Janis told me the story like this: "RCA sent me up to Canton, Ohio, to open this big show for Pat Boone in the summer of '57. I had a lot of relatives who lived up around there, and they all came out to this show. Well, I got a real good reception and all, and all the kids loved my show, but all the girls had come to see Pat Boone. After I finished my show, they wheeled out this great big old cage from behind the curtains and put it out in front of that stage, and when it was time for Pat Boone to come on and sing his songs, he ran out from behind those curtains, jumped in that big old cage from the backside of it, and stood at the microphone and went on to "Wop-Bop-A-Lu-Bop" and then croon all his other songs while the girls just all screamed their lungs out. I thought it was the funniest thing I'd seen up till that time in show business. What I thought was even funnier, a guy put a lock on the cage after Pat had jumped in, and I was thinkin', 'Boy, it'd be funny if they couldn't get it opened after he

got done, and they had to put him in a truck and take him to the next show and town in that cage.' I guess Pat wanted to be in that cage 'cause he thought he was gonna get hurt or somethin', but it sure was a sight to see."

Later in 1957, Janis Martin put her own band together and began to tour the nightclub, theater, and fair circuit all across the U.S. and Canada. RCA Victor Records dropped Janis from her contract in 1958, after they found out she had been secretly married to her childhood sweetheart since she was fifteen years old. He was in the Army from 1955 to 1958, and the blow to RCA in Nashville came in '58 when they found out Janis was not only married, but pregnant also. Janis had her first son in late 1958, but continued to perform until early 1959, at which time she went back to Virginia to raise a family. A year later, in 1960, she signed with Palette Records, after turning down deals from Decca and King Records, and recorded four songs for this new label. After those two records were released and Janis went out on the road for more shows, she retired for the next fifteen years or so, 'cause the music business just interfered too much with the raising of her growing family.

During the mid 1970s, Janis put a new band together around Danville, Virginia, and started playin' weekend show dates across the state. In 1977, she had one 45 record released on Big Dutch Records, where she sang a rockin' version of Hank Snow's classic "I'm Movin' On" and Marty Robbins's old hit "Begging to You." After Bear Family Records in Germany released most all of the 1950s rockabilly songs she'd recorded for RCA Victor on two 1979 albums, Janis began to tour all over Europe in 1980, two to three times a year. She's continued to do so right to the present day. In 1994, Hydra Records in Holland released a CD of all new recordings by Janis.

I'd recommend any of Janis Martin's rockabilly recordings I've mentioned. That basically means about every song Janis has out there. I only named the ones that I think are her greatest, but all of 'em are the best examples of rockabilly music by a female artist anywhere around. On the latest Hydra Records album, you'll find a song that Janis co-wrote with an old friend of hers by the name of Ed Bayes, called "Hard Rockin' Mama." This song was written in the late seventies, and it's pure female rockabilly dynamite.

I never got to see Janis Martin perform during 1956 and '57, and to be honest, I can't remember seein' her on TV. I think if I had, I would-a sure remembered. But all of her RCA Victor records got a lot of airplay on the radio stations I listened to around Washington, D.C., and I bought 'em all, 'cause they were easily found. Even her four-song EP album. The only record she was on that it would take me until the mid 1970s to get my hands on, which I didn't know had come out in late 1956, was a ten-inch, twelve-song album called *Janis & Elvis*. This album only came out in the country of South Africa, and it wasn't out but for a very short time, because even though Elvis had given his endorsement to Janis Martin, which Colonel Parker couldn't do anything about, the old Colonel wasn't about to have his boy share billing with Janis Martin, especially when her name was put first. Parker had RCA Victor of South Africa pull this album off the market when he found out about it. It's a hard and rare album to find today.

Janis came up to do a live show in Severna Park, Maryland, for me on February 23, 1990. Janis brought her husband, Wayne, plus her oldest son, who played drums behind her, and a real good rockin' piano player named William from her hometown in Virginia. I got her two other hot rockabilly musician friends of mine from the Washington, D.C., area to complete her band, Pedro Serra on lead guitar and Jimmy Cavanaugh on bass. Janis was only doin' shows in Europe at this time, and she was good enough to come up and prove not only to me but also to the almost 300 fans that were there that she was definitely a hard-rockin' mama. Janis could finallly cut loose and rock out to a young audience of U.S. rockabilly fans the way she wanted to, with no one to tell her what to do. The crowd loved every minute of it, 'cause she proved she's the #1 1950s female artist still performing today. In early 1994, Janis went out to Los Angeles and San Diego and did a few shows out there. But today, she's mainly content with still doin' occasional tours overseas a couple times a year, where she's constantly in demand. Since I was recording again, and occasionally performing live, Janis after several tries finally talked me into going overseas in the fall of 1994 to do several shows with her. I wouldn't go all that way with just anybody, but Janis Martin knows how to rock, loves the fans like I do, and still knows how to have fun, so I wound up on that plane with her.

Just as an update, heading into 1998 Janis and I will be doing more shows together, this time in the far Northwest. I've had many conversations with Janis over the past several years, and I like her a whole lot, 'cause she is what she is, just a good ol' real hard-rockin'

country girl who loves rockabilly the most of all and ain't got no use for all the new manufactured high-tech music comin' out of MTV and TNN.

Brenda Lee

I'll go with Brenda Lee next. Brenda is the #3 all-time top pop female artist of the rock 'n' roll era. Only Brenda had fifty-two songs reach the *Billboard* Top 100 singles charts between 1957 and 1973. Brenda also had nine of her albums reach the *Billboard* Top 40 pop albums charts between 1960 and 1965. Twelve of her *Billboard* singles chart hits made it into the Top 10, with two of those reaching #1, both of those in 1960, her big year. All her Top 10s were between 1960 and 1963. Brenda Lee was an international pop teen queen and on the cover of most teen-type magazines between 1960 and 1963. I should also mention that Brenda had a total of thirty-four songs chart on the *Billboard* country singles charts. She had one country chart hit in 1957, and the other thirty-three came between 1969 and 1985. Over the past forty years, Brenda Lee has sold right at 100 million records, by most accounts. Those are all pretty good numbers for a poor little country girl who was born Brenda Mae Tarpley on December 11, 1944, in the charity ward of Grady Memorial Hospital in Atlanta, Georgia.

Brenda Lee's life story or musical career can be found in other major books, so I'm mainly gonna stick with the basics on the dozen or so great rockabilly-styled songs Brenda's incredible voice belted out at such a young age. I'll just sketch out her background as quickly as possible. By age eleven she was a regular on Red Foley's network TV show "The Ozark Jubilee" and was signed to Decca Records. Paul Cohen was the head of A&R for the Decca country division in Nashville, and he's the one who signed her to his label, in May 1956. In August, Cohen took Brenda Lee into Owen Bradley's barn studio in Nashville, and, along with Bradley, produced the first of five recordings on her. Six songs were recorded at that first session. Four of 'em were released as her first two 45 singles. Brenda recorded two Hank Williams classics, "Jambalaya" and "Your Cheatin' Heart," one called "Doodle Bug Rag," two newly written childish Christmas songs called "I'm Gonna Lasso Santa Claus" and "Christy Christmas," and one song now considered Brenda Lee's first rockabilly classic, "Bigelow 6-200." The latter song is real good, but Brenda's best rockabilly songs would come over the course of the next two and a half years. Out of these six songs, they chose "Jambalaya" for the A side and "Bigelow 6-200" for the B side of her first single. This 45 was released on September 17, 1956, and although it got a fantastic review by *Billboard* magazine upon its release, it failed to sell that well and didn't make in onto either the country or the pop singles charts in *Billboard*. Only six weeks later, at the end of October, Decca Records released "I'm Gonna Lasso Santa Clause" b/w "Christy Christmas" for the upcoming Christmas season. Once again, the same results: low sales, very little radio airplay, and no chart success. During the course of these two record releases, Brenda continued to appear on "The Ozark Jubilee," as well as on tour with all the top country stars, such as Faron Young and Mel Tillis, on the road tours the Ozark Jubilee show performed throughout the South, Southwest, and Midwest. It should be noted that though Brenda Lee was eleven years old when her first two 45 singles were released, for whatever marketing reasons, Decca Records billed her on the labels as "Little Brenda Lee (9 years old)."

Paul Cohen and Decca Records changed directions for Brenda Lee's next recording session, in January 1957. It proved to be a good and successful move when they sent Brenda Lee to New York City then, to have two songs for her next 45 single produced by Milt Gabler. Gabler was the person responsible for the first #1 rock 'n' roll record in the history of the music when he earlier produced "Rock Around the Clock" by Bill Haley and His Comets, which also came out on Decca Records and was recorded in New York City. Decca Records' New York City house band plus The Ray Charles Singers were used to back Brenda Lee up on the two songs she recorded there under the guidance of Milt Gabler. Those two songs were "One Step at a Time" and "Fairyland." Now, "Fairyland" was just a silly little kid-type syrupy song, but the A side of this 45, "One Step at a Time," vocally proved that twelve-year-old Brenda Lee had the rip-roaringest, most unique stutter/stammer style on a solid rockabilly tune that anyone had ever heard by a female singer up to this point.

"One Step at a Time" debuted on the *Billboard* pop charts on March 2, 1957, and reached a peak of #43 the following month, but had a nice ride of eleven weeks on those charts. On April 6, "One Step at a Time" also was on the *Billboard* country charts, but for only one week, at #15. In 1957, teenagers were buying over 80 percent of the 45 single records in America, and

Brenda Lee's first big chart success with "One Step at a Time" sent a message to Paul Cohen and Owen Bradley in Nashville that this was gonna be the kind of material, rockabilly, that they would for a few years record on her. After the success of "One Step at a Time," Brenda Lee did all of her recording from 1957 to 1976 in Nashville. The pop success of this song also led to appearances on top-rated network TV shows, such as the Steve Allen show and the Perry Como show, along with others.

Paul Cohen and Owen Bradley did the next recording session on Brenda in April 1957, back at Bradley's barn in Nashville, and that resulted in her follow-up single to "One Step at a Time." This new one had the strong, rockin', fast-paced rockabilly song "Dynamite" on the A side and a solid mid-tempo stutter-style rockabilly tune called "Love You Till I Die" on the B side. "Dynamite" debuted on the *Billboard* pop charts on July 15, 1957, and only climbed to a peak position of #72, but stayed on those charts for a seven-week ride. "Dynamite" failed to reach the *Billboard* country charts, though Brenda continued to perform weekly on the Ozark Jubilee TV shows and tours and performed mostly for country audiences into the fall of 1959. Brenda Lee was known as "Little Miss Dynamite" from this time on. She and her family moved permanently to Nashville, in July 1957, and she has made her home there ever since. Brenda wouldn't see another song of hers reach anywhere on the *Billboard* country charts until 1969, though she recorded in Nashville and made her home there.

Even though Brenda Lee's next six 45s and one album between the fall of 1957 and the summer of 1959 all failed to reach the *Billboard* pop charts, Decca Records continued to stick with this little girl with the big, gutsy, gritty voice, as Owen Bradley did when he took over Paul Cohen's position at Decca Records in the spring of 1958. Brenda's greatest moments in rockabilly music really came on those six 45s that failed to make the national charts. Her songs such as "Ain't That Love," "One Teenager to Another" (1957), "Ring-a-My Phone," "Little Jonah" (1958), and "Let's Jump the Broomstick" (1959) are all great female rockabilly songs. Even though they didn't hit the national charts here in the U.S., several were big chart hits in many foreign countries where Brenda Lee was touring between 1957 and 1959. I thought so much of Brenda Lee's 1958 single "Little Jonah" b/w "Ring-A-My Phone" that I put both those great rockabilly tunes on LesLee "Bird" Anderson's 1988 album *Runnin' Wild*.

Brenda Lee finally cracked into the mainstream world of pop music, and there was no lookin' back from then on, when on December 21, 1959, "Sweet Nothin's" (which was written by fifties rockabilly artist Ronnie Self) debuted on the *Billboard* pop singles charts, and while it only reached a peak position of #4 in the spring of 1960, it stayed on *Billboard* for twenty-four straight weeks. Brenda never had another song ride those charts longer than that one did. Brenda Lee had just turned fifteen years old when "Sweet Nothin's" debuted on the charts, and even though this song had a rockin' edge to it, it was the beginning of 1960, and rock 'n' roll was pretty much dead. Teen idols, both male and female, were the in thing that year. Teen idols of the early sixties sang dreamy love ballads, and that's how Brenda Lee's career was marketed for a few years, until the British Invasion either wiped everybody out or, at least, as was Brenda Lee's case, slowed 'em down as far as high-ranking *Billboard* chart success went. But Brenda Lee's pop teen queen magazine years are made for another book. I want to tell you what made Brenda Lee one of the greatest girls to ever sing rockabilly. All it boiled down to was the natural way she had of doin' those wild-soundin', hiccuppin', stutter/step tricks where she split words in two, but while she was doin' it, she was able to go on to drive the song home with the raunchiest, rawest, gutsiest, throatiest vocal sound out there. Brenda Lee was pure dynamite with her delivery on a song, any song. Even in the early sixties, when she had strings and pop instrumentation behind her on an up-tempo song, you could still hear her beltin'-out style come through. I'm sure glad we had Brenda Lee out there all during the 1960s and on the *Billboard* charts, 'cause she always belted out a certain number of up-tempo songs with not much change in her astounding vocal range. Even as late as 1966 and 1967, Brenda was still into the *Billboard* pop Top 40 with great songs like "Comin' On Strong" and "Ride, Ride, Ride."

I met Brenda Lee once in late 1959 and four times during 1960 when she came on the Milt Grant TV dance show to promote her latest records. She was nice to me every time, as she also was in 1972 when I talked to her after her show at The Stardust in Waldorf, Maryland. The last time I spoke with Brenda was in November 1988. She was still the nice person she'd always been. I was still a fan of her music and guess I always will be. I've seen Brenda on TNN (The Nashville Network) since then a number of times, and I remember I taped one interview show back in 1989 where they went into her home and asked her about her life and career. I recently watched that video tape again, 'cause I wanted to be sure she said what I'd remembered when I first saw it. Brenda told the TNN interviewer and audience that only one thing annoyed her about Nashville, and that was that after living her entire adult life in Nashville and recording all her music there, along with donating her time and coming out for every charity and fund-raiser the country music industry has asked her to be a part of, she still felt as if she'd never been fully accepted as a part of Nashville's country music family. That really seemed to bother Brenda then. All I can say to "Little Miss Dynamite" is that you've got to have warehousefuls of more international and U.S. awards, plus sold more records and accomplished more in your long career, than most all of yesterday's and today's country or pop stars. You've always been a real great natural singer, Brenda, and can still outsing 'em all. Most important is, old and new fans of all ages still love ya!

Wanda Jackson

Well, you know a chapter on women, or chicks, whichever you prefer, who sang rockabilly music wouldn't be complete without the lady who fans around the world that love rockabilly music all consider the main queen of rockabilly music in the fifties. That bein' Wanda Jackson. Let me say this before I get rockin' on Wanda. From 1956 into early 1962, I bought all fifteen 45 singles, along with her first four albums, that all came out on the Capitol Records label during that time period. My personal favorite Wanda Jackson rockabilly songs, which I think are some of the finest examples of female rockabilly music that you'll hear almost anywhere, are, in order, "Riot in Cell Block #9," "Fujiyama Mama," "Mean, Mean Man," "I Gotta Know," "Tongue Tied," and "Man We Had a Party." Out of these really fabulous rockers, only "I Gotta Know" made a national *Billboard* chart. It was #15 for one week on *Billboard*'s country charts on October 20, 1956. There's quite a few other late-fifties rockabilly and even country songs I enjoy by Wanda Jackson, but the ones I just named all just completely blow me away even today. On those songs, Wanda no doubt proves she had the raunchiest, scorchin', raw, growlin' vocal ability on a 1950s rockabilly song, more than any of the other country chicks that released rockabilly songs on a pretty regular basis back at that time. Though, in a different way, Brenda Lee had just as raw a vocal delivery as Wanda did on a rockabilly tune.

But to be real honest, I've always had a real problem with how Wanda Jackson has been hyped over the past ten to fifteen years on the liner notes of so many reissues and a couple newer more recent record albums. Plus, it's always bothered me that in everything I've read on her in magazine articles, Wanda is listed as the all-time, ultimate Queen of rockabilly music. Before I get into what I know to be the facts, let me give you some background on Wanda Jackson.

Wanda was born in Maud, Oklahoma, on October 20, 1937. She was the only child of Tom and Nellie Jackson. Her full name is Wanda Jean Jackson. There was hardly any work around Maud, Oklahoma, and Tom was barely able to keep food on the table for his wife and newborn daughter. He kept takin' odd handyman jobs, along with playin' piano in local hillbilly honky honks. In 1941 Tom Jackson packed the family's belongings in his old car and moved his family to Bakersfield, California. Tom was able to get a job as a barber there and settle his family into a fairly decent home. Young Wanda loved the country music that was real popular in the Bakersfield area, and she listened to a lot of it on the local country radio stations throughout the 1940s. Wanda learned how to play the guitar by age six and learned how to play the piano by age nine. She did a lot of singin' in church while living in Bakersfield.

In 1949, Tom moved his wife and daughter to Oklahoma City, Oklahoma, where he took a job selling used cars. In 1950, after winning a local talent contest, Wanda was given a fifteen-minute radio program of her own on station KLPR after school each day. Hank Thompson also made his home in Oklahoma City, and he and his western band played every Saturday night there. Hank Thompson was Wanda Jackson's idol and favorite singing star. She sang a lot of Hank's songs on her radio program. One day after Wanda's program went off the air, Hank called the radio station and invited Wanda to

sing with his band there in Oklahoma City. This led to a close friendship as Hank Thompson encouraged Wanda with her music and singing. Within a few years, Wanda became a regular member of Hank Thompson & His Brazos Valley Boys and started touring with the group in between her high school days.

During the early part of 1954, Hank Thompson tried to convince his label, Capitol Records, to sign Wanda to a solo contract, but Capitol turned him down, even though his band was backing Wanda up on a four-song demo Hank had recorded on Wanda. After Capitol Records turned Hank down, he approached Paul Cohen at Decca Records in Nashville, and Cohen decided not only to sign Wanda but also to release those four songs as her first two 45 singles. One song was a duet with Billy Gray, who was also on the Decca Records country artists roster at the time. The first 45 off that demo that Decca Records released clicked and went into the Top 10 *Billboard* country charts during the late summer of 1954. It was the duet side with Billy Gray, called "You Can't Have My Love," that debuted on the *Billboard* country charts on July 24, 1954, and peaked out at the #8 position, while staying on those charts for an eight-week run. It wasn't a bad song at all for 1954 country music. It was just the standard-type country song that was popular back then. It was upbeat and on the fast side, also.

Wanda entered her senior year at Capitol High School with a Top 10 country chart hit under her belt. Through to the end of 1955, she recorded fifteen songs for Decca Records, which resulted in a total of seven 45 releases, but after the first duet country hit single with Billy Gray, all the others failed to make the national charts. Not to say Wanda wasn't a popular country music attraction at live country shows, 'cause she certainly was.

Forgettin' to Remember to Forget

During the late fifties, I got to see Wanda Jackson sing rockabilly on "The Ozark Jubilee" and also on the California-based "Ranch Party" shows, when she was on 'em as a special guest. I even seen Wanda once at a big country music package show in 1957 that my parents took me to at the Washington, D.C., armory. Wanda sure was terrific on that show. She also was one great-lookin' chick, with her long black hair, big silver long drop earrings, and I remember how I loved it back then watchin' her belt out "Hot Dog, That Made Him Mad" while she strummed on the strings of her great-lookin' big old guitar and bumped her rump in time with the music. Wanda was definitely the highlight of that country show for me.

Shortly after graduation from high school, Wanda became a regular member of Red Foley's "Ozark Jubilee," out of Springfield, Missouri. Wanda stayed there on a regular basis until 1960, when she had her first *Billboard* pop chart hit. Wanda has said on TV shows in recent years that it was Elvis, who Wanda worked with as a supporting act on a good number of shows he did in late 1955 and early 1956, who told her it was rockabilly and rock 'n' roll that was gonna be the next big thing in all of music, and that she better jump on it. Wanda went on to say she told Elvis, "I'm doin' straight country and feel I'm gettin' hotter all the time, and I really don't feel I can sing that kind of music." But Elvis persisted and went on to tell Wanda he knew she did have the voice for it, and according to Wanda, Elvis even went so far as to help try and find her rockabilly/rock 'n' roll type songs.

I know Elvis musta liked Wanda Jackson in those early years of his career to help her that much. Why wouldn't he? Wanda was one fine-lookin' eighteen-year-old chick with a great shape, as all her mid- and late-fifties photos prove. Wanda has been a born-again Christian since 1973, and I respect that, but she won't talk about her and Elvis's personal relationship back in 1955 and early '56. Wanda definitely took Elvis's advice, though.

With her two-year recording contract with Decca Records completed, Wanda signed on with Hank Thompson's manager Jim Halsey in the spring of 1956, and Halsey had Wanda signed to a solid contract with Capitol Records within about a month. By this time, Capitol Records was havin' boomin' success with Gene Vincent & His Blue Caps and their rockabilly style. Wanda was produced by Gene Vincent's producer, Ken Nelson. Wanda's first 45 single was "I Gotta Know" b/w "Half as Good a Girl." The A side, "I Gotta Know," starts off like a sad, sappy country ballad, and then all of a sudden Wanda just roars into the meat and potatoes boppin' rockabilly sound. It really took you by surprise back in the late summer of 1956 when you first heard it. Elvis was as right as rain has to fall when he said Wanda Jackson had the voice for a rockabilly tune. Those grooves in that record didn't lie.

"I Gotta Know" made it onto the *Billboard* country charts for one week at #15 on October 20, 1956. From then on through to the end of 1961, for Wanda's next eleven straight 45 singles, Capitol Records continued to couple a rockabilly or rock 'n' rollish teen-type oriented song on one side with a straight-soundin' country song on the flip side.

Except for one show with Ricky Nelson in the late 1950s, Wanda Jackson only toured with country stars of the day and performed for country music audiences, such as Janis Martin and Brenda Lee also had during the late 1950s. Wanda Jackson's first love then was country

Forgettin' to Remember to Forget

In 1995 all this hoopla was goin' on here in Nashville with fans of rockabilly music because Wanda Jackson was gonna be appearing live with Rosie Flores to help Rosie promote her latest album, called *Rockabilly Filly,* on Hightone Records. Rosie has played clubs in Nashville many times, doin' both country and rockabilly music. She has a lot of friends here, but it was Wanda Jackson who was the big attraction that almost everyone came out to see. Well, I was warned by rockabilly friends and fans I knew in Austin, San Antonio, and Corpus Christi, Texas, that when Wanda and Rosie played in San Antonio a week earlier, they all had been disappointed (to put it nicely), 'cause neither Wanda nor Rosie did what they considered to be a rockabilly show. But I figured I'd go, as I knew there'd be a lot of people there who were friends of mine. Well, I got there in time to catch the whole last set and saw Wanda and Rosie do what they do. The show was billed as Wanda Jackson and Rosie Flores's "Rockabilly Tour '95." My friends in Texas were right. I hate to say it, but to Wanda Jackson, rockabilly today is just singin' a bunch of her old songs in a fifties revival way and lettin' it go at that. (As for Rosie Flores, I'll talk more about her in Chapter 13.) On top of that, Wanda and Rosie did way too many plain country songs in what was called a rockabilly show. But most of those who were there had never seen Wanda, and I guess were just happy to be in the presence of the fifty-eight-year-old lady who was been touted as being the ultimate female rockabilly woman of the 1950s.

music, and there's certainly nothin' wrong with that, and she made a lot of good solid country records into the early sixties. But it would take until the summer of 1961 before Wanda had another song on the country charts of *Billboard*, although she did have regional radio country chart success in southern markets.

Wanda's great version of "Fujiama Mama" was a big hit in Japan in 1958, and she went over and did a tour over there in the Far East. But after more than four years of tryin' and hopin' that one of Wanda Jackson's rockabilly-type songs might catch on in the teenage market, it finally did happen during the summer of 1960. Though don't get the wrong idea, Capitol Records were all pushing their country artists foremost towards the mainstream of country radio during the late fifties, 'cause they were primarily havin' success playing to country audiences. But there was always a good chance one side of the record might catch on in the big-selling teenage record buying market. Capitol Records had big success with Sonny James and Ferlin Husky, among others, during the late fifties, so Wanda Jackson was no different. They did the same thing with them by putting a country song on one side of a 45 single and a teenage-type or rockabilly/rock 'n' roll song on the other side. Well, it was on Wanda Jackson's eleventh Capitol Records 45 single that she made it onto the *Billboard* pop charts with a real big-selling national hit. It was on a cover of an Elvis Presley song he sang and had out on the soundtrack album and in the movie *Loving You*, from 1957. The song was called "Let's Have a Party."

Wanda had recorded this song in April 1958, and she's stated in interviews that it was just a throw-in extra cut for her first Capitol Records album in 1958. Wanda also admits if it wasn't for this disc jockey in Iowa playin' this song from her old album two years later and gettin' requests from teenagers to hear the song on an everyday basis, Capitol probably wouldn't have come out with it at all in 1960. But when Capitol Records heard about this, they decided to go with "Let's Have a Party" as Wanda's next 45 single in the summer of 1960. Wanda Jackson's version of "Let's Have a Party" was really a bright spark for me and thousands of others who all loved rockabilly and solid real hard-hittin' rock 'n' roll. But a real geat rockin' song like "Let's Have a Party" by a singer comin' out of the country music field of entertainers was destined only to make it so far up the pop music charts at this late date. "Let's Have a Party" reached a peak position of #37 by early October 1960, and stayed on those charts for a total of ten weeks.

What the song did, though, was put momentum into Capitol Records to release two albums in a row by Wanda Jackson geared directly at the teenage market. The first one, *Rockin' with Wanda*, had her best rockabilly/rock 'n' roll material on it. They followed that one up in 1961 with *There's a Party Goin' On*, which were all newly recorded cover songs that were pretty weak versions of the originals. There were a few good bright spots, such as "There's a Party Goin' On," "Tongue Tied" (which was great), and "Man We Had a Party," but Wanda's versions of "Kansas City," "Tweedlee Dee," "It Doesn't Matter Anymore," "Lonely Weekends," and the rest just didn't come close to hittin' the mark on an album that on the front cover said, "An album of great rockin' songs by Wanda Jackson." When this album was recorded and released in 1961, you can tell Wanda wasn't into rockin' or rockabilly like she had been several years earlier. The times had changed, and she was goin' back into what she loved most after that. Country music.

After "Let's Have a Party" broke her onto the pop mainstream *Billboard* charts, Wanda had even bigger country or country/pop hits on those charts with her next four straight 45 singles that Capitol Records released. "Let's Have a Party" never made *Billboard*'s country charts. There was no way that was about to happen back in those early days. But because of that great old rockabilly song, Wanda was able to rack up a long streak of country chart hits on *Billboard* pretty consistently through early 1972.

Wanda Jackson's biggest pop *Billboard* hit was the follow-up to "Let's Have a Party." That was called "Right or Wrong." This was a country ballad song that reached #29 on the *Billboard* pop charts and #9 on the country charts. This came during the summer of 1961. Throughout the 1960s Wanda Jackson recorded and had released by Capitol Records quite a few good country songs that were all *Billboard* country chart hits back then. Of course, I think everybody could have done without Wanda's hit versions of songs like "A Little Bitty Tear," "If I Had a Hammer," and "By the Time I Get to Phoenix," but just chalk it up to the trends during those times.

Around 1972, Wanda remarried and became a born-again Christian. Over the next ten years or so, she recorded a good amount of gospel, religious, and Christian music on record labels such as Myrrh Records. During the early 1980s, the European promoters enticed Wanda to come back over there to perform all her great old rockabilly songs. Wanda had done many tours of these foreign countries from the late fifties and throughout most of the sixties.

Wanda recorded an album called *Rockabilly Fever* for a Swedish label in 1984 that was released by Rounder Records here in the U.S. in 1986. I have to say it: The spark, the fire, everything that was great about Wanda Jackson's raw and raunchy rockabilly songs of the 1950s was completely gone. This is no more than an oldies slice-of-nostalgia album, and not a very good one at that.

When this album came out on Rounder Records in 1986, I happened to see Wanda was listed as one of the guests on Ralph Emory's old "Nashville Now" TNN network cable TV show. I figured, great, I'd tape the show. I'm glad I did. For two reasons. First is that it showed me sometimes a once-great artist doesn't know when to quit. Second is I found out how Wanda Jackson really felt about rockabilly music. First off, I felt sorry for Wanda Jackson when she sang her best-known 1961 classic country song "Right or Wrong," 'cause her voice went off key and cracked when she tried to reach for the notes she needed. Wanda then sang the title track from the Rounder album, "Rockabilly Fever" (which is a lame song Carl Perkins wrote in 1980, where he'd used the title of a great rockabilly tune Tex Rubinowitz and Billy Hancock had given him a year earlier in Bethesda, Maryland, that he told 'em he was gonna record). When Wanda finished the song, she came back over and Ralph Emory asked her about her recent European tour, and the rockabilly fans over there that came out to see her perform her old rockabilly songs, and what she thought of it after all these years. Wanda replied, "All the kids over there love that music, and I just try to have fun with it, because that's what they're payin' to see. I don't take it too seriously, 'cause I'd rather be singin' country music."

In conclusion on Wanda Jackson, I've only told you the truth as I see it 'cause I don't want any rockabilly fan bein' disappointed or blamin' me if they went to a rockabilly show. If you wanna see good older artists that put on great rockabilly shows like they did in the 1950s that all rockabilly fans seem to love, then go catch Sleepy La Beef, Janis Martin, Ronnie Dawson, or The Collins Kids (Larry and Lorrie). They'll all rock you real good. Wanda, I'm sorry if I hurt your feelings. From now on, though, I'll just keep listenin' to your great old songs.

The Collins Kids

Those are the three ladies that all charted one or two rockabilly records on the *Billboard* pop charts between 1956 and 1960, and they're all the best remembered today for the dozen or so great rockabilly songs they recorded back at that time. But another duo, who were an enormously popular act that recorded and had released a whole lot of great rockabilly-oriented songs, but were never on any national charts, were Larry and Lorrie Collins. Better known to rockabilly fans around the world today as The Collins Kids. The two were equally important, but I'm puttin' 'em in this female chapter because Lorrie Collins was one of the best out there on her delivery of a rockabilly tune. I only saw The Collins Kids on the TV show "Ranch Party" from 1956 through '58 or '59, but they were the main reason I watched that show, which came out of Compton, California, but was broadcast in Washington, D.C., where I lived then.

Lorrie Collins was born in Tahlequah, Oklahoma, on May 7, 1942, and younger brother Larry was born in Tulsa, Oklahoma, on October 4, 1944. They had one older sister. Their father was a dairy farmer for a short time and then went on to take a job as a crane operator at a nearby steel mill. They lived in the little town of Pretty Water, Oklahoma, during their childhood years. Their father had no musical background whatsoever, but their mother was an amateur singer who also played the mandolin. Their older sister Sherry Collins thought about a career in music for awhile but married when she was fifteen years old instead.

Lorrie was the first to show an interest in music, and although the area they grew up in was dominated by both male and female country music performers, Lorrie has stated that her favorite singers around 1950 and '51 were Kay Starr and Teresa Brewer. Both were pop singers of that era, but really good ones. Lorrie won her first talent contest in 1950. The contest was hosted by Leon McAuliffe, who had a popular western swing band around that area. McAuliffe encouraged Lorrie's mother Hazel to take her eight-year-old daughter, who he felt was real good, to California if she really wanted to give her a real chance at pursuing a professional career in the music industry. For a short while in 1952, Hazel Collins took her daughter to Los Angeles, and they made the rounds of talent contests and managerial agencies, and Hazel was told if she moved out to that area, they felt sure Lorrie stood a good chance at makin' it in the music business. When they returned from Los Angeles, they finally convinced Lorrie's father, Lawrence Collins Sr., the family should move permanently to California.

Lorrie's younger brother Larry hadn't really showed much interest in music up to this point, but one of his presents on Christmas Day, 1952, was his first guitar. Larry's mother showed him how to play a couple chords on that guitar. The Collins family made the move to California in 1953. All through the end of that year, Larry and Lorrie Collins separately entered many talent contests, winning a good number of 'em. Just as Larry and Lorrie's parents were thinkin' about maybe movin' back to Oklahoma at the end of 1953, a local disc jockey named Squeekin' Deacon advised Hazel Collins to take Larry and Lorrie over to audition for Bill Wagnon, who booked "Town Hall Party" (which was later known as "Ranch Party" when it went into syndication around the U.S.). By this time, Larry and Lorrie's father had suggested that the two of 'em should practice their singin' and guitar playin' together. Larry had already taught Lorrie how to play the guitar. After practicing together, they came out as a duo act with Larry singing the high harmony parts and Lorrie singin' the lead vocals.

After Larry and Lorrie Collins entered a "Town Hall Party" talent contest in February 1954, the two kids were hired to perform on the TV program the next day. Tex Ritter was the host of this show, and other regulars on the program when The Collins Kids first joined were Johnny Bond and Freddy Hart. One other regular member, who would be the biggest influence on young Larry Collins's phenomenal lead guitar playin', was guitarist Joe Maphis. This was already a popular show and had originally begun in 1951. Throughout the rest of 1954 and into 1955, The Collins Kids were a popular act among viewers of "Town Hall Party." The two kids also did other TV and radio work during this period.

The top A & R man for Columbia Records in Nashville, Don Law, made a number of trips to California to scout out talent for the label. At the insistence of Johnny Bond, Don Law signed The Collins Kids to a short-term six-month contract on July 25, 1955. The Collins Kids' first recording session was held at Radio Recorders in Hollywood, on October 4, 1955, and was produced by Don Law, who would continue to produce every Collins Kids recording from then on, until the act broke up in 1961.

From that first session came two songs that became The Collins Kids' first 45 single. They were "Hush Money"

and "Beetle Bug Bop." In late October 1955, when this record was released, although it failed to make any national charts, it musta sold pretty well, as Don Law renewed The Collins Kids' recording contract with Columbia Records in January 1956, and continued to keep renewing it into the early 1960s. This first record by The Collins Kids was a kid-oriented country record, as were their next several 45s in 1956. But hey, that's just what they were then. Kids! Through most of 1956, Larry was eleven years old, and Lorrie was thirteen and then fourteen years old. During 1956, they were both kids just like I was, and I watched 'em every time they came on TV through 1958. They sang a lot of cover rock 'n' roll and rockabilly songs all during that time, and let me tell you, the outfits they wore looked phenomenal to me. They were the straight-fringed, spangled country cowboy/cowgirl-type show clothes that a lot of top country artists like Carl Smith wore back in '55 and '56.

Larry Collins was the outgoing, spunky, biggest ball of fire, with so much energy it was unbelievable. Larry would dance, jitterbug, and hop in circles all around Lorrie when she sang. All the while, he kept knockin' out the greatest guitar licks in a ninety-mile-an-hour speed limit you could ever dream of. Sister Lorrie was a cute little girl in 1956, who by 1958 turned into one luscious and vivacious-lookin' sixteen-year-old chick, and let me tell you, they both could rock out on some of the best rockabilly music from that period. Larry and his double-neck guitar goin' nuts, and Lorrie just had the most perfect voice on any kind of song. Especially as 1957 and '58 came in, when I believe all their greatest rockabilly tunes were done. Neither one of The Collins Kids was ever threatening to Nashville's country music industry, even though they were both singin' and performing some of the best rockabilly music of that period. The reason is simple. The two of 'em, once again, were just looked upon as the kids that they were.

As a duo, The Collins Kids recorded ten sessions at Columbia Records, which resulted in fourteen 45 single releases between late 1955 and mid 1961. Larry recorded four other sessions for Columbia through mid 1962. The first one, on September 25, 1957, resulted in two instrumental releases on Columbia Records with the great Joe Maphis tradin' licks with Larry on guitar. The best and most exceptional, fabulous, tear-it-up, rockin' instrumental off these two 45s is a song Larry Collins wrote called "Hurricane," which is an appropriate title. Larry had two other solo instrumentals released under his own name in 1960, and then after Larry and Lorrie ended the act in 1961, Larry had three more 45 singles released that he sang on in 1961 and 1962.

I was a Collins Kids fan in the late fifties. I bought their first eleven 45 records, right when they first came out between late 1955 and early 1959. They were on Columbia Records, and Washington, D.C., was a big-selling area for the country music industry then, so their 45s were easy enough for me to find. The final record I bought by The Collins Kids in '59 was called "Sugar Plum" b/w "Kinda Like Love." The reason that was the final record I bought by 'em was because I could hear the change in what was once some of the best hard, lightnin'-speed rockabilly music you could find that was nowhere on the charts. These two songs released in 1959 were both on the silly, love, teeny bopper theme that was startin' to come in at that time. Hey now, it was a whole lot better than Frankie Avalon's big hit "Gingerbread" from around the same time, but it was the final Collins Kids record I bought without hearin' it first.

What I consider the five greatest rockabilly songs The Collins Kids ever had released, during their relatively short recording career as a duo, came from '57 and '58. They were the fantastic "Mercy" and "Whistle Bait," both from 1958, and both hot, scorchin', frantic rockabilly all the way, "Hop Skip and Jump," "Hoy Hoy," and their version in their own style of Elvis's early '57 song "Let's Have a Party," which were released in 1957. Lorrie Collins had one great voice, and it was in no way a high-pitched, nasal, irritating voice that some of the female country singers had during those years. While Lorrie could sound at ease blastin' out a raunchy, raw, speedy rockabilly tune such as "Mercy," she could also give a young teenage boy like me goosebumps back in '57 and '58 on her sultry, sexy, mid-tempo rockabilly songs such as "Rock Boppin' Baby" and "Heartbeat."

The Collins Kids were perfect for all my tastes in the kind of music I loved, and that was rockabilly, rock 'n' roll, and good fifties hillbilly. I'm really glad I got to enjoy all their great late-fifties 45s. But by 1959, I was fifteen years old, and Larry and Lorrie Collins were fifteen and seventeen, respectively. Oh now, I did watch Lorrie Collins on quite a few of the "Ozzie and Harriet" TV shows, where she'd occasionally appear as a guest. She would usually sing, or on two shows I taped in recent years from the reruns, Ricky would sing his love ballads to her. This was during the 1958 to 1959 TV season. It only made sense that Lorrie Collins was on the TV show

at that time, as Lorrie and Ricky became engaged to be married during 1959. The reason the two were never married was that The Collins Kids had been touring pretty steady with Johnny Cash and his show. Lorrie Collins evidently grew more than fond of Johnny Cash's road manager, Stew Carnall, during 1959, as the two of 'em eloped and were married in Las Vegas in the fall of 1959. Lorrie was still only seventeen years old then. Talk about tough luck. Ricky wound up readin' about their marriage the following day in the Los Angeles *Herald Examiner*.

Lorrie Collins and Ricky Nelson were on the covers and in a lot of TV, teen, and movie magazines all during that time. But this marriage caused the two Collins Kids (who were both growin' up fast) to split up for about six months. When they got back together, they went back out on the road touring again with Johnny Cash. Lorrie's husband Stew Carnall was now managing the two Collins Kids. By February 1961, The Collins Kids as a duo pretty much ended, because Lorrie had her first child that month, although they did continue on for awhile through the rest of 1961, performing some shows together, as well as doing a couple foreign tours of Europe and the Far East.

Lorrie and Larry Collins did their final recording session for Columbia Records in June 1961. Though The Collins Kids had no national chart records, their 45s sold well enough for Columbia Records to stay with 'em for a long time. Their two biggest-selling records, as everyone seems to agree, were "Let's Have a Party" and "Whistle Bait," from 1957 and 1958, respectively. Besides the "Town Hall Party" shows, these two talented, energetic rockabilly kids were seen on many national network TV shows between 1956 and 1958. The Arthur Godfrey, Dinah Shore, Steve Allen, and Perry Como network TV shows were some of the ones The Collins Kids appeared on back then.

In late 1961, after Lorrie Collins had left this once-great child duo, Larry Collins on his own became a solo artist and had three releases on Columbia Records before he was dropped by the label. While Lorrie was being a housewife and raising a family, little brother Larry continued to stay in the music business in Nashville. Larry had worked with virtually every top country star in the business by the early sixties, so he had a lot of friends in Music City. Larry was barely eighteen years old when he left the Columbia Records label, but he went on to record for Monument Records in 1963. Throughout the sixties and into the seventies, Larry worked as a song-writer for music publishing companies in Nashville.

Larry and Lorrie Collins got together again for a DJ convention in Nashville in 1971 and performed a new song Larry had written, called "Delta Dawn." They sang this song a number of times at various locations in Nashville around that time, but nothin' happened for them as a team, at least on this song. But a year later, during the summer of 1972, "Delta Dawn" became the first Top 10 country song for the thirteen-year-old Tanya Tucker. Tanya's version also crossed over onto the *Billboard* pop charts. On September 15, 1973, Helen Reddy took "Delta Dawn" all the way to the #1 spot on the *Billboard* pop charts and received a Gold Record for the song. Larry Collins was a golf instructor by this time but had one more huge success as a songwriter when a song he wrote about his home state, "You're the Reason God Made Oklahoma," hit the #1 spot on the *Billboard* country charts by David Frizzell and Shelly West during the spring of 1981. The success of that song led Larry Collins to record an album and play Las Vegas for awhile before he went back to his life again, doin' what he loved, that was playin' a lot of golf.

Right after the decade of the 1990s came in, The Collins Kids first played The Hemsby Festival to thousands of screamin' rockabilly fans. Greg Wolski, who spent five years producing the film *Tear It Up: The Rockabilly Documentary* (which is now available through Lasso Productions, out of Columbus, Ohio), included a piece of footage from The Collins Kids' first 1990s live show. They both look terrific, sound terrific, and put on one of the liveliest rockabilly shows out there today. The Collins Kids have gone back to Europe several times, playing to packed audiences everywhere. They've also done rockabilly shows on the West Coast. Everywhere they perform is packed today. Larry and Lorrie use my buddy Dave Stuckey and his band The Dave & Deke Combo to back 'em up now.

When I spoke with Larry Collins in March 1996 by phone, he told me he couldn't be happier with the way his life is today. Lorrie feels the same way. Lorrie's first marriage ended years ago, and she's been happily remarried now for quite a number of years. Larry told me now that their kids are grown, they're just happy that a whole new generation of rockabilly fans remember their original music. When I told him I had bought the two-CD complete collection of all The Collins Kids' songs of the fifties and early sixties, which came out on

Bear Family Records in 1991 (which I highly recommend to any lover of real rockabilly music), Larry laughed and then said, "Man, you gotta be a real friend, 'cause it's unbelievable the prices they get for that over here." I just told him it was well worth it in their case, as they'd made some of the best rockabilly music during the original days when rockabilly and real rock 'n' roll ruled. Larry then said, "We would have recorded more of it, too, but Columbia Records at that time was a little scared of the incoming rock 'n' roll music, so we were only allowed to do so much of it at the time." When I said to Larry, "You were really lucky to work with all the great performers and guitarists you did back in the fifties," he responded by saying, "I really do consider myself a lucky man, and I wouldn't trade those memories for anything."

I'm really glad Larry and Lorrie Collins survived this crazy music business and are happy with their lives today. I'm also happy that they're back out there performing their original music once again to a whole new generation of fans and performin' it in the original vibrant way they did in the 1950s. The Collins Kids are the only great original fifties rockabilly act still alive, in good health, and performing that I would love to perform with, for three reasons. They are and have always been professionals, they still love rockabilly music, and they both treat rockabilly music with the respect it justly deserves, and you can't ask for any more than that.

Other Female Artists

I stated at the beginning of this chapter the word "wild" should not be used in reality when describin' the performances of women in the 1950s who recorded rockabilly music, but there is one exception. Before I start on who I consider the wildest, rockin'-est live performing, most threatening (at least to adults and old people) rockabilly chick who recorded a substantial amount of rockabilly and rock 'n' roll between 1956 and 1962, I'm gonna run down a list of other girls and women who recorded at least one or two rockabilly (or what some fans of the music today consider to be rockabilly) songs that I think are great, good, or at least passable. None of these rockabilly girls ever saw a national chart with any rockabilly songs I'm mentioning, and quite a few were country girl singers or acts and came out of that background. I'm gonna leave out some I know, such as the country music singers like Bonnie Lou and others, because they were just country girls dressed up in their cowgirl hats and getup just trying to figure out what rockabilly was back then, which, in my opinion, they never did find out, so they went back to doin' country music in the fifties.

First off, The Davis Sisters, Betty Jack Davis and Mary Francis Penick (the latter sister today is a well-known Grand Ole Opry regular member who became Skeeter Davis later). On October 17, 1953, The Davis Sisters had a #1 country *Billboard* chart hit called "I Forgot More Than You'll Ever Know," but on the B side of this 45 was a hillbilly boogie jump tune called "Rock-a-Bye Boogie." This song has appeared on many rockabilly collections for over twenty years now. I don't understand why, 'cause it's just real good hillbilly boogie, like a lot of other country acts and artists were doin' during the early 1950s.

Sam Phillips on his Sun Records label in the fifties and early sixties only released a handful of records on girls or women. Only a few are worth mentioning. The others, like Sherry Crane and Maggie Sue Wembly, either did novelty-type songs, straight country, or country/pop. The first female act on Sun Records to cut a rockabilly-type tune was The Miller Sisters (Elsie Jo Miller and Mildred Wages). In March 1955 The Miller Sisters recorded a song called "Someday You Will Pay," which was first released on Sun Records' affiliate label Flip Records, and then a little later on the Sun Records label, in 1955. The Miller Sisters had two more 45 releases in 1956 on Sun Records, but along with "Someday You Will Pay," only one song from these two 45 releases keeps showin' up on rockabilly collection albums up to this day. That song was called "Ten Cats Down." It was released on Sun Records on August 3, 1956.

Jean Chapel was known in Las Vegas showrooms, where she appeared a lot during late '56 and throughout 1957 as the female Elvis Presley. That's what the press dubbed her then, because of her glittery and flashy style of dress and her on-stage movements that she was takin' from Elvis's act at the time. Jean was born in Nashville. She was in her late twenties when her first record came out on Sun Records in June 1956, "Welcome to the Club" b/w "I Won't Be Rockin' Tonight." Sam Phillips sold her contract to RCA Victor Records soon after this record came out on Sun, and RCA obtained the rights to release these two Sun recordings on their label. Jean had one other rockabilly-type release, called "Oo-ba La Baby," that has also appeared on many rockabilly collections. Jean performed at the Paramount on an Alan Freed Show

one time in 1957. It should be noted that before rockabilly and rock 'n' roll became popular, Jean Chapel was in many early hillbilly bands as a singer of country during the late forties and early fifties. After 1956, her recording career started up again. Between 1963 and 1969, Jean had many country releases on labels such as Smash, Challenge, and Kapp Records. She always made her home in Nashville and became a successful songwriter there into the 1970s. Jean passed away in Nashville in August 1995.

Barbara Pittman probably had the best example of a female wailin' out a rockabilly song on Sun Records when Sam Phillips released the song "I Need a Man" on September 24, 1956. This was Barbara's only Sun Records release, though she did have three other 45 releases on Sun's subsidiary label Phillips Records between 1957 and 1960, but each one got weaker after the terrific rockabilly song "I Need a Man," and none of the others are really considered rockabilly music today. Those were Barbara's only record releases, but on the strength of "I Need a Man," she was able to do many rockabilly shows in Europe throughout the 1980s.

Rose Maddox was another country singer out on the West Coast, who was in her early thirties by the time she had three of the best examples of primitive rockabilly released on Columbia Records in 1955 and 1956. These songs, "Hey Little Dreamboat," "Wild Wild Young Men," and "My Little Baby," are all great examples of a country female artist who was able to sing early rockabilly music with great ease. Rose Maddox was always able to sing and record great hillbilly boogie before and after rockabilly's heyday.

Then, of course, there was Patsy Cline, who turned out several great rockabilly-style songs during that same time, including "Gotta Lotta Rhythm (In My Soul)," "Love Me, Love Me Honey Do," and "Deal the Cards Slowly."

In 1957, I saw someone called Alis Lesley (another singer billed as "the female Elvis Presley") perform a raw rockabilly tune on "The Milt Grant TV Teen Dance Show" in Washington, D.C. The song she sang was "Heartbreak Harry," and when I saw this crazy, wild-eyed chick rockin' on TV, I went out and found that 45 record within a week. Alis had high, pomped-up dark hair, she wore guys' clothes such as pegged black slacks, cool white shoes, had her collar turned up in the back and down on the sides, and wore a man's sport jacket. Her hair was swept back in a long cool ducktail. She was pretty wild lookin' for a teenage girl, and she rocked on "Heartbreak Harry." The other side of "Heartbreak Harry" was called "He Will Come Back to Me." It was rockabilly also, and I liked it too. The record was on Era Records back in '57.

Sparkle Moore was the one rockabilly chick who definitely had the tough girl teenage look, with her cool-lookin' blond hairstyle and leopard skin jacket. Sparkle (whose real name was Barbara Jordan) only made two 45 singles on Fraternity Records in 1957, but all four of those songs, "Skull and Crossbones," "Rock-a-Bop," "Killer," and "Ooh Ba Ba La Baby," have all been reissued on many rockabilly compilation albums in the 1980s and 1990s.

Laura Lee Perkins had two 45 releases in 1958 on the Imperial Records label that also keep turnin' up on the many rockabilly compilation albums that continue to be released today. Laura Lee's three best rockabilly songs from those 45s are "Kiss Me Baby," "Don't Wait Up," and "Oh La Baby."

Connie Francis was certainly never considered at all a female rockabilly artist, but two songs of Connie's have turned up on some rockabilly compilation albums, such as *MGM's Rockabillys*, released during the 1980s. One of the songs I'm speakin' of was a Top 30 *Billboard* chart hit in 1958. It was called "Fallin'." The other song is called "Robot Man," which was released by MGM Records only as a DJ promo 45 here in the U.S., but the song got a full release in Europe. Connie Francis told me she didn't prefer to sing rock 'n' roll back in 1959, but honey, you're still on these reissue rockabilly albums today.

Jackie Johnson made one great hot-rockin'-all-the-way, scorchin' rockabilly song in 1958 for Imperial Records, called "Starlight Starbright." This song knocked me off my feet when I was fourteen years old and still does today. I don't know whatever happened to Jackie, but she sure can light you up on this great rockabilly tune.

At the same time Connie Francis had out "Robot Man" in 1959, another female rockabilly singer by the name of Jamie Horton had the same song out. Jamie's version of "Robot Man" came out on Joy Records. I met her and saw her sing on the Milt Grant TV show at that time, and she did a good version of it also.

Rockabilly may have been almost dead by 1959, but nobody could convince these final five rockabilly chicks of that back then. Penny Cancy had a solid rockabilly

song on a number called "The Rockin' Lady (From New Orleans)" in 1959. This record came out on the Flippin' Records label then. She was another rockabilly chick I met down on the Milt Grant show at that time.

Jackie Dee (before she became Jackie De Shannon) had one of the roarin'-est, growlin'-est rockabilly songs in 1959, called "Buddy," on Liberty Records when she was only fifteen years old and just startin' out. This has also been reissued on various rockabilly compilation albums, and it's a must.

Linda & The Epics were from the West Coast, and Linda rocked hard on one great rockabilly song in 1959 called "Gonna Be Loved." This is raw, raunchy, garage-soundin' rockabilly all the way. It originally came out on Blue Moon Records back in '59.

One final song in 1959 that's considered rockabilly today but not really the strongest, though it's worth pickin' up on a compilation album, is one called "Puppy Love" by — you ready for this? — Dolly Parton. Dolly was thirteen years old when she made this, her first, 45 record for the Goldband record label, and yep, it's rockabilly.

The Infinity record label was pretty well distributed, at least in the Washington, D.C., area, and in 1962 I heard a song from this label playin' in the record store in D.C. where I bought most of my records then, and it knocked me out. I asked Eddie, the salesman who worked there, what was that he was playin', and he told me it was a brand-new record they'd just gotten in that day. I told Eddie I had to have a copy of that one. I never heard it on the radio back in '62, but I still got it today, and it's finally startin' to turn up on some rockabilly compilation albums now in the nineties. The female rockabilly singer's name was Joyce Harris, and this dynamite screamer of a rockabilly tune is called "No Way Out." By 1962, you hardly ever stumbled across a great rockabilly number like this one. I've loved this song so much throughout the years, me and LesLee "Bird" Anderson went into the studio and recorded a duet on "No Way Out" in January 1995.

There's a whole lot more I could have mentioned, but at least I feel I've given some prime examples of some of the best rockabilly music done by some rockin' chicks that never made it onto the national charts during the golden years of rockabilly. Turn to Chapter 13 to read about the rockin' chicks that are still carrying on rockabilly music wholly or at least partly in their recordings and live shows today. For now, it's on to one final rockin' lady of the late fifties.

Jo Ann Campbell

It might have all been called rock 'n' roll back in 1958, but since the late seventies Jo Ann Campbell and her music have been called rockabilly on varous compilation albums, as well as a few of the six vinyl LPs and three CDs that have all been released on albums solely by her between 1983 and 1994 of her music from the fifties and early sixties. Now, I'm sure there's a lot of forty-year-old and under rockabilly fans readin' this that are all sayin', "No way." You think that Jo Ann Campbell

did a few good rockabilly-type songs in the fifties and then moved on in the early sixties, where she finally had three *Billboard* pop chart hits with silly teen songs of that era. Well, today, I'll guarantee you there's still hundreds of thousands of fifty-year-olds and older that are still alive and still remember her frantic, sexy live performances during the fifties and early sixties, not only in and around New York City, but all up and down the East Coast. Jo Ann Campbell's live performances in the late fifties and early sixties would make her the only rockabilly honey of the fifties the word "wild" could be applied to.

Forgettin' to Remember to Forget

Let me take you back to the first week of January 1958. This here almost-fourteen-year-old kid comes home from St. Francis De Sales seventh-grade class to watch "The Milt Grant TV Teen Dance Show" from 4:00 to 5:00 p.m. before dinner, as he's been doin' for a year or so by now. When it was time for the special guest star on the program, Milt said the name as he introduced this singer, who he said was from New York City and had a new record out that was in the Top 10 there. I'm thinkin', "Gee whiz, it's a girl singer that's from New York that I ain't never heard of and'll probably sing some sappy pop-type song." But when this teenage girl came on the screen of our old black-and-white TV set, this thirteen-year-old's hormones were sent higher than they'd been since the summer before when I'd seen Jayne Mansfield in the color movie *The Girl Can't Help It*. When I was watchin' this teenage chick on Milt's show, I couldn't even remember what name he'd called her. She came on that old TV screen with a guitar slung around her neck, wearin' a skin-tight one-piece spangled toreador pants outfit that glittered on the TV screen.

It wasn't just the outfit. This young chick was gorgeous to me that day. She had blond hair, a beautiful face that had the sexiest looks a cat would want to see, plus the most perfect shape in this outfit that looked like it had been painted on her and was topped off with what looked like shiny four-inch gold high-heeled shoes.

It wasn't just that outfit and them great looks. It was also what she was doin'. I knew even back then she was lip-synchin' to her rockin' song, but it didn't matter, 'cause the way she rocked, shook, bumped, and moved while playin' and slingin' her guitar around, as well as turnin' sideways and pointin' it atcha with a pout on her face while she was growlin' out this rockabilly tune I'd never heard, was just a killer memory that's lasted a whole lifetime for me. That was my first introduction to the wildest live stage female performer ever to belt out a rockabilly tune.

When the song was over, Milt Grant walked over to her while the audience clapped and shouted their approval. He said "How 'bout Jo Ann Campbell? They call her the Blond Bombshell in New York. Isn't she great, kids?" Once more, the whole audience cheered and whistled. When Milt went on, as he always did, and interviewed Jo Ann, she sounded just nice, sweet, shy, and humble when he brought up about her fans in the New York area going wild over her live shows she was regularly doin' at the Apollo, New York Paramount, Brooklyn Fox, and other theaters all around the New York area.

As was normal, Jo Ann Campbell came back later in the show and again got rousing screams and applause for another song she lip-synched, called "Come On Baby." This was a mid-tempo, sexy-sounding rocker I really like a lot, too. I still have my old notebook that I wrote her name down in on that day and the name of the two songs she sang. I wasn't about to forget it. On that page in that old notebook, I got written also "Gone Records," which Milt Grant had said her new record that she sang first, "Wait a Minute," was on. The only other thing I wrote on that page was, "This chick is really gone! Gotta find her records."

Even in the sixties, Jo Ann included songs like "Jailhouse Rock" in her set, 'cause that's what's been in her heart since she was a young teenager, rock 'n' roll, rockabilly, and rhythm & blues music. Right up to today, that's what Jo Ann Campbell only listens to, 'cause all that was real music. Thanks to Jo Ann, I can finally, for the most part, put it into her own words and explain why she has chosen not to perform live since 1967. Although if this still fine-lookin' lady ever does decide to do another show, which is as unlikely as snow in July in Austin, Texas, she'd make a few others that are still out there think about hangin' up their rockabilly shoes.

Jo Ann Campbell was born in Jacksonville, Florida, on July 20, 1938. From her earliest remembrances, she wanted to dance. As a young child, she would dance all the time. By the time she was four years old, her parents enrolled her in a school in Jacksonville for dancing lessons. This came natural for this young child, so she practiced hard throughout the rest of the 1940s. When Jo Ann entered junior high school at the end of the 1940s, her ambition in life was to someday become a professional dancer and move to New York City. By the time she started her freshman year at Fletcher High School in Jacksonville in September 1952, this fourteen-year-old girl was not only the top drum majorette in and around Jacksonville, but she had also gone on to win the Florida State Baton Twirling Championship.

Jo Ann told me she listened to the local pop radio stations in Jacksonville during her first year and a half at Fletcher High School, which would have been during late 1952 and 1953. She said her favorite singers then were Johnny Ray and Kay Starr. Jo Ann went on to say, "I really liked Johnny the most. He was the first singer I went to see when I got to New York City. I screamed like all the rest of the teenage girls back then. I liked some of Kay Starr's songs, too. Especially 'Wheel of Fortune.' That was my favorite."

I asked Jo Ann, "When you were still in Jacksonville, did you listen to any country music?" She quickly answered, "No. I'd never heard any kind of country music then. After school, me and my girlfriends would all listen to the pop music then, but rock 'n' roll type music was just startin' to come in around 1953, and there was this one black station we'd all turn on and get excited when we heard the songs they were playin' by groups like The Orioles, Drifters, Clovers, Five Keys, and others. I remember hearin' Fats Domino then, too. All us girls loved that music, but we had to sneak it on the radio,

'cause our parents didn't want us to listen to those kind of songs. 'Lawdy Miss Clawdy' by Lloyd Price was played a lot on that station, and all us girls would dance around in our bedrooms to songs like that when our parents weren't home. We were all just havin' innocent fun drinkin' Cokes and munchin' on peanuts and candy, but that kind of music was looked on as really bad for young girls like us to be listening to, so we could only hear it until one of our parents came home." I persisted and said, "So you really never heard any country music at all when you were a teenager in Jacksonville?" "No, really. I didn't know what it was or even existed, because the group of kids I was friends with never listened to it, and I don't remember my parents listening to it either. In fact, even after I went to New York City and became a dancer in 1954 and went on to sing rock 'n' roll a couple of years, I'd still never heard a country music song. It just wasn't on the radio in New York City. Pop music and then rock 'n' roll and rhythm & blues was all you heard by then." Well, that was more than a bit surprising to me, but learning about her early years, it does make sense to me now.

After Jo Ann completed her sophomore year at Fletcher High School in June 1954, she went to Europe on a big USO tour of Army bases, performing as a dancer for the U.S. troops stationed there. When she returned in the late summer of 1954, the then sixteen-year-old Jo Ann Campbell moved with her parents to New York City to go for that dream of becoming a professional dancer. Enough attention had come her way by this time that before she even got to New York City, she had been signed by an agent there who had a regular spot for her as one of The Johnny Conrad Dancers, which was a modern jazz ensemble of dancers. With The Johnny Conrad Dancers, Jo Ann appeared on many of the top-rated network TV shows of that period, such as "The Milton Berle Show," "The Ed Sullivan Show," "The Colgate Comedy Hour," and many others.

Jo Ann stayed with this group of dancers throughout the rest of 1954, but when 1955 came in, she and her male dancing partner formed a dance duo team and called themselves The Haydens. Throughout 1955, they were a popular dance duo and went on tour with many of the top pop stars of that day. The one that she liked the most and said was extremely nice to her was Tony Bennett.

After Jo Ann's junior year in high school was completed in June 1955, her and her dancing partner in The Haydens had so many bookings, she quit school. If fate hadn't-a stepped in and changed this seventeen-year-old's life forever during the fall of 1955, Jo Ann Campbell was sure to go on to become a top professional dancer in all the major Broadway musicals of the fifties and sixties. She was just about to make that move in November 1955 when she happened to attend her first Alan Freed rock 'n' roll show at the New York Paramount Theater.

Jo Ann recently described it like this: "It was all just so exciting. There I was, just a kid myself, moving up in the line while I was eatin' my little bag of peanuts until it was my turn to buy my ticket and go inside and find a seat. I loved the rock 'n' roll artists and groups I was hearin' on the radio in 1955, 'cause it was really hot in New York then with all the other kids, but I'd never seen a live performance before. There's just no way to explain the thrill of seeing Alan Freed and his big band with the great Sam the Man Taylor on sax. When the lights went down and Alan Freed and the band came on and the stage lights went up, all the kids went wild, screamin', jumpin' up and down in their seats, and I did too. As that show went on and Alan Freed kept bringin' on acts like Frankie Lymon & The Teenagers, The Moonglows, The Cadillacs, Bill Haley and His Comets, Chuck Berry, and all the rest, it made me jump up and down and scream till I was dizzy. I mean kids were all out in the aisles and in front of the stage dancin' and just goin' crazy. Those kids all loved Alan Freed, and he loved them and all that music, too, with all his heart. I know that for a fact. Well, when I came out of that first Alan Freed rock 'n' roll show, I knew my days as a dancer were over, even though at the time I was up for parts in Broadway plays then. I was determined I was gonna sing rock 'n' roll and be on Alan Freed's stage one day.

"The next morning, I went into my manager's office and told him I wasn't gonna dance anymore, and that I wanted to make a rock 'n' roll record. He was my personal manager and had been since right after I came to New York. His name was Mike Gendell. He was really a nice sweet man who helped my career a lot, but he was an older man and astonished by what I told him I wanted to do. My partner in The Haydens was also up for dancing parts on Broadway, which he went on to get later, so me and him parted as good friends. We had both been trying out for Broadway all along and knew one day soon we'd have to go our separate ways anyhow. But my manager, Mike Gendell, didn't know anything about this new music that was drivin' kids crazy at this time, but he knew somebody who had a little record

label in New York called RKO Point Records, so in February 1956, I was put in the studio and recorded two songs, 'Wherever You Are,' and 'I'm Coming Home Late Tonight.' My Lord, I'll never forget it, 'cause they both sound so terrible to me today, I just can't stand the thought of 'em.

"I went back and was thrilled again and again watchin' more Alan Freed shows from December 1955 to February 1956, and I'd practice singin' rock 'n' roll, 'cause I really was determined to be a good singer. I already knew how to play the piano, and I knew all the basic chords on the guitar at the time, but the way I sounded on that first record is just awful. But when it came out, shortly after, my manager got me some bookings in some of the New York nightclubs, where I sang it and other rock 'n' roll songs."

I then asked Jo Ann how her first record sold, and if it made any of the New York regional charts. Jo Ann said, "I don't think it sold much at all, but there was one disc jockey by the name of Phil Guilding in New York that liked it then, so he played it quite a bit, but I don't think it ever got on any charts. It sounds terrible to me today." I then said, "Well, the two 45s that came out on you on Eldorado Records in 1956 sure sound good to me today, so how did that come about?"

Jo Ann said, "In the spring of 1956, two guys who had just started a new record label called Eldorado Records came out to see me in a New York nightclub I was performing in. Their names were Bill Buchanan and Dickie Goodman. They had big hits on their own with all those flying saucer records they did in '56 and '57. They liked me and wanted to sign me to their new label. They had mostly black rhythm & blues artists comin' out on their Eldorado label, and they were booked by the Gayle Booking Agency in New York, so I signed with them to book my shows. Gayle was booking all the big stars of rock 'n' roll and rhythm & blues then, and I think I was one of the only or few white artists they booked."

I went on to ask Jo Ann how her first two records did on Eldorado Records, how she came to writing her first song, "Come On Baby,", and if the Gayle agency got her a lot of bookings, and here's what she told me: "At Eldorado, they really liked the first song I ever wrote, 'Come On Baby,' the best out of the five songs we cut on that session. So when they released it in June 1956, the biggest black disc jockey in New York City, by the name of Jocko, liked it a lot, so he played it on his show over and over for the first week it was out. Jocko had a lot of listeners, and outside of Alan Freed, who had a daily radio show on WINS in New York, he was the top disc jockey in that city then. I worked steady all the time from then on. It was on a lot of the charts in New York City, Connecticut, and New Jersey when it came out. Jocko was responsible for that record doin' so well, and all the airplay I was gettin' from it was what got me booked into the all-black Apollo Theater in Harlem. The only other white artist that I remember playing the Apollo during the whole time I played there from 1956 to 1958 was Lillian Briggs. There could have been others, but she's the only one I remember. It didn't matter whether they were black audiences or not, 'cause they just loved my shows. I've always thought of myself as an entertainer, and I moved, rocked, and danced a lot when I sang, and back then, blacks and whites liked to see that, so I guess that's why they kept bringin' me back for shows at the Apollo as late as 1958.

"When Jocko started playin' 'Come On Baby' and kept gettin' more requests for it, that's when Alan Freed started playin' it on his radio show. Alan came out to see me sing it in the summer of '56, and it was really a big thrill when he came backstage to meet me after the show. Whenever he played 'Come On Baby' after that, Alan always called me the Blond Bombshell. Alan gave me that nickname then, so the Gayle Agency started usin' it wherever I did a show or whatever big bill I was on from that time on to promote me. When Jocko played my records on Eldorado, he always referred to me as 'the little ofay chick.' Ofay meant white to black people in the fifties, but not in a bad way at all.

"I worked all the time up and down the East Coast in 1956 and '57, from Washington, D.C., to Boston, Massachusetts. I worked wherever the Gayle Agency sent me throughout that whole period. I must have worked with every top star in rock 'n' roll during those years. All the really great ones. Even though most of the artists I worked with were black and a lot of the audiences were mostly black, it didn't bother me, 'cause back then there was no rivalry or racism when it came to those artists or to the audiences. They all had the same love for great rock 'n' roll, no matter what color you were. The old fuddy duddies blew a lot of things out of proportion then, 'cause they didn't want or like this new music and really didn't like seeing white teenagers go wild over black performers. The older people were the racists, and they were the ones who created the problems. Not the performers and kids who were at all these shows in droves."

Before I let Jo Ann continue here, I have to say once more that because of the records she made from 1956 to 1962, she's considered a female rockabilly singer by fans around the world today, but what rockabilly fans everywhere don't realize is that Jo Ann Campbell was on the same bills and shared the stage with more legendary or lesser-known rockabilly artists than virtually any other male or female artist ever in the history of rock 'n' roll and rockabilly music. She appeared numerous times with every single one of them that ever mattered in rockabilly, with the exception of Elvis Presley and Carl Perkins. Jo Ann Campbell not only did shows with 'em, but most of 'em she toured with on big-bill package shows.

The reason is very simple why Jo Ann Campbell toured with more of the greatest performers and legends in rockabilly, rock 'n' roll, and rhythm & blues than any rockabilly chick of the fifties. That reason being Jo Ann was Alan Freed's wild, rockin' girl from 1957 to 1961. She's proud of it today and says with much pride and satisfaction, "Connie Francis was always Dick Clark's girl, and I was Alan Freed's. He was my hero, and I was there for him whenever he called."

Even throughout 1959 and '60, when Dick Clark was in total control, had killed off real rock 'n' roll, and had his no-talent, lily white, pet pretty boys croonin' to white American teenagers on his Caravan of Stars across the U.S., Alan Freed's popularity in New York City at least survived, and Jo Ann Campbell was one of the few original rock 'n' roll artists who remained loyal enough to keep performing on every big Alan Freed show into 1961. This was after Jo Ann had her first national *Billboard* pop chart hit. While many of the other, both black and white, rock 'n' roll and R&B stars had jumped onto Dick Clark's Caravan of Stars road shows, Jo Ann was one rocker who didn't do any of his road tours at that time. Jo Ann did appear on Dick Clark's "American Bandstand" many times from 1957 through 1964 and twice did his half-hour Saturday night weekly ABC network TV show from New York City, but all artists had to do those and local shows of that kind to promote their latest records.

I'm gonna stop right here and let Jo Ann continue to tell you the rest of her story through the greatest years of rock 'n' roll and rockabilly music. "When Eldorado Records decided to release the next 45 on me because of the success of 'Come On Baby,' [they picked] two songs from the one session I'd done earlier in the year for them. Those songs were the old standard 'I Can't Give You Anything but Love' and 'Funny Thing.' 'I Can't Give You Anything but Love' was the one that took off in New York. It had a modern rock 'n' roll arrangement to it. Again, Jocko was the one who really loved my version of it. Both Jocko and Alan Freed were both still playin' 'Come On Baby' when 'I Can't Give You Anything but Love' was released before Christmas 1956. Jocko gets all the credit for sendin' 'I Can't Give You Anything but Love' to #1 on every chart in New York City, and Connecticut too. Jocko played that song constantly for three or four months straight every day, over and over, until it hit #1 on all the charts. Alan Freed played it a lot, too, all during the early months of 1957.

"I continued to tour, being booked by the Gayle Agency, and kept playin' shows at the Apollo, but the first really big show I was on where all the kids went wild for me, that just thrilled me to death at the time, was at Jocko's Giant Rock 'n' Roll Revue show at Lowe's State Theater in New York City." This was Jocko's Christmas show in December 1956. "The Diamonds, The Platters, Bo Diddley, Little Richard, and all the big names were on the bill. I was just so excited, 'cause they loved both the songs I did. I was only eighteen years old then, but I was still determined to be the best singer and performer I could be.

"When my contract was up with the Gayle Agency, I signed with GAC [General Artists Corporation], who were a top major booking agency that booked artists worldwide. Mike Gendell was still my personal manager, though. I was working constantly and with all the big stars I loved so much all through the spring and summer of 1957, plus I was still doing the Apollo shows.

"The next big show I played on was the one I'd been waitin' for so long to do. It was Alan Freed's Ten-Day Easter Holiday Spectacular Line-Up of Stars show. The day before this big event, I was driving back to New York from a show I'd done in New Jersey, and it was raining and I had a wreck. It was the other driver's fault, but I was taken to the hospital and told I had a concussion. Well, it didn't matter to me, because there was no way I was gonna miss the chance to be on the same stage with Alan Freed. This was what I'd been waitin' for. I only had the two records out on Eldorado at the time, but had offers from other New York labels that I still hadn't decided on.

"Well, this show was at the New York Paramount, and the whole ten days was sold out. I was only supposed to sing one song on it, because there were fifteen or twenty big-name stars who [mostly] had national hits. The only song Alan Freed's Big Beat Band knew that we'd rehearsed the day of the show was 'Come On Baby.' That was the only song I'd planned to do. I always moved around a lot whenever I sang, and the kids all loved it. They went wild during the whole song, and when I finished, I waved and blew a kiss to the kids and ran off behind the curtains, but they just kept bangin' on the front of the stage, screamin' in their seats and hollerin' for me to do another song. Well, backstage, as soon as I got there, Alan Freed said, 'You better go out and do another song for the kids, Jo Ann.' I told him that 'Come On Baby' was the only song I knew that The Big Beat Band knew that we'd rehearsed beforehand. Alan said, 'Well they're not gonna stop all the commotion out there until you do one more, so just go out and do 'Come On Baby' again.' So that's what I did, and they all went just as wild as they had before. From that time on, I always had three to four songs of mine that the band knew how to play. From then on, Alan Freed wanted me as much as possible for all his biggest shows and tours."

When I asked Jo Ann how she came to decide on Gone Records for her next record label deal, she told me this: "Gone was a big independent label in New York that had national hits by The Dubs and other acts before I signed with 'em in the fall of 1957. George Goldner owned the label, and George was friends with Alan Freed, so I signed with them because they seemed like the best rock 'n' roll label to go with at the time. I stayed with them for two and a half years, and I really shouldn't have left when I did, because all my Gone releases made the Top 10 in a lot of markets up and down the East Coast. Some even hit #1. It was a big mistake on my part for leaving Gone. The reason I left probably sounds silly today, but by early 1960, I'd go to big important functions and parties where there'd be a lot of important people there, and someone would always ask 'What label are you with?' I always felt embarrassed when I'd have to say, 'Gone.' It had such a negative-type ring to it. Their subsidiary label was called End Records, and that was a negative name too, or so it seemed to me.

"So in 1960, when my manager told me ABC Paramount Records wanted to sign me, I jumped at the chance. The top female artist then, Connie Francis, was with MGM Records, and Brenda Lee was having her first big hits on Decca Records, so I just wanted to be on an established big major label like they were at the time, and ABC Paramount Records was a major label with a lot of hits behind 'em by that time. But it was a mistake, because I was pretty happy with the songs I recorded for Gone Records, because they were the kind of rock 'n' roll I loved and did the best. The songs I went on to record for ABC Paramount and later Cameo Records weren't me. Especially the ones on Cameo. There were only a few songs I did for ABC Paramount that were ones I wanted to record. I wrote a couple of those, and there were a couple others I got to do that I felt comfortable with and liked a lot, but I just didn't have the freedom, or the fun either, that I had with the songs on the Gone label.

"Sid Feller was in charge of all the sessions for ABC Paramount at the time. He wasn't the producer, but he chose all the song material, and he couldn't stand rock 'n' roll. He was an older man from the Tin Pan Alley days of pop music, and he picked the silliest songs that I still can't stand to listen to for me to record. Even though 'A Kookie Little Paradise' was my breakthrough national chart hit, I never ever sang that song in any of my live shows in 1960, when it was on the charts. I went on 'American Bandstand' and lip-synched it for the camera like I did on other local teen TV dance shows around the country to promote it when it first came out, but I never sang it live, 'cause it was just silly, and I was embarrassed by it then, but rock 'n' roll had changed to a lot of those kind of silly songs by 1960 and I had to sing a lot of things I didn't want to when I recorded from then on if I wanted to stay in the business and keep performing."

That's only a tiny fraction of what Jo Ann Campbell has opened up her kind heart and told me about her rockin' years as one of the few female rock 'n' rollers who lasted a long time for back then doin' real rock 'n' roll. A lot of the music Jo Ann had released back then is by today's generation of rockabilly music fans considered to be female rockabilly music, and they're the ones who are buying the newer reissue albums of her old songs. But I want to fill in a lot of holes that are important and haven't been touched on as yet.

I want to go through her recording career as a solo artist first. Jo Ann's talked about her first three records on the Point label and the two others on Eldorado Records that were released in 1956, so I'll start with her Gone record label releases.

Jo Ann had seven 45s released between December 1957 and August 1959 on Gone Records. All of her greatest rock 'n' roll and rockabilly hard-drivin' songs came out on this label. On each of these seven releases, at least one side shows you why today there's more interest in her early music than ever before. Jo Ann had a raw, raunchy, gritty "You Better Take Me Serious, Jack!" vocal style that made you want to listen up on hard-drivin' songs such as "You're Driving Me Mad," "Wassa Matter with You Baby," "Tall Boy," "Nervous," and "Wait a Minute." Two other songs, called "I Really, Really Love You" and "Beachcomber," are today considered two of the best mid-tempo female rockabilly songs out there, mainly because Jo Ann has such a sexy, sensual passion on her vocal delivery of these tunes. Marti Brom, who was voted Top, #1 Female Vocalist in Austin, Texas, for the year of 1995, considers Jo Ann Campbell the perfect example of what a female rockabilly artist should be.

Jo Ann Campbell's first five or six 45 single records on the Gone record label had to sell a whole lot of records, mostly in the middle Atlantic and northeastern states, or George Goldner would never have released a full-length twelve-song album by Jo Ann Campbell, called *I'm Nobody's Baby*, on his subsidiary label End Records in March 1959, with a full-color front on the album. Back in the late 1950s, unless a rock 'n' roll-type artist had a national chart record on the *Billboard* pop singles charts, it was awfully rare if their label released an album on 'em. Jo Ann was seen in theaters and drive-ins during the summer of 1959 performin' a Bo Diddley-penned song, "Mama (Can I Go Out Tonight)," in the Hal Roach film *Go Johnny Go*.

Like Jo Ann said, today she feels it was a mistake to have left the Gone Records label. By the time Jo Ann did her first session for ABC Paramount, goofy and silly songs were really startin' to hit it big, such as "Alley Oop," which had already gone to #1 and soon would be followed by "Itsy Bitsy Teenie Weenie Yellow Polka Dot Bikini" close behind, eventually reaching #1 on the *Billboard* pop charts. So Sid Feller had Jo Ann Campbell record one, too. It was the first record they rushed out on Jo Ann, called "A Kookie Little Paradise," and it became her first *Billboard* pop chart hit. It debuted on the *Billboard* pop charts on August 15, 1960, only reaching a peak position of #61, but it had a good run of nine weeks on those charts.

Although Jo Ann was made to record a few more really dumb songs that were released on her on the other six 45s that ABC Paramount Records released between that summer of 1960 and the spring of 1962, such as "Puka Puka Pants" (which was the worst) and one or two others, most of her songs were really pretty darn good for that late of what was still bein' called rock 'n' roll. The instrumental arrangements and vocal backup singing always hurt the overall sound, but that was all part of the big thing goin' in those days. None of these records charted nationally, but as was the case of her Gone 45s, all sold well enough to get up into each city's regional charts throughout the northeastern states and other parts. Some of those other parts were places Jo Ann Campbell didn't realize, such as the Philippines, where the flip side of "A Kookie Little Paradise" went to #1. The song was called "Bobby, Bobby, Bobby." Jo Ann's ABC Paramount songs made the charts in England with "Motorcycle Michael," "Duane" in Australia, "Puka Puka Pants" in Hawaii, and several other countries during the early sixties. By early 1962, ABC Paramount released Jo Ann Campbell's second album — the first on that label.

"The Twist" song and dance craze got hot all over again by the fall of 1961. The first go-round during the late summer and fall of 1960, "The Twist" was big with teenagers, and throughout 1961, "The Twist" never really died out completely. Well, during the summer and fall of 1961, "The Twist" started catchin' on with adults, parents, and even grandparents, as well as the entire International Jet Set around the world. Jo Ann Campbell wound up involved in the revived "Twist" craze also. During the late fall of 1961, Jo Ann flew to Hollywood to star in one of those low-budget, quickie "Twist Flicks" that came out during the spring and summer of 1962. There were a bunch of 'em made then by both independent and top major movie studios. The film Jo Ann starred in as the top female lead behind Joey Dee & The Starlighters was called *Hey Let's Twist*. The film was made by a major studio, Paramount Pictures, and even had a soundtrack album of the same name to go with it. Jo Ann is seen on the cover of the soundtrack album that came out on Roulette Records in 1962, along with Joey Dee and the other stars all billed under Jo Ann, such as Teddy Randazzo and Kay Armen. Jo Ann only sings one song on the album, but it's the best one on there. That's for sure. It's called "Let Me Do My Twist." The main reason it's good and listenable is because Jo Ann shouts and growls it out in a female rockabilly vocal style.

By the time this movie and soundtrack came out in early 1962, Jo Ann had finished what would be her final session at ABC Paramount Records, and they had a dozen songs that were gonna go onto her 1962 album.

This album is not all that bad of an album for 1962, because what Sid Feller and ABC Paramount chose to put on it were six songs that had been released on Jo Ann's first five 45 singles that came out on their label between the summer of 1960 and December 1961. The other six songs were unreleased up to that time. Out of the twelve songs on the album, ten had boys' names in 'em, such as Johnny, Donnie, Bobby, Eddie, Willie, Jimmy, and so on. Jo Ann told me she was trying to convince the record label to call the album *Boy Crazy*, but because "The Twist" craze was at an all-time high, the label instead called her album *Twistin' and Listenin'*, even though the only song out of the twelve on the album that had the word "Twist" in it was one called "Mama Don't Want No Twistin'."

Without a doubt, the best song on this whole album is the hard-drivin' rockabilly/rock 'n' roll tune called "Crazy Daisy," which was Jo Ann's second 45 release on ABC Paramount Records in late 1960. What hardly any fans knew back then or even today is that Jo Ann Campbell wrote that song under the name of Doris Hatcher. Jo Ann wrote quite a few of her classic rockabilly-type songs on the Gone label as well as some of the ones for ABC Paramount under her own name, but Jo Ann told me she was told back in 1957 by her management or someone in charge to pick another name to put on some of the songs she wrote that they were recording at the time. They just told her you did that in the music business then, and that it was perfectly all right, so Jo Ann chose the name Doris Hatcher, because it was her mother's maiden name, to write great songs like "Crazy Daisy," "I Really, Really Love You," and several others. The only completely new original song that had never been released up until the time this album came out was one Jo Ann wrote that I've always thought is a great New York-styled fifties-type rock 'n' roll ballad with a kind of a doo wop style to it, called "Donnie." Jo Ann wrote this song as well as one of the other really good ones on this album, a bluesy rock 'n' roll song called "Duane." "Motorcycle Michael," which had been Jo Ann's third 45 single released on ABC Paramount Records, was also a solid rock 'n' roll/rockabilly song that rocked hard on this album. As I said, "Motorcycle Michael" had gotten into England's Top 50 singles mainstream pop charts during 1961, although Jo Ann never performed there. The rest of the *Twistin' and Listenin'* album was made up of covers of songs that had been hits on the *Billboard* pop charts by other artists in the fifties.

On Jo Ann's final session for ABC Paramount Records, she recorded five songs. Only four got released at that time. She did this session in late 1961, and the four songs that were released on two 45 single records came out between December 1961 and April 1962. The first 45 single they released in December 1961 was a good rockin' number called "I Changed My Mind Jack." It was the female answer song to Ray Charles's #1 *Billboard* pop and R&B hit called "Hit the Road Jack," which was still on the charts and radio at the time Jo Ann's answer version came out. Both records were on ABC Paramount Records at this time. Jo Ann's answer version, "I Changed My Mind Jack," didn't crack into *Billboard*'s charts, though she sure gave a gutsy, rockin' vocal performance on it, and even on the flip side, "You Made Me Love You," which was an old pop standard even at that time, Jo Ann's updated vocal treatment is pretty good get-down and hard-rockin'.

Her final 45 single on ABC Paramount was "I Wish It Would Rain All Summer" b/w "Amateur Night." Both sides were just your common songs that appealed to young teenage girls during the spring of 1962, when they were released.

There was a fifth and final song recorded on that session that would take twenty-five years before it would see the light of day on a vinyl record. It was Jo Ann's version of "Boogie Woogie Country Girl," a fifties classic by "Big" Joe Turner, who was one of Jo Ann's idols. It finally came out in 1987 when MCA Records here in the U.S. released two albums called *Rockabilly Classics, Volume 1 & Volume 2*. There were ten songs on each album, all recorded or released between 1956 and 1961. On the back of each album, it states, "All selections recorded at Bradley's Film & Recording Studio (Quonset Hut) in Nashville, Tennessee." While both these albums were great albums for a U.S. record label to release at the time, filled with mostly obscure rockabilly songs on 'em that only with two exceptions had never seen a *Billboard* chart when they were first released, I knew for a fact by 1987 that there was one song on there that had definitely not been recorded in Nashville at any studio there. That song being Jo Ann Campbell's version of "Boogie Woogie Country Girl." By 1987, I knew better than to believe what I read in the liner notes on a lot of albums, although I was certainly glad to have this great song by Jo Ann Campbell at this late date. Out of the twenty songs on the two albums, her song plus one by Roy Hall were the only unreleased songs on these albums.

After leaving ABC Paramount Records, Jo Ann went on to sign with Cameo Records in Philadelphia in the early summer of 1962, and the first thing she did, which was also recorded where she lived in New York City, was sing an answer version of the second-biggest *Billboard* country chart hit that year, which was also headin' for the Top 10 *Billboard* pop charts, called "Wolverton Mountain," by country artist Claude King. Jo Ann's record was released in July 1962, and by August 18, Jo Ann's answer version, called "(I'm the Girl On) Wolverton Mountain," debuted on the *Billboard* pop charts and quickly reached #38 while havin' a seven-week run on those charts. Jo Ann's answer version also debuted on *Billboard*'s country charts on September 22, and reached a peak position of #24 there but dropped off after only three weeks on those charts.

I've had a number of fans and people I know tell me Jo Ann's Campbell's picture and a brief article is in a recent book about female country singers who sang rock 'n' roll. I haven't seen the book, but if that's the case, they've got it backwards, because Jo Ann Campbell was one female rock 'n' roll/rockabilly chick that only happened by accident to record two out of the more than eighty songs she recorded between 1956 and 1964 that could even be considered country music.

Right after Jo Ann's answer version to "Wolverton Mountain" debuted on the *Billboard* charts, Cameo Records put her in the studio and had her and the New York session band knock out ten or so easy cover versions of recent big hits of the day, so they could rush out an album on her that they titled *All the Hits of Jo Ann Campbell*, with "(I'm the Girl On) Wolverton Mountain" in the biggest print on the front cover. Jo Ann is really embarrassed by this album today, 'cause it was just silly music to her.

Jo Ann had two final releases on Cameo Records. One was during the fall of 1962, "Mr. Fix It Man" b/w "Let Me Do It My Way." The final one that gave Jo Ann her last *Billboard* pop chart hit as a solo artist was "Mother, Please!" It was released in March 1963 and debuted on the *Billboard* pop charts on April 27, reaching a peak position of #88 and only staying on the charts for three weeks. "Mother, Please!" though it has silly lyrics, holds up as the best and closest thing to strong rock 'n' roll from that time, only due to the fact once more of Jo Ann's gritty-soundin' rockabilly vocal style.

Before I completely conclude my story on Jo Ann, I have to fill you in on some little-known facts about her days as the hardest-drivin' rockin' chick I ever seen before The Beatles changed music forever. I'll start off with her relationship with Bobby Darin. Throughout 1959 and early 1960, she was on the covers and inside stories of so many movie and teen magazines with Bobby Darin, and most of the articles in those magazines had Jo Ann and Bobby as bein' engaged to be married. This was all totally false. The truth on this is that Jo Ann met Bobby Darin in 1957, and they immediately became good friends. They started dating by 1958, but by 1959 they were workin' so much their schedules just didn't allow them to see each other, so they parted as friends.

Jo Ann started workin' with her future husband Troy Seals sometime during the fall of 1962. Troy had a great rock 'n' roll and rhythm & blues band then, and around that time, he and his band went out on the road and backed Jo Ann up on all her live shows through 1963 and into 1964, at which time Troy and Jo Ann signed with Atlantic Records as a duo.

Jo Ann also told me she never expected Alan Freed to ever fall or be banned completely as he eventually was in 1962. She said in 1960 and '61, she knew he was in trouble because of the payola scandal goin' on, but she never imagined he'd wind up, within a year, takin' the fall and becomin' the main scapegoat for what almost

Forgettin' to Remember to Forget

I met Jo Ann Campbell in September 1962, when I came to watch her perform every night of a six-night stand at The Rocket Room in Washington, D.C. I was a collector in 1962, and I had never given anything to an artist, no matter how much I liked or loved 'em, but I thought so much of Jo Ann Campbell for bein' the nice person she was, on the final night of her engagement I brought down about thirty magazines that had her and Bobby Darin either on the cover or in stories inside, and I handed all of 'em over to her.

Jo Ann Campbell was the first artist I'd met that was a real person and had no ego. For six nights in a row after her shows ended, she sat and talked with me about what I loved most, as she did also: real rock 'n' roll and rockabilly. She had the bubbliest, perkiest, most upbeat, and happiest personality of anyone I'd ever met in rock 'n' roll music. I couldn't take my eyes off this classy lookin' rockin' chick. I would have never told her back in 1962, but after seeing her for six nights straight, I had fallen head over heels for Jo Ann Campbell. She was perfect in every way, as a person, rockin' singer, and performer. But I was still only eighteen years old then.

I made sure me and whatever friends I had brought to these shows with me all had a front table every night. On about the third or fourth night, she got me up on stage to dance with her when she was singin' "Johnny B. Goode." I'll admit to it now, I was nervous as hell, but the two friends I had with me got a big kick out of it. On that final night in her dressing room after the show, Jo Ann wrote my name and address down and told me she wanted to stay in touch, and she'd be sure to write to me from wherever she was on the road. But I'd heard that before from other artists, although she really did sound like she meant it when she said it. I think I'd been the only fan of hers that showed up with all three of her albums that week, which she autographed for me, plus she signed the backs of the three small publicity photos of her she gave me.

Jo Ann had made that week real special for me and gave me a memory that's lasted all these years. I was real surprised that over the course of the next five or six weeks Jo Ann did write to me in her own handwriting on three postcards from cities she was performing in at the time. They were Cleveland, Pittsburgh, and Milwaukee. On the last one, she put down her address in New York City and asked me to please write her back soon at that address. But I went on with my life and the teenage girls I was either datin' or goin' steady with. I didn't write a whole lot back then, so I just never stayed in touch with Jo Ann after that.

In 1962, I knew I didn't stand a chance with the most gorgeous rockin' chick I'd ever laid eyes on, but I never forgot her and kept buyin' her records through early 1965, 'cause she took the time, for awhile at least, to encourage me in the music business. Jo Ann honestly cared then, and I never forgot that.

every disc jockey in the country was doin' and considered common business practice in the music business at that time. She told me, "When I saw Alan Freed go down and have to leave New York in 1962, a big piece of my heart went with him, and [I knew] that New York radio and all of rock 'n' roll would never be the same again."

While pop music continued to go from one fad to the next, Jo Ann and Troy just kept beatin' out their brands of rock 'n' roll. By 1964, real rock 'n' roll performers such as Jo Ann Campbell turned to black-style rhythm & blues music. Jo Ann had the perfect duo partner for this kind of music in Troy Seals, who she married that year. What's been written over the years is that Troy Seals was a producer in New York for Atlantic Records. For the first time, I can tell you that's totally untrue. It was only because of his relationship with Jo Ann from the fall of 1962 on that he was also based out of New York City. All of his family and friends were from Kentucky, Indiana, and Ohio before that. Troy was born in Kentucky.

At the end of the summer of 1964, Atlantic Records, which was primarily always a black artist label, signed Jo Ann and Troy to a recording contract. Atlantic recorded fifteen songs in two separate sessions on 'em by the end of 1964. Their first 45 release came out in late October 1964, and was called "I Found a Love, Oh What a Love," which was a song Jo Ann wrote under the name of a girlfriend of hers. The B side of this great song was Jo Ann and Troy's pumpin' version of the R&B classic "Who Do You Love?" "I Found a Love, Oh What a Love" debuted on the *Billboard* pop charts on December 12, 1964, reached a peak position of #67, and stayed on the charts for six weeks. It also made it into the Top 40 of the *Billboard* Rhythm & Blues charts by January 1965, and stayed on those charts for eight weeks. Atlantic Records followed this first hit up in the spring of 1965 with the old Lloyd Price #1 R&B classic song "Just Because" b/w "Same Old Feeling," which was another song Jo Ann had written under her girlfriend's name. When this record failed to chart, there were no more releases.

Jo Ann and Troy had been married for a while and continued to tour, but Jo Ann became pregnant with her only son, T.J., around the time the second 45 on Atlantic was released. About this same time, Jo Ann and Troy received a call from the G.A.C. booking agency, who told them that Dick Clark wanted to use them as regulars on

his new daily afternoon TV show, called "Where the Action Is." This is another fact that's never been in print until now.

From June to August 1965, Jo Ann and Troy performed as regulars on "Where the Action Is," which was broadcast nationwide by the ABC network. Jo Ann was four or five months pregnant when she and Troy left the show.

Jo Ann would have probably quit performing altogether after this to raise her son T.J., but in September 1965, Troy and his band got an offer from the Inner Circle Nightclub & Showroom in Cincinnati, Ohio, to become the house band there. Troy took this gig, and Jo Ann told me that it was the perfect situation to continue for her to perform with Troy and not have to travel across the country. Shortly after T.J. was born in late 1965, Jo Ann performed with Troy and his band regularly at nights while she could still care for her son the rest of the time. Jo Ann and Troy, along with his band, stayed at the Inner Circle as the regular house band and performers for over two years, until the end of 1967. Until now, not many lovers of real rock 'n' roll ever knew Jo Ann Campbell went on performing through 1967. Everything in print up to now has her out of the business by early 1965.

By the end of 1967, even though Jo Ann and Troy were both only twenty-nine years old at the time, they decided to settle down and get out of the business altogether so Jo Ann could raise their son, who was then two years old, and Troy would just get into workin' a regular daily job. He worked in the concrete business for a couple years, but then got back into the music business, recording demos and writing songs. Jo Ann was now able to be a homemaker and raise her son under a normal environment.

Troy went on to become one of Nashville's top songwriters. Some of the hits he wrote or co-wrote are "Lost in the Fifties Tonight (In the Still of the Night)" by Ronnie Milsap, "Who's Gonna Fill Them Shoes" by George Jones, "Country Girls" by The Bellamy Brothers, "Drinkin' and Dreamin'" by Waylon Jennings, and "Seven Spanish Angels" by Willie Nelson. Troy and Jo Ann's son T.J. is now a young man, a songwriter and fine musician in his own right doin' his own thing in today's music.

Before I close this part on Jo Ann Campbell out, I have to answer this question: Why haven't you seen her perform (at least in Europe) or haven't heard anything about her much over the years? It's because Jo Ann Campbell wants all her fans to remember her for the thousands of fine shows she performed during the late fifties and well into the sixties. She was young then, as the music she was doing then also was. Literally over a million fans witnessed these shows during that time, and she wants them to remember how great all her shows were, because she was totally professional and a perfectionist. I can tell you personally today Jo Ann Campbell still looks better, can sing rock 'n' roll and rockabilly better, and can outperform and out-rock any of the female artists from the 1950s rockabilly music I've mentioned up to now. Jo Ann knows this also, but the lady is too modest to admit it.

It's not that Jo Ann Campbell hasn't been asked to perform for rockabilly and rock 'n' roll audiences here is the States, 'cause she has. But she's declined offers from the biggest rock revival promoter, Richard Nader, along with others, as she has a happy, busy life outside of music. Besides her close ties with her family, Jo Ann has devoted much of her time as a volunteer at a local animal shelter over the past twenty-five years or so.

I believe Jo Ann Campbell has survived to look so great and keep an upbeat attitude and vibrant, happy personality on rock 'n' roll because she went on with the important things in real everyday life. To me, this lady proved all she ever had to. That she was the best hard-rockin' female artist in rockabilly music. She really did love it and still loves it. On top of which she and her husband Troy are just two great, sincere, nice people. On the music side, just check out Jo Ann's rockabilly tunes on the reissue CDs out of Europe, and you'll find out how hard she rocked and why in my book she's #1.

A Change on the Air:
The Pretty Boy Bobbys Arrive

It's been said many times the two things in life that are always inevitable are death and taxes. Well, there's also another one. That's change. Nothin' ever stays the same. As far back as anyone alive today can remember, trends in pop music have always been aimed toward the young generation. And as a new batch of youngsters comes along, the music they listen to isn't the same as what the previous batch listened to. (But the ones in charge who made the decisions were always adults anywhere from thirty years old and up. With the ones in control, it's all the business of making money that comes first. It seems it has to be that way in any business; whether the product you're selling suffers or not, it doesn't matter as long as it sells.)

By the early fall of 1958, all forms of original rock 'n' roll, rhythm & blues, and rockabilly were gone from the Top 10 national charts forever. In their place were the oh-so-mellow sounds of manufactured teen idols. I've talked in previous chapters about those who I feel were made the scapegoats for the supposed evils of rock 'n' roll — those being Elvis, Little Richard, and Jerry Lee Lewis. I'd like to mention a couple others here.

Chuck Berry and Alan Freed

Chuck Berry, who I'll remind you was promoted by his record company in 1956 and '57 as a rockabilly artist, had to be the greatest lyricist ever in rock 'n' roll history, along with being the most influential rock 'n' roll guitarist of the 1950s. Between the fall of 1955 and the summer of 1958, he charted five songs in the Top 10, and he had many others that received heavy airplay. His live performances were so wild back then they made parents of white teenagers shudder to think their innocent daughters witnessed this sort of thing. They didn't mind too much somebody like a friendly, well-dressed, chubby black man like Fats Domino, who sat there and had a nice smile, swaying back and forth while he was singin' and playing a little boogie-woogie rock 'n' roll

on his piano. That they could tolerate. But Chuck Berry, with his long legs spread out as far as he could get 'em, drivin' his guitar between 'em while he moved and sang while making strange head-bobbin' moves and menacing faces, was too much for them and city officials to stand for by the summer of '58. So "Johnny B. Goode" would end Chuck Berry's string of Top 10s in the summer of '58, and it would take another six years, when The Beatles took America by storm with their own new sound along with mixing in the sounds of Chuck Berry and other artists of the fifties, for Chuck to have a new Top 10 record. While Little Richard and Jerry Lee Lewis were both mainly responsible themselves for losing their power of staying up in Top 10 ranks on all the national charts, Chuck Berry really wasn't, at least not in the summer of 1958. Chuck Berry's downward slide out of the national Top 10 in the summer of '58 could be attributed to his close association with the man given the credit for coining the music phrase "rock 'n' roll," disc jockey Alan Freed.

Most rock 'n' roll and rockabilly fans know Alan Freed's story. But to make it short, in July 1951, Freed accepted a job at WJW radio in Cleveland, Ohio, playing black rhythm & blues records. The sponsor of the program was Leo Mintz, the owner of Record Rendevous, a large downtown record store in Cleveland, who was noticing a growing number of white faces among his primarily black customers buying R&B records in his store. Freed was the perfect personality to promote these records. He nicknamed himself the "Moondog" and howled like a dog and would smack away on his desk or a phone book along with the beat of the record while it played. In the beginning all his listeners were black. They didn't even know Freed was white. In 1952, Freed held what is considered to be the first rock 'n' roll concert in Cleveland. It was an all-black audience there and turned into a riot before it ended. But his listening audience was growing and picking up more white listeners. By early 1953,

Freed called his radio program a rock 'n' roll show that spotlighted the best in R&B records. In 1954, Alan Freed had the #1-rated radio show in Cleveland. He had gotten too big for Cleveland, Ohio. WINS radio in New York City offered Freed a deal to move his radio show there, which had the biggest listening audience in the country, and by the summer of 1955, Alan Freed became the first king of rock 'n' roll. Before 1955 ended, independent and major labels alike knew it was Alan Freed who could make a record bust on the *Billboard* pop and R&B charts just by playin' it.

This is where Chuck Berry comes in. His first record, "Maybellene," was released by Chess Records of Chicago, one of the biggest independent labels in the country that specialized in releasing R&B and blues records by black artists. Alan Freed was given partial writer credit on the song, which was common practice throughout the fifties with powerful DJs in big markets. "Rock Around the Clock" by Bill Haley and His Comets was the first #1 rock 'n' roll record when it hit that spot on the *Billboard* pop charts on July 9, 1955, and it stayed at the top for eight straight weeks. But Chuck Berry's record of "Maybellene" reached #5 on the *Billboard* pop charts and #1 on the R&B charts in late September 1955, selling (no matter what's been said to the contrary) over a million copies by year's end. This made it the first genuine rock 'n' roll (or rockabilly) song to make it this high on the pop charts until that time. This record started a long association between Berry and Freed that would last through 1959, when the Payola Scandal would eventually make Alan Freed the primary victim of the entire music business, which had always been corrupt anyway and in various other ways continues to be that way to this day.

From the summer of '55 to the summer of '58, Alan Freed pretty much ruled real rock 'n' roll, but in '58, when Freed took his Caravan of Rock 'n' Roll Stars road show into Boston for a one-night show (which was headlined by Chuck Berry), there was a fight outside the Boston Arena, which was located in a bad section of the city, in which a young white sailor was stabbed by a black man who was never caught by police. The next day's newspapers blew this incident out of proportion. All the TV news channels said there were colored teenagers runnin' through the streets of their lovely city with weapons and destroying property. Though city officials had no witnesses or filmed account of this, and there was no proof the stabbing had anything to do with the rock 'n' roll show inside the Arena, this was all they

needed to indict Alan Freed with "inciting a riot." Freed was found *not* guilty, but because of the nationwide coverage in papers, TV, and radio news, this was definitely proof enough to convince other city officials and parents of teenagers that Alan Freed was the head honcho who was promoting the ever-increasing onslaught of juvenile delinquency in our country every time he put on one of his shows. Shortly after all this negative publicity, WINS radio in New York fired Alan Freed, even though his radio show was still #1 in the ratings.

Chuck Berry stuck it out with Alan Freed almost to his demise. I'm sorry if it seems like I might be giving you a history lesson, but some things just need to be said. Alan Freed was ahead of his time. Between 1955 and 1958, during rock 'n' roll and rockabilly music's beginning and best years, his rock 'n' roll shows had not only black and white performers starring on them, but the fans who attended were also a mixture of both races. You may think, well, most of his big shows were in northern cities, so what's the big deal. Well, let me tell ya, there was as much racism in cities like Boston, Philadelphia, Pittsburgh, Baltimore, and Washington, D.C. (where I was living), in the mid-to-late-fifties as there was in Atlanta, Little Rock, Memphis, or Shreveport. The only inroad blacks had made in this country by 1958 was when President Eisenhower integrated public schools in 1954, and that was still causing riots, not in the South, but in prudish Boston, as late as the early seventies. From '55 to '58, Alan Freed didn't care if you were black or white; if you made rock 'n' roll, rockabilly, R&B, or music with "the Big Beat" he brought to nationwide prominence and loved so much, you were usually somewhere on his show bill, whether you had a big national hit or not. When the press relentlessly went out in full force to get rid of Alan Freed in 1958, that was what really killed all forms of great rock 'n' roll as we had known it.

After '58, hard-core rockabilly, rock 'n' roll, R&B, street corner doo-wop, etc. would either never reach the national Top 10, or it would be delivered in a milder, softer-soundin', lily-white way to please the adult establishment. It would take another year or so for it to completely disappear from the national charts altogether, but when Alan Freed finally got brought down altogether in 1960 when he was arrested on twenty-six counts of commercial bribery, everything to do with any form of great rock 'n' roll bein' heard on your radio was only wishful thinkin' in a teenager's young mind. What's really never been written that much is the real reason the federal government was able to crucify Alan Freed for something that was being done by virtually every DJ in the country is because commercial bribery (a form of payola) was only illegal by federal law in two of the now fifty states in this country. New York happened to be one of 'em. Freed was an easy target for the feds to make an example out of.

When Freed was fired by WINS radio in 1958, his radio show was picked up by WABC radio in New York City, and he had a TV dance party show on WNEW-TV, also in New York. But he was fired by the time those charges came down on him. Alan Freed was a bold, outspoken renegade of a man who really did love the music he played and promoted. Oh, yeah, he also loved the money and the fame it brought him, but in April 1960, when he was finally forced (which before he had refused to do) to testify in secret in front of a Washington House subcommittee investigating bribery in radio and TV broadcasting, he didn't walk around the truth like others did. He spelled out in plain words what were the common practices in all of the entire music business. Freed admitted being on the payroll of a number of record manufacturers and distributors, but quickly shot back with, "You may call that payola in the music business, but in Washington it's called lobbying." The subcommittee did not find this truthful statement to be humorous in the least. He also told them he'd never taken any money to play a record on the air, and he never would. He admitted to accepting gifts. He said, "If I do somebody a favor and they give me a gift later, sure I'll accept it. It's the backbone of all American business, and every one of you know it, but as I said, I'll never take a dime to plug a record." When a member of the subcommittee asked him, "If someone were to send you a gift of a new Cadillac, would you send it back?" in his typical flamboyant style, Freed answered, "That would depend on what color it is." The subcommittee was not amused. But that's why you should love Alan Freed as much as I do. He gave us real rock 'n' roll, and when forced to, he told the truth, and it ultimately became his downfall. Later Freed made a public statement in front of the press and cameras stating, "You creeps may think payola stinks, but it's always been here, and I didn't start it." It took the feds another two years to finally convict him in 1962, when he was found guilty on three counts of the original bribery charges. He was fined $300 and given a suspended sentence. By this time, he was completely blackballed in all New York broadcasting circles. At the time of his death in January 1965, the IRS was after him for failing to report the payola income from his 1962 convictions. He died from uremic poisoning in the Palm Springs Desert Hospital at forty-three years of age. Penniless and completely broken. Forsaken by his old friends for the most part.

Before Dick Clark went on national TV in '57, Alan Freed was the host of the very first network TV rock 'n' roll music show in late '56 for ABC, and his CBS "Camel Rock 'n' Roll Party" was the first coast-to-coast rock 'n' roll radio show. That was also in 1956. I don't want to get into Dick Clark bashin', but he had it easy by the time "American Bandstand" went nationwide on ABC-TV in August 1957. Alan Freed had paved the way.

Dick Clark

For all you real rockabilly and rock 'n' roll fans who love the great songs and artists of the fifties and want the straight scoop about Dick Clark, go out and see if you can find his 1976 autobiography, called *Rock, Roll & Remember*. In it he makes clear that he was a man on a mission: to make the most money he could at what he did best. What he did best in August '57, when "American Bandstand" went on network national TV on a daily basis, was to be able to convince white American teenagers of the middle to upper class that he was on their side with music that was theirs, and that he also loved it.

Before 1957 ended, "American Bandstand" was the #1-rated daytime program on TV, and Dick Clark was the top daytime personality. Rockabilly artists were still a force to be reckoned with, and many of the top stars, such as Buddy Holly and The Crickets, Eddie Cochran, Gene Vincent, Jerry Lee Lewis, Chuck Berry, Buddy Knox, etc., appeared on the program. Other rockabilly artists with Top 10 regional, but not national, hits also appeared on the show during that period, including D.C.'s own Vernon Taylor and New York City's top rockabilly chick Jo Ann Campbell. But by the end of 1957, Dick Clark had become the most powerful person in all forms of music that teenagers were attracted to. So he did what any other good business person would do in his field at that time. Here are the facts that Clark has always admitted to, and it must be said that everything I'll list were normal business practices that were not illegal at that time.

In mid July 1957, a few weeks before "Bandstand" went coast-to-coast, Clark formed his first two major music publishing companies. After this, he accepted 25 percent of the publishing rights to the song "Butterfly" by Charlie Gracie, which went to #1 on *Billboard* and sold a million copies. Bernie Lowe was one of the primary owners of the Cameo label, which had struggled in Philadelphia up until this hit song. Soon after this took place, Clark, Lowe, and another business associate formed Chips Distributors, a record distribution corporation. Clark owned one-third interest. Jamie Records was another struggling record company in Philadelphia in late 1957. Clark went into equal partnership with three other Philadelphia businessmen. One was a lawyer, one was a record promotion man, and the final one owned a record pressing plant. Shortly after Clark became a partner, a guitarist working on the West Coast, who up until this time had not had a big major hit record in the pop field, was signed to an exclusive contract to Jamie Records. The guitarist I'm speaking of is Duane Eddy. Shortly after signing Eddy, Clark and a talent manager friend formed SRO Artists Company for the sole purpose of becoming Duane Eddy's managers. They later managed other artists in '58 and '59. In December 1957, Clark took his biggest step into the independent record label business when he and two music business friends formed Swan Records in Philadelphia. Clark owned 50 percent of the label, and each of his other two partners owned 25 percent. Dick also gladly accepted 50 percent of the copyright on the song "At the Hop" by Danny and The Juniors in December 1957, as the owners Artie Singer and Larry Brown insisted he deserved it, since when they first came to him with the song it was called "Doing the Bop," and Clark told them they should redo the song and call it "At the Hop." Clark felt there was nothing wrong with accepting half the copyright, as, in his own words, it was just something in return for using his creative energies. This song hit #1 nationally in early '58 and went on to sell two million copies back then. "At the Hop" was on Swan Records. In February 1958, besides "Bandstand's" daily show on ABC-TV, Dick Clark was given a Saturday night half hour prime-time TV show, broadcast from a theater in New York City. The show, like "Bandstand," was live. Clark agreed to do this show only if he had total control of the entertainers who appeared on it. During 1958 and most of 1959, Clark acquired two more independent record labels, managed certain artists, formed a couple more music publishing companies, bought his own record pressing plant, and formed his own TV production company.

By the summer of 1958, Dick Clark was dominating the new trend to come in rock 'n' roll. I believe he was the real downfall and the real reason great rock 'n' roll,

rockabilly, and rhythm & blues were all virtually dead by late 1959 and pop music was in a different way, almost back to where it'd been before real rock 'n' roll and rockabilly started to bust out in 1955 — with silly teenage pop songs for white America. In 1958 and 1959, whatever Dick Clark played the most was what sold the most to teenagers in America. His teenage audience watched him promote what he chose to play not only five days a week but now also on Saturday nights.

One big question I've always had in my mind was would Duane Eddy have become the #1 rock 'n' roll instrumentalist of all time if it hadn't been for Dick Clark becoming his manager. Duane was definitely a good guitarist with a unique sound, but what made him better than, say, Link Wray, who was also an excellent guitarist with a unique sound? When Dick Clark was asked during the payola hearings in early 1960 why he played more of Duane Eddy's songs on his TV show than even Elvis Presley's, his answer to the congressmen was because he closed his show each day with an instrumental song, and with the exception of "So Rare" by Jimmy Dorsey, there just weren't that many instrumental hit songs to choose from at that time. Definitely not true. For one thing, "So Rare" was off the charts and had been a hit over a year before Duane Eddy charted with his first hit. "Honky Tonk" was a classic rock 'n' roll instrumental that stayed on the national charts into the early months of 1957. It peaked at #2 and was loved by all teenagers throughout the fifties. Other huge hit instrumentals in rock 'n' roll between '57 and '59 were "Raunchy" by Bill Justis, "Topsy" by Cosy Cole, "Tequila" by The Champs, "Rumble" and "Rawhide" by Link Wray and His Wraymen, "Patricia" by Perez Prado, "Smokie" by The Bill Black Combo, "Walkin' with Mr. Lee" by Lee Allen, and dozens more. All in the teenage rock 'n' roll-type field. 'Nuff said on that.

When Dick Clark gave his testimony at those payola hearings, he came out smellin' like a rose and went on with the business of making money, only he had to do it in a different way, which he had already begun. He had been told in November 1959 by Leonard Goldenson, the president of American Broadcasting-Paramount Pictures, which produced "Bandstand" and the Saturday night show, to immediately get rid of every music business property his name was on, unless he wanted to find work elsewhere. By that time, though, the damage Dick Clark had done to real rock 'n' roll music was beyond repair.

Nineteen fifty-nine and 1960 were the two peak years for the no-talent teen idols who showed up every week on "American Bandstand." Three of the biggest teen idols of 1959 came out of Philadelphia and were on Philadelphia-based labels. They were Frankie Avalon, Bobby Rydell, and Fabian. The music was still called rock 'n' roll, but none of these three singing teen idols ever made a rock 'n' roll song in '59 or '60. Nor did Jimmy Clanton, Edd "Kookie" Byrnes, Paul Anka, Freddy Cannon, Bobby Darin, or The Fleetwoods. These nine artists dominated the top of the *Billboard* pop charts throughout 1959. Four of them held Billboard's #1 spot for almost half the year, twenty-four weeks to be exact. Only two of these artists would go on to prove they had lasting talent as pop music entertainers or songwriters. Those were Paul Anka and Bobby Darin. None of them ever had a rock 'n' roll song that would influence future rock artists, the way the real rock 'n' roll, R&B, and rockabilly artists of 1955 to 1958 did. Those great first-generation rockers were all true artists. They all made music that has continued to stand the test of time. Dick Clark's bandwagon of fly-by-night pretty bandstand boys only made a lot of money in a short period of time doin' mostly silly, trite songs that were specially written for them by others so they could make money. None of these songs had any artistic value whatsoever.

When the teen idols ran their course, Clark went into any trend that came along, startin' with "The Twist" and other dance crazes. In early '64, he moved his show out to California to cash in on the surf sound. Then in the mid sixties he started doin' a new TV show called "Where the Action Is" to get in on Beatlemania. By 1967, he came up with another short-lived teen show, with Paul Revere and The Raiders, titled "Happening." Over the past twenty years, Dick Clark has done whatever it took, from TV game shows to TV blooper shows to opening restaurants to teaming up with Ed McMahon to do advertisements for Publishers Clearing House sweepstakes.

If you're a rockabilly fan and go to a Ronnie Dawson show, please ask him about his experiences and feelings about Dick Clark. Dawson is one of the last few good artists who made rockabilly records in the late fifties who can still put on as good a rockabilly show as you'll ever want to see in the nineties, and he had firsthand experience with Clark. Ronnie had two action-packed 45s come out on independent labels in the Dallas area in '58 and early '59. Both were solid rockabilly. The second record, "Rockin' Bones," broke into the regional charts in a number of major cities and received good airplay. This came to Dick Clark's attention by the summer of '59, so he sent two scouts down to Dallas, where Ronnie had a steady following of kids who loved his brand of rockabilly. Clark's scouts were impressed, and when they reported back to Clark, Ronnie got a call shortly thereafter saying Swan Records wanted to sign him, but he had to come up to Philly to record his music. They told Ronnie he'd be allowed to do it the way he always had. But by the time he did the session for Swan, the songs and musicians were already chosen for

Forgettin' to Remember to Forget

*E*ven though I never thought Fabian could sing a lick to save his life, he didn't really upset me. When I sat down and talked with him in the spring of 1960, I actually felt sorry for him. He was on Milt Grant's TV show promotin' his next-to-last Top 40 record. His big hits (and for the most part his music career) were behind him. By this time, he was no longer bein' mobbed by girls. There weren't more than a few waitin' for him when he came in and out of the hotel. When I first started talking to him, I thought he was stuck up, but after we talked for a couple minutes, I found out he was just nervous and suffering from the twenty-four-hour-a-day schedule he'd been kept on for the last year and a half. I remember him tellin' me he was glad his records were slippin', 'cause he was tired and had almost been killed by thousands of girls trying to get to him the year before. He said he was glad his managers were putting him into serious movies now. Fabian was only two years older than me. At the time, he was eighteen and I was sixteen. I thought he had it made. He was a big star. It was the first time I realized bein' a big star sometimes wasn't everything you thought it was. Fabian was more controlled by his managers than Elvis ever was.

him, and they were not the type of music he loved the best. He had two 45 releases on Swan, and if you ask him, he'll tell you they're his most embarrassing records.

After doin' Dick Clark tours with the likes of Bobby Rydell and Freddy Cannon, Ronnie (or the "Blond Bomber," as he's always been called) had enough of this silly music and lip-synchin' his Swan releases for the teenage audiences and went back to Dallas by his own choice in 1960. He's been happy ever since 'cause he got to go back to playin' real rock 'n' roll, R&B, and rockabilly music and continues to do it and is bigger than ever in the nineties.

Vernon Taylor

Rockabilly music was out of the Top 10 throughout all of 1959, but it wasn't completely off the national charts, and by all means it was still alive and well in and around Washington, D.C., in large part because we had one local rockin' hero in our town that me and my friends thought was in the Top 10 all over the country. This cat's name was Vernon Taylor.

Vernon was born and raised in the country hills of Montgomery County, Maryland, in the late thirties, when that county was nothin' but pure country. He got his first guitar when he was eight years old. In the late forties and early fifties, Vernon was influenced by the sounds he heard on Saturday nights either on WWVA's "Jamboree" radio show out of Wheeling, West Virginia, or WSM's "Grand Ole Opry" out of Nashville. In those days on AM radio after sundown you could actually pick up a radio show as far away as Nashville.

During his last year in high school in late '54 and '55, Vernon formed his own band, started playing dances, and for a while had his own morning radio show. By 1955, the area around Washington, D.C., was a mecca for country music, mainly due to the efforts of Connie B. Gay. Connie was responsible for the huge success of Jimmy Dean's daily afternoon "Town and Country Time" TV show and Jimmy Dean's weekend family country dances at places like Turner's Arena. During 1955 and '56, Vernon Taylor and his band played on a lot of Dean's regular country dances around the Washington area.

Now back in those days, Vernon and all the other members of his band had to work day jobs. When Vernon graduated from high school, he went to work as a printer. Today he's still workin' as a printer, and, believe it or not, forty years later, at the same place.

Though for a few years when it looked like he'd make it big in rockabilly he took about a three-year leave of absence. But never actually gave up that day job. Smart move, Vernon!

Between 1955 and 1957, Vernon was workin' anywhere from four to six nights a week singin' and playin' various places on a regular basis. By this time, he was throwin' in a few rockabilly tunes with his normal country cover songs, and as rockabilly got bigger and bigger all during 1956, his popularity grew all over the Washington area. He had a regular decent-paying gig every Saturday night that he really liked a lot, but but he had to give it up in the summer of 1957 when "The Don Owens TV Jamboree Show" began on local television, and Owens hired Vernon as a regular performer on the show. It would become the biggest thing up to that time that happened to Vernon in music. A few months prior to the start of the TV show, Owens signed Vernon to a personal management contract. By that time, Don Owens had not only become the top country music disc jockey in the Washington, D.C., area, but also one of the top country DJs in the entire nation.

Don had a regular show on WARL radio, a country music station owned by Connie B. Gay. He was friends with a lot of the top country artists out of Nashville and would book these artists on the many shows he promoted in and around Washington, D.C. Even though his first love was old-time bluegrass and hillbilly music, Don supported the earliest, most primitive forms of rockabilly music comin' out of Memphis in the mid 1950s.

There were a number of other local D.C. country disc jockeys, but it was Don Owens who would play Elvis while he was still on Sun Records and still wasn't known outside of the South. Tomcat Reeder, who went on to become another legendary disc jockey in country music, remembers well that it was Don Owens who first played "Baby, Let's Play House," which made it to #5 on the *Billboard* country charts in the summer of '55, and then went on to play Elvis's final record on Sun, "I Forgot to Remember to Forget," which reached #1 on those charts all during the fall of the same year. Reeder remembers Don as being very broad-minded, especially with this new rockabilly style of music that was comin' in out of Memphis via the Sun label, and givin' each record a shot to see if his listeners liked it, and if they did and he got requests for it, he would continue playing it. According to Reeder, a lot of other country DJs at that time wouldn't touch the stuff, but Don wasn't like that at all.

Around the time his TV show started, Don Owens called his old friend Mac Wiseman, who, besides being a performer and recording artist for Dot Records, out of the Nashville area, was also a producer and A&R man for the label. Don worked out a deal for Dot Records to sign Vernon to a recording contract. Shortly after, Don and Vernon went to Nashville, and Vernon recorded four songs with Nashville's top session men: "Losing Game," "I've Got the Blues," "Satisfaction Guarenteed," and "Why Must You Leave Me." Dot Records released Vernon's first record, "Losing Game" b/w "I've Got the Blues," in August 1957.

The A side, "Losing Game," was probably the biggest selling record he had in the early fall months of 1957. Even though this song is not a rockabilly song, it still couldn't be considered a pop song or a trite teen song either. It's more of an easygoin', smoothly sung, country flavored, almost mid-tempo ballad. That's one of the strangest analyses of a song I've ever had to give. But it's the best way I can describe it. The B side, "I've Got the Blues," was more in a rockabillyish vein, though. "Losing Game" not only became Vernon's biggest hit in Washington, D.C., and surrounding areas, but it also broke onto a whole lot of radio station charts in other markets up and down the East Coast, from Atlanta to Buffalo. It sold well enough and made it onto the regional charts in enough big cities that Dick Clark took notice, and Vernon went on his way to Philadelphia and appeared on "American Bandstand."

Dot Records for the most part was promoting Vernon's record towards the pop and teenage market, but Vernon was mainly on shows with country stars in the Washington area throughout the rest of 1957. This was because his manager, Don Owens, had all his main ties with Nashville and the country market. Vernon remembers one instance in October 1957, when Don Owens took him down to the Country Music Disc Jockey convention. Vernon said, "I met all the big names in country music. Don knew 'em all well by then. One evening me and Don went out to dinner with Jim Reeves, and I remember him tellin' us all of Nashville's top country acts were really worried 'cause Elvis and rock 'n' roll had brought country music down to its lowest level in the past few years. The whole industry and business of country music was bein' wrecked by what Elvis had started. None of the top established acts were drawing big audiences at their live shows like they were only a few years earlier. Even the "Grand Ole Opry's" attendance was down. I was shocked to hear this, 'cause Jim

Reeves was just comin' off the biggest hit he had to date on the song 'Four Walls.' It even crossed over big into the pop charts." Well, friends, I reckon that's why (as of this writing, anyway) Elvis has never been honored as a member of the Country Music Hall of Fame. Even though he placed eighty-four songs on the *Billboard* country charts, including eleven #1s and thirty-six others that made Top 10. It's only his car they've decided to honor there.

"Losing Game" did well enough for Dot Records that in January 1958 they released the other two songs he had recorded for them, "Satisfaction Guaranteed" b/w "Why Must You Leave Me." "Satisfaction Guaranteed" was a bouncy up-tempo rockabilly styled number written by Don Owens, while "Why Must You Leave Me" was on the country side, sung with just a touch of country soul. Vernon wrote this song. After this song was released, Vernon went out on a ten-day promotional tour of local teen dance shows and visits to Top 40 radio stations to promote the record in various major market cities. But for the most part, he spent practically all of his time during 1958 working in and around the Washington area, where he was best known, drawing big audiences, as well as becoming one of the most popular acts on Don's TV show.

Don Owens kept Vernon mostly on country music shows in and around the D.C. area for the most part of his recroding career, which lasted only a short two years between the summer of 1957 and the summer of 1959. Vernon only had four record releases during this period, but it was his final two that have secured him a place in rockabily music's history overtop many other artists considered by some as rockabilly artists. The reason being that Vernon's final two 45 records were recorded at the original Sun Recording Studio. This came about as the result of Vernon's manager Don Owens striking up a lasting friendship with the now legendary and flamboyant Jack Clement, engineer and producer at Sun.

The way Jack puts it, "I got a job at Sun Studios late in 1956. Well, I hadn't kept in touch with Don that much over the past few years, but sometime in 1957, I called him up one day and I told him what I was doin' and I found out that he loved Elvis and all that kinda stuff. He called me awhile after that and said he had this boy in the D.C. area that was goin' pretty good with the young crowd around Washington and wanted to bring him down to Memphis and cut some songs there. I told him come on, let's do it, so he booked some studio time and Don and the boy, Vernon Taylor, drove down, and we cut a bunch of songs both on Vernon and on Don 'cause he had his own label up in D.C. at that time."

Jack Clement remembers only two sessions Vernon and Don recorded at Sun, probably due to the fact that the four songs that were released on Vernon's two Sun 45s came from two different sessions. Vernon remembers he and Don made four trips down to the Sun Studio, between late August 1958 and early March 1959.

By the time Vernon Taylor's first record on the Sun label was released in November 1958, the glory days of rockabilly music and the Sun label were over. There would be no more Top 10 national pop charts for either the music or the label. But don't take that wrong; Sun would still continue to chart Top 40 hits on the pop charts and sell millions more records through 1961. But with Jack Clement doin' practically all of the production work and mixing, the sound of Sun was not what it was a year earlier in 1957. Jack Clement was doin' his best to compete with the ever-changing commercial sound in music by late '58. It showed on Vernon's first 45.

Out of all the songs they recorded, the two they chose to release were "Today Is a Blue Day" b/w "Breeze." "Today Is a Blue Day," written by Jack Clement, may not have made the national charts, but Vernon and me both remember during late 1958 and early 1959 it was not only in the Top 10 in Washington, it also broke onto the charts in Baltimore, Richmond, Wilmington, and other cities. In the liner notes on the backs of reissue albums in the late seventies to late eighties, it's been written that the sales on both Vernon's Sun 45s were not very good at all, but whoever wrote this could be going by Sun Records' accounting files on his records. All I know is "Today Is a Blue Day" not only got a lot of airplay (more than any release Vernon had), but also record stores in D.C. couldn't keep it in stock the first month it was out, and it's always been his easiest 45 to run across for me when I've gone through old records for sale in the D.C./Maryland area during the seventies and eighties. Vernon also believes it was probably his biggest selling record. It definitely sold enough for Sam Phillips to release a second 45 by Vernon in July 1959.

Vernon remembers that for the last of his four Sun sessions, Sam Phillips himself was at the controls. Sam chose two of the songs from that session for Vernon's final record, "Mystery Train" b/w "Sweet and Easy to Love." I'm sure Sam chose those two titles because his

music publishing companies owned the rights to both songs. No doubt in my mind that Sam always loved the music and loved gettin' the sound right to what he heard in his own creative mind, but has never been no dumb hillbilly when it comes down to business. "Mystery Train" was Vernon's best rocker, and Vernon Taylor has the distinction of bein' only one of three artists in the 1950s to have a release on Sun Records on that song. Of course Elvis in '55 is the one who made it famous, and the other one is the writer of the song, Little Junior Parker, in 1953. But when Vernon's updated rockin' version of "Mystery Train" came out in the summer of 1959, it didn't stand a chance of hittin' the national charts. Of course, again, all over the Washington, D.C., area, you heard it pretty regularly on the radio, and it was in all the record shops in the area.

Vernon appeared several times on the Milt Grant TV show, where I got to see and talk with him. The last time I remember was in April 1960. Vernon can't remember why he was on the show that late, 'cause he didn't have a new record out, but both me and him remember the other guest star that was on the show that day. It was Charlie Rich. Charlie's first national hit, "Lonely Weekends," on Phillips Records, was climbing up the charts and stayed on for twenty-one weeks, eventually peaking out at #22. This record refused to die. The reason "Lonely Weekends" by Charlie Rich refused to die was because it was a good rockabilly/rock 'n' roll type record that probably sold a million copies. But as I said, it only reached a peak of #22. I believe the politics of the music business kept Sun and Phillips records out of the Top 10 by this time, and though they kept 'em down someplace on the charts, they couldn't keep 'em off completely because of all the airplay and sales they were receiving. In fact, at twenty-one weeks, "Lonely Weekends" lasted not only longer than any of the Top 10 teen garbage of the day, it even outlasted anything The Beatles recorded throughout the sixties.

It wasn't only Charlie Rich that seemed to be discriminated against in the early months of 1960. Around December, 1959, former great Sun artist and session man Billy Lee Riley became partners with another legendary Sun Records session man, Roland Janes, who played guitar on almost every song Jerry Lee Lewis recorded at Sun Records between 1956 and 1963, to form their own Memphis record label, Rita Records. The first record they put out on their new label was a smash hit. Every DJ in the country loved it, and it was commercial enough to be geared directly at the teenage audience. You may not recognize the artist's name unless you're a big rockabilly fan, but you're sure to remember the hit song from 1960, called "Mountain of Love." The original artist's name is Harold Dorman. After its debut in late February 1960, "Mountain of Love" by Harold Dorman only reached a peak position of #21, but remained on the *Billboard* pop charts for nineteen straight weeks. Johnny Rivers hit the *Billboard* pop Top 10 a little over four years later with a cover of "Mountain of Love" that reached #9, but fell off the charts after only eleven weeks. In 1960, it was just a plain and simple fact that no matter how good distribution, airplay, and songs got, if they were comin' out of Memphis-based labels with artists or people connected previously to Sun Records, they were not ever gonna get into the Top 10. One final example is the song "Rockin' Little Angel" by Ray Smith on Judd Records. This was another big seller. After its debut on the *Billboard* pop charts in 1960, it only reached a peak position of #22, but it stayed on the charts for sixteen straight weeks. Again, longer than almost all the teen junk that was up into the Top 10 at the time. In 1958 and '59, Ray Smith had three good rockabilly releases on the Sun label. Judd Records was owned and operated by Sam Phillips's brother Judd Phillips. By 1961 and '62, both Harold Dorman and Ray Smith went back to Sun Records and both had a couple releases each, but of course with no success.

The Four Star record label wasn't out of Memphis, but they hit big from early May to mid October 1960 with one of the all-time classic teenage hot rod-type car songs. It's best remembered by the great rock 'n' roll/rockabilly styled group Commander Cody and His Lost Planet Airmen. The song was "Hot Rod Lincoln." Cody's group did a great version of that song, and it went on the *Billboard* pop charts on March 25, 1972, where it stayed for fourteen weeks, reaching a peak of #9. Charlie Ryan and The Timberline Riders did the original version of this song, which is still being sung in clubs today by current rockabilly bands. Charlie's version stayed on the *Billboard* pop charts for a nineteen-week ride, and it's totally unbelievable to me that it only reached a peak position of #33.

I believe I've made my points on the politics of the major charts back around 1959 and 1960. Fabian, Bobby Rydell, Freddy Cannon, Frankie Avalon, Paul Anka, and all the rest of those teen idols' records are practically worthless to professional record dealers and collectors today, but Charlie Rich's, Ray Smith's, Harold Dorman's, Jerry Lee Lewis's, The Johnny Burnette Trio's, Buddy Holly's, Gene Vincent's, and Vernon Taylor's records from around the same time all bring high dollar prices. Why? 'Cause they made real rock 'n' roll and rockabilly music that's lasted and has been re-recorded by later and current artists.

It wasn't long after Vernon's final appearance on Milt Grant that the "Don Owens TV Jamboree" was taken off the air, sometime in the late summer of 1960. A final note on Don Owens, though. While it's true Connie B. Gay started the D.C. country music scene back in the mid to late forties and turned it into the biggest outlet that far north for the music comin' out of Nashville, he went down in country music's history for all of his accomplishments, but Don Owens has never really been given the credit I believe he deserves. Don Owens was more receptive to the changing times, even though old-time country music would always remain his first love. Don would always have local entertainers such as Bobby Metzler and Sonny Dixon doin' rockabilly type songs on his TV show.

Don Owens has never been given any credit for how important he was in the careers of both Patsy Cline and Roy Clark. Don managed and booked both those artists and released them from his contracts at a time when they had real chances to go on and leave the area to get into the big time in country music. In Patsy Cline's case, though she went to Nashville in late '59, during the previous years she spent doin' most of her shows in and around D.C., she could rock with the best of 'em. A good number of the records she had released between '55 and '59 while still in the D.C. area have always been considered rockabilly songs among fans of the music. Songs like "Deal the Cards Slowly," "Let the Teardrops Fall," "Love, Love, Love Me Honey Do," "Got a Lotta Rhythm in My Soul," and especially "Stop, Look and Listen" are all forms of good female rockabilly. In some of these songs you can hear at certain times or sometimes throughout the whole song a gravelly growl, a squeal, and even a few hiccups in Patsy's vocal style. She could belt this stuff whenever she wanted. She made it sound easy. I've heard female rockabilly singers in the eighties and nineties, such as LesLee "Bird" Anderson, Virginia Veatch, Martí Brom, and Rosie Flores all include at least one of the songs I've mentioned in their sets. I believe Patsy's early rockin' sides will always be included in future sets and be recorded by young female rockabilly singers. As for Roy Clark, when he left D.C. to join Wanda Jackson's band in 1960, Wanda was at that time really startin' to hit it big with what fans know today as her greatest rockabilly period. After her only real rockabilly *Billboard* pop chart hit in the late summer months of 1960, a cover of the Elvis song "Let's Have a Party," which reached a peak of #37 and stayed on the charts ten weeks, she went in the studio to cut songs in the same vein. Roy Clark played some of the hottest rockabilly guitar licks you'll ever hear on some of Wanda's best rockin' songs, like "Hard Headed Woman," "Riot in Cell Block #9," "Tunnel of Love," "Man We Had a Party," "There's a Party Goin' On," and others. Wanda shined with her cuttin', raunchy vocals, but Roy's guitar solos stand as the best forms of rockabilly guitar work you'll hear on just about any Wanda Jackson rockabilly song.

Don Owens was a country and bluegrass disc jockey, but had the foresight to see you couldn't stop the incoming rock 'n' roll and rockabilly music in the mid to late fifties, and he didn't discriminate against it like so many country DJs did at that time. He knew it was done by young country boys, so he embraced it, though it wasn't his first love in music. Nashville's music business may have hated what Elvis had done to 'em, but Don Owens continued to program Elvis records until well into 1960 on his radio show on WARL, until the station changed formats. After Don lost his TV show, he continued to be involved in radio and in the music business. But in the early morning hours of August 21, 1963, Don's life would end when he fell asleep at the wheel and his car crashed into a tree. I never met Don Owens, but I wish I had, 'cause he was truly dedicated to the kind of music he loved. It's really too bad there's not a whole lot more like him in the music business today.

A short while after Don Owens's TV Jamboree went off the air in 1960, Vernon Taylor went back to his day job as a full-time printer, but continued to play music part-time in various clubs around D.C. on the weekends until just about the end of the 1960s. But Vernon definitely had his "day in the sun" where others had failed. By 1958 and '59, Vernon Taylor was so big, he had a national fan club of more than 2,000 members, and in 1959, he not only headlined shows over Patsy Cline in Washington, D.C., but also George Jones. During the summer of 1958, Vernon was listed third on the bill on one of the biggest 1950s rock 'n' roll shows ever held at the Ritchie Coliseum on the campus of Maryland University. Bill Haley and His Comets were the main headliners, The Diamonds were listed second, and Vernon Taylor was right behind them. Even Link Wray and His Wraymen were listed behind Vernon's name, and

they had already had a Top 20 national hit with "Rumble." Other local acts were the first great rockabilly band to come from D.C., Terry and The Pirates, who made one forever-lasting great rockabilly song in 1957 called "What'd He Say."

Vernon did his last actual show in 1969. Then he got out of performing for good (he thought). In 1978, I was just gettin' involved with a local entertainer who I'll talk more about later, and during that time he signed a management contract with a local rock 'n' roll promoter by the name of Rudy Callicutt. Rudy was the manager and cousin of D.C. rockabilly's great one-record wonder Dudley Callicut, known to rockabilly record collectors for the rare "Get Ready Baby," on D.C. Records. I was around Rudy on a number of occasions from late 1978 to late 1979, and during one of our conversations about rockabilly's glory days in the D.C. area during the late 1950s, I asked him whatever happened to Vernon Taylor. Rudy told me he's still working at the same printing company in Montgomery County he's always worked at except when he had his records out. One day not long after our conversation I was headin' over that way anyway, so I decided to stop in at the printing company Vernon worked for. But he had just left to go get lunch, and I didn't feel like hangin' around, so I just left. I had just picked up an extra copy of an import album from England called *Sun Sound Special: Raunchy Rockabilly* that had a song that had never been released by Vernon that he had cut at the Sun Studios, called "Your Lovin' Man." It was the strongest hard-driving rockabilly song I'd ever heard him do. I didn't leave the record for him that day 'cause I figured I'd just come back or call him about it. This was sometime in January 1979. Well, I just became really busy as time went on and never got back over there to drop in on Vernon Taylor.

Vernon never really crossed my mind until I got a call in early December 1984 from Joe Sasfy, a local writer who did a lot of articles and reviews in support of all the new rockabilly singers and groups that had sprung up since 1977 when Robert Gordon revived interest in rockabilly music on a national scale. Joe wanted to do an article on Vernon Taylor and wanted to know if I knew where he was, so I told him to call the printing company where he worked at. Shortly after this, I met Vernon by chance in a record store. We struck up a long conversation and exchanged phone numbers and both said we'd keep in touch. We did stay in touch, mostly by phone, over the next few years. But I was so absorbed and completely over my head working on dozens of projects between 1985 through early 1989 that Vernon Taylor didn't cross my mind that much. Plus during our phone conversations he seemed reluctant anytime I'd mention he ought to maybe give some thought to doin' a live show 'cause a lot of older fans around D.C. still remembered him. But in early March 1989, I called Vernon up and told him I was puttin' together a big rockabilly show to benefit Charlie Feathers, and all the money raised was goin' to pay for Charlie's ongoing medical bills, and I'd really like him to come out and do some songs. Vernon was still hesitant, but within a few weeks he agreed to do it, 'cause I told him I'd put a solid professional band behind him, and I'd even go with him and the rest of the band for a couple rehersals to help him get through it and make him feel more secure. By 1989, the rockabilly revival of the late seventies and early eighties had fizzled out on a national scale, but I knew in the Washington, D.C., area, if you put on a great rockabilly show and load it up with names like Charlie Feathers (who came up from Memphis), Robert Gordon, Narvel Felts, Vernon Taylor, Tex Rubinowitz, Billy Hancock, and a dozen other local and New York City acts, it had to work. Vernon thought he was rusty, but the crowd loved him. It was Charlie Feathers's night, and he performed eight songs at the end, but it was Narvel Felts and Vernon Taylor who stole the show, 'cause the overflow crowd from nineteen states and three foreign countries was not aware of these two guys who could still pull off a good rockabilly song.

Vernon saw that it worked that night, and he agreed to perform at three more of the rockabilly concerts I put on through January 1990, before I moved to Nashville. Vernon loved bein' on the bills with the likes of Jack Scott, Janis Martin, Becky Hobbs, and others, and I loved having him on those shows and watchin' him gain more confidence. When British rockabilly artist and promoter Dave Travis heard that Vernon was alive and well and still performing, he tried to get him over to England. He finally succeeded, and Vernon appeared at the Hemsly Festival, right outside of London, in May 1995.

Ronnie Dawson's the same age as Vernon, and Sleepy La Beef and Sonny Burgess are a little older. Sleepy, Ronnie, and Sonny are still makin' a living doin' young music that appeals to young crowds both in this country and overseas. Ronnie Dawson has told me and others that's what keeps him young. All three continue to record new songs that appeal to the young crowd 'cause the songs they record and do are hard-drivin' rockabilly tunes. They're all in demand for more than 150 shows a year. Sleepy's

been doin' this almost constantly since 1956. He's never slowed down. I think Vernon's finally gotten it through his (to put it bluntly) thick skull that he needs to be doin' the same thing — to be in front of young people playin' and singin' still-current real rockabilly music that he either wrote or created.

By the time you read this, there'll be a new CD album out on all the songs Vernon Taylor recorded at Sun Records. Quite a few new titles of some hot rockabilly numbers nobody's ever heard are on it. Also, Vernon now has become the newest and freshest rockabilly discovery for fans in Europe since Ronnie Dawson in the late eighties. I'm sure he'll be makin' many more trips to Europe and other parts of the world, and they'll be as well received as his first one, 'cause Vernon's a true professional and 'll give those kids over there just what they want to hear.

On the personal side, it's rare for me to strike up a new friendship with an original rockabilly artist from the 1950s who meant so much to me back in those days who's not lookin' to use me now for their own personal gain. Believe me, I had 'em comin' out of the woodwork for awhile, and I got in trouble a few times because I've always been a fan and thought too much from my heart instead of usin' my head. Just when I got disgusted with those types I had on pedestals for so long, then along comes Vernon Taylor. Just a guy that's happy and almost humbly embarrassed that someone like me remembered and thought so much of his recordings and live performances thirty-five to forty years ago. Vernon's a rare breed in this business.

Jack Scott

To me, along with practically all of the long-time fans of rockabilly music I continue to communicate with today, the most important part of a great rockabilly song, without question, is the style, approach, or unique frantic type dynamics the lead singer or artist on the record puts across to the listener. The music and backup band and backup vocalists and screamers are always secondary. Jack Scott had every one of those qualities as a rockabilly singer. Jack is not known as a rockabilly star here in the U.S., but in almost every other country in the western world, that's exactly what he is looked upon as.

Jack Scott was the last really big rock 'n' roll/rockabilly star of the late fifties and early sixties, because he had a longer string of *Billboard* chart hits between June 1958 and November 1961 than almost any other artist in rock 'n' roll or pop music that you can think of during that time. He racked up nineteen Top 100 chart songs in a short period of three years and five months. Jack wrote sixteen of these nineteen chart songs solely by himself. Between 1958 and 1960, four of these songs made it into the Top 10, and another five made the Top 40 on *Billboard*. Jack Scott definitely left his mark, making some great records at a time when pop music was going back to the silly or softer sounds in the music being promoted to teenagers. Jack was also the best rockabilly vocalist of any artist outside of the southern states. No other artist I've ever heard to come out of the northern states, especially as far north as where Jack was at, could ever do it as well as Jack Scott could. Jack Scott came from about as far north as you could get. Actually, completely out of this entire country. Jack was born in Windsor, Ontario, Canada, in 1936. Jack's parents moved to suburban Detroit when he was ten years old. He had been given a guitar a year earlier, which his father taught him how to play.

Jack's real name was Jack Scafone. He came from an Italian background. That's why to me it's really interesting that he developed a huge interest in the country music he listened to in the late forties and early fifties. In 1952, while he was still in high school, Jack formed his first band. He continued to sing and play out with his band whenever he could at any of the country nightspots around the Detroit area into early 1956. He'd always try to sound like the big-name country artists when he sang their songs, and when Elvis's music came along, he liked it and tried to sing it like Elvis did. Jack adds, "It was around this time I got serious with writing my own songs, and on those I didn't have nobody to copy, so they all just turned out soundin' like me."

By early 1957, Jack Scott was doin' well playin' rockabilly and rock 'n' roll in Detroit, and he had written a dozen or more of his own songs by this time. Jack went into a local studio and recorded an acetate demo recording of two of these songs. One song was called "Greaseball," and the other was "My True Love." The acetate found its way to Joe Carlton, head A&R man for ABC Paramount Records in New York City. Carleton liked what he heard enough to sign Jack to the label, but also wanted to hear the other songs Jack had written. Carlton put Jack into the studio in the spring of 1957, where Jack recorded four of his own compositions, which were released on two 45 records on the ABC Paramount label during the summer and fall of 1957.

It's always been written that neither of these two releases sold very well and both failed badly, but Jack Scott remembers it this way: "The very first ABC Paramount release sold pretty well. Especially in the Detroit area. The A side was 'Baby She's Gone,' and it got enough airplay and sales to make the local charts, not only in Detroit, but in Cleveland too. I remember goin' over to Cleveland and doin' all the local radio promotions and a TV show there. The second release didn't do as well, though. I don't believe the label got behind either of 'em with enough promotion to push 'em over the top at the time." Whatever the case may be, and although "Baby She's Gone" never became a national chart hit, this classic rockabilly number has become Jack Scott's most requested song among rockabilly record collectors and fans around the world today. Over the past two decades, Jack continues to open up his live shows with "Baby She's Gone," 'cause that's always the one that gets the fans rockin'.

In early 1958, Joe Carlton decided to start his own independent label in New York City, and he was confident that Jack Scott could become a big star, so he bought out the rest of Scott's contract from ABC Paramount Records, and Jack was the first artist he signed up to his new label, called Carlton Records. Joe let Jack use his regular band from Detroit for all the recordings he would make over the more than year and a half he recorded for the Carlton label. Even when Jack Scott left the Carlton record label in late 1959 and moved on to the Top Rank record label, where he would continue to stay for over a year until the early months of 1961, he was still given the freedom to use his regular band.

Carlton liked the song "Greaseball," which had gotten him interested enough in Jack to sign him to ABC Paramount Records a year earlier, but he told Jack that he needed to change the title, 'cause it would offend too many people. Jack changed it to "Leroy," and Joe released it in May 1958 as the A side of his first record on the Carlton label. "My True Love," a great fifties love ballad, was the B side. "Leroy" first hit the *Billboard* pop charts on June 9, 1958, and this song was surely destined to reach the Top 10, and it holds up today as one of the hottest examples of the rockabilly sound in music to come out as late as the summer of 1958. But it wasn't meant to be, because of a decision that the top promotion man for Carlton Records decided to make on his own about a month or so after the record was released. I'll let Jack Scott tell the story exactly the way it happened. "The way I remember it, the head promotion man for Carlton at the time was a guy named Juggy Gales, and I didn't really realize what was goin' on at the company at the time, but I know 'Leroy' was doin' really well and goin' over good at all the shows I was doin'. I found out later from Juggy that he had called Joe Carlton, and he told him he had decided to have all the DJs around flip the record over and start playin' 'My True Love.' Joe Carlton told him, 'Don't do that, 'cause "Leroy" is doin' so well, so just leave the record alone.' But from what Juggy told me afterwards, 'I'm either gonna get a pat on the back or I'm gonna get my walkin' papers,' you know, so he just took it on his own and had 'em all flip the record over, and by the time he came off the road and got back to New York later in the summer, Juggy got a $5,000 bonus from Joe Carlton. He took a chance and it worked." The outcome of this was "My True Love" breaking onto the *Billboard* charts three weeks after "Leroy" first debuted on 'em. "My True Love" hit the charts on June 30, 1958, and by early September 1958 would rise all the way up to #3 on *Billboard* and stayed on the charts longer than any other record Jack Scott would ever have. A total of nineteen weeks. "Leroy" was real popular, though, and had a good ride of thirteen weeks on the *Billboard* pop charts, but only reached a peak of #25. "My True Love" also became a Top 10 record on the major charts in England, reaching #9, though Jack never toured there during the fifties and sixties.

Today, Jack Scott's great pop ballad chart hits are better known than his name. Rockabilly fans always preferred the rockin' sides of Jack Scott's 45s, but yet most are not turned off by the ballad sides, 'cause they always seem to have a distinctive sound and edge to 'em that no other artist was able to capture between 1957 and 1961. Even by the time Jack got to Capitol Records in 1961 and '62, and the label took control and added strings for a more commercial sound on most of his songs, Jack was still able to put across a certain edge in his terrific vocals that still made all his songs listenable. Jack Scott also holds a unique distinction that I can't think of any other artist in rock 'n' roll history has. That distinction is that all of his early records between 1957 and 1962 are not only collected and cherished by rockabilly and rock 'n' roll record collectors, but also by collectors of vocal group, or now what's called doo-wop, music. Not to take anything away from The Jordanaires, who backed up Elvis on a lot of great songs in the fifties, The Chantones' work backing up Jack Scott on his songs has more real, raw chemistry.

Jack also wrote most all his songs solely by himself. No co-writers. That was real unusual. Jack Scott should be considered up there with some of the greatest all-time writers of early rockabilly/rock 'n' roll and doo-wop type ballad songs, in my opinion. To me, he's definitely in the league with Buddy Holly, Fats Domino, Chuck Berry, Johnny Burnette, and Little Richard. Most of those great writers all just wrote their songs in one style. Jack wrote and continues to write today in all styles of music, including country, even rockin' gospel.

Without a doubt, Jack Scott's all-time greatest rockabilly songs came out on the Carlton record label between 1958 and 1960. Just as "My True Love" started to descend out of the Top 10 on *Billboard*, Jack's second record was released. Again, both songs were penned by Jack. The A side had almost the exact same sound of "My True Love." It was called "With Your Love." This song debuted on the *Billboard* pop charts on September 29, 1958, but only reached a peak of #28 and dropped off the charts after a ten-week run. But the B side of this record made it onto the *Billboard* pop charts also. This was a fast rockabilly tune called "Geraldine." It was only on the charts for one week, on October 13, 1958, at the #96 position, but that still musta meant somebody out there wanted to hear Jack's brand of rockabilly.

Jack Scott recorded his first album, titled simply *Jack Scott*, during the fall of 1958, and it was released shortly thereafter. It was a mixture of six rockabilly tunes, all written by Jack, and six on the ballad side, four of which Jack wrote. This album today remains a high-dollar collectible among record dealers, as there were not many albums being released at the time, especially to the teenage market, that were recorded in stereo.

Jack's third single release hit real big after its debut on the *Billboard* pop charts on December 15, 1958. The song was a real good, solid mid-tempo rockabillyish song Jack had written called "Goodbye Baby (Bye Bye)." During the early months of 1959, this song reached a peak position of #8 and stayed on those charts for sixteen straight weeks. The B side, "Save My Soul," is a wild, scorchin', hard driving rockabilly/rock 'n' roll, old time, tent revival screamer written by Jack with biblical-type lyrics. "Save My Soul" debuted on the *Billboard* pop charts on December 29, 1958, and reached a high of #73 before falling off after three weeks. Jack Scott had done something that had never geen done before and would never be done again. He wrote a wild rockabilly/gospel song and it made it onto the *Billboard* pop singles charts and was requested by teenagers who heard it on their local teenage music radio stations. Elvis had a hit on "Peace in the Valley" in 1957, but it was a traditional gospel song sung in the reverent standard way. What made Jack Scott's "Save My Soul" so unusual for becoming even a minor hit with teenagers is that even as late as 1958 and early '59, according to most adults, all teenagers were headed for hell and goin' to the devil because of this new kind of music. Also, what puts "Save My Soul" in the rockabilly category of music is it had the hard-drivin, slappin', thumpin' sound of bass player Stan Getz bein' noticeably brutal on that upright bass of his. This bass sound always stood out on all Jack's rockabilly Carlton Records recordings. By 1959, a lot of upright bass players in mainstream rock 'n' roll had switched over to electric bass, but Getz continued to use the upright, and that's just part of why Jack Scott's recordings hold up so well today to rockabilly fans around the world. Other things that rockabilly and rock 'n' roll fans today consider important factors in the great sound he got on all his recordings even through 1962 was not only his standout, raw vocal ability that was always in all of his songs, but the cuttin' edge in the acoustic guitar he played. Then of course there was the backup group The Chantones, who at times added handclaps in certain songs Jack wrote. There was also a solid hard-hittin' drum sound added, and last but not least, through the early sixties, whenever there was a sax used on one of Jack's songs, even if you didn't care for a sax in some songs, you loved it on his recordings, because it always seemed to fit the song and have that certain kind of raw, tortured, scorchin' sound the song called for.

Between February and May 1959, Jack Scott did a short hitch to fulfill his army induction and duty. This was right at the time "Goodbye Baby" was in the Top 10 on *Billboard*. Carlton Records released one record on Jack while he was in the service, and it debuted on the *Billboard* pop charts on April 6, 1959, but only reached #78 and fell off the charts afrer a four-week run. The song they went with for the A side was titled "I Never Felt Like This." One of Jack's all-time best rockabilly songs. If Jack wasn't in the army at the time it came out and was out in front of the public, I'm sure this song would have risen higher up on the charts than it did. The B side was one of Jack's oddest releases of the fifties, but at the same time is still classic Jack Scott ballad fare. The song's title is "Bella." The only way to describe it is it's a country-flavored Italian song with mournful, pleading lyrics about lost love.

After Jack's return from the service, his first 45 release on Carlton Records was "The Way I Walk" b/w "Midgie." Well, there was just no way "Midgie" was even gonna crease the national charts, 'cause it was a fast, gritty, hard rockin' rockabilly tune at its best with some screachin', honkin' sax work on it. Both songs, again, were solely written by Jack Scott. The record company had to go with the A side, and it would wind up being Jack's final classic rockabilly song to make the *Billboard* pop Top 40. After "The Way I Walk," a solid mid-tempo rockabilly number with fabulous backup vocals and strong slappin' upright bass sound, debuted on the *Billboard* pop charts on June 29, 1959, it only reached a peak of #35, but stayed on the charts for fourteen weeks. This rockabilly tune had stayin' power on the charts and over the airwaves throughout the summer and early fall of 1959, and it remains one of Jack's most requested and most recorded rockabilly songs by rockabilly bands and artists in the seventies, eighties, and nineties.

In late September 1959, while "The Way I Walk" was still on the *Billboard* charts, Carlton Records released what would turn out to be Jack's final new 45 release for this label. They went with the ballad for the A side, a song called "There Comes a Time." As always up to this point, both sides again were penned by Jack. By the fall of 1959, there was no way they could have tried to push a raw, raunchy, fast rockabilly song, both musically and frantically sung with pure grit evoking from Jack's vocals, onto the airwaves of all the radio stations now firmly embedded into playing the soft sounds of The Fleetwoods, The Browns, Frankie Avalon, Santo and Johnny, and others that had taken over what we were being forced to hear at that time. "There Comes a Time" is one of Jack's standout ballads. Much better than any the artists I just mentioned had ridin' on the top of the charts at the time. But for whatever reason, after this song debuted on the *Billboard* pop charts on October 12, 1959, it only reached #71 and fell off the charts after only five weeks.

I've read in the liner notes on a couple of Jack Scott's reissue albums that came out of Europe during the 1980s that Joe Carlton and his Carlton Records label were nearing the end of their existence by the fall of 1959, so that's why Jack moved on to another record label. This was not the case, and in no way close to the truth. Carlton Records and its subsidiary label, Guaranteed Records, released over sixty 45 singles and over a dozen LPs after Jack Scott left the label in

November 1959. Joe Carlton not only stayed active with his labels through at least the end of 1962, but had two dozen or more *Billboard* chart hits between 1960 and 1962. A few rockabilly-type artists Carlton had after Jack Scott left who had some chart success were Gary Stites, Jesse Lee Turner, and Danny Peppermint, among others.

The Top Rank record label was just gettin' started in late 1959, and they made Joe Carlton a good offer to buy out the rest of Jack Scott's contract from him. Carlton agreed to it. This was definitely a good move for Jack Scott's career. Maybe not as a classic rockabilly artist (though his overall sound didn't change a lot), but the Top Rank label gave Jack some big ballad commercial success. On November 25, 1959, Jack Scott brought his band and backup vocal group The Chantones from the Detroit area where Jack had continued to live to New York City and recorded his first session for Top Rank Records. One of the songs, "Baby, Baby," which they chose to release for the B side of his first single, was still in the rockabilly vein. It's classic Jack Scott rockabilly all the way through. But it was the A side that remains today Jack Scott's signature song by all styles of record and music fans and collectors. That song was "What in the World's Come Over You." It's this song that most nostalgia, oldies, or pop music fans over the age of forty-five remember, but nary a one can ever tell you the name of the artist who sang it.

Nineteen sixty was probably Jack Scott's biggest year as a top commercial record star. He still wrote most of the songs that were released on the four 45 singles, and you

Forgettin' to Remember to Forget

The first time I booked Jack Scott in the D.C. area, in 1988, he came over to my house. We had a big recreation room, and my wife Pepper had the walls covered with mostly personal photos I had taken over a thirty-year or so period of a lot of the artists I had met or worked with during that time. The walls were lined with photos of Elvis, Gene Vincent, Buddy Holly, and so on, but Jack zeroed in on one particular picture after lookin' at them all. It was a photo I had enlarged to an 8x10 of me with Annette Funicello, taken in 1963. It's a good picture. Annette (as always) looked fantastic standin' there in her pretty dress holdin' her pink poodle pocketbook. I was standin' beside her with my arm lightly around her waist (in reality back then almost afraid to touch her, 'cause she looked like a living doll that might break), and I was dressed neat as a pin with my white sport jacket, black pegged slacks, black shirt, and white thin tie, plus my crepe-soled snap bomber loafers that made me 5-foot-11 instead of 5-foot-9.

Jack stared at that picture at a few different intervals over about a ten-minute period and finally looked over at me and said, "You really like Annette, huh?" I said, "Well, yeah. Back in '55 when I was a kid, I used to watch 'The Mickey Mouse Club,' and it was mainly to see her." Then Jack said, "Well, that picture was taken after '55, so you musta liked her then too, huh?" I said, "Well, Jack, she was gorgeous in '63 when that picture was taken, what's not to like?" Jack then said, "Did you collect her records too?" I then gave up and replied, "OK, Jack, you got me. I was a closet Annette Funicello fan, and yeah, I did buy her records back then too, what in the hell you leadin' up to?" Ignoring my question and deep in thought while still staring at the photo and then lookin' over at me, Jack smiled a sly smile and said, "I bet you still like her now, eh?" I said, "Jack, Annette is no longer at the top of my play list anymore by any means, but I've got some fond memories of when I met her 'cause she was always real sweet to me at the time, and to answer your question or any further ones you may come up with, back then I had a bit of a crush on her, and yeah I still like her today. Anything else?" Jack replied, "You know, I did a couple of big Dick Clark tours with her back then. The first one was when 'The Way I Walk' was a big hit for me." I said, "That's really cool." Jack then said, "After I get back home, I'll send you somethin' I think you'll really like." I said, "Well, I really appreciate that."

I didn't really give it any more thought after that until a few weeks went by and in the mail here comes a large brown envelope from Jack Scott. I had so much on my mind by then I'd forgotten about that game of twenty questions Jack played with me. Well, I opened the envelope up and here I find this great personal 8x10 photo of Jack Scott sitting next to Annette Funicello. Jack's wife, Barbara, wrote in a short letter that Jack really wanted me to have this picture 'cause he was sure it would mean a lot to me (which it does).

could tell by the B sides that Jack was Jack when you heard him do one of the rockabilly/rock 'n' roll type songs on those records. But from the time Jack's song "What in the World's Come Over You" debuted on the *Billboard* pop charts on January 11, 1960, and took off up the charts like a rocket, finally peaking out at #5 in March and staying on the charts for a total of sixteen weeks, the pattern was set that all of Jack's songs from then on that you would hear on the radio would be in the ballad style. But Jack had such a great, different-sounding deep voice on all those ballads, rockabilly fans in those days found themselves liking most of 'em a lot. "What in the World's Come Over You" reached a peak of #6 in England's major music charts by early April 1960, and it was a Top 10 hit in most other countries around the world also, even though Jack Scott never toured over there during the late fifties and sixties. Top Rank Records released Jack's first album for their label sometime in late March 1960, while "What in the World's Come Over You" was in the Top 10. It was a tribute to Hank Williams, Jack Scott style. It holds up well.

Jack's next 45 single on Top Rank was "Burning Bridges" b/w "Oh Little One." "Burning Bridges," a ballad written by a British writer named Walter Scott, was one of only three of Jack's nineteen consecutive *Billboard* pop chart hits that Jack didn't write. Within two weeks after "Burning Bridges" was released, it debuted on the *Billboard* charts on April 18, 1960, shot up to a peak of #3 in June, and stayed on the charts for seventeen weeks. It became Jack's fourth gold record. Two weeks after "Burning Bridges" debuted on *Billboard*, the B side of the record, "Oh Little One" (written by Jack), hit the *Billboard* pop charts on May 2, eventually climbing up to #34 and staying on the charts for seven weeks. Most B sides of 45s by 1960 were pretty bad, but "Oh Little One" is one of the best you'll find anywhere around. It's an easygoin' mid-tempo song with a vocal group/doo-wop feel to it.

Jack Scott was so hot and burnin' up the top of the *Billboard* charts all during the spring and summer of 1960, Joe Carlton, at Jack's old label Carlton Records, issued two 45s plus an album by Jack featuring some of the songs he had recorded on Carlton Records that had never been released. In May, Carlton released a 45 called "What Am I Livin' For," written by the great late R&B artist Chuck Willis, and which had been a Top 10 *Billboard* pop hit for him in 1958. Jack's version of this song was done in his own driving solid way. The B side

was "Indiana Waltz," a classic country song that was on Jack's first Carlton album but had never been out on 45. In August, Joe released one of the wildest, rawest rockabilly songs Jack ever recorded, called "Go Wild Little Sadie." It's again one of the best rockabilly songs Jack ever wrote. The B side on this 45 was another one that appeared on Jack's first Carlton LP. It was another country standard, titled "No One Will Ever Know." Both these 45s were issued on Joe Carlton's subsidiary label Guaranteed Records. Neither one of these 45s hit the charts when they were released, because by the summer and fall of 1960 those charts were dominated by the soft, silly sounds of the Bobbys, Freddys, and Frankies. But I know these two 45s had to sell fairly well, because they were well distributed and easily found at the time of release, and I still see copies of 'em every once in a while today for sale at conventions and yard sales. Joe Carlton also released a second album by Jack Scott on his Carlton Records label in early June, titled *What Am I Livin' For*, with a dozen mostly rockabilly gems from Jack's 1958 and '59 period with the Carlton label.

Not to be outdone, Top Rank Records released a fresh album in late July 1960, while Jack was still ridin' high on the charts. This second album for Top Rank was titled *What in the World's Come Over You*. It contained Jack's first four songs that had been his first two singles for the label, plus two more songs that had just been released as his third single, as well as six new ones. Seven of the twelve songs on this album were written by Jack. Even in 1960, Jack Scott was in no way abandoning hard-core rockabilly music like some others were. It was a rockabilly lover's delight to hear Jack Scott rockin' hard on two of the songs from this LP in mid 1960, "Cruel World" and a gospel one called "My King." Top-notch, wild, fast-movin' rockabilly at its best once again. One other rockabilly song with a Cajun feel to it that drives pretty good is another country standard, called "Good Deal Lucille." The way Jack does it, you don't even think country, 'cause he makes it all his own.

On August 1, 1960, Jack's third 45 for the Top Rank label debuted on the *Billboard* pop charts. The A side was called "It Only Happened Yesterday," which Jack wrote, and was in his now typical sound of haunting, tough-edged ballads. The B side was a traditional cowboy/western song "Cool Water." Jack put his own thumpin' beat sound to it that made it unique. It's sort of a mid-tempo rocker classic Jack Scott once again. Jack's version was so different, it wound up that both sides of his new record hit the charts and received a whole lot of airplay. Both debuted on *Billboard* the same week. "It Only Happened Yesterday" only reached a peak of #38 in September 1960, and only had a nine-week ride on the *Billboard* pop charts. "Cool Water" only reached #85 and dropped off the charts after three weeks.

Two unusual things that occurred between January and September 1960 proved Jack Scott to be not only one of the nation's top record-selling and true concert stars in pop music, but also the last of the 1950s rockabilly artists to still have the record stores flooded with new, unheard material at that late period. (He had more fresh rock 'n' roll/rockabilly-type material out at that period than even Elvis.) First, between January and August 1960, the Top Rank, Carlton, and Guaranteed record labels released three full-length LP albums, three four-songs-each EP records, and five 45 singles on Jack Scott, with five songs goin' into the *Billboard* charts — two of 'em goin' Top 5. Second, during 1960 Jack Scott arranged and put together two of his own package tours. They were called the Jack Scott Caravan of Stars tours. The one he remembers most had The Champs, Danny and The Juniors, Sonny James, and Oliver Coal as supporting acts for himself as the headliner. Of course, Jack did the Dick Clark and Irvin Feld tours that year as well, but it's pretty incredible today to think he was that big a star that he could headline his own tour and be in competition with the big moguls of that time.

Jack Scott's fourth 45 single for Top Rank debuted on the *Billboard* pop charts on October 17, 1960. Only one side made the charts. The song was called "Patsy." Jack didn't write it. It's an up-tempo song, and Jack sings it real well, but the lyrics are silly and trite. "Patsy" only made it up to #65 on the *Billboard* pop charts and dropped off after only four weeks. The B side was a solid, raw, rockin' version of the gospel classic "Old Time Religion," done once again in the great unique style of Jack Scott. In January 1961, "Old Time Religion" was one of the twelve songs included on Jack Scott's final LP for Top Rank, called *The Spirit Moves Me*. Which of course was an all-gospel album. It was a great one, though, with both rockin' gospel and traditional spiritual songs all done with the superb backup of the fabulous Chantones. Jack's fifth and final 45 for Top Rank debuted on *Billboard* on January 9, 1961. It was a great classic Jack Scott ballad called "Is There Something on Your Mind." It only reached #89 and dropped off after only that one week. The B side was a good mid-tempo rockabilly-styled tune called "Found a Woman."

Top Rank went out of business in the spring of 1961, but the major label Capitol Records picked up the remainder of Jack Scott's contract and purchased all of the master recordings he had done while at Top Rank. Jack's first three 45 record releases for Capitol Records, between the late spring and late fall of 1961, all hit somewhere in the bottom end of the *Billboard* pop charts, at peak positions of #91, #83, and #86. The A sides were all ballads Jack wrote in his same great style. But two of the B sides, "Strange Desire" and "One of These Days," were typical Jack Scott rockin' rockabilly tunes. On November 20, 1961, rockabilly may have been all but dead and buried in the mainstream of teen dance music that was dominating at that time, but you never knew it when you flipped a Jack Scott chart record over. That was the last time he was on the *Billboard* 45 charts.

Though the hits quit comin', Capitol Records didn't give up on Jack. Jack had five more 45 releases on Capitol through the spring of 1963, but out of the 10 songs, only three of those were written by Jack. The best is a tough rockabilly B side song called "Grizzly Bear," issued in early 1962. Capitol Records, for whatever reasons, waited until 1964 to release their only LP on Jack, *Burning Bridges*.

After Jack's contract expired with Capitol Records in the spring of 1963, he signed what would be his last long-term major label recording contract with RCA Victor out of Nashville. This was in the early fall of 1963. In the beginning, Jack's releases would be on the subsidiary Groove Records. Groove back then was marketed to the pop music field, even though the recording sessions were all done in Nashville. Another rockabilly artist, Charlie Rich, was on the Groove label around the same time Jack Scott was. Jack's first record on Groove, "There's Trouble Brewin' " b/w "Jingle Bell Slide," was released in time for the Christmas season, as both sides were rock 'n' roll/rockabilly soundin' Christmas songs. While Jack would go on to record two or three more songs during 1964 that some consider to be rockabilly songs, these two Christmas songs would turn out to be his final really good rockabilly sounding records. Jack had four single releases in 1964 on Groove and three more in 1965 on RCA Victor.

It seems Jack Scott was given every chance Nashville and RCA Records could give him to break through with another hit record right through to the end of 1965. But 1964 and 1965 saw a lot of changes in mainstream music, the likes of which haven't been seen since. It wasn't only the British Invasion. All these years later, I can't lay all the blame on just that. By the end of 1965, the whole world as we had known it only two years prior had been turned upside down.

After Jack Scott's final release on RCA had run its course by early 1966, he was content with just staying at home with his family and buddies in and around Detroit. He had occasional new 45 records released on various labels, including his own Ponie Records.

By the early seventies, Jack's old fans and ones from Europe were comin' to Detroit to see him live in action once again with the renewed interest in rockabilly music. Jack Scott never quit writing new songs that fit his unique style, so he had plenty to offer old and new fans alike by 1977. Jack Scott was the first American artist to headline the biggest fifties rockabilly revival tour in England in 1977. This package tour included not only Jack Scott, but also Sun Records rockabilly legends Charlie Feathers and Warren Smith, along with Buddy Knox, and sold out everywhere it played. Somebody recorded their biggest show, at the Rainbow Theatre in London. EMI Records in England released it as a live album in early 1978. It's a rare, high-dollar album here in the U.S. today. Since that tour, Jack Scott has been in demand for festivals and concerts in dozens of countries around the world. For eighteen years now, Jack has continued to tour all of these foreign countries, but only on his own terms. Some European promoters haven't been too happy with Jack Scott at times over the years because, according to them, he demands too much. But in his own words, "The fans who pay to come see me sing my old hit songs expect them to sound exactly the way they remember them, and if I don't sing 'em in the same keys, and the band and backup group aren't very good, the fans'll go away disappointed, and I can never let that happen, 'cause if the music and sound is not exactly right, then it's not worth doin', and the fans have been cheated. I've always tried to give 100 percent to my music and my fans through the years. I'm one of the few white rock 'n' roll and rockabilly artists who has always written his own material, and also I was never part of the rock teen idol factory of New York City and Philadelphia that was so influential in the late fifties and early sixties. The reason I maintained such a low profile despite all of my major chart successes was that I really didn't care to tour all that much. In fact, at one point on a Dick Clark caravan, I left the tour because I just wanted to be with my family." That's the kind of man he is, and there's nothin' wrong with that!

Ricky Nelson

Anybody that tries to tell you Ricky (or later Rick) Nelson never was a rockabilly artist don't know what they're talkin' about. It's always bugged me when I'd hear some fool say, or even worse, put down in print, "Ricky Nelson had it made 'cause his parents had a TV show." Let me tell you something. If you don't live, breathe, and love music and always put it first, as Ricky's brother David has stated Ricky always did from the beginning until the end of his life, there is just no amount of money, no matter how large, and no weekly TV show, no matter how popular, that will allow you to sustain a successful musical career like Ricky Nelson's, which gave him fifty-three *Billboard* pop chart hits, including seventeen Top 10 singles, and ten Top 40 albums between 1957 and 1973. If you don't have the raw talent and love for the music you're doin', all the connections and money in the world won't keep you stayin' around that long and allow you to be listed as one of the Top 15 artists of the rock 'n' roll era over the past forty years. Contrast Ricky Nelson with the likes of Nancy Sinatra or Gary Lewis and you'll get the point: money and connections won't get you very far without drive and talent.

Ricky Nelson not only had talent, but he also loved, learned, and studied this new rock 'n' roll and rhythm & blues music that he was hearing as early as 1953, when he was only thirteen years old. Both his parents had a musical background, with Ozzie being a big band leader and Harriet being a singer, so music was always part of Ricky's life. This new music he loved fit him perfectly. In the early fifties, Ricky was the cute, sassy little kid who irritated his older brother David in the TV show. But in late 1956, Ricky was now a good-lookin' sixteen-year-old that young teenage girls were attracted to. At this time, Elvis's first movie, *Love Me Tender*, had just been released, and shortly thereafter Ozzie filmed a show centered around Ricky and David going to a costume party. Ricky dressed as Elvis (with fake sideburns and the whole bit). He had a guitar slung around his neck and stood there with a sulky look on his face. He then hit the guitar strings a few times while singin' a couple lines of "Love Me Tender." That's all it took. The show ended on that scene, and more than 10,000 pieces of fan mail poured in the following week from teenagers wantin' to hear and see Ricky do more. So ask yourself what would you have done if you were Ozzie or Ricky Nelson. If you were Ozzie, you'd run out and get your boy a record contract and let your boy be seen singin' the new music of the day, because that's what a large part of your audience said they wanted to see each week on your TV show. If you were a sixteen-year-old Ricky, you were gonna get to do what you loved most anyway.

So when the network ran this episode in late January 1957, and the mail kept pourin' in during the early weeks of February, Ozzie made, from what I've heard and read, a verbal deal with the mostly jazz-oriented label Verve Records to record Ricky and put out his first records. Ricky cut his only session for Verve Records in early April. Verve rush-released the first two songs on his first 45, and Ricky was seen singin' both of 'em, "I'm Walkin' " and "A Teenager's Romance," on "The Ozzie and Harriet Show" in late April, and that's all it took. On May 6, 1957, two days before Ricky's seventeenth birthday, "I'm Walkin' " debuted on the *Billboard* pop Top 100. A week later, "A Teenager's Romance" bounced onto those same charts. Ricky Nelson had a two-sided smash, which, within a month after it hit the charts, had sold over a million records. Ricky's rockabilly version of Fats Domino's "I'm Walkin' " only peaked out at #17, but stayed on the *Billboard* pop charts for a seventeen-week run. The flip side, "A Teenager's Romance," went all the way up to #2 on *Billboard* by July. It's definitely worth mentioning Fats Domino's original version of "I'm Walkin' " was on the *Billboard* pop charts at the same time as Ricky's version and hit a peak position of #4 and had a long twenty-five-week run.

After that first session for Verve Records and his first two songs became big hits, Ricky knew exactly the kind of music he wanted to do from then on. Ricky wanted to rock. Both Ricky and Ozzie knew he needed the right band to back him up. Ozzie made Bob Luman's backup band an offer they couldn't pass up. So Ricky now had a top-notch, first-rate rockabilly and rock 'n' roll band, which included the great talents of James Burton on lead guitar and Jim Kirkland on upright bass. Today, James Burton seems to be more well known as Elvis's lead guitarist from 1969 to 1977, but James actually spent more time recording, performing live dates, and being seen on the Nelsons' weekly TV show between 1957 and 1966 with Ricky than he did with Elvis later on. One more ballad release, titled "You're My One and Only Love," on Verve Records, hit the *Billboard* pop charts on August 26, 1957, made it up to #14, and stayed on the charts for twelve weeks.

Lew Chudd, the president of Imperial Records, knew during the late summer of 1957 that Ricky Nelson was up for grabs and Ozzie was looking for a solid record contract for his teenage rocker. Imperial was a major contender in rock 'n' roll, having had a long string of successes with Fats Domino alone, as well as many others. Chudd offered Ozzie the kind of lucrative deal he was lookin' for, and Ricky went on to enjoy his most successful and what I consider his most creative output of rockabilly songs and big chart hits over the next five years. Between the first week of October 1957 and the early spring of 1963, Ricky Nelson charted thirty-two consecutive songs on the *Billboard* pop charts with only seventeen 45 single releases. On fifteen of these seventeen singles, both sides of the record hit somewhere on the charts. This was surely because he was seen on TV almost every week during this period, singin' both sides of the record. It's been said and written over the years that when a top pop music recording artist gets his own TV show or is seen every week on TV singing, it hurts their career by way of record sales and chart success. But that wasn't true with Ricky.

In 1958, another advantage of seeing Ricky on TV each week for those who were buying rockabilly records and loved the music was you got to see Lorrie Collins (one half of The Collins Kids) sing on the show, as well as seein' Ricky sing a few songs to her. Lorrie Collins had been around with her brother Larry, and Lorrie could really belt out a rockabilly tune, which The Collins Kids had always been known for. But by the fall of 1958 and into the early months of 1959, when Lorrie was on the TV show, rockabilly music and The Collins Kids' career were both slippin' fast. Lorrie appeared on the Nelsons' TV show a half dozen times or so during this period, as Ricky and Lorrie were not only doin' some heavy datin', but Ricky had even given her an engagement ring. But while The Collins Kids were out on tour with the Johnny Cash show during the summer of 1959, Lorrie eloped with Cash's road manager.

Now, there ain't no way I got space to go through all Ricky Nelson's great rockabilly songs throughout the years. There's just way too many, and a lot more than the average music fan could imagine. I know a lot of hard-core rockabilly fans may think Ricky's early records on the Imperial label were his best, but at times you could hear Ricky gettin' better as he got older, and the rockabilly music he continued on to record was bein' done in his own style. On his first three records for Imperial, four of the six songs, while they had solid rockabilly music backing all the way, had teen-oriented lyrics. "Be Bop Baby," "Stood Up," "Waitin' in School," and "Believe What You Say" lyrically were songs about goin' steady and waitin' for the school bell to ring so you could go home and call your steady girlfriend to meet her at the soda shop. Ricky fires 'em at 'cha with a lotta drive, and remember this was late 1957 and early '58, and Ricky was still in high school himself, and all these lyrics coincided with the lingo and slang words in teenage music at that time. The B side of Ricky's third record on Imperial is about the best shoutin'-out rockabilly version of "My Bucket's Got a Hole in It" that you'd ever want to hear. All these songs were million-sellers and up in the *Billboard* Top 10 charts.

It was on Ricky's fourth record for Imperial where you found the A side was a mid-tempo, well-polished song called "Poor Little Fool." On the B side was the first song Ricky Nelson wrote, called "Don't Leave Me This Way." This song is also a mid-tempo song. But there's a great acoustic sound on the guitar, and Ricky's flowin' vocals give it sort of a rockabilly edge. "Poor Little Fool" (written by Sharon Sheeley, who became Eddie Cochran's girlfriend) was Ricky's first #1 record, in August 1958, and it sort of set a trend from then on out that it would be Ricky's ballads that would be pushed the most and put on the A sides of his 45s, even though both sides usually charted. Like I've said, by the late summer of 1958, the fast rock 'n' roll and rockabilly songs were bein' replaced by either teen sounds or the ballad sounds of the day, and Ricky Nelson could certainly handle the ballads as well as or better than most any of the newer breed of eighteen- to twenty-year-olds on the pop music scene. But it was always evident with his 45 and LP releases that Ricky loved to rock, well on into the sixties.

From the fall of 1958 to the fall of 1959, Ricky Nelson had three 45 releases where all six songs reached well into pop Top 10 on *Billboard*. The A sides "Lonesome Town," "Never Be Anyone Else but You," and "Sweeter Than You" were all ballads, but all the B sides, which reached equally as high or only a notch or two under the A sides, were good rockabilly numbers: "I Got a Feeling," "It's Late," and "Just a Little Too Much." By the summer and fall of 1959, Ricky was the only one anywhere who could consistently break into the Top 10 with rockabilly songs. The Fabians, Avalons, and Rydells were all havin' their first of only two really big years, but Ricky was continuing to chart just as high as they were during this whole year. Though even with Ricky, it wouldn't last.

Ricky continued to choose good material to release all during 1960. With the eight songs released on four 45 records, all of the A sides once again were the ballad songs, which were the bigger hits, all charting between #12 and #27. But all four of the B sides were still in the rockabilly vein, and all of them charted somewhere between #34 and #79. One song in particular was Ricky's rockabilly version of "Milk Cow Blues Boogie," which debuted on the *Billboard* pop charts on December 31, 1960. It only reached #79 in January 1961, but it proved Ricky was still able to chart records of songs he loved that were in the rockabilly vein.

Some of Ricky's best rockabilly songs were just extra cuts on his late-fifties and early-sixties albums. You can't beat songs like "Shirley Lee," "You Tear Me Up," and "One of These Mornings" for hot kickin' rockabilly. Ricky always put it across real good, and when we needed it most into the 1960s. "Shirley Lee" was originally put out on ABC Paramount Records by a rockabilly artist from Arkansas by the name of Bobby Lee Trammell in 1957. It failed to chart, but got good distribution and broke out locally in a number of cities across the U.S. Trammell wrote the song and did a wild version of it. Bobby Lee was also a crazy, wild, live artist to witness back in the late fifties doin' some killer rockabilly songs. Ricky heard Trammell's record and cut his own version and performed it when I saw him live in concert in 1958, and he did the song justice to say the least. Ricky Nelson wasn't seen movin' around the stage on his weekly TV show much, but he sure rocked and moved when I saw him sing "Shirley Lee" back in '58.

Ricky's final record that was under the name Ricky Nelson was "Travelin' Man" b/w "Hello Mary Lou," which had the two sides hittin' #1 and #9, respectively, in the late spring and early summer of 1961. Ricky had now turned twenty-one and was now known as Rick Nelson. But I didn't care, 'cause back then and even today I've always thought of him as Ricky. He continued on as the musical times continued to change throughout 1962 and had several Top 10 ballad hits, one of which was "Teenage Idol," which reached #5 in the early fall of 1962. The title of this song could be why some writers over the years have put Ricky in the same class as the pretty boy Bobby, flash-in-the-pan types. But those that have done this have all done Ricky a big injustice, 'cause Ricky always had real, raw, creative talent in most all the music he chose to record. The B side of Ricky's final record for Imperial (not counting the ones issued after he left the label) was a good rockin' cover version of the 1956 Top 10 pop hit by Fats Domino called "I'm

In Love Again." Ricky's version hit #67 on the *Billboard* pop charts in the early spring of 1963.

Elvis had recorded a rockabilly version of the Ray Charles R&B classic "I Got a Woman" back in 1956 that was an extra cut on his first RCA Victor album. Ricky Nelson's first record release after he signed with the Decca label in early 1963 was "You Don't Love Me Anymore" on the A side, but "I Got a Woman," done in a rockabilly style, on the B side. The A side ballad only reached #47 on the *Billboard* pop charts in the late spring of 1963, but surprisingly for the period and the changes in music trends by then, "I Got a Woman" got up to #49 on those same charts at the same time.

From an early age, Ricky Nelson grew up on R&B, real rock 'n' roll, and rockabilly music. Ricky never gave up on this music, but the times they were a-changin'. For this period, his last Top 10 record was in February 1964, and his final chart record on *Billboard* that broke his eight-year string of consecutive chart hits was in March 1965. Ricky told me later that he wasn't all that unhappy when the Nelsons' long-running weekly TV show went off the air in the late spring of 1966, because he could devote full time to the kind of music he really wanted to do. That kind of music was gettin' back to the roots of rock 'n' roll and country that he said he always loved the most. Ricky Nelson was really ahead of his time when it came to the country rock music movement. In 1966 he recorded a couple dozen country songs that were released on two albums (and later combined into a double album) by Decca Records, one in 1966 and the other in 1967. These two country albums were really full of songs Ricky Nelson liked and wanted to do, but they didn't do well. In 1968 he took a more folk/country direction; he formed The Stone Canyon Band to back him up and started performing and recording Tim Hardin and Bob Dylan songs. Ricky had let his hair dry out. The Brylcream and Wild Root Cream Oil was long gone by '68, but he still had that youthful look even with his shoulder-length hair at this time.

Ricky continued to tour and record with his Stone Canyon band, and in 1969 and 1970 broke back onto the charts with a couple of country/folk rock songs. "She Belongs to Me," written by Bob Dylan, only made it up to #33, but stayed on the charts for an incredible eighteen straight weeks. The follow-up song, "Easy to Be Free," was the first of only two songs that Ricky wrote himself that hit the *Billboard* pop charts. It got up to #48 but dropped off after only a short six-week run.

By this time Ricky was a total and complete artist and also a top-notch showman who knew what his fans expected, and he didn't let 'em down. He knew there were old fans in his audience who were there to hear his big hit classic, more rockin' songs, but contrary to what's been written throughout the years, even those older fans were still able to accept this new Ricky Nelson sound. He gave his audiences some of both. Ricky had one bad experience with an audience, which was really blown out of proportion, that turned into his final Top 10 *Billboard* chart record. In late 1971, he did his first fifties oldies revival show, booked by Richard Nader into New York City's 20,000-seat Madison Square Garden. There was a small portion of the audience that booed Ricky and didn't want to hear any of his new songs. They were real vocal about it. Well, most of you know what happened. Ricky Nelson went on shortly thereafter to write his million-sellin', Top 10, protest-type song called "Garden Party," based on his bad experience at Madison Square Garden. The B side of that 45 single is a really good up-tempo country rocker I've always liked, called "So Long Mama."

"Garden Party" hit the charts on July 29, 1972. Interestingly Chuck Berry's "My Ding-A-Ling" debuted a week later. And then two weeks later, Elvis's "Burning Love" came on the charts. Three singles released by three 1950s legends known as rockabilly artists when they started. Now, it had been over eight years since either Ricky Nelson or Chuck Berry had been in the pop Top 10. And even though Elvis had never been out of the Top 40 since 1956, he was in a bit of a slump, as he hadn't made the Top 10 for over two years. It's odd enough these three original rockers were on the charts at all as late as 1972, but what is most fascinating of all is that for one week, on October 21, 1972, Chuck Berry held down the #1 spot with "My Ding-A-Ling" (his first and only #1 pop record), Elvis Presley was in the #2 position with "Burning Love," and Ricky Nelson was at #6 with "Garden Party." This would be the final time any of these three great fifties rockers would ever see the *Billboard* pop Top 10. While "My Ding-A-Ling" stayed on the pop charts for seventeen weeks and "Burning Love" for fifteen weeks, "Garden Party" outlasted both. It had a nineteen-week run. I shouldn't have to tell you that Elvis went on to chart another twenty songs on the *Billboard* pop charts up until and after his death, but Chuck Berry only had one more, and it was the same way with Ricky Nelson.

Another odd thing that happened during the fall of 1972 was that Johnny Rivers also debuted on the charts, with

Forgettin' to Remember to Forget

In the fall of 1968, Ricky still wasn't able to break back onto the *Billboard* charts, but he was out doin' a cross-country tour of mostly small nightclubs with his fresh, new-sounding band. One of the clubs he was scheduled to play at was a legendary folk music club in Washington, D.C., called The Cellar Door. It wasn't a place I ever went to at this time, but when I heard Ricky Nelson was gonna play there, I was planning to be there. But it wasn't meant to be. Two days before Ricky was to appear at The Cellar Door, I had a run-in with several members of a former outlaw biker gang that caused me to land in the hospital, where I was in traction for two weeks. I didn't think it was all that bad (as far as my physical condition went) at the time, 'cause the doctors kept me stoned on painkillers. But I wasn't so out of it that I forgot about Ricky's show.

There was a phone on the table next to my bed. Around four o'clock in the afternoon on the day of the show, I asked my soon-to-be-wife Pepper to call information and get the number for The Cellar Door, then dial the number and hand me the phone. Pepper said, "For what?" I said, "Just do it." Me being six years older than Pepper and being in and around the music business, especially the club scene, I knew something she didn't. When big-name acts came in to do a show, even in 1968, they usually did a soundcheck during the early or mid part of the afternoon. Inside what brain I had left from all the drugs I was on, I had a story I could lay on whoever worked at the joint that was good enough for them to put Ricky on the phone.

I remember a girl answered the phone, and I could hear the music in the background, so I had to talk loud, but she got the message. A good five minutes or more went by, but then the music stopped and shortly afterwards I had Ricky Nelson on the phone. I told him what the deal was on why I couldn't be there and how hard I'd tried to get out of the hospital 'cause I figured I'd never get another shot at seein' him in a small club setting like the one that night. I also told him I'd seen him back in 1958, and that I still listened to his old records as well as buying his more recent ones. I told him also that if I didn't make good sense it was because of all the dope they put in me. I remember Ricky asking me how I got him on the phone, 'cause he wasn't supposed to be interrupted. I said, "Didn't they tell you?" He said, "No. They just told me it was an important call from L.A. that I had to take immediately." I said, "I told the girl that answered that I was Deke Rivers [which was Elvis's name in the film *Loving You*] and worked for Rick's booking agent, and I had to talk to Rick himself, no road manager, because his agent had just booked him in a club in Wilmington, Delaware, two days from now to fill one of the gaps in his northeast tour schedule. Pretty good, huh?" Ricky broke up laughin'. He told me if he didn't have to leave right after the show to do another one the next night, he'd-a liked to come by the hospital and see me. I asked him if he still did any of his old rockabilly songs, and he said he still did "I'm Walkin'" and "Believe What You Say," so I told him to dedicate one of 'em to me that night, 'cause there were some friends of mine who would be at his show and that it would blow their minds. He said he'd do it. I know he didn't forget that, 'cause I got two calls the next day from people I knew who were at the show who told me he dedicated a song to me and said I'd called him from the hospital.

Ricky told me rockabilly music would always be what he'd prefer to do, and he still played and sang the old Elvis and Eddie Cochran songs just for fun when he was at home. He also gave me his home telephone number in California and told me to call him in about a month, after he came off the tour. But I was screwed up and goin' through a lot of changes back then too, and I never did call him. Just one of my way-back regrets. For two guys who never met before, we hit it off so well, that phone call turned into lasting at least about forty-five minutes.

Pepper had been sittin' next to my bed for a good ten minutes while me and Ricky were talking, and she said, "I know you didn't get Ricky Nelson on the phone. This is just another crazy stunt you're pullin'." So I said to Ricky, "Hey, man, do me a favor and just say a quick hi to my girl, but make sure you tell her what your name is." Ricky said, "Sure, I'd love to." I handed Pepper the phone and she said, "Yeah, hello." Well, Pepper's jaw dropped, and she didn't really know what to say, but she knew by the voice on the other end it was the same Ricky Nelson she'd watched and loved to see singin' on TV.

an old New Orleans R&B song called "Rockin' Pneumonia and the Boogie Woogie Flu." Now, I know Johnny Rivers is best remembered for ridin' the wave of the "Go-Go" craze back in the mid sixties. Johnny Rivers put the Whiskey a Go-Go Club in Los Angeles on the map back at that time. Between the summer of 1964 and the fall of 1967, he had fourteen straight single releases make the *Billboard* pop Top 40, including one #1 and six others that reached the Top 10. But he started out as a rockabilly artist. His first recordings were for the Suede record label in 1956 with a group called The Spades. At that time he went by his real name, John Ramistella. He made some real good rockabilly records for Gone, Cub, and several other labels in the late fifties and early sixties. So it's no wonder by 1964, when he signed with the label Ricky Nelson had practically all of his biggest hits on, Imperial Records, that Johnny was recording old rockabilly songs with a different sound to fit the new sounds in pop music then. But by the fall of '67, the "Go-Go" craze was dead, and so were Rivers's big hits. He left Imperial in 1970 and signed with United Artists, but after a few folk-type things that landed in the bottom of the charts and disappeared quickly, he musta come back to his senses to do "Rockin' Pneumonia and the Boogie Woogie Flu." It peaked out at #6. He'd never see another song of his reach that high on the *Billboard* pop charts again. Also, it stayed on the charts for nineteen weeks. Longer than any of his previous twenty-three *Billboard* pop chart records. He did a good rock 'n' roll version of this classic tune. He followed this up in the spring of 1973 with the Carl Perkins rockabilly classic "Blue Suede Shoes," and his version made it to #38 and stayed on the charts for ten weeks.

So what's all this prove? Well, not that the powers that be will ever listen to me, *but* it proves that every time you dish out solid-soundin' real rock 'n' roll and rockabilly music and the artist comes across with a true-to-the-music feel, it'll outsell and go farther than any of that lame, quick-buck junk they keep dumpin' millions of dollars into. As long as it's promoted and is able to get on mainstream radio, rockabilly and rock 'n' roll will always be music that young people, even in the 1990s or 2000s, will want to snatch up and grab onto.

In the late seventies, Johnny Rivers was able to come back one final time with three bottom-end songs on *Billboard* and one that got to #10, and that was the end for him.

Ricky Nelson, on the other hand, was able to put only one more song on the *Billboard* pop charts. It was the

follow-up to "Garden Party," called "Palace Guard." It only reached #65, in March 1973, and fell off the charts after a short five weeks. It's no wonder; it was a dreary song anyway. The Decca record label was now called MCA Records, which it remains today. Ricky had five more singles and a couple more albums released on MCA Records during 1973 and 1974, but the label dropped him by the end of 1974. He kept touring with his Stone Canyon Band until the end of the 1970s. In 1977 and '78, he had several 45 releases and a couple of albums on Epic Records. They all failed to chart, and unless you're a hard-core Ricky Nelson fan, there's really nothin' out of all of 'em that special to mention. In 1981 and '82, Ricky got another major record deal with Capitol Records. One album and a few singles were released. This stuff was better than the Epic material, but it also failed.

Between the late seventies and early eighties, rockabilly music was just startin' to happen all over again. During the early 1980s, Ricky performed live at various L.A. nightspots. One of the people he became friends with during this time was a local rockabilly singer and musician by the name of James Intveld. James was not only a popular rockabilly singer in the L.A. club scene, but he also had the best and tightest raw rockabilly band backing him up out there during this period. By 1985, Ricky Nelson had decided he wanted to go back to his roots and record and perform rockabilly music again. After all, he was there in the beginning. He needed a solid backup band that knew how to play rockabilly the right way, and James Intveld had the best one, so that's the one Ricky wanted and got. It didn't bother James at all, 'cause he's an easygoin' guy and too much of a professional to stand in anybody's way to move up the ladder, plus he knows that's just the way the music business works. James Intveld is without question in my opinion and that of other rockabilly fans around the world the best young pure rockabilly vocalist anywhere on the West Coast. You'll read more about him later. James's younger brother Rick Intveld was James's drummer, and now in 1985 he was Ricky Nelson's drummer.

In 1986 Polygram Records released an album called *The Class of '55*, which reunited Carl Perkins, Johnny Cash, Jerry Lee Lewis, and Roy Orbison, the four biggest stars that had started out on Sun Records doin' rockabilly music in the 1950s who were still alive in the 1980s. It was to be recorded in the fall of '85 in the original Sun Records Recording Studio, where these four artists had recorded their first hits and other early songs. To put it bluntly, this album was a lie and a farce to any rockabilly fan, as they made sure they took the photos and cut some of the tracks at the original Sun Studios, but other tracks were done across town at producer Chips Moman's American Studios. Everything was also mixed at Moman's recording studios. It really had nothin' at all to do with the original 1950s Sun Records sound that was so special then and now.

The finale song for the album was written by John Fogerty. It was called "Big Train (from Memphis)." And Ricky Nelson was one of the big-name artists brought in to sing backup on it. Others, such as Dave Edmunds, were also legitimate rockabilly artists, but what were The Judds doin' on what was being called a true rockabilly masterpiece? I don't need to go on anymore about it, only to say this album was the biggest overproduced piece of garbage that Polygram Records sunk millions of dollars into that flopped so bad it sent all major labels at the time running in the other direction if you were trying to get a legitimate rockabilly music record deal. That's all it takes is one major disaster like the *Class of '55* album to set rockabilly music back so far the big boys don't want to touch it.

After Ricky Nelson finished his part on that one song in Memphis, he did a recording session and went out on tour with his new rockabilly band. I don't have to tell you what happened. In the early morning hours of December 31, 1985, Ricky Nelson's private airplane crashed in De Kalb, Texas, on the way to a big New Year's Eve concert. Ricky, his fiancée, and his entire band (which included James's brother Rick Intveld) were all killed in the fiery crash. Not that this really matters, but Ricky Nelson had purchased this airplane from Jerry Lee Lewis, and as the story goes, The Killer was afraid to fly in it anymore because it was old and needed repair work desperately. That's the first time I've ever heard of Jerry Lee Lewis bein' afraid of anything.

I would have gotten drunk and happy that New Year's Eve, 1985, but when I heard and saw on the evening news of Ricky Nelson's death, I just got drunk and real sad. I stayed up all night and listened to all his great rockabilly records. Ricky was only forty-five years old, and him and his music had always meant a lot to me. They always will. He was not just another teenage idol, I can tell you that much. He was a whole lot more. He had real talent. Sure, when rockabilly and real rock 'n' roll went out of style he tried out other styles of music, but you can't name me one other rockabilly artist who

ever had even one minor hit in the 1950s on any of the *Billboard* charts that didn't experiment with other forms of incoming music to try for another hit. So don't hold it against Ricky Nelson. Ricky was as good or better a rockabilly artist than most.

The very first song Ricky recorded in early 1957 was a rockabilly version of "I'm Walkin'." It was a million seller then. The very last song that he recorded in 1985, which was released on an MCA 45 single, was called "Do You Know What I Mean?" It was with his new band, and it was released right after his death. This new song was pure hard-hittin', upright-bass-slappin' rockabilly all the way through. The best rockabilly song he'd done in over twenty-five years. And the very last song Ricky Nelson ever sang live on stage, in Gunnersville, Alabama, on December 30, 1985, only hours before his death, was Buddy Holly's rockabilly classic "Rave On." So what more can I say? Ricky Nelson was always a rockabilly in his heart.

Conway Twitty

Knowin' Conway Twitty even as little as I did on the personal side, he wouldn't have cared if he wasn't even mentioned at all in this book. His first and last real love was country music. But between 1956 and 1964, Conway Twitty recorded and had released so many great rockabilly and rock 'n' roll songs that are today still being collected, listened to, and loved by rockabilly fans young and old all over the world, that he has to be given some space.

Conway Twitty was always one of my favorite artists in rockabilly and rock 'n' roll. I know I saw him more times down at "The Milt Grant TV Teen Dance Show" in Washington, D.C., than any other artist that came through promotin' their latest record. To be exact, it was nine times between November 1958 and January 1961. Right after the Milt Grant Show went off the air in April 1961, I went down to the Casino Royale nightclub to catch a great live rockin' show Conway did. I booked him on January 12, 1967, in Palmer Park, Maryland, just as he was starting out in country music, but on my booking, he was forced into doin' a great rock 'n' roll show, which you'll read about later. I next saw him do an all-country music show in Gaithersburg, Maryland, in October 1970, and saw him and talked with him last in March 1992, down at the TNN Studios in Nashville. So I reckon you could say I dug Conway Twitty. Especially the rockin' side of Conway, which came through in a good number of his up-tempo country songs — mostly buried on albums throughout the seventies and eighties.

Conway Twitty was born Harold Lloyd Jenkins on September 1, 1933, in Friars Point, Mississippi. He was named after Harold Lloyd, who was a popular silent screen comedian during the 1920s. At age four he was given his first guitar, and he learned his first chords from an old black man that everyone called Uncle Fred, who was nearby where Conway's family lived in their houseboat on the banks of the Mississippi. Conway said he sang southern gospel music with his family in church and heard the colored folks singin' black sharecropper blues-type music while workin' in the fields, but that when he was a kid, he thought the only kind of music on the radio was country music, and that the only station on the radio was WSM in Nashville, because every Saturday night his family went over to his grandmother's house to all get together to listen to "The Grand Ole Opry."

He played and sang gospel and country music growin' up, and after he was drafted in 1954, formed a country music band with some fellow servicemen in Yokohama, Japan, where he was stationed. When Conway's hitch in the Army was over and he landed in San Francisco on March 14, 1956, he remembers clearly the first thing he heard comin' out of the radio: "When I first landed back in the States after bein' overseas for two years, I didn't have no idea how much the music on the radio had changed. The first person I heard singin' on the radio was Elvis. The song was 'Heartbreak Hotel.' I'd never heard nothin' like it. It just floored me, man. A couple weeks later, I got settled in back home in Helena, Arkansas, and saw Elvis on national television singing and shakin' all over. I couldn't believe it. It changed my whole life. Then when I heard this cat open his mouth to talk, it gave me goosebumps and made the hair on the back of my neck shoot straight out. I knew right then if a young guy from seventy miles down the road from where I lived could make it doin' this new rockabilly music, then I could too."

In July 1956, Conway put together an all-rockabilly band called Harold Jenkins and The Rockhousers. They started playing all the local dances and nightspots. Conway signed his first management and booking contract with the bass player in the band, by the name of Bill Harris. By the early fall of 1956, Conway and the group went where every would-be rockabilly at that time was headin': right to the doorstep of Sun Records in Memphis. Conway got to Sun Records too late, though,

'cause Sam Phillips and his label were well into the black by this time with Elvis, Johnny Cash, and Carl Perkins already havin' scored huge successes, and Conway was just one of the hundreds he had comin' by to show him they had what it took to be as big as Elvis. Sam Phillips told me in 1990 that he heard something special in Conway, but couldn't ever put a handle on it. Sam put it this way: "I knew Conway had real talent or I would-a never spent a sizable portion of two to three months trying to find what I was lookin' for, and that was something different. Back then, I never felt I really came up with that on what Conway was layin' down on tape. But I knew he'd go on to do great things in music, 'cause I could see that cat had the drive in him to make it and make it big." The several months Sam was speakin' of spanned from October 1956 through January 1957. Nobody really knows (except for maybe Sam Phillips himself) how many different songs Conway recorded while trying out for Sun Records, but out of the ones that surfaced and have come out over the past twenty years, Conway proves on 'em that he could do rockabilly music with the best of 'em. Especially on songs like "Give Me Some Lovin'," "I Need Your Lovin' Kiss," and "Crazy Dreams." Today they may sound primitive, raw, and spontaneous, but hey, that's what always made rockabilly music sound great to begin with.

Another recently discovered song Conway recorded at Sun Records was one he called "Rockhouse." Conway was writin' a lot of rockabilly songs by the summer of 1956, and he cut quite a few at Sun Records. Sam Phillips released a new song by Roy Orbison called "Rockhouse," where the writer credit was given to Roy Orbison and Sam Phillips. Sam evidently let Orbison hear Conway's version, and Roy changed most of the words, but the melody on both songs is basically the same. To put it mildly, back in '57, Conway was not pleased. He wanted a release on Sun Records real bad at the time and felt Sam had treated him badly. After Conway became a superstar in country music, he and Sam mended their differences. Most rockabilly fans around the world agree both Roy's and Conway's versions of "Rockhouse" are great examples of rockabilly music.

In January 1957, while Conway was still trying out for Sun Records, he was contacted by Don Seat in New York, who had heard about Conway from some guy who had been with him in the Army. Seat asked Conway if he was doin' this new kind of music that was comin' out of Memphis. Conway told him he sure was, and Seat told him to send a demo tape to him. Which Conway did. Seat contacted Conway a week or so after he got the tape and told him he could put him on any major record label he wanted to be on. Conway told Seat he wanted to be on Sun Records, but Seat told him, "No, they're just too small, and the bigger labels will do more for you." So Don Seat went on to sign Conway up to Mercury Records in February 1957. It was at this time Seat told Conway that he needed a name change, as up until that time he was still going under his given name, Harold Jenkins. There's two different versions of how Conway came up with his new, unusual name, which back in 1957 sounded as different and crazy as Elvis Presley's had to most people. Don Seat's version is that him and Conway sat down with a roadmap of the South and Southwest and after a number of tries of picking names, they each stuck a pin in Conway, Arkansas, and another pin in Twitty, Texas. Conway's version is that he himself sat down with a road atlas and studied it closely, and after hours of picking out dozens of terrible-sounding names, he finally decided on Conway Twitty after seein' those same two towns. Whatever the case, Conway Twitty was born in the music business in February 1957.

Don Seat was one shrewd businessman. He not only signed Conway Twitty to an exclusive personal and business management contract, but went so far as to secure for himself the full legal rights to the name Conway Twitty. He owned that name in 1957. After Conway broke ties with him around 1964, Seat made Conway buy that name back from him before he could go out and do anything under it. Don Seat, though, did make things happen fast for Conway. Only a little more than a month after the final session Conway had done at Sun Records, he was now doing his first of two sessions for Mercury Records in late February. Seat also had him out on tour and had Conway's first record out and in the stores by late March. The first 45 was "I Need Your Lovin'" b/w "Born to Sing the Blues." "I Need Your Lovin'" was stutter-style, hiccuppin' rockabilly vocals at its best. Conway's always said when this record came out he thought he'd be as big as Elvis within a few weeks. It wasn't meant to be. The record did make an appearance on the *Billboard* pop charts for one week at #93, on May 20, 1957. Mercury Records followed this up with "Shake It Up" b/w "Maybe, Baby," both written by Conway. This 45 was released during the early summer of 1957, and even though both sides were strong rockabilly songs, the record went nowhere.

Conway went in and did one final session for Mercury during the late summer of 1957, which produced three songs, but these songs weren't released in 1957. Two of 'em, "Double Talk Baby" b/w "Why Can't I Get Through to You," did come out as a 45 single in the fall of 1958. But this was only because Conway Twitty was then sittin' in the #1 spot on the *Billboard* pop charts with his first song on MGM Records, called "It's Only Make Believe."

In late 1959, Mercury Records also put out a compilation album, titled *Singin' and Swingin'*, on its budget Mercury Wing label, which also featured "Double Talk Baby" and "Why Can't I Get Through to You." This compilation album featured six artists or groups, all doin' two songs each. One of them was another rockabilly artist at the time who would go on to also meet with his greatest success in country music during the 1970s, by the name of Narvel Felts. Narvel and Conway were both with Mercury Records at the same time during 1957. But Narvel stayed with Mercury through to almost the end of 1958. Though none of Narvel's Mercury 45s hit the *Billboard* charts, several of the songs, such as "Foolish Thoughts," "Kiss-a-Me Baby," and "Little Girl, Step This Way," were some of the best examples of frantic, or stutter, step, hiccuppy, quiverin' rockabilly music that a teenager would want to grab onto back at that time. "Kiss-a-Me Baby" was one of the two songs on this Mercury Wing compilation album. Narvel was probably included on this LP in late 1959 because he was on the independent label Pink Records by this time and was starting to have some minor chart success.

It was a long dry spell for Conway Twitty after the failure of his second Mercury 45 single in the fall of 1957, although his manager Don Seat had Conway and his band on tour both in the U.S. and Canada. Conway was a popular act in early 1958 at quite a number of his Canadian nightclub appearances. During the early months of '58, though, Don Seat was shoppin' Conway to all the major labels, looking for a new recording deal for Conway, as Mercury had dropped him. Seat had a tougher time this go-round finding the kind of major record contract he wanted for Conway. There were a number of companies interested in Conway during the early months of 1958, but Conway was known to them as a rockabilly singer, and both rockabilly and rock 'n' roll were startin' to lose some of their steam by the early spring of 1958. The softer sounds of new acts like The Everly Brothers were starting to attract teenage audiences by this time, plus the labels wanted to hear fresh material. Don Seat finally found the deal he was lookin' for by April 1958, with Jim Vienneau, who had recently become the new head of A&R at MGM Records in New York City.

Don Seat got Jim Vienneau to agree to go to Nashville and cut a one-day session on Conway. Four songs came out of that first session on May 7, 1958, for MGM Records, all co-written by Conway and Jack Nance. Producer Jim Vienneau was happy with the way the session went and felt they really had a major hit with one of the songs, called "I'll Try," which was put on the A side of the first single. He put "It's Only Make Believe" on the B side. Conway recalled years later, "That record had been out for almost three full months, and I knew in my mind they were puttin' the push on the wrong side. I believed that 'It's Only Make Believe' could hold its own against any song that was on the charts back in '58. Me and my band were playin' clubs up in Canada, where 'It's Only Make Believe' was a big hit and in the Top 10 charts up there by July 1958. But nothin' was happenin' in the States 'cause they were still pushin' 'I'll Try.' By the end of July, I was sick of waitin' for something to happen and tired of playin' the clubs, so I just broke the band up, quit, and went back home. A couple weeks later, I was out in the field driving a tractor on my father-in-law's farm in Arkansas when I was called into the house to take this phone call. On the other end of the line was this top disc jockey in Columbus, Ohio, who called himself 'Dr. Bop,' and he told me, man, I should head up to Columbus, 'cause I had the #1 record in that town with 'It's Only Make Believe.' So I got ahold of all the guys in my band, and we got in my broken-down Mercury and drove straight to that radio station in Columbus. They treated me like I was Elvis. Then when this 'Dr. Bop' disc jockey had us show up that night to lip-synch the song at this drive-in restaurant, there were thousands, and I mean thousands, of wild, screaming teenagers there, and I thought, 'I'm gonna be killed.' When we drove up to this drive-in restaurant, we had no idea what it was gonna be like. I had a sign on my old Mercury that said 'Conway Twitty, MGM Recording Star.' When all these kids saw that, they started grabbin' at us through the windows, so I said, 'Roll 'em up,' and then they started rockin' the car. When we finally got about a quarter-mile from the restaurant, the police came to our rescue, and they had to get us onto the top of this drive-in restaurant building. The only way they could do it was carry all four of us overtop of their heads through thousands of screamin' teenagers who were all tearin'

at us. Funny thing, thinkin' back, is none of 'em really knew which one of us was Conway Twitty. When we got up onto the top of that building and 'Dr. Bop' told the crowd 'It's Only Make Believe' was gonna be the biggest hit of 1958, and then he introduced me, and the song started and I began lip-synchin' it, those thousands of kids all went wild. The noise was deafening, man, I was in shock and just couldn't believe it. I remember it like it was yesterday. You would-a just had to have been there and gone through this wildness to even imagine what it felt like."

Well, after being out for almost four months, "It's Only Make Believe" made its debut on the *Billboard* charts on September 15, 1958. With Conway's constant promotions at radio stations, teen dance shows, live shows, and national TV shows such as "Ed Sullivan" and "American Bandstand," it only took "It's Only Make Believe" eight weeks to wind up in the #1 spot on the *Billboard* pop charts on November 10, 1958, where it stayed for two weeks and had a twenty-one-week run before it finally fell off the charts in February, 1959. Conway had worked hard for over two and a half years to reach this kind of success. It had finally paid off, and he wasn't about to slow up now. Sam Phillips had been right. Conway Twitty certainly did have the drive to make it big. He also had the drive to make it last longer than most doin' his brand of rockabilly and rock 'n' roll between 1958 and 1964, when it wasn't in fashion and was losin' strength among the ever-changing, fickle younger record-buying public. I've been told "It's Only Make Believe" topped the charts in twenty-two countries around the world and sold two million copies the first four months after it hit the *Billboard* charts. By 1963, MGM Records declared it ultimately sold a total of eight million copies.

Don Seat did a smart thing when he negotiated Conway's contract with MGM Records. Seat had seen how much money Elvis's first three movies had grossed, so he had a clause in Conway's recording contract with MGM Records that if any one of Conway Twitty's recordings for their label topped one million copies in sales, Conway would have to be given a starring role in at least one MGM film. Seat made sure MGM lived up to their obligations by 1960, when Conway was given the part of Billy Jack Barnes in the low-budget MGM teenage delinquent flick *Platinum High School*. This was a typical film geared right at the teenage market. Conway stayed a busy boy out in Hollywood in 1960, co-starring in two more films that, lookin' back, were even worse than the first. His second film was titled *College Confidential* and was released by the major film company Universal Pictures. His final appearance on the big screen, released by Allied Artists Pictures at Christmas time, 1960, was called *Sex Kittens Go to College*. All in all, for having virtually no acting experience, Conway didn't do that bad, but then again, most of the "major" stars in these three films couldn't act any better than Conway. All three films, though, served their purpose. They all made money then.

Like I said, Conway Twitty worked hard at keepin' his star shinin' bright doin' his best to rock 'n' roll his way through the teen idols that had taken over during 1959 and 1960, when Conway had ten more consecutive songs on the *Billboard* pop charts following the success of "It's Only Make Believe." Two of those ten made it into the Top 10 on *Billboard*, and another five made it well up into the Top 40 during that period. On most of 'em, what you noticed was that raw, gutsy, throaty growl on his mid-tempo bluesy rockers. You knew instantly it was Conway. Conway had success on the charts with rockin' numbers like "Hey Little Lucy," "Mona Lisa," and "Danny Boy," but he was really at his best when he did the slower or mid-tempo bluesabilly songs. "Lonely Blue Boy," Conway's Top 10 song from early 1960, and "Is a Bluebird Blue," his Top 40 song also from 1960, both come through with the pure, raw vocal sound that made Conway great and that no one could ever duplicate. Conway had twenty-five single releases and ten album releases during his rockabilly and rock 'n' roll period between 1957 and 1964.

The following twenty-eight years, from 1965 to 1993, when Conway suddenly passed away, to the shock of both the country music world and real rock 'n' roll fans, were spent singin' what Conway loved most, country music. But even in country music, Conway's rockabilly growlin' vocal style shined through, especially on the Eagles song that he had a Top 10 country chart hit of in 1983, titled "Heartache Tonight." There's many other examples of Conway's rockin' days buried on his country albums of the seventies and eighties.

Conway Twitty has been and will always be regarded as a rockabilly and rock 'n' roll artist in England, Europe, and other parts of the world. He toured England in 1959, and not only did "It's Only Make Believe" hit #1 there early that year, but his two rockers "Hey Little Lucy" and "Mona Lisa" also reached #20 and #6, respectively.

Bear Family Records out of West Germany released an eight-album boxed set called *Conway Twitty: The Rock 'n' Roll Years*, which covers his 1956 Sun demo recordings, 1957 Mercury recordings, and everything he recorded for MGM from 1958 to 1964. This set came out in 1985 on vinyl; I'm not sure if it's available on CD. There's 144 of Conway Twitty's rockabilly and rock 'n' roll songs on it. It's a well-put-together package, and I highly recommend you seek it out. There's songs on there that future generations will be redoing.

When I remember Conway, I like to think of something he said to me the last time we talked, in March 1992. Conway said, "I never thought my rockabilly and rock 'n' roll stuff was very good, but I wanted to do it at the time 'cause it was really happenin'. But then along comes another person like you that tells me how great you think it is and how it made a big difference in your life. Anymore when I hear talk like that I can appreciate it. I always loved the blues like I did country back in the forties and early fifties, and rockabilly came out of those two music styles. Plus I think too, if it makes you and so many others feel so good, it can't be all that bad. From the beginning, all the kinds of music I've done through the years I've always given 100 percent and laid it down the very best I could do, and I'd let guys like you decide on it from there." Well Conway, you did just fine in my book.

Other Artists from the Late Fifties

To close out the fifties, which was the greatest period in rockabilly history, I feel I have to touch on a number of other artists or bands who charted records on the *Billboard* pop charts that are usually found on rockabilly compilation albums today. Practically all these artists I met between 1958 and 1961 down in Washington, D.C., on "The Milt Grant TV Dance Show."

Dale Hawkins was an eighteen-year-old crazy rockabilly cat who was born in Goldmine, Louisiana, who Leonard Chess (owner of Chess Records) signed up in the early months of 1957 and placed on his Checker Records label, which was a subsidiary to Chess Records. Between 1957 and 1961, Dale Hawkins had fifteen 45 releases and one album release. But what would stand as his finest moment in rockabilly and rock 'n' roll history came during the summer and fall of 1957, when his second 45 release, "Susie-Q," blasted over the radio stations around the country, and teenagers all over went for Dale's swampy, vibrant vocals and James Burton's raw, unique guitar sound. "Susie-Q" reached a peak position of only #27, in September 1957, but it stayed on the *Billboard* pop charts for nineteen straight weeks. Dale went on to have two follow-up 45s released in late 1957 and early 1958, but neither one found any success on the *Billboard* charts then. One of the songs is a wild, jumpin', rockabilly-all-the-way tune called "Little Pig," which has been performed and recorded by countless rockabilly artists and bands from the late seventies up to the present. Buzz and The Flyers and Tex Rubinowitz are two rockabilly names that come to mind immediately that did the best rockabilly revival versions on "Little Pig." This song, as well as other great rockabilly songs like "Tornado," "See You Soon Baboon," "Mrs. Merguitory's Daughter," and others were all included on Dale Hawkins's only big 1950s rockabilly album, which was released in early 1958. This album was reissued on vinyl in the 1980s here in the U.S. by Chess Records and has since come out in the nineties on CD. It's Dale Hawkins's best work as a rockabilly artist. Dale had three more *Billboard* pop chart records in 1958 and '59 on the Checker Records label, but these and the ones that followed never measured up to "Susie-Q" or all the great cuts on that album. Dale was still young, though, and when Checker Records gave up on him in 1961, he made some 45s for Atlantic Records in late '61 and early '62, then cut a "Twist" album for Roulette Records in the summer of 1962. He also had releases on ABC Paramount Records in 1965 and Bell Records in 1969, but that was about it. During the past ten years or so, he has performed in parts of Europe on several occasions, 'cause fans there don't forget great rockabilly artists like Dale Hawkins.

Another artist who also over the past fifteen years has made a number of trips to large, appreciative rockabilly audiences in Europe is Ronnie Hawkins. Ronnie was born in Huntsville, Arkansas, on January 10, 1935. He formed his first band in 1952, calling them The Hawks. In 1958 he moved to Canada (where he still lives today) with his drummer, Levon Helm, and formed a new group of Hawks to back him up. Ronnie and The Hawks had one 45 release on a small independent label called Quality Records. But it was in the spring of 1959, when Ronnie signed a deal with Roulette Records in the U.S., that he found his greatest success. His first 45 release, called "Forty Days" (which is actually a direct steal of Chuck Berry's "Thirty Days," a rockabilly song from 1955), which Hawkins claimed co-writership on, debuted on the *Billboard* pop charts on June 8, 1959, and reached a peak position of #45, while stayin' on the charts for eight weeks. The flip side of "Forty Days" was

called "One of These Days." Both songs were hard-drivin', high-powered, frantic examples of rockabilly music. Ronnie Hawkins put across a gruff, raw vocal sound laced with all the high squeaks and hiccups that make for a great rockabilly song. Ronnie's follow-up to "Forty Days" was a rockabilly version of the R&B classic "Mary Lou." This song was an even bigger hit. "Mary Lou" climbed to a peak position of #26 by October 1959 and stayed on the *Billboard* pop charts for sixteen weeks. Ronnie Hawkins was not only seen on Milt Grant's TV show when I was down there, but he was on all the others around the country, including "American Bandstand." By the fall of 1959 on these TV shows, guys who were still doin' this kind of rockabilly music (and there weren't too many) and were able to get on the *Billboard* pop charts with it were not goin' as crazy on TV as they had been a couple of years prior. Jack Scott, Conway Twitty, and others rocked pretty good in 1959, but man, Ronnie Hawkins was still doin' those crazy, wild, shakin' movements right on "American Bandstand" in late '59. These kind of actions were supposed to be dead and gone with the incoming, fresh-faced, bubble-headed brand of boys and girls that had taken over what teenagers were listening to. I guess that's why that was the final time Ronnie Hawkins saw the *Billboard* charts until February 1970, when he had his final pop chart record with another R&B classic song, called "Down in the Alley." The times had changed by then, and his song only reached #75 at the time. Roulette Records continued to release nine more 45 singles after "Mary Lou," which all failed to chart, and they put out five albums on him through 1963. But it was Ronnie's first two albums, *Ronnie Hawkins* in 1959 and *Mr. Dynamo* in 1960, that had all of his great rockabilly tunes on 'em. After those in 1961 and '62, Ronnie mostly got into doin' the folk music bit, which was big at the time. He ultimately would come back to his rockabilly, screamin' roots, 'cause that's what outlasted all the other kinds of music he tried out well into the early seventies on various record labels.

Ronnie Hawkins went back to workin' the nightclub circuit in Canada after he and his band The Hawks split up in the mid 1960s. A few years later, in late 1967, The Hawks all got back together in Woodstock, New York, and formed a new band. They called themselves The Band. These were the exact same guys who backed Ronnie Hawkins up in the late fifties. Robbie Robertson, Levon Helm, Rick Danko, Richard Manuel, and Garth Hudson. The Band did a lot of recording with Bob Dylan until the late seventies, when they split up.

The final thing I want to say about Ronnie Hawkins is that it was he who invented the "Moon Walk." You know, that slidin' style of move that Michael Jackson became famous for in the mid eighties. No kiddin'! A promotional film short on a Ronnie Hawkins song from 1959 called "Need Your Lovin' " shows that he did the exact same "Moon Walk" dance movement in his 1959 song, only in a slower motion, and much cooler, I must say.

The Everly Brothers have at times throughout the years been called rockabilly by some writers. Now, I don't personally agree, but because I think very highly of their early country/pop up-tempo songs, and because Phil Everly was one of the nicest big teen stars I ever met in 1959 and 1960, I think they should be alotted some space. There's no question these two young country boys had the greatest harmonies in rock 'n' roll music history with some of their biggest hits. Nobody can touch them in that department. It's been written The Beatles were so influenced by their music that at one point early on they even called themselves The Four Everlys. In 1975, Linda Ronstadt peaked at #2 with a solid version of an Everly Brothers classic, "When Will I Be Loved?" which had been a Top 10 hit for brothers Don and Phil back in 1960. The Everlys also had a major influence on super producer and major rockabilly revival artist Dave Edmunds, when, in 1980, Edmunds, along with Nick Lowe, had a four-song EP album of all Everly Brothers songs released. I could always hear a softer kind of rockabilly sound in their up-tempo numbers. Especially ones like "Hey Doll Baby," "This Little Girl of Mine," "Claudette," "Poor Jenny," "When Will I Be Loved?" and a few others. They even did, and charted with, their own version of Gene Vincent's classic "Be-Bop-A-Lula." Their hearts were in the right place. Hey, I bought most of their records back in the late fifties. Whether you like 'em for their early teen-oriented songs such as "Wake Up Little Susie" or "Bird Dog," or for their great harmony ballads such as "Let It Be Me" and "All I Have to Do Is Dream," you got to like 'em and their music, 'cause they were young country boys who were the most important duo in rock 'n' roll history. Most rockabilly fans, you'll find, will have Everly Brothers records in their collections, so that says enough in itself. In early 1976, the hard rock group Nazareth, from Scotland, put an Everly Brothers song called "Love Hurts" into the *Billboard* pop charts, and it reached #8 then and stayed on the charts for twenty-three weeks. It wasn't too bad, but up against The Everly Brothers' 1960 version, it was no contest. The Everly Brothers' harmonies wind up makin' you really feel how "Love Hurts." Between 1957 and 1967, they had thirty-seven *Billboard* chart hits. They split up for ten years between 1973 and 1983 and made several comeback albums and 45s between 1984 and 1988. The best two were produced by rockabilly producer Dave Edmunds. He was able to bring out, at that late date, the true essence of what The Everly Brothers still had left in 'em. It was always their great harmonies, and it shines through on the Edmunds-produced albums, which were also the most successful. The Everly Brothers are still out there occasionally doin' shows. If they come to your town, you better catch 'em before it's too late. You won't be disappointed.

Tommy Sands has always been put in the class of a teenage idol of the late 1950s. Which, I can't argue, he was. In fact, I guess Sands was the first of the teen idol stars in the early months of 1957, when his first record for Capitol Records, called "Teenage Crush," zoomed up the *Billboard* pop charts and was sittin' in the #2 spot on 'em for two weeks during April 1957. But he was more than that. If only on a handful of songs, Tommy Sands falls under the rockabilly banner. In fact, he had one rockabilly chart song, "The Worryin' Kind," which made it to #69 on the *Billboard* pop charts, staying on those charts for nine weeks. When I first met Tommy in October 1959, I had one question on my mind: After he had done and been successful with so many mild-mannered and silly teen/pop-oriented songs like "Teenage Crush," "Fantastically Foolish," "Ring-A-Ding-A-Ding," "Ring My Phone," and "After the Senior Prom" all throughout 1957 and '58, how come he turned out several really great songs with a rockabilly feel and sound to 'em like "The Worryin' Kind," "Is It Ever Gonna Happen," and "I Ain't Gittin' Rid o' You" during the first six months of 1959, and now he had a new pop ballad out of the old song "I'll Be Seeing You"? When I laid that question on him (and I was barely fifteen years old then), Tommy said, "I'm glad to hear you like rockabilly music, 'cause man, it's what I've always loved to do the most. But you see, my record label decides what comes out on me. I was lucky enough to hook up with this rockabilly band called The Raiders about a year or so back, and we recorded some great-soundin' rockabilly songs, but after the last one we did that Capitol Records put out on us didn't make the charts, they wanted me to go back to singin' these pop ballads, 'cause Capitol figures the rockabilly and old rock 'n' roll style is dead now. But man, I'd rather be singin' it, I swear, than any other kind of music." I told Tommy back then I thought he did a really great job on 'em as well as others like "Sing, Boy, Sing" and "Your Daddy Wants to Do Right." Tommy was a real nice guy, and I got his autograph, and he gave me a publicity card photo he had at the time. All those silly songs Capitol Records had him do in the early sixties (most all of which failed to chart) are long forgotten. But I was glad to read and hear that in the early 1990s, rockabilly promoters in England, Holland, and other countries were bringin' him over there for shows. At last Tommy Sands was gettin' to sing the songs he loved the most: the rockabilly songs. They had stood the test of time and held up the best, as rockabilly always has done. He was received well by the European rockabilly fans. His best material was bein' released and sellin' well all over the world again. Robert Gordon recorded "The Worryin' Kind" in 1979 for RCA Records, and Texas rockabilly legend Ronnie Dawson has recorded it in the nineties and includes it regularly in his shows. "I Ain't Gittin' Rid o' You" was also recorded by a number of rockabilly artists in the 1980s. So I'd say Tommy Sands left his mark on rockabilly music.

Another group, called The Rock-A-Teens, also laid down some of the finest rockabilly music you'd ever want to hear at the end of the music's ride back in 1959. They managed to chart one great song on the *Billboard* pop charts for twelve weeks, from mid October 1959 to the first week of January 1960, and they were able to reach a peak of #16 with it to boot. There weren't many great rockabilly songs that got up that high on the charts by this late date. But the fantastic rockabilly song "Woo Hoo" by The Rock-A- Teens was one that sure did. The song was really a wild, rantin', guitar-crazy instrumental rockabilly number with the exception of those title two words "Woo Hoo" bein' sung throughout most of this two-minute song. The label they were on, Roulette Records, was located in New York City, but all six young men in the group come from Virginia. On The Rock-A-Teens' only album, from early 1960, titled *Woo Hoo*, ten of the twelve songs were written by three of the members of the group. The lead singer, Vic Mizelle, wrote seven of the ten. One rockabilly song Mizelle wrote was called "Janis Will Rock." This was sort of a frantic rockabilly tribute song to the first female artist who hit the *Billboard* pop charts with a rockabilly song in 1956. That female rockabilly artist was Janis Martin. Martin was sixteen years old in 1956, and though she only charted with one song, she had a lot of 45 releases on RCA Records through 1958. Janis was a popular artist in Virginia, where she was born, raised, and still lives today. The only cover song The Rock-A-Teens did on this

album was the Gene Vincent late 1957 and early 1958 hit rockabilly song "Dance to the Bop." Gene Vincent was also born and raised in Norfolk, Virginia, and did a lot of shows in the state. His original group The Blue Caps all came from the Norfolk area. The Rock-A-Teens in no way copied Gene Vincent and The Blue Caps like other bands had done and were continuing to do even in 1959, but in their wild music you could certainly hear some resemblances of Gene and The Blue Caps' 1956 sound, with some of the hollers and screams members of the band were doin' either in the background or in the middle of guitar and sax solo instrumental breaks. The Rock-A-Teens proved on this twelve-song album that a saxophone works great in raunchy rockabilly. And they proved this back as early as 1959. Their follow-up 45s, such as "Twangy," "Doggone It Baby," and others, were all great, but they were released in 1960, at a time when the spontaneous, wild craziness that The Rock-A-Teens drove across to the ears of the listener on this one album was lost in the mass of come-and-go, smooth croonin' pretty boys. But boy did The Rock-A-Teens leave us in a flash with one great rockin', raunchy, raw album. They sounded possessed on the song "Lotta Boppin'." Others, like "I Was Born to Rock," "Story of a Woman," "That's My Mama," as well as "Janis Will Rock" and "Doggone It Baby," showcased Vic Mizelle's southern rockabilly vocal style, as well as the raw rockabilly sound of the band. On instrumentals like "I'm Not Afraid" and "Pagan," they've got a sound like Cliff Richards's backup group The Shadows made famous during the early sixties. The Rock-A-Teens were doin' it first in 1959. There ain't a bad song on this whole album. "Woo Hoo" was a big chart record, and thanks to that, The Rock-A-Teens left us with what might be considered the last really great raw all-rockabilly album of the 1950s.

There were so many artists that made records and touched my life during the 1950s, there's not enough room to list 'em all, but from here on out, I will at least list all the ones that charted with different forms of rockabilly music before I completely close out this decade.

There was a group (a trio to be more exact) that left their mark on rockabilly music that came out of Metamora, Illinois, called The Rockin' R's. They had a great successful instrumental rockabilly tune called "The Beat," which made it up to a high position of #57 during the spring of 1959. (Remember earlier I said that Dick Clark said there wasn't hardly any instrumentals except for Duane Eddy's for him to play back in those days. Ha!) Not only was "The Beat" a good raw example of rockabilly music that hit big and got a lot of airplay, but you also couldn't have asked for a better rockabilly song on the flip side of this 45. It was called "Crazy Baby." The vocals were raunchy sounding, as was the rest of the band. The West Coast rockabilly revival band The Blasters did a good cover over twenty years later that came out on their very first (and now very rare) album on Ronny Weiser's Rollin' Rock Records. Billy Miller's Norton Records label also put an entire album out on The Rockin' R's in the late eighties. But it was the song "The Beat" that was the group's only national chart hit, back in 1959.

Huelyn Duvall was a rockabilly singer from Huckaby, Texas, who made one brief appearance on the *Billboard* pop charts with a song called "Little Boy Blue" on the Challenge record label. "Little Boy Blue" only reached #88, in June 1959, and then dropped off the charts after only three weeks. "Little Boy Blue" was more teen-oriented rockabilly, but its flip side was a better example of good rockabilly, with the song "Three Months to Kill." Even though the lyrics were geared at the high school set, Duvall put 'em across good, and the band behind him was drivin' with a solid rockabilly beat. Huelyn Duvall made four 45s for the Challenge label, and a few of those songs were good rockabilly ones, but the slow-to mid-paced "Little Boy Blue" would be his only major chart appearance.

Ray Sharpe was a black artist born and raised in Fort Worth, Texas, who on July 20, 1959, debuted on the *Billboard* charts with a good song called "Linda Lu." "Linda Lu" only made it up to #46, but it had a nice run of thirteen weeks on the *Billboard* pop charts before it fell off in late October. Back in 1959, "Linda Lu" had a white sound to it. I never really considered it rockabilly, but since that time, rockabilly revival artists like Tex Rubinowitz and Robert Gordon have either included it in their live performances or recorded it. Back in '59, I bought it 'cause it was definitely a good rock 'n' roll song at that date. A couple interesting notes are that it came out on Jamie Records, and Duane Eddy was one of the guitarists on the song. Dick Clark, as I've stated and he readily admits, owned a sizable portion of Jamie Records. By the summer of '59 (when this record hit), Duane was already a huge star. The only thing I can figure is that Duane could have been responsible for bringing Ray Sharpe to the attention of Jamie Records. Whatever the case, "Linda Lu" holds up as a great song today and is still being sung by new, young rockabilly artists.

Jesse Lee Turner was a rockabilly artist from Bowling, Texas. But during the early months of 1959, from early January to early April to be exact, Jesse had a silly novelty song that reached #20 on the *Billboard* pop charts called "The Little Space Girl." It had a twelve-week run on *Billboard*. But back then as well as today, rockabilly fans all collect his records, and they can be found on numerous rockabilly reissue collection albums. The flip side of "Little Space Girl," on the Carlton record label, was a roarin' rockabilly tune called "Shake Baby Shake." Great ones that followed, like "Please Don't Tease," all failed to chart, but Jesse Lee Turner continued to turn out some great rockabilly numbers on various labels through 1962.

The Monument record label was cofounded by top Baltimore teen dance show host Buddy Deane, who was immortalized in the John Waters film *Hairspray* in the late 1980s. The label's first record, in the fall of '58, was by country artist Billy Grammer. It made the *Billboard* pop Top 10. The song was called "Gotta Travel On." It wasn't a rockabilly song, but it sold well to the teen market. Their second release has been considered rockabilly; it was "The Shag," by Delaware-born singer Billy Graves. "The Shag" reached #53 and stayed on the *Billboard* pop charts from late January to early April in 1959. For a nine-week run. It was a popular dance-type number with a bit of pop/rockabilly feel to it. It was real popular up and down the East Coast and especially in Baltimore and Washington, D.C., where both Billy Graves and Billy Grammer did many live shows at that time. Both of these guys had been regularly seen on Jimmy Dean's short-lived CBS network television show out of New York in 1958. "The Shag" is well remembered around Washington, D.C., but that song was Billy Graves's only dabble into rockabilly-type music.

Fraternity Records released what I guess you'd call a novelty rockabilly song in early December 1958, called "All American Boy." This was a really big record. It was patterned after Elvis and the Colonel. You know, about a rock 'n' roll star, his manager with a big cigar, and then he gets drafted by Uncle Sam. It was perfect timing, as Elvis was still at the top of the charts, but now he was over in Germany in the U.S. Army, and that was slowin' him up a bit. The teenage public loved it so much it stayed on the *Billboard* pop charts for sixteen weeks, until mid April 1959, and got up to a high position of #2. The artist who actually sang the song was Bobby Bare, who when the record started to hit was out of the country himself serving in the U.S. Army. The artist they listed as the singer for the record on the label was Bill Parsons. Parsons was also signed to Fraternity Records. Months later, after this record sold a million copies and was off the charts, and Bobby Bare found out about all this, he of course questioned the record label. Fraternity Records told Bobby Bare it had made a label error on the name of the artist. What Bare knew, though, was that Fraternity Records sent Bill Parsons out all over the country lip-synching "All American Boy" on shows like "Ed Sullivan" and "American Bandstand." Hey, that's show biz!

Rusty York made some good rockabilly records for over a half-dozen different record labels between 1958 and 1963. He spent a good portion of his time recording for the Cincinnati-based King Records, doin' some of his best rockabilly songs there. But he found his only *Billboard* pop chart success with Chess Records, in late July 1959, when his screamin' rockabilly number called "Sugaree" made it up to #77 but then quickly fell off the charts after only three weeks. Rusty York established his place in rockabilly history, 'cause his version of "Sugaree" sure holds up as one of the best examples of wild-soundin' rockabilly you'd ever want to hear. It's a shame that King Records never could break through with a big hit rockabilly song, 'cause man, no label tried any harder between 1956 and 1960 to do so. They'd have to wait twenty years for the great music they recorded by such artists as Charlie Feathers, Mac Curtis, Hank Mizell, Bob and Lucille, and a lot of others to really be appreciated. I reckon in the late fifties they were recordin' rockabilly the right way, raw and tough, and that turned out to be wrong in the eyes of the powers that controlled the music industry. But it's held up over the years, while the rest really haven't.

Gene Summers was born and raised in Dallas. He made several great rockabilly 45s for the local Jan record label. None ever made the *Billboard* pop charts, but his song "Straight Skirt" was a big hit in Washington, D.C., where I was in 1959. I bought all three of Gene's Jan Records singles back then. Every one of 'em was pure, hard-drivin', fanatical rockabilly at its best. Songs like "School of Rock 'n' Roll," "Gotta Lotta That," "Straight Skirt," and "Twixteen" were more than a rockabilly fan could ask for back in 1959. In 1979, Robert Gordon covered one of Gene Summers's best bluesy rockabilly numbers from that period when he did the song "Nervous." Robert's version came out on RCA Records and was a big audience pleaser. Rockabilly bands still cover Gene's songs, though he never had a national hit.

All three of Gene's Jan rockabilly 45s have meant a lot to me since 1959, 'cause they're the perfect examples of what a great rockabilly vocalist should sound like, yesterday or today.

During the late summer and fall of 1958, Robin Luke had a song called "Susie Darling," which has been called rockabilly on some reissue albums in the past fifteen years. To me, it's not rockabilly, but for those who consider it to be, the song reached #5 on the *Billboard* pop charts and had a seventeen-week run in late 1958. After that, Robin Luke never was on any of the *Billboard* charts ever again.

Then there was a guy they put under the rockabilly banner in the spring of 1959. His name was Stan Robinson. He was the new, next guy to have a release on Monument Records after Billy Graves's song "The Shag" died out. Stan's song was called "Boom-A-Dip-Dip." For four weeks, from the end of March till the end of April 1959, "Boom-A-Dip-Dip" was on the *Billboard* pop charts and eventually got to a high position of only #83. Robinson, like Luke, was also never to see another major chart record again.

Even though Link Wray and His Wray Men had a big *Billboard* pop Top 30 hit with "Rumble" in 1958 and "Rawhide" in 1959, I want to leave Link go until later chapters, because he was important in the D.C. area during the 1960s and 1970s in helping keep rockabilly music alive and well.

Although country superstar George Jones don't like to talk about his great rockabilly song "Rock It" on the Starday record label back in 1955, where he sounds like a half-crazed Texas wildcat tryin' to grab a slice of the pie Elvis was then enjoying, Buck Owens don't mind talkin' about his days when he was startin' out doin' rockabilly down in Texas. He's not ashamed one bit of his great rockabilly song called "Hot Dog," on the tiny Pep record label, which he cut down in Texas in 1956. British rockabilly revival artist Shakin' Stevens redid the song in the late 1970s for Epic Records, released both in Europe and here in the States, and Buck Owens himself even recut "Hot Dog" back in the late eighties. Ole Buck still sounded great on it. Buck Owens told me in 1991, "Hey, rockabilly was happenin' in '56, and I did it. What's the matter with that? The folks still sometimes ask for it, and I still do it. I like doin' it, and I feel I ought to give my audiences what they want to hear most, no matter what it is." Way to go, Buck!

Dickie Lee had two 45 releases on Sun Records in 1957 and 1958. Both, I guess, come under the rockabilly banner 'cause they had that distinctive Sun studio sound, but they were in a vein that's more teen/pop rockabilly. They didn't have any kind of a raw edge to 'em like others in '57 and '58 did. Dickie went on in the sixties to find success on the *Billboard* pop charts with a couple of teen/tragedy songs, "Patches," which reached #6 in late '62, and "Laurie (Strange Things Happen)," which reached #14 in the summer of '65. Then from '71 to '81 he had a string of twenty hits on the country charts. He also wrote some of the biggest hits in country music since the early 1960s, starting with George Jones's 1962 #1 country classic "She Thinks I Still Care." Though never really thought of by most as a rockabilly artist, Dickie Lee did start out at Sun Records when it was still shining bright, and he certainly did go on to leave his mark in both the pop and country fields. Also, I've got to say that he's just a plain and simple real nice genuine person. He still works today as a writer for one of Nashville's biggest publishing companies.

That's pretty close to every rockabilly-soundin' song I can think of that made it onto the *Billboard* pop charts between 1955 and 1959. Plus, I've put plenty of detail into the artists who were influential (especially to me) in rockabilly music during that period, even if they didn't make the charts. I know there's probably some others you think I should have mentioned, but you may be surprised when you find their names later in this book. A lot of space had to be given to the decade of the 1950s, because that was when rockabilly music was at its peak. But I don't feel you'll be disappointed by the remaining chapters in this book. Though some may be a bit shorter, you'll find that rockabilly music has always been influential, not only in my life, but in many others' around the world also. To round out the decade of the 1950s, I'll mention some local and national acts that never had big chart hits but were important to me when I saw 'em on "The Milt Grant Teen TV Dance Show."

In June 1959, a guy and a girl were down on the Milt Grant show, and before they went on the air, the guy told me they had a rockabilly record out and asked me if I'd like one. I didn't know who they were, so I told this teenage guy sure. I didn't know who they were, but I'd always take a free record. He also wanted to give me a fan club card of theirs and wanted to put me in their fan club. Well, I accepted the card as well as the record, but I was never a fan club joiner and wasn't about to start with somebody I'd never heard of. I didn't care if they

were on Decca Records. They called themselves Jamie and Jane. The record he gave me was called "Snuggle Up Baby." I got it home and played it, and it sounded like maybe teen rockabilly, but not the real kind of rockabilly I was into. It was over ten years later that I found out this teenage Jamie guy who was singin' with his Jane girl on the record was actually Gene Pitney!

Dudley Callicut was real popular around D.C. in 1958 and 1959 with his great song "Get Ready Baby," on D.C. Records. I saw him at that time on "Milt Grant" and at a couple of live record hops. Dudley's rockabilly killer song became so popular in the eighties and nineties, it's still bein' bootlegged on 45s today. I'll bet it sold more in the past five years than it ever did when it was first released in the late fifties.

Of course, Jerry Dallman was on "The Milt Grant Show" in 1959 when his record of "The Bug" was hot. Jerry did all the local record hops. Terry and The Pirates were still singin' their great song "What'd He Say," one of the toughest rockabilly records to ever come out of D.C., and the first that I can remember by a local group. They were still great in 1959.

There was this crazy guy known as "The Cat" who had a record out in 1959, and it was good rockabilly, too. Maybe that's why my copy got stolen at a party shortly after "The Cat" gave it to me. To this day, I still can't remember the record label it was on, but the rockabilly side of the 45 was a song called "Calhoun." I liked him enough to take pictures of him at a local record hop back in '59.

As far as rockabilly or solid rock 'n' roll music in the fifties goes, the best group to come out of Baltimore was without a doubt The Chavis Brothers. They achieved some national recognition in the late fifties and early sixties with major record releases on the Clock and Brunswick record labels. Their records really sound great and hold up today as well as any wild rockabilly sounds you'd ever want to hear. Several of their hottest songs have been reissued on various European import compilation albums. The group turned to country music in the early seventies but stayed together, regularly playin' various Baltimore clubs, until the early eighties.

Barry Darvel was a local singer who was on the D.C.-based Colt 45 record label and made some real good rockabilly and rock 'n' roll records in 1959 and 1960, like "Geronimo Stomp" and "Have Gun, Will Travel." I liked him back then, and he became real popular on the

D.C. scene. In the early and mid sixties, he recorded for major labels such as Atlantic, Cub, Columbia, and World Artists. In 1959 and 1960, Milt Grant used him quite a bit at his hops all around D.C., Maryland, and northern Virginia. I got to know Barry pretty well back then, and later booked him for dances into the mid sixties.

Mark Damon was a movie star who starred in low-budget teenage juvenile delinquent films between 1958 and 1960. Well, during the summer of 1959, he came on "The Milt Grant TV Show" also. Mark signed a picture to me and gave me some record he had out with The Jordanaires on the Wynne record label. He seemed like a nice guy, and later that night I went out and saw him at a local record hop and shot some photos of him. He was being billed as rockabilly also.

The Rockabilly Attitude

Back in the 1950s and even into the 1960s, rockabilly wasn't just the music. It was a new, daring, defiant lifestyle with a touch of exciting danger in it that you had to live and breathe every day. The frantic drivin' beat and lyrics of the music was the fuel to keep the blood runnin' through your veins so your motor would run hot, hard, and fast. If you were between twelve and twenty back then, you didn't care what price you had to pay, you had to take the chance, even if you were flirtin' with danger. For a fourteen-year-old kid like I was in 1959, it meant flushin' a lit cherry bomb down a toilet at the Catholic school — and never admitting it, no matter how much the nuns beat or threatened me. You find out when you get older like me, I mean in your forties and fifties, that the only things in life you'll come to regret are the chances you didn't take. If you think rockabilly is just music, you're wrong. Rockabilly's always been an attitude.

I don't like to use movies for an example, 'cause they're pretend. But when teenagers in the fifties and early sixties were watchin' Marlon Brando in *The Wild One*, James Dean in *Rebel without a Cause*, Elvis in *Loving You* and *Jailhouse Rock*, and Robert Mitchum in *Thunder Road*, they were witnessing the rockabilly attitude. These were all actors portraying young cats who were goin' against the grain, were tired of the greedy crooked establishment they lived in, they all wanted to be free of the chains that bound 'em in the past and weren't gonna take no grief from nobody. When you heard Johnny Burnette screamin' out to you to "Tear It Up," he wasn't just talking about a dance floor, he was talkin' about how you wanted to live your life. Presley, Burnette, Vincent, Perkins, Lewis, and all the other original fifties rockabillys played some mean, tough juke joints. They smoked cigarettes, drank a lot, took some amphetamines, and did some other wild, hairy things.

I know some of the bands that call themselves rockabilly today in the nineties think that by copying the old fifties cats' rockabilly music, puttin' on a motorcycle jacket, stackin' your hair up a foot high and wearin' tattoos makes 'em a rockabilly. Well, I'll give 'em credit for takin' the chance to be different, but that just ain't all there is to it. If you're a true rockabilly, you play it, do it, and live it, 'cause you love it. And you stick to it. It's always stuck with me my whole life, and it always will.

I got into all aspects of the rockabilly business in the sixties and later on, but from the beginning, I've always been and stayed a fan of both the true rockabilly music and attitude that was created back in the 1950s.

The Sixties:
Down but Comin' Back

Going Pop, to Europe,
or Headin' Back to the Country

The big event in rock 'n' roll and rockabilly music early in 1960 was Elvis's discharge from the Army, which came in early March. Music had changed drastically since June 1958, when Elvis recorded his final session shortly before leaving for Germany with his Army unit. During those twenty-two months, the powers that be in the music business had stopped everything that sounded like rock 'n' roll or rockabilly from making it into the *Billboard* Top 10. Looking back now, there's no way anyone could blame Elvis for the death of rockabilly and solid rock 'n' roll music during the short time he'd been away. But at the time, in March 1960, I did expect something more rockin' than his first new single, "Stuck On You." I knew Elvis could do whatever he wanted and blow off any of the new silly teen, pop, no-talent bunch. It had only been a short five months since October 1959, when his last new 45 single record, "A Big Hunk o' Love," was still on the *Billboard* charts. This song was everything rockabilly and rock 'n' roll music were all about. It was screamin', scorchin', blisterin', frantic, blood-and-guts Elvis at his best.

Even though over the years it's been written that Elvis always chose the music he recorded (except for songs used in his sixties movies), and I know that to be true, Elvis could only choose from what he was given to choose from. And from a business standpoint, Colonel Parker made sure during the 1960s that Elvis would only hear and choose from songs where the publishing rights either all or mostly went to the two publishing companies Elvis owned with him. When his album *Elvis is Back* was released in April 1960, it's clear that Elvis did make great choices on the songs he decided to record. This album is not a rockabilly album, but what it turned out to be is the last great down-and-dirty rock 'n' roll album Elvis would ever do. The youthful hillbilly and rockabilly cat of 1954 and '55 proved on *Elvis is Back* in 1960 that though he had matured, there wasn't a white man alive who could deliver black blues classics such as

"Reconsider Baby," "Like a Baby," and "Such a Night" the way he could do it. "Dirty, Dirty Feelin' " and "Make Me Know It" also proved he was still better than anyone out there who was still tryin' to lay down rock 'n' roll the right way. Elvis had no choice in what his record label would push as the 45s to be played on radio, so of course it would be many years before later-day music critics and historians realized how great some of his 1960s songs really were. Even though I never gave up on Elvis's music and even his mostly stupid movies of the mid to late sixties, which he himself publicly admitted many times during the seventies he hated making, it was real clear that his rockabilly days were gone forever. But there were still quite a few others who were not ready to give up on rockabilly as yet.

Ray Smith

One of my personal all-time favorite rockabilly artists, Ray Smith, finally broke through on January 4, 1960, when "Rockin' Little Angel" debuted on the *Billboard* pop charts and reached a peak position of #22 but had a long ride of sixteen weeks on those charts. Ray Smith was now on Judd Records, which was owned by Sam Phillips's brother, Judd Phillips. Ray had three of the best rockabilly 45s released on Sun Records in 1958 and '59. Those rockabilly tunes on Sun, including "Right Behind You Baby," "So Young," "You Made a Hit," and "Rockin' Bandit," all got the spirit of what rockabilly music's all about. Although they failed to chart at the time they were released, twenty years later and up to the present day they're now being appreciated by new generations of rockabilly fans around the world.

Ray Smith's follow-up record to "Rockin' Little Angel" debuted on the *Billboard* pop charts on May 9, 1960. It was a rockabilly version of the old pop standard song "Put Your Arms around Me Honey." This song is great, but it wasn't quite as strong as "Rockin' Little Angel." It only stayed on the *Billboard* pop charts for two weeks, reaching a peak position of only #91. What made this song, as well as most of Ray Smith's songs from the late fifties throughout the sixties, rockabilly was Ray Smith's tremendous rockabilly vocal style. This cat was always able to come through with one of the best southern rockabilly vocal styles you'd ever want to hear. I could always feel it! That's what rockabilly's always been about since Elvis stumbled onto it: the feel. Ray Smith was one cat who definitely had that feel.

"Rockin' Little Angel" stayed on the charts so long and sold over a half million records the first three months after it hit the charts that Judd Records released a real good rockabilly album on Ray Smith in the spring of 1960, called *Travelin' with Ray*. Judd Records released two more 45s that failed to chart. But all four of the songs couldn't be beat for late 1960 and early 1961. "Makes Me Feel Good," "One Wonderful Love," "Blonde Hair and Blue Eyes," and "You Don't Want Me" are all worthy to be in any rockabilly fan's record collection.

After Ray Smith left Judd Records, he went on to record for well over a dozen record labels between 1961 and 1979. Throughout the 1960s, Ray's releases on labels such as Sun Records (which he came back to in 1961 and '62), Warner Brothers Records, Infinity Records, Tollie Records, Smash Records, Celebrity Circle Records, and Diamond Records were mostly all in the rockabilly/rock 'n' roll vein. Ray had some outstanding rockabilly songs released on some of those labels during the 1960s. But as the seventies came in, pop music sure

didn't want any part of southern rockabilly cats. By 1973 and '74, Ray Smith finally succumbed to Nashville's country music sound.

Ray first recorded for ABC Records in Nashville before moving over to Cinnamon Records during 1973 and '74. Cinnamon Records was having a lot of success then with another old rockabilly artist from the late fifties who had also tried out for Sun Records, Narvel Felts. From having been around both Narvel Felts and Ray Smith, it's easy for me to see why Narvel Felts found his greatest success in Nashville and country music and Ray Smith couldn't achieve the same thing. Narvel's a nice, easy-going, willin'-to-please-you kind of guy, and that's what you have to be if you stand a chance of makin' it in Nashville. Ray Smith, on the other hand, was a whole different personality.

After his try in Nashville failed, Ray had 45 and LP releases on Corona and Wix Records between 1975 and '78. The rockabilly revival thing hit big both in the U.S. and Europe in the late seventies, and in '78 and '79, Ray made several trips to audiences who remembered him and loved his rockabilly music of the late fifties and early sixties. There's no need to get into what happened or why, but on November 29, 1979, Ray Smith took his own life at the age of forty-five. By this time, a lot had changed in both music and life around us. I know music certainly got worse, for the most part.

One of my favorite Ray Smith songs has always been "So Young," which came out on Sun Records in 1958. When

Forgettin' to Remember to Forget

I first met Ray Smith on a bitter cold January day in 1960 when he came in and lip-synched "Rockin' Little Angel" on Milt Grant's teen dance TV show. I knew ahead of time he was gonna be one of the guests on the show that day, so I brought in his Sun Records 45s for him to autograph. Ray flipped out when he saw I had all three of 'em. It really made him feel good that teenagers in the North, like me, liked his music a lot. Ray was warm, friendly, and on top of the world that day. He gave me his home address and a couple of phone numbers I could reach him at around Memphis, where he and Judd Records were both based at the time. Ray Smith made such a lasting impression on me of being a cat that just loved hard-drivin' rockabilly and real rock 'n' roll that I got ahold of him by phone during Christmastime 1965 and asked him if he'd come up to the Washington, D.C., area and headline an all-rockabilly/rock 'n' roll show I was planning to put on in April 1966. Ray was more than happy to agree to do the show for me, but I'll wait until the next chapter to get into that.

I think of and remember Ray Smith and all the great rockabilly music he gave us, "So Young" is how I'll always remember him.

Memphis, Tennessee

As far as Memphis went, which was where rockabilly music was born, by 1960 Sun Records and Sam Phillips were no longer the force and power they had been only a couple years earlier in mainstream music. In the early and mid 1950s, Sam Phillips had virtually no competition in the city of Memphis as he continued to release blues, R&B, rockabilly, and hillbilly 45s and build his little studio and record company into a power in the music industry like no one else in Memphis had ever seen before. But by 1960, Sam and Sun's light had dimmed considerably. Even though Sam opened the largest, most advanced studio Memphis had ever seen in 1960, leaving behind his old tiny one at 706 Union (which he readily admits today gave him his greatest sound ever), he couldn't withstand the competition of the new labels in Memphis during the first few years of the 1960s that would go on to have huge hits in pop and R&B music throughout the sixties and into the seventies.

Though Judd Records had only short-lived success with Ray Smith, as did Rita Records out of Memphis with another Sun rockabilly reject, Harold Dorman, and his 1960 *Billboard* hit "Mountain of Love," other labels, such as Hi Records, had consistent *Billboard* pop chart hits, most notably with the Bill Black Combo. As you probably know, Bill Black was Elvis's original rockabilly bass player from 1954 to 1957, but from the beginning of 1960 into early 1965, the Bill Black Combo charted seventeen instrumental singles on the *Billboard* pop charts. Bill Black died from a brain tumor on October 21, 1965, but Hi Records kept releasing new 45s and lots of instrumental albums for another ten years or so after his death.

The Bill Black Combo remained a big-time lounge and club act well into the 1970s, after Sun Records had long been gone from Memphis. After Bill Black's death, the group charted one final record on the *Billboard* pop charts in 1968. During the decade of the 1960s, the Bill Black Combo had more *Billboard* chart hits than any other instrumental rock 'n' roll band. That means they had more than Duane Eddy, Booker T. and the MG's, or Junior Walker and the All Stars. The others may be better remembered, but the Bill Black Combo had more chart hits, and some big ones, like "White Silver Sands," "Don't Be Cruel," and "Smokie."

Hi Records had a couple of *Billboard* pop hits on rockabilly artists also. One was Gene Simmons. Gene was from Elvis's home town, Tupelo, Mississippi. After doin' several sessions at Sun Records for Sam Phillips during 1956 and '57, Gene finally had one release on Sun in April 1958. Gene's wild, rampaging, passionate singin' on one of the songs on that Sun 45, "Drinkin' Wine," certainly earns him a place in rockabilly music history. "Drinkin' Wine" failed to sell very well outside the South, and it didn't come close to makin' the national charts, so Gene did a short stint with Checker Records in 1960 before comin' back to Memphis in 1961, where Hi Records soon started issuing 45s on him. Gene Simmons was nicknamed Jumpin' Gene Simmons because of his wild stage act. It took awhile, but Gene Simmons finally hit the *Billboard* pop charts on August 8, 1964, with about the closest thing to rockabilly music you could find right in the middle of Beatlemania and at the height of the British Invasion. The song he finally hit with was called "Haunted House," which as the years went by turned into a Halloween classic. "Haunted House" peaked out at #11 and stayed on the *Billboard* pop charts for eleven weeks. Hi Records released an album at the time, titled *Jumpin' Gene Simmons,* but Gene's follow-up 45 record, called "The Dodo," only reached #83 on *Billboard* and fell off the charts after only three weeks. Gene continued to have releases on Hi Records into 1967 with no chart success.

Hi Records was still puttin' out rockabilly-oriented records through the late sixties. Most had no chart success, though, such as some real well-done songs Narvel Felts recorded. Narvel's only *Billboard* chart record up until this time had been when he hit the pop charts with a rockabilly cover version of the Drifters' 1954 R&B classic "Honey Love." Narvel's version hit the *Billboard* pop charts on February 8, 1960, but only reached #90 and was only on the charts for two weeks. "Honey Love" was on the Pink Records label, where Narvel also had several other fine rockabilly releases.

Narvel may have failed to chart with the now-changing sound of rockabilly music, but Arkansas-born rocker Jerry Jaye did manage to have a big rockabilly hit in 1967 on Hi Records. Jerry's rockabilly cover version of Fats Domino's 1960 hit song "My Girl Josephine" debuted on the *Billboard* pop charts on April 15, 1967, and reached a peak position of #29, staying on the charts for nine weeks.

While Hi Records took on a lot of the rockabilly and rock 'n' roll sound and artists that Sam Phillips started and controlled during the fifties, another Memphis label took over the black R&B and blues sound that Sam Phillips had also nurtured. Stax Records began the new sound of R&B, which soon turned into soul music. Former Sun Records artist Rufus Thomas was among those that had many big hits for Stax Records, along with his daughter Carla Thomas and the group Booker T. and the MG's, among many others. Stax Records had many big hits from 1961 through the late 1970s on the *Billboard* pop charts. But there were many other labels, both major and independent, that continued to chart with older and new rockabilly artists throughout the sixties in other parts of the U.S. besides Memphis.

I want to tell you next about four artists that are all considered today for makin' some of the greatest rockabilly music in the 1950s, but found their major national success later in pop or country music: Johnny Horton, Roy Orbison, Warren Smith, and Bob Luman.

Johnny Horton

Rockabilly and country legend Johnny Horton is best remembered on oldies radio stations for his three most famous country/pop and movie songs, "The Battle of New Orleans," "Sink the Bismarck," and "North to Alaska." All three made the *Billboard* pop charts, reaching highs of #1 (for six weeks straight), #3, and #4, respectively, all between April 1959 and February 1961. They all had long runs of four and five months each on the pop charts, as well as doin' the same on the country charts. But music fans don't really buy those big hit songs of the late Johnny Horton today. What rockabilly fans buy and steadily collect are all Johnny's rockabilly songs that he recorded for Columbia Records in Nashville between 1956 and 1958.

Johnny Horton was born on April 10, 1925, in Los Angeles. He made his first country records for the L.A.-based Cormac and Abbott record labels. His manager at the time was Fabor Robinson, who was able to obtain a regular weekly spot for Johnny on the famous "Louisiana Hayride" show starting in May 1952. By early 1953, Fabor Robinson got Johnny a new record deal with the major label Mercury Records. During September 1953, Johnny Horton married Hank Williams's second wife and widow, Billy Jean Jones. Starting in October 1954 and goin' all the way through 1955, Johnny witnessed the rise of the biggest rockabilly (or any) star "The Louisiana Hayride" ever had: Elvis Presley. Horton saw the hysterical reaction Elvis was gettin' and he felt like he could put across the same kind of music.

In 1955, when he approached the producers with Mercury in Nashville about doin' rockabilly, they told Johnny there was no way they would incorporate the kind of trash Presley was selling into country music. But by early 1956, when Johnny got out of his deal with Mercury after having no chart hits, he signed a new record deal with Columbia Records. Don Law was his new producer, and Johnny Horton laid down some of the finest rockabilly songs to ever come out of Nashville for the next two and a half years. His first five songs all made the *Billboard* country charts. Today, all five are considered rockabilly. In 1956, "Honky Tonk Man" reached #9 and "I'm a One Woman Man" reached #7. In 1957, the frantic "I'm Coming Home" made it to #11 and "The Woman I Need" hit #9. The fall of 1958 saw Johnny's final rockabilly chart song, "All Grown Up," reach #8 on the country charts.

He recorded many other great songs that are known around the world by rockabilly fans today. Songs like "Lovers Rock," "Honky Tonk Hardwood Floor," "Got the Bull by the Horns," "Let's Take the Long Way Home," and others are Johnny Horton at his rockabilly best, and today new young fans are discovering just how great his pre-"Battle of New Orleans" songs were. Around the world, this is the stuff that's marketable on Johnny Horton, and it's what keeps sellin'. 'Cause it was real, and you can feel it.

Even after Johnny Horton's death on November 5, 1960, in an auto accident, it was the rockabilly songs that were reissued and hit the charts. "Honky Tonk Man" was re-released in early March 1962 and not only made #11 on the *Billboard* country charts, staying for twelve weeks, but also for two weeks in early April 1962 made it to #96 on the pop charts. The following year, in February 1963, Columbia Records re-released "All Grown Up," and it reached a high of #26 on the *Billboard* pop charts.

Johnny Horton was one of the most influential rockabilly artists ever to come out of Nashville. Little did Dwight Yoakam's mama know when she was still carryin' Dwight in her belly in 1956 that Johnny Horton's new hit "Honky Tonk Man" would be the song that her baby boy would release exactly thirty years later, to the acclaim of both country and rock critics as the "new" sound in country music. After Dwight, George Jones, Marty Stuart, and others started recording Johnny Horton's rockabilly songs. Nashville has always seemed to find out too late what was sittin' in their vaults the whole time. Rockabilly bands and artists here in the States and overseas have been singin' Johnny Horton's rockabilly songs since the mid seventies, and even if Nashville gets onto somethin' new, which they're likely to, rockabilly kids all around the world will still always keep singin' Horton's rockabilly songs, 'cause those'll always be the ones that count the most when it comes to real, feel music.

Roy Orbison

Another artist who started out as a flat-out, hot rockabilly singer was Roy Orbison. Roy would find his greatest success between 1960 and 1964 as a pop vocalist. He was one of the all-time best and most talented pop vocalists right up to his death in 1989.

Roy was born in Vernon, Texas, raised in Wink, Texas, and formed his first band, called The Wink Westerners, in 1951 when he was thirteen years old. Roy and his band played shows and dances all during the early fifties, not only doin' the songs of Lefty Frizell, Webb Pierce, Slim Whitman, Roy Rogers, Gene Autry, and others, but also throwin' in some Glenn Miller and Benny Goodman pop standards, as well as Bob Wills's music.

After his high school graduation in 1954, Roy made a trip up to Dallas to see what all the fuss was about with somethin' called Elvis Presley, who was causing pandemonium by early 1955, when Roy saw Elvis perform on Dallas's "Big D Jamboree." Roy remembered, "I didn't like him at all back then. He just looked like a greasy punk kid to me, but all the girls were screamin' and trying to tear his clothes off, while their boyfriends looked like they were gonna knife him in the parking lot after the show. What I didn't like about him most of all back then was he told some really dirty, crude jokes in between his songs, and he talked like he had a mouth full of mush. He really did have a whole lot of energy and jumped around a lot back then. Later, during the sixties, when I met him, we became friends, and I found out he was a pretty decent guy."

Whatever Roy thought when he first saw Elvis early in '55, it made enough impact on him to start thinking about changing his direction in the music he was then doing. By the spring of 1955, The Wink Westerners were now called Roy Orbison and The Teen Kings. By the time Roy Orbison started his second year of college in September 1955, Roy Orbison and The Teen Kings already had their own local TV show on KOSA-TV in Odessa, Texas. Roy was the show's host. They played their music as well as having special guests from the area

and others better-known from other areas. Both Elvis and Johnny Cash were guests on Roy's TV show during the latter part of 1955. Johnny Cash liked Roy and told him that he should get in touch with Sam Phillips at Sun Records, though when Roy contacted Phillips in late 1955, Sam told Roy in no uncertain terms, "Johnny Cash don't run my damn record company."

Also in late 1955, Wade Moore and Dick Penner, who were students with Roy at North Texas State College, brought him this song they had written, called "Ooby Dooby." They thought Roy should try it out. These same two guys, Wade and Dick, later had one release on Sun Records called "Bop, Bop, Baby" in the spring of 1957, which was a pretty good rockabilly number, though it had no success at the time. Roy liked "Ooby Dooby" enough to go up to Dallas and do a demo session at the request of Jim Beck, where an acetate was made and forwarded to Columbia Records in Nashville. This was sometime in December 1955. The Columbia Records people in Nashville didn't care for the singer, but they gave the acetate of the song to a country group that was doin' some material to try to reach the new teenage audience. The group they gave "Ooby Dooby" to was a popular Texas group they had under contract on Columbia Records, called Sid King and The Five Strings. They cut "Ooby Dooby" on March 6, 1956. A day earlier, on March 5, Roy Orbison and The Teen Kings cut "Ooby Dooby" once more, at Norman Petty's studio in Clovis, New Mexico. An executive at the Gulf Oil company had a small record label in Texas called Je-well Records, which wanted to release the song immediately, as Roy Orbison and The Teen Kings were real popular in a lot of parts of Texas.

"Ooby Dooby" was on the radio and in record stores within ten days of when Roy recorded it. It started sellin' well right away, especially in the record shops in Midland and Odessa, Texas, that Cecil Holifield owned. Holifield had booked Elvis on shows in his area and was selling records on a number of Sun artists at the time. He called up Sam Phillips, played "Ooby Dooby" over the phone for him, and told him it was sellin' big. Sam Phillips told him to send him a copy right away. Sam and Sun were ridin' high in both the pop and country charts then with Carl Perkins's "Blue Suede Shoes" and Johnny Cash's "Folsom Prison Blues," but when he got the Je-well version of "Ooby Dooby" and heard it, he contacted Roy Orbison and told him to come to Memphis right away, as he wanted to recut "Ooby Dooby" and release it on Sun Records. Sam told him to bring his group The

Teen Kings with him. It had taken Sam Phillips five years of hard work with Sun Records, and now after sellin' Elvis over to RCA Victor Records, he was finally out of debt and had made a name for himself and his label, especially in rockabilly music, and he wasn't about to take any chances that a little label in Texas might break out big with a song that easily fit into the sound of music he started. So by mid April 1956, Roy Orbison and The Teen Kings recut "Ooby Dooby" for the third and final time, along with several other songs. Sam released "Ooby Dooby" in early May 1956, and within two weeks it was in the Top 10 in Memphis and several other big markets.

Roy Orbison and The Teen Kings went home to Texas after the recording session, and a month later they got a call from Sam Phillips to get back up to Memphis, 'cause "Ooby Dooby" was sellin' and breakin' into the charts, and he was puttin' 'em out on tour with Johnny Cash, Carl Perkins, and Warren Smith. Sam had arranged for Bob Neal, who had managed and booked Elvis from the fall of 1954 to the fall of 1955, and went on to do the same thing for virtually all of Sun Records' top and rising new stars, to manage Roy and his group. Neal and Phillips were old friends, had a deal worked out, and worked closely, so Roy Orbison and The Teen Kings were out on the road on the Memphis and Sun package shows starting in May 1956.

"Ooby Dooby" debuted on the *Billboard* pop charts on June 16, 1956, reaching a peak position of #59 and staying on the charts for eight weeks. They say it sold somewhere around 200,000 copies during the summer of 1956. The version by Sid King and The Five Strings on Columbia Records failed to chart. It didn't hold up near as well or have the punch that Roy Orbison's had and what was expected in rockabilly music at the time. But in July 1956 RCA Victor released a version of "Ooby Dooby" by Janis Martin that certainly did hold up against Roy's version. Though it failed to make the national charts, it had as good a feel and spontaneity as Roy Orbison's version had. But it was Roy Orbison who had the major chart record and got the big sales on "Ooby Dooby."

Sam Phillips wanted a follow-up record, so in between Roy's constant touring, he brought Roy and The Teen Kings back in the studio during the summer of '56 and cut another session, out of which came two great rockabilly songs. "Rockhouse" was put on the A side of the resulting single, and one of the two greatest rockabilly

songs Johnny Cash ever wrote, called "You're My Baby," was used for the B side. Sam released this record in late September 1956. The record got rave reviews in both *Billboard* and *Cash Box,* and though it broke out in several major markets and sold fairly well, it failed to chart on the major charts. The sound was still the older, though high-energy and wild, more primitive sound of rockabilly music, which was just startin' to change and mature a little by the fall of 1956.

Roy Orbison had started writing songs while he was out on the road tourin'. He had written a lot of 'em by the time he went in to record his next session at Sun Records, which would produce the two songs for his next 45. One was called "Devil Doll," which is what I call an excellent rockabilly ballad, and the other was a mid-tempo rockabilly number called "Sweet and Easy to Love." Roy knew Elvis had The Jordanaires backing him up, so he brought in a backup vocal group he knew in Texas, called The Roses, for these two songs. They're both great rockabilly songs, but once again, after Sam Phillips put this new 45 out in late January 1957, it failed to chart and didn't sell as well as "Rockhouse" had, even though Roy continued to tour promotin' it during the late winter and spring of 1957. It was at the start of this session in December 1956 that Roy's band, The Teen Kings, got into a heated disagreement with Roy because they were no longer getting equal splits in pay and royalties. When Sam Phillips signed Roy Orbison to a contract on Sun Records, and Bob Neal signed Roy to an exclusive booking contract, it was only Roy who was signed, not The Teen Kings. But according to several members of his band, Roy had agreed right from the beginning that all the money they made would be split equally, five ways, among each of 'em. Well, Roy didn't see it this way anymore by December 1956, so the four Teen Kings left the Sun studios and headed back home to Texas. Roy did his session with the regular Sun house band of Roland Janes, Stan Kesler, and James Van Eaton. When Roy went back out on tour during 1957, he just used other artists' backup bands, such as Warren Smith's. His fans didn't know the difference.

Roy went on and kept writing songs, touring, and doing several more sessions for Sun Records until the spring of 1958. From a session Roy did during October 1957, Sam Phillips would release two songs by Roy that would turn out to be his fourth and final release while he was still contracted to Sun Records, "I Like Love" b/w "Chicken Hearted." Today, if you collect Sun Records and find this single, you'll have to pay more for it, because it not only never came close to hittin' the charts, but it also sold way less than any of his three previous records at Sun.

Early in 1958, Roy married his first wife, Claudette Frady, who lived in Odessa, Texas, and he was tired and disgusted at how his career had been handled for the almost two years he had been at Sun Records. So when the spring of 1958 rolled around, he wanted out of the remaining time left on his Sun Records contract. Sam Phillips's concentration now was with Jerry Lee Lewis (which was about to end up a disaster), but he only agreed to give Roy his release if he relinquished all his copyrights and gave Sam full rights to everything he wrote and recorded while at Sun. Roy agreed to give 'em all up with the exception of the song "Claudette," which he had given to the Everly Brothers. Sam agreed to that.

Roy and his wife moved back to Odessa. After several months in Texas with only occasional live performances, Roy signed a deal with Wesley Rose of Acuff/Rose Publishers in Nashville. They published all of the Everly Brothers songs, and the song "Claudette" by the Everly Brothers had reached #30 on the *Billboard* pop charts as the B side of "All I Have to Do Is Dream" during the early summer of 1958. Acuff/Rose would wind up publishing all of the songs Roy wrote from then on. Wesley Rose also got Roy signed to a one-year contract with RCA Victor by the late summer of 1958. Roy had two pop/teen-sounding 45 singles released in late '58 and the spring of 1959. After both 45s failed badly, and RCA wasn't going to renew Roy's contract, Wesley Rose signed Roy to Monument Records.

Roy's first 45 on the Monument label was released in the early fall of 1959. That 45, "With the Bug" b/w "Paper Boy," failed to chart, but Roy's second release, "Uptown," debuted on the *Billboard* pop charts on January 18, 1960. "Uptown" is considered by some as a mid-tempo rockabilly song. Rockabilly revivalist Robert Gordon certainly thought so when he recorded "Uptown" on his first album for RCA Victor in 1979. Roy's version only made it up to #72 on the pop charts, staying on the charts for six weeks, but it was the start of twenty consecutive *Billboard* pop chart songs for him on

Forgettin' to Remember to Forget

I first met Roy Orbison during the fall of 1960 when he came through the Washington, D.C., area and appeared on the Milt Grant show to promote his follow-up hit to "Only the Lonely," called "Blue Angel." Even back then he seemed like a quiet, reserved, almost shy kind of guy. He seemed genuine and seemed to appreciate the fact that I liked his Sun Records from a few years earlier as well as his new recordings at the time.

It would be another twenty-two years before I'd get to talk to Roy Orbison again. He was singing at the Bayou Nightclub in Washington, D.C., in 1982. The place was packed to capacity, with around 500 screamin' fans in attendance. One of D.C.'s top rockabilly vocalists and musicians, Billy Hancock, and his group The Tennessee Rockets opened up the show with, as always, an energetic set of solid rockabilly music. Roy's two sets really were great, as he of course did all of his big hit ballads, but mixed 'em in with a few of his rockabilly tunes, such as "Ooby Dooby," "Mean Woman Blues," and of course "Oh Pretty Woman."

After the show, I got to go backstage and talk with Roy in his dressing room. He was still the same calm, gentle, and sensitive person I'd met twenty-two years earlier. I asked him if he'd always done "Ooby Dooby" in his shows. Roy said, "I just started doin' 'Ooby Dooby' a few years ago when I started goin' back to Europe. I really hadn't sung any of those songs since the fifties. When I got to Europe, though, the new generation of fans there knew 'em all, so I put 'Ooby Dooby' back into my sets. The couple years I spent with Sun Records were a learning experience. Rockabilly music was what the big thing at the time was, and it gave me a chance to break into the music business, but I always wanted to write and sing good, strong songs with a meaning behind them. I still love all the old rockabilly songs, though, and I'm glad a lot of people remember them. But I'm always looking ahead, and trends in music change all the time, so I just always try to come up with something fresh and new, and it's always been the ballads I've been most fond of."

Monument Records, going through to the summer of 1965. The hits that followed "Uptown" all made the *Billboard* Top 40 charts, with two reaching #1 and nine others reaching the Top 10. Though Roy left Monument Records in 1965 and moved over to the MGM Records label, which would only produce a half dozen mediocre *Billboard* chart hits and songs through 1967, he had left his mark as not only a big pop ballad singer of the early 1960s, but also one who could deliver the best rock 'n' roll and rockabilly songs that became big hits between 1960 and 1964. I'm glad we had Roy Orbison during that period to hear on the radio.

Roy scored a #2 *Billboard* pop hit with "Only the Lonely" during the summer and fall of 1960. His follow-up song, "Blue Angel," reached #9 in November 1960. As his next 45 single on Monument, "Running Scared," was headin' for the #1 spot on the *Billboard* pop charts in spring 1961 (it hit #1 on June 5), Sam Phillips released Roy's first and only rockabilly album, appropriately titled *Rockhouse*. Even before Sam released this great album, he had reissued Roy's third release for his label, "Sweet and Easy to Love" b/w "Devil Doll," in late November 1960 to cash in on Roy's newfound pop success. While teenagers like me in 1961 were happy to get our hands on a new album with five of Roy's best songs Sun had released on 45s plus seven new ones, which included two of the best rockabilly numbers Roy ever did in "Problem Child" and "Mean Little Mama," this move by Sam Phillips really upset Roy Orbison. It's been said that Roy got so mad that he drove down to Memphis and walked up to Sam and told Sam he'd better hand him over every unissued master he had on him. Of course that was a joke as far as Sam was concerned at the time. Roy didn't get the tapes. But Roy, to say the least, didn't like the exploitation of his hard-earned success. Roy Orbison, though, even as early as 1961, had learned the hard way, music was a business first.

After Roy's classic ballad hits, which he always preferred over the rockers, quit comin' in the mid sixties, other artists started havin' *Billboard* pop chart hits with 'em. First Jay and The Americans hit #25 in the late spring of 1966 with "Crying." In February 1969, Sonny James hit #92 with "Only the Lonely." Sonny's version hit #1 on the *Billboard* country charts around the same time. During the fall of 1977, Linda Ronstadt took "Blue Bayou" to #3. Then Don McLean had his second and final *Billboard* Top 10 pop hit with "Crying" during the late winter and early spring of 1981, when it got all the way up to #5. Then one year later, the hard rock group Van Halen, which had been selling millions of *Billboard* chart top albums since 1978 but weren't having much luck on the singles charts for radio airplay, had their biggest pop chart success up to that time with Roy Orbison's classic 1964 rockabilly or rock 'n' roll (whichever you prefer) #1 hit "Oh Pretty Woman." Van Halen's rock version reached #12 during the spring of 1982. After Roy's death, "Oh Pretty Woman" by him remains probably his best-remembered song since the release of Julia Roberts's hit film *Pretty Woman*.

One other interesting note for rockabilly fans was that when "Blue Bayou" was released as the A side of Roy's new 45 single in the late summer of 1963, the rockabilly tune "Mean Woman Blues," from Elvis's 1957 film *Loving You*, was used for the B side. Now, all six of Roy Orbison's previous Top 10 *Billboard* pop chart hits had been ballads, with the exception of "Dream Baby," which was a solid mid-tempo rocker. But when "Blue Bayou" came out backed with "Mean Woman Blues," the disc jockeys here in the U.S. picked up on the B side during a time when Roy Orbison was on tour with The Beatles in Europe. "Mean Woman Blues" by Roy broke onto the *Billboard* pop charts on September 7, 1963, reached a high position of #5, and stayed on the charts for thirteen weeks. "Blue Bayou" came on the *Billboard* pop charts a week later, but only reached #29, staying on the charts for ten weeks. The rockabilly side (and by today's standards of rockabilly music, it is rockabilly), "Mean Woman Blues," was a much bigger hit than "Blue Bayou," but over the years "Blue Bayou" has always been thought of as the big hit for Roy. "Mean Woman Blues" is best remembered by Elvis from back in 1957. Roy Orbison did one whale of a rockin' version of "Mean Woman Blues" for this late date, when rockabilly music was all but dead on the *Billboard* pop charts. But most of the time, through rockabilly music's hardest times, whenever a major label puts it out there and gives it half a chance of doin' something on the big-time charts, it usually always comes through.

Throughout the seventies and eighties, every rockabilly song Roy Orbison ever even fooled around with was released, mostly in Europe, and went on to sell millions of records. Bands both in the U.S. and in other parts of the world continue to cover Roy's rockabilly songs. They all know that Roy was no wild, hip-shakin' rockabilly cat of the late fifties, but the rockabilly music he did and left behind can't be denied. Roy Orbison could rock with the best of 'em.

Warren Smith

I like all types of rockabilly music as long as I can feel it and it's done the way it was meant to be. But I have to admit that the kind of rockabilly I like the most from the fifties rockabilly artists was the "billy" sound of rockabilly. Not that I don't like the "rock" side of rockabilly, but the side with a hillbilly edge has always been my personal favorite. Warren Smith was one of the first early rockabilly artists who captured and shined on both of these sounds. Warren had five 45 releases between April 1956 and February 1959, while he was one among the many up-and-coming rockabilly artists on Sun Records. Although Warren was only able to put one rockabilly song, called "So Long, I'm Gone" (written by Roy Orbison), on the *Billboard* pop charts for only two weeks in June 1957, peaking out at #72, that was still one more than great talented rockabilly artists such as Jack Earls (who was also one of my favorites), Billy Lee Riley, Sonny Burgess, Ray Harris, Edwin Bruce (later known as Ed Bruce to country music fans), Gene Simmons, Vernon Taylor, Ray Smith, and so many others who all had strong rockabilly releases on that golden Sun Records label between 1956 and 1958, but never saw any of theirs get onto the *Billboard* pop charts.

I was fortunate enough to meet and talk with Warren Smith in May 1978, when rockabilly music was startin' its revival here in the U.S. Warren was one of the Sun rockabilly artists of the 1950s that turned out for the "Memphis in May" street music festival that was held annually in Memphis for a number of years during the seventies and early eighties. Charly Records in England had released a sixteen-song album of Warren's 1950s rockabilly songs in 1977. There were seven songs on it that had never been released until then, and they were all great. Warren, along with Charlie Feathers, performed in England in April 1977, and Warren was headin' back over there for more shows later in 1978 with Ray Smith. When I talked to him I had no idea of the terrible, serious problems and troubles he had endured for about ten years between 1965 and 1975. I'd just as soon not get into that, 'cause Warren Smith left too much of a good impression on me in May 1978. He was one of the warmest, friendliest, most down-to-earth people I'd ever met, and he was excited about and looking forward to the future.

Warren Smith, who (like most early rockabilly artists) started out in country music, was the first fifties rockabilly that broke back into country, back in early 1960. He told me, "Shortly after my last record on Sun was

released, I packed up everything we had, and me and my family moved from Jackson, Mississippi, out to California. I guess that was in the late spring of '59. Rockabilly wasn't doin' too good anymore, so Sam let me out of my contract, and I wanted to get back into doin' country anyway." I interrupted Warren at this point and said, "Yeah, but you made a couple o' records for the Warner Brothes label in '59 that were on the pop/rockabilly side before you signed with Liberty, right?" A surprised look came over Warren's face, and he said, "Damn, you got those records." I said, "Yeah." Warren laughed and said, "Good Lord, I've tried to forget about those and hoped everybody else had, too. You're the only one who's reminded me of those. But I guess I gotta tell ya then that that's the reason I went out there. Warner Brothers was a big company, and I signed a contract with 'em right before I left, and when we recorded those songs, I didn't like the way they turned out, and when they didn't sell that much I went back to playin' country music in the clubs out there. Johnny Cash was living out there at the same time I was, and we did quite a few shows together. Liberty Records had just formed a West Coast country division to put out records in the country market, and when Joe Allison, who was the head man, came up to me after a show once and told me he'd like to sign me to the label, I couldn't-a been happier. I loved doin' the rockabilly songs, but I guess country was always my first love."

Warren went on: "Yeah, I was sure lucky to have a half dozen or so big hits for a few years at Liberty, but here after all these years it's kinda funny, 'cause it's all come back to where it started happenin' for me. Doin' rockabilly music all over again. That's what they remember the most. I had to go out and learn the songs all over again. Even the one rockabilly song I wrote, 'Miss Froggie.' I had to learn that all over again, too. I'm just glad they remember and still want me to do rockabilly, 'cause I had some great times doin' it for a few years."

I took Warren Smith's words from an old tape I had runnin' when we were talkin' on that spring day in Memphis in 1978. After listenin' to this old tape after all these years, it makes me a little sad, 'cause Warren really felt great things were gonna happen all over again, even though he was forty-five years old at the time. He'd had some troublesome times, like I said, and when he was given a second chance in 1977, he made the most of it. He was living in Longview, Texas, at the time he made his first trip overseas in April 1977, and when he came back, he was excited enough to put a band together and start playin' music in various towns and cities around where he lived.

Warren did get one more chance to go back to Europe in November 1978, for a number of shows with Ray Smith, and the audiences loved him once again, 'cause he proved he could still deliver his classic rockabilly songs as good as he ever could. By that time, a second live album was released in Europe from the first time he'd been over there in '77, and he was signed to do another tour in April 1980. But on January 30, 1980, Warren went to his doctor with chest pains. His doctor sent him to a clinic for tests. This was around one o'clock in the afternoon. After the tests at the clinic, they transferred him to the main hospital in Longview, Texas, and he was put in the intensive care unit. Warren's wife,

Jean, had been called and went to the hospital, but the doctors told her not to worry, that Warren was in stable condition, and for her to go home and come back when visiting hours started again at 5:30 p.m. His wife wanted to stay, but hospital personnel told her she definitely had to leave at around 3:30 p.m. Jean returned at 5:20 p.m. to find that Warren had a massive heart attack at 4:45, and doctors had worked to save him for a good, solid thirty minutes, but he had passed away three or four minutes before she returned. Warren Smith was one week shy of his forty-seventh birthday. When he died, I remember thinking this cat still had more great rockin' left to do, 'cause he still wasn't all that old. But here we are more than fifteen years later, and now everything known to exist by Warren has been released on some format of recording around the world, and I still enjoy

Forgettin' to Remember to Forget

Though Johnny Cash may not have had the voice for rockabilly music, it was Johnny's hand that wrote the first classic rockabilly song Warren Smith recorded in February 1956, called "Rock 'n' Roll Ruby." Or was it? Here's the story the way Warren told it to me:

"After 'Rock 'n' Roll Ruby' had been out for a while, there was this story goin' around that Johnny Cash hadn't actually written that song. Guys in Memphis were tellin' me that Johnny bought the song off George Jones while he was doin' shows down in Texas in '55. A year later, in '56, after 'Rock 'n' Roll Ruby' came out and was sellin' real well and all over Memphis radio, this story kept floatin' around. Johnny was a close friend of mine back then, so I wasn't about to bring it up. Johnny was with Sam Phillips the first time they ever came to see me in late '55 over at the Cotton Club in West Memphis, Arkansas, when I was singin' straight country music, and Johnny encouraged Sam to sign me to Sun Records right after that.

"That story was kinda hard for me to believe back then, 'cause when I first went in to cut 'Rock 'n' Roll Ruby,' Johnny was right there in the studio, tellin' me how he wanted me to sing it. He was kinda coachin' me through it, with the other musicians playin' along, 'cause I'd never sung none of this new rockabilly music up to that time. I was nervous as all get-out, but I was determined I was gonna do it the way Johnny wanted it done, 'cause this was my big chance. Well, at the end of the day, Johnny and Sam, and I think Carl Perkins was there too, whatever, I mean they were really all excited about how well I'd took to this new song, and they told me to come back the next day and we'll cut it. Well, when I come back the next day, everything just fell in place, and when Sam got the take he wanted, I remember him saying, 'Boys, what we now have down on tape is the next big hit for Sun Records, 'cause y'all just created magic, and I snatched it and caught it, and now it's right here on tape waitin' for the world to hear.' So because me and Johnny were such good friends, I wasn't about to ask him if he bought that song off George Jones. There was just no way, 'cause Johnny had been too good to me out on the road after the record took off and we started tourin' together.

"It was after I had a couple hits on Liberty, I guess sometime in '61, when me and my group were touring in Texas, and we were on the same bill with George Jones one night. Well, before the show, I was on his bus and we got to talkin' 'bout different things, so I asked him if he wrote 'Rock 'n' Roll Ruby.' George just reared back, looked at me, and said, 'Damn sure did.' I laughed and said, 'C'mon George, you're puttin' me on.' George came back with, 'Naw, I ain't! I sold that song to John back then for forty bucks cash!' Well, we both laughed. All I can tell ya, Billy, is I wasn't there when it was wrote. I can only tell ya what was told to me."

it more than ever. As early as 1974, Billy Hancock sang one of Warren's best rockabilly songs from 1956, called "Ubangi Stomp," when he was lead vocalist for Danny Gatton's band, Danny and The Fat Boys. "Ubangi Stomp" is also on their first album, from the same year. Since then, "Ubangi Stomp" and "Rock 'n' Roll Ruby" have become two of the most covered and recorded songs by rockabilly bands and artists, both here in the U.S. and in other parts of the world.

"So Long, I'm Gone" was Warren's only rockabilly *Billboard* pop chart hit, in June 1957. "Rock 'n' Roll Ruby" had been a #1 hit in Memphis and several other big cities. "Ubangi Stomp" had been the record in between those two, and according to the accounting department at Sun, it only sold a mere 8,000 copies. But record companies have always had a funny way of dealing with numbers when it came to the amount of records sold. "Ubangi Stomp" was distributed all over the country. Sun Records had big-time distribution in 1956. It's real hard for me to believe that with a big label like Sun Records, as it was in 1956 and '57, that "Ubangi Stomp" only sold 8,000 records.

One other thing on the personal side of Warren Smith. It's been written he reneged on deals, cheated musicians, had a big ego, and could be downright mean at times. Well, let me tell you something: So what! Warren Smith was human like everybody else, and he was a tough country boy like all the other great rockabilly artists of the fifties. He wasn't any meaner and didn't cheat anybody any more than just about any other rockabilly artist that ever recorded at Sun Records. Big egos? Sure, they're all bound to get 'em. I've seen that with no-talent little rockabilly artists and bands around the country during the revival in the early eighties. Again, so what! Warren Smith was no different than any of the rest of 'em on the personal side. The real difference is that Warren left behind one big-time chart hit rockabilly song and more than a half dozen of the finest honky tonk *Billboard* country chart hits you'll ever want to hear.

Sam Phillips, when asked to comment on Warren Smith over the past twenty years, has always given this same reply: "Warren Smith was always the best pure-soundin' country singer I've ever heard in my whole life. You could feel his soul comin' through in his voice. He could also handle rockabilly with the best of 'em, too." Warren Smith's rockabilly songs and honky tonk country'll never die. He left behind more than two dozen great rockabilly songs and another two dozen or so early-sixties honky tonk country songs that keep being repackaged

around the world, and now thousands of new fans are discovering what a tremendous talent and important artist Warren was to rockabilly and real country music. As recently as 1988, when Barbara Mandrell's musical hit career was nearing its end, she turned to Warren's first big honky tonk soundin' Top 5 *Billboard* country hit of 1960, called "I Don't Believe I'll Fall In Love Today." Barbara hadn't had a Top 10 hit in two years, but her version of Warren's song, sung with the exact same melody and retitled "I Wish That I Could Fall In Love Today," also made it up to #5 on the *Billboard* country charts in late '88. It was Barbara's final big hit. Warren did it better, but at least Barbara's version was good to hear at the time. Do yourself a favor. Go out and find rockabilly and pure honky tonk country music from when it still had a feel and was real. Buy something by Warren Smith, 'cause he could do both as good as any of the rest that came later.

Bob Luman

Rockabilly artists such as Charlie Feathers, Sleepy La Beef, Ronnie Dawson, and others are well-known names today for either their continuous string of record releases or their live personal appearances in nightclubs and festivals held around the world. But by the early 1960s, these artists and many others were virtually unheard of nationally, as they were held to having only regional success. When rockabilly died out in the early sixties, artists such as these usually went back to playin' country music or boogie woogie. Their biggest acclaim would be recognized later on, in the 1970s. By then, we'd find out that the ones I just mentioned, along with a number of others, had made some of the most creative rockabilly music of the late 1950s, but failed to gain national attention. Bob Luman was one of the exceptions. Even though listeners of oldies radio remember Bob only for his sole *Billboard* pop (and country) Top 10 hit "Let's Think About Living," which debuted on the pop charts on September 5, 1960, and climbed to #7, remaining on those charts for fourteen weeks, there's a whole lot more to Bob Luman and his music than that one novelty hit.

When I booked Bob Luman in September 1965, I knew he was from Texas. I didn't bother to ask him which town he was born in, 'cause we had too many other good-time things to talk about. It's mostly been written Bob was born in Nacogdoches, but I've also seen it in print he was born in Blackjack, just over the state line from Louisiana. Doesn't really matter. Bob Luman was Texas-born and bred, and his two biggest loves in life when he was a kid growin' up during the forties and early fifties were country music and baseball. Not necessarily in that order at first. He told me, "I was workin' hard at playin' baseball in all my spare time, and I was a pretty good ball player and was hopin' to play in the big leagues someday." Well, Bob continued with that dream, but his interest in country music was growin' some.

By the time he was in Kilgore (Texas) High School, Bob formed a little hillbilly band and started playin' a few dances, high school functions, parties, etc. He was singin' the big hits of the day and had a knack for soundin' just like the big, top country artists. Bob said, "I was only mostly doin' it on weekend nights, 'cause I was a first-string all-star ball player at Kilgore High and was still hopin' for a crack at the big leagues." Well, Bob's head really got turned around early in 1955,

during his final year in high school. The Pittsburgh Pirates had sent scouts to Kilgore to check Bob out at that time and were somewhat interested in him, when a girl he knew told Bob about a singer he should go see called Elvis Presley. So he did, and that was all it took. Like he told me in 1965, "From then on it was rockabilly with me. They don't like it in Nashville, but I still slip it in every chance I get, and I will till the day I die I guess, 'cause I've always loved it the most since that first time Elvis showed me that's the way to go."

Bob Luman was to go on and prove he was one of the best that ever sang and played rockabilly music back in the fifties. In '65, when I had him play the Bladensburg, Maryland, fire hall, the main fifties rockabilly records I had by Bob were his three 45s on Imperial Records and one on Capitol Records. These four 45s had come out in 1957 and '58. I was also collecting all his MGM

Forgettin' to Remember to Forget

Out of all the shows I booked between 1963 and 1967, Bob Luman's has to hold up as my favorite one. His agent let me speak to him on the phone ahead of time to let him know this show he was gonna do for me was not a country music show, and that he had to sing and perform rock 'n' roll and rockabilly songs, 'cause people that came to my shows were not into country music in 1965. They wanted to hear rock 'n' roll, 1950s style.

By no means was Bob Luman's show or any of the other six shows I promoted between October 1963 and January 1967 ever looked upon as oldies or revival-type shows. In the area I lived and hung out, which was the northern tip of Prince George's County, Maryland, there was a large group of lovers of 1950s rock 'n' roll music between the ages of eighteen and twenty-five that were all lost and left out in the cold the first several years after the British Invasion took over the radio airwaves of America. We also couldn't relate to the Beach Boys and Jan and Dean's surfin' music. It wasn't just the guys, either. I wanted Bob Luman to know all this, plus the audience that was gonna be at the show didn't want to hear any of the country music he was now doin'. When he called me in early June 1965, and I later talked to him in late August, Bob Luman couldn't have been happier about the kind of show I had planned for him to do. Bob couldn't believe that there was still an audience that wanted to hear good rock 'n' roll and rockabilly music, and that I had a band he could work with that could back him up on his old rockabilly songs. Bob said, "Man, this'll be fun and a breath of fresh air to be able to do what I love the most."

What I need to tell you right here is, while Bob Luman loved hillbilly and country-style music, and by the time of his death in 1978 he had charted thirty-nine songs on the *Billboard* country charts, including five Top 10s, country music wasn't nowhere close to being Bob Luman's first love in music. And on that night in September 1965, for over an hour and a half, Bob Luman sang over thirty of the best rockabilly and rock 'n' roll songs you'd ever want to hear. That set included songs Bob was known for, such as "Red Cadillac and a Black Mustache," "All Night Long," "Red Hot," "Your Love," "Make Up Your Mind," "Whenever You're Ready," "Buttercup," "The Fool," and a few others. After it was over, Bob told me, "Billy, I can't say enough thanks for the good time that you gave me by bringin' me up here to do this show. I can't remember the last time I was in front of a young crowd like you got in here tonight, and they all went wild over the rockabilly and rock 'n' roll songs I laid on 'em. It's just unbelievable, man! If I could make a good livin' for me and Barbara [Bob's wife] doin' 200 of these kind of shows a year, I swear I'd do it. Even though I'm in Nashville now and doin' all country records, I'll always love rockabilly the best."

Records from 1959 to 1963, which were a little on the pop side of country/pop. In 1963, Bob signed with Hickory Records and started doin' the country music of the day. Even though the Hickory records weren't as good, I could always find something good in the sound and feel in Bob Luman's voice, so I bought 'em all.

I asked Bob in '65 how he wound up recording in Nashville after doin' all his records out in L.A. between 1957 and 1959. He said, "It was when I seen the Everly Brothers out in California right after they'd signed with Warner Brothers. I had already had a couple releases on Warner Brothers by early 1960, but back then neither one of 'em sold that well and didn't chart, and I was about ready to throw in the towel and say the hell with all this. Phil Everly convinced me I guess sometime in May or June 1960 to go down and see their publisher, Wesley Rose, about a song they'd passed on but that they thought it would be perfect for me and would be a big hit too. So as a favor to them, 'cause I really liked both Don and Phil, I agreed to go down and cut this song called 'Let's Think About Living.' I didn't even hear it till I got to Nashville. I told Don and Phil I'd do the song and the session, but afterwards I was gonna concentrate on baseball. Well, when I got there for the session and heard the demo of 'Let's Think About Living,' I couldn't stand it and thought it was the silliest song I'd ever heard. That shows you how much I know. Ever since then, I've cut all my stuff in Nashville. Me and Wesley Rose always got along pretty good even though he didn't care for the rockabilly side of me, so after Warner Brothers dropped me a few years ago, Wesley signed me over to Hickory Records."

Bob left Hickory Records in '68 and signed with Epic Records. It would be on Epic Records that Bob would have his biggest success, with four Top 10 singles in 1972 and 1973. Three of these 45s were country/pop-type tunes that Nashville was pushin' at the time. But his last Top 10 song, "Still Loving You," was a fifties-style rockabilly ballad with an old Elvis sound to it. Especially in Bob's voice. You knew it was Bob Luman, and I could tell he enjoyed doin' this song. "Still Loving You" had been written by Troy Shondell, who had a Top 10 Billboard pop hit in 1961 called "This Time," which was good for its time, actually holds up well today, and some consider to be a rockabilly ballad. Billy Hancock certainly did when he recorded a terrific rendition of "This Time" for Ripsaw Records in 1979. Bob Luman, though, had recorded "Still Loving You" for Hickory Records in the late sixties, but when he kept chartin' hit after hit on

the Billboard country charts after he signed with Epic, Hickory released their version of Bob doin' "Still Loving You" in the spring of 1970, and it reached #56 and stayed on the charts for eight weeks. Three and a half years later, in the fall of 1973, Bob's new version for Epic Records reached #7 on the Billboard country charts and had a fifteen-week ride all over again.

In 1970, Bob Luman took Johnny Horton's "Honky Tonk Man" up to #22 for fourteen weeks. In late 1971, Bob hit #40 on the Billboard country charts with a rockin' version of "I Got a Woman," and even only about a year before Bob passed away, he hit #33 with a rockabilly-soundin' tune called "I'm a Honky Tonk Woman's Man" in 1977. These are only a few of the big chart examples of Bob Luman's lifelong love for and dedication to the music he loved the best, rockabilly music. There are many more buried on his old albums.

For thirteen straight years, from 1966 to 1978, Bob Luman had at least one song on the Billboard country charts. His last performance on "The Grand Ole Opry" was on December 15, 1978. Four days later, Bob was admitted to a Nashville hospital and put into the Intensive Care Unit with severe pneumonia. He passed away eight days later, on December 27, 1978. Bob had overcome life-threatening health problems a few years before, during the mid seventies, when he almost died due to a blood vessel rupturing close to his stomach. In 1976, Bob's friend Johnny Cash produced one of Bob's last albums, titled Alive and Well. The title was meant sort of as a joke, because Bob kept overcoming his health problems. That's not the worst and biggest joke in Bob Luman's life. The two worst jokes are that Bob is mainly remembered for his one big Billboard pop Top 10 hit, "Let's Think About Living," and that Nashville's new changin' country music industry has totally forgotten about what a great artist and human being he was. One artist that's still hangin' on in Nashville that hasn't forgotten is Steve Wariner. Steve was in Bob's band for a lot of years, and they were very close. About ten years ago, I heard him say he was sort of a protege of Bob's.

Bob Luman was only forty-one years old when he died. It's a shame he couldn't have lived just a few more years into the early 1980s and seen the European bootleg releases of all his released and unreleased recordings from the fifties. By 1983, I had found five different albums on four different labels from various countries in Europe. The best legitimate releases of Bob Luman's rockabilly songs have come out on the Bear Family

Records label in Germany. They released five albums between 1979 and 1988 of more than eighty of Bob Luman's best rockabilly-type songs recorded between 1955 and 1966.

I love Bob Luman's music and always will. I've never heard a bad or unkind word said about him. Even in Nashville! I'm glad we had some laughs together thirty years ago. To me, Bob Luman was the best true-to-the-bone rockabilly cat that ever came out of the great state of Texas.

Instrumentals

Bob Luman'll probably be the last fifties rockabilly that I needed to give that much space to. Some of the other important artists who recorded great rockabilly songs in the fifties would have to wait another twenty years or so to be acknowledged and appreciated. I'll cover some of those later. I'm gonna try to condense it from here on out, because I'm sure there's gonna be rockabilly fans that'll remind me I should have talked more about a Joe Clay or Groovy Joe Poovey or Rudy "Tutti" Grayzell or Mac Curtis, etc., but keep in mind that none of the above had rockabilly-type *Billboard* pop chart songs. They only had regional success in the fifties and are now only heard of because anybody that ever made a rockabilly-type song in the fifties and sixties, includin' me, is now bein' dug out someplace in some country in the world and bein' re-released.

Between 1960 and '63, there were still some rockabilly-sounding tunes either making the lower end of the *Billboard* pop charts or doin' well in certain regions. There were some good instrumentals that could be considered rockabilly during this time, and some did get high up on the *Billboard* pop charts during this period. I was never into instrumentals all that much, but these were some of my favorites during that time. Not just in rockabilly music, but also in rock 'n' roll, if an instrumental was great, I bought it, startin' I guess with Bill Doggett's "Honky Tonk" in 1956, which reached #2 on the *Billboard* pop charts.

In early '58, another R&B act, Lee Allen & His Band, had a gutsy feel to "Walkin' with Mr. Lee." It only reached #54 on the *Billboard* pop charts, but it was in the Top 10 in Washington, D.C.

I can tell you that Duane Eddy & The Rebels made some real good instrumentals in the late fifties that were all big chart hits I liked, such as "Rebel Rouser," "Ramrod," "40 Miles of Bad Road," and a number of others. Duane

was always a great guitar stylist, and I liked most of his records on the Jamie Records label, but when the times changed and he started doin' stuff like "Dance with the Guitar Man" on RCA Victor Records in 1962, I was losing interest in his songs. He was also having less success on the national charts.

Of course, I bought all the records by Link Wray & His Wraymen, startin' with "Rumble" in 1958. There was no doubt from 1958 to 1968 Link Wray was the King of the Guitar Wildmen in the Washington, D.C., area. But then again, in 1958 he was the only one, so I guess that's why he ruled. His style was copied, but never duplicated, as the sixties went on, but I gotta give it to ol' Link, he came up with a unique, grungy, echoey, trebley sound on his guitar before anyone else I ever heard. I'll get into Link later. I could write a whole book on him alone between '63 and '68, 'cause that sucker was crazier than I was during that time.

The first rockabilly instrumentals that really lit my fire, though, were two that never made the charts, from 1959. I had gone to see this teenage movie at the Queens Chapel Drive-In Theater in Hyattsville, Maryland, called *The Ghost of Dragstrip Hollow,* during the summer of 1959, and the band playin' at the teenagers' party in the film was called The Renegades, and they played two wild-sounding instrumental songs. Both songs were just frantic, thrashin', trashin', spontaneous rock 'n' roll or garage rockabilly instrumentals. One song was called "Charge," and the other was called "Geronimo." *The Ghost of Dragstrip Hollow* was made by American International Pictures. They had their own record label in the late 1950s, and after searchin' for awhile back then, I finally found The Renegades 45 of "Charge" b/w "Geronimo" on American International Records. In the late sixties, American International Pictures made a string of real popular outlaw motorcycle films, including *The Wild Angels, Devil's Angels, Hell's Angels on Wheels,* and *Hell's Angels '69.* And for a while there, the outlaw bikers and the music they listened to were the only rockabilly rebels left.

Another good rockabilly-soundin' instrumental was The Virtues' version of an old song by Arthur Smith called "Guitar Boogie Shuffle." The Virtues' version peaked out at #5 in the summer of 1959 and stayed on the *Billboard* pop charts for sixteen weeks.

The Ventures were one of the most popular instrumental bands of the 1960s. They did a variety of styles-of-the-days songs during that decade, but they did have a couple of big *Billboard* pop chart hits that had a bit of a rockabilly sound to 'em. Their first hit, the biggest hit they'd ever have, "Walk, Don't Run," reached #2 during the fall of 1960 and had a long ride of eighteen weeks on the *Billboard* pop charts. Then their third record on the Dolton Records label, "Ram-Bunk-Shush," got up to #29 in late February 1961, and stayed on the charts for nine weeks. I'd say those two had a rockabilly feel to 'em.

There were four or five instrumental groups from the late fifties to the late sixties that went under the name The Revels. In December of 1959, one group called The Revels reached #35 and stayed on the *Billboard* pop charts for ten weeks with a song called "Midnight Stroll." That was a pretty good rock 'n' roll-type song. But in 1960, a different group who called themselves The Revels had one 45 record on the Impact record label that really knocked me out. It was called "Church Key." It never hit the *Billboard* charts, but it sure got some good radio airplay by Don Dillard on WDON radio out of Wheaton, Maryland, back then. By the early sixties, Don was the only DJ in our area who was goin' against the grain and still playin' solid rock 'n' roll, rockabilly, black and white doo wop, rhythm & blues, etc. Well, the instrumental "Church Key" definitely fell into that class. Don played the dickens out of it. This song went over great at parties back then. It was everything garage rockabilly or rock 'n' roll should be. It had a menacing guitar and sax in it, and it was wild and spontaneous, but what made it exceptional was this girl named Barbara Adkins, who was listed underneath The Revels' name on the record, had this evil laugh; the couple times that the music would come to a stop, then you'd hear a church key pop open a beer can, the hiss would flow out, this deep guy's voice would say, "Church key," and then you'd hear this real evil laugh like it was comin' from the depths of hell. That's all this Barbara Adkins did on this song. But that chick nailed it.

There were other good rockabilly-type instrumentals throughout the early and mid sixties that made the *Billboard* pop charts. Really too many to mention. Lonnie Mack had a couple big ones during the summer and fall of 1963. First Lonnie brought back an instrumental version of Chuck Berry's classic song "Memphis" and took it to #5 for thirteen weeks on the *Billboard* pop charts. Then his follow-up record "Wham!" reached #24 for nine weeks.

Of course, probably my favorite rockabilly-soundin' instrumental of the early 1960s (1963 to be exact) is Link Wray's "Turnpike U.S.A." I'll never tire of listening to that one. It was his follow-up to his last big hit, "Jack the Ripper," and it never made the charts, but it's still probably my favorite rockabilly instrumental.

Before Link had those records on the Swan record label, that label had a huge hit with a rockabilly-soundin' instrumental called "Wild Weekend." The group that did it called themselves The Rebels. "Wild Weekend" debuted on the *Billboard* pop charts on December 29, 1962, and got all the way up to #8 and had a nice long ride on *Billboard* for seventeen weeks. Great song!

Keepin' the Flame Burning

As far as other male singers that were still doin' rockabilly throughout the early sixties, there were some that had been around a few years trying for that *Billboard* chart record, while there were always a few new ones poppin' up, trying to rekindle the flame of this fiery music that was gettin' stamped out or watered down by 1960.

After more than three years of trying, Narvel Felts finally broke onto the *Billboard* pop charts for two weeks in February 1960, reaching a peak of #90 with a rockabilly remake of The Drifters' classic song "Honey Love." Narvel had made the *Cash Box* charts in 1959, but this was his first of three *Billboard* pop chart entries. The other two would be during the seventies, after Narvel turned to Nashville and country music, becoming one of country music's biggest chart stars of the seventies. Even in Nashville, Narvel never strayed far from his rockabilly roots, as he kept covering old rockabilly songs on his many albums. In 1960, I had Narvel's Mercury 45s and was sure glad to find some new ones on the Pink record label.

Carl Mann had two *Billboard* pop chart records in 1959 on the Phillips label in Memphis. Carl's considered a rockabilly singer and piano player by many fans around the world today. "Mona Lisa" reached #25 and stayed on the charts for sixteen weeks. Then Carl's follow-up record, "Pretend," peaked out at #57 and stayed on the charts for seven weeks. This was between June and November 1959. Carl, along with Charlie Rich, had quite a number of 45s released on the Phillips label between 1960 and 1963, but those were his only two to make it onto the *Billboard* pop charts.

After being banished to low-life, juke joint dives down South in 1958, Jerry Lee Lewis managed to score Sun Records' final Top 40 *Billboard* pop chart hit during the spring of 1961, when he took a rip-roarin', rockin' version of the Ray Charles classic "What'd I Say" up to #30 for an eight-week ride. The Killer would make more appearances for only one to three weeks and never make it above #91 on the *Billboard* pop charts with rockin' songs in 1963 and 1964, but his record releases were all pretty much doomed, as pop music tastes had changed big-time by then.

Black singer Ron Holden had a *Billboard* pop Top 10 song called "Love You So" during the spring and summer of 1960, and this song was all over the radio and eventually rose up to a high position of #7 during the summer of 1960 and stayed on the charts for nineteen weeks. Where I was, I heard the B side of that record quite a lot on the radio. It was a frantic rock 'n' roll/rockabilly blood-and-guts screamer called "My Babe." During the early 1980s, several rockabilly revival bands recorded "My Babe" and sang it in their live shows. Local D.C. rockabilly artist Bob E. Rock was just one of quite a few who did this great song.

There was a group called The Beau-Marks who I thought at least vocally had a rockabilly sound to their one and only *Billboard* pop chart hit. On May 16, 1960, The Beau-Marks' song "Clap Your Hands" debuted on the *Billboard* pop charts for a fourteen-week run. It was on a small independent label called Shad Records. "Clap Your Hands" only reached #45, but it was a good song to have around at that time 'cause it had a rockabilly-type sound in the vocals for sure, and even the backup music was in somewhat of a rockabilly vein.

"Dear One" by Larry Finnegan might not be exactly what today's young rockabilly fans would consider to be a rockabilly song, but it had somewhat of a rockabilly feel when I first heard it, when it climbed up to #11 on the *Billboard* pop charts during the spring of 1962. It was Larry's only chart song, and it had a fourteen-week ride on *Billboard* at the time. It was on the Old Town Records label, which was mostly known for releasing great rock 'n' roll and R&B songs by black artists such as The Fiestas, Billy Bland, and others. In 1962, "Dear One" may not have been hard-core rockabilly, but it was about the closest thing we had to it. I heard Larry Finnegan moved to Sweden to live for quite a while during the late sixties, and they tell me he's remembered well over there to this day.

In 1962, three or four years before Felton Jarvis ever dreamed he'd be producing all Elvis Presley's records at RCA Victor Records for the last ten years of Elvis's life,

Felton produced two artists for the ABC Paramount Records label. The two singers he produced came from the Atlanta, Georgia, area. Between 1962 and 1964, Felton produced both of 'em startin' out in great rockabilly styles that had long since passed and were nowhere to be found on the *Billboard* pop charts. At least not up in the Top 10 in the year of 1962. One of these artists succeeded, and the other didn't.

The one that did was Tommy Roe. Tommy had first recorded for Judd Records in Memphis in 1960 with no success at all. In 1962, Felton Jarvis put a Buddy Holly vocal and musical rockabilly style to the song "Sheila," and after its debut on the *Billboard* pop charts on July 28, 1962, it was soon sittin' in the #1 spot for two weeks, starting on September 1. "Sheila" had a fourteen-week run on the *Billboard* pop charts. It was Tommy Roe's best effort with a fifties rockabilly sound. It was all downhill from there, at least on the creative side of music. Tommy Roe went on to place twenty-one more songs on the *Billboard* pop charts between 1962 and 1973. It's too bad his best-remembered songs on oldies radio from the mid to late sixties are his big Top 10 hits, such as "Sweet Pea," "Hooray for Hazel," "Dizzy," and "Jam Up and Jelly Tight." All of these songs were examples of some of the worst trite trash of that decade. "Sheila" was a good rockabilly-style song for as late as 1962.

The other guy from Atlanta who Felton Jarvis produced was Vince Everette, which wasn't his real name, but this name was placed on him 'cause that was the name Elvis had used in the hit movie *Jailhouse Rock* in 1957. In 1962, a lot of fans still remembered. This singer Vince Everette was real good at copying Elvis's early style. He didn't make it onto the *Billboard* charts, but his four 45s between 1962 and 1964 were certainly some good examples of the early Elvis Sun Records sound, as well as Elvis's better early-sixties sound. Several of the eight songs on the four records are outstanding. Production-wise and all. The first one I remember hearing on local radio in the D.C. area was the third 45 single, released in 1963. It about knocked me for a loop then. Here I heard someone called Vince Everette singin' the best poundin', rockabilly-soundin' version I'd ever heard of "Baby Let's Play House" since Elvis had first done it. Also, I don't think I've heard any that were better in the past thirty-plus years than Vince Everette's cover version from 1963. Yeah, it was done exactly like Elvis's, but it had the real rockabilly feel to it. You couldn't find that nowhere around in 1963. Musically and vocally, "Baby Let's Play House" by Vince Everette is about as close as

you can come to perfection when you're doin' a rockabilly cover song.

After gettin' my hands on Vince Everette's "Baby Let's
Play House" in '63, I special-ordered his prior two 45s.
Then the following year, I got his last 45 on ABC
Paramount. In 1965 I even found a record on the Lawn
record label called "Buttercup" by Vince Everette in the
discount 45 bins. Today, you can now find the best of
Vince Everette's early 1960s rockabilly songs on various
European rockabilly compilation LPs and CDs. Vince
pulled off some great ones. Besides "Baby Let's Play
House," there was "I Ain't Gonna Be Your Low Down
Dog No More," "Livin' High," "Such a Night," and "Sugar
Bee." Elvis had left rockabilly music in the dust by 1963
with tacky songs like "Bossa Nova Baby" and "The
Bullfighter Was a Lady," so I for one was glad to hear
somebody doin' the real sound of rockabilly music that
had first made Elvis a star.

Ral Donner

The most successful Elvis sound-alike who also comes
under the rockabilly banner these days is Ral Donner.
Ral made five separate trips onto the *Billboard* pop
charts in 1961 and 1962. All of Ral Donner's *Billboard*
pop chart records were on the Gone Records label out
of New York City. "Girl of My Best Friend" reached #19
and had a ride of eleven weeks on the *Billboard* pop
charts from mid April to early July 1961. "Girl of My Best
Friend" had been recorded by Elvis and came out only
as an album track on his first album after his Army
release in the spring of 1960. But it was a pretty strong
song, as RCA Victor released it over in England as the
follow-up to Elvis's "Stuck On You" (his first 45 after his
Army release), and it rose up to #2 on the major British
charts during the summer of 1960. But it was unheard
here in the States until Ral Donner hit with it on his first
of five straight *Billboard* pop chart hits for the Gone
label. It was really a first also, as before this no one had
dared cover a song Elvis was known for if they were
trying to have a big hit record, 'cause Elvis's versions
were always considered better. "Girl of My Best Friend"
was really the only Elvis song Ral Donner recorded and
released throughout the 1960s.

Ral Donner's next record was his biggest. The song "You
Don't Know What You've Got (Until You Lose It)" hit
Billboard on July 10, 1961, and by the first week of
September had reached a high position of #4. It stayed
on the *Billboard* charts for twelve weeks. His follow-up,
"Please Don't Go," only got to #39 between late

September and early December 1961, and had a nine-
week ride on *Billboard*. His next release, "She's
Everything (I Wanted You to Be)," got Ral back up to
#18 by early February 1962, after its debut on *Billboard*
on December 25, 1961. It had an eleven-week ride on
the charts until mid March 1962.

Ral's final *Billboard* chart record debuted on March 24,
1962, and only reached #74, but it did manage to stay
on the charts for seven weeks, until early May. The
song was called "(What a Sad Way) To Love Someone."
When Ral Donner met Elvis in 1962 out in California, it
thrilled Ral to no end when Elvis started singing the
words to "(What a Sad Way) To Love Someone." Elvis
told Ral it was his personal favorite out of all of Ral
Donner's songs.

There's a whole lot more to Ral Donner than these
Billboard pop chart songs, which were not rockabilly
songs but were still good solid examples of ballad and
mid-tempo serious pop/rock 'n' roll of the early sixties.
There wasn't much of that goin' around then. Ral
Donner was more than just an Elvis sound-alike. On his
only album during his big hit streak, called *Takin' Care
of Business* on Gone Records, which was released
during the fall of 1961, there were two songs that come
to mind right away that are real good examples of high-
energy rockabilly music. Those are "Nine Times out of
Ten" and "For Love, nor Money." Sure, Ral sounded like
Elvis on 'em, 'cause they were written for Elvis, but Elvis
had turned 'em both down.

Ral Donner was born in Chicago in 1943. He was only
thirteen years old when Elvis hit it big in 1956. He loved
Elvis, and he loved rockabilly music. He made his first
record in 1959, when he was sixteen. It was called "Tell
Me Why." It sounded a little like Elvis. But not that much.
It was on the rockabilly side. I spoke both with Ral
Donner's wife and son Ral Jr. in January 1992. They both
told me Ral never gave up on rockabilly and rock 'n' roll
music. Ral loved Elvis from the beginning to the end of
both their lives. Ya see, Ral passed away at the young age
of forty-one on April 6, 1984. Ral died from cancer. His
wife told me Ral only got one doctor's opinion and
should have gotten a second, 'cause it could have saved
his life, as he was misdiagnosed by the doctor.

Ral's biggest fan and admirer has to be Rip Lay, out in
California. During the late seventies, Rip and Ral produced some of Ral Donner's best rockabilly and rock 'n'
roll songs, which Rip Lay released on his own Starfire
Records label during that time. Rip named the label after

Ral's backup band on his Gone Records recordings, The Starfires.

A few years before Ral passed away, he was chosen to be the speaking voice of Elvis in the 1981 documentary theatrical release film *This Is Elvis*.

Pye Records in England was probably the first to release a legitimate collection of all Ral's best songs during his career, in 1978. There have been at least five or six bootleg albums on Ral released between 1976 and 1989. Murray Hill Records released a nice fourteen-song album here in the U.S. in 1988, and as recently as 1991, Sequel Records in England released a double CD set of forty of Ral Donner's best songs, with quite a few unreleased tracks on it. I should also mention Ral Donner wrote quite a few solid rockin' songs over the years. One of 'em was the rockabillyish "I Got Burned," which was released on Reprise Records in 1963.

As a human being, Ral Donner was a gentle, kind, sincere, and honest person. He was a loving husband and father. He was a friend to Alan Freed to the very end for Alan. He performed on Alan's final live shows in 1962 after other artists had deserted Alan. Ral Donner was always called upon to do Elvis-type projects on the major level. He may have been an Elvis sound-alike for most of his career, but what rockabilly fans know is Ral was a rockin' cat who was a good musician that had real talent.

Matt Lucas

The only other U.S. artist I want to touch on who cut some rockabilly tunes around this time is Matt Lucas. Matt had several songs that made the *Cash Box* charts in 1963, but he only had one major hit on the *Billboard* pop charts. That was with a wild, scorchin', revved-up cover version of the #1 country hit from 1950 by Hank Snow called "I'm Movin' On." Matt's version rose to #56 after it debuted on the *Billboard* pop charts on May 4, 1963. "I'm Movin' On" by Matt had a nine-week ride back then on the *Billboard* pop charts. Matt also had big regional successes with rockabilly classics of the fifties shortly after that with songs like "Maybellene" and "Ooby Dooby." They sold a lot of records, especially in the South.

I've gotten to know and like Matt Lucas real well over the past several years, because he's about as real an original rockabilly cat as there is left anymore. Oh, if so-called normal people talked five minutes with Matt Lucas, they'd run like hell, 'cause they'd think he was a full-blown crazy and plum out of his mind. But this cat's as real as they come, 'cause he'll tell you, with no bitterness at all, about the pure hell he's gone through in his life.

Matt Lucas was and still is a rock 'n' rollin' singer and drummer. That in itself is unusual. I can't think of any others back in the fifties. Matt knew he was born in Memphis on July 19, 1935. But what he didn't know for a long time, as he puts it, was "I was born a bastard. The people I thought were my parents had actually adopted me. When I was about eight years old, I went snoopin' through a drawer and found the papers. It just knocked me for a loop, I tell you. We were livin' in Poplar Bluff, Missouri, at the time."

Well, when Matt was about twelve or thirteen, he started doin' some real hell raisin'. When he was fourteen, he got busted for stealin' a truck and takin' it for a joyride before wreckin' it. He then spent about a year in reform school. When he got out, Matt kept playin' the drums in various joints around the South for several years. He had quit school at sixteen and by 1954 had worked his way west and wound up out in Hollywood, where he spent some time playin' drums and singin' in various jazz and blues bands in the bad areas of town. Matt told me he was on the set and used as an extra in the 1955 juvenile delinquent movie *Blackboard Jungle*. He hung out with Nick Adams, Vic Morrow, and other wild hellions who were just startin' to break into movies in the mid fifties. Matt was always a hustler. He wanted to break into movies, music, whatever, and the timing was right, but it just didn't work out.

Matt don't mind tellin' ya when he left California in 1956 and worked his way back to Memphis, he was already hooked on booze, broads, amphetamines, tranquilizers, and anything else in tablet or capsule form. Back in Memphis, Matt just went back to playing all the low-life, rough black and white juke joints throughout Arkansas, Mississippi, and Alabama. Matt was playin' and singin' some rock 'n' roll, rockabilly, and R&B all through the late fifties in these places. They were all the same joints rockabillys like the Burnette Brothers, Billy Lee Riley, Sonny Burgess, Roy Orbison, Ronnie Hawkins, Elvis, Charlie Feathers, Jack Earls, Carl Perkins, and so many others either worked before or at the same time Matt was workin' his way through 'em. Matt Lucas met and worked with just about every white and black artist and musician in and around Memphis, where he stayed based out of between 1956 and 1963.

In 1959 Matt had his first record come out on the Good record label in Memphis. The A side was called "Tradin' Kisses" and sold pretty well around Memphis at the time, but it really didn't get any farther than that. The song had a rockabilly edge to it, probably thanks to Roland Janes, who produced it at Fernwood Studios in Memphis and played guitar on it. Roland is best known for playin' on all of Jerry Lee Lewis's biggest hits and best songs on Sun Records.

After that first record, Matt was back in the beer halls and joints around Memphis and surrounding states until 1962 and early '63, when he went into Sonic Studios in Memphis and self-produced about a dozen wild rockabilly, blues, and soul screamin' get-down songs. Roland Janes engineered these sessions, and Matt used some of the best backup musicians in Memphis music history, including Narvel Felts and Travis Wammack on guitar, J.W. Grubbs and Fred Carter on bass, Jamie Isinhood on piano, Billy Lee Riley on bass and maracas, and of course Matt Lucas played drums and sang all the wild vocals. These were the sessions that produced Matt Lucas's only *Billboard* pop chart hit, "I'm Movin' On."

The follow-up record was "Ooby Dooby." Once again done in a scorchin', wild, frantic style for its time. This record made the *Cash Box* charts and sold real well. Some say better than Roy Orbison's did in 1956. It did well enough that Dot Records released several more 45s well into 1964 that were all recorded at those 1962 Memphis sessions. The first Dot release sold well enough to hit the *Cash Box* charts, but the following two releases, "Put Me Down" and "Turn On Your Lovelight," failed to do as well. So after a couple of good high-rollin' and wild-livin' years on the road of ridin' up at the top in the big time, Matt Lucas would start the worst decline ever in his whole life between 1965 and 1970.

Matt did some soul and R&B recordings in 1965 in Detroit. He kept doin' booze and dope all the while he was giggin' in blues joints, and in 1970 he wound up in Toronto, where he spent the next five years. Matt's told me he was at his lowest point in life in 1970. He was livin' in a fleabag apartment on the bad side of town. His fifth wife was about to take the kids and leave him. They'd shut the heat off 'cause he was broke and hadn't paid the bills, and he'd about destroyed his body with drugs and alcohol by this time. This was a cat that five and six years earlier was drivin' new Cadillacs.

But around 1971, Matt came back, workin' his way at gettin' clean in his body and mind with the help of his sixth and current wife, Barbara. Matt started gettin' regular gigs again with old pal and rockabilly artist Ronnie Hawkins and cut a blues album in 1972 called *I've Paid My Dues*. Ronnie Hawkins and Matt Lucas were both hangin' out with Xaviera Hollander, more widely known as "The Happy Hooker," around this time. Matt says, "Yeah, she was 'The Happy Hooker' and I was 'The Happy Hustler.' " Matt and his wife Barbara left Canada in 1975 and relocated in Florida, where they live today. Matt went to Chicago in 1983 and recorded two albums. One was a blues album, and the other is a pretty strong rockabilly album.

The reason I like Matt Lucas as a friend today is 'cause he's an honest cat who has nothin' to hide about his past, 'cause like he says, "You can't change it." Matt can still deliver one of the wildest live stage acts in rock 'n' roll or rockabilly I've ever seen. He can still drive an audience of young fans nuts. I've seen him do it. He's still giggin' wherever he can down in Florida, and the nightclub and rockabilly world is really missin' out by not bookin' this ol' original wild cat, who still knows how to rock, more often than they do.

Tex Rubinowitz and me both agree it kind o' makes us sick, and get mad when we see some young twenty-two-year-old punk, about 5-foot-4, who weighs about 110 pounds soakin' wet, that comes from an upper-class family, swaggerin' all around on stage singin' all these classic blues songs about how tough times have been and he's seen so much blues in his life it's a downright sin, and so on. Just forget it! All you wannabe young blues singers need to talk to Matt Lucas, 'cause Matt can tell ya all about the Delta, Chicago, rock 'n' roll, rockabilly, and soul blues for real, 'cause Matt Lucas has lived it most of his life as much as any black or white man. He's got a right to sing 'em, and he's damn lucky and grateful to have lived through 'em where so many others didn't.

Billy Fury

In 1960 I found out I had a sixteen-year-old cousin in Ireland, named Brian Murphy, who liked American rock 'n' roll. We wrote to each other and traded records for a while until early 1961. I'd send him American records I thought he'd like, and he'd send me ones by British rockers. One of the ones he included was a guy I'd never heard of, named Billy Fury. After he sent me a couple of Billy Fury's 45s, I told him in a letter I really liked him a lot, so in early 1961, I got in the mail from him a ten-inch album called *The Sound of Fury*. Here it is over thirty-five years later, and I've still got that album today, 'cause I consider it the first and best rockabilly and rock 'n' roll album ever done by a British rocker. Even when I listen to it today, it sounds as good as when I first got it. Every one of the ten songs on it are all pure rockabilly and rock 'n' roll. Even the two ballads are great. My favorite song has always been "Turn My Back On You." Helped along by the first great rock 'n' roll guitarist in England, Joe Brown, and the solid upright bass work of Bill Stack, Billy Fury delivered the best ten rockabilly songs of his fairly long career in Europe.

Though Billy never had a chart hit here in the States throughout the 1960s, anytime I'd see one of his 45s, which were on the London record label over here, I'd buy it. In 1959 and '60, Billy Fury looked like a rockabilly cat, and he was the only one in England that I've heard that continued throughout the sixties to have that certain sound and edge in his vocals where, at least to me, he sounded like he felt whatever type of song he was doin'.

Billy Fury's early rockabilly songs are the greatest ones he ever recorded. I don't know if he felt that way or not before he passed away of a heart attack in January 1983 at the young age of forty-one. Most singers and artists I've talked with over the years think their earliest recordings were their worst. But even though Billy Fury went into doin' and coverin' a lot of pop-type songs from 1961 on and had twenty-nine top British chart hits till the late sixties, most all of those songs, or at least the B sides of 'em, were more than listenable. By the late sixties, I couldn't find his records in the U.S. anymore, and I didn't hear any more about him until 1973, when I went to see a British film called *That'll Be the Day*, which starred David Essex. The reason I went to see the movie was because I noticed Billy Fury's name listed down about third or fourth as one of the stars. I knew it had to be the same Billy Fury, and it was.

From the late seventies to late eighties, I bought about twenty European-issued albums on Billy Fury. In 1987, I produced one of his songs that was on that first *Sound of Fury* album from 1960, called "Allright Goodbye," on my favorite California rockabilly girl and friend LesLee "Bird" Anderson.

Whenever anyone asks who I think was the best original rockabilly artist to come out of England, I always say, "No question. It was Billy Fury." I hope British rockabilly fans never forget him.

The Trend-ells

The first four years of the 1960s, meaning 1960, '61, '62, and '63, hard-core rockabilly music was rarely on the radio, much less on the charts, although with each passing year I'd keep finding records of fifties rockabilly artists at cheap prices on independent record labels as the one thing that's never changed. But mainstream popular music was constantly changin', and new teen idols and dance trends were comin' and goin' as each year passed.

In September 1959 I started high school at De Matha Catholic High School in Hyattsville, Maryland. It was a "prep"-type school. After my first year there, when it became clear that I wasn't exactly college-bound, my parents transferred me to Northwestern High School, a public school. I liked that a lot better.

I could always find something to do by early 1961 that had to do with music. My friends and I always made the rounds of all the local teen clubs around Prince George's County to check out local bands and girls. Right after exams and I got out of the tenth grade and was headin' into the eleventh grade at Northwestern High School, during the first week of June 1961, I was over at the teen club in Green Meadows, Maryland, to see these three local guys who had a little band that played all the good rock 'n' roll songs like "Stagger Lee," "Money (That's What I Want)," "Johnny B. Goode," "Blue Monday," and a ton of others. They called themselves The Bel-Airs. I would get up on stage and sing a couple songs with them at some of their record hop, teen club, and party-type shows they were doin' once in awhile when I was out ridin' around drinkin' on the weekends.

That night during the first week of June 1961, I got up at the Green Meadows Teen Club with The Bel-Airs and sang four or five songs with 'em. After I come off the stage, some man in a suit who was I guess in his late twenties came up to me and asked me if I wanted to make some money singin' in a professional rock 'n' roll band that he managed. He said, "We're playin' a dance with Link Wray and his band at the Camp Springs, Maryland, fire hall tomorrow night and then headin' north on tour all the way up to Albany, New York. One of the guys in my group quit on me the other day and went back home to Kentucky. I've got four guys left in the group, but only one who can sing lead vocals. The boy who left was one of the two lead singers. Link Wray told me the singer in this group was good enough to replace the boy who left." I said, "But the lead singer in the band The Bel-Airs that I sang with tonight is a whole lot better and has a lot more experience than I have. I just do this for kicks." He then told me, "I watched both of you tonight, and you're better for some of the songs we're gonna record in a couple weeks." I said, "Record! You mean make records?" This sucker had my head spinnin'.

He arranged to come over to my house the next day, which was Saturday, and talk things over with my parents. Which he did. My mother was hard to get over on, but this guy, whose name was Tommy Mattaso, was good. Really good. It took him a good two to two and a half hours, but my mother was impressed by his good

manners, his well-groomed look, the suit and tie he was wearin', and all the promises she demanded he make to her before she'd agree to allow her underage seventeen-year-old son, as she put it to him, to go trampin' around the country for the summer, singin' with his rock 'n' roll band. He wanted her to sign a six-month contract, but she'd only agree to sign a ninety-day one, because I was damn sure goin' back to school in September.

My father took up for me as usual in cases like this, and he was really thrilled to death with what he was hearin' from this guy about me makin' records, bein' seen on TV, and all. He was more than willin' to sign and let me

Forgettin' to Remember to Forget

$\mathcal{T}$ime moved on, and things rapidly changed as 1961 came in. "The Milt Grant Teen TV Dance Show" finally came to a screechin' halt the first week of April 1961, when it was taken off the air for good. So the end of a regular era of seeing my favorite rock 'n' roll, rockabilly, and R&B stars had come to an end. This show didn't end because of the payola scandal, though. Buddy Deane's TV dance show would continue for several more years up in Baltimore. Milt's show didn't go off the air because of falling TV ratings, either. I was right there when all of us regular dancers were told the show was being canceled within two weeks.

Milt Grant told all us teenagers that the station, WTTG, channel 5 in Washington, D.C., had succumbed to pressure either to take the show off the air or let black couples become regular daily dancers on the show along with all of the white kids. Not that blacks and whites would dance as partners together, but they would have to be on the show each day dancing with their own race with all the rest of us and others from the surrounding guest high schools. Up until this time, blacks were only seen on the show one day a week dancing. The white kids had the other four days. But by 1961, Washington's black population had really grown, and blacks were finally startin' to make a lot of progress in obtaining equal rights. Washington had a much larger population of blacks in the early sixties than Baltimore did. But I can understand the TV station not wanting blacks and whites, even though dancin' with their own race, being seen live, shoulder to shoulder each day together in the same audience. There was a whole lot of white racists in and around Washington, D.C., at that time, and I'm sure all hell would-a broke loose. But in life all good things sooner or later have to come to an end.

Milt Grant went on in the mid sixties and either bought or started another independent local TV station in Washington, D.C. I know it was on channel 20. I believe the call letters were (and maybe still are) WDCA. Milt never had any of his own shows on it, but he was president of the station or whatever when it first started. Sometime in the seventies, Milt sold his interest in it and left the station, from what I've heard. Before he did, though, we had a reunion of as many regular dancers as could be found in early 1971, ten years after his show had been off the air. Local TV disc jockey and promoter Barry Richards had a rock dance show on channel 20 each week at the time, and it was his idea to do this thing. When I got contacted and was told Milt Grant and a lot of the old regular dancers I had known would be there, me and Pepper went down for the taping of it.

The show was an hour, Milt was the guest of honor, and they played all the old popular songs of the late fifties, from Link Wray's "Rumble" to Jerry Dallman's "The Bug." Milt Grant's hair was all white by this time, but he still looked good. Milt and a few of the regulars couldn't believe I'd collected all those hundreds of autographs of various artists that were on the show between '58 and '61. Most of us down there all still loved the old real rock 'n' roll music the best. We had a great time. I sure wish I could find a copy of that show.

go off with this guy. But my sister would be the first to tell ya he was always a pushover as well as bein' a sweetheart of a person.

My mother did check out all of Tommy Mattaso's credentials with some union offices in New York and the whole bit before she let me go two days later, on Monday afternoon. I went with him that Saturday night to the show. Link Wray and his brother Doug both told me Tommy Mattaso was straight and OK. They said they'd dealt with him before. That was good enough for me.

I met the four guys in Tommy's group. They called themselves The Trend-ells. I hit it off pretty good with all four of 'em at the time. Three of the guys were from Louisville, Kentucky, and one guy, Steve Claypool, was from Pittsburgh, Pennsylvania. All of us were between fifteen and seventeen years old then. Tommy Mattaso told the group I was the replacement for the guy that quit and would take on the lead singer parts on the songs he had done plus sing harmony backup behind the other lead singer, Jimmy Gunther.

Tommy right away had me practicing constantly with the other four guys on the songs where I sang backup harmony and Jimmy Gunther sang lead. Then there were four songs Tommy told me I had to really concentrate on as we were goin' in a New York studio and two of these songs would come out on a new 45 on the Tilt record label.

For the first week or so, The Trend-ells just mostly played record hops, movie theaters, teen dances, drive-in restaurants, drive-in movie theaters, a couple of bowling alleys, and places like that. Nothin' glamorous. But after we did this four-song recording session on a weekday morning and part of the afternoon and then did a photo session, we were billed as rock 'n' roll's newest recording stars, The Trend-ells. I was into it, but it all happened so fast, it blows my mind to think about it today.

We recorded that first session on June 25, 1961, and DJs had their copies by the Fourth of July. Then I guess it hit the stores, 'cause we were in a different city or town every night, doin' local radio or TV promotions and interviews, along with all kinds of live appearances. Most of 'em opening for better-known artists or groups at the time.

The four songs we recorded at that first session were: "Don't You Hear Me Calling Baby," by fifties rockabilly artist Ronnie Haig; "Love Is My Business," by Cliff Gleaves, another rockabilly artist, who also worked for

Elvis from about 1957 to 1972; "I'm So Young"; and "Please Say You Want Me." I sang lead on the first two songs. Jimmy Gunther sang lead on the last two, which were mid-to-late-fifties teenage vocal group, or now known as doo wop, songs.

The two songs they chose to release for that first record were "Don't You Hear Me Calling Baby" b/w "I'm So Young." After Tilt Records released it, Tommy Mattaso had us booked throughout the rest of the summer and into the fall on all kinds of shows with a lot of big names and some I still haven't heard of to this day. Most of the shows we did were in the Northeast, but we went as far south as Charlotte, North Carolina, and as far west as St. Louis, Missouri. I know this record did really well in the New York City, Pittsburgh, Cleveland, Louisville, Baltimore, and Boston areas, 'cause I remember seein' it on some of the local radio station charts when we were out on tour.

That was one of the fastest summers of my life. All of us in The Trend-ells smoked, as well as Tommy Mattaso, but there wasn't any time for drinkin' much beer, partyin', or girls. That's one thing that bothered not only me but the other guys in the group as well. Still, I hung in there, not only 'cause my parents had signed me over to Tommy until mid September, but also 'cause I got to meet a lot of rock 'n' roll stars I really liked at the time. The biggest show we were ever on was one at the Steel Pier in Atlantic City. That's the best memory I got. It was on Labor Day weekend, 1961. There was well over a dozen big acts on that show, as well as a couple like us. The major hit artists they had on the show that day were Freddy Cannon, Larry Hall, Teddy Randazzo, Clarence "Frogman" Henry, Brian Hyland, The Fleetwoods, Bobby Lewis, The Jarmels, Bobby Comstock & The Counts, Gary U.S. Bonds, and the two big headliners, Dion and Del Shannon.

After that show and some more to follow, my ninety-day stint was about up, and to tell you the truth, back then I really didn't care, 'cause too many restrictions were bein' put on me. Rock 'n' roll and rockabilly music to me was about bein' free to do whatever I pleased, even in '61. Well, right before that ninety-day stint was up and my mom thought I'd be on my way home shortly, Tommy Mattaso talked her into signing an extension till my second semester started at Northwestern the third week of November 1961. He did this by raising the weekly check he sent her from $50 to $75. I was less than pleased, to put it mildly, 'cause I wasn't seein' none of that money.

Tommy Mattaso kept workin' us right on past November 1961. He scheduled another recording session for mid November to put out a second 45 on Tilt Records, and we went and recorded five more songs. I sang lead on three rockers and Jimmy Gunther sang lead on the two slow ones. The three I sang lead on were "You Got Me Goin' " and "It'll Be Easy," two songs Tommy had that I'd never heard before, and one I'd written, called "Cool, Cool Baby." I had started writing a few songs while we were travelin', and Tommy liked this one. I didn't know nothin' about copyrightin' back then, and I don't think it ever got released, but if anybody readin' this knows of a copy of it even on cassette, I sure wish they'd forward it to me. The two songs Jimmy Gunther sang lead on were "Moments Like This" and "Can I Come Over Tonight." Two more songs from black vocal groups of the late fifties. I should add right here, Tommy was managin' a second group by this time, called The Sultans, and members of The Trend-ells kept changin' on a weekly basis. After I left The Trend-ells, two of the songs I sang lead on both came out on a 45 single on Tilt Records. They came out under the name The Sultans, but it was actually three members of the then-Sultans and me and a backup singer from The Trend-ells, on the songs "You Got Me Goin' " and "It'll Be Easy."

Tommy kept me out there with The Trend-ells right until January 2, 1962, and when it got way past the date I was supposed to be home, my mother told him over the phone in no uncertain terms if he didn't send me home immediately, she was gonna have him arrested for kidnapping, 'cause he didn't have a contract any more. So two days after New Year's Day 1962, after many more nasty calls from mom, Tommy gives me a bus ticket from Columbus, Ohio, back to D.C., and $50. I never told mom about the fifty. Tommy could afford it, though, 'cause when I got home, I found out he hadn't sent the past two weeks of money to her, which added up to $150. I was sure glad to be back home, though, I can tell you that much. It was then I was thinkin' if I ever get back into the music business I was gonna be a manager, 'cause they must see all the money. I sure didn't.

I'll end this chapter on that note. Throughout 1962 and '63, I just went on collectin' records, and after I turned eighteen in February '62, I was hittin' all the local nightclubs and beer joints to see all the good rock 'n' roll bands like Link Wray that were still rockin' D.C. There were lots of 'em, too.

By October 1963, I started a three-and-a-half-year stint of booking shows myself. Things were really gonna change fast after that. More than I'd ever seen before in my life. It started with President John F. Kennedy being gunned down and killed on November 22, 1963. That was really a first-class tragedy that nobody had ever seen in their whole lifetime, no matter how old they were. Right after that, The Beatles and the rest of the British Brigade took over and dominated music like we hadn't seen since Elvis started. Livin' through all that stuff was tough for a rockabilly cat like me, but it's all comin' atcha on the following pages.

The British Invasion Hurts,
but Link Wray Eases the Pain

Through the Stray Cat revival period of the early eighties and sometimes even today, the rockabilly scene has seemed to be a fashion show of how cool you're dressed and look. It wasn't in my neighborhood back in the early sixties. We weren't playin' dress-up cool for the night to show. This was our way of life. And sometimes we got hassled for it, or even beat up. But that's just the way it was back around '63. Those were the dark days of ridin' waves with surf music that was pretty silly, along with the "Wah Watusi" or "Puff the Magic Dragon." You weren't cut any slack back then for stickin' by somethin' you believed in.

Link Wray

In the summer of 1963 I graduated from Northwestern, got my first steady job as a stock clerk, got my very own first car, an old two-tone green 1953 Chevy, and just kept right on rockin' mostly to the real rock 'n' roll bands that were still throwin' in rockabilly music from five or six years back. Link Wray & His Wraymen were definitely the top, standout, premier hard-driving rock 'n' roll band from the old 1950s school in the D.C. scene back then. They certainly helped me get through that first wave of the British Invasion between 1964 and 1967 more than any other group or artist, 'cause they were always playin' in some joint on almost any night of the week around D.C. throughout that period. Most rock 'n' roll and rockabilly fans in the D.C. area always took Link Wray for granted.

I first met Link along with his brothers Ray Vernon and Doug Wray down on the Milt Grant TV show in late 1958. Link Wray & His Wraymen already had their first great instrumental *Billboard* pop chart smash hit with the song "Rumble," which had gotten up to a peak position of #16 during the summer of 1958 and stayed on the charts for fourteen weeks.

"Rumble" had been on the Cadence record label, which was owned by Archie Bleyer, who was basically a pop musical director in the late forties and early fifties until he founded Cadence Records around 1953. Cadence is best known for all of the Everly Brothers' first and biggest hits between 1957 and 1960. That sort of pop-soundin' country, rockabilly, or soft rock 'n' roll was OK with Archie Bleyer, but he was dead set against any of this new-soundin' hard-edged rock 'n' roll. After Milt Grant, who was Link Wray & His Wraymen's manager for a little over three years, from late 1957 to early 1960, sent Archie Bleyer a tape of "Rumble," he just let it sit in a pile of rejected tapes. It was only at the insistence of Archie's teenage daughter that he eventually released the record. But Bleyer didn't want to be known for that kind of music, and he didn't need it because of the huge success he was havin' with the Everly Brothers and other more wholesome acts and artists at that time. It's hard to believe, I know, but after "Rumble" sold around a million copies, Archie Bleyer told Milt Grant he didn't want to put any future records out on Link Wray.

Well, Milt didn't have any trouble gettin' Link signed to a new label in late 1958. Maybe Bleyer had a certain code of ethics about what kind of music he was gonna release on his label, but Epic Records in New York was lookin' at it from how much money Link could make for 'em when they signed Link to a three-year record deal. Milt Grant had sent Epic a demo of two songs, "Rawhide" and "Dipsy Doodle," which they released as his first 45 single for this label. "Rawhide" debuted on the *Billboard* pop charts on January 26, 1959, rose up to a peak position of #23, and stayed on the charts for thirteen weeks. This would be Link Wray & His Wraymen's last national chart hit for over four years, although Epic Records brought Link and his group up to their New York studios for several sessions in 1959 and 1960, which resulted in six more single releases into 1961, plus one LP release simply called *Link Wray and His Wray Men*, which came out in 1960.

There's just no way I'm gonna give you a whole history of Link Wray's recording career during the 1960s. Though that, in my opinion, was his prime time period on wax. Between late 1958 and early 1961, I was actually better friends with Link's brothers, Ray Vernon and Doug Wray. I liked 'em both a lot. Link was fine, but he was a little more distant than Ray and Doug. Of course, I liked Ray because I had his 1957 Cameo 45 release "Evil Angel," which I always thought was a really good record. "Evil Angel" was a Top 10 hit in Washington, D.C., and a number of other major cities, though it never broke into the *Billboard* national pop charts.

Doug Wray had one 45 release out in 1959 called "Goosebumps" on Epic Records which was kinda silly, but I never really told him then, 'cause he was a good guy. He gave me that record at the time. When I used to go down and see Doug during the mid seventies when he was playin' at a place called Howard's Restaurant in Waldorf, Maryland, we talked a lot about the crazy clubs in D.C. him, Link, and The Wraymen had played at during the 1960s. One night I brought up to him that I still had his record that he gave me back in '59. Doug laughed hard and said, "Damn, man, burn that thing. It was really awful." We just had a good laugh over it.

Watchin' Doug do his thing was kinda sad, when I think about it. Here was one of the best, solid rock 'n' roll drummers sittin' on a stool on top of a long rectangular bar singin' Merle Haggard songs while he played an acoustic guitar and there was no mike. Not many of the dozen or so drunks sittin' around the long bar were even listening to him. But this was on Wednesday nights each week, and it was 1975. Doug owned a barber shop down there at the time and cuttin' hair was his regular job. I enjoyed the talks we had then, and I know he did also. That was probably the last time I saw Doug.

I guess the last time I saw Ray was at The Stardust club in Waldorf, Maryland, sometime during the summer of 1971. Link had a new album out that I always called "The Indian Cover" album. The real title was just *Link Wray*. To be honest, I really didn't like this new album at all. It was completely out of left field, but I guess Link was tryin' to change with the ever-changing times then. I do know Ray Vernon engineered and co-produced it. And from what Danny Gatton told me later, he—that is, Danny—played some guitar parts on that album that Link took credit for. But that summer of 1971 was the final time I'd get to see and spend some time with Ray Vernon. I hadn't seen him in almost five years, and as always, he was as happy to see me as I was to see him.

Ray was always just one of the friendliest and nicest guys I'd ever met, and he was real easy to talk to, and he'd take time to listen. When a local promoter named Rudy Callicutt told me Ray had taken his life in the late seventies, I found it hard to believe and felt sad 'cause Ray was always a special person and a guy who always seemed upbeat. But as the years go by, I guess this music business gets a lot of us down.

After Link Wray finished his deal off with Epic Records in 1961 and he was out from under Milt Grant's management, he still played the local D.C. scene and continued to release records on various labels. All of 'em sold well in the D.C. area, I can tell you that much. Atlas, Mala, Rumble, and Vermillion Records were all independent labels between 1961 and 1963 that released records by Link Wray & His Wraymen. Both 45s and LPs were released by the group then. Rumble and Vermillion Records were owned by Ray Vernon, and Link's 45s and LPs on those two labels were mostly only sold in local record shops and at the steady stream of gigs Link continued to play. A couple of these 45s were released under Ray Vernon's name, as Link was still under contract to Epic Records at the time.

Around late '62, Ray Vernon bought a house and some property down in Accokeek, Maryland, and built a recording studio in his basement, and that's where Link & His Wraymen would record most of their future gut-bustin' songs till close to the end of the 1960s. Up to this time, startin' in 1959, Ray had been renting space in office buildings in the downtown section of Washington, D.C., and always had problems with other occupants in other offices on various floors of the buildings complaining about Link & His Wraymen makin' too much racket.

Back in 1956, both Link and Doug Wray came down with tuberculosis. Link's case was the most severe, and he lost a lung to the disease. He spent a good part of 1956 in a T.B. hospital. When he was finally released, his doctors told him he should stick to his guitar playin' and leave singin' alone, but by the early sixties, after two major instrumental hits with "Rumble" and "Rawhide," Link started to tackle some vocals on his records, as evidenced first on his 1960 Epic 45 release "Ain't That Lovin' You Baby." Link's gravelly vocal style was a good match for his demonic, grungy guitar sound. But it would never be Link's vocals that grabbed your attention. It was always that shocking, electrifying, ahead-of-its-time guitar work he was layin' down like nobody had done before that caught your ears.

"Jack the Ripper" was the proof of the puddin' that nobody had ever come up with a sound like this before Link. Most fans would remember "Jack the Ripper" when it became a big-sellin' *Billboard* pop chart hit from mid June to mid August 1963, reaching only #64 but stayin' on the charts for eight weeks then. It was on the Philadelphia-based Swan record label by then. But to fans of real rock 'n' roll in the D.C. and Baltimore area, "Jack the Ripper" was just a great old song you always wanted to hear again by '63. Ray Vernon had cut it over two years before at his Vermont Avenue office building studio and released it on his own Rumble Records label, and it was a big local hit and one of Link's most requested songs during the spring and summer of 1961. Even while I was tourin' with The Trend-ells throughout the summer and fall of '61, I'd hear "Jack the Ripper" on various radio stations in the mid-Atlantic states and even up in some of the far northeastern towns we played in. Through most of 1962, whenever I'd go out and see Link & His Wraymen, even though they'd released newer songs by then, "Jack the Ripper" was always in their set lists. Ray Vernon musta sold a lot of copies at live shows around the D.C. area, because when I really got into huntin' down rockabilly and rock 'n' roll 45s during the early 1970s, "Jack the Ripper" would show up on the Rumble label as much as on the Swan label in all the 45s I was diggin' through at the time.

I know if I ever end up in the nut house and some shrink's lookin' at my musical background and is givin' me a word association test and he says, "Link Wray," I'd come back and say, "Jack the Ripper." If he wasn't happy with that and wanted another answer and said "Link Wray" again, I'd have to come back with "Run Chicken Run." The reason being is because between late 1962 and late 1967 Link always sent the drunken patrons in his audience completely out of their gourds with those two guitar scorchin' tunes. During those five years, I saw Link Wray & His Wraymen more times than any of the other local bands around D.C. The weird thing is that Link Wray had national chart hit records and was on either major labels or the big-time independent labels like Swan Records who were more than able to compete with the majors throughout the early to late sixties. And he was playin' in the same sleazy dumps that the no-hit and even no-record bands were also playin' in. It's well documented in the recent Norton Records releases on Link that he preferred to play these steady gigs for sometimes weeks and even months at a time as the sixties moved on. He felt comfortable in 'em, and he could play whatever he chose to in 'em. But I can tell you this

much, between 1964 and 1967, I saw Link in some of the meanest damn joints I ever been in in my life.

In my opinion, this was also the time of Link Wray's most productive and artistic output, as all of his Swan recordings indicate today. It was probably due to the fact that Link and his older brother Ray Vernon were given a free hand at what they wanted to come up with, lay down on tape in Ray's studio, and hand over to the Swan Records people for release.

And release it they did. After Link's final *Billboard* pop chart national hit recording of "Jack the Ripper" in the summer of 1963, Swan Records went on to release one album in the fall of '63, called *Jack the Ripper,* and a dozen more 45s into 1967, when Swan Records finally shut their doors and closed up shop for good. Though none of Link's many 45 releases after "Jack the Ripper" hit it big or ever made the national charts, they all sold well and were all heard on a number of local radio stations in the Washington, D.C., area during that whole period.

The Fab Four

Now, to put it mildly, I was no Beatles fan when they broke on the American scene in 1964. But as early as March 1964, when I heard the song "All My Loving," which was written by John Lennon and Paul McCartney, I could hear musically it had a rockabillyish sound to it. It was the first song I heard by them, though I hated to admit it back then, that I liked.

I certainly didn't like The Beatles' versions of Carl Perkins's rockabilly classics such as "Matchbox," "Honey, Don't," and "Everybody's Trying to Be My Baby," or their versions of Chuck Berry's "Roll Over Beethoven" that were all over the radio and charts throughout 1964 and early '65, along with a couple dozen of their own songs and other covers of songs such as "Please Mr. Postman." I still prefer the original versions of these songs to this day. But as the years went on and the more I read and listened to, especially John Lennon, I grew to respect where they were comin' from when they first started this group. With a few exceptions, even today, I'm still not all that crazy about their music, although it sounds great up against what's on the *Billboard* pop charts today.

Even though John Lennon's weirdness and politics annoyed me at the time during the late sixties and early seventies, I always liked him the best out of the four of 'em. The main reason bein' is he was the defiant one, and he'd say what was on his mind. It was John Lennon who was the true rock 'n' roller out of that group. He took the heat for it, too. Probably the best example I can give you to prove that fact is with The Beatles song "The Ballad of John and Yoko." Now, if you don't listen to what the words are sayin' to you and just listen and get down on the music Lennon and them boys laid down, you're deaf if you can't hear that music was more true, original rockabilly and rock 'n' roll than anything Charlie Gracie or Buddy Knox ever recorded in the 1950s.

Forgettin' to Remember to Forget

In May of '63, I was approached one night by local WDON radio DJ and promoter Barry Richards (who I had known for a couple years) to go in with him and co-promote a big rock 'n' roll show he wanted to put on at the Bladensburg Fire Hall in Maryland. I'd never gotten involved with this before, but Barry knew the ropes 'cause he'd been successful at it for several years working with Don Dillard, who was the owner of WDON. He was bringin' in Bo Diddley to headline, and I had no problem gettin' Link Wray & His Wraymen to do the show, which was on the first weekend of August. Link and Barry had recently had a falling-out over finances.

That show went so well that I told Barry I'd be willin' to go into another one of his shows with him. He told me he already had the ones that were comin' up in other areas covered, but that he would pay me to help promote and spread the word on an unknown group he was bringin' into the Bladensburg Fire Hall sometime in mid January 1964. Now, you can believe this story or call me the biggest liar livin' on the face of this Earth. When I told Barry, yeah, I'd help him on it, he then went into his suitcase of stuff that he was promoting and handed me two big rolls of stickers that he told me to pull off and stick everywhere possible to get the word out on this hot new act. He said he had just gotten the contract back on this group, and he had a lot of money ridin' on this act.

Well, I looked at these two rolls of stickers and pulled one of 'em off and stuck it up on the wall in the back room where we were at the Fire Hall and just stared at it and said to Barry, "What the hell is a Beatle?" Barry said, "They're from England, and they're the hottest group all over Europe, and they're causin' riots everywhere they play. They're gonna be really big over here, and me and Don have put up a lot of money to start their first U.S. tour right here for us."

Well, these stickers were on rolls of brown paper, and when you tore 'em off, they were rectangular, had a white background, and had the now-famous four mop-top haircuts, but without any faces on 'em. There were two mop tops in the middle and two more underneath those, printed in red. Circling the four were simply the words "The Beatles Are Coming" in bold red print. Barry said, "When you run out, let me know."

Well, after stickin' 'em all on everything from pool hall windows to mail boxes, I didn't call him to get any more, that's for sure. That is, I didn't call him back until right after the New Year of 1964 came in and I heard some strange-soundin' song on the radio comin' home from work one day, and when it was finished, the disc jockey on WPGC radio said, "That's a brand-new platter we just got in by a new group from England called The Beatles, and they want to hold your hand, so watch out, 'cause they're gonna be big, big, big!"

When I finally talked to Barry on the phone, he told me their manager had sent his deposit back to him in early December and canceled the deal out. Well, you know the rest. The only thing I can add is I wish I knew where that contract was with Brian Epstein's signature on it. The first show The Beatles performed live in this country was only about ten miles from that old Bladensburg, Maryland, Fire Hall. It was at the Washington Coliseum. I went and checked 'em out, and I couldn't believe what I was seein'. I couldn't hear a thing, really, except shriekin', screamin' twelve- to fourteen-year-old girls. They were all goin' into spasms when The Beatles did their "Yeah, Yeah, Yeah," mostly silly songs while they flopped their mop heads from side to side, dressed in funny-lookin' suits and playin' even funnier-lookin' little guitars. But it didn't matter what me and a couple of others I was with thought on that cold Tuesday night, February 11, 1964, 'cause the pop music world was witnessing the biggest change it had seen since Elvis stormed into it.

According to rock historian Greil Marcus, the fifteen-year-old John Lennon met the thirteen-year-old Paul McCartney at a church social sometime in 1955. Other sources say it was in 1956. But in 1955, Lennon had his own skiffle music group called The Quarrymen. McCartney joined The Quarrymen in 1956 and throughout '56 and '57 began writing rock 'n' roll and rockabilly songs, together with playing and singin' versions of all the original American rock 'n' roll songs that were now infiltrating the British charts, spawning British rock 'n' roll imitators such as Tommy Steele. During that period, John Lennon preferred Elvis and Paul McCartney's favorite was Little Richard. Later with Paul it would be Buddy Holly, though he continued his love for Little Richard's music.

In 1958, fifteen-year-old George Harrison joined The Quarrymen. George was a guitarist who was most influenced then by Scotty Moore's, Buddy Holly's, and Chet Atkins's guitar work. Over the next couple years, The Quarrymen had a number of name changes. Some of which were Johnny & The Moondogs, The Rainbows, and The Silver Beatles. They decided permanently on The Beatles when they left for a string of long, all-night gigs at rough joints in Hamburg, Germany. By this time, Stu Sutcliffe, a Liverpool art student, had joined the group, and Pete Best was picked up to play drums.

In 1961, The Beatles recorded their first record, "My Bonnie," in Hamburg. Sutcliffe left the group shortly after to go back to painting and concentrated on becoming an artist. During '61, The Beatles started playin' and soon became a popular act at The Cavern Club in Liverpool, England, though they continued their all-night gigs in Germany.

In November of 1961, Brian Epstein, who owned a local record store in Liverpool, went out to see The Beatles at The Cavern Club, mostly out of curiosity because of the many requests he was getting for their record of "My Bonnie." The following month, Epstein signed The Beatles to a management contract.

In January 1962, The Beatles were voted the #1 pop group in Liverpool. They auditioned for Decca Rcords in England, but Decca passed on the group. Stu Sutcliffe died from a brain tumor in April 1962. Around that same time, Brian Epstein was telling and writing to British music news journalists that his group would soon be bigger than Elvis. Though they chuckled at the time, Epstein turned out to become the only manager in rock 'n' roll history to be right!

By the summer of 1962, The Beatles had an enormous following in England, and EMI Records signed 'em to a recording contract in August of that year, but EMI's label in America, Capitol Records, refused an option to release their records in the U.S. That was a big mistake on their part, but Epstein didn't need 'em.

The Beatles' first record, "Love Me Do," debuted on the major British charts on December 15, 1962, and reached a peak of #17. But Pete Best wasn't on it. Right when they were about to sign with EMI Records in August, he was thrown out of the group. It's that simple, but it's complicated also because of all the different reasons as to why. And Best as well as all The Beatles had their own stories, so I Best leave that one for another book. Anyway, Ringo Starr joined the group on drums in August 1962.

After their next record hit a peak of #2 in England in the spring of 1963, every other record The Beatles put out on 45 till 1969 topped the British charts. But what has enlightened me the most was in 1993, when I bought a nine-CD album box set imported from Italy on Great Dane Records that had over 200 songs on it, called *The Beatles: The Complete BBC Sessions*. Except for the first six songs from March and June 1962, which had Pete Best on drums, all of the rest were from between January 26, 1963, and June 7, 1965, with Ringo Starr on drums. I got a deal on this thing, and I wanted it out of curiosity, because the song titles blew me away. Many unreleased and well-hidden until then. After listenin' to this thing, I know now John, Paul, George, and even Ringo were comin' out of the fifties school of raw rockabilly, rock 'n' roll, and solid rhythm & blues. It blew my mind.

Except for the first six songs, all the rest were studio recordings. There were a lot of duplicate versions, also. Sure, there was the "She Loves You" and "I Want to Hold Your Hand" stuff on there, but that was this new style they'd created that I hated so much in '64. But in between these are four early Elvis rockabilly songs which are all pretty obscure. The unbelievable track is George Harrison's lead vocal on the Charlie Feathers/ Stan Kesler song "I Forgot to Remember to Forget." Harrison is as serious as a heart attack when he's singin' this song. You really can't hear his British accent that these boys were known for. The whole band is playin' the song straight. Copying the original the best way they knew how to. And this was recorded on May 18, 1964.

There's six Carl Perkins songs that Carl cut at Sun Records between 1955 and 1958. Now I know everybody knows The Beatles recorded, released, and charted with three of Carl Perkins's best rockabilly classics, but what most rockabilly fans didn't know all these years is they also recorded three additional ones, "Glad All Over," "Lend Me Your Comb," and an unbelievable hillbilly-soundin' version of "Sure to Fall."

There were a couple Buddy Holly songs, "Cryin' Waitin' Hopin' " and "Words of Love." Of course, there were nine Chuck Berry songs and other rockabilly songs that were recorded in the late fifties by artists such as Chan Romero and Eddie Fontaine. There was the best of mid to late fifties and early sixties pure rock 'n' roll and black rhythm & blues, also. There were two Coasters songs. They weren't the silly "Yakkety Yak" and "Charlie Brown" novelty songs The Coasters are known for, either. The Beatles did solid renditions of "Young Blood" and "Three Cool Cats." Four of Little Richard's best fifties songs are on there. Other great black rock 'n' roll artists from '60 to '62 were on there, such as Barrett Strong, Arthur Alexander, Smokey Robinson & The Miracles, and a few others.

But another cover song by The Beatles that blew me away was The Johnny Burnette Rock 'N Roll Trio song "Lonesome Tears in My Eyes" from 1956. Now this was cut on July 23, 1963, and John Lennon in his lead vocal is trying real hard to duplicate the great stutterin', stammerin', hiccuppin' style Johnny Burnette had on his original. John was sure tryin' his damndest to lay down a rockabilly vocal, and the rest of the group rocked pretty good on it, too. So what else can I say, except that I'm sure John and The Beatles could have easily covered Johnny Burnette's 1960 Top 10 pop hit "Dreamin'," which was a bigger hit in England than in the U.S. But they didn't, 'cause "Dreamin' " was just that. A teeny-bopper pop hit. It didn't have the guts of The Johnny Burnette Trio rockabilly songs. Those are the ones that have outlasted and by now outsold all Johnny's early sixties pop hits. I didn't hear any Paul Anka, Freddy Cannon, Buddy Knox, Bobby Vee, Bill Haley, or Boyd Bennett songs on there, either. All of them made the charts during the mid to late fifties.

Sure, the Fab Four went through all kinds of musical changes over the years, John Lennon especially. He started out playin' and singin' rockabilly and rock 'n' roll, and even after The Beatles split up, he came back to it on his 1975 album simply titled *Rock 'n' Roll*. It's not a particularly good album. There's several rockabilly classic songs on there, as well as rock 'n' roll and R&B songs. The first song on side one is Gene Vincent's

"Be-Bop-A-Lula," and the album cover pretty much says it all. On it you see John Lennon dressed in a black leather jacket, jeans, and motorcycle boots, with his hair up and combed back, with a brooding look on his face. He's standin' alone in the dimly lit doorway of a sleazy joint with the words "Rock 'n' Roll" in old neon lights. So I wonder what John Lennon could have been thinkin' in the mellow music days of 1975 when he had this album cover shot. Could he have been thinkin' about his idol, the Black Leather Rebel, Gene Vincent, when they toured together thirteen or fourteen years back, and who had died a few years earlier? Maybe, 'cause it seemed he was tryin' to look the part of Gene Vincent on that album cover. Or could John have been thinkin' after almost twenty years of goin' through so many different musical, personal, and political changes in his life, he wished he could go right back where he started before everything around him got complicated? Back to the rockabilly days in Liverpool when the music and times were good, and you always had fun, with something to look forward to? Whatever he was thinkin', that goin'-back-to-his-roots album would be his last one for five years. When John came out of semi-retirement in 1980, he was forty years old. Then he'd record his final album. Which still holds up as a better pop album than anything the other three Beatles had recorded since their split. I'll always believe John Lennon was a rocker in his heart.

It goes without sayin' Lennon and McCartney were great songwriters in both pop music and some rock 'n' roll, but when The Beatles hit and hit hot and hard, all of U.S. pop music was hurt worse than even when Dick Clark had his Philadelphia boys into high gear. For three years, between early 1964 and early 1967, the U.S. was hit so damn hard on the pop music charts with the worst bunch of silly, no-talent, freaky-lookin' British groups, the likes of which had never been seen before, like Herman's Hermits and Freddie & The Dreamers. It didn't stop there. It even rolled over onto the American bands who took on the new British sound and look, such as The Monkees and Gary Lewis & The Playboys. Of course, when this three-year period was up, the only ones that would prove to last, 'cause they had talent, were The Beatles and The Rolling Stones.

I don't care what some rock historians have written about the first wave of the British Invasion and how wonderful it seems to them; most of the British music of 1964 and '65 was as hokey and pathetic as anything Johnny Crawford or Paul Peterson had hit with a few years earlier. Those years 1964 – 1967 were just a period of really silly, wimpy music that dominated the *Billboard* Top 10 pop charts. FM radio was just beginning to come in, but it was still Top 40 AM radio that everyone listened to. At least young people in their teens and twenties. The Motown sound and some of the other new black music was about the only relief you were able to get from the garbage the major record labels were dumpin' out at that time. That is, if you wanted to hear some form of rock 'n' roll. I mean, Gene Vincent's "Be-Bop-A-Lula" and Little Richard's "Tutti Frutti" may have had silly words to 'em, but there was real fire, soul, and passion in their music.

Now, when The Beatles first hit and brought a whole new look and sound to pop music, in some ways it helped some of the true rock 'n' roll, rockabilly, and R&B fifties legends. It probably helped Chuck Berry the most. Besides The Beatles in '64, Johnny Rivers was also havin' big chart hits with Chuck's original fifties rockers. Chuck had served his time in jail and was out now, so him and Chess Records (his original fifties label) wasted no time in slammin' out six new 45 singles between the spring of '64 and the spring of '65 that were all recorded in the same old fifties style of rock 'n' roll and rockabilly that made Chuck's music so great. It was all newly written music and words, but it was still all solid American rock 'n' roll and rockabilly. The first three records were Chuck's biggest comeback *Billboard* chart hits. "Nadine" made it up to #23 in the spring of '64, "No Particular Place to Go" reached #10 during the summer of '64, and "You Never Can Tell" peaked out at #14 in the early fall of '64. Chuck's next three records weren't as successful, not because they were any less rockin' and solid, but times were constantly changin' and America was bein' flooded by every weird little guy with a Beatle haircut by then. When one of Chuck's best artistic rockers hit *Billboard* on December 12, 1964, it was only able to make it up to #41 in January 1965. The song was "Promised Land." How much better can Chuck get? But he'd have to wait another seven years or so to come back with his #1 novelty hit "My Ding-A-Ling." Then that was pretty much it as far as hearin' him on Top 40 radio. But Chuck could always be found playin' live somewhere over the years.

The Beatles were doin' Little Richard's songs early on in '64 here in America, so he set the Bible aside for awhile to teach these English boys how the real thing was done with his music. During July and August of 1964, Little Richard smacked back onto the *Billboard* pop charts with a great new screamer called "Bama Lama Bama Loo." This new song was in the same scorchin' rock 'n' roll style of all his great fifties classics. It holds up against any of 'em. It was on his old original 1950s record label, also, Specialty Records. It only made it up to #82 and dropped off after only four weeks, but Little Richard stayed out there again for a couple more years. Then he went back to preachin', and then again in 1970 he came back, this time on Reprise Records, with a couple new songs that hit the bottom end of the *Billboard* pop charts but were then more about the racial conflicts and imprisonment of blacks in a white-dominated America at the time than they were about great rock 'n' roll.

Roy Orbison was another one during the spring and summer of 1964 that saw his final hit record when "Oh, Pretty Woman" went all the way up to #1. Great rock 'n' roll and rockabilly like that always holds up and'll always come back by some new artist. Roy had toured with The Beatles before they hit it big in America. When they got over here, in the beginning they were doin' all kinds of great old rockabilly and rock 'n' roll songs, but not after 1965. After "Oh, Pretty Woman," Roy Orbison wouldn't come even remotely close to the *Billboard* pop Top 10 charts, on his own, and others I failed to mention from '64 and early '65 wouldn't either. It would take Elvis himself over four years after The Beatles hit to come back and prove he was still the coolest rockin' fiery-eyed cat rockabilly or rock 'n' roll music ever saw, when he did his legendary '68 comeback TV special.

Bobby Fuller

I was still a subscriber to *Billboard* in the spring of 1966 and always followed what was high up into the charts. With only a very few exceptions, by that time there was a new form of music that was just starting to build a stronghold on radio airwaves. The hippie drug culture movement and its music were now comin' on strong. The best exception and true example of the 1950s rockabilly sound that made it up into the *Billboard* pop Top 10 charts came in March 1966, when The Bobby Fuller Four took the old Sonny Curtis-penned song "I Fought the Law" up to #9. You could maybe look on "I Fought the Law" as the final rockabilly song that came out of the old school of the 1950s that was able to inch its way into the *Billboard* pop Top 10 charts that was sung and played by an artist and group who grew up influenced by West Texas 1950s rockabilly and released by a label owned by the man, Bob Keene, who was responsible for releasing some of the final original rockabilly songs that made the *Billboard* national charts in the late 1950s.

Bobby Fuller was born in Goosecreek, Texas, in 1943. His family moved to Salt Lake City until 1956, when they moved again to El Paso, where Bobby's father found steady work at the El Paso Natural Gas Company. Bobby Fuller was twelve, not quite thirteen, when they first got to El Paso, and driven by the sounds of Elvis all throughout 1956. But from 1957 on, Buddy Holly's music would make an impact that would last till the end of Bobby Fuller's short life. According to Bobby's mother, he was totally obsessed with the best of Buddy Holly's rockabilly music his entire life. To Bobby Fuller, that was the only kind of rock 'n' roll that really drove him and that was true to the bone. When Buddy Holly was killed in early February 1959, it was Bobby Fuller who carried on Buddy's poundin' rockabilly beat in practically all his future live and recorded songs. Bobby Vee would only use it for a short time as a launchin' pad or short-lived vehicle to achieve his short-lived teenybopper success, but Bobby Fuller would live and breathe it for the rest of his short life.

I can't give Bobby Fuller and his group the space they so justly deserve, but if you want to read (and you should) the best and most in-depth and honest story on Bobby Fuller's short life, I believe it's still available in *Kicks* magazine #6, written by Miriam Linna back in 1988. Miriam got all the facts straight, and a more accurate story could never be written on Bobby Fuller's personal and musical life than this one. I'm only gonna give some bare facts on The Bobby Fuller Four.

After havin' his first 45 record released in 1961, Bobby Fuller was billed as only Bobby Fuller until 1964 and had seven or eight 45 releases under his own name, 'cause that was during a time when solo artists ruled the charts. These 45 releases were on various small labels in the Southwest. By 1964, Bobby Fuller had become the "Rock 'n' Roll King of the Southwest." By then, he was in constant demand, playin' every teen club, community hall, high school gymnasium, and nightclub throughout Texas and neighboring states.

Bobby first recorded "I Fought the Law" in 1964, and it was released on the Exeter Records label then. By late 1964, after Bobby and his band had played as far west as Fresno, California, he came to the attention of Bob Keene, who had started and owned Del-Fi Records since early 1958. Bob Keene was the first one to take a chance on a sixteen-year-old Ritchie Valens back then and charted several big songs on him before Ritchie's death in early '59. Keene had regional chart success in '59 with Chan Romero and was in the *Billboard* Top 10 once

again in 1960 with Ron Holden's "Love You So" on Del-Fi Records' subsidiary label, Donna Records. Keene kept churnin' out pretty good rock 'n' roll and rockabilly-type material on his various labels throughout the early 1960s. In late '64, Keene released one 45 on Bobby Fuller on the Donna Records label. By now, The Beatles had hit it big, and group names were the "in thing" in pop music, so the record came out under Bobby Fuller & The Fanatics.

Keene had recently started another subsidiary record label to his Del-Fi Records family and called it Mustang Records. A very appropriate name in California at the time, due to the huge popularity of the new classic Mustang cars the Ford Motor Company had just come out with. So in 1965, Bobby Fuller had four 45 releases on the Mustang label, the last of which was called "Let Her Dance," which never made it onto the *Billboard* pop charts, but was a huge success all over the West Coast. Liberty Records even licensed it from Bob Keene and released it at the time.

In late 1965, The Bobby Fuller Four were about the hottest real rock 'n' roll nightclub act out on the Sunset Strip in Hollywood. Bobby Fuller was totally committed to keeping true American rock 'n' roll alive in 1965. When he was asked by a journalist out there to describe or define the music he sang and played, he simply replied, "Just Texas rock 'n' roll, and it's nothin' new. We've been playin' it for years all in the same way. It's the same thing The Beatles have been trying to play but can't. They come close, but they ain't from West Texas." The Bobby Fuller Four's next 45 release after "Let Her Dance" was a newly recorded version of "I Fought the Law." That's the one that catapulted him into the *Billboard* pop Top 10 charts, put him on "Shindig," "Hullabulloo," "Where the Action Is," and every other national teen TV show at the time. The group was also in one stupid movie singin' one stupid song at the time. This forgettable movie was called *The Ghost of Bikini Beach*.

The Bobby Fuller Four's follow-up to "I Fought the Law" was a remake of a great old fifties Buddy Holly rockabilly tune called "Love's Made a Fool of You." After debuting on the *Billboard* pop charts on April 16, 1966, it climbed up to a peak of #26, which is more than respectable for a great American rockin' song at this date during this dreary musical period. No one will ever be able to redo the song "Love's Made a Fool of You" better than Bobby Fuller. He sounds so much like Buddy Holly on it, it's uncanny, and his passion and love for that music comes through in a heavy way.

Bobby's next 45, "The Magic Touch," released shortly before his untimely death, failed to chart. But Bobby Fuller didn't have much time to promote it, either. His death came on July 18, 1966. It was said Bobby died from asphyxiation. He was found dead in his car by his mother outside the home that they shared together in Hollywood. The newspapers reported Bobby's death as a suicide, and the Los Angeles Coroner's report called it "due to undetermined causes." It remains an unsolved mystery to this day. But anyone who was there will tell you it reeked of foul play and an L.A. Police cover-up. Which, due to recent outcomes of Los Angeles prosecution trials, is very believable. When his mother found him early that afternoon (his car wasn't there in the mid morning), Bobby was badly beaten up, burned, doused in gasoline, and gasoline was later found inside his body. So, from what the authorities concluded, it came down to Bobby Fuller drivin' himself home about ten or eleven o'clock in the mornin', then beatin' himself up, throwin' gasoline all over his body while takin' a few swigs, and then takin' his Zippo lighter out to light up a Lucky Strike and, gee whiz, he accidentally killed himself. Yeah, right! Like I said, that small part, and much more, plus his whole great career, is all in *Kicks* magazine #6, from the people at Norton Records. In the story, band members and close friends are quoted as sayin' Bobby Fuller was involved with drugs and the new drug scene that was pickin' up speed the first six months of 1966 out in L.A. It wasn't just in L.A. then. It was goin' on in every major city and smaller ones all over the country at the time. It was sure gettin' in high gear around the Washington, D.C., area where I was in the summer of 1966.

Booking Shows

After the first show I co-booked with Barry Richards in the late summer of '63, I struck out on my own. In December '63, I'd put my own $100 deposit down with the guy who rented out the Bladensburg Fire Hall for a Friday night show in April 1964. The rhythm & blues group The Clovers were a popular act and always have been in the D.C. area, where they always stayed based out of, so I booked them along with TNT Tribble & His Band to back up them and Barry Darvel. Barry also got his start in D.C. and had made some solid rock 'n' roll and rockabilly 45s on the D.C.-based Colt 45 record label in 1959 and '60. His best songs were "Geronimo Stomp," "How Will It End?" "Have Gun Will Travel," and "Run Little Billy." Barry had bounced around doin' mostly teenage pop tunes for various record labels with

no real major success, but he was still recording and performing in and around the D.C. and New York areas throughout 1965 at least. Even some of Barry's teenage pop tunes weren't all that bad, 'cause you could hear a bit of a doo wop flavor to 'em. Barry still dug doin' fifties-type rock 'n' roll in '64 and '65, though. That show went real well, 'cause like I said, there was still this whole age group between eighteen and twenty-five that thought all this new British music sucked. So again the place was packed. This trend continued for the next couple years. I was havin' some success and havin' fun myself doin' these shows, so I continued puttin' on two a year until the spring of 1966.

I guess I'd always wanted to someday buy me a motorcycle after first seein' Marlon Brando in the film *The Wild One* in 1954. And I'd rationalize in my head that why wear a motorcycle jacket and boots if you didn't own a motorcycle? So in February 1964 I bought my first Harley. And that spring I joined my first motorcycle club, The Roaring 20—not an outlaw gang, but a group fully sanctioned by the American Motorcycle Association. They weren't completely innocent by no means, but a well-organized club of guys who helped out and supported each member. I stayed, rode, and partied with 'em about as long as I did or longer than any of the outlaw clubs I joined or formed later on. I know all the members of The Roaring 20, along with their wives, girlfriends, and other friends, all showed up to support the three final shows I put on at the Bladensburg Fire Hall. They loved all the rock 'n' roll and rockabilly artists, their music, the dancin', drinkin', and good-time fun. With these guys and the usual group of other friends and young people around the Bladensburg and Hyattsville area I could always count on for these shows, it wound up makin' all three of 'em pretty successful.

I didn't lose any money on any of the three of them, although on the first out of the three after I joined The Roaring 20, I came close to losin' money, 'cause I'd brought in Charlie Rich to headline a show that also featured Link Wray & His Wraymen, along with The TNT Tribble Band. This was in September 1964. Charlie Rich had left Sun Records by this time and had only one *Billboard* pop chart hit under his belt, but I'd been buyin' his records on RCA Victor's subsidiary label Groove Records in '63 and '64, and still thought he sounded pretty good and was doin' some solid rock 'n' roll on a few of the numbers. But when I talked with his booking agent, they wanted $500 plus airfare, motel room, transportation, etc. Well, at first I turned it down, but when they cut out the motel room and knocked the price back to $400 (which was still too much for 1964), I agreed to send 'em their deposit. They wouldn't let me talk to Charlie Rich himself but assured me he'd do whatever songs he'd recorded in the past that I wanted him to do, just so long as the backup band knew the songs. Of course, I had to provide the piano for Charlie, which wasn't a problem.

Charlie did an hour-and-a-half set. He was a nice guy and really wasn't a problem for me either. We got along good at the time. Charlie did most of the rockabilly-type songs I wanted to hear, such as "Whirlwind," "Gonna Be Waitin'," "Rebound," "Lonely Weekends," and a few others, but there were a few others I wanted him to do that he told me he just didn't want to do and that was that. He recorded 'em, but he had others he preferred to do. I told him what his booking agent had said, but he didn't care, so after that I either talked to the artist about that part of it or got it in writing (with one exception in late '66, which you'll read about shortly). Now, Link Wray, on the other hand, I knew was more than willin' to play or by now even sing anything he knew that I wanted to hear. Anyway, after payin' Charlie Rich the rest of his money, along with Link, TNT Tribble, and the other expenses, I doubt if I made over $20. It was only like two bucks to get in for a show like that back then.

The TNT Tribble Band either was booked on another gig or was about to hang up their rockin' shoes when I booked my next show in March 1965. I had met Crash Craddock back in 1959 and 1960 on three or four occasions down at the Milt Grant show. His first records in 1957 and '58 on the Colonial and Date record labels were good rockabilly songs. I really like those. Two of his best on those labels were "Aw Poor Little Baby" and "Lulu Lee." Crash still had a rockabilly sound when he got a major record contract with Columbia Records in 1959. Crash almost made it big in late '59 and '60. Columbia Records was promotin' him in a lot of the teen magazines in '59 as the new upcoming teen idol. Crash did a lot of touring for almost two years with the likes of The Everly Brothers, Paul Anka, Frankie Avalon, and others, but it only resulted in one song, "Don't Destroy Me," that would make the *Billboard* pop charts for one week during November 1959.

Crash was suprised to find out when he did a tour of Australia with a couple of the top acts of '59 and '60 I just mentioned that he had a #1 record over there and the 1,000 or so teenage girls who were all waiting for the plane to land at the Melbourne airport were all awaiting his arrival. The other big-name hit record artists all thought they were the ones who'd be mobbed by these girls, but it was Crash they all charged straight for at that time. While he was still on Columbia in 1960, Crash, I'm pretty sure, was the first pop artist to record the song "One Last Kiss," which a few years later would become famous in the Broadway play and then major motion picture called *Bye Bye Birdie*. I'd liked most of his Columbia Records. Practically all of 'em either had the rockabilly or Elvis fifties ballad style to 'em.

After Columbia released him in late 1960, he had a few 45s released on Mercury Records in 1961 and '62. After they failed, Crash got out of the business and went back home to Greensboro, North Carolina, where he was originally from. In 1964 he tried to make a comeback doin' some rock 'n' roll and country-type material and had several 45s released in '64 and '65, again with no success to speak of. So back to Greensboro he went. After a lot of phone calls, that's where I finally got hold of him in the early months of '65, and he was only too glad to come up and do a one-night show in late April 1965 for me. He had recently gone back to laying sheet rock down in Carolina, and I'm sure this was a nice break from that work.

I got Danny Denver & His Band to back him up and also used Barry Darvel. Danny Denver always put on a great show of his own back in those days, and as usual, the night went well. Crash was really a great guy and a hell of a good rocker, too. He was still only about twenty-six years old at the time, and he loved doin' a lot of his old rockabilly songs, along with other great rock 'n' roll and rockabilly classics. The whole crowd loved it.

By early '65, Crash and his other original fifties rockabilly contemporaries were right in the middle of their darkest days. Warren Smith and Bob Luman had already turned themselves over to Nashville and country music, and soon after would come Conway Twitty and even Jerry Lee Lewis. Others like Narvel Felts and Charlie Rich would follow later in the seventies to also meet with huge success. Many other talented ones such as Billy Lee Riley, Ray Smith, Hayden Thompson, etc. also gave valiant tries but without much success.

Crash Craddock was one of the fortunate ones, though, who racked up seventeen *Billboard* country charts hits that all went Top 10, along with three others that made it to #1, between 1971 and 1979. In 1974, he had two records cross over onto the *Billboard* pop charts when "Rub It In" made it up to #16 and when he covered The

Drifters' classic fifties rhythm & blues hit "Ruby Baby." Through 1983, Crash racked up a total of 40 *Billboard* country chart hits. Like with Narvel Felts' 1970s country hits, you could always find some great old fifties rocka-billy classics buried somewhere on his albums. During his country hit period, he was goin' under the name Billy "Crash" Craddock.

Well, The Roaring 20 motorcycle club members and their wives, girlfriends, and other friends all supported the show in a big way, and in addition to once again packing the hall, they all sure enjoyed seein' great rock 'n' roll that we all still loved.

The same held true with the next show I did at Bladensburg Fire Hall, in September 1965, with Bob Luman, Barry Darvel, and Danny Denver & His Band. I already told you in Chapter 7 that this show remains my all-time personal favorite one.

By the end of 1965, I had become disenchanted with The Roaring 20 and joined an outlaw club that called themselves the Kamikazes. At the same time, in December 1965 was when I got ahold of Ray Smith to come up and do his brand of rockabilly music over at the Bladensburg Fire Hall. At least that's where it was scheduled to take place. But after ridin' with the Kamikazes biker club for about three months, I joined the Pagans. When I joined this outlaw group, I had no way of knowin' what their major goal was at the time. That was for the Pagans to become as big in number and as powerful as the Hell's Angels were on the West Coast. Over the next couple years, they'd almost wind up accomplishing that goal, with all the media attention that would be thrown upon 'em after certain things the group did.

After becoming a member of the Pagans in March '66, I was mainly concentrating on pullin' off this Ray Smith rock 'n' roll/rockabilly show the following month. But when the guy who booked the Bladensburg Fire Hall saw I was flyin' Pagan colors (wearin' their insignia), he told me he couldn't let the show go on, 'cause the police wouldn't stand for it. He told me I was in for real trouble with that bunch. He returned the deposit I had given him on the hall for the upcoming show. I didn't want to cancel for various reasons. One was I'd already sent Ray Smith half his money to get up here and had Danny Denver and his band scheduled to back him up. I didn't know where I could put the show at this late date. When I told the officers in the Pagans of this problem, they told me not to worry, I could hold it at Vista Motorcycle Raceway, which was in Palmer Park, Maryland.

Ray Smith drove up from his home in the South so he could bring in a couple of buddies he had to back him up. Danny Denver's drummer also backed him up, and Ray alternated with Danny's piano player on some of the songs he chose to do, which were all great, and the mixed crowd of both blacks and whites loved both acts. Though they'd really never heard of Ray Smith. This was a completely different audience than the ones at the Bladensburg Fire Hall shows. Nevertheless, it was still a full house, and just about everybody was more than happy to pay to see a top-class rock 'n' roll and rocka-billy show of some great music from the 1950s.

Ray Smith and his buddies, along with Danny Denver and his band, were more than happy with the reception they got from this wild bunch of bikers and their outlaw women when they sang the songs of Elvis, Jerry Lee Lewis, Chuck Berry, Fats Domino, Gene Vincent, Ray Charles, Eddie Cochran, Little Richard, Dale Hawkins, Jackie Wilson, and many others. We all went home happy that night, and the next mornin' I woke up on the floor of Ray Smith's motel room with one hell of a hangover.

After Ray Smith and his boys headed back home, I didn't know it at the time, but I was headin' into deep trouble. The real trouble with the Pagans didn't begin till around December 1966. Up till that time, it was all one big good time party with me, and it was a way to escape the British Invasion music and the phony hippie love music of groups like The Mamas & The Papas. The Pagans were at least into solid American rock 'n' roll. A good bit of which I didn't care too much for at the time, though. I guess that's why I decided to try another rock 'n' roll/rockabilly-type show when I looked up in the *Billboard* yearly book for music promoters on who I'd like to book.

I decided to call the Bob Neal Agency in Nashville in September 1966, to see how much Conway Twitty would cost me to bring up for a show. Bob Neal, who had been Elvis's first real professional manager over a decade earlier, was now exclusively booking Conway. I knew Conway had just recently switched over to singin' country music, but he had been on the *Billboard* country charts in 1966 with only two minor hits that barely made the Top 40, and I figured he could still do a good rock 'n' roll/rockabilly-type show.

When I asked Bob Neal how much Conway would cost to come up and do two hours of music, he told me $1000. I told him he or Conway had to be out of their minds, and that I could get Brenda Lee for around that much, and she still had real hit records. I went round and round with Bob Neal and his son Sonny Neal, who finally called me and said these were Conway's final conditions: He'd fly into Washington's International Airport from Oklahoma on the morning of January 12, 1967, which was the date of the show, I'd have a car waiting to pick up him and his three-piece backup band, The Lonely Blue Boys, with their luggage and equipment, and then proceed to take them to a respectable hotel or motel with a restaurant on the premises. Conway would pay the overnight hotel expenses himself, and I would then see to it that he and his group had transportation to and from the show that night and back to the airport the following morning. The lowest price he would do this show for was $750, but that was only under the condition that he would choose all of the songs he would do, which would only be country songs with the exception of "It's Only Make Believe," and that the entire $750 had to be paid in full to the Bob Neal Agency two weeks prior to the date of the show.

Well, I told Sonny I only had two slight problems with all of that. One was if the only damn rock 'n' roll type song Conway was willin' to do was "It's Only Make Believe," why in the hell was he still callin' his backup band after one of his few Top 10 rock 'n' roll hits, "Lonely Blue Boy." I told Sonny nobody knew or cared to listen (at that time) to country songs by a fifties rock 'n' roll and rockabilly artist. They were gonna want to hear his rockin' hits, plus other rock 'n' roll songs he sang so well. Well, as booking agents usually do, Sonny told me not to worry and to talk with Conway when he got there, and he was sure he'd do whatever the crowd or audience requested, whether it was rock 'n' roll or country. I'd heard that before, but reluctantly I said OK. So that solved one problem. The other was that I knew it was standard to only send half the artist's money prior to the show and the other half before he went on stage. I told him I had done that with both Charlie Rich and Bob Luman and never had a problem. Well, I was then told it was because Conway was givin' me a break on his usual price (yeah, right!) that he wanted it all in full before he got there. So again I reluctantly agreed.

So when all the dust settled and they said they'd get the union contracts off to me right away, I proceeded to find a real nice hall to put this expensive fifties rocker into. There was no way I intended at that time to put Conway Twitty in at Vista Raceway. Within a few days, I put a sizable deposit down at a big hall on G Street in N.W.

Washington, D.C., located inside The Presidential Arms Hotel. I figured it had a restaurant, and he was payin' the high cost of stayin' there that night anyway. Of course I cleaned my act up and went in there neatly dressed, as I planned to be for the night of the show, which I was going to spend some money to advertise to open for the general, average, normal public, in hopes they would attend in masses.

Well, things got a little crazy over the next couple months, though I did manage to receive the contracts, but only sent $375 of the full amount back with the contracts early in November '66 and told 'em either take it or leave it. They took it. Then I proceeded to book an opening band. Because Conway was now into country music, I chose a local group from the Beltsville, Maryland, area called The Frank Gosman Band. I had my tickets printed up and my all-important newspaper advertisement finished by mid December '66. Then the whole damn roof caved in on me. A Christmas Eve party with the Pagans in Newark, New Jersey, got out of hand and landed a bunch of us—me included—in jail until New Year's Day 1967. When that happened, I made my mind up I was quittin' the Pagans as soon as possible.

I was finally released on New Year's Day and went to the bus station and got back to the downtown D.C. Greyhound terminal and then caught a local bus back to Brentwood, Maryland. I got home about nine o'clock at night on New Year's Day, 1967, and I got to tell ya, to put it mildly, mom wasn't too happy to see me. The first thing I was shown was the *Washington Daily News,* which had all of the local Pagans' names in it. Mom had mine underlined, of course. But that was only the start of some new troubles I wasn't prepared for.

After cleanin' my act up and lookin' as good as I could, I rode down to my job around noon the next day. At least I had a paycheck comin' that I'd missed. I got it, but it was the final one, as my boss told me they knew I was involved in the Pagans' Newark disaster, so papers had been put in to terminate me, but they agreed to let me resign so it wouldn't go on my record. After I left there I rode down to G Street to The Presidential Arms Hotel, where I had a room reserved in Conway Twitty's name, plus I had the deposit on the hall and the advertisements were now really in the local newspapers, so I wanted to make sure everything was OK on that front. It wasn't. The guy I'd booked the hall with had also heard or seen my name involved with the Newark fiasco, so he returned my deposit very quickly, even though I tried my hardest to assure him that the Pagans didn't even know of this show, none would be present at it, and it was a completely straight-type show for the general public. Which the Pagans and all outlaw bikers during the mid and late sixties referred to as "citizens."

When I was ridin' back from there that day, I felt like my life was crumblin' around me. Conway Twitty and The Lonely Blue Boys were arriving in ten days. I didn't have but one choice, option, or whatever you want to call it. I went over and seen the president of the Pagans and told him that I was bringin' in Conway Twitty and his band in ten days and needed a place to put him. Well, by this time the Pagans had so much control at Vista Raceway, it only took one phone call from him to get it OK'd for the night of January 12. He seemed at least to understand I had a lot of money invested in this show and basically only wanted straight "citizens" there who'd pay the money that I needed to go over the top on it. Plus this was a former rock 'n' roll/rockabilly singer who wanted to sing primarily country. That it wasn't like the previous Ray Smith show at all. So he told me he'd take care of it, and for me not to worry, that it would all work out. He made the call and the show was set for Vista. But he did tell me Conway would be singin' rock 'n' roll that night, whether he wanted to or not. That was enough to give me plenty to worry about, 'cause I knew what it meant.

I did go back down to The Presidential Arms Hotel twice, until I found out what doorman would be working on the evening of January 12, so whoever was gonna show up down there to see Conway, he could at least give them flyers I had quickly printed up for this last-minute change that had directions on how to get to Vista. I was worried, I can tell you that much. I did have a little money from my last paycheck, so I gave this nice black doorman $10 to do this favor for me. He swore he could get it done without gettin' into trouble or anybody findin' out. I know he did pass some out as some real brave unknowing "citizens" showed up that night, all dressed up very nicely, I might add. But a whole lot more musta showed up at The Presidential Arms and decided not to make the trek out to Palmer Park, Maryland. I believe it was only the handful of really die-hard Conway Twitty straight rock 'n' roll fans that did come all the way out when the location of the show was changed. I was sellin' all tickets at the door that night of the show. I didn't sell any in advance like I had done at the Bladensburg Fire Hall shows.

Another problem I had was I knew I had to get a straight-lookin' normal, "citizen"-type person who had a big car to pick up Conway Twitty and his three Lonely Blue Boys and their equipment at the airport the morning of January 12. There was no need (I felt) to have Conway in a bad mood until he saw the place he was playin' in that night. The one person who seemed perfect to do this big favor for me at the time, which over all these years I have been eternally grateful for, was my older sister, Anna Mae. The best part was she drove the biggest and most impressive looking car of anyone I knew. It was a big shiny 1960 gold Cadillac. So Anna Mae, with some reservations, agreed to drive me over to the airport, where Conway had landed his private small plane after flying in from Oklahoma, and pick up him and his three band members and their equipment and take them to a motel.

When me and Anna Mae met Conway and his group at the airport, they had quite a bit of equipment, such as guitar and bass amps, several of their guitars, and a Big Bull stand-up acoustic bass. We weren't able to fit everything in her trunk. Well, I sure wish I had a picture of what it looked like inside that Cadillac on the ride over. The trunk was half open and tied down in the back, but the craziest memory is to see Anna Mae drivin' these three big healthy ol' country boys in the back seat, all scrunched up with that big old bass fiddle layin' across 'em along with part of their luggage. Conway was in the front seat on the passenger side, and he even had an acoustic guitar in its case between his legs, and I was in the middle with another piece of equipment on my lap. It was one hell of a sight, I can tell you that much. One that my sister clearly remembers to this day.

Finally, we all arrived at the motel. But they didn't accept the kind of credit card Conway had. By this time he was fuming. So it was back in the car and down the road to a different motel. I helped get 'em unloaded and get everything into their rooms, and Conway had calmed down by then. After a few choice words to me, Anna Mae quickly split from that motel, leaving me there with Conway and his boys.

I made a few phone calls from Conway's room and got one of the guys in the Pagans to come and pick me up over at the Howard Johnson's restaurant. I didn't feel Conway needed to see what his audience was going to look like just yet. Though I was forced to tell him the location had to be changed at the last minute because the room was taken away from me for some political fund-raiser for the city of Washington, D.C., and I couldn't fight city hall. Conway understood that. He didn't understand when I told him he'd be playing in front of an audience that I didn't think he had ever played in front of before. Plus the place was nowhere near as nice, but it was all I could come up with at the last minute. Conway told me not to worry about the people he'd be playin' for, that he'd played in front of every kind of audience that there was. When he said that, I was thinkin', "That's what you think." He only wanted to make sure I had the P.A. system and the other conditions we'd agreed on taken care of, which I did, and he seemed satisfied with that.

While Conway went on to get some rest, I left there around 2:00 p.m. and told him I'd be back there with at least two cars to pick him and the boys back up around 6:30 p.m. That's when I arrived back there with a couple old straight-lookin' friends. And I was flying my Pagan colors. Between their two cars, I was able to get Conway, his boys, and all their equipment out to where the show was. On the ride over, I reminded Conway his agent had told me he'd sing and play mostly rock 'n' roll, 'cause that's what the audience would be expecting. Conway told me his agent ain't got nothin' to do with what he's gonna sing on stage, and he still insisted he was gonna do mostly country with some rock 'n' roll thrown in.

Well, to make it as short as I can, we arrived at Vista Raceway's indoor ballroom (and I use that word lightly) a little after 7:00 p.m. Frank Gosman and his country band were already there. The P.A. was set up, and the lights were on the stage. There weren't many people there except for the bartenders and a few cleanup people who worked there, along with a dozen or so Pagans and a few of their girlfriends, who were called their "old ladies" or "property," and a few of the regular girls who were always open to being with anybody in the club. They were always referred to as the club's "mamas."

I introduced Conway to Frank Gosman and his group, who Conway seemed to like. Then I went around the bar and a couple tables and collected whatever little money I could from some of the Pagans who were willing to fork it over. Around 7:30 I went over to the door to again collect whatever money I could from those club members that were slowly starting to come in around that time.

Frank Gosman and his band started to play their brand of country right at 8:00 p.m. like they were supposed to, but it didn't matter, 'cause it was still early. The room was gettin' crowded by the time they quit playin' shortly before 9:00. I don't know how they were able to last that long, as during their last several songs, this crowd of about 200 or so Pagans were all booin' after each song, and some were yellin' out that they wanted to either hear rock 'n' roll or to turn the damn jukebox on so everybody could dance to rock 'n' roll, at least.

It was Conway's turn next. After he and the band got set up, he got in front of the mike and said, "Good evening, my name's Conway Twitty." There was instant applause, screams, and whistles. When it started to die down Conway then said, "I used to do a lot of rock 'n' roll a few years back and I'm gonna do some for you tonight." (More wild screams of delight.) "But first I'm gonna start off with one you might remember that's the kind of music I do now." Conway then started out with the Leroy Van Dyke 1961 country/pop crossover hit "Walk On By."

Practically the whole crowd started booing and yellin' for rock 'n' roll. A couple guys down front crushed their beer cans into the edge of the stage and threw 'em up onto the stage. Conway did the shortest version of "Walk On By" I've ever heard. He only sang the first verse, the chorus, then repeated the last lines of the chorus and ended it and immediately turned to his band and gave them a quick title for the next song while the boos were still comin' and then went directly into, of all things, The Beatles song "I Saw Her Standing There." And boy, did he ever rock that song to this wild crowd's approval. I'm thinking, "You've finally seen the light and you're not gonna die tonight."

As soon as Conway ended that one, without sayin' a word, he broke into a great, wild rockin' version of Bo Diddley's "You Can't Judge a Book by the Cover." After that one, Conway could do no wrong. He had this crazy wild bunch of drunken and drugged-up maniacs in his back pocket from then on, doin' almost every Chuck Berry, Little Richard, Elvis, Buddy Holly, Joe Turner, Sam Cooke, Gene Vincent, Jackie Wilson, Jerry Lee Lewis, etc. song he could think of, as well as throwin' in his own rockin' hits such as "It's Only Make Believe," "Lonely Blue Boy," "What Am I Living For," "Danny Boy," "Is a Blue Bird Blue," and a few others.

When he finally finished about an hour-and-fifteen-minute set, Conway was wringin' wet with sweat and his tie was long gone. He just looked at me, grinned, and said, "That felt pretty good. I'm goin' back up and we're gonna play up till midnight. They got my adrenaline runnin' in high gear and I'm gonna keep on givin' 'em what they want." Which he went on to do.

After the show, Conway told me Frank Gosman and his band were gonna take him and his boys back to their rooms, plus come by and drive 'em to the airport in the morning. Which was fine by me. I was just glad this nightmare was finally coming to an end. I told him OK, I'd meet him back over there.

When I got back to his motel room, I told him I could only give him about half of the remaining money I owed him because of the circumstances that were not my fault that happened that night. I told him I'd contact his agent Bob Neal and send him the rest at a later date. Conway seemed to understand and didn't seem at all upset when I only paid him $175 of the $375 that I owed him.

Conway Twitty was genuinely a really nice guy, but he was all business. Even back then. He was doin' things the right way. Conway used his head instead of his heart when it came to takin' chances on the music you love. The music he'd always loved first and foremost was country music, which he went on to become one of the greatest legends and hit makers ever in during all of the 1970s and eighties and even up until June 1993, when he suddenly passed away.

That may have been the last full rock 'n' roll show Conway Twitty ever gave on that night in January 1967. If it was, it was damn sure a great one. It took about a full year after that show for Conway to get his remaining $200 I owed him, at a rate of about $20 a month for ten months starting in March 1967. I made the first few payments, and my mother, much to her dismay, paid off the rest.

In the fall of 1970, me and my wife Pepper went to see Conway at a concert in Gaithersburg, Maryland. He was not only the hottest act in country music at this time, but he was also crossing over onto the pop charts with songs such as "Hello Darlin'." While I stood in the background, Pepper got in a line after the show for autographs. I had told her about the show he did for me and she knew it was true, as my mother and sister had been talking about it around her for about two years now. But when she mentioned her husband had promoted that show with the Pagans in attendance, Conway told her he had never performed in this area since he got into country music, and he certainly was sure he never performed a rock 'n' roll type show for a motorcycle club. Pepper didn't press the issue, but she told me Conway looked uncomfortable when she brought it up to him. But about a year before Conway passed away, during the spring of 1992, I got to talk with him (thanks to Danny Amis) when he was a guest on the old "Nashville Now" live TNN TV show here in Nashville. I brought a copy of

the contract and a letter from Bob Neal on making payments to him on what I owed from that show, and when he saw that, he sort of got a kick out of it. I remember him telling me, "At least you paid the balance of what you owed me. Back then some others didn't. I'm just happy you wound up gettin' out of that wild bunch you were runnin' with back then. That was sure one crazy night. I've told people over the years about that show and said, boy, I never wanted to be put in that position again." Conway told me he didn't have any ill feelings towards me because of it, and that made me feel good. I'm glad I had a chance to confront him with it, and we both left that night feeling all right about each other.

Conway to this day remains one of my all-time favorite rockabilly, rock 'n' roll, and country artists. He did it all!

Ridin' Out the Sixties

As for me, after that January 1967 show, and with the thoughts of spendin' those eight days behind bars in Newark, New Jersey, still fresh in my mind, I was concentrating most on trying to find an easy way to somehow quit, resign, or disassociate myself from the Pagans. I've always tried to do things in a way that made the most common sense to me, which didn't always turn out to be the right way. I had been secretary of the Pagans since July 1966, and had kept all the notes I had taken from each monthly meeting through March 1967. So in early April 1967 I met with the president of the Pagans. I turned over the nine months or so of notes I had taken at meetings and told him I just had to get out. He said quittin' is not allowed. He made it real clear in no uncertain terms if I was serious about quittin' that I would wind up in the underground group. He wasn't talkin' about in hiding, either; he was talkin' about puttin' me six feet under the ground of God's green earth, and I knew it. He told me I better give it some serious thought before I made a final decision. I was young and a whole lot dumber back then, 'cause I told him I already had been thinking about it long and hard, and that I quit and was outta here. Last thing he said to me was, "We'll see ya around, Billy."

I went on to organize a new outlaw gang with some bikers in Montgomery County. I decided the name of this new group would be the Renegades. I took the name from the rock'n' roll/rockabilly-type instrumental group that I had that one great 45 by and had seen perform the two songs in the 1959 flick *The Ghost of Dragstrip Hollow*.

To make a long story short, the Pagans were on the lookout for me, and in January 1968 they caught up with me. Landed me in the hospital with a concussion and twenty-four stitches. I quickly traded my bike for a sleek black two-door '62 Cadillac and left town. I took along with me a girl who had hung out with the Renegades. Her name was Pepper.

We ended up in Nashville, 'cause some of the old rockabilly singers I liked were down there and I wanted to see 'em.

From the time we got to Nashville, the main radio station I listened to was WSM, which has always been the home of "The Grand Ole Opry." Besides doin' continuous nights of drinkin' at Dass' Bar, Tootsie's, The Midnight Hour, and too many others to recall, on Saturday nights me and Pepper always would wind up at Ernest Tubb's Record Shop for the weekly live broadcast of his "Midnight Jamboree" right after "The Grand Ole Opry"

ended. Boy, the country legends Ernest Tubb had on that stage were great, and what was even better was after it all ended, you could go up and meet and talk to 'em. I really dug that back then. They were all just down-home country singers then. I don't remember any I met that had big egos at all. I met so many of 'em, most of whom were young then also, there's no way I could mention 'em all. Of course, Ernest Tubb and Justin Tubb were always there, but besides the regular stars of the Opry, there were a lot more recent stars, such as Willie Nelson, Bobby Bare, Jerry Reed, Connie Smith, Charlie Rich, Jack Greene, Roger Miller, Merle Haggard, Henson Cargill, Melba Montgomery, Bobby Lord, Ernest Ashworth, Charlie King, Warner Mack, etc. Ernest had 'em all, and they were all great back then. The two I remember the best, and, boy, was the record shop packed to the rafters on these nights, were when we saw Johnny Cash and Loretta Lynn. On two separate nights, of course.

Forgettin' to Remember to Forget

𝒮leepy La Beef, I think, was living in Nashville at the same time I was during the spring of 1968, and although our paths never crossed then, I heard a song on the the radio called "Every Day" played quite a bit that I liked, and they said it was sung by Sleepy La Beef. I only had one 45 (and I had it with me then in Nashville) by a singer called Sleepy La Beef. The one I had I'd picked up in Washington, D.C., about ten years before, in the late fifties. It was a great rockabilly song that I played a lot over the years, called "All the Time." It was on Mercury Records in the late fifties. It was rockabilly at its best. Now, this "Every Day" was real good, though not as good as "All the Time," so I went to Ernest Tubb's Record Shop down on Broadway and they had it, so I picked it up. I figured in 1968 there was only one Elvis Presley and one Conway Twitty and one Narvel Felts in the world of music, so there had to be only one Sleepy La Beef. You just don't forget names like those.

"Every Day" was on Columbia Records, and it hit the *Billboard* country charts on April 13, 1968. It reached a peak of #73 and stayed on the charts for three weeks. That was the national charts, but it had to do better in Nashville, 'cause it sure got a lot of airplay for a couple of months during that time when I was living down there.

A few days before I left to go back to Maryland to check on the Renegades for a few days, after this DJ played "Every Day" by Sleepy, there was an advertisement that came on the radio advertising some scary horror movie that was playin' at a local drive-in on the upcoming weekend, called *The Exotic Ones*. The radio ad said one of the stars in this movie was Sleepy La Beef. Well, Pepper loved horror movies back then (and still does), so we went out to this drive-in, 'cause I was interested in seein' what Sleepy La Beef looked like. I'd never seen even a picture of him at the time. Well, man, was I in for a surprise, 'cause it wasn't long before me and Pepper figured out Sleepy La Beef was this swamp monster that only growled and came out at night to strangle people. Sleepy looked about eight feet tall on that old drive-in screen back then. Sleepy's a big man anyway, but they musta used five-foot-two-inch actors and actresses (and I use those words lightly) in that B-rated flick. I'm glad Sleepy stuck to singin' good country, boogie woogie, and rockabilly, 'cause him and everybody else in that film would-a starved to death if they thought they could act. It would be 1976 before I finally found out what Sleepy La Beef really looked like.

In those late winter and early spring months of 1968 in Nashville, another thing me and Pepper enjoyed doin' was goin' over to the old WSM studios and visiting with Ralph Emory, who had an all-night radio show at that time. Ralph had it for a lot of years, I believe, but when we were goin' down there, things couldn't-a been better. Evidently, Ralph would let almost anybody hang out in the studio in those days, 'cause he let us come in there. Once he got to know us, he really enjoyed our company. I've always liked ol' Ralph a lot. I think he started his all-night radio show around 11:00 p.m. or 12:00 midnight, and it ran till at least five the next mornin'. Me and Pepper would usually show up around two or three in the mornin', after a night of drinkin'. I know we went up there and hung out with Ralph at least a couple dozen times. It was great, too. Hell, back then you could not only smoke, but you could slip some beer in and drink a few, too. Hey, Ralph Emory was young then, too. That's just the way it was up there in those days. I remember givin' Merle Haggard one of my beers up there one night when he stopped by for Ralph to interview him. I liked Merle and his music a lot back then and still do. The night Dolly Parton came in there for an interview was really somethin' else, too. Marty Robbins, Dottie West, Del Reeves, Bill Anderson, and all of 'em still stick out in my mind from seein' 'em up there at the old studios at WSM in the early hours of the morning. I didn't know it then, but those were some of the best times of my life, and I bet if Ralph Emory thought real hard, he'd probably think they were pretty damn good days for him, too. Country hadn't gone big-time, uptown then, and everything was in a relaxed atmosphere with no pressure.

During the summer of 1968, Pepper and me worked at Frontier Town in Madison, Tennessee. She was a saloon girl and I was a gunfighter. I got to meet a lot of the country artists who'd show up once in awhile during the weekdays. The one I liked meeting the most at that time was Jimmy Edwards, who recorded a classic rockabilly record for Mercury Records called "Love Bug Crawl" that made the *Billboard* pop charts for three weeks in late January and early February 1958. This was ten years later, and Jimmy looked like he was a little down on his luck, but he really cheered up when I told him I had that old record and still played both sides of it. Jerry Foster was another cat who'd made some decent rockabilly-type records for the Back Beat record label between 1959 and '61, and he kept recording through the early

seventies. He was also surprised I had his old records, as he never did have a national chart hit. I believe Jerry worked at Frontier Town for a portion of that 1968 season. The other one I loved talkin' to there was Waylon Jennings when he showed up down there one weekday morning. Waylon had a great new song at the time, called "Only Daddy That'll Walk the Line." It would wind up bein' his biggest hit up to that time. Waylon really looked great. I remember he was wearin' a black cowboy hat and totin' a six-gun on his hip that day. We both really enjoyed talkin' to each other, especially when I brought up Buddy Holly. Boy, Waylon sure loved Buddy Holly and his music.

The manager at Frontier Town wanted both me and Pepper to come back the following year and work there again, but it just wasn't meant to be. Pepper went to the doctor right after Labor Day and found out what we both thought. That she was pregnant. So we just packed up and headed back home to Maryland. Neither one of us really wanted to leave Nashville then, and I always said someday I'd move back there (it took a long time, though). We got married on November 23, 1968. By that time the Renegades outlaw motorcycle club was no more, and the Pagans had a whole lot more things to think about than me. I got back with some good old drinkin' buddies and I just let the good times roll on right into the next decade. Drinkin', partyin', and goin' to clubs to see old rock 'n' rollers whenever they played in the area. The motorcycle was history, but crazy times continued.

There was real hope in music once again when I saw The Hillbilly Cat (Elvis) turned into a wild panther in early December 1968, in his now-famous comeback TV special. Boy, did he ever prove he was back. After watchin' him on that TV special, I knew Elvis, like me, couldn't give a hoot about the incoming "Woodstock" generation. Also, it's worth noting that Charlie Feathers was down in Memphis, oblivious to what was goin' on in mainstream music, when he went in and recorded a 45 of two of the greatest rockabilly classic songs ever recorded at this late date in 1968, called "Stutterin' Cindy" and "Tear It Up." The great Marcus Van Story was on upright slappin' bass with Charlie on those sides. Charlie knew somethin' the pop music world didn't know in '68: that this rockabilly music was on the way back big-time when the seventies would arrive!

The Seventies:
The Sun Shines Once More

Mainstream Music Stars Cover the 'Billys

Before the new decade of the 1970s even began, everyone in America could see there was definitely a "Bad Moon a-Risin'." During the summer of 1969, John Fogerty's words in that great hit song couldn't have been more on the money than at any other time in this country's history up to then.

Liberalism was at an all-time high by the end of the 1960s. It was an all-out war between blacks who wanted and deserved equal rights, along with the free-spirited, bra-burnin', draft-dodgin', doped-up hippies and yippies who all wanted to run amok and do whatever they damn well pleased, up against the old hard-line political leaders like J. Edgar Hoover, Richard Nixon, and others who weren't about to give in to these young upstarts and weirdos who were trying to change and ruin everything that had been good in this country till they came along.

By the end of 1969, everybody was sick of the Vietnam War that was on national television in new living color. But the outrage had all started with Martin Luther King's assassination in April 1968, with the riots in numerous cities across the U.S., then escalated when the sure-to-be next president of the U.S., Robert Kennedy (John Kennedy's younger brother), was assassinated in June 1968, and it was capped off by Jerry Rubin and his band of yippies and hippies rioting at the Democratic National Convention in Chicago two months later. It would all continue to get worse right through the first three to four years of the 1970s. It was the first really terrible and most completely out-of-control period up to this time in any of our lives in this country.

Looking and thinking back, all sides were wrong. But back in '69, when I had to watch a bunch of hippie freaks at the now-glorified Woodstock festival on national TV do nothin' more than get stoned out of their minds on acid and other hippie drugs while they slid through mud naked, listening (but not really hearing) some of the worst noise called rock 'n' roll up to that time, it was pretty damn hard to take. Between 1969 and 1974, a whole lot of innocent people, especially college students, wound up dyin' when they weren't even on one side or the other of all the war, civil rights, and other protests. For those who think the Woodstock period was the great time of peace and love, I'm here to tell you that you have been snowed. All this crap caused a lot of killin', dyin', and drug overdoses to happen every single day. It all came in a lot of the dark music of The Doors, Jimi Hendrix, Janis Joplin, and others.

Motown and black music was changin' fast and not really for the better at the start of the seventies. While Diana Ross was leavin' The Supremes and they would go their separate ways, Motown would give us the silly teenybopper sounds of The Jackson Five. Shortly after The Jackson Five started dominating the top of the *Billboard* pop charts, along comes the lily-white version of this group. Something called The Osmonds. The Osmonds were worse than The Archies, 'cause The Osmonds were real. The Archies went away quick after the gimmick ran its course.

John Fogerty and CCR

But all hope was not lost as far as real rock 'n' roll and rockabilly music went. There was always an underground revival of good music by new and older artists takin' place, which I guess started with Elvis when he was filming his 1968 TV special during late June 1968. At that same time, a new group called Creedence Clearwater Revival were in the studio layin' down some damn good versions of rockabilly songs and newly written ones that came under the same banner. Their leader, John Fogerty, took Creedence and defied the odds by puttin' real American rock 'n' roll and rockabilly back on the radio and at the top of the *Billboard* pop charts for the next four years into 1972. They may have been in California, but they weren't doin' no surfin'. They were rockin', and rockin' hard. They also may have looked scruffy with their long hair and beards, but even that was OK, 'cause John Fogerty (who to me was Creedence and didn't need the rest of those guys) at least looked like a real man, and he wrote and they laid down more solid rockabilly music than even The Stray Cats would a decade later. The Stray Cats were good, with some of their rockabilly songs, there's no denyin' that, but Brian Setzer and his two other cats capitalized more off of their teenage punk, tatooed, wild-haired look than they did with delivering rearin'-back, hard-rockin' rockabilly music. No doubt, The Stray Cats did a whole lot to bring rockabilly music to the mainstream masses all over again around the world, but John Fogerty did it a lot better and stayed on top with it longer at a time when we first really needed it more than ever.

Creedence had the old sound down from the late sixties into the early seventies. Whether it was on old cover rockabilly and rock 'n' roll songs like "Ooby Dooby," "Susie-Q," "My Baby Left Me," "Hello Mary Lou," "The Midnight Special," and others, or on creatively written John Fogerty original rockabilly and rock 'n' roll tunes such as "Lookin' Out My Back Door," "Bad Moon Rising," "Don't Look Now," "Lodi," "Travelin' Band," "It Came Out of the Sky," and a whole lot more. Creedence had a roots Louisiana/country/swamp rock sound in a whole lot of their songs, but it all holds up today as good as it did back in the late sixties and early seventies. John Fogerty was to Creedence Clearwater Revival what John Lennon had been to The Beatles. He was the real, original rocker in the group.

Whenever a rock, pop, or country top artist can get a rockabilly-soundin' song on the radio and it's pure to the roots, it will stay around a long time. What Creedence Clearwater Revival brought in between 1968 and 1972 was the kind of gutsy swamp rock 'n' roll and rockabilly that the partyin' college-age group between eighteen and twenty-two and others a little older wanted to hear. Real music that rocked.

The *Billboard* pop charts between '68 and '72, with a few exceptions, were dominated by just that—pop music. Rock 'n' roll and rockabilly sounds were real hard to find with the onslaught of the new teenybopper heartthrobs such as Bobby Sherman and David Cassidy both solo and with The Partridge Family. I've already mentioned The Osmonds and the Jackson Five. New ones just kept poppin' up all the time on the other side of pop throughout the early seventies. You had The 5th Dimension; James Taylor; Carly Simon; Helen Reddy; Paul Simon solo but still with Simon & Garfunkel;

Crosby, Stills, Nash & Young; Neil Young solo; John Denver; Maureen McGovern; The Carpenters; Judy Collins; Carole King; Tony Orlando & Dawn. The list could just go on and on. There were always a few shining rays of hope for rock 'n' roll and rockabilly, as Creedence proved this great music still sold millions. By the time Creedence broke up in 1972, a few new artists would continue to break high up into the *Billboard* pop charts with a big hit every so often. But none would ever match the success that Creedence Clearwater Revival had with the solid rock 'n' roll and rockabilly-style music they drove at us for four straight years during some of the worst troubled times in this country's history.

Creedence only had twelve new 45 single releases and seven new album releases while the band was together between the summer of 1968 and the summer of 1972. Their first album, simply titled *Creedence Clearwater Revival,* gave birth to their first two 45 *Billboard* pop chart hits, "Susie-Q" and the Screamin' Jay Hawkins classic "I Put a Spell on You." They reached #11 and #58, respectively. The album reached #52 on the *Billboard* pop charts in late 1968.

After that first album, their remaining six albums all went gold, along with a greatest-hits album released in early 1973 titled *Creedence Gold.* The second, third, fourth, fifth, and sixth albums all reached the *Billboard* pop Top 10 album charts, with the third reaching #1. Their fifth album, *Cosmo's Factory,* from 1970, stayed #1 for nine straight weeks, and it was the second-longest #1 album of the year. Simon & Garfunkel's *Bridge over Troubled Water* only beat *Cosmo's Factory* out by one week when it stayed #1 for ten weeks. Creedence's seventh and final new album would have probably made the Top 10, but Tom Fogerty had left the group to pursue a solo career, and the group had about quit tourin' by this time. That final album, *Mardi Gras,* did manage to peak out at #12, though.

Creedence dominated consistently high up in the *Billboard* pop singles charts as well, from their very first release, their cover version of the Dale Hawkins rockabilly classic hit song "Susie-Q" during the late summer and fall of 1968. Creedence took "Susie-Q" higher than Dale Hawkins had back in 1957, when they peaked out at #11 with it in the fall of 1968, along with a twelve-week run on the charts. Eleven of their twelve 45 single releases hit somewhere in the Top 30. All twelve made the pop charts during their four-year run. Not only the A sides, but also the B sides were so strong they also charted. All in all, they had a total of nineteen songs on the *Billboard* pop charts, with four songs reaching #2 and five others reaching high up into the Top 10.

The record label Creedence Clearwater Revival was on was Fantasy Records. They were an independent label out of Berkeley, California. Four years after Creedence broke up, Fantasy Records released "I Heard It through the Grapevine" by the group, and in March 1976 this song peaked out at #43 on the *Billboard* pop charts. It had an eight-week run back then, with no touring and very little promotion behind it. The song hadn't been released as a 45 single before, but had been released already in 1970 on their *Cosmo's Factory* album. As recently as 1982, Fantasy Records released another album of all previously released material, called *Creedence Country.* They released a single in December 1981, and the updated version of the old song "Cotton Fields" reached #50 during the early months of 1982 on the *Billboard* country charts after an eight-week run.

Today, both U.S. and European labels continue to reissue, now on CD, everything Creedence Clearwater Revival ever recorded during their glory years of doin' the best rockabilly and rock 'n' roll sounds around. Their songs continue to sell in the millions around the world today. A whole new generation of fans have discovered Creedence, and they can't get enough of 'em. Older ones like me continue to buy in the new formats we've been forced to switch over to. Creedence Clearwater Revival and the music they gave us will never be considered an oldies group, though some oldies cover bands do some of their material, as it sounds so close to fifties songs. Their music sounds as fresh today as it did almost thirty years ago. That's because it was real, gutsy rock 'n' roll and rockabilly. Played and sung the way it should be, because John Fogerty loved it.

After Creedence broke up, John Fogerty continued to succeed. After the success of *Creedence Gold,* Fantasy Records released a second greatest-hits album later in 1973, called *More Creedence Gold.* This album sold well enough to climb up to #61 on the *Billboard* pop charts. You could be wondering why a rock 'n' roll band that played and sung a whole lot of rockabilly and country in the greatest way possible at the time would split up. The answer is easy. John Fogerty started and formed this great band, and he was the leader. This was during a time in America when all young people were really rebelling against anybody who was a leader. Even in music. Since rock 'n' roll and rockabilly began in the early fifties, if you had a band name, it was almost inevitable that when you really succeeded and were at

the pinnacle of success such as Creedence was, there were bound to be internal problems within the group. It mattered not that John Fogerty had been the creative genius behind the group since it started in 1968. John wrote, produced, arranged, and picked all of the cover material the group did until 1970. It worked fine for a couple of years. All the other three members of Creedence got to ride along on John Fogerty's hard working ability to make this group the top real rock 'n' roll group in the country and at the top of the charts consistently. But after the other three members of Creedence had reaped more financial rewards than they ever dreamed possible from John Fogerty's work and creative ability, they decided they wanted more creative input.

John Fogerty gave in somwhat in the fall of 1970, but they managed to still get things done his way on their next-to-last album, *Pendulum,* which came out shortly before Christmas, 1970. Up to then, the group had been averaging two albums a year, which was about the norm back then. But during the recording of their final album, *Mardi Gras,* John's brother Tom Fogerty quit the group and John gave in to the remaining two original members of Creedence, Stu Cook and Doug Clifford, and allowed them to have an equal part in all of the writing, arranging, and performing on the album.

Mardi Gras demonstrates just why John Fogerty was Creedence Clearwater Revival. It was their weakest album creatively they'd ever do. For the most part, it's soft rock. The cuttin' edge they'd had that made 'em great was now gone. John Fogerty only wrote and sang three of the songs on this last album that took over a year to get finished and come out. Neither Stu Cook nor Doug Clifford could come close to writing as well as John Fogerty, and their singin' abilities were lackluster at best. It was their last album, and the first since their debut album that hadn't made the *Billboard* Top 10 pop album charts. Once again, musicians' egos killed a great band.

But John Fogerty went into his next album project for Fantasy Records where he wouldn't have to argue with anybody. As soon as Creedence parted for good in October 1972, John was in the studio with what would be his new group, called The Blue Ridge Rangers. He'd be the only member, pick all the material, play all the instruments, arrange, produce, etc. Sure can't have no arguments that way. The engineers are only there to get paid. This album, simply called *The Blue Ridge Rangers,* may not be as great as *Cosmo's Factory* was, but it sure beat the hell out of the last two albums by Creedence. It also showed where John Fogerty's roots really were in the early seventies. They were comin' from the same places that the rockabilly artists in the mid to late fifties were comin' from. Everything from bluegrass to stone hillbilly to old-time gospel to sixties country to a great rhythm & blues classic that John put a scorchin' rockabilly arrangement on. That song was called "Hearts of Stone."

John Fogerty had beat the odds from 1968 to 1972 when, as rock music writer Ellen Willis wrote in the 1976 *Rolling Stone Illustrated History of Rock 'n' Roll,* "He made Creedence the White American dance band. No one else came close." This was an unbelievable feat, as Fogerty was living in the worst city in America to be laying down and garnering millions of sales on some of the best rockabilly and rock 'n' roll music of that time period. San Francisco, California, at that time was at its peak with hippies, black and white radicals, drugs, homosexuality, etc. Fogerty was right in the middle of all this and writing and singing about the fun and more understandable and simplistic things in his music. It didn't fit in at all, in, of all big cities, San Francisco, where they were all wearin' flowers in their hair. But Fogerty and his music outshined and outlasted all of 'em then and now.

On March 31, 1973, when John Fogerty landed his new updated hard-drivin' arrangement of "Hearts of Stone" on the *Billboard* pop charts, he proved once again you could take a great rhythm & blues song and turn it into one of the finest, gutsiest examples of rockabilly music you'd ever want to hear. Oh, now, it wasn't called rockabilly back in '73 when it first hit, but the song "Hearts of Stone" by Fogerty today still has more of an authentic rockabilly sound both musically and vocally than anything the later well-known (exclusively for rockabilly music) group The Stray Cats ever recorded. I can feel Fogerty's soul comin' out of that song. That's all I need now, and I really needed it back then.

"Hearts of Stone" under The Blue Ridge Rangers name had a twelve-week run on the *Billboard* pop charts during the spring of 1973. When it peaked out at #37 in May 1973, the #1 song in the country was "Tie a Yellow Ribbon Round the Old Oak Tree" by Tony Orlando & Dawn. They had a TV show all America was watchin'. John Fogerty didn't go out and promote or do shows behind the four 45 singles and one album that came out under the name The Blue Ridge Rangers on Fantasy Records between the fall of 1972 and the fall of

1973. But the records still sold well, because people still wanted to hear real rock 'n' roll.

Fantasy Records released four 45 singles by The Blue Ridge Rangers, beginning with "Blue Ridge Mountain Blues" b/w "Have Thine Own Way" in October 1972. This first 45 failed to chart at all, so they quickly released "Jambalaya (On the Bayou)" b/w "Workin' on a Building" next, and this Hank Williams song with a new poundin' hillbilly rockabilly beat to it entered the *Billboard* pop charts on December 2, 1972. "Jambalaya (On the Bayou)" had a sixteen-week run and peaked out at #16 during February 1973. John Fogerty put a new sound (that still sounded like Creedence) on one of the all-time classic songs in country music history and took it higher on the *Billboard* pop charts than any other artist or group had done before or has done since.

The *Blue Ridge Rangers* album was released in the spring of '73 along with the "Hearts of Stone" hit 45, and there was only one other 45 single, which wasn't on the album, that came out later in '73, which failed to chart mainly because John Fogerty had a real bad falling out with the owner of Fantasy Records over a royalty money dispute, which over a decade later, in the mid eighties, John Fogerty would become very outspoken about. Like I said earlier, it's always money first with record companies and their owners. At least in 99 percent of the cases. But on John Fogerty's 1973 *Blue Ridge Rangers* album, there were other great classic songs done in the Creedence style he was responsible for creating. From the Blue Yodeler Jimmy Rodgers to Webb Pierce to Hank Locklin to George Jones to Merle Haggard and others. Fogerty gave new fresh treatments to all of the great songs these artists had written or done before him.

After leaving Fantasy Records, John Fogerty did one album for Asylum Records in 1975, simply called *John Fogerty.* This album may not be great, but it was sure plenty good enough for 1975, when disco was startin' to thrive. It was still rock 'n' roll, and even by most fans' standards had a few songs on it that come under the rockabilly sound. Not the original, pure old sound, but the newer, more modern sound of rockabilly. This album only reached #78 in the fall of 1975, but it did result in three *Billboard* pop chart singles. The first two were the best. The first single, "Rockin' All Over the World," reached a peak of #27 in October 1975, and had an eleven-week run on the *Billboard* pop charts. In December, the second single (although great) only made it up to #78 and had a short three-week run. This song was called "Almost Saturday Night." It's better known today among rockabilly fans, because six years later, during the rockabilly revival, in 1981, "Almost Saturday Night" was even a bigger hit single on the *Billboard* pop charts by Dave Edmunds. John Fogerty's final chart appearance during the seventies was when the song "You Got the Magic" had a four-week run during May 1976, but only reached a peak position on the *Billboard* pop charts of #87.

John Fogerty wanted (and knew how with the best of 'em) to write, sing, play, record, arrange, and produce real rock 'n' roll, but it was pretty hopeless by the dark and down disco days of the mid 1970s, plus he felt he'd been ripped off bad by the music business, which I have no doubt that he had been, one among the many. So he got out of all of it for close to a decade. But John came back one last time, soundin' at times real close to Creedence. This was right before Christmas, 1984. John Fogerty had a new deal with Warner Brothers Records and had a new song, "The Old Man Down the Road," being consistently played on all formats of rock radio —album-oriented rock, college, pop/Top 40, etc. It was a good one, too. The rockabilly revival here in the U.S. that Robert Gordon had started back in the spring of 1977 was over by the time "The Old Man Down the Road" debuted on the *Billboard* pop charts on December 22, 1984. The Stray Cats had recently split up, but Fogerty was a true original, and his new song climbed to a peak position of #10 on the *Billboard* pop charts in March 1985, and had a nice eighteen-week run on those charts.

Less than a month after "The Old Man Down the Road" debuted on the *Billboard* pop singles charts, Warner Brothers released an album on John Fogerty called *Centerfield.* Fogerty produced and wrote all the songs on this new album. It was good to see him back, and it really is a pretty good album. At least it was rock 'n' roll. Everybody was sick of disco after about a ten-year run. Fogerty's *Centerfield* album was sure what old and new fans of real rock 'n' roll wanted to hear. It debuted on the *Billboard* pop album charts on February 2, 1985. Seven weeks later, it hit #1 when it knocked the pop duo Wham! out of the #1 slot after their three-week run. *Centerfield* went on to become a platinum album. John Fogerty proved America still wanted real rock 'n' roll in a year that was dominated with the hit sounds of everything from Madonna to Phil Collins to Prince. Every time a Bruce Springsteen, Bob Seger, Billy Joel, or John Cougar gave young fans even a dose of something close to real rock 'n' roll or rockabilly, it sold big-time.

Warner Brothers Records had controversy on their hands with *Centerfield,* 'cause there was a real rock 'n' roll song on the album that Fogerty sang live during that period about his former record label owner at Fantasy Records. The song was called "Zanz Kant Danz." The main whole line that was repeated throughout this song was "Zaentz can't dance, but he'll steal your money." Zaentz is the last name of the owner of Fantasy Records. A lawsuit was quickly filed right after the album came out, and Warner Brothers had Fogerty rush in and overdub to change the first word of the title of the song to "Vanz."

Several more 45 singles were released through the end of 1985, but only the follow-up to "The Old Man Down the Road" hit the *Billboard* pop charts. The A side was a solid rockin' tune done in classic John Fogerty style, called "Rock 'n' Roll Girls." It debuted on the *Billboard* pop charts on March 16, 1985, and started rising up the charts right after "The Old Man Down the Road" had peaked and was just beginning its downward slide. Well, "Rock 'n' Roll Girls" would have probably made it into the Top 10 like "Old Man Down the Road" had done, but the B side of the 45 had a strong commercial appeal, and DJs around the country all started playing that side during May 1985. That side was the title track of the album *Centerfield.* Well, in 1985 baseball was still America's favorite pastime. Recent developments between greedy owners and players have now turned a whole lot of nineties baseball fans sour on all of major league baseball. This wasn't the case between late May and late August 1985. "Rock 'n' Roll Girls" quit rising during mid May 1985 and peaked out at #20, and a month later it was completely off the *Billboard* pop charts after a twelve-week run. The B side, "Centerfield," debuted on the *Billboard* pop charts on May 25 and though it only reached a peak position of #44, it had a longer ride of thirteen weeks than "Rock 'n' Roll Girls" had, primarily due to the fact that the song was not only all over the radio but was consistently played throughout the rest of the summer of 1985 in every major-league ballpark in America. You still hear it in the background today at major-league baseball games. But that was pretty much the end of it.

John Forgerty, for whatever reasons, changed directions in his music on his follow-up album on Warner Brothers Records, called *Eye of the Zombie,* and when the first 45 single was released, of the title cut from the album, it debuted on the *Billboard* pop charts on September 6, 1986, only reached a peak position of #81, and dropped off the charts after only four weeks. After the album debuted on the *Billboard* pop album charts October 18, 1986, it did manage to reach a peak position of #26 and was certified gold. This was probably due to the fact that like me, other lovers of solid rock 'n' roll would go out and buy an album by a consistently dependable artist such as John Fogerty without even hearin' it first, because you knew thare was gonna be at least a couple or more solid tunes that really knocked you out on it. This wasn't the case on Fogerty's *Eye of the Zombie* album. It was his most disappointing album of his career as far as solid rock 'n' roll music went. But that was OK. John Fogerty was forty-one years old by that time, and he gave us enough true rock 'n' roll, rockabilly, hillbilly, swamp rock, and all the other forms of real rock 'n' roll to last us a lifetime.

It would be eleven more years before John Fogerty came out with a new album. That's OK, too. He don't owe anybody anything. I'm just thankful he gave us what he did, when he did, 'cause it was real, man. And it looks like on his latest album, *Blue Moon Swamp,* which came out in 1997, ol' John's returned to his musical roots. All I can say is, for a lot of years, what he's given us has been a whole lot better than the noise, complicated crap, and dull music that most all the other artists who called themselves rock 'n' roll gave us and tried to force us to listen to.

Commander Cody

Commander Cody & His Lost Planet Airmen hit big-time on the *Billboard* pop singles charts during the spring of 1972 with their cover version of a song that comes under the rockabilly banner 'cause it's always been revered, loved, and collected by rockabilly fans. It was the old Charlie Ryan & The Timberline Riders' hit from the spring of 1960, "Hot Rod Lincoln," which was also a hit for Johnny Bond later in the same year of 1960. It was great to hear a new version of "Hot Rod Lincoln" all during the spring and early summer of 1972. Cody and his group gave this old classic rockin' car song a great new treatment. It debuted on the *Billboard* pop charts on March 25, 1972, quickly shot up to #9 during May, and stayed on the charts for fourteen weeks.

Before their breakthrough on this song, Cody had his group based out of San Francisco at the same time Creedence Clearwater Revival started hittin' the *Billboard* charts in 1968. Being in California, Commander Cody & His Lost Planet Airmen were fortunate enough to be on the same shows with Gene Vincent,

as well as do some live recording with him shortly before his death in October 1971. I had no way of knowin' this until after "Hot Rod Lincoln" became a national Top 10 hit for the group and I was reading an article on 'em in *Rolling Stone* magazine. That was enough for me. If they were good enough for Gene Vincent, they had to know how to play rock 'n' roll and rockabilly. But Cody and his group played other forms of American roots music also that were indicated on their various albums between 1972 and 1977 that I was buying. They gave you heavy doses of old-style hillbilly and Bob Wills-type western swing music. They fused it all together and played and sang it right.

Commander Cody & His Lost Planet Airmen never had another big national hit like "Hot Rod Lincoln," and I really don't know when the group finally broke up. But I kept finding their albums in stores and buyin' 'em into the late 1970s. Their follow-up 45 single to "Hot Rod Lincoln" only made it up to #81 during the summer of 1972 but stayed on the *Billboard* pop charts for seven weeks. This song was another cover version, of an old Will Bradley 1940 hillbilly/boogie/swing song called "Beat Me Daddy Eight to the Bar."

Cody and his group were a real popular touring rock 'n' roll group during the early and mid 1970s. I remember 'em playin' at either clubs or places in D.C., though I never went out and seen 'em during that period.

Cody and his group did chart two more 45 singles at the bottom end of the *Billboard* pop charts into 1975, but that was about it. The guy that sang lead vocals for the Commander Cody group, Bill Kirtchen, moved to the Washington, D.C., area I believe in 1982 sometime. I last saw him in January 1995, at Tornado Alley in Wheaton, Maryland, with his current band, Bill Kirtchen & Rents Due. Bill was still singin' and playin' the same good-time rock 'n' roll, rockabilly, and hillbilly swing he'd always done. He's still recording and playin' all over the Washington, D.C., area. He's a good cat. But Washington, D.C., never really let rockabilly and roots rock 'n' roll die. There's just too many rockabilly rednecks and now even sons and daughters of rockabilly rednecks that always seem to keep it goin'.

Elvis's Comeback

Elvis had not been taken seriously since the British Invasion arrived in early '64. But when his 1968 comeback TV special was first broadcast in early December 1968, on NBC TV, Elvis was taken more seriously by both music industry people and both young and older music fans alike at that time. That's because Elvis took this TV special more seriously than anything he'd ever done up to that time. Elvis had somethin' to prove to himself for the first time in his career. That was to see if he could appeal to a new generation of pop music fans that were now embracing a whole new crop of pop artists from The Monkees to The Doors.

In '68, Elvis was still sellin' millions of records and had never missed a year since '56 of havin' at least a Top 40 release on every new 45 or album on the *Billboard* pop charts, 'cause he had a more loyal following than anyone ever had in music. They'd buy it as long as it was Elvis. It didn't matter if it was rock 'n' roll or opera he sang. His die-hard fans bought it just as they'd been goin' to the drive-ins during '66 and '67 to see his movies that were becoming sillier than ever before. It was still Elvis on the big screen.

It wasn't that rock 'n' roll had passed Elvis by in 1968, or even that he had given up on rock 'n' roll by then. It was just that there was no rock 'n' roll music at the top of the *Billboard* pop singles or pop albums charts throughout the year of 1968, when he came back on TV and showed America he was the only one who could still do rock 'n' roll music better than anyone alive. All you have to do is look at the top of the *Billboard* pop charts and the facts are there. Every album and every 45 single that topped those charts during 1968 was either a new form of "rock" music, straight pop music, or the newer

sound of soul music. No such thing as a rock 'n' roll song or rock 'n' roll album anywhere on the *Billboard* pop charts in 1968.

So Elvis Presley, as all America watched, came out and proved one more time he could do it all better than the new crop. He hit that screen then like the Tasmanian Devil. He was breathin' hard raw sex and drivin' through with every bit of hard-hittin' rock 'n' roll like he hadn't done in over ten years. He was still in his prime at thirty-three years old, never looked better, and now he was in full control, not just smokin', but burstin' into flames. He was decked out in black leathers and ready for the challenge.

Later during the mid seventies and up until he died in 1977, he may have compiled his classic rock 'n' roll songs into medleys and almost seemed to treat 'em as a tired old joke, but not in 1968. He rocked then on raw, raunchy, updated arrangements of "Heartbreak Hotel," "Jailhouse Rock," "Hound Dog," and others. He didn't forget his rockabilly roots, either, when along with Scotty Moore and D.J. Fontana, you saw him in top form on songs like "That's All Right, Mama," "Lawdy Miss Clawdy," "Trying to Get to You," and others. Sam Phillips'll tell ya Elvis could always handle blues and rhythm & blues with the best of 'em. He proved that on our TV screens back in '68 on songs like "One Night," "Tiger Man," "Baby What You Want Me to Do," and others. He also couldn't be touched on rockin' south-ern gospel when you saw him do "Up Above My Head"

Forgettin' to Remember to Forget

When me and Pepper were married on November 23, 1968, my motorcycle and outlaw gunfighter days may have been behind me, but I was still a crazy twenty-four-year-old. I still had a lot of wild young rockabilly blood runnin' through me then. Between 1968 and 1977, we did a lot of partyin' and saw a lot of great shows, as well as a lot of local bar bands.

The Crossroads, during those late sixties and early seventies, was always a favorite place that we went a lot, mostly because Danny Denver and his band had a regular gig there through most of that time. His regular lead guitarist in the band was a guy named Roy Buchanan during a good part of those years when we went out to see him. I knew from the shows I'd booked Danny on during the mid sixties that he hadn't given up on rockabilly and real rock 'n' roll, and everybody that went there during that time hadn't either. During the days of disco in the mid seventies, Prince George's County couldn't-a been a better place to be, 'cause there were a whole passel of redneck rockabillys around like me. So it was always there or down in Waldorf that I was always found listenin' to the same old music I'd always listened to. I had all of Creedence's and Commander Cody's records I could find.

and "Saved." You forgot all about the way you saw Elvis sing the song "Trouble" in his 1958 film *King Creole*. Ten years had gone by, and "Trouble" and the look on Elvis's face told you what him and this song was definitely all about.

The reason Elvis Presley lasted high on the music charts is because he proved up until his death, even in the terrible shape he was in by then, that he was like no other artist in the history of pop music. He could sing any and every style of music and do it better than anyone that had come before or would come later. He was never an oldies or revival act. For the first time, in this 1968 TV special, he definitely proved he could compete in that day's current market of pop music. He proved it when he delivered one of the most powerful pop songs he'd done up until that time with "If I Can Dream." He also proved it again during that special with the mellow, soft, sensitive singing he did on the song "Memories." From Jerry Lee Lewis, Chuck Berry, Fats Domino, and Little Richard to The Beatles, The Rolling Stones, Elton John, Bruce Springsteen, The Eagles, and Boyz II Men, there's just no comparison between any of 'em and Elvis. They're all great at what they do, but they're all limited at what they do best. Elvis Presley did every style of music better than the rest. Paul Simon recently came out in an interview and said the way that Elvis recorded his song "Bridge over Troubled Water" was the actual way he had intended it to be done. He said he was unable to do it that way.

Elvis proved everything he had to with that TV special. Even though his "Aloha" 1973 TV worldwide special was good, and he looked great, it still pales in comparison with his '68 TV special. By 1973, Elvis had nothin' left to prove, though he kept on churnin' out great big hit rockers such as "Promised Land" all through the seventies.

A new form of good rock 'n' roll music was takin' ahold on the American charts from 1969 on through the whole decade of the seventies. You could just feel it in the air after Elvis's 1968 TV special. A month after it aired, Elvis went into the American Studios in Memphis and recorded over three dozen fresh soul, R&B, rock 'n' roll, pop, and country numbers. Elvis's pure rockabilly Sun sounds were nowhere to be found here, as we'd find out over the next couple of years, but there was still enough strong new vibrant rock 'n' roll and R&B like we hadn't heard from this original cat in many a year.

Elvis had just had a birthday, and he was the best-lookin' thirty-four-year-old cat on this planet in 1969. After these session dates, he finally finished his last couple of dumb movie scripts, but all the while he was thinkin' of goin' back to live performing again at the International Hotel in Las Vegas in August 1969. When Elvis hit that Vegas stage, he once again proved he was still the King of rock 'n' roll as well as the first King of pop music, when an eleven-year-old Michael Jackson was still a little kid in Detroit waiting with his older brothers for his first record to chart on *Billboard*. In August 1969, Elvis didn't have to self-proclaim himself anything. Everyone knew then he was back, and it was just a fact he was the King of music.

The numbers on the *Billboard* charts are all there. On the *Billboard* pop album charts between 1969 and 1973, eight of Elvis's albums with new song material all went gold. All nine made the Top 40, plus one of the many rehashed albums on the budget Camden Records label even reached #22. All of these new song albums contained a mixture of pop, rock 'n' roll, blues, R&B, country, and soul music. On the *Billboard* pop singles charts, all thirty-three (an astounding number in a four-year period) new songs RCA Records chose to release on Elvis for the pop radio market were mostly just that. Pop music. Songs such as "In the Ghetto," "Don't Cry Daddy," "Kentucky Rain," "The Wonder of You," "You Don't Have to Say You Love Me," "Rags to Riches," "I'm Leavin'," "Until It's Time for You to Go," "Separate Ways," etc. A few, such as "I Really Don't Want to Know" and "There Goes My Everything," leaned towards the country side of pop. Now all of these songs and others hit big. Way up in the charts. All reaching the Top 40 and a good portion of 'em reaching the Top 10 and Top 20. But what's puzzlin' is why more new-style rock 'n' roll or rock 'n' roll with an old feel to it wasn't released as the A sides of Elvis's 45s. He sure recorded enough of it between 1969 and 1973, and on the few occasions it was released on 45, it always reached a higher position than the pop material. The two best examples being Elvis's final #1 45 single, "Suspicious Minds," in the fall of 1969, and his final Top 10 45, "Burnin' Love," which peaked at #2 in the fall of 1972.

In late 1970, when Elvis started his grueling pace of U.S. cross-country tours that lasted up until seven weeks from his death in 1977, his live shows were loaded with high-energy rock 'n' roll, blues, and R&B, along with gospel, pop, and country songs. From December 1968 up until the time Elvis died, he was the primary reason there was a back-to-basics move toward fifties style and new roots-oriented rock 'n' roll music, even though the vast majority of his *Billboard* chart singles were in the pop vein. Not only Elvis fans, but the general music-buyin' public were into buyin' and wantin' solid rock 'n' roll. Elvis fans would buy everything. Even as late as September 1974, when RCA Records released Elvis's version of the 1965 Chuck Berry rocker "Promised Land," it peaked out at #14 on the *Billboard* pop charts in December 1974 and stayed on the charts thirteen weeks, until late January 1975. In the broad sense of the word, the way Elvis rocked on and delivered his new rockin' version of "Promised Land," it would be considered rockabilly today.

For the rest of his short life, and releases that followed after his death, such as "My Way," Elvis was doomed never to have a song reach as high on the *Billboard* pop charts as "Promised Land" had. He was always somewhere in the Top 40 with powerful pop ballads such as "My Boy" or "Hurt," and other mild-mannered, mid-tempo rockers such as "I've Got a Thing About You Baby" and "Moody Blue," but none of 'em would reach as high as "Promised Land" had. Chuck Berry wrote a great song, as most of his songs were, but Elvis blew Chuck Berry's 1965 version out of the water.

In conclusion on Elvis's years between 1969 and 1977, in the very beginning when he did his comeback live month-long shows in Las Vegas, he was dressed in black slacks, regular shoes, black shirt, and sports jacket. It's a tragedy that a man who had a twenty-three-year career in music that's unequalled in rockabilly and rock 'n' roll music to this day seems to be most remembered by the gaudy jumpsuits and capes that he wore the last five years of his life from 1972 to '77. The jumpsuits the first two years of 1970 and '71 weren't that bad-lookin'. Most of Elvis's music will never become a joke. But most of the fans and the no-talent imitators who are still seen on television over twenty years later have certainly turned his image, and incorrectly so I must say, into one.

Cub Koda and Brownsville Station

After Elvis and Creedence proved roots rock 'n' roll and rockabilly music was a consistent sellable music form once more during the early 1970s, new roots artists and groups such as Brownsville Station wound up having million-selling records in this same vein. "Smokin' in the Boys Room" was a roots rock 'n' roll song by Brownsville Station that not only teenagers but guys and girls in their twenties could relate to in the fall of 1973 when it debuted and had a long run of nineteen weeks on the *Billboard* pop charts, eventually peaking at #3 in early 1974. Brownsville Station continued to chart their brand of rock 'n' roll music on the *Billboard* pop charts through 1977.

The leader of this three-man group, Cub Koda, struck out on his own, touring and recording some of the best rockabilly, hillbilly, and roots music you'd want to hear during the 1980s. In 1983, Cub proved he knew the real thing when it came to fifties rockabilly when he was on the same bill as an artist I was managing at the Psyche Delly club in Bethesda, Maryland. I enjoyed Cub's choice of obscure rockers in his set more than I did my artist,

Forgettin' to Remember to Forget

I won't go on about Elvis after this part here, because me and Pepper were too close to him between Labor Day weekend 1970 and June 1977, having seen thirty-eight concerts in nine states, meeting with him on eleven occasions, and sitting down and talking with him about normal things in everyday life on six other occasions during that six-year-and-nine-month period. I'm probably the only person during the 1970s that was offered a job by my childhood hero and shocked him by turning him down flat. But he understood when I told him I had too much respect for him and I'd rather be a friend that would tell him the truth. If I took a job from him I'd become like most of the rest the last couple years of his life. Just another leech. Besides, I always had a life outside of Elvis during that period, even though Elvis was always the top priority. The Elvis I talked with and knew during the 1970s is a whole different book that I'll never write.

Johnny Seaton, mainly because Cub reminded me of a few old great rockabilly songs I'd forgotten about. He did a great energetic set that night.

Today, as far as I know, Cub still records, tours, and occasionally writes roots music columns for various publications.

Lookin' Back

From the time Elvis's 1968 comeback special was broadcast originally in early December 1968 and then repeated in August 1969, there was a revival of fifties music, styles, clothes, and memorabilia, well into the late 1970s when the rockabilly revival started.

Besides Richard Nader's popular rock 'n' roll revival shows (and by 1972, Dick Clark also got into this big-money action with his own string of oldies shows around the country), there was Don McLean's huge hit from late 1971 and early '72, "American Pie, " which made us all think of how much we not only missed Buddy Holly and rockabilly and real rock 'n' roll, but made us long for those better times during the fifties. In 1972, Elvis, Chuck Berry, and Ricky Nelson were all back in the *Billboard* pop Top 10 singles charts.

In 1973, George Lucas (of *Star Wars*) made his first film, and it became the top-grossing film of that year. It was called *American Graffiti*. It was filled with pure rock 'n' roll, rockabilly, and rhythm & blues, all from the 1950s. The soundtrack album of all these old songs reached the *Billboard* Top 10 albums charts during the fall of '73, and it went on to be certified gold. It was a double-album set, which meant you paid twice as much for it. The rockabilly-styled character in the film, Big John, with his yellow vintage hot rod, seemed to be the most popular character in that film. The film and that character were so popular, *American Graffiti* was the inspiration for one of the most popular TV series of the mid seventies to early eighties, called "Happy Days." Henry Winkler played the new rockabilly-type "Big John" character, and he soon became the most popular actor in that series. The theme song, "Happy Days," by Pratt and McClain, reached #5 on the *Billboard* pop charts during the early summer of 1976. This show spawned a spin-off that was a big hit TV show for seven years during the late seventies and early eighties, called "Laverne & Shirley." Rockabilly music of the fifties was all dominant in these TV shows and movies during the early to mid seventies.

Rockabilly music was actually dominant all throughout the 1970s in both TV shows and films after the big success of *American Graffiti* in 1973. Along with other popular rock 'n' roll artists and groups as well as rhythm & blues artists and groups, the rockabilly music of Buddy Holly, Gene Vincent, Jerry Lee Lewis, Carl Perkins, Eddie Cochran, Jack Scott, Buddy Knox, and others from the 1950s was heard mixed in the background for certain scenes in these films. All these old sounds were so popular during these times when people in America were trying to forget about the Woodstock era, which was about gone by now, and the terrible killings of four Kent State college students by police and National Guardsmen in 1970 during the protests against the Vietnam War, which was also about over by 1973, that record labels, movie studios, and TV networks all jumped on the bandwagon to capitalize on all this old music.

After the popularity of *American Graffiti,* MCA Records released the original version of "Rock Around the Clock" by Bill Haley & His Comets. Now, in 1955 this record became the first #1 rock 'n' roll record and had a twenty-four-week run on the *Billboard* pop charts. But after Elvis and a few others took over by the spring of 1956, Bill Haley & His Comets were only able to chart one more *Billboard* Top 40 hit. And that was in 1958. After that, Haley had to either play his style of rock 'n' roll in Europe (where some always considered him a treasure) or in dives here in the U.S. But sixteen years after his last Top 40 *Billboard* hit, he winds up back on those same pop charts with the same song and version he'd recorded almost twenty years prior. On March 16, 1974, "Rock Around the Clock" entered the *Billboard* pop single charts one more time. By late May 1974, it peaked out at #39 and wound up having a fourteen-week run on this second go-round.

This would be Bill Haley's final appearance on the major charts, but it kept Haley and a re-formed group of Comets out on the road doin' revival shows through 1976. Haley also recorded several new albums during this period, mostly redoing new versions of his old songs. In 1975, Bill Haley & His Comets even had a guest appearance on the hit TV show "Happy Days," where they were seen singin' "Rock Around the Clock" during one spot in one of the early episodes. Bill Haley was fifty years old at this time, and fifties music and styles of dress were startin' to appear all around us once again.

Haley's brief second fling of success was short-lived, as was he. Less than six years after his appearance on "Happy Days," Bill Haley passed away of a heart attack at his home in Harlington, Texas, on February 9, 1981.

He was fifty-five years old. By 1981, the rockabilly revival was in full swing both here in the U.S. and in Europe. When that first started to catch on in the U.S. in 1977, Bill Haley couldn't find a way to fit into it, as the rockabilly image and music was always personified by the Gene Vincent and Elvis greasy delinquent look of the mid to late fifties. Bill Haley always had the misfortune of dressing and looking like some kid's favorite uncle.

While new young artists and groups of the early seventies such as John Fogerty and Creedence, Commander Cody, Brownsville Station, and others took their brands of roots rock 'n' roll and rockabilly seriously and seemed to keep it on the artistic side, other popular groups like Sha Na Na and Flash Cadilac & His Continental Kids turned it into a joke. That was the downside of this revival of all kinds of fifties rock 'n' roll style music.

But I grabbed onto every decent slab of vinyl I was findin' in the record stores and goin' to see any movie that was built around fifties rock 'n' roll, because there was always rockabilly music, and sometimes the original artists, included in the films. One of those films in the early seventies was a British rock 'n' roll movie called *That'll Be the Day.* I only saw it because the only real British singer that ever pulled off rockabilly and rock 'n' roll the way I like had a sizable part in it. That being Billy Fury. I saw it at the Greenbelt Theater in Greenbelt, Maryland, around 1972. David Essex was the star, but Billy Fury played a rock 'n' roll singer called Stormy Tempest. The film wasn't great, but it wasn't too bad either for its time. I remember Billy Fury singin' several songs in it, and I was just glad that he was at least somewhere in the world singin' rock 'n' roll-style still.

Another film that was released in 1974 but could have been made right after the success of *American Graffiti* in 1973 was one called *The Lords of Flatbush.* I enjoyed this flick a lot at the time. It was set in the fifties and had the teenage delinquent motorcycle jacket image and a rockabilly-type edge to it. It also had a good musical soundtrack of vintage fifties music of all styles, as well as a couple new songs in the fifties mold of rock 'n' roll that were pretty good. There were two unknown actors at the time who'd later become household names. One, Henry Winkler, who only had a very small part in the film, soon gained instant success as Fonzie on the TV series "Happy Days," but the second one, Sylvester Stallone, who had one of the starring roles, soon became a superstar in movies such as *Rocky* and *Rambo.*

A few years later, both Tim McIntire and Gary Busey would give outstanding performances respectively in their roles of Alan Freed in *American Hot Wax* and Buddy Holly in *The Buddy Holly Story.* Jerry Lee Lewis and Chuck Berry were both seen singin' in *American Hot Wax,* and Gary Busey, as well as doin' an outstanding job as an actor portraying the late Buddy Holly, also did the singing on Holly's songs and did another outstanding job in that department as well. Busey got an Academy Award nomination for best actor in the film, though he didn't win. Busey was basically unheard of before this movie. While these two movies had outstanding actors in the lead and title roles, Alan Freed and Buddy Holly fans, family, and friends were all highly upset, as neither of these two films came remotely close when it came to the truth and the actual events and facts in Alan Freed's and Buddy Holly's lives. This part was all distorted crap, but both movies and their soundtracks were immensely successful.

Many more films such as these would continue throughout the 1980s and into the nineties both on the major and low-budget scales, and even though the facts were wrong, all of 'em did big business at the box office. Just to name a few, there was *Grease, The Idolmaker, Roadhouse 66, The Loveless, La Bamba,* and *Great Balls of Fire.*

But goin' back to the musical front and artists puttin' songs on the *Billboard* pop charts, Elton John was one who capitalized on the fifties music revival that was in full swing during the early seventies. Elton first hit the *Billboard* pop charts during the summer of 1970. Over the next two and a half years, through 1972, he charted seven songs, three of which managed to reach the bottom half of the *Billboard* pop Top 10. But on December 9, 1972, his fifties-soundin' "Crocodile Rock" debuted on the *Billboard* pop charts. Even though lyrically "Crocodile Rock" is a bit of a silly song, it wound up racin' up the *Billboard* pop charts and hit #1 on February 3, 1973, and stayed #1 for three straight weeks. Through 1976, when Elton's #1 streak in *Billboard* ended for good, he only had one other song that stayed #1 longer, and that was only by one week.

The song "Crazy Little Thing Called Love" by the pop/rock group Queen was actually one of the best rockabilly-sounding songs of this period. It debuted on the *Billboard* pop Hot 100 in December 1979 and stayed on those charts for twenty-two weeks — four weeks at #1, which was longer than any other record Queen ever had. This song was also covered by the masked Elvis Presley impersonator Orion, who also recorded under the name Jimmy Ellis, and it reached #63 on the *Billboard* country charts in the spring of 1981 on Shelby Singleton's Sun International Records.

Linda Ronstadt

The one artist from the early to late 1970s who charted consistently with good cover versions of solid rockabilly, rock 'n' roll, R&B, and soul songs from between 1957 and 1965 was Linda Ronstadt. Now, Linda was born in Tucson, Arizona, on July 15, 1946, and had been influenced by the folk music that was comin' on strong during the early sixties. While she was still in high school in 1962, she formed a folk trio called The Three Ronstadts with her sister and brother. After graduation in 1964, Linda moved to Los Angeles and got involved in the coffee house folk scene out there.

Linda recorded one lone 45 for the independent Sidewalk Records label in LA in 1965. Soon after, she formed a folk rock group called The Stone Ponies. Capitol Records signed up Linda's group in late 1966, and after a couple of singles that went nowhere, the group had their first *Billboard* pop chart hit. That song was called "Different Drum." After its debut on the *Billboard* pop charts on November 11, 1967, it reached a peak position of #13 during February 1968 and had a run of seventeen weeks on the charts. The follow-up 45 only reached #93 on the *Billboard* pop charts for two weeks during the early spring of '68, and The Stone Ponies' next and final 45 failed to even chart. So, in late 1968, Linda split from the group to become a solo artist.

Capitol Records immediately signed her up, as they had the good sense to know Linda was the sole reason The Stone Ponies had achieved the minimal success they had. Her first three solo singles failed to chart in 1969 and early 1970. But Linda Ronstadt was startin' to zero in on the kind of music that would make her the top female rock 'n' roll belter and seller of the 1970s. Linda's third single that failed to chart was the old Shirelles classic "Will You Love Me Tomorrow" b/w "Lovesick Blues," the Hank Williams classic. Linda Ronstadt had a great voice at a time when there weren't many out there; she could handle country, pop, R&B, soul, rockabilly, or rock 'n' roll in whatever soulful manner it called for. By 1971, Linda was beginning to get into this groove of music, especially the country side that she was well aware of from growin' up in Arizona. She was also aware of the rockabilly sound she had heard during her childhood years.

Linda's fourth 45 single as a solo artist broke onto the *Billboard* pop charts on August 15, 1970. The song was called "Long Long Time." During the fall of 1970, it reached a peak position of #25 and had a twelve-week ride on the charts. Linda had three more 45 releases on Capitol Records in '71 and '72 after "Long Long Time," but all ended up well in the bottom half of the *Billboard* pop charts, though she was doin' solid credible covers of country classics such as "I Fall to Pieces" and "Crazy Arms."

So, with lack of big chart success, Linda jumped ship in 1973 and signed with Asylum Records. There was only one problem. Linda still, according to her Capitol Records contract, owed Capitol one more album. By the time Linda got this news, she had already recorded her first sessions for Asylum Records, and her first release for Asylum debuted on the *Billboard* pop charts on December 1, 1973. It was a song called "Love Has No Pride." It still only reached #51 on the *Billboard* pop charts. The follow-up 45, the classic country song "Silver Threads and Golden Needles," didn't fare even as well, only reaching #67 on the *Billboard* pop charts during the spring of 1974.

Up until the early months of 1974 when she finally went in the studio and recorded enough tracks to fulfill her obligation on her Capitol Records contract, Linda Ronstadt had stuck with recording her own brand of country, folk country, folk rock, and country rock music since she had become a solo artist for Capitol Records. The trend continued on her early releases after she signed with Asylum Records. She was so into these styles of music that in 1971 she formed and hired a backing band that consisted of Glenn Frey, Don Henley, Randy Meisner, and Bernie Leadon. This backup band only stayed with Linda a little less than a year, because in 1972 these four guys signed with Asylum Records and became known as The Eagles. They definitely left their mark between 1974 and 1980 on both the *Billboard* pop singles and albums charts. But while Linda Ronstadt's early 45s and first album on Asylum didn't fare well, it was the one last Capitol Records album she had owed that became the breakthrough she'd been waiting for. The album was called *Heart Like a Wheel*. It was a departure from the music she had previously been doing. This was Linda's first album that included good doses of solid rock 'n' roll, R&B, and rockabilly classics done with the great vocal ability she was blessed with.

When the first 45 single, "You're No Good," which was a solid rockin' cover version of Betty Everett's 1963 R&B hit that had reached #51 in late 1963 on the *Billboard* pop charts, was released in the late fall of 1974 and debuted on the *Billboard* pop charts on December 7, 1974, it shot all the way up to #1 on February 15, 1975, giving Linda Ronstadt the only #1 *Billboard* singles chart hit of her entire, long career in music. The album *Heart Like a Wheel* debuted on the *Billboard* pop album charts a week after the single debuted, on December 14, 1974, and by February 15, 1975, it was also sitting in the #1 slot on the *Billboard* pop charts. It was certified gold shortly thereafter.

"You're No Good" had a sixteen-week ride on the *Billboard* pop charts. By the time its run was finished, Capitol Records released the follow-up single, "When Will I Be Loved." This was the final Top 10 hit The Everly Brothers had on the Cadence record label. The Everly Brothers were on Warner Brothers Records in 1960 when their 1959 recording of "When Will I Be Loved" was released and reached #8 during the summer of 1960 on the *Billboard* pop charts, and it was really the last solid song they'd have in a rockabilly vein. Linda Ronstadt's new, updated, more rarin', rockin' version of "When Will I Be Loved" debuted on the *Billboard* pop charts on April 12, 1975, and by the third week of June 1975, it sat in the #2 position on the *Billboard* pop charts for two weeks. Ronstadt's cuttin' vocals on "When Will I Be Loved" kept this song on the charts for a fifteen-week ride.

The odd thing that happened during that summer of '75 was as soon as "When Will I Be Loved" started fallin' down the charts during July, the DJs around the U.S. flipped the record over and began playin' the B side, which was a cover of Buddy Holly's final U.S. chart song (which charted after his death), "It Doesn't Matter Anymore." Ronstadt had given this song a fine treatment as well. Right after "When Will I Be Loved" dropped off the charts, "It Doesn't Matter Anymore" popped on and debuted on July 26, 1975. It only reached #47 and dropped off the charts after a short four-week run, but the stage had been set for future Linda Ronstadt releases.

A lot of the credit had to go to Peter Asher, who produced *Heart Like A Wheel* and would continue to produce Linda's recordings. Asher had seen his own share of big success between 1964 and 1967 when the British Invasion first came in and he was one half of the Peter & Gordon duo that racked up fourteen *Billboard* pop chart hits, which included three in the Top 10 during that period. But when he became Linda Ronstadt's producer in 1974, the music scene had changed, and he was smart enough to know Linda

Ronstadt had the vocal ability to handle the great rock 'n' roll, rockabilly, R&B, and soul classics of the past. Asher was able to get Ronstadt to lay down some raw, raunchy vocals on some of these classic tunes, and every time she did, it turned out to be solid gold.

Ronstadt and Asher kept this trend of bringing back classic songs from rock 'n' roll's Golden Era of the fifties and early sixties right through 1980 on the Asylum Records label. Every time these songs were released as singles, they jumped up high up into the *Billboard* pop charts, goin' Top 10 or at least Top 20. Martha & The Vandellas' Top 10 1963 Motown hit of "Heat Wave" reached #5 for Linda Ronstadt in 1975. Buddy Holly's 1957 #1 hit "That'll Be the Day" reached #11 for Ronstadt in 1976. Roy Orbison's classic "Blue Bayou" only reached #29 for him in 1963, but Linda Ronstadt took it all the way up to #3 in 1977.

Asylum Records quickly followed up "Blue Bayou" with a Buddy Holly & The Crickets song called "It's So Easy," which, when it was first released during the fall of 1958, was the first 45 single that failed to even make the *Billboard* pop charts for Holly. It had the old rockabilly sound that was slippin' at that time, but it still remains one of Holly's best rockabilly songs. Linda Ronstadt's updated rockin' version, which I believe would have made Buddy Holly smile, raced up to #5 in December 1977.

So after "Blue Bayou" and "It's So Easy" had high chart numbers and long runs of twenty-three and eighteen weeks, respectively, on the *Billboard* pop singles charts in 1977, what does Asylum Records decide to do? On Linda's first two 45 releases in 1978, they almost put her off the radio when they released "Poor Poor Pitiful Me" and "Tumblin' Dice." "Poor Poor Pitiful Me" only reached #31 and fell off the *Billboard* pop charts after an eight-week run. Then came the song "Tumblin' Dice," which had been a Top 10 *Billboard* pop chart song for The Rolling Stones only six years earlier, in 1972. Linda's new rockin' cover version only reached #32 during the late spring of 1978. By this time, most of Linda Ronstadt's fans, at least the majority who were buying her 45s and albums, wanted to hear rockin' updated versions of great fifties and early sixties songs. They just weren't buying any kind of new modern rock, folk rock, or rock 'n' roll by her, even at this late date.

By '78, some purist fifties or hard-core rockabilly fans referred to Linda as "Linda Repeat Ronstadt." But the *Billboard* pop chart numbers didn't lie. Asylum should have known this by then, as after "That'll Be the Day" peaked out at #11 but had a long run of sixteen weeks on the *Billboard* pop charts, they followed it up with a new song that nobody'd remember but a Ronstadt fanatic, called "Lose Again." That song only reached #76 in 1977, which was her lowest *Billboard* chart number since she'd been with The Stone Ponies nine years earlier. It quickly dropped off the charts after a five-week run.

Linda's albums through 1980 were all filled with solid covers of fifties and early sixties solid rock 'n' roll, rockabilly, R&B, and soul. After "Tumblin' Dice" didn't stay on the *Billboard* pop charts long and didn't come anywhere near the Top 10 or even Top 20, the folks at Asylum Records went back to the fifties rockabilly and rock 'n' roll bag. They released Linda Ronstadt doin' a killer cover version of Chuck Berry's final Top 40 hit from the 1950s. The song was called "Back in the U.S.A." Chuck's version had only reached #37 during the summer of 1959. Linda's new updated version (but with the same real feel as all of her cover versions had) reached a peak position of #16 during the fall of 1978 and had a respectable run of thirteen weeks on the *Billboard* pop charts.

They followed this up with the 1965 Smokey Robinson & The Miracles Motown soul hit "Ooh Baby Baby." In '65, it only reached #16 for Smokey & The Miracles, but in January 1979, Linda Ronstadt took "Ooh Baby Baby" all the way up to #7 and had a sixteen-week run with it on the *Billboard* pop charts.

Linda's final cover song was one by another group and artist who'd first started havin' rhythm & blues hits on the *Billboard* pop charts but had survived the British Invasion and continued to chart Top 40 hits on the *Billboard* pop charts through 1965. Linda covered Little Anthony & The Imperials' 1965 final Top 10 pop hit,

"Hurt So Bad." Little Anthony had reached #10 during the spring of '65 with this song, but during the spring and early summer of 1980, Linda took "Hurt So Bad" up to a peak position of #8 on the *Billboard* pop charts, and gave it a fourteen-week run on those charts.

Between 1974 and 1980, Linda Ronstadt came out with seven good albums with a lot of solid covers of great old songs she turned into big-time 45 single hits. The first two albums, in 1974 and '75, went gold. The Record Industry Association of America (RIAA) didn't start givin' awards for or certifying records as platinum until 1976. If they had started in 1974, Linda's first two albums would have certainly been certified as platinum albums, as her five other albums between 1976 and 1980 all were.

By 1980, Linda Ronstadt had changed directions in her music and was involved in Broadway and movie projects. She was off the charts completely in 1981, and when she did her next new album, titled *Get Closer,* in 1982, it only reached a peak position of #31 on the *Billboard* pop album charts. Between 1974 and 1980, three of the seven albums she put out reached #1, and the other four all reached peak positions of between #3 and #6. Linda's *Get Closer* album did go gold, though, and the title track did reach #29 on the *Billboard* pop singles charts, and they turned that tune into a Close Up toothpaste commercial on TV.

During '83 and '84, Linda turned to recording lush, 1940s-type Big Band music. That's pretty much it. I know some rockabilly music fans of today don't think too much of Linda Ronstadt's covers of their heroes' songs, but hey, don't write Linda Ronstadt off that quickly. Linda's music was one of the best things we had goin' until the U.S. rockabilly revival really caught hold in 1978 and '79.

Europe Begs for and
Brings Back Original Fifties Rockabillys

Ronnie Weiser and Rollin' Rock Records

Between 1970 and lasting well into the early 1980s there was one guy on the West Coast, out in the Los Angeles, California area, who had a passion for rockabilly music in its purest form, who started recording and then releasing records on just about every obscure and unknown artist he could find who'd started out recording and performing rockabilly music during the late fifties. His name is Ronnie Weiser.

Ronnie was born in Milan, Italy. When he was barely a teenager there in 1957, the first glimpse of rockabilly and rock 'n' roll he saw was the faded blue jean and motorcycle boot look of Elvis in *Loving You*. In his homeland he searched out the rock 'n' roll and rockabilly recordings of Elvis, Gene Vincent, Chuck Berry, and others. Ronnie had a desire and dream to come to America, where this great music was comin' from. That dream came true during the 1960s. Here in America, he went to UCLA and received a Bachelor of Science degree in electrical engineering. But the young Ronnie Weiser didn't want go be an electrical engineer for the rest of his life. After college, he set his sights straight at rockabilly and obscure rock 'n' roll music. He knew that all over Europe there were thousands of fans who loved this original music of the fifties, so in 1969, Ronnie started publishing *Rollin' Rock* magazine. This was the first fanzine devoted entirely to rockabilly artists of the fifties.

Ronnie built a small studio in the garage behind his house in Van Nuys, California, shortly thereafter and started recording older rockabilly artists that he was searching out. By 1970, he started releasing singles and albums on these artists. During the days of psychedelic music and the Woodstock generation, Ronnie Weiser's Rollin' Rock Records label was the first and only American record label recording new rockabilly music by the original fifties music artists. Before he built his garage studio, Ronnie recorded these artists right in his living room.

A month before Gene Vincent died, during early September 1971, Ronnie Weiser recorded four songs by Gene. Gene was in terrible health at the time, and his once great, smooth but vibrant, high-energy voice was probably at its lowest point during this session, but these four songs are still worth a listen, even today, as Gene Vincent was still doin' his best to sing real rock 'n' roll as he knew it right up to the end of his life.

Ronnie Weiser was a one-man operation with his Rollin' Rock record label when he started it, and when I say he was the only one strictly devoted to releasing records on pure, authentic rockabilly music from 1950s original artists, I'm excluding Sun International Records in Nashville.

Shelby Singleton and
Sun International Records

In July 1969, Sam Phillips sold his legendary Memphis-based Sun Records label to Shelby Singleton, who was now located in Nashville and having huge success with his independent Plantation Records label. During the fall of 1968, Singleton had sold over a million copies on the song "Harper Valley PTA" by Jeannie C. Riley.

The real benefit of Shelby Singleton purchasing Sun Records was that now rockabilly music fans here in the U.S. would be flooded with material on artists we'd never even heard of during the 1970s. A lot of this stuff was songs and artists Sam Phillips in the 1950s didn't think were up to his standards to release records on. Singleton, being the shrewd businessman that he was, immediately started releasing 45s and LPs on the two biggest-selling recording stars Sun Records had in the 1950s. Those being Johnny Cash and Jerry Lee Lewis.

Actually, Singleton's first Sun release was a Memphis soul-style song by Billy Lee Riley, called "Kay." It failed to chart, but it was a great record. Billy Lee Riley poured more grit, true feel, and soulful emotion into "Kay" than you could imagine hearin' comin' out of the grooves of a 45 record.

The next release on Sun International Records that Shelby Singleton decided to release was in that trove of golden unreleased 1950s masters by none other than The Killer himself, Jerry Lee Lewis. Jerry Lee had been on a roll about a year and a half, racking up six straight *Billboard* country chart Top 10 hits, which included one song that reached the #1 spot, when Shelby released the never-before-heard song "Invitation to Your Party" the first week of August 1969. This song debuted on the *Billboard* country charts on August 16, 1969, and reached a peak position of #6. Jerry Lee's follow-up record on Sun, "One Minute Past Eternity," even did better and reached #2 on the *Billboard* country charts and had a longer ride there than Jerry Lee's new country 45s on his current label at the time, Smash Records, which were also topping out between the #2 and #3 positions on the *Billboard* country charts during late 1969 and into the early months of 1970.

These were the first two big chart successes for Shelby Singleton's new Nashville-based Sun International Records label. They were only the beginning. It was like hittin' the ultimate jackpot, and a big bonanza for all rockabilly fans and lovers and collectors of all music that was recorded by the biggest legends of rockabilly music who had first started out on the original Sun Records label between 1955 and '57. For the first three years after Shelby Singleton took over the old Sun Records catalog, he released more than two dozen 45s, along with another two dozen or more full-length albums, on the likes of Jerry Lee Lewis, Johnny Cash, Carl Perkins, Roy Orbison, Charlie Rich, and others. All this was between 1969 and 1972. Elvis was the only one Shelby Singleton couldn't release material on, as RCA Victor Records had purchased everything Elvis had done while he was with Sun Records when they bought his contract from Sam Phillips.

Johnny Cash was hotter than at any time during his entire career between 1969 and 1971. Not just in country music, either. His novelty song "A Boy Named Sue" reached #2 on the *Billboard* pop charts in September 1969, and he had just started the first year of his own major network national TV variety show. It lasted two seasons, until 1971. Sam Phillips had released practically every song Cash had recorded while at Sun from 1955 to 1958, and the few things that hadn't come out on the original Sun Records label wouldn't be found until many years later. Shelby Singleton didn't need anything new in late 1969 and '70, 'cause anything by Johnny Cash was selling large amounts of 45s and LPs to not only country fans but also pop and rock 'n' roll ones. Singleton made a great choice with his decision to reissue one of Cash's best songs from 1956, which had been the B side of "I Walk the Line" at the time and made it onto the *Billboard* country charts then. That song was "Get Rhythm." It made it up to #23 on the *Billboard* country charts after its debut on October 11, 1969, but then on November 15, 1969, it crossed over onto the *Billboard* pop charts, where it reached a peak of #60 and had a six-week run there. On the *Billboard* country charts, it had a twelve-week run.

Singleton released "Rock Island Line" by Cash in late January 1970. The song was never an original 45 single on Sun by Johnny. It had been released on a 45 EP album and a full-length album when it was recorded in 1956. This song only made #93 on the *Billboard* pop charts, but it did get up to a high of #35 on the *Billboard* country charts for a seven-week run.

Cash and Lewis both were so hot between 1969 and 1971, not much promotion was even needed. There was no recording cost, and once again you could hear on the radio how great these artists really were in the 1950s. Singleton was also licensing his newly acquired Sun masters to labels such as Pickwick Records. They were a budget-priced album label in the early seventies.

Besides releasing the more than two dozen 45s and numerous LPs on Sun International Records, Singleton consistently kept his Plantation Records label alive and well, releasing about a hundred 45s and a couple dozen albums between 1968 and 1973 alone. On the Plantation label, Shelby would release country-oriented material, while on Sun International, it would be mostly on the rockabilly-soundin' side of music.

Sleepy La Beef had releases on both Plantation and Sun International records between 1969 and 1979. One of Sleepy's 45s for the Plantation record label made the *Billboard* country charts during the summer of 1971 and had a five-week stay there. Sleepy's version of "Blackland Farmer" reached #67 at that time. When I recently asked Sleepy why he stayed with Shelby Singleton's two record labels probably longer than any other recording artist, Sleepy replied, "Because I was free to record whatever I wanted to. During those years I cut everything from rockabilly to boogie woogie to gospel to western swing to blues. I loved it all. I know we cut somewhere between 150 to 200 songs during the years I spent there, and Shelby consistently released records on me, 'cause I stayed on the road 300 nights a year workin' live shows, and I was sellin' those records to the fans at the shows."

While Sleepy seems to have no regrets or bitterness with his dealings all the years he spent with Shelby Singleton, many other older rockabilly artists don't even want to hear you mention his name today. Whatever the case, some of these older artists who seem to complain the most did wind up benefiting the most between the late seventies and even up to the present day.

Europe Calling

It all started around 1973 when Shelby Singleton started licensing all of the old Sun-issued and unissued masters to a record company in England called Charly Records. As a fan wanting to hear anything and everything that had ever been recorded at Sun Records, I was overjoyed at the sight of finding these unknown treasures of rockabilly music from 1973 on, which started with an album titled *Sun Rockabillys: Put Your Cat Clothes On*. Even though I had to pay a higher price for these import albums, it didn't matter. I just wanted to hear all this great music Sam Phillips had decided not to release even though some of these songs were actually better and hotter rockabilly songs than ones he did choose to release in the fifties.

British and European fans in general whose first love was American rockabilly and true fifties rock 'n' roll music have always had a much greater respect for this music than Americans did. The Americans, young and old alike, will go right with whatever new trend or fad that becomes popular. But it's been different with a whole lot of rockabilly fans all over Europe and especially in England. With the British fans, rockabilly and rock 'n' roll music never died. For the most part, like it has always been with me, rockabilly wasn't just the music. It was a way of life.

The British were so dedicated that I remember seein' on the network TV world news sometime in the late sixties a segment about two gangs in England called the Mods and the Rockers who were having gang fights (or rumbles, as they were called in the fifties) with chains, ball bats, etc., because of the music each group liked. This must of been some heavy-duty battlin' that the Bobbies (English police) were havin' a tough time tryin' to control. It had to be serious for me to see this on the TV news back then, 'cause with the Vietnam War,

protests, riots here, the civil rights movement, and everything else the news had to cover then, why would it be on national TV? From what I remember about it, this one group, the Mods, rode these dorky little motor scooters, dressed in the new clothes fashions of that period that The Beatles had popularized, and were on the side of the new British sound in pop music. The rival group, the Rockers, rode big manly or macho motorcycles such as Triumphs, Harley-Davidsons, or BSA's, dressed in the Marlon Brando "Wild One" garb such as leather Harley jackets, leather pants, and motorcycle boots, and wanted to stamp out all those Mods and the fairy music they liked that was dominating the British airwaves at the time. The Rockers wanted true original rockabilly and rock 'n' roll music. Today they refer to lovers of this form of music as "Teddy Boys." When I watched this news show thirty years ago, it looked like they had a full-scale war goin' on over in London to keep real rock 'n' roll and rockabilly alive and on the radio.

So after Shelby Singleton inked that deal around 1973 to license all of the old Sun recordings, released and unreleased, within the next four to five years, the European label Charly Records, who he had licensed 'em to, flooded the market with 45s and EPs, but mostly LP albums, of released and unreleased rockabilly songs by practically every singer, good or bad, who walked through Sam Phillips's doors back in the mid to late fifties.

While Charly Records released, like Shelby Singleton had, all the Cash, Lewis, Roy Orbison, and Charlie Rich material on solo albums, they also released solo albums on artists such as Billy Lee Riley, Warren Smith, Sonny Burgess, etc., during the mid and late seventies. These albums included great unreleased songs such as Warren Smith's "Uranian Rock" and "Red Cadillac and a Black Moustache" and Billy Lee Riley's "Open the Door Richard." In 1975 and '76, Charly also put out seven-inch, four-song EP albums on artists such as Roy Orbison, Charlie Feathers, Warren Smith, Billy Lee Riley, and others. There were so many of these records in select record stores here in the U.S. by 1977, it was hard to keep up with it all. But it was grabbed up quickly over here by fans like myself, so I can't even imagine how many records were sold around the world on these and various compilation albums. Some of these compilations included artists such as Dean Beard, Junior Thompson, Narvel Felts, and many other artists that never even had an actual release on the original Memphis-based Sun Records label.

So while European bands and artists had always kept rockabilly music alive and well throughout the years, the releases of these Charly Records Sun artists only made fans over there hunger for a chance to see some of their favorite artists come over there and perform live on stage. The first big live rockabilly stage show was in April 1977, at The Rainbow Theatre in London, when promoters brought original fifties rockabilly stars and artists Jack Scott, Warren Smith, Charlie Feathers, and Buddy Knox over there. After the huge success of that show, almost any artist who recorded a rockabilly-soundin' record during the 1950s has wound up performing in some foreign country right up to the present time. The list of these entertainers is a mile long.

Just about every artist who recorded rockabilly music in the fifties that I've mentioned thus far in this book, with the exception of Elvis, has wound up performing live shows in Europe and other foreign countries since 1977. Jack Scott has been over there every year since 1977 between one and three times each year. Sleepy La Beef started goin' overseas in 1979 and hasn't missed a year since. Sleepy's probably done more rockabilly shows and festivals in foreign countries than any

Forgettin' to Remember to Forget

I made my first trip over to Holland during the spring of 1984 and saw how serious the British and various other European rockabilly fans took not only rockabilly but the lifestyle that surrounded it. Me and my wife were there with the rockabilly artist I was managing and who I had gotten to record a 45 and album of rockabilly music that I chose, produced, and released on my record label, Renegade Records, in 1982. The record and the artist, Johnny Seaton, were doin' real well over here, and by late 1983 I licensed the album to Rockhouse Records in Holland. So a seven-day promotional tour was set up with four live shows.

In the spring of 1984, the new breed of rockabilly fans I was seein' at shows in the U.S. were mostly the fly-by-night kind that had just gotten into rockabilly music during the past year and a half since The Stray Cats had become the big new act in pop music starting during the summer and fall of 1982. These new rockabilly fans played dress-up in the 1950s clothes fashions when they went out to see a rockabilly band or a show. The hair was stacked in overexaggerated fashions, and it was just one big game. But I found out over in countries like England, France, Germany, Holland, Finland, Sweden, Spain, Ireland, etc., the older rockabilly fans around my age or a little older had not only never given up on this music of the 1950s they loved so much by Gene Vincent, Elvis, Carl Perkins, Eddie Cochran, etc., when they were all young teenagers, but they'd also raised their children up with it. Not only on the rockabilly music, but also the rockabilly delinquent style of dress from the fifties. It was being carried down from one generation to the next over there. I mean these first-generation rockabilly fans were doin' something I had even slowed up on doin' by the early eighties. From the beginning since the fifties, a whole lot of 'em I talked with looked at me like I was crazy when I said, "You mean you don't just wear these clothes and hair like this for these shows, that you really go to work every day lookin' and dressin' like that?" They most all told me of course they did and had been doin' so since the fifties. Most of these guys around my age were all blue-collar workers over there like myself. During the early 1980s, I was still wearin' my hair in a pompadour and wore my jeans and motorcycle boots, but if I had-a showed up where I was workin' with my shirt collar turned up and a motorcycle jacket studded and layered with chains, my supervisors would have really thought I'd gone off the deep end. But in Europe, it's always seemed to be a way of life.

Plus they've always had a total respect for the great artists of the 1950s who helped invent rockabilly music. They've known all along there never would have been a Robert Gordon, The Stray Cats, or Shakin' Stevens, or maybe even The Beatles, without Elvis, Carl Perkins, Gene Vincent, Eddie Cochran, Buddy Holly, and a lot of lesser-known artists who all came before 'em.

What was really the highlight for me on that seven-day trip was what I'd already heard about European rock 'n' roll and rockabilly fans was completely true. None of 'em seemed to give a good damn about The Stray Cats. One British fan said, "Aw, they're no more than Elvis imitators. Why should anyone want to hear them copy Gene Vincent and Johnny Burnette songs when you have the original records? Those are the ones that'll last." I told this guy he really said a mouthful there.

rockabilly artist alive today. Sleepy also has performed more rockabilly shows here in the U.S. than any other artist, period. Sleepy just keeps goin' and goin' and goin'. Once you see his live show, you'll know why they keep bringin' him back. That heavy-duty cat is hard to beat.

It was the release of all these Charly Records recordings plus the other independent record labels such as Big Beat Records in France, Rockhouse Records in Holland, Ace Records in England, Star Club Records in Sweden, and Bison Bop and Bear Family Records, both in Germany, that started releasing 1950s obscure, mostly unheard-of, or high-dollar 45s by original rockabilly artists that created a demand to see these original fifties artists live on stage over there from 1977 on. The White label in Holland was also another early label from about 1974 that also started pourin' out material that you just couldn't find any more on 45s.

All these labels I just mentioned started puttin' out material during the 1970s. There were many others, but that list also is too long. With the success of these labels, others, such as Sunjay Records in Sweden and Goofin' Records in Finland, would spring up during the 1980s. All of the above continue to release original rockabilly music, old and newly recorded by the original artists of the 1950s.

After the rockabilly revival got in full swing by 1978 and '79, some of the above-mentioned labels would begin issuing records by younger newer artists who were now doin' this music. From 1970 to 1976, rockabilly and true fifties-style rock 'n' roll kept garnering a bigger and bigger group of fans, especially in England. By 1976, rockabilly music and the new bands and artists who were performing it in the clubs and putting out records was reaching the highest peak it had been at in well over a decade in all of Europe, but especially throughout England.

Something happened in 1976 in England that had never or could never happen here in the U.S. There was a frantic, great rockabilly 45 record released in the U.S. in 1957 on the King Records label, called "Jungle Rock," by an artist by the name of Hank Mizell. Now, King Records out of Cincinnati released some really great, I mean some of the finest examples, of raw, exciting, primitive, wild rockabilly 45s on the likes of Charlie Feathers, Mac Curtis, Bob & Lucille, Joe Penny, Bill Beach, and others. All of Feathers's and Curtis's King records remained the finest examples of 1956 and '57 rockabilly music you'd ever want to hear. But the really only crazy,

wild rockabilly song this artist Hank Mizell ever recorded back in the 1950s was the song "Jungle Rock." He was basically an older country artist who was in his thirties at the time he recorded it. He was just another of the many standard, southern country music singers that decided to take a stab at this new teenage music that was sweepin' the U.S. back in '57. Well, at the time King Records released it, the song flopped, like all the Charlie Feathers and Mac Curtis records had done before it. But over in London in 1976, this nineteen-year-old record started bein' played by DJs in various discos that were popular at that time. Within a short time, "Jungle Rock" by Hank Mizell was one of the most requested songs in all the clubs all over London by new music fans and the "Teddy Boy" group of fifties rockabilly fans as well.

King Records was now owned by the Nashville-based Gusto Records Corporation. "Jungle Rock" had first come out on EKO Records, but King picked it up shortly thereafter. Gusto Records licensed "Jungle Rock" by Hank Mizell to a major label in Europe, and upon its release, the original 1957 recording shot all the way up into the Top 10 on the major British charts, as well as doin' the same in a number of other countries in Europe. I mean, here was this wild rockabilly song perched in the same Top 10 charts in various countries all through Europe as the likes of Elton John, The Bee Gees, Queen, and other top artists of the day.

Everybody wanted this artist over in Europe in 1976, but nobody in Nashville had a clue of not only where he was and if he was still alive, but even who he was in the first place. By the time they located him living deep in the hills of northwest Tennessee, it was well into 1977, but they still wanted to see him in Europe live on stage, even though the song had long dropped off the charts. Well, let's just say that at that late date, ol' Hank was pretty much out of step with the wild rockabilly sounds of this earlier record of his. But "Jungle Rock" becoming a huge hit overseas opened a lot of eyes and ears both in Europe and here in the U.S. During 1976, a large group of rockabilly-lovin' "Teddy Boys" marched on the BBC, demanding that they give more air time to rockabilly and fifties-style rock 'n' roll.

Shakin' Stevens

Young new rockabilly artists such as Shakin' Stevens and his band The Sunsets were becoming immensely popular in England all during the period from 1970 to 1976. Dave Edmunds produced Shakin' Stevens's first professional recordings in 1970. Nineteen seventy-six was a breakthrough year for Shakin' Stevens, when he signed his first major record contract with Track Records that would give him major distribution. Track Records in England had been the first to discover and sign The Who and Jimi Hendrix. In early 1976, they felt Shakin' Stevens could also become a gigantic mainstream star. He already had a large "Teddy Boy" following of devoted rockabilly fans on the nightclub circuit and was extremely popular in a number of European countries by then.

Whenever an artist, meaning singer, signs with a major record label, they have to make concessions. One of those concessions was that Track Records was signing Shakin' Stevens alone. His longtime band, The Sunsets, had to go elsewhere. From what I've read and heard over the years, the hard-core, purist "Teddy Boy" rockabilly fans of Shakin' Stevens & The Sunsets felt then and even now that Shakin' Stevens had deserted pure rockabilly music and went mainstream. A lot of 'em turned against him. But it sure helped him in the long run.

Shaky, as he's referred to, stayed with Track Records for two years, until 1978, recording practically all covers of old rock 'n' roll, rockabilly, and rhythm & blues songs from the 1950s. He had been doin' that all along with his band, The Sunsets, also. With his old group, Shaky recorded Carl Perkins, Johnny Burnette Trio, Billy Lee Riley, Jack Scott, and tons of other rockabilly songs from the fifties. When Shaky moved over to Track Records and later to Epic Records, he was doin' basically the same covers even as the early eighties came in. They may have been more polished and had a little slicker sound, but Shaky's energetic vocals (which sold the millions of records later) sounded pretty good to me.

While Shaky was still at Track Records, he got the lead role in a stage show in London, and when it opened in December 1977, Shaky started to achieve a lot of acclaim by critics and fans alike. This show was called *Elvis,* and that's who Shaky portrayed. Here in the U.S., that's always made a lot of money for artists such as Johnny Seaton, but it's wound up bein' a curse in the long run for an original artist. That moniker of portraying Elvis always sticks with you. Shaky was more than able to overcome this image, though.

After Shaky signed with Epic Records in the late 1978, he'd go on to his greatest success. While he was with Track Records, though, I felt Shaky recorded better and rawer rockin' versions of Buddy Knox's "Somebody Touched Me" and The Righteous Brothers' "Justine"

than the fifties and sixties originals. But it was when Shakin' Stevens recorded "Marie, Marie," which had been pitched to Epic by Ronnie Weiser, as he had cut this song by The Blasters in 1979, that put Shaky into the mainstream Top 20 charts in England and other European countries. The Blasters were signed to Rollin' Rock Records at the time, and their lead guitarist, Dave Alvin, wrote "Marie, Marie." The Blasters would achieve their own success during the early eighties, when they went on to sign with Slash Records, a subsidiary label of Warner Brothers. They'd become an important group when the rockabilly revival was at its peak here in the U.S. "Marie, Marie" by Shakin' Stevens reached a peak position of #19 on the mainstream British charts in early 1980. The following 45 was a rockabilly version of an old Rosemary Clooney hit from the early fifties, called "This Old House." It shot straight to #1 all over Europe on every chart, and for the rest of the decade of the 1980s so did just about every other new 45 Shaky put out.

Shaky had many 45 single records released on him between 1980 and 1990 on Epic Records, and like I said, they all were gigantic hits through that time period. During the summer of 1990 I read an article in the "International News" section of *Billboard,* which covered the biggest artists around the world. What it said totally shocked me at the time. It had a list of the pop and rock artists for the decade of the 1980s who had actually sold the most 45 singles and LP albums during that decade in all of Europe combined. On that list Shakin' Stevens placed second, only behind Madonna, for selling the most total 45 single records for the decade of the 1980s in all European countries. That meant Shaky was the top-selling 45 singles male artist for the entire decade, in which he had sold more 45s than superstar artists such as Michael Jackson, Lionel Richie, Prince, Bruce Springsteen, Elton John, Daryl Hall & John Oates, Phil Collins, Billy Joel, and so many other pop and rock artists who became legends in the U.S. Shakin' Stevens did it all with his brand of rockabilly and original rock 'n' roll. Even though as the eighties grew on it became more polished, but it was much better than any of the above so-called legends that we had to hear on pop and rock radio here in the U.S. during that decade.

Epic Records tried hard, I believe, to break Shaky here in the U.S., as they consistently released 45s and LPs by him here through at least 1987. The closest Shaky came to havin' a real chart hit was when on April 21, 1984, his song "I Cry Just a Little Bit" debuted on the *Billboard* pop charts and reached a peak position of #67 in May. The song had a six-week ride on the *Billboard* pop charts, then dropped off. I remember seein' him when he came over to promote "I Cry Just a Little Bit" on a half dozen TV shows, such as "Solid Gold." The cat still looked more rockabilly to me than The Stray Cats had, who went their separate ways around this time. Plus he moved and rocked in the way real rock 'n' roll and rockabilly singers had in the past as I remember 'em. He was good, and he had a whole lot of energy. Country artist Sylvia (What ever happened to her?) covered the song "I Cry Just a Little Bit" and took it up into the *Billboard* country Top 10 later that year.

Even though Shakin' Stevens never made it big in America, a whole lot of American rockabilly and rock 'n' roll fans bought anything they could find on him throughout the 1980s. As late as 1985 and after, you could still find his solid rockabilly-soundin' versions of classics such as Billy Fury's "Don't Knock upon My Door," Joe Turner's "Lipstick, Powder, and Paint," and even solid covers of another Dave Alvin/Blasters song, "So Long Baby Goodbye." Shaky also recorded good rockabilly-type originals such as "Bad Reputation," "Diddle I," "As Long As," and many others. I think Europe should be happy at least that they had Shakin' Stevens consistently on their pop radio stations for over ten years. It was a lot better than the junk we had to hear on those same type stations here in the U.S.

I haven't heard much from Shakin' Stevens since 1990, but he was the biggest star around the rest of the world who was still layin' down some pretty damn good rockabilly music for quite a few years.

Back in the U.S.A.

While we had Sun International continuing to release U.S. rockabilly albums on older artists through to the end of the 1970s (except when Shelby Singleton decided to exploit and milk the lowest caliber of Elvis fans who still believed Elvis was out there among us from 1978 to 1981, when Shelby had this masked Lone Ranger character who he dubbed Orion sellin' records, and a lot of 'em to those dummies, too), we also had a lot of other companies here in the U.S. starting to get a piece of the action.

Gusto Records in Nashville released albums on a lot of the obscure rockabilly artists who had recorded rockabilly songs in the 1950s on the King, Federal, Starday, and Dixie record labels. These records sold many more than they'd ever sold when they were first released in the mid and late fifties.

By 1978, many others would spring up here in the U.S. Ronnie Weiser out in California recorded and continued to release new 45s and LPs on the likes of Ray Campi, Mac Curtis, Jackie Lee Cochran, Charlie Feathers, Pat Cupp, Whitey Pullen, Chuck Higgens, Sonny Cole, Tony Conn, and many others through to the end of the 1970s.

Forgettin' to Remember to Forget

The best example I can give Americans who may have never heard of Shakin' Stevens and all the big hits he had during the decade of the eighties in Europe is when in March 1988, while I was still Johnny Seaton's personal manager, me, Pepper, and Johnny had an appointment at the Capitol Centre in Landover, Maryland, to meet with Abe Pollen and Mike Evans, his right-hand man for concerts at the Centre. After the meeting, me, Johnny, and Mike started talkin' about rockabilly music. When I brought up the name Shakin' Stevens, Mike Evans popped up and said, "Man, do I ever remember that name. In 1983, I was the road manager for The Rolling Stones, and we had a show in London then on a world tour they were doin'. I couldn't figure out why the hall we were playin' in there was only about half full. I asked one of the British road crew why the place hadn't sold out. The guy told me, 'Because Shakin' Stevens is performing tonight at the biggest hall here, and he always sells out.' I asked the guy, 'What the hell is a Shakin' Stevens?' He looked at me funny and said, 'That guy's the biggest star over here, mate, and no act can outdraw him.' It blew my mind, 'cause I'd never even heard of this character."

During the early eighties, Ronnie was still releasing and now licensing his own produced material to overseas labels and ones like Rhino Records right here in the U.S. Around 1979, after a decade of recording the original artists Ronnie loved so much, he began recording newer groups and artists on a more frequent basis and releasing records on them also.

Ronnie was surely in the rockabilly game to make money, but unlike Shelby Singleton, Ronnie was totally dedicated and devoted to all this pure rockabilly sound in music that was really grabbing ahold by the end of the 1970s. Ronnie Weiser was a good businessman, and he took some chances before anyone else back in '69 and '70. Sure, you want to make as much money as you can when you're gamblin' yours as Ronnie was back then, but he completely loved the original rockabilly music he was producing, and that's what's always counted with me first.

The older fifties artists that complain the most because they've been cheated or never received any money from their 1950s rockabilly songs that have been reissued over and over again don't want to talk about the other side of that. Though I'll always believe it's wrong they never received the royalties they justly deserved, on the other side of the coin is no one would have heard of 'em in Europe or here in the U.S. if these reissue albums hadn't come out during the seventies and eighties. The final fact is the artists who complain the most are the ones who constantly have continued to make a good deal of money by going abroad for rockabilly shows since the late 1970s.

All that aside, if you were a rockabilly music fan in 1976, it was one great time to walk into your select record shops and find all this unreleased rockabilly music you'd never heard before. I loved it all!

Charlie Feathers: The Only Original Early Fifties Rockabilly Who Has Remained True Blue

As 1977 rolled in, disco music was in high gear and all over pop and rock radio, along with heavy metal, straight pop, and the sounds of Funkadelic music. College radio stations were playin' alternative music, though, and new wave and punk bands were really popular at that time, also. In some ways, while most of these new wave and punk bands sounded like a lot of noise to me, they owed what they were playin' to rockabilly music. These bands were experimenting and takin' their music way out into left field at the time. A group like The Cramps back in '77 looked weird and freaky, but they were still doin' some old rockabilly songs that almost didn't sound half bad.

But for me, as '77 began, I was still into buyin' the real rock 'n' roll and rockabilly music that was easily found, plus I was travelin', for as much time as I could get off work, to see Elvis in whatever city or town I could, 'cause by this time, even though Pepper didn't want to hear it, I was sayin' to my mother, friends, and guys at work, I was goin' out there as much as I could to see this cat, who'd turned into a friend by then, because I could see he was killin' himself by this point. People that have known me a long time'll tell you I kept sayin' the cat was gonna die before long at the pace he's goin'. I was never one of the naive ones who believed Elvis had been in the hospital because of exhaustion, colon, or glaucoma problems. I knew what the real problem was then. I only wanted to see and be around him, no matter how bad a shape he was in then. Me and Pepper were there pretty close to the end, at least up until seven weeks before he died on August 16, 1977. That's when Elvis finally got the peace in death that he could never seem to find during those last four years of his life here on this earth. Elvis's death on that hot August day in 1977 was sort of a turning point in my life.

I was never your typical Elvis fan. While seein' Elvis wherever I could throughout the 1970s until he died was at the top of my list of priorities, I had a whole outside-

Elvis life goin' on from 1970 to '77. Most of it all centered around real rock 'n' roll and rockabilly music. I was always trying to go see as many live shows as I could during this period, as well as keeping up with all the new records that were coming out. But of course there was always my regular day job I had to be on five days a week.

The first real jolt in my life was when my father passed away in April 1974. The only other time in my young life I had to deal with personal immediate family death was when my grandmother Nanny, on my mother's side, had died back in 1963. I was only nineteen and had recently completed my final year of high school then, and while her death stunned me at the time, I was more ready for it, because she was ninety-four years old and had been ill for what seemed like quite awhile to somebody as young as me then. I got over my grandmother's death pretty quick. It was eleven years later now, and it was hard to accept my dad's death. After I got out of the whole outlaw biker scene, and me and Pepper got married, I got closer with my dad during the last five years of his life. We'd always been close, but I guess it's just that from '69 to '74, I was around him more than I had been since the 1950s when I was a kid.

My father had instilled in me a great love for the southern states and all its music. I also inherited his sarcastic humor. My father was exactly what he was. Real! He didn't put on no airs. He didn't care what people thought about him, either. I'm about the same way.

Background

Three years before Elvis died, on one of my trips to Memphis to see if I could catch Elvis at Graceland, I'd meet an original rockabilly artist by the name of Charlie Feathers who was also real. Especially in his great music. It was three months after my dad died, during July 1974. I had heard of Charlie Feathers because I had bought a 45 by him on King Records back about '58 or '59, and there was this local disc jockey by the name of

Dick Lillard who had a late-night "Roots of Rock 'n' Roll" radio show for about four hours that I listened to regularly in the past couple years on a Washington, D.C., oldies station called WMOD. Everything I'd heard Dick play by Charlie Feathers sounded great. I also knew that while he was still on Sun Records, Charlie had co-written Elvis's fifth and final Sun record, "I Forgot to Remember to Forget," which was Elvis's first actual #1 song on the *Billboard* country charts, and it stayed on those charts for thirty-nine straight weeks, longer than any other song Elvis ever had in his entire career, and that it was also the song that got Elvis signed to RCA Victor after Colonel Parker became his manager.

Well, on that trip to Memphis, not only did I find and buy some rare old singles by Charlie Feathers on the Sun, Meteor, and Flip labels, but I also found out he still lived around town and had just bought a nightclub, called the Phoenix Club. So I went out there. Charlie, in addition to being owner, bartender, and bouncer at the Phoenix Club, also got up and sang a set of rockabilly classics that night before closing time. Afterward I got a chance to talk with him, and he persuaded me to extend my stay in Memphis to visit him at his house the next day.

On that 1974 July day, Charlie took me in his house, and we went back in his bedroom where he had his reel-to-reel recorders set up, and I was amazed by what he was playin' for me and the stories he was tellin' me behind each one of the old songs my ears were hearin'. From that first meeting in 1974 through to the end of the 1970s, Charlie's stories were pretty much right on the money, even though at that time I felt some of 'em weren't or just couldn't be. Into the 1980s, though, Charlie seemed to delight in overexaggerating some of these early stories, which were all about his early days at Sun Records between 1953 and '55.

First off, Charlie told me he first met Elvis during the summer of 1953, when Elvis was workin' at the Crown Electric Company in Memphis. Elvis was only eighteen years old, and Charlie was twenty-one at the time. Charlie said Elvis had already went into what was then called the Sun Recording Service and recorded a couple of songs on an acetate that Elvis paid for himself to see what he'd sound like on a record. He said Elvis was just a shy, timid kind of backwards young boy at that time. Charlie said in late '53 and early '54, Sam Phillips started gettin' into recording some white artists doin' hillbilly music of the day. It's a fact by early '54 Charlie was bein' paid by Sam Phillips to do some engineering and help out on arrangements on certain songs that were bein' cut at

Sun, 'cause Charlie's wife has shown me a receipt signed by both Charlie and Sam Phillips, dated December 9, 1954, for the weekly paycheck Sam Phillips had paid Charlie for this work during this period. Stan Kesler, who Charlie was co-writing songs with during the early fifties down at Sun, and was also the co-writer of "I Forgot to Remember to Forget," was also drawing weekly paychecks from Sam Phillips by 1954.

Charlie told me Elvis was always hangin' around the Sun studio from the summer of 1953 to when Sam decided to start recording him with Scotty Moore and Bill Black in July 1954. By this time, Elvis had already made and paid for a second acetate of two more songs for his own personal reasons down at the Sun studio. Charlie said he was in there when these were cut. That these early Elvis songs were pop songs like the Ink Spots and such, from what Charlie said. Years later, this proved to be true when RCA Records and the Elvis Presley Estate obtained the rights to release these first recordings by Elvis. They were songs the Ink Spots had done, such as "My Happiness" and "That's When Your Heartaches Begin." These songs finally surfaced twelve to fifteen years after Elvis's death and proved his goals were to be a pop music singer when he was a teenager, 'cause that seemed to be where the real money could be made. But Elvis was stuck right in the middle of all the blues records that Sam Phillips was recording in the early fifties. In 1974, Charlie confirmed that's what Elvis was singin' in the beginning. Charlie also told me that on a whole lot of Friday nights during late 1953 and into 1954, Elvis, Charlie, and Charlie's older brother Shorty would go down to the old Princess movie theater in Memphis.

Now I know there's gonna be doubters on some of these claims of Charlie Feathers's early association with Elvis before he ever officially recorded for Sun Records starting in July 1954. European writers and so-called experts have written over the years that Charlie Feathers has only made these claims to inflate his own early importance at Sun Records. Well, there is only one thing I can be totally sure of in my mind. That is that Charlie Feathers's wife Rosemary, a religious, God-fearing woman, who I know would never tell me a lie to back one of Charlie's stories up, will speak out on the stories that she knows are positively true and that she witnessed, and that's one of 'em. There's plenty others.

By early '54, Charlie Feathers was playin' clubs in and around Memphis at night, and he was regularly down at Sun Records during the day, so I'm sure Elvis was more than glad to hang around. Both Elvis and Charlie wanted the same thing, and that was to get a record out on the only label in town, Sun Records. Of course, later on Elvis would definitely stand the best chance, because he'd do whatever it took or whatever he was told to do to achieve his goal. On the other hand, I'm sure Charlie was about as outspoken and brash when it came to his ideas on how the music he was doin' ought to be done for it to be right (the way he heard it) back in 1954, as he was in 1974 and even today. Also, by all accounts (except Charlie's), Sam Phillips always saw Charlie Feathers as a great country singer, and after Elvis and rockabilly took off in late '54 and '55, Sam was determined he was only gonna release country records on Charlie. In 1990, Sam himself told me, "Charlie Feathers could have been as big as George Jones back then, 'cause Charlie had that pure country soulful voice that only comes along once in a great while, but he just wouldn't listen to anybody. He was the first great country singer I ever cut and probably the pure best, but when he saw Elvis take off, he wanted to jump on the rockabilly stuff, and I just never heard him makin' it doin' that, but he could-a-made it big, man, if he'd-a-stuck with the country stuff like I wanted him to. But back then, he just wouldn't listen."

I can believe all that Sam said, with the exception that Charlie Feathers really did come around to defining the true art of pure, authentic, mid-1950s raw rockabilly songs, even though some time would have to go by before this was completely recognized by rockabilly fans around the world. But what can't be denied Charlie Feathers is that, at least by the summer of 1953, Charlie and Elvis were in that Sun recording studio quite a bit, and by early 1954, Charlie was bein' paid by Sam Phillips for his talents as a unique arranger and possibly engineer on various sessions.

For the most part, when Charlie told me a ton of stories at his house, before takin' me back to the Phoenix Club on our first meeting, he was at that time on the humble side (which is hard to believe for those who'd meet him later on), not braggadocious, and basically said everything about his and Elvis's early days in a just plain matter-of-fact way. I wasn't anybody important. By this time, the European rockabilly fans were just starting to make pilgrimages to Memphis to try to find Charlie Feathers. But this was still early on, and Charlie was still scrapin' it out in the local places. He had only recently purchased the Phoenix Club, which he didn't keep for too long. Charlie had no reason to make things up as early as 1974.

What has always led me to believe Charlie Feathers's stories on his and Elvis's early days at Sun and Charlie's involvement with Elvis recording sessions at Sun was several of the old reel-to-reel tapes he played for me in July 1974. Now, Charlie has told me and many others he was at all of Elvis's recording sessions at Sun. I wasn't there, so I can't say if this is true or not. Charlie also claims that when they couldn't find the right arrangement on the rhythm & blues classic "Good Rockin' Tonight," he was the one that came up with it, and Elvis recorded it exactly that way. This I have no reason not to believe, because at his house back in '74, Charlie played me not only his original September 1954 version done in the Sun studio, but also a version by Elvis on another reel of tape he had on the same type arrangement of "Good Rockin' Tonight" that was sung by Elvis that I'd never heard before in my life and have never heard since. Charlie ran both versions back a couple o' times and let me hear over again with the in-between studio chatter and comments that were all comin' from Charlie, Sam Phillips, Scotty Moore, and Elvis himself. Now I had been listening to Elvis's voice for about twenty years by this time, and there was no doubt then or now that it was Elvis on that reel of tape, and Charlie on the other one. Also the version of "Good Rockin' Tonight" by Elvis was when he was just beginning to learn the song in the arrangement Charlie had put on it for him, and it sounds considerably different on that early take of "Good Rockin' Tonight" than the one that Sam Phillips released after they'd all fine-tuned this great song by Elvis.

If that wasn't enough to blow my mind (and Charlie could see it by the look on my face), he then gets another reel of tape and plays me some song by him that I'd never heard, called "We're Gettin' Closer to Being Apart." Charlie tells me he recorded it back in '55, and him and Stan Kesler wrote the song, and Sam Phillips was gonna release it as the follow-up to "I Forgot to Remember to Forget," but that Sam sold Elvis's contract over to RCA Victor right after Elvis cut it, so the song wasn't able to come out. I told Charlie back then, "Get outta here, you gotta be kiddin'." With a sly look on his face and a gleam in his eye, Charlie then said to me, "You think so, do ya? Well, you just listen to this next song and tell me who it is." Charlie then puts on another reel of tape, and as the same song starts playin', I didn't believe what I was hearin', but I didn't say a word until Charlie said about halfway through the song, "Now, you tell me who that is. Come on, you know." I just looked up at Charlie and said, "Ain't no doubt. That's Elvis. But how in the hell did you wind up with it?" Charlie just said, "Lotta things I got, boy, that nobody else has got, and nobody else is gonna get 'em, either." After the song finished, I said to him, "Play it back one more time and just let me hear it to be sure it was Elvis, so that you ain't puttin' somethin' over on me." I asked Charlie not to say anything. To just let me listen real close to it all the way through from the beginning. Which he did. After about a three-second false start, I could hear Sam Phillips say, "Take two," and then the song started again. There was no doubt right then and there that I knew Charlie Feathers was definitely tellin' the truth. That was Elvis singin' "We're Gettin' Closer to Being Apart" from start to finish.

While I was at Charlie's house that day, he played me quite a few old rockabilly songs of his I'd never heard up until that time, but it was that alternate version of Elvis singin' "Good Rockin' Tonight" and Elvis singin' the never-before-heard song "We're Gettin' Closer to Being Apart" that I'll always remember more than anything else. Only Charlie and maybe his family knows if he still has those two songs by Elvis that were cut at Sun Records. The way I've grown to know Charlie, he probably does still have 'em. But by now, he's probably buried 'em somewhere that nobody'll ever find 'em. If so, good for him.

When I went down on a trip to Memphis during the early spring of 1978 specifically to see Charlie for a few days, he introduced me to a guy named Johnny Bernero, who Charlie said was Elvis's first drummer and the only one ever used on Elvis's Sun recordings. I asked him if he remembered recording "We're Gettin' Closer to Being Apart" with Elvis. Bernero showed no hesitation when he told me he did. He also told me he came to Sun Records to play on sessions during the summer of 1954, and Charlie was either workin' on various sessions or recording his own songs when he first got there. I don't believe I have to go on much farther on the facts of Charlie Feathers's importance to rockabilly music. I've either seen or have proof or have heard it from the ones who were there as early as 1953 and '54. Johnny Bragg, lead singer for The Prisonaires, is another one.

The reason I've written this much that contradicts what other so-called historians and experts on Sun Records have written is because Charlie Feathers has made a lot of enemies during the past twenty years or so. Some of these are influential writers who either own or own interests in independent record labels that have put out Charlie's early recordings, plus they are also paid tidy sums of money to write liner notes for major record labels, as well as top music publications. I agree with a few things they write, such as Charlie Feathers has probably been his own worst enemy where the music business has been concerned. I didn't know this in July 1974, when I first met Charlie. I also didn't know then when we left his house, and he took me back to the Phoenix Club, and we parted after we exchanged phone numbers, took a couple more pictures together, and he signed an 8x10 photo of himself for me, that my family and Charlie's family would have a close friendship that would turn out to last more than twenty years now. More importantly, I didn't realize then that Charlie would be the one who would inspire me the most within a few years of this meeting to go back into the music business full-time. Charlie taught me more about recording and producing rockabilly music the only way it should be done (the right way!) than anyone I ever met.

Sure, Charlie Feathers has made a lot of enemies. Charlie don't like music writers, booking agents, promoters, producers, music and record company executives, and so on. Why should he like a writer that on the liner notes of a European album wrote, "Charlie's only real contribution to early rockabilly music is the fact that he made a handful of brilliant records and until recently his convictions for gambling outnumbered mentions of his music in the files of the local newspapers in his adopted hometown of Memphis where Feathers was rarely more than an underground figure in the 1950s." I don't think I'd like that either, especially when this particular writer at the time he wrote this was part-owner of the record label that released this album of mostly all unissued recordings Charlie had made during the fifties and sixties. Why should Charlie like any music writer after reading this and seein' it on the back cover of a full album of songs, most of which he wrote and all of which he arranged, that this now highly touted music writer had obtained from someone who was one of Charlie's regular band members between 1955 and 1958? Charlie knew that he wouldn't see a penny from this album in the way of artist or publishing royalties from the sales of it or from the other two albums and CDs between 1986 and 1990 that were put out by this writer's label. This writer I'm speakin' of is definitely in the small minority of some really fine music writers not only here in the U.S. but in parts of Europe also. But with Charlie Feathers, all it takes is one like this to turn him against all of 'em.

It's been in print before that Charlie Feathers is illiterate and is only able to sign his name. Charlie was born in a hard year, 1932, and grew up in a poor, hard place, Slayden, Mississippi. Back during this Depression period, when you were a kid in the Deep South, there was no time for school. You had to work like Charlie did, and work hard long hours, too, if you wanted to eat at the table with the rest of your family. Charlie, like so many other kids in that region of the country and during that time, worked at every hard-labor job he could find, from pickin' cotton to workin' on the pipelines they were layin' in the ground. It didn't matter if the color of your skin was black or white back in the thirties and forties, everybody had one thing in common, and that was bein' poor. But where Charlie was, both blacks and whites alike sang about it. An old black man named Obie Patterson taught Charlie how to play the guitar when he was about nine years old. Charlie seen Bill Monroe around that time and liked what he heard, but couldn't play that kind of music. Charlie only knew how to play and sing what the many black people, who worked on all the same farms he did, played and sang. Charlie calls it "cottonpatch blues." In Mississippi, when Charlie was just learnin' to play and loved his guitar and the music that came out of it, he went to black churches on Sundays, where he said they had picnics, shot dice, and did all sorts of things, but he was mostly there to watch 'em when they started rappin' on their guitars and singin' the cottonpatch blues. Years later, what Charlie learned from these black men would be much more important in his world than anything that would have been taught to him in a schoolhouse at that time. That music got inside Charlie's soul and never left him.

Charlie wound up moving to Memphis in 1949. A year or so later, he met and then married his wife Rosemary. But in 1951, Charlie came down with spinal meningitis and wound up in the hospital with this serious illness for over a year. By the time Charlie moved to Memphis, Hank Williams was the biggest singer in country music. Charlie will tell you today Hank was the greatest country singer who ever lived. Charlie was influenced by the country sounds of not only Hank Williams but Bill Monroe as well during those early fifties. In 1952, by the time Charlie got out of the hospital, Sam Phillips and his Memphis Recording Service were starting to release blues records on Sam's newly formed Sun Records.

Sam tested the country music market as early as the fall of 1953 with a release by The Ripley Cotton Choppers and then again during the spring of 1954 with releases by Earl Peterson and Doug Poindexter. But after "Baby Let's Play House" broke out all over the South in sales and radio play in the spring of 1955 and was followed shortly with "I Forgot to Remember to Forget," which

reached #1 on the *Billboard* country charts before the end of 1955, Sam's days of recording black artists were just about completely over. Rockabilly music was then a "Mystery Train" that was racin' full-speed ahead.

So after all the artists and musicians I've spoke with over the past twenty-plus years who were present at Sun Records in 1953 and '54 have confirmed Charlie Feathers was not only present at the Sun studio then but was workin' there and recording there, it's been written that a lot of Charlie's early songs were recorded over to save tape in the early fifties. This may be, and who knows, they might magically appear on some new foreign CD album someday. I guess I've spent so much time writing what I know to be the truth about Charlie's early years at Sun because of several nerdy, British, so-called expert historians on Sun Records who have put out books, magazine articles, liner notes on their albums, and others that are all filled with bullshit I've had to read saying that Charlie Feathers's early 1950s musical contributions at Sun Records are no more than fabrications in his own mind. Well, many others who were there totally disagree, including the late Marcus Van Story and one of The Miller Sisters, who were there as early as '54, at least. The one that disagrees the most, though, is none other than a man that was not only inducted into the Country Music Hall of Fame in 1980, but also was recently inducted as well into the Rock 'n' Roll Hall of Fame. That man's name is Johnny Cash.

After Charlie had recorded his first-ever new major label album for Elektra Records here in the U.S. during August 1990, writer Ben Sandmel was the one who wrote the liner notes for it. When Sandmel interviewed Johnny Cash in late 1990 and asked Cash what he thought Charlie Feathers's importance at Sun Records was, Cash replied, "Charlie Feathers is the main reason there is, and was, Sun Records. His songs were recorded by all of us there, and he has never been given the credit or recognition he deserves. I will always be a Charlie Feathers fan." That is an exact quote, word for word, right out of the mouth of Johnny Cash. He'll tell you the same thing today. That was also only what was chosen for Elektra Records to use as part of the promotions for Charlie's 1991 release on their label. Cash didn't get paid or had nothin' to gain by how he described Charlie's importance to all of Sun Records. Johnny Cash came to the Sun Studio in the fall of 1954, so he knew what went on from then on until 1958. That's when Cash left Sun.

After I moved to Nashville, and Charlie's Elektra Records album came out during the summer of 1991, I spoke with Johnny Cash here in Nashville, and he not only backed up what he had told Ben Sandmel, but also told me quite a bit more. He said Charlie had been workin' for Sam Phillips for over a year before he got there, and he knew for a fact that from Elvis's second record on, Charlie contributed more ideas on the rest of Elvis's Sun songs than Sam or anybody else in the studio. Cash admitted maybe Elvis did stumble onto rockabilly music during a break in a session when he started goofin' around, but it was Charlie who'd always pick up somethin' like that and figure out how to take it out into left field somewhere. Sam Phillips was always lookin' for something out of left field anyway, and Charlie's mind in those days was always out in left field when it came to music. Cash went on to tell me he wasn't trying to take anything away from Elvis, 'cause Elvis, not Charlie, was the only one at the time who could put this new sound across the way he did, but it was mostly Charlie Feathers's ideas that helped get it there to begin with.

When I asked Cash, as I have so many others, why he thought Charlie never had a big hit record in the fifties, Cash chuckled a little when he simply said, "'Cause he's Charlie Feathers." By 1991, I knew what he meant by that. Cash went on to say, though, Charlie had to do his music his way, and nobody else thought like he did when it came to the way he heard things, and him and Sam clashed a lot on that. Cash said, "Even after Charlie left Sun and went and signed with other labels, Sam always let Charlie come back, 'cause he knew he could use some of Charlie's ideas on songs he was cuttin' on other artists then." Cash said whenever Charlie wasn't out playin' shows on the road, he could usually be found down at Sun workin' on somethin'. Cash also said during '55 and '56, after he had his first releases on Sun, him and Charlie probably played more than a hundred or so shows together. He said most time they'd be in the same car and Carl Perkins was with 'em on a lot of those tours through the South and Southwest.

Then I asked Johnny Cash one thing I was already sure of, just to see what his answer would be. I said, "I know you were there, but didn't sing, during what they now call the 'Million Dollar Quartet' sessions, but was Charlie Feathers in there that day, too?" Cash said, "Yeah, Charlie was in there when I stopped by, and he was still there when I left. I'm sure he was in there even after Elvis had left. Charlie was always in that ol' studio when he was in town."

Well, if there's anybody readin' this who has never heard of this now-famous Million Dollar Quartet session

recorded down at the old Sun Records Studio, here's what it's all about. On Tuesday, December 4, 1956, Elvis Presley was home in Memphis, and for whatever reasons he might have had, probably to see what was goin' on, decided to stroll into the old Sun Records Studio that he had left behind a little over a year earlier. Elvis had a girl with him, as well as a couple friends. When Elvis and his friends walked in, there was a Carl Perkins recording session goin' on. Well, when Elvis walked in, everything came to a dead stop.

Either Sam Phillips or Jack Clement, who had been engineering the Carl Perkins session, decided to capitalize on the moment when one of 'em put in a quick call to reporter Robert Johnson at the Memphis *Press Scimitar* newspaper, and he dropped everything to come down to Sun to snap photos of Elvis, Cash, Perkins, and Jerry Lee Lewis, who was there to play piano on the Carl Perkins session. This was the first time Elvis had met Lewis. Johnson ran a picture and a short story on this event the following day in the Memphis newspaper, with all four artists in the picture together. According to the newspaper article, when Elvis first sat down at the piano and started singin' "Blueberry Hill" and other songs, Johnny Cash, Carl Perkins, and Jerry Lee Lewis all drifted over and started singin' along.

It's definitely evident by now Elvis just wanted to jam together with his old friends, but what wasn't publicly known was if this session was recorded and where was it, or who had possession of it. Well, two things are for sure. Both Sam Phillips and Jack Clement knew that tape machine was rollin' that day, and that it would maybe someday be a valuable piece of property.

These reels of tape were safely tucked away for the next twenty-four years. It was 1980 then. Elvis had been dead for three years. The first half of what Sam Phillips had recorded on the Million Dollar Quartet appeared on an album put out on a German label. Germany has no copyright laws that the U.S. can prosecute against. Not long after the German release, the same exact album of seventeen songs by Elvis, Perkins, and Lewis singin' along together on was released in England in 1981 on "Sun Records." Charly Records in England was behind this release, as they had licensed the Sun logo for all the Sun albums that they were releasing by this time, but the Charly Records name was nowhere on this first release of theirs. Numerous lawsuits followed, to no avail. Six years then goes by, and right when all the hoopla was comin' up in the media about all the great things planned for the celebration in Memphis in August 1987 to celebrate Elvis Death Week, what happens but a double album of almost forty songs appears on the market, called *The Complete Million Dollar Session*. It was both on vinyl and the new CD format then. This time, it was boldly released on the Charly Records label in London, England. Three years later, in 1990, the Elvis Estate and RCA Records finally released it in the U.S. on RCA. The same exact release.

After almost two years of laying down songs on tape in the Sun Studio, Sam Phillips decided to release two songs by Charlie on a new subsidiary label of Sun he called Flip Records. Sam had planned to release only country artists on this new label, from what he told me in 1990. So during the early months of 1955, Charlie Feathers had his first 45 record released on Flip Records, called "Peepin' Eyes," which was a bluegrass-tinged up-tempo country tune. It was backed with a haunting country ballad titled "I've Been Deceived." Personally, these two songs don't knock me out. This first 45 of Charlie's has always remained his rarest and most sought-after record by his many fans.

Charlie Feathers had to finally leave Sun Records to reach his quest at gettin' a pure, authentic rockabilly record released during the mid 1950s. Before Charlie walked out on Sam Phillips and Sun Records, though, Sam released a second 45 on Charlie, "Defrost Your Heart" b/w "A Wedding Gown of White." This time on the Sun label in December 1955. Again both sides were country. But this time, both sides were two of the purest and greatest songs that you'd ever want to hear in country at the time. There was so much soul bleedin' through Charlie's vocals on the A side, "Defrost Your Heart," it's incredible.

During the early months of 1956, Charlie had a rockabilly song he'd written and recorded at Sun by then he wanted Sam Phillips to release, called "Tongue Tied Jill." When Sam said, "No way. That song could offend people with speech impediments," Charlie went to Sam's competitor across town in Memphis at the time, Les Bihari, who owned Meteor Records. Meteor was more than glad to have Charlie record this song for them, and they quickly released it. According to what Charlie has told me (and probably others) over the years, Sam got so damn mad when "Tongue Tied Jill" came out on Meteor, he came over to Charlie's house one day and told him, "I'll personally see to it you never have a hit record in this business." I don't know for sure if that's true or not, but what I do know is "Tongue Tied Jill" b/w "Get With It" went on to become the closest thing Charlie ever did

have to becoming a hit. It became the biggest-selling record the small Meteor Records label in Memphis ever had, and it received many good and positive reviews in a whole lot of the music trade magazines and newspapers of that day. This record proved Charlie Feathers was by no means copying or following in Elvis's footsteps. That he had developed by then his own unique brand of rockabilly music, that, though primitive, could possibly do well if given the chance. Meteor gave Charlie more success than he'd ever achieved at Sun Records with country releases.

"Tongue Tied Jill" got so much attention it led to a contract with King Records later in 1956, where Charlie recorded and had released four 45 singles during 1956 and '57, that me and most other rockabilly fans around the world consider to be some of the greatest examples of 1950s rockabilly music ever released. Charlie really got to define his now-famous hiccup style of this music that was hard-drivin', thumpin' rockabilly at its best. Songs he did for King, such as "One Hand Loose," "Bottle to the Baby," "Nobody's Woman," "Can't Hardly Stand It," "Too Much Alike," "Everybody's Lovin' My Baby," "When You Come Around," and "When You Decide" are all true artistic examples of how to write, arrange, and record rockabilly music when it's your only true love. Those eight songs on those four records never went on to chart nationally, but by the time Charlie Feathers left King Records in 1957, he knew in his mind that he was one of the few that really knew how to lay down rockabilly music with the crazy, free, wild, exciting sound it called for that could set a young person's soul on fire.

After Charlie left King Records in 1957, he went back to Memphis and continued to play the local circuit of clubs, record hops, school houses, etc. around Memphis and other parts of the South. Charlie Feathers's next 45 release was on the small Kay Records label in Memphis. In 1958, when the two songs, "Jungle Fever" b/w "Why Don't You," were released, they sold only moderately around Memphis and other areas of the South. Rockabilly music was changin' and was about to soon disappear from the charts and die out eventually. Charlie Feathers wasn't about to change in his ways of doin' his brand of rockabilly. For a generation of newer rockabilly fans along with punk and new wave fans that would come along during the late seventies and early eighties, the song "Jungle Fever," which was written by Charlie Feathers and Raymond Maupin and arranged by Charlie, was as much ahead of its time as Link Wray's "Rumble" instrumental hit that same year in 1958. Charlie put a jungle beat drum sound on this song which he'd choose to use later in the late seventies and eighties. That, along with his bizarre vocal sound on this 1958 recording, put it as far out in left field as some of Danny Gatton's guitar licks would be some twenty years later.

The B side of "Jungle Fever" was another example of straight-ahead rockabilly. The song was called "Why Don't You," and once again, it's Charlie's fast hiccupin' vocal style that's able to change and smooth at times that turns this song into another classic loved by Charlie Feathers fans around the world.

In 1958, when Kay Records released "Jungle Fever" by Charlie, they also released two songs called "Jody's Beat" and "My, My." Charlie played guitar on the record, as the artist it came out on was one of his band members, Jody Chastain. This record by Jody on the Kay label had the same fate as Charlie's back in 1958. It was never really heard of outside of the South. Now today, you got certain people that would like to convince rockabilly fans around the world that Jody Chastain's one record on Kay was a really important and great record in the history of rockabilly. But everybody knows when they hear it that just wasn't the case.

Charlie had one other 45 release before the 1950s closed out. In 1959, Charlie wrote a song called "Dinky John." This was a nickname, at the time, that Charlie used to call his then three-year-old son, Bubba Feathers. Now you won't find "Dinky John" on hardly any of the over forty albums on Charlie Feathers that have come out in the past twenty-three years or so. It's an odd song, but it's not a rockabilly song, and definitely not your standard hillbilly, country, or blues song such as Charlie has been known to do in his own unique way. Charlie Feathers today will tell you it's a folk song. There was a small label in Memphis at the time, Walmay Records, and they wanted to release it, so Charlie recorded it, and they released it in 1959. But Charlie didn't want to become known for that sort of music (the way he told me), so Charlie had the Walmay label put it out under the artist's name of Charlie Morgan. But this one also failed to sell or get much airplay at the time, except around Memphis. The B side of "Dinky John" is actually a pretty good hillbilly tune called "South of Chicago." "South of Chicago" can be found on recent albums by Charlie Feathers, as it's closer to the sound of the kind of music he's always done.

Charlie stayed, lived, played his kind of music in the various clubs, and went on to continue to raise and support a family right there in Memphis, Tennessee, after rockabilly music died out in late '58 and '59. Yeah, rockabilly music died completely when the 1960s came in, at least on the pop mainstream charts like *Billboard*. But all throughout those changin' times of the 1960s, when trends in pop music came and went quickly, Charlie Feathers just kept right on recording and makin' a livin' playin' rockabilly and pure hillbilly right there in all those Memphis nightclubs. That's why his fans, first in Europe and later in the U.S., are so passionate about his music and the man himself. It's because Charlie Feathers was the only genuine, original 1950s rockabilly artist that continued to do rockabilly-type music his own way. Every single other artist that started out doin' rockabilly or had some success with it either quit, went to Nashville to try their luck in mainstream country, or went into pop music either in Los Angeles or New York City. I'm not one to say they made the wrong choice. Usually people will do what they have to do, like these original rockabilly artists you've read about up to now did. They did what they did to make the most money they could from the 1960s on. No matter what they had to sing. Charlie Feathers was the stubborn one. But on the artistic level in rockabilly for the last forty years, Charlie's turned out to be the most highly respected one today, because his fans around the world know that he never sold rockabilly music out. Charlie Feathers records and appearances at live shows, especially in Europe, are more in demand and bring higher prices than any rockabilly artist alive today. Although since 1987, when Charlie fell upon bad health, he's only performed maybe a dozen or so shows. It's easy to figure out why his music is in demand, when you listen to it from the beginning right on through his forty years of recording.

The Sixties

Charlie Feathers only had three 45 record releases in the entire decade of the 1960s, although he spent a lot of time in several Memphis studios constantly recording his and others' songs. The studio he spent the most time in was owned by Sam Phillips's brother, Tom Phillips. Charlie said he knows he had to have recorded over a hundred songs down at Tom's studio in Memphis between 1961 and 1970. Charlie didn't know a thing about how to copyright his songs back then. He wrote songs that he thought had somethin' to 'em, he went into Tom Phillips's studio and just laid 'em down on tape, either with himself just playin' guitar or with whatever musicians were there to back him up. They'd just lay there on those reels of tape. There's no tellin' how many he might have recorded during those days.

One story some readers won't believe or might choose not to believe that I'll go to my grave believing is true is that Charlie Feathers wrote the song "Hold On to What You Got" sometime in 1963, recorded it, and left it layin' on a reel of tape down at Tom Phillips's studio. At the time, whoever was there just wasn't interested in the way Charlie did it. Charlie, according to his wife Rosemary, wrote the same melody and every word of that song. The only difference was Charlie's title for the song then was "One, Two, Three." Those three words, if you're aware of this hit song, are repeated as much as the title it was finally given, "Hold On to What You Got." More than a year after Charlie recorded and left this song on a reel of tape down at Tom Phillips's studio, Charlie and Rosemary were driving in Memphis, when they heard "Hold On to What You Got" by a black soul singer by the name of Joe Tex. This was in late 1964. There was nothin' much Charlie or Rosemary could do about it. This kinda thing was common in the music business back then, where uneducated or naive young artists are concerned. Legendary female rockabilly artist Janis Martin has even got a more horrible story than that. She swears that she wrote and originally recorded "Are You Lonesome Tonight?" at RCA. "Hold On to What You Got" went on to launch Joe Tex's long career in soul music. That song reached #5 on the *Billboard* pop charts in early 1965 and remains Joe Tex's second-highest-ranking *Billboard* pop chart hit.

Charlie Feathers's first of three 45s during the 1960s came out on the Memphis record label in 1961. Side A is a great strong up-tempo number called "Wild Wild Party," sung with the passionate true feel and the same drive Charlie's earlier 1950s rockabilly tunes all had. The writer credits are given to Charlie Feathers and Jerry Huffman on this solid rockabilly tune that went nowhere nationally at the time, 'cause this kind of authentic rockabilly was even dead in Memphis by 1961. The B side of "Wild Wild Party" was a mid-tempo rockabilly-type song called "Today and Tomorrow." Charlie's great vocals on this tune are why it's always been considered a rockabilly song. It's not as wild as "Wild Wild Party," but it's still one of the best B sides on a record you could ask for. Somehow, Charlie Feathers received sole writership on this tune.

Charlie's second release during the sixties came out on the Holiday Inn label that Sam Phillips had started, according to Charlie, 'cause Sam was one of the original stockholders in this motel/hotel chain. Holiday Inn's home office was right there in Memphis, and after it started in 1955, it had become one of the fastest-growing motel/hotel chains across the U.S. It didn't turn out this way, but the original idea was to place records that were released on this new label in the Holiday Inns and have the artists who were on the Holiday Inn label play in the hotels' lounges that had live music. At least this is what Charlie told me.

The two songs Holiday Inn Records released on Charlie were "Nobody's Darlin'," which is a real good mid-tempo rockabilly tune done once more in classic Charlie Feathers style, and on the B side was an old blues tune called "Deep Elm Blues." Charlie does a fantastic, strange arrangement, with a stutterin', stammerin', hic-cupin' vocal on it. A lot of artists have cut this song, but Charlie's version has to be heard to be believed. Charlie's vocal treatment on it is gut-wrenchin' and like no other you'll ever hear. Of course, in 1963, this record didn't stand a chance of sellin' outside the Deep South. It was in no way commercial, like the sounds of Buck Owens, Marty Robbins, and Johnny Cash that were dominating country radio that year. While all their songs from that era hold up well today and still sound great, they had the polished sound for commercial country radio. Charlie Feathers's Holiday Inn 45 was scary, man. It was too damn real for the top radio stations. But none of this bothered Charlie. He just kept right on playin' his kind of music in all the clubs and juke joints that were still goin' in Memphis and surrounding states like Mississippi and Arkansas.

It would be five years before Charlie got his third and final 45 release of the 1960s, and Charlie was being booked by The Gene Williams Booking Agency in clubs around the South. This agency booked quite a few Memphis artists right through the 1970s. But Charlie Feathers was able to do somethin' on his new 1968 45 record that no rockabilly artist had been able to do in over ten years. These two songs were recorded once more at Tom Phillips's studio, which, by the way, was called Select-O-Hits Studio. Charlie had the longest relationship with this studio, between at least 1961 and 1970 (he might have recorded some even as late as '73 there), than any other studio in his entire long recording career. But when Charlie went in there in 1968, Charlie was definitely an artist on a mission. Charlie wound up coming out of there producing and arranging the greatest two-sided rockabilly-soundin' record, in its most pure, frantic form, that he'd come up with since he left King Records in 1957. The two songs I'm speakin' of that Charlie came up with on this 1968 session were a rip-snortin' rockin' treatment of the 1956 Johnny Burnette Trio song "Tear It Up" and a frantic, wild, new, original pure rockabilly song he wrote, called "Stutterin' Cindy," which went on to become one of Charlie's most requested songs during his many live performances in the seventies and eighties.

I've said many times over the past twenty years that "Tear It Up" and "Stutterin' Cindy" was the LAST rockabilly record ever made with the original sound that made Sun Records and rockabilly music famous in the mid 1950s. Charlie Feathers took every great, pure, wild ingredient and was somehow able to duplicate it. I'll give you an example and proof of how close it was to the sound of 1950s Sun. To begin with, Charlie knew he could deliver the vocal treatment and put the right arrangements on these songs. He made sure he was gonna do the mixing on the songs, and he was gonna use the original musicians on these songs. On upright, slappin' bass, Charlie used the great Marcus Van Story. Marcus had played bass on Charlie's first record, "Peepin' Eyes," in early '55, and they worked a lot of other sessions together after that. Marcus was Warren Smith's regular bass player while Warren was at Sun Records, and from the mid 1980s until his untimely death in 1992, Marcus was always one of the standout musicians and singers with the group The Sun Rhythm Section. Marcus was a personality in his own right and one hell of a rockabilly bass-slappin' original. Plus he was always a good close friend of Charlie's over the years. So Charlie made a great choice with Marcus Van Story. Another good choice was Raymond Maupin on lead guitar. Charlie had worked with him since the late fifties. Raymond was given co-writer credit on "Jungle Fever" in 1958. The drummer Charlie used was Bubba Fuller. Charlie told me he used him because this cat was the only one left in Memphis in 1968 that could get the true feel for what these two great songs needed.

The real proof, though, that Charlie Feathers had once again found the original, true-blue soul of rockabilly music that was invented in that little Sun studio in Memphis came around January 1992, when the Smithsonian Institution's Collection of Historic Recordings department contacted me. They told me that a friend of mine, Pat Carroll, at a local record shop outside Washington, D.C., had given them my phone number in Nashville, and I was possibly their last hope at finding out the information they needed on one song they were planning to use on a forthcoming compilation rockabilly album. The Smithsonian told me at that time they were working on this project in conjunction with

the Center for Southern Folklore in Memphis, Tennessee, and it was to be called *Rockabilly in Memphis in the 1950s*. There were eighteen song titles chosen, by thirteen different artists that all recorded these songs in Memphis during the 1950s, from what they had been told by the Center for Southern Folklore in Memphis. Their problem was that they had found seventeen of the eighteen song titles, artists, session details, recording dates, studios, etc., but they were puzzled because of one song that no one in Memphis knew anything about that they were all sure was recorded at Sun Records during the fifties, but Sun Records International, now located in Nashville, had no record in its files on it like the other seventeen songs they had given them, which were all recorded at Sun during the fifties. I laughed when the man from the Smithsonian told me the song they needed the information on was "Stutterin' Cindy" by Charlie Feathers. He was completely baffled when I told him it was recorded and released in 1968. I asked him on that first of several conversations, "You mean to tell me that the 'experts' and people in charge of this Center for Southern Folklore [which I'd never heard of at the time] in Memphis don't know this?" The man told me, "No." I thought, "Here we go again. More big shots (or wannabe big shots) gettin' into somethin' they don't know a damn thing about." I told the guy at the Smithsonian to call me back in a couple days, and I'd call Charlie and find out for him some of the details I didn't already know. I did know the year it came out, I had the 45 record so I knew the label it was on, as well as knowing Charlie wrote the song, but I had to call Charlie to find out where he'd recorded it and the drummer who played on it. I called Charlie, and he gave me the rest of the information the Smithsonian needed. He also told me somebody in Memphis called him about it, but he hung up on 'em. I know why that was. Charlie don't have nothin' to do, really, with these kinds of people in Memphis. Some of the older ones, by 1991 and '92, had ripped him off over the years in the music business, and now those older ones are workin' together with younger ones to make money off his great music still. It's too long to get into. But it's true.

When the Smithsonian finally released this compilation CD album in late 1992, they had retitled it. They called it *Rockabilly in Memphis, 1954 – 1968: Memphis Rocks*. Seventeen of the eighteen songs that were included on it were recorded at the Sun studio between October 1954 and January 1959. "Stutterin' Cindy" by Charlie Feathers was the only rockabilly song there that was recorded as late as 1968. The final interesting fact about this compilation album is that out of the thirteen different artists that were on this CD, only five of those artists evidently were deemed great enough, for the most part for marketing appeal, to be chosen to have two songs each on the compilation. Those were Carl Perkins, Johnny Cash, Jerry Lee Lewis, Warren Smith, and Charlie Feathers. Other artists that got one song on this compliation were great names at Sun Records, such as Roy Orbison, Billy Lee Riley, Sonny Burgess, Ray Smith, Carl Mann, etc. Every one of those artists had dozens more recordings of rockabilly music during the 1950s than Charlie Feathers did, but I know it's that Charlie Feathers was the most unique, artistic, and sellable name on that CD is why those in Memphis behind this album wanted to place two songs by this old cat on there.

Beyond Memphis

After "Tear It Up" b/w "Stutterin' Cindy" was released on Philwood Records in Memphis in the summer of 1968, it would be another five years before Charlie would see his next 45 release come out. In 1973, the Pompadour record label in Memphis released a song that another fifties Memphis rockabilly artist, Eddie Bond, had written, called "Uh Huh Honey" b/w "A Wedding Gown of White," which Charlie recut in '73. "A Wedding Gown of White" was originally recorded and released by Charlie on Sun Records back in '55. Charlie put an unusual and outstanding hiccupin' rockabilly-style vocal arrangement on "Uh Huh Honey," and it went on to become another of his most requested songs by his many fans around the world between 1977 and 1987.

This would be the last time Charlie would have to rely on local Memphis labels to get a record released. By 1973, word had gotten out on Charlie Feathers some-what, especially in Europe, that his tremendous ability to put a rockabilly song across couldn't be touched by practically any artist alive at that time. Besides, in 1973, most artists, if not all, that had done rockabilly music in the fifties had since given up on it long ago. So the parade of not only European record label owners, but also ones in this country as well, began.

The first U.S. label to approach Charlie Feathers, to cut a twelve-song album, was Cowboy Carl Records, out of Plano, Texas. Charlie cut a dozen songs for this label on August 18, 1973. Charlie's told me many times over the past several years that he likes this album, from his outlook, better than any other album he's ever done. The twelve songs on the album cover a wide range of rock-abilly musical styles sung and arranged in Charlie's own

unusual way. Eleven of the twelve are covers of old songs made famous by other artists, but when Charlie sings 'em, they become fresh again. Cowboy Carl Records released this album by the end of 1973, but it virtually got no distribution. That makes it a hard record to find. It's called *Rockabilly Rhythm*. In just about all the record collectors' record price guides I've seen over the past twenty years, I've yet to see this one listed.

In 1973, the European independent record company owners who were approaching Charlie in Memphis were lookin' for Charlie to give up some fifties recordings he'd made (and he wasn't about to do that). George Paulus came down from Chicago and he offered Charlie a deal that he took to go into a Memphis studio and cut enough songs for a full-length album. Paulus owned a record label at the time in Chicago, called Barrelhouse Records. So, on November 20 and 21, 1973, Charlie went into Allied Studios in Memphis with George Paulus and laid down fourteen songs that Paulus took back to Chess Studios in Chicago, where he mixed them and mastered them, resulting in a full-length album on Barrelhouse Records that was titled *The Legendary King of Rockabilly: Charlie Feathers, Good Rockin' Tonight*. Unlike the Cowboy Carl album, this one on Barrelhouse got pretty good distribution, as I was able to locate it by the fall of 1974. I didn't find the Cowboy Carl album until 1976, and it was in Memphis where I found it then.

By 1973, when all this interest started to develop in the authentic rockabilly style of Charlie Feathers, he had already taught his oldest son Bubba (who was seventeen years old then) exactly how he wanted the lead guitar work played, right to the letter. So when Charlie played his live shows or was in the studio recording from 1973 through 1992, Bubba was on that lead guitar or Charlie just wasn't doin' it. I only know of a couple exceptions over all those years where this didn't take place. It should also be noted his firstborn child, Wanda Feathers, was usually found singing on Charlie's live shows, as well as some of his new recordings, between 1973 and 1979.

George Paulus had to know he was onto something here that it would later take years for others to discover and realize. That's why only a little over a month after Charlie cut enough songs for the first planned album on the Barrelhouse label, George Paulus was right back in Memphis. This time he was there to capture Charlie doin' a live show with his band, which included his son Bubba. It was in a local Memphis club called The Silver Dollar Bar on December 28, 1973. Paulus recorded a set of live music that came out on his Barrelhouse

Records label in 1976, which was titled *Charlie Feathers: Live in Memphis, Tennessee*. Like on the studio album, Paulus recorded the only kind of music Charlie had been doin' since 1954, rockabilly music. On those two albums, you'll find Charlie singin' songs in the purest of the original rockabilly sound, such as "Good Rockin' Tonight," "Corrine, Corrina," "Tongue Tied Jill," "Baby Let's Play House," "Matchbox," "I Wonder Where She's at Tonight" (which they chose to title "Rain Keeps on Falling" back in '74), "Mean Woman Blues" (which they also mistitled as "I Got a Woman"), "Shake Rattle and Roll," "Hello Josephine," "Wild Side of Life," "Blue Moon of Kentucky," and others, including "Honky Tonk Man" done rockabilly style. This was thirteen years before Dwight Yoakam ever dreamed this Johnny Horton classic would launch his million-dollar career in "new" country music. Charlie Feathers was the only one in America who not only was performing these songs on a regular basis in 1973, but also had been doin' so regularly since rockabilly died on the national charts in the late fifties.

Most of these were forgotten songs; at least they weren't being done in a primitive rockabilly style throughout the sixties and early seventies. Proof of this was when George Paulus had the foresight to come back to Memphis during the mid seventies and purchase fourteen songs from Tom Phillips that Charlie had recorded at Select-O-Hits Studio in Memphis between 1967 and 1969. Paulus released these songs on his third and final album on his Barrelhouse Records label by Charles Feathers, titled *That Rockabilly Cat!* By 1979, it was easy to sell Charlie Feathers records. He was the most sought-after original 1950s artist during the rockabilly revival goin' on then. But on that 1979 album, you found out that between 1967 and 1969, Charlie had been recording classic rockabilly tunes such as his own "Tongue Tied Jill," Carl Perkins's "Gone, Gone, Gone," Eddie Bond's "Uh Huh Honey," and others, such as ones he'd been writing, like "Mama, Oh Mama," "Cherry Wine," "Cold Dark Night," "Do You Know," and a few others.

I kept in regular touch with Charlie Feathers after first meetin' him in July 1974. Now, when Elvis died, I took it pretty hard, even though I saw it comin'. When I passed by that casket on August 17, 1977, and saw Elvis finally restin' in peace (and it was Elvis and no wax dummy in that casket, I'm here to tell all you non-believers), it hit me like a boulder fallin' right on top of my head. And after I got back home, it took me awhile, probably a month, to figure out, though Elvis had given

me a lot of kindness, sincerity, and love throughout the years, he was dead now, and I had to go on livin'.

What I'd always loved the most outside of my family was music. The music I loved the most was rockabilly music. The greatest rockabilly artist I knew in the early fall of 1977 was Charlie Feathers. So it was Charlie Feathers who I called in September 1977. He'd been steadily workin' on the road with his band then, but he was gonna be home for a week or so in October, so me and Pepper drove down to Memphis, and after several days of goin' around Memphis clubs and talkin' with Charlie, he said he thought I belonged in the music business, 'cause of everything I knew about rockabilly and rock 'n' roll then. I'd told Charlie I'd been in a rock 'n' roll-type group back in the early sixties and done some bookin' of shows a little later in the sixties, and I was thinkin' about startin' a record label and maybe doin' some producing. I remember Charlie tellin' me at one point then, "Well, boy, don't you know that you were born to do it, then, 'cause that's what you love the most, and a man's gotta do what he loves the most and is inside his soul, or he ain't never gonna be happy. That's the best advice I can give you, Billy Poore. Just do it!" Sometimes when I think back on Charlie's words from so long ago, I don't know whether to thank him and hug him or cuss him out. Mainly 'cause I've seen it all. Or at least all I care to see in this crazy rockabilly world I've been in. But the good times do outweigh the bad.

I've learned more from Charlie Feathers about how to figure out this music business than anybody I've known, and when I didn't listen to his advice, sometimes I got screwed for it. After more than twenty years, I've found out Charlie was not right by far about everything he told me about this music business, but he was right many more times than he was wrong. That's why Charlie Feathers is not very well liked by many people in the music business today. Especially some in Europe. But he don't care, and I don't either. The truth is, it's the fans who continue to buy his records and CDs right up to this day. They all know that Charlie Feathers has recorded and had released more rockabilly music which holds up today in bulk as being not only the most, but the greatest in the history of this music. To try to sum it up and give you proof of the points I've made, from 1973 through 1996 there has never been a year go by that Charlie Feathers has not had at least one 45 or album release somewhere in the world. He didn't have to rely on his old fifties recordings, either. From 1973 through 1987, Charlie Feathers recorded and had released more freshly recorded rockabilly music than any other artist in the history of this music.

Charlie found out he had diabetes during the mid seventies, and by 1987 it had turned into diabetic neuropathy. This disease turned so severe, within months Charlie could no longer perform or play the guitar, as it affected his entire nervous system. Through most of 1988, Charlie was confined to either his sofa, his bed, or his wheelchair. He was in and out of the hospital and back and forth to the doctors. The bills began pilin' up. Charlie's wife Rosemary called me in late May 1988 and said Jerry Lee Lewis's latest father-in-law, Bob McCarver, wanted to put on a big benefit to be held at the Vapors Club in Memphis, which holds about 1,000 people. She said McCarver wanted to help Charlie and his family raise money to help pay some of his escalating medical expenses, because like so many artists of the 1950s, Charlie had no hospital insurance. Rosemary told me that Charlie told her to call me, 'cause he wanted me and Pepper there, 'cause for more than ten years we'd been comin' down to Memphis on a once-a-year basis to at least visit him, and we'd stayed with Charlie and his family on most of those trips, and he considered me, Pepper, and my daughter Stacy like family to him, so if we could, he'd just like to see us, 'cause he didn't know how much time he had left.

She also told me to tell Tex Rubinowitz, who both Charlie and his son Bubba loved not only as an artist but as a person, and see if he could come down and perform on this benefit. She told me Bob McCarver was puttin' this whole thing together, and for me to call him up and tell him that Charlie wanted us involved in this benefit show. I told Rosemary to tell Charlie somehow me and Pepper and I'm sure Tex would all be there, then I called Bob McCarver. McCarver more than welcomed my assistance on this benefit show and was lookin' for more authentic rockabilly artists, old or recent, so I told him I could bring LesLee "Bird" Anderson down also, who I'd been workin' with on a new album that was comin' out the last week of July 1988. My main problem, though, was this benefit was bein' held during the busiest month of the year at that time for me. The date it was on was Sunday, July 17, 1988, with continuous music from 4:00 p.m. to 2:00 a.m. It was a tight schedule for Tex Rubinowitz as well.

When it came to great rockabilly music in the Washington, D.C., area, Tex Rubinowitz ruled and fueled the fire between 1978 and 1990. Some in the area still won't admit it, but during those years, Tex could outdraw any local act in the whole surrounding areas, 'cause Tex always remained true to the original rockabilly music of the fifties. Tex had bookings all around Sunday, July 17, 1988, including a big Blue Bayou Festival of Roots Rock 'n' Roll Music that Sleepy La Beef and Tex were headlining on July 16. I had many things goin' on, such as managing and booking LesLee "Bird" Anderson, who was playin' a club up in Baltimore on Friday, July 15. I was still involved with Johnny Seaton, who was in Las Vegas at that time, performing the lead role in a theatrical extravaganza that was endorsed by the Elvis Presley Estate, titled *Elvis: An American Musical*. My biggest immediate problem was that I had the legendary great rockabilly and rock 'n' roll fifties hit artist Jack Scott comin' in for a series of six shows in Virginia and Maryland two days after the benefit for Charlie. Jack Scott bein' the top professional he is, I knew he demanded perfection, and I had two local radio interviews prior to his first show set up for him to do in Washington and Baltimore, plus there was all the music newspaper media I had to deal with. If I hadn't-a quit drinkin', I could-a never pulled all this off. By the time I put Jack Scott on that plane back to his home in Detroit on Monday, July 25, 1988, I had lost nine pounds in twelve days, probably from hardly any sleep and very little food. But on Sunday morning, July 17, 1988, me, Pepper, Tex, and LesLee were on a plane headin' south to Memphis. We were joined by music writer Joe Sasfy. All of us really enjoyed this trip.

Charlie was really in bad shape when we got there. He was on a lot of medication and confined to a wheelchair, and after all the local Memphis bands that were performing the current day's Top 40 country music had finished playing, they brought Charlie into a dressing room around 8:00 p.m., where the group that came with me all got to visit with him, and by the time some of the headliners of the show came on stage around 9:30 p.m., they wheeled Charlie out so he could witness this great event. It really was a once-in-a-lifetime chance to be able to see more fifties Sun Records artists on stage than at any other function I've ever heard of, before or since. The best part was these artists and musicians were relaxed, because they were playin' in Memphis.

The two main star names that were performin' that drew in the most local Memphis people were Jerry Lee Lewis and Charlie Rich. The Sun Rhythm Section, which had performed at the Blue Bayou Festival in Upper Marlboro, Maryland, the day before with Tex Rubinowitz, Sleepy La Beef, and others, also were a big part of this benefit. On that night, this band consisted of Sonny Burgess (fifties Sun Records artist), Marcus Van Story (fifties Sun Records musician), Stan Kesler (fifties Sun Records musician and songwriter), Paul Burlison (The Johnny Burnette Trio's 1950s lead guitarist), D.J. Fontana (Elvis's fifties and sixties drummer on RCA Victor), and Smoochie Smith (Memphis musician). Barbara Pittmann, who had one 45 release on Sun Records and three other 45s on Phillips Records in the late fifties, performed a set with Bubba Feathers and his band Big City backing her up. Bubba and his band backed up most of the artists who'd come in from out of town or who lived in Memphis but didn't have a backup band. Mack Vickery, who recorded a session at Sun Records back in '57 and later went on to write many huge country hits in Nashville, was also there and backed up by Bubba and his band. As was rockabilly artist Dave Travis, who came over from England to perform. Tex Rubinowitz and LesLee "Bird" Anderson were others that were also backed up by Bubba's band on that night. Marion Keisker, who was Sam Phillips's secretary at Sun Records during the early and mid fifties, was also there that night, and Bob McCarver, who was the M.C. of this benefit, got Marion up to mostly talk about her early years workin' at Sun Records.

The highlight of the evening for me, Pepper, Tex, LesLee, Joe Sasfy, and others who really cared personally for Charlie Feathers was when Charlie was wheeled up onto the stage, and after he thanked the audience, Marcus Van Story got Charlie to sing the first song Charlie had released while recording at Sun Records, "Peepin' Eyes." Marcus had played upright bass back in '55 on this song, and Marcus sang along with Charlie as Bubba and the band played in the background. So if you were just there as a fan, this was one tremendous night of music. Memphis music and rockabilly, for the most part.

In 1990, I asked Sam Phillips why he didn't attend it that night. When I was talkin' to him at that time, he was down at his studio, where Charlie Feathers was recording his first major album for Elektra Records, so the reason Sam wasn't at that benefit couldn't-a been because of Charlie. Sam's answer to me then was, "I wasn't about to be anywhere where there is a show promoted under the pretense as a benefit to raise money to help pay someone's medical bills, when it's really bein' put on and done by people who only want to bask in their own glory." I knew exactly what Sam meant by this time. Charlie's wife Rosemary told me Bob McCarver only gave her $1,600 and said that was all they were able to raise. That pissed me off when she told me several months later. It was $10 a head at the door that was collected. They could cram anywhere from 800 up to 1,000 people in the club. So let's say 300 to 500 got in free. That means they still took in $5,000. Bob McCarver made sure he had his people goin' to everybody in the place with cardboard buckets the whole night, and he kept announcin' for everybody to put in as much as they could to help Charlie Feathers out. The later the night got and the more people drank, the more money they put in the buckets. Me and Tex stood there watchin' this go on for hours. The bar at Bad Bob's Vapors Club that night hadn't seen a night where they'd made this much money since eleven months prior, when they held their tenth anniversary, once-a-year shindig to determine who the greatest Elvis imitator was in the world during Elvis Death Week that's celebrated each August. And the barmaid told me a percentage was goin' to Charlie. $1,600? Give me a break. When I did a benefit for Charlie Feathers in August 1989, with seventeen acts that included Charlie himself after he was able to get better and was up walkin' with the help of a cane, I didn't collect any money from the audience. I only took in the 400 people who had paid at the door, plus I pooled it together with my own rockabilly records I was sellin' that night, and at the end of the night I was able to give Charlie Feathers $3,500. I had to pay Narvel Felts and Robert Gordon, who were also on this benefit, plus their airfares from Memphis and New York, along with takin' out for the hall rental and sound and lighting people, but Charlie wound up gettin' over twice as much. I guess none of that's all that important, but it's all true.

Discography

I get letters from around the world still askin' me for a complete discography of everything I know that's been released on Charlie Feathers around the world. Well, I'm certainly not gonna have space to list 'em all before I end this chapter. Now, these are only the ones I know of between 1955 and 1996. I'm sure there's a few that have been released in certain countries around the world that I haven't located as yet. I'm not gonna list song titles. There's not enough space. I'll only list labels, countries, years they were released, and whether they were newly recorded songs, unissued old songs, or rehashed old songs.

First the 45s: Flip Records, U.S. (1955); Sun Records, U.S. (1955); Meteor Records, U.S. (1956); King Records, U.S. (1956 and 1957, four 45 singles); Kay Records, U.S. (1958); Walmay Records, U.S. (1959, this is Charlie Feathers under the name of Charlie Morgan); Memphis Records, U.S. (1961); Holiday Inn Records, U.S. (1963); Philwood Records, U.S. (1968); Pompadour Records, U.S. (1973); Rollin' Rock Records, U.S. (1975); Vetco Records, U.S. (1976, two 45 singles); Charly Records, England (1976, this is a four-song EP with a color picture sleeve, of songs Charlie Feathers recorded in 1973); Feathers Records, U.S. (1979 to 1983, a total of thirteen 45 singles were released during these years); Maverick Records, U.S. (1984 and 1985, three 45 singles); Renegade Records, U.S. (1992 and 1993, two 45 singles); Norton Records, U.S. (1992, one previously released song from 1973 and one unreleased alternate take of a song from Charlie recorded in 1978); Norton Records, U.S. (1994, this is a four-song EP 45 with a hard picture cover, with the two songs previously released in 1958 on Kay Records by Charlie Feathers, along with two songs credited to Jody Chastain that Charlie Feathers played guitar on); Nashville Records, U.S. (1996). All of the above 45 singles and EP 45s were all new releases during the years listed, except where noted.

Now for the LP and CD albums: White Label Records, Holland (1973, this is a rehash of some of Charlie Feathers's 1950s 45 releases); Cowboy Carl Records, U.S. (1973); Barrelhouse Records, U.S. (1974); Barrelhouse Records, U.S. (1976); PolyGram Records, England (1977, this is a rehash of Charlie Feathers's 1950s 45 releases); Gusto Records, U.S. (1978, this is a rehash of Charlie Feathers's 1950s 45 releases); EMI Records, England (1978); Barrelhouse Records, U.S. (1979, contains fourteen unreleased songs Charlie recorded in Memphis between 1967 and 1969); Charly Records, England (1979, side 1 consists of five songs Charlie Feathers recorded at Sun, four of which were released on 45 singles, plus one unreleased track with Charlie singin' harmony vocals with lead vocalist Mack Self; song 6 on side 2 was recorded in 1973 and had been previously released on an earlier U.S. LP; all six songs on side 2 had also been previously released and were recorded between 1967 and 1978); Feathers Records, U.S. (1979, two volumes); Lunar Records, U.S. (1980); Redita Records, Germany (1981, a rehash of recordings Charlie Feathers made between 1956 and 1973 that had all been previously issued on earlier LPs); Bear Family Records, Germany (1985, 1950s and sixties recordings by Charlie Feathers, some of which had never been released up until this time); Zu Zazz Records, England (1986, unreleased demo recordings Charlie

Feathers had recorded between 1954 and 1956); Rockstar Records, England (1987, side 1 of this LP consists of songs recorded by Charlie on a 1979 tour he did in England; they were recorded well in the studio and hadn't been heard or released up until this time; side 2 of the LP consists of eight of the songs on the previously released Lunar Records LP from 1980); New Rose Records, France (1987, six-song LP with previously released songs Charlie had released on 45s on Feathers Records between 1979 and 1983); New Rose Records, France (1988, eight-song LP with previously released songs Charlie had released on 45 singles on Feathers Records between 1979 and 1983); New Rose Records, France (1988, all fourteen of the above-mentioned previously released songs on one CD album); Zu Zazz Records, England (1989, mostly unreleased songs and alternate takes of songs Charlie Feathers recorded between 1954 and 1964); Zu Zazz Records, England (1990, twenty-five-song CD that consists of songs Charlie Feathers recorded between 1954 and 1973; all songs except for one had been previously released on previous albums. Even that song had been previously released on Feathers Records when Charlie Feathers recorded it in 1979; the song is called "Walkin' the Dog," and when Charlie and his son Bubba heard it when I gave it to them in 1991, they knew as I did the master tape of this song had been speeded up to make the listener believe they were hearing an earlier version of it.); Elektra Records, U.S. (1991, CD and cassette only); Charly Records, England (1991, this twenty-four-song CD album consists of all previously released songs by Charlie recorded between 1955 and 1974); Norton Records, U.S. (1992, LP and CD; on this album, you find twenty-plus songs Charlie recorded between 1965 and 1975; most had been previously reissued, but there are four or five never-before-issued songs on this album); Sunjay Records, Sweden (1993, this is a twenty-song CD-only album of all newly recorded songs that I produced on Charlie Feathers in October 1991; up to the present day, it remains Charlie's final full-length album of new songs recorded in late October 1991); Demon Records, Japan (1993, a CD-only album of previously released songs on the Barrelhouse Records albums); Edsel Records, England (1994, a twenty-five-song CD-only album of the first two LPs released on the Barrelhouse Records label); Norton Records, U.S. (1995, a collection of a couple dozen raw demo recordings, all unreleased, that were recorded by Charlie Feathers during the 1960s; most are just Charlie singin' with only his guitar for accompaniment; there's a few gems on this one); Fever

Records, Germany (1996, sixteen unreleased songs Charlie recorded between 1975 and 1985; great suff, but I'm bewildered at where they came up with these).

That's pretty much as close as me or anybody can give you on a complete discography of Charlie Feathers record and CD releases over the past forty-plus years. This man that never had a national hit record in his entire career of four decades of continuous recording of more than 400 different songs still remains the most sought-after rockabilly artist of all time. The reason being is record label owners around the world can just come up with one or two never-before-released songs by this man that fans know has devoted himself to rockabilly music solely, they can put it on an album of already released material, and sell who knows how many records around the world. The downside is Charlie doesn't know, most of the time, these records and CDs even exist. Most of the ones involved don't even send him a copy of the CD or album, 'cause they don't want him to find out. Even if he does, they don't pay him. In recent years, I must say, the only record labels that have done Charlie right (according to Charlie) are Renegade Records (my label), Norton Records, and Nashville Records. Nashville Records is owned by a Nashville attorney who Charlie was continuing to record for as late as the summer of 1997.

Knowin' Charlie

Charlie Feathers never fully recovered from his diabetic neuropathy, but he's one real tough old bird. Though in excruciating pain at various times since 1987, he's continued to fight hard for his family, and now especially his latest grandchild, Charlie Jean Feathers. I've known him now for twenty-three years. I've had a number of older artists, musicians, promoters, and record label owners ask me how I could remain friends with a man as stubborn, ornery, and sometimes downright mean, even to me, for all this time. Those people don't have a clue of the real personal nature of Charlie Feathers. In the earlier years, I'll admit Charlie Feathers made me so damn mad I could have at least tried to beat the tar out of him. Every time I booked him or went in the studio to record him back then, I swore it would be the final time. I was never really a glutton for punishment. It just took me a lot of years to realize why he did some of the crazy things he did. I'm just gonna give you a quick (as I can) rundown on some of the humorous and crazy events that I witnessed that took place over the years.

Charlie sold the Phoenix Club the year after I'd first met him. I went down to visit him and talked to him on the phone a lot during '75, '76, and '77. Robert Gordon had brought the rockabilly revival movement in heavy by the

Forgettin' to Remember to Forget

In the fall of 1979, Charlie Feathers had two album releases on the Feathers label. I get a package in the mail from Charlie; I open it up, and there's two new albums in there, and no explanation. The albums were gatefold albums. They were called *Charlie Feathers Volume 1* and *Charlie Feathers Volume 2*. I personally only cared about the music on the albums, so the first thing I did was play 'em. Inside the albums there were some liner notes in Charlie's own words, but in each of the albums, on both sides of the gatefold, they were mostly covered with old photos from Charlie Feathers's career. I only glanced at the photos.

I had the albums about a week and then called Charlie. He wasn't home the day I called. His wife, Rosemary, answered the phone. I thanked her for sending me the albums and told her they were great. She said, "What did you think of your picture inside?" I said, "What picture?" She said, "The picture from a few years back." Again I said, "What?" She said, "There was a picture you sent Charlie of the first time you all met, of you and Charlie, and he insisted on using it in the *Volume 2* of the two albums." When I got off the phone, I sat down and looked at every single photo, and there were approximately a dozen in each album, and every single photo in these two albums was a picture of Charlie with musicians he had worked with or of Charlie and his immediate family, except for one, and that one was the first picture ever taken of me and Charlie, at the Phoenix Club in Memphis in 1974, in front of the jukebox. Rosemary explained later that Charlie insisted on using it because I was his biggest fan. That was a real honor to me.

summer of '77, and local D.C. artist Billy Hancock was always incorporating rockabilly into his shows then, along with the blues and R&B he loved the most. Billy had also brought older R&B artists such as Amos Milborn into the D.C. area for shows at local clubs. I had recently met Billy around that time, and he asked me for Charlie Feathers's phone number, 'cause he'd like to bring him up to the D.C. area to do a show. So I gave him Charlie's number.

I remember Charlie callin' me up and askin' me if I thought he could trust this guy Hancock. I told Charlie, "Well, I've been out to see him perform a few times, he's a likeable guy, so I guess he's all right." I remember Charlie sayin', "I don't care nothin' 'bout that, I just want to know if I come all the way up there with Bubba to do that show, is he gonna pay me the money he says he will?" I told Charlie, "I can't really say. That's your call, Charlie. I just know I ain't heard he's ripped anybody off up to now." Charlie said, "Well, has he got a good band?" I said, "I think they're pretty good." Charlie then said, "Well, I guess I'll do it. I don't like to fly, but Hancock wants me to fly up there and use his band, but I told him I had to bring Bubba with me on lead guitar, 'cause he's the only one who can play rockabilly the way I do it. Hancock said OK, and that he'd pick me up at the airport in Washington when I got there. He said me and Bubba are gonna stay at his house, but I don't know what kinda boy he is, so Bubba's gonna take your phone number in his wallet, and if we don't like it, Bubba's gonna call you to come and get us." I told Charlie, "It'll work out OK, man, but if it'll make you feel any better, me and Pepper'll drive over to National Airport and meet you when your plane comes in." Charlie said, "I'd sure appreciate that, 'cause you and your wife are the only ones we know up in that part of the country."

When Charlie and Bubba arrived at the airport, me, Pepper, and a friend of mine and his girlfriend were waiting for him around 10:30 p.m. on January 27, 1978, when he got there. It bothered Charlie that Hancock had sent a friend of his, Ken Briley, over to pick him up. He told Charlie that Billy Hancock had told him to bring him back to Hancock's house, where him and Bubba would be stayin' the next two nights. Charlie asked me if I knew this guy here, and I told him no, but I'm sure it'd be all right. When I was tellin' Charlie me and Pepper'd just see him over at the Psyche Delly Club in Bethesda, Maryland, around six o'clock the next day, when they'd do their soundcheck, Charlie said, "OK. But you listen for that phone, 'cause I don't like the looks

of this, so if we need you, we'll call you." I just said, "Don't worry, it'll work out all right."

Well, I'll be damned if my phone didn't ring at 8:30 the next mornin', and it was Bubba on the phone, talkin' in a soft, low southern drawl, tellin' me, "Daddy wants you to come over here to get us right now." I said, "Why? What the hell's wrong?" Bubba said, "Well, Daddy's real mad 'cause Hancock put us down in the basement of his house where he keeps his dogs, and it was cold down there, but we slept for awhile, and Daddy always wakes up early, and when we went up the basement steps, Hancock had the basement door locked, and we couldn't get out, and Daddy was hungry and wanted to go find a place to get breakfast. He thinks Hancock's crazy or somethin' and locked that basement door on purpose to keep us down there till he decided to let us out. I can't talk loud, 'cause we found Hancock upstairs in his bedroom sleepin', and Daddy don't want to wake him. He just wants you to come and get us and take us away from here." I said, "OK, Bubba, but you gotta tell me two quick things. How'd y'all get the basement door unlocked to get upstairs?" Bubba said, "Well, Daddy had me hold my cigarette lighter while he kept pickin' at the lock on the door till he finally got it opened." I said, "How long did that take?" Bubba said, "I guess about a half an hour. That's why he's so hoppin' mad now." I said to Bubba, "Look, tell him to calm down, and I'll be over there as fast as I can get there, but I've never been to Hancock's house. So here's what you gotta do, Bubba. I know Hancock lives in Alexandria, and I got a street map of it, so you hang up now and go outside and tell me the address on the outside of the house and walk up to the end of the street and find out what street Hancock lives on." Bubba said, "OK, but I'll call you right back, 'cause I'm gonna run up there to find the name of the street."

Bubba hung up and called me back in no more than five minutes. I woke Pepper up and told her to get dressed quick, 'cause we were headin' for Alexandria to get Charlie and Bubba. Well, when Bubba called right back, he gave me the house number and told me it was on French Street and that I wouldn't have no trouble findin' 'em, 'cause Charlie said they'd be out on the street waitin'. I then said, "OK. But tell Charlie I live over an hour away in Laurel, Maryland, but I'm on my way, and I'll get there as quick as I can." Bubba said he'd tell him, and then we hung up.

It took me a good hour to get there, and I was drivin' at breakneck speed. When I turned the corner, though, the first thing me and Pepper saw was Charlie and Bubba with their bags of luggage beside 'em, standing on the sidewalk outside Hancock's house, waitin' and ready to go. Charlie was glad to see me but was still mad, cold, and hungry. After he threw their luggage in the back of my '74 Ford van, I asked Charlie what he thought was a stupid question. I said, "Why didn't you wait in the house to get out of the cold?" Charlie snapped back at me and said, "I ain't goin' in no place to stay where that boy'd put me, 'cause he ain't right in the head. Just get me to a place where I can get some breakfast." I went to the closest diner, and after Charlie ate, he calmed down and said he wanted me to take us back to our place, and he'd stay there till he got on that plane when he finished his show and was headin' back to Memphis. I told Charlie that'd be OK with me and Pepper, but we lived in a mobile home park, and I'd have to take my kids over to my mother's house or sister's house so him and Bubba could have their bedroom. Charlie said, "Naw, y'all don't have to do that, we can sleep on a couch or anything. I just want to be in a place where I can get out the door when I want to." I laughed and said, "Well, you ain't gotta worry about that, plus I got a couch that opens into a bed anyway." Charlie even laughed by this time and said, "Well, that's all me and Bubba need. I already know you and Pepper, and your family are good people, but if there's any more like that Hancock fella up in this part of the country, I sure don't want to have nothin' to do with 'em."

Well, I got Charlie settled down in our mobile home with the help of Pepper, and him and Bubba took a nap that afternoon and felt a lot better when they got a shower and got dressed and ready to go to the show. Thinkin' back after all these years, this was one of the funniest experiences I ever had with Charlie. Charlie thought Billy Hancock was a lunatic then and had escaped from what he called a place where they put crazy people. I told him that I'm sure that wasn't the case, but he insisted I didn't know the boy, so there was no way for me to know. Today, I just wish I had a video of this rockabilly legend pickin' that lock at the top of Hancock's basement stairs, tryin' to escape.

What capped all this now-funny lunacy off was while Charlie and Bubba were sleepin', my phone rang, and it was Billy Hancock on the other end, and he had a real scared and worried tone in his voice when he said, "I've been trying to call you for hours, because Charlie Feathers and Bubba disappeared sometime this morning, and I've been all over the place trying to find 'em, but they must be lost or could-a-been kidnapped,

and I'm gettin' ready to call the police." After gettin' to know Billy Hancock in the years that would follow, if I had this to do over again, I'd-a told him, "Well, I don't know where they are. But you better find 'em, or you'll be in big trouble." But I told him the truth, and that Charlie wanted me to come and get him 'cause he locked him in the basement with his dogs. Well, Hancock told me then that he didn't lock him in the basement. That Charlie or Bubba musta accidentally locked themselves in. I figured I wasn't gonna tell Charlie this, 'cause I knew that would get him mad all over again. I just told Hancock I'd have him and Bubba at the club in time for the soundcheck. Billy was relieved that I had Charlie and he didn't have to call the police and the show would go on as scheduled. And what a show it was. Charlie did two sets of rockabilly music to a full house of young fans at that time who were just gettin' into the rockabilly revival that had begun. Billy Hancock played bass, and I believe it was Jeff Lodson who was on drums. Charlie was satisfied with Hancock and his drummer backin' him up.

I could write a whole book of stories on this great artist, but I'm gonna give you, as brief as I can, some of the adventures me and Charlie had together during the eighties and early nineties. Except for what I've covered, this is what took place. In March 1978, I started a Charlie Feathers Appreciation Society and advertised it in *Goldmine* magazine for six months and began to communicate with Charlie's fans around the world. On September 8 and 9, 1978, I had Charlie bring his whole five-piece band, which included his daughter Wanda, up to Maryland for two big shows at the Public Playhouse theater in Cheverly. Charlie brought his wife Rosemary along, and this was the first time I paid to book an Elvis imitator by the name of Johnny Seaton. Both shows sold out. In early 1979, I went in the studio with Charlie and Bubba and recorded some songs that still remain unreleased. In February 1980, I brought Charlie and Bubba up to D.C. for two live shows. Johnny Seaton got up and sang a couple Elvis Sun Records songs at those shows. The shows went well. In July 1980, I was back in Memphis to record Johnny Seaton in Reno Studios, which Charlie was part owner of, and I paid Charlie and his band to produce Seaton's first rockabilly songs, along with me producing a few on Charlie.

For eleven days, starting on June 9, 1981, Charlie Feathers brought his whole band, along with his P.A. system, for a long series of shows I had booked for him, which me and Pepper went along with 'em on, that ran between Richmond, Virginia, and New York City. The highlight of this tour was Charlie's first appearance ever in New York City, at the Lone Star Cafe on Fifth Avenue, though by the time he finally got up on that stage, I felt like throwing him in the Hudson River, what with his temper and his crazy demands and his repeated threats to turn around and go home to Memphis and all. I got a young strugglin' band I knew called The Zantees to open for Charlie at The Lone Star. The Zantees of course changed some members in their group to the A-Bones later in the eighties, when they really had *Kicks* magazine goin' and then started Norton Records after that. But I was more than happy to help Billy Miller and Miriam Linna out at the time, when they were just startin' out. Miriam, by the way, was the original drummer for The Cramps, who were sort of a psychobilly band back in the late seventies and early eighties. The Cramps are still around today. After The Zantees finished their set, Charlie finally went on, but only after insisting that I spend at least five minutes introducing him and telling this packed-to-the-rafters audience, who by now were shoutin' his name, about what he'd done in music. Well, when Charlie at last did his two sets to the largest night-club crowd of rowdy rockabilly fans he'd ever played to in a nightclub in the North up to this time, they loved him. Though he talked too much in between songs. Robert Palmer wrote in *The New York Times* two days after the show that Charlie Feathers did the kind of rockabilly music on that night that every young band in the current rockabilly revival that was takin' place then was trying to capture but never would be able to, because Charlie was the original master of it. We had a few more minor dates to play in Maryland at clubs like Zip's and the Turf Club in the Beltsville and Laurel areas, plus a private party, but we all got through it.

I swore I'd never book Charlie again. But I did. I had a short memory back then (and at least I can laugh about it now) when it came to who I knew was the greatest rockabilly artist alive. So in June of 1983, I brought Charlie Feathers back up to the Washington, D.C., area for a series of several special-event shows straight in a row that I titled "Three Generations of Rockabilly." I had my problems with Charlie, but they were nowhere as severe as that long 1981 tour. I also have to say that I could have never put this extravaganza of shows on or pulled this whole thing off without the invaluable assistance of Tex Rubinowitz, who I had gotten to know through Billy Hancock, and who by now was a real close friend of mine. Tex was the one who put the backup band together to back Charlie up. Bubba couldn't make

this trip, 'cause he couldn't get away from his regular gig at Bad Bob's Vapors Club at the time.

Charlie brought his youngest son, Ricky Feathers, up with him, and the two of 'em once again stayed with me and Pepper in Laurel, Maryland. I had Johnny Seaton open the show, as I was managing, booking, and doing everything for him at that time, and he was pretty much on a roll in the rockabilly scene by this time. I had Danny Gatton, who was pretty regularly backing Seaton up on guitar by then in Seaton's band, on the show. Danny was a star in his own right on guitar in D.C., and during Seaton's set, Danny rocked out on three rockabilly instrumentals. Tex Rubinowitz had put a great band together to back both him and Charlie Feathers up. The band consisted of Tex on rhythm guitar plus backup vocals for Charlie, Bob Margolin on lead guitar, Evan Johns on upright slappin' rockabilly bass, and Jeff Lodson on drums. Charlie of course headlined the show, and we had a finale at the end of the night and brought Charlie, Tex, Danny, and Johnny Seaton back out to do a medley of "Mystery Train" and "That's All Right, Mama." The first show was held at The Wax Museum, and with a lineup like this, every show was sold out.

All these shows were great if you were a fan of true rockabilly, and both me and Tex Rubinowitz survived these four nights. Though Tex is like me, and we always worried every night somethin' was gonna happen to piss Charlie off, but that was mostly my department to straighten out. Me and Tex split the bill on filming one of the shows, hopin' PBS would be interested in it, but it remains collecting dust to this day.

After this series of shows, I continued to stay in touch with Charlie, and when me and Johnny Seaton had the first of what became many fallin' outs, I went down and cut some tunes in the studio on Charlie in March 1985. After that, until 1988, I only kept in touch mostly by phone.

Charlie recovered slowly somewhat after that 1988 benefit in Memphis, and I was still working hard with LesLee "Bird" Anderson and managing and booking her, as well as bookin' other artists like Bobby Smith, who was doin' rockabilly. But when Charlie called me in early March 1989 and told me he was thinkin' about doin' a show for an arts organization at the University of Massachusetts in Boston, if he felt up to it, he asked me if I'd go along with him and show him where Boston was, 'cause he'd never been that far North before. He said he was able to get around now with the help of a walker, but he was still in constant pain, so he'd have to wait and see.

Well, they were paying him good money to do one show, and he needed it then, so he called me back and said he was gonna come up there to my house, which was now in Severna Park, Maryland, and pick me up and give me $100 to show him where Boston was. Charlie asked me to find him a good upright bass player and a drummer who could play his songs. He told me what he'd pay 'em, and as usual, I could count on Jim Cavanaugh to play the upright bass the way he wanted it, so I got him, along with Buddy Grandel on drums. Charlie was happy with both musicians. I knew he would be.

Even in terrible health, with Charlie having to sit down while he performed, I was able to witness this man do the best pure set of rockabilly music of anybody alive today. Charlie was only contracted to do an hour but actually did an hour and ten minutes. The whole audience was on their feet clappin' and cheerin' in this good-sized hall, 'cause all these young people knew they'd heard the best from the man that was there at the beginning of rockabilly music. Charlie did two encores. Charlie knew he wasn't playin' to a bunch of drunks out for a good time on this night. They loved him, and he loved them back. He finally had an intelligent audience that gave him and his music the respect they deserved.

After Charlie came up for my benefit for him in August 1989, I'd see him again on Father's Day, 1990. Me and my daughter Stacy went down to Memphis, 'cause Ben Vaughn, who is a recording artist but also a producer for Elektra Records, had called me, 'cause him and Elektra wanted to come to Memphis to record an album on Charlie in August 1990. They wanted me to be a consultant on it and negotiate and explain the contract to Charlie. Ben Vaughn said they were willin' to pay me for my trouble (which I knew would come into it somewhere down the line) if I could find out Charlie's price for it, and if Charlie would be up for it.

Well, Charlie was up for it, all right. But the advance money he wanted for it was the problem. Ben Vaughn said Elektra wouldn't pay that much. The other artists they had signed to do what they were callin' "The American Explorer Series," such as Johnnie Johnson, Jimmy Dale Gilmore, Vernard Johnson, and Boozoo Chavis, were only being paid half that much, and they were all happy to have a new album on a major label. I told Ben Vaughn, "Charlie don't care, really, he told me

y'all could take it or leave it. That's just the way Charlie is, Ben." They took it, but Ben Vaughn, who loved some of Charlie's great music and wanted desperately to produce this album, had to do some finaglin' to get the deal through.

It really wasn't worth the small amount of money they paid me for my part in this project. I was given the title "consultant," but the real reason Ben and Elektra needed me was word had gotten out (Ben told me this) that I was considered (as Ben put it) Charlie's lion tamer. I told Ben that Charlie trusts me as much as anyone outside his family, but I can't work miracles. Charlie does things his way, and I can't make him do anything he don't want to. I just know how to talk to him and understand better than most people why he chooses to make the decisions he does, but if he says no or backs out, I ain't gonna be held responsible for it. It's all up to y'all and Charlie. But Ben told me they really needed me if Charlie got out o' hand in the studio, so I told him I'd do it.

Even though Charlie was gonna get the money he wanted, he didn't like a lot o' things in the contracts, but he signed 'em after awhile anyway, and Ben set the dates up at Sam Phillips's studio. I got to Charlie's house five days before the session was supposed to start. I arrived on Wednesday, August 1, 1990. The session was due to start on Monday, August 6. But Elektra Records was supposed to have had Charlie's advance of half the money there a week before the session started. It didn't come, and Charlie called me and said he wasn't gonna do this album, 'cause Elektra were liars like every other record company out there. I called Ben Vaughn and told him to get that money there from Elektra, or there wouldn't be no Charlie Feathers album. Ben assured me it would be there no later than Friday, August 3. Charlie was mad anyway, 'cause it was in Elektra's contract he'd signed that it would be there by a certain date, and it wasn't there.

When Ben Vaughn got there on Friday, August 3, he came over to Charlie's after me, and Charlie had been waitin' outside all morning for the mailman to come, and when he did, the check wasn't there. So, in Charlie's viewpoint, those Northerners had lied to him again and were all crooks. Now he wasn't doin' the damn album, even if the check did come on Saturday, 'cause in his mind it wouldn't be any good. Ben Vaughn came by again on Saturday, and the check finally came. Ben had some final contract he needed Charlie to sign, but he wouldn't do it. Ben left the contract with me. Charlie said he ain't signin' nothin' else, he wasn't gonna do the album, 'cause they lied, and they wouldn't pay him the other half of the money, anyway, after they took the album back to New York. Well, after me and Charlie had a screamin' match out in his front yard, which even Rosemary joined into, Charlie finally agreed to sign the contracts. He called Jerry Phillips (who engineered this session), and Jerry, who is Sam Phillips's son, assured Charlie he'd make sure Charlie would get the rest of his money.

Charlie still wasn't happy, and Ben Vaughn was worried, but the session got started, a day late. Rosemary told me before I left Memphis after the session was over that Charlie told her the only reason he signed that final contract was he knew if he didn't, Billy Poore would be mad at him. I think Rosemary would have been, too.

The session was recorded on August 7, 8, and 9, 1990, and there were problems in the studio. Elektra had agreed to let Bubba play on the album, but Charlie wanted to use his Memphis drummer, bass player, and piano player. Elektra was promotin' this as a Memphis project being sung by the greatest rockabilly music artist still alive. They had paid James Van Eaton to play drums and Roland Janes to do some guitar work. Charlie didn't want no part of that, 'cause they didn't get to Sun Records to play on sessions until 1956, after him and Elvis had moved on, and in Charlie's eyes, they couldn't play rockabilly the pure right way it was supposed to be done. Charlie didn't mind Stan Kesler bein' there, 'cause he was at Sun Records in '54 when Charlie was. He played steel guitar and some bass on it. Well, between not likin' Van Eaton's drummin' on his music and Ben Vaughn wantin' to do more of the jungle beat rockabilly music Charlie recorded in the eighties that Charlie didn't want to do anymore, Charlie walked out of the studio to quit three times during the first two days. I went out and brought him back each time, tellin' him he wouldn't get the other half of his money if he quit now, and Elektra would sue him for the half they'd paid him.

I rode from Charlie's house and back those three days with him in his car, and boy, I was sure glad when this whole session was through. I lost another five pounds or so that week. But the album came out in June 1991. By then, I was livin' in Fairview, Tennessee, and involved in other music projects. Ben Vaughn did a good job mixing the album, and Charlie was proud as a peacock by then to have an album out on a major label. Elektra Records vice president Danny Kahn, who'd I'd been talkin' to quite a bit, said they'd pay my expenses if I'd go to Memphis to help keep Charlie under control,

'cause they wanted to send a major photography company down to shoot some photos for the press. That only took one day, and Pepper was there to help me out with Charlie, and though there were again some minor problems, they were easy enough to handle at the time.

Two months after this album was recorded, in August 1990, Charlie went into the hospital, where he had to have an entire cancerous lung removed. He had just done a festival in England a couple weeks earlier. Charlie almost died during this operation, and his recovery took quite a while. In October 1991, Charlie brought his band up to a studio near where I lived and recorded an album of great songs for me that I licensed to Sunjay Records in Sweden.

I went to Memphis for Charlie's sixty-first birthday on June 12, 1993, after bein' invited, and brought my buddy Laurence Beal and his band The Hot Dice to play at it. Danny Kahn at Elektra Records told me a year after the album by Charlie had been released that it sold more copies than any other album in their five-album series, with the exception of Jimmy Dale Gilmore's album. All four other artists toured extensively to promote their albums, while Charlie didn't do one show the whole first year it was out. That's a fact. Charlie did open a show for Charlie Rich, at Charlie Rich's request, on New Year's Eve, 1992. This took place in Memphis.

During 1994 and '95, Charlie had three heart bypass surgeries performed, and today he may not still be performing, but I'm sure glad he's still with us. His last show in Europe was during the fall of 1992, where he played at the Hemsby Festival in England.

I still see and call Charlie Feathers, and both him and his family know that me and Pepper'll be there if he needs us. So why, after a lot of what I've just told you about Charlie Feathers (and there's a ton more), do I still love and stay devoted to him and his family? Because Charlie Feathers has overcome more abuse and handicaps in this music business than anyone I ever met in my life. It took me till late in life to realize how many valuable lessons he's taught me about this business. While other rockabilly stars and artists'll tell you bullshit about the early rockabilly days, Charlie'll tell you the truth, 'cause he saw it. It's all in his forty years of rockabily music. His fans know it. Charlie Feathers is the closest I'll ever come to knowin' and workin' with the greatest musical genius ever to record a rockabily song. No matter all his faults. His music don't lie.

July 4, 1956.
Elvis on stage with bass player Bill Black at Russwood Park in Memphis. *(courtesy of Brenda Johnson)*

August 2, 1956.
The cat who broke it wide open, Elvis Presley, outside his home on Audubon Drive in Memphis. Elvis had just purchased this coat only a few hours before this photo was taken. He was showin' it off to fans gathered outside his house. A little over a month after this photo was taken, Elvis made his debut on "The Ed Sullivan Show." *(courtesy of Brenda Johnson)*

March 1955.
Johnny Burnette, singing and playing guitar to his son Rocky, who went on to have a Billboard Top 10 hit in 1980. Just look at those greased-back ducktails on little Rocky's head. *(courtesy of Rocky Burnette)*

1957.
Rockabilly comes to the big screen. All three of these low-budget films, and many others, capitalized on the popularity of rockabilly music during its peak year.

May 1956. An advertisement from Stars, Inc., featuring prominent Sun Records artists. This agency, which Bob Neal ran, booked most of the Sun package shows in the South.

Christmas 1956. Promotional shot featuring Eddie Cochran, from the movie *The Girl Can't Help It*.

Best Wishes
from
EDDIE COCHRAN
Currently Featured in 20th Century-Fox
"THE GIRL CAN'T HELP IT"
Personal Management
JERRY CAPEHART   GENERAL ARTISTS CORPORATION   Representation

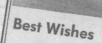

1958. Jo Ann Campbell performing "Jailhouse Rock" on an Alan Freed show at the Brooklyn Fox Theater. Hot stuff! *(courtesy of Jo Ann Campbell)*

May 4, 1958. A handbill from Alan Freed's Big Beat Show, headlined by three rockabilly artists: Jerry Lee Lewis, Buddy Holly, and Chuck Berry. This six-week bus tour sold out during the spring of 1958. This particular show, in Montreal, caused a riot. *(courtesy of Jo Ann Campbell)*

Early 1960. Jo Ann Campbell still rockin' in the night clubs. *(courtesy of Jo Ann Campbell)*

Christmas 1957. "Mister Rock and Roll," Alan Freed, with Jo Ann Campbell at the New York Paramount Theater Christmas Show. Today Jo Ann Campbell still says with much pride, "Connie Francis was Dick Clark's favorite girl, but I was Alan Freed's. He was my hero." Her last show with Alan was his Christmas Show of 1961. *(courtesy of Jo Ann Campbell)*

Fall 1959. Gene Vincent's first tour of Great Britain. This tour would influence a generation of rockers, including the lads from Liverpool.

Fall 1958. One of rockabilly's greatest performers, Gene Vincent, on stage in Wisconsin. *(courtesy of Melody Jean Vincent)*

1958. Publicity photo of local Washington, D.C., singer Dudley Callicutt. Today, Dudley is a minister.

1958. Publicity photo of Gene Summers. In 1959, Gene's recording of "Straight Skirt" was a big hit in D.C. *(courtesy of Crystal Clear Sound Records)*

Summer 1959. I took this snapshot at a record hop in Hyattsville, Maryland. Here Dudley Callicutt may be performing his big hit, "Get Ready Baby."

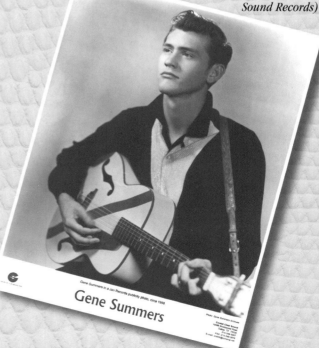

1957. Conway Twitty and his first band, The Rockhousers, performing in the Midwest. On one of his stops during the summer of 1959, Conway gave me this great wild shot of him with his rockabilly band. *(courtesy of Conway Twitty)*

June 1959. Jack Scott and Annette Funicello backstage at the Hollywood Bowl, where they were both headliners on Dick Clark's Caravan of Stars. Jack totally shocked me when he gave me this never-before-seen, phenomenal photo of him and Annette. *(courtesy of Jack Scott)*

January 1960.
Eddie Cochran live on stage in London. This photo was sent to me by Trevor Cajiao, who publishes the #1 European rockabilly magazine, *Now Dig This.* (*courtesy of* Now Dig This)

1960. I surprised Brenda Lee with this snapshot as she signed autographs after a performance on "The Milt Grant Show." She had just started her long string of Top 10 pop chart hits when I snapped this photo.

September 1961. This photo was taken in New York during a touring break with my group The Trend-ells.

February 1960. Me with Connie Francis after her performance on "The Milt Grant Show." By the time this picture was taken, I had talked to Connie Francis a half a dozen times at the show.

September 1968. Jerry Lee Lewis giving the camera his "Killer" pose with me after a show in Jessup, Maryland.

July 31, 1976.
Here I am with Elvis Presley in Hampton Roads, Virginia. My wife Pepper snapped this photo right after we got inside his suite on the top floor of the Sheraton Hotel. Before I left that night, Elvis said, "Billy Boy, here's a hundred-dollar bill; now gimme that damn Sun T-shirt, 'cause I'm tired of lookin' at it." Well, I took his hundred bucks, took the shirt off and gave it to him. Elvis proceeded to tear that T-shirt all to hell and looked at me and laughed hard when he said, "Now, Billy Boy, that's finally the end of Sun Records, ain't it?" I told Elvis, "You'll never get rid of Sun Records!"

December 1977. Robert Gordon, Bruce Springsteen, and Link Wray backstage at the Ritz in New York City. I had been photographing my old friend Link Wray on this night with popular revivalist Robert Gordon. While Link was showing Robert some guitar licks, some guy that I'd never seen before walked up and just stood between the two of 'em. I think he picked up a few ideas.

July 1979. One of rockabilly's pioneers, Carl Perkins, with me before a show I booked him on at The Bastille in College Park, Maryland.

February 1974. Fifteen-year-old firecracker Tanya Tucker on stage at the Stardust Night Club in Waldorf, Maryland. As you can see from this shot I got of her in action, she was the wildest and hardest-rockin' chick I'd witnessed in many a year.

August 1974. Me with Waylon Jennings at the Stardust Night Club in Waldorf, Maryland. Waylon and his "outlaw" country music were just hittin' big when this photo was snapped.

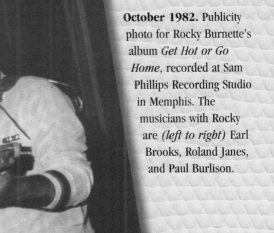

October 1982. Publicity photo for Rocky Burnette's album *Get Hot or Go Home*, recorded at Sam Phillips Recording Studio in Memphis. The musicians with Rocky are *(left to right)* Earl Brooks, Roland Janes, and Paul Burlison.

Summer 1982. Musician, producer, and great performer Dave Edmunds *(center)* with Johnny Seaton and me in Washington, D.C.

October 1982.
Johnny Seaton live on stage at the Bayou Club in Washington, D.C. In a short ten-month period, I was able to teach and guide D.C.'s most talented Elvis impersonator into being the top live rockabilly stage performer anywhere. This picture captures his look.

June 16, 1983. The amazing Danny Gatton performing at my first big Rockabilly Extravaganza at the Wax Museum Night Club in Washington, D.C.

December 29, 1983. Tex Rubinowitz *(left)* and Link Wray backstage at the Wax Museum in their home town of Washington, D.C.

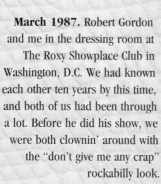

September 1, 1985. Ricky Nelson *(left)* and James Intveld backstage at the legendary Palomino Club in Hollywood. A short four months later, Ricky, along with James's former band members (including his younger brother Rick), were all tragically killed in a plane crash.

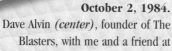

October 2, 1984. Dave Alvin *(center)*, founder of The Blasters, with me and a friend at Girard's, in Baltimore.

March 1987. Robert Gordon and me in the dressing room at The Roxy Showplace Club in Washington, D.C. We had known each other ten years by this time, and both of us had been through a lot. Before he did his show, we were both clownin' around with the "don't give me any crap" rockabilly look.

1989. Publicity photo of the most successful rockabilly revival group, The Stray Cats. I met bass player Lee Rocker in June 1997, when we were both in Indianapolis performing at the fifth annual Rockabilly Rebel Weekend. *(courtesy of Lee Rocker)*

September 6, 1986. Dwight Yoakam and me at the 930 Club, Washington, D.C. I was the manager of the opening act. We talked a good bit before he went on stage, and I found him to be a real down-to-earth guy.

September 1989. Me with Colonel Tom Parker, Elvis's controversial manager, in Las Vegas. This photo was taken at a private party after the final night of a four-week run of *Elvis: A Musical Celebration* at the Hilton Hotel.

1991. Rockabilly and country star Narvel Felts with my wife Pepper *(right)* and our daughter Stacy in Nashville. Narvel is one of the nicest, most genuine cats I've ever met. This photo was taken after Narvel appeared on a TNN television show.

September 29, 1986. A couple of rockabilly sweethearts, LesLee "Bird" Anderson *(left)* and seventeen-year-old Kelly Willis, in the vocal booth at Glass Wing Studios in Hyattsville, Maryland.

August 12, 1989. A great reunion shot that I used as my official postcard for Rollabilly Music. *Left to right:* Me, Vernon Taylor, Charlie Feathers, Narvel Felts, and Robert Gordon. This was taken after the most successful show I held at the Elks Lodge in Severna Park, Maryland. I had a total of seventeen artists and bands on this all-rockabilly festival, which lasted ten straight hours and brought in rockabilly fans from nineteen different states and three foreign countries. I felt it was my greatest achievement for the rockabilly artists, the fans who attended, and the music itself.

June 2, 1990.
Becky Hobbs and me after the second annual Rockabilly Music Festival in Severna Park, Maryland.

August 8, 1990.
Me with legendary producer Sam Phillips. Sam looks terrific, but he wasn't the one in his Memphis studio trying to keep Charlie Feathers from going berserk on the visiting producer. This picture shows how ragged I looked after only the second day.

January 28, 1991.
Marty Stuart and me in Nashville. We've known one another since 1988. Marty has purchased a lot of rockabilly memorabilia from me over the years. This photo was snapped right after he finished taping a show for TNN.

April 22, 1994.
Me, Martí Brom, and Ronnie Dawson at Chukkers Club, Tuscaloosa, Alabama.

214

August 10, 1991. Billy Lee Riley, still rockin' hard, at Vino's Club in Little Rock, Arkansas. I traveled with Billy on several shows we did between Little Rock and New York City.

August 13, 1993. Rosie Flores, James Intveld, and me at a Nashville studio. They performed on my first recording in over thirty years.

August 24, 1991. High Noon, with Finland's #1 rockabilly band, The Hal Peters Trio, diggin' the latest issue of my *Rockabilly Revue* at Club Parisitar in Helsinki. *Left to right:* Kevin Smith, Shaun Young, Hal Peters, Sean Mencher, Jussi Huhtakangas, and Eino Rastas.

THE COLLINS KIDS

Collector's Edition

April 1996. Collector's edition of The Collins Kids publicity photo sent to me by Larry Collins.

December 15, 1995. Ruthie Noone *(left)*, lead singer of the group Ruthie & The Wranglers, with Wanda Jackson at the Birchmere in Alexandria, Virginia. *(courtesy of Ruthie Noone)*

July 20, 1995. Sleepy La Beef *(left)*, me, and D.J. Fontana (Elvis Presley's drummer from 1955 to 1968) at Sleepy's sixtieth birthday party at the Ace of Clubs in Nashville.

November 1995. Nashville's sensational rockabilly group BR5-49 with me on the stage of Robert's Bar and Night Club. *Left to right:* Jay McDowell, Shaw Wilson, me, Don Herron, Chuck Mead, and Gary Bennett.

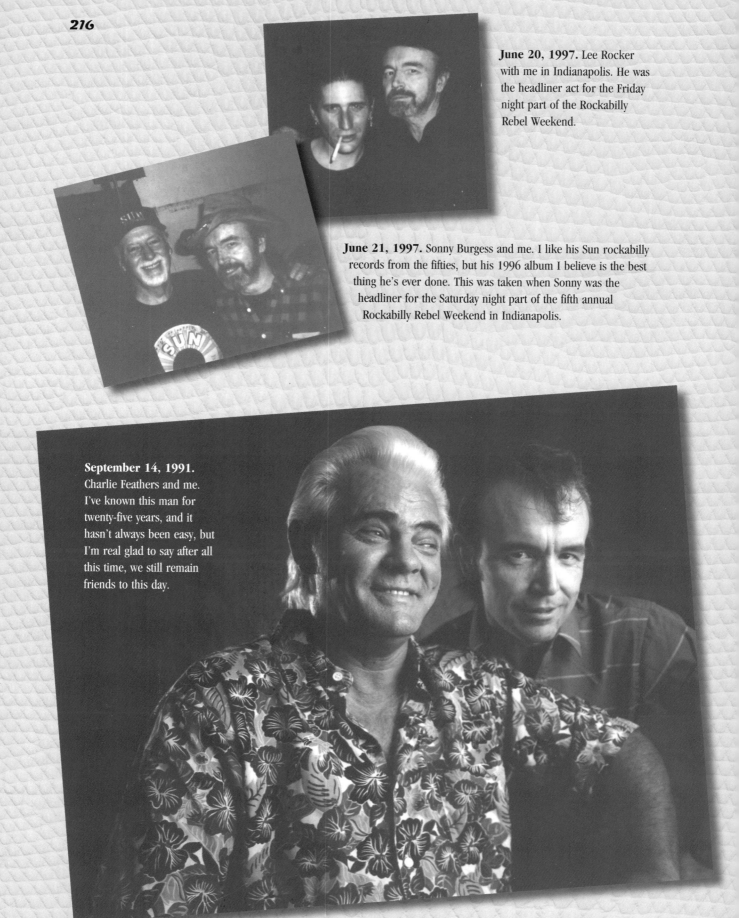

June 20, 1997. Lee Rocker with me in Indianapolis. He was the headliner act for the Friday night part of the Rockabilly Rebel Weekend.

June 21, 1997. Sonny Burgess and me. I like his Sun rockabilly records from the fifties, but his 1996 album I believe is the best thing he's ever done. This was taken when Sonny was the headliner for the Saturday night part of the fifth annual Rockabilly Rebel Weekend in Indianapolis.

September 14, 1991. Charlie Feathers and me. I've known this man for twenty-five years, and it hasn't always been easy, but I'm real glad to say after all this time, we still remain friends to this day.

The Eighties: Second-Generation Cats

A New Breed of Punks and
Cats Hits the Scene with an Old Sound

*R*obert Gordon

The rockabilly revival began in Europe with young bands and artists covering the classic rockabilly music at least several years before it began here in the U.S. As I've previously mentioned, the one person who has to be given total credit for reviving rockabilly music on a major scale here in the U.S. is Robert Gordon. Robert Gordon was not only the first, but in my opinion, which is shared by many other rockabilly fans around the world, the best new rockabilly artist who wound up makin' it on a national scale.

There were five new albums released on Robert Gordon between 1977 and 1981. There was one additional album by Robert released in 1982, but it only contained four new songs. The rest had been previously released. Robert Gordon's first two albums were on the Private Stock record label, out of New York City. Robert's final four major-label albums were all on RCA Records, also out of New York City. These six albums spawned more than a dozen 45 singles between 1977 and 1982. Only two of those singles made it onto the *Billboard* national pop charts. Robert's first 45 single release, "Red Hot" (the fifties rockabilly classic that Billy Lee Riley is best remembered for), debuted on the *Billboard* pop charts on October 1, 1977. It only reached #83 and stayed on the charts for only three weeks. Robert's other *Billboard* chart song came with the Marshall Crenshaw-penned "Someday, Someway." This song debuted on the *Billboard* pop singles charts on June 27, 1981. It only reached #76 and was on the charts for a short four weeks. I should also note that between those two *Billboard* pop chart songs, Robert had two songs that reached the bottom of the *Billboard* country charts. His cover of Conway Twitty's "It's Only Make Believe" reached #99 for one week on March 31, 1979, and a cover of the Leroy Van Dyke pop and country Top 5 hit "Walk On By" reached #98 for one week on June 23, 1979. Both were sung in a rockabillyish style. All of

Robert's recording was done in New York City, but on these two I just mentioned, The Jordanaires overdubbed backup vocals in Nashville, so I'm sure that helped them to reach the *Billboard* country charts.

All of Robert Gordon's five newly recorded albums reached somewhere at the lower end of the *Billboard* pop album charts. On Robert's first two Private Stock albums, he was teamed with legendary rock 'n' roll guitarist Link Wray. On Robert's first two albums for the RCA Records label, he used Chris Spedding, who was at the peak of his great guitar style at that time. On Robert's final new RCA Records album, the now-legendary Danny Gatton handled all of the lead guitar work. On Robert's final album for RCA, all three of these great guitarists can be heard.

Now, those are all the basic facts. But there's a whole lot more to Robert Gordon and the great music he released during those short five years or so than just statistics and facts. I wish I had the space and time to cover it, but I'm gonna do my best to let you know what an important rockabilly artist he is.

Robert Gordon was born in Washington, D.C., in late March 1947. He grew up in a suburban county of D.C., Montgomery County, Maryland, where he was a singer in a local rock 'n' roll group called The Confidentials that played area teen clubs and record hops in the early sixties. Robert was fifteen and sixteen years old at the time. In 1965, Robert served in the National Guard in Maryland. He got married to his childhood sweetheart in 1967. He took a regular job, and they began to raise a family. Robert loved rock 'n' roll, though. Tough, real rock 'n' roll. Today, he still has a clear memory of the first time he heard "Heartbreak Hotel" and "Be-Bop-A-Lula" on the radio, when he was only nine years old.

Robert wanted to be in the music business, and he knew if he was ever gonna make it in it, he had to get the hell out of D.C. So in 1970, he moved his wife and two sons to New York City, where the real music business was. Again he had to take a regular job, but eventually started his own business. With trying to support his own family, he was for the most part out of music for about four years or so. His marriage fell apart, and Robert and his wife split up in late 1975. From what Robert's told me, this was when he joined a group called The Tuff Darts. They were one of New York City's first punk bands. Robert stayed with the group for about a year. Robert recently told me, "Man, I was depressed when I was with The Tuff Darts. Me and my ole lady had just split up, and she went back to D.C. with my kids and all, but those were screwed up times for me then. I wasn't meant to be in a group like that. I knew I could sing good rock 'n' roll, and all they wanted me to do in The Tuff Darts was scream my damn brains out. I wanted a solo career. Larry Uttal at Private Stock Records gave me a shot and signed me to the label in February 1977. I got with producer Richard Gottehrer, and we got along great 'cause he had grown up with and loved the same music I did. Fifties rock 'n' roll and rockabilly music. We both hated Sha Na Na and all the damn revival groups that were popular then who were treatin' the music we loved like a joke. I wanted to do it with every ounce of raw energy I had in me and give it the respect it really deserved. Richard was right in tune with that, and we both thought it would be a good idea to get Link Wray for my first album. Link was an original fifties rock 'n' roll legendary guitarist, plus he was a D.C. home boy too. Me and Link got along great, and it worked real well at the beginning." Robert not only loved the music, but he had the whole "I don't take no shit" rockabilly attitude that went along with what rockabilly music was all about in the 1950s. He was there like I was.

On his first album, titled simply *Robert Gordon with Link Wray,* Robert recorded six cover rockabilly songs that were all obscure in 1977 in America except for "Summertime Blues" (which Robert sang with rawness and force, something Sha Na Na and others didn't do). Three of the other four songs were written by Link Wray, and the one other song was co-written by his producer, Richard Gottehrer. This first album was recorded in April 1977 and released at the end of the summer of 1977. This album was great when I first heard it. But what made Robert unique was, in most cases, an artist's first album is usually their best if it's rockabilly, as far as I'm concerned. But in Robert Gordon's case, each album got better. Another thing that to me ranks Robert Gordon #1 on the list (which is only a handful) of other artists and bands that made it big on the major-label scale and into the mainstream music charts is that Robert Gordon could handle a classic obscure cover of a Gene Vincent rockabilly ballad like "I Sure Miss You" better than all the ones that followed. Robert had the great voice and the feel for it. He put emotion in it, 'cause he loved it. Other national groups that came later only did rockabilly music because it was the in thing at the time to do.

"I Sure Miss You" was on his first album. I was sold on him right there and then. That's why when Robert and Link Wray played The Cellar Door nightclub in the Georgetown section of Washington, D.C., in October 1977, me and Pepper were right there in the middle of an overflow crowd. Rockabilly music was alive and well in the right way once again to a whole new generation of kids between eighteen and twenty-two who didn't even know or had never heard songs like "Red Hot," "Twenty Flight Rock," "The Fool," "Five Days, Five Days," etc. It was all new music they could go wild to. I felt about as old as Link Wray that night, but it sure was a great sight to see, and a hell-raisin' good time was had by all who were there. After the show, me and Pepper went upstairs to see my old friend Link Wray, who was glad to see me and seemed to be havin' the time of his life, and to meet Robert Gordon. I'm glad I took some pictures at the time of Link, Robert, and a few members of his backup band, which he called The Wildcats. After talking about old times with Link Wray, Link introduced me to Robert and told him how long I'd been around D.C. and how much I'd been in rockabilly music my whole life. Me and Robert hit it off right away. I'm gonna say right here and now, because in recent years a lot of things have been said about Robert's bad shows, mean attitude towards promoters, musicians, etc., that the first time I met Robert, the guy was a decent, nice, down-to-earth cat. Robert stayed that way for a good while. The mainstream music business has a way of makin' you mean. Not that Robert was a saint or anything close to it, but in the beginning, he was doing the music he loved the most, partyin' and havin' a ball, and a nicer guy couldn't be found.

Me and Pepper went up to New York City, which was only a three-and-a-half-hour drive from where we lived in Laurel, Maryland, at Robert's invitation to see him once in November and twice in December 1977. Bruce Springsteen got up and sang a couple rockabilly songs with Robert on one of the nights in December. I didn't even know hardly who he was at that time. I had only heard the name and heard one or two of his songs on the radio by then, which, to be honest, I really didn't care for. When I went backstage to see Robert and Link, I snapped some photos off of the three of 'em, which I'd done when they were on stage also, but I just had to ask this guy Springsteen a question. So I said to him, "Man, you seemed like you were havin' a ball up on stage with Robert and Link, and you were kickin' ass pretty good, knockin' out some hot rockabilly sounds. I've heard a couple of your songs on the radio, and they're damn sure better than disco shit, but they ain't near as good as what you were into on stage with Robert and Link. So how come you don't record some solid rockabilly and true rock 'n' roll?" Springsteen got a sheepish but polite grin on his face and said, "I record rock 'n' roll. It's just that I write all my own songs, and on those I hear so many different things in all kinds of ways, but I really love the kind of stuff we did tonight more than any other music, 'cause I was a kid when all this stuff first came out. I've just never written anything close to it yet. Someday I might, though, 'cause I love performin' it. It really turns me on and puts me into high gear." I told him, "Good luck, and I'll be listenin' for it." He just said, "Thanks." Bruce Springsteen finally did try his hand at writing rockabilly-type songs. At least when they came out on the B sides of his string of Top 10 songs from the biggest commercial rock 'n' roll album of his career, *Born in the USA*, fans at the time called 'em rockabilly songs. One was titled "Pink Cadillac," and the other was "Stand On It." "Pink Cadillac" is OK. But his song and delivery on "Stand On It" is phenomenal. To me, that song would rate as one of the all-time Top 10 rockabilly songs of the 1980s. Mel McDaniel reached #12 on the *Billboard* country charts with it from September 1986 to February 1987. Yeah, that's right! His version refused to go away. It rode those charts for a long nineteen weeks. Since that time, Mel McDaniel has only had one other song that reached a few notches higher. In Mel's version, he changed one word from Springsteen's version. Bruce had a line in his version of "Stand On It" that said, "Grab a girl, go out and see a rock 'n' roll band." Mel McDaniel sang the line, "Grab a girl, go out and see a rockabilly band." Both versions are great, but Springsteen's will never be topped.

After the third time in New York City that I saw Robert Gordon and Link Wray, I wouldn't see 'em again until April 1978, when they came back to Washington, D.C., and played once again at The Cellar Door to promote Robert's second album for the Private Stock label, called *Fresh Fish Special*. (The title was taken from a line used in Robert Gordon's favorite Elvis Presley movie,

Jailhouse Rock.) This album had been recorded in December 1977, and I read recently in some European liner notes on a recent Robert Gordon CD that Link Wray left Robert Gordon shortly after this album was recorded and was replaced by Chris Spedding on lead guitar. Now, I don't know how shortly was meant by the writer of those notes, but Link was sure there in D.C. on that show, and there's still a lot of Robert's fans in the D.C. area who'll attest to that fact. Again it was a great show, and Robert kept pickin' up momentum. Even though Robert wasn't rackin' up high numbers on the charts, his records were sellin' well, and he was drawing packed houses wherever he played. And he was playing around the U.S. constantly from then on into early 1983.

On *Fresh Fish Special*, which included obscure classic rockabilly cover songs such as the Johnny Burnette Rock 'N Roll Trio's "Lonesome Train (On a Lonesome Track)," Jack Scott's "The Way I Walk," Warren Smith's "Red Cadillac and a Black Mustache," etc., there were also three others that were either new or for the most part totally unknown at the time. One was an obscure Link Wray song, and another was a song Link had recorded sixteen years earlier that was written by his brother Doug Wray. But the standout song on this album was a new song Bruck Springsteen had written especially for Robert and given to him, called "Fire." Bruce even came into the studio in December 1977 and played piano on Robert's version of "Fire." Robert did a haunting vocal on this tune that chills you to the bone. Robert Gordon's version of this song got enough radio airplay to attract the attention of The Pointer Sisters' producer, and their pop version of "Fire," which had absolutely no guts to it, reached #2 for two consecutive weeks on the *Billboard* pop charts and became the group's first million-selling 45 single and had a run of twenty-three weeks on the charts between November 1978 and April 1979. But Robert Gordon was "Red Hot" all over the club, auditorium, and college concert circuit with his brand of rockabilly music all throughout 1978. So hot that RCA Records in New York signed him to a multiple-album contract by the late summer of 1978.

Robert recorded three sessions in New York for RCA between November 1978 and January 1981, which resulted in three new album releases: *Rockabilly Boogie* in 1979, *Bad Boy* in 1980, and *Are You Gonna Be the One* in 1981. On the first two albums, there were twenty-two classic obscure rockabilly cover songs. Chris Spedding handled all the lead guitar work. The only new original song on these two albums was a song co-written by Robert Gordon, called "The Catman." This was Robert's tribute song to the late, great Gene Vincent, who he idolized. Robert had the voice and power to put across in an original, raw, but also fresh way rockabilly classics such as "Rockabilly Boogie," "Love My Baby," "I Just Found Out," "Black Slacks," "Nervous," "Sweet Love on my Mind," and others. On these two albums, Robert also covered pop and country classics in his own rockabilly arrangements. One knockout song for me was called "Need You," which was a ballad on the *Bad Boy* album. Donnie Owens had reached #25 with this song in 1958. When I heard Robert put his feelin' into "Need You," neither me or Pepper ever wanted to hear Donnie Owens's version again, which I had liked, because Robert's was far superior to it. There's just too many to mention, though.

Like I said, the only national chart success Robert had on these first two RCA albums were with "It's Only Make Believe" and "Walk On By," which made it to the bottom of the *Billboard* country charts in 1979. So when Robert went in to do what would be his final new album for RCA Records, he changed directions somewhat by gettin' a new producer, a whole new group of professional studio musicians, with the exception of Tony Garnier, who played both upright slap bass and electric bass on his second RCA album, and only recording one older cover song, which was the Don Gibson country classic "Look Who's Blue," which Robert turned into a solid rockabilly tune. The nine other songs on his final (new) album, *Are You Gonna Be the One,* were all newly written for this project. Robert Gordon co-produced this album with Lance Quinn and Scott Litt. The three of them would also co-write, along with now-lead guitarist Danny Gatton, a powerful, fresh, modern-day rockabilly song called "Too Fast to Live, Too Young to Die," which would wind up becoming the title of Robert's fourth and final album for RCA Records, which would be released in 1982.

Most Robert Gordon fans then and now all agree as I do that *Are You Gonna Be the One* was Robert's greatest, best, and most artistic album. Every track is great. Robert Gordon and his new band of Wildcats toured extensively behind this album throughout 1981. But like I said, the only minor *Billboard* pop chart hit he had from it was "Someday, Someway." This song should have put Robert high up into the national charts. It had the guts, and it had the most powerful guitar player on the planet playin' the perfect rockabilly licks on it. That bein' Danny Gatton. But I guess it wasn't meant to be. This was before there was MTV. Another killer rockabilly

song, co-written by Billy Swan and given a solid rockin' treatment by Robert Gordon, was one called "Drivin' Wheel." It was a monster of a rockabilly song by Robert Gordon, and it too got a lot of airplay, but again it also failed to chart. Emmylou Harris knew a great song when she heard it, 'cause she took her weak, but good for her, version of "Drivin' Wheel" up into the *Billboard* Top 10 country charts. It was one of the few rockin' songs Emmylou ever did. Other songs like "Lover Boy," "Are You Gonna Be the One," and "Too Fast to Live, Too Young to Die" all had hit potential. It was definitely Robert Gordon's finest hour, with the greatest backup band he ever had. He promoted the hell out of it, sellin' out shows everywhere he played from New York to California, but it just didn't happen. Robert was disgusted, and for good reason, too. 'Cause the yuppie crap that was at the top of the *Billboard* pop charts was just that, too. Crap and gimmicks in 1981. Air Supply, Stars on 45, Christopher Cross, etc. No real rock 'n' roll there. It's been written Robert Gordon was dropped by RCA after this great album, but according to Robert, who I got to know very well as the years went on, and who I know has never lied to me when it came to his career, RCA wasn't planning to give up on him at all and was planning to put him in the studio again in late 1981 or early '82 and do a whole new fresh album once again. But RCA was only willing to put $150,000 into the budget to record it. Robert recently admitted to me that he blew it at the time by demanding $250,000 and wouldn't take anything less. Like he went on to tell me, that was a whole lot of money in those days just to cut an album, so when RCA wouldn't meet his demands, Robert took a walk, and they released him from his contract.

By the beginning of 1982, Robert Gordon had a lot of personal problems, which I'm just choosing not to get into. They're irrelevant to what he had accomplished in a short five years. Even if you're a nice guy when you first start out, like Robert definitely was, at least to me, a lot of times the demands put on you by the major music business can make you crazy, hard, and mean. Even though Robert may have brought some problems on himself, it just don't matter. Robert Gordon was and still is a real talent, and on account of him more young artists and bands around the country started singin' and playin' rockabilly music the real way it was meant to be. But things weren't over for Robert by any means in 1982. The album *Too Fast to Live, Too Young to Die* came out that year, and he was still selling out all the clubs he played. He toured and did a whole lot of shows throughout 1982 and well into 1983. Danny Gatton had pretty much bowed out by then and was only doin' Robert's shows periodically that year between Washington, D.C., and Boston. Robert went back to using Chris Spedding on lead guitar from then on, for the most part.

During the spring of 1983 when Robert was in town for a show, Danny got him to go into Omega Studios for me and record five rockabilly tunes. Danny did this as a favor for me. Robert didn't mind at all. I paid Danny, Robert, and the drummer. That was basically it, except for the eight hours studio time and tape. Danny played all the guitar parts, along with the bass parts on five easy songs they all knew, such as "Bertha Lou," "Gonna Romp and Stomp," "Linda Lu," and a couple of others. After 1983, I didn't see Robert too much for a couple years, though he still continued to do shows, just not as many, right on up to the present day. I'd go out and see him at least one to two times a year between 1983 and 1985 when he played the D.C. area. From 1986 through 1989, I saw him more often, though. We stayed pretty tight and became closer friends. I'd go down to the Roxy Showplace in N.W. Washington, D.C., where Robert Gordon played when he came to town during those years. That was basically his home club. The owner, Tesfly, was a really decent club owner, also. I can't say that about most of 'em. But during that four-year period, Robert played the Roxy on about a twice-a-year basis. Besides Johnny Seaton, I was booking Billy Hancock, LesLee "Bird" Anderson, Bobby Smith, Kelly Willis, The Fireballs, and other local groups in the Roxy, as well as other area venues. I even booked Tex Rubinowitz in there once. But most of those rockabilly acts I just mentioned I'd have booked on Robert Gordon's Roxy Showplace shows mostly between 1985 and 1988.

I met Robert's two sons in March 1987, when Robert did a split-bill show at the Warner Theater in D.C., which held about 2,000 people, with Dwight Yoakam. Dwight was able to walk on both ends of the fence back then and play to both country audiences and rock/punk audiences. Me and Pepper got good memories from partyin' backstage with Robert and his band that night. Robert did a good show and was in a great mood, I guess because he was around his two sons, who were about seventeen and nineteen years old at that time.

I booked Robert on two big shows at the Severna Park Elk's Lodge Hall in Severna Park, Maryland, where I was living at the time, in 1989. One of the shows was the sold-out benefit I had for Charlie Feathers with seventeen acts and performers on it. That was August 12,

1989. The second show that I brought Robert down for was on September 29, 1989. I was bringin' Jack Scott in just for a one-night show, and I was hopin' I could get Jack and Robert up on stage at the end of the night to do a duet of Jack's song "The Way I Walk." Robert Gordon had done this song on his second Private Stock Records album, and by 1989, he was opening a lot of his shows with it, and his fans knew him for it, rather than Jack Scott. But it wasn't meant to be on that night.

Robert Gordon was the first and the last U.S. major record label rockabilly solo star of what's now considered the rockabilly music revival period from 1977 to 1984. Robert is also the first artist since the 1950s described in Joel Whitburn's books of *Top Pop Singles* and *Top Pop Albums* solely as a solo rockabilly singer. He was booked by the biggest booking companies in the world and sold more records than any other solo rockabilly artist. Robert is a great singer who stayed with rockabilly music longer than any of the other Johnny-come-latelys that followed his lead. He was on major record labels and sold more records than any of the other artists or acts in the so-called rockabilly revival, with the exception of The Stray Cats. He was devoted to rockabilly music. Robert just barely missed out on the MTV generation. He didn't have the luxury and advantage of that kind of promotion, as The Stray Cats would have over five years later. But Robert was seen on some of the most popular and biggest national television shows of their time, such as "The Midnight Special" (with Link Wray) hosted by Wolfman Jack (1978), "Second City TV" (1979), "Late Night with David Letterman" on NBC (1984, 1986, 1987, and 1988), and many others I don't remember. In 1980, Robert Gordon also had a starring role in the movie *The Loveless*.

A lot of top mainstream artists would capitalize on the revival Robert Gordon started here in the U.S. by trying out rockabilly music. Most succeeded big-time on the charts, too. One artist who failed terribly that always comes to mind was Neil Young. He was always way up high in the charts from 1970 on, doin' that lame, forgettable, soft schlock rock he's known for. But during the early eighties, Young comes out with this album called *Pink & Black* with him on the cover with his hair slicked down and back and fifties-type cat clothes on. If he didn't make a big enough fool of himself on the cover, every rockabilly fan I ever talked to sure agreed he did on the grooves of that record album. I guess what I'm saying is steer clear of this piece of garbage. It ain't rockabilly. It didn't sell at all, was panned by critics, and hit the discount album bargain bins real quick. Another one that comes to mind right away was folk singer Joni Mitchell. Joni had been off the *Billboard* pop charts for six years in 1982. From 1970 to '76, Joni had charted eight songs on the *Billboard* pop charts with her brand of coffee house music that was dead in the days of disco by then. But in the fall of 1982, Geffen Records gave Joni one last shot at the top of the charts. With the rockabilly revival goin' on, Geffen Records released, of all things, one of the best rockabilly songs Elvis sang in the 1957 movie *Jailhouse Rock,* called "(You're So Square) Baby I Don't Care," by Joni Mitchell, in her own style. If Elvis had-a been alive in 1982, he would have shot the radio out when he heard this crap. It did somehow reach #47 for a nine-week run on the *Billboard* pop charts, but then it was adios, Joni.

In 1989, New Rose Records in France released a four-teen-song album on Robert Gordon called *Robert Gordon at The Lone Star.* The Lone Star Cafe was always Robert Gordon's New York City home base club for more than a decade. This album was all pure rock-abilly music and included five new songs never before available before this time by Robert. One of which was his version of the Elvis Sun classic "I Forgot to Remember to Forget," which Robert had been singin' in his shows regularly since at least 1979. In 1990, Bear Family Records in Germany released two separate single-CD albums of fifty of the best songs Robert Gordon had released on the Private Stock and RCA record labels between 1977 and 1982. They're both fine collections, with discoveries that I'd highly endorse for fans to pick up. These collections of songs led to Robert Gordon going overseas for the first time in his career, 'cause European rockabilly fans know great music when they hear it. Robert did shows in England, France, Sweden, Finland, Japan, and other countries between 1991 and 1993. In 1994, Robert had his first new studio album released here in the U.S. in more than a decade on Viceroy Records. It was called *All for the Love of Rock 'n' Roll.* This label didn't have major distribution, so I wasn't able to obtain a copy of it, so I've never heard it. I've been told it was a departure from the straight-ahead solid rockabilly music Robert had always done, and people I know that had it said they didn't care for it. I can't say until maybe someday somebody will send me a tape of it or send me the CD.

I've spoken with Robert by phone several times since February 1995, and he continued to perform his same brand of rockabilly and rock 'n' roll music up until the fall of 1995. Through most of '95 he toured the Northeast, as well as doin' shows as far away as Los Angeles and Seattle. But in the fall of '95 Robert's life almost came to an end, when he was mugged, robbed, and sliced up in the face and throat so badly that it took 173 stiches to put his face back together. This happened on a street in New York City not far from where he's always had an apartment on West 57th Street. He was on his way to the store by himself late one night to get a pack of cigarettes. He almost bled to death before the ambulance got there. When I last spoke with him in March 1996, Robert told me, "I thought I was gonna die right then and there, Billy, I really thought I'd bought it this time. I'm livin' on borrowed time, and I know it. I'm not usin' [Chris] Spedding no more. It's been a long healing process, but I just did my first live show here in six months, and it went over good. I've changed, and I'm seein' things in a whole new light. Thanks for hangin' in there with me, pal." Robert married his longtime steady girlfriend, Mary Lee, in December 1995, after goin' with her for more than ten years. Robert also told me there's a whole lot more great rockabilly music and shows left for him to do 'cause that's what he loves the most, and when given the chance, he'll be doin' 'em. I believe him this time, and eventually I'll give him that chance. 'Cause he was the best from '77 on who never deserted the true music. Without Robert Gordon you would have never heard of The Stray Cats.

The Stray Cats

The Stray Cats without a doubt were the biggest record-selling rockabilly band during the early 1980s, and also had the biggest, highest-ranking U.S. chart success of any rockabilly group or artist on the *Billboard* pop charts between September 1982 and February 1984.

First the facts. The Stray Cats were three suburban middle-class teenagers who lived in Long Island, New York, which is just outside New York City. When they first got together and formed their rockabilly band in late 1978, New York City was a hotbed for the thriving rock-abilly scene that Robert Gordon had goin' in full force by then. They weren't known as The Stray Cats when they first started playin' anywhere they could in New York City by early 1979. They had several different names through to the end of 1980. In early 1980, they were called The Tom Cats.

The three Tom Cats went to England in 1979 and met Dave Edmunds. But they returned to the U.S. during the first part of 1980 and after having no success here in the States, they went back over to England later in 1980, got with Dave Edmunds once more, and were eventually signed to a major-label contract there with Arista Records in 1981. By that time the group, which consisted of Brian Setzer on lead guitar and lead vocals, Lee Rocker (real name: Leon Drucher) on upright slappin' bass and backup vocals, and Slim Jim Phantom (real name: Jim McDowell) on drums and backup vocals, had changed their name to The Stray Cats. Brian Setzer had written a song for their first album they'd recorded, called "Stray Cat Strut." I've often wondered, if they'd-a kept the name The Tom Cats, if that song might have been called "Tom Cat Strut." Interestingly, when Dave Edmunds appeared as a rock singer in the 1974 major motion picture *Stardust*, The Stray Cats was the name of his band in the film.

In 1981 this trio of Stray Cats burst up into the top of the English major charts as well as every other major music chart in all of Europe with their first several 45 releases and first album release. They were all hot, wild, skinny young guys who were performing their new brand of rockabilly music to thousands of screamin' fans all over Europe. They had an energetic, vibrant, shakin', screamin', all-over-the-stage live show act. I saw it when they first came back and did their first tour of America. That's exactly what they had to do, 'cause even though they were playing to tens of thousands of fans everywhere, they went and were selling millions of records all over Europe, there's an old sayin' for as long as I can remember, if you don't make it big in America, you didn't make it. Well, The Stray Cats did make it. In late 1981, I had bought their first European album, and I liked about half the album. "Rock This Town" was the song I liked the best, 'cause it was pretty true to the original sound I loved the most in rockabilly music. Other songs like "Runaway Boys" I didn't even think sounded like rockabilly songs to me. I was listening the most at the time to WHFS-FM radio, who played progressive rock music then, and they were playin' a lot of cuts off The Stray Cats' first European album.

When they first arrived here in the U.S. in the spring of 1982, they didn't even have a record deal in this country. But what they did have was a whole lot of momentum and money behind them, and they were placed on a short-lived, but heavily watched, network late-night comedy show in the vein of "Saturday Night Live" that each week spotlighted hot new rock and pop musical artists and groups. The show was called "Fridays." It was on each Friday night. I videotaped that one-hour show

on which The Stray Cats performed four songs. In fact, they closed out the show, and at the end, right before they started to roll the credits, they put up a notice about The Stray Cats. It read, "The Stray Cats are an unsigned recording group in America and do not have a U.S. recording contract." Well, it didn't take no time until EMI Records in New York City signed 'em to a contract. Their material was already recorded, and their first 45 and album were rushed out immediately, and they began to tour all over the U.S. right away. I saw 'em at an old movie house down in N.W. Washington, D.C., during the summer of 1982 on their first tour, and this place was jam-packed. I was lucky to get in. I didn't like all their music. What I did like was that they were turnin' on young sixteen- to twenty-two-year-old kids to old obscure rockabilly songs by The Johnny Burnette Trio, Gene Vincent, Eddie Cochran, and others. Every local Washington, D.C., rockabilly singer or band really wanted to be the opening act on that show. But I remember when I called about gettin' Johnny Seaton the opening act slot for the show in D.C., the promoter told me they couldn't use any act or artist that was even close to a rockabilly act, as it was in The Stray Cats' contract everywhere they played that all of their opening acts had to be ones that played hard rock, blues, heavy metal, or some other form of music not connected to rockabilly or old rock 'n' roll.

But The Stray Cats beat the odds and made all the pop/rock and hard rock radio stations have to come to finally makin' the decision to play what they all considered outdated music. Rockabilly music. They didn't have much choice. After The Stray Cats' first American album debuted on the *Billboard* pop charts on September 4, 1982, it raced up those charts and reached the #2 position by late November. Their American album was called *Built for Speed,* and it would surely have been a #1 album on *Billboard,* as it was certified platinum here in the States, but it had the unbelievable misfortune of going head-to-head up against the biggest album of 1982, which was the *Business as Usual* album by a now-forgotten group called Men at Work, which stayed #1 for fifteen straight weeks, from early November 1982 to late February 1983, only to be replaced by Michael Jackson's *Thriller* album in late February, which was the biggest-selling album of all time, staying #1 for a total of thirty-seven weeks. The Stray Cats' first album stayed on the *Billboard* album charts for over a year, and they wound up havin' two Top 10 *Billboard* pop singles off it. The first, "Rock This Town" (which I personally always felt was their best), debuted on *Billboard* on

September 18, 1982, and reached a peak position of #9 in December 1982, and had the longest ride for any one song The Stray Cats would ever have on the *Billboard* pop charts. It stayed on the charts for twenty-one straight weeks, until February 1983. The follow-up 45 single to "Rock This Town" was "Stray Cat Strut." It debuted on the *Billboard* pop singles charts on December 25, 1982, and went on to reach a peak position of #3 and stay on the charts through April 1983. It was odd, but The Stray Cats' two follow-up 45 singles failed to even reach the *Billboard* pop charts at all.

It wouldn't be until their second American album, called *Rant 'n' Rave with The Stray Cats,* was released during the summer of 1983 that The Stray Cats would once more reach high up onto the *Billboard* pop charts. Their first 45 single release off this album was called "(She's) Sexy + 17." This song debuted on the *Billboard* pop charts on August 6, 1983. MTV was really startin' to get hot, and there was a video on "(She's) Sexy + 17" that received really big-time heavy MTV air time. After its debut, this song reached a peak position of #5 on the *Billboard* pop charts. Shortly after this song was released and started climbing up the charts, I was given tickets to go see The Stray Cats at Merriweather Post Pavilion (an outdoor and indoor 7,000-seat amphitheater in nearby Columbia, Maryland), where the big top national acts played. I was still buying The Stray Cats' records and all, but I wasn't real heavily into 'em as much as the fans in their teens and early twenties that were the bulk of their audiences. I'd seen 'em once, and that was pretty much enough for me. I would have probably given those two tickets away, but me and Pepper decided to go, because The Stray Cats' special guest on this show was Dave Edmunds, who was responsible for their success then, as the only major chart songs I've mentioned and the couple that followed were all produced by Dave. I'd met him a year earlier and at that time could watch this guy perform almost any song. I thought he was great back then and still do. He's a phenomenal producer of not only rockabilly music but other forms of roots rock 'n' roll as well. In my opinion (and many others'), Dave and his band blew The Stray Cats away on that show.

"(She's) Sexy + 17" quickly reached #5 on the *Billboard* pop charts in October 1983 and stayed on those charts for a total of fifteen weeks. Their follow-up single from the second album was a nice-soundin' ballad with a doo-wop feel to it, called "I Won't Stand In Your Way Any More." This is a really good song. But it wasn't rockabilly. Brian Setzer, who I have to say is a really fine guitarist, proved he could handle a ballad pretty well. But the young fans The Stray Cats had evidently didn't like this departure from the new sound of rockabilly music they'd been dishin' out for over a year around the U.S. "I Won't Stand In Your Way Any More" only reached #35 on the *Billboard* pop charts but had a decent run of thirteen weeks on those charts from late October 1983 to late January 1984. That was also the time The Stray Cats' final chart 45 single, "Look at That Cadillac," debuted on the *Billboard* pop charts, which was on January 28, 1984. Even though this song was one that was back in the same style which The Stray Cats had first succeeded with, it only reached #65 and had a short five-week run on the *Billboard* pop singles charts. Their second album, though, *Rant 'n' Rave with The Stray Cats,* was certified gold and after its debut on the *Billboard* pop albums charts climbed up to a peak position of #14, and it had more than a six-month run on the charts, until the early spring of 1984. By then, though, the excitement they'd stirred up among young fans had faded.

While they stayed together through most of 1984 and were committed to EMI Records for more albums, The Stray Cats at the time were having internal trouble, and they wanted to do other kinds of music besides rockabilly. Which they did. In 1985 and 1986, Brian Setzer did solo albums with 45 single releases. He toured behind 'em, but the public didn't buy it. Brian was trapped as a Stray Cat. He was the King Stray Cat. It should have been easier for Slim Jim Phantom and Lee Rocker. They were just backup musicians. EMI Records gave them a chance, like they had Setzer, when Phantom and Rocker got a singer and guitarist by the name of Earl Slick and they had an album released called *Cover Girl* by Phantom, Rocker & Slick, as they were then known. It was a weak album and failed miserably. So by 1986, The Stray Cats reunited and went back in the studio and cut yet another album of mostly cover songs. None of which are memorable, and most of which are lame. Especially a lazy, tired-soundin' version of the Charlie Feathers classic rockabilly song "One Hand Loose." When you listen to this EMI Records album, titled *Rock Therapy,* and compare it to their early music, you can tell they either didn't want to have to resort back to doin' rockabilly music, or they just wanted to get it over with and get away from each other.

When this album also failed, EMI Records gave Brian Setzer another shot, where he put out another solo album with his "Stray Cat Look," complete with leather pants and boots with chrome tips and studded straps, leanin' on an old restored classic Indian motorcycle and doin' twelve new songs mostly with the Stray Cats sound. The album was called *Live Nude Guitars*. Most of the songs were written by Setzer, and most were either produced or co-produced by him. A few songs on this album are actually pretty good. But again it failed to even dent the national charts, and the 45s released from it also failed. Only leftover hard-core Stray Cats fans bought it. That was enough, 'cause they were becoming fewer and fewer by this late date in America. So, back to the drawing board once more. Like most acts in pop music that had the success The Stray Cats had, they wanted control over their music, as well as producer credits, etc. Well, Brian Setzer sure got it after 1983. Like I said, when you think of The Stray Cats, he's the one that comes to mind right away. But it was Dave Edmunds who had produced every one of their 45 single *Billboard* pop chart hits for the year and a half they were at their peak.

So there was only one thing left to do. EMI Records would give The Stray Cats one final shot on their label, but they'd bring in Dave Edmunds to produce it. Edmunds had already had a lot of success during the mid and late eighties producing movie soundtrack albums such as *Porky's Revenge*, which were geared toward the teenage music market, and those albums all contained various forms of rockabilly and roots rock 'n' roll music. Dave Edmunds also had his own career as a solo artist goin' on in 1989 and was still a big concert draw on his own, as he had a faithful audience still. But Dave came in again and produced what would be the final new album on The Stray Cats, for EMI Records at least. He produced every one of the ten songs on it and engineered eight of them. The album was much better than the last one they had done as a group some four years earlier. At least this one had some fire behind it. EMI put a good bit of promotion behind it, puttin' the old Stray Cats cartoon drawing on it, as well as having the group do a nationwide tour across the U.S. But this time they were back to the nightclub circuit, for the most part. The 45 singles released failed to reach the *Billboard* national charts, as did the album, but there were a few good solid songs sung and played with energy on it. The album was titled *Blast Off*. That was the first song on side one. That was a good rockabilly number, as was the Buddy Hollyish song "Gina." There was a tribute song to Gene Vincent and Eddie Cochran, "(We're Gonna Rock with) Gene and Eddie," and though it was a little tacky 'cause the lyrics were mainly titles

from Vincent's and Cochran's great rockabilly songs, I liked it for the reason it was at least bringin' attention once more to two of the greatest artists in rockabilly and rock 'n' roll history. "Slip, Slip, Slippin' In" was another pretty good song off this album.

Just to finish up on The Stray Cats. They have to be given a lot of credit, as I've stated, for takin' the term "rockabilly" and having it become well known on a national scale here in the U.S. After their 1989 album failed, they reunited once more with Dave Edmunds as their producer and had an eleven-song album released on Great Pyramid Records which was distributed by BMG Records. So it got major distribution, but it still failed once more. This album was called *Choo Choo Hot Fish* and was released in 1992. In the early nineties, the three Stray Cats toured Japan, where they had a large following. Brian Setzer did a solo big band orchestra album that also failed to chart. The other two Cats have also done solo projects in the early nineties, but for the most part, The Stray Cats' days have passed. At least on the national charts. And hey y'all, if you dig The Stray Cats' music, that's fine with me. You just keep right on rockin' away to it, 'cause at least it's better than most things you hear on the radio today.

Dave Edmunds

During the late seventies to mid eighties, Dave Edmunds was one of the most important and consistent roots rockabilly and rock 'n' roll artists. But he first broke through when his great updated cover version of the Smiley Lewis 1955 rhythm & blues hit song "I Hear You Knockin'" debuted on the *Billboard* pop charts on December 26, 1970. Dave's drivin', poundin' beat and gritty vocals were great to hear on Top 40 pop radio goin' into the early months of 1971. That's when Dave's version of "I Hear You Knockin'" soared up the *Billboard* pop charts and reached a peak position of #4, in February 1971, staying on those charts for twelve weeks. This record came out in the U.S. and in Europe on the independent Mam record label. When it became Dave's biggest hit ever in early 1971, I'd never heard of him, but I knew I liked what I was hearin'. "I Hear You Knockin'" went all the way to #1 on the major British charts and also in other countries in Europe.

Dave Edmunds was born in Cardiff, Wales, but was based out of England when this record became a worldwide hit. Even though he had a Top 5 instrumental hit with his band Love Sculpture in 1968 in England, Dave was still treatin' his love and passion for roots rock 'n' roll music as a hobby when "I Hear You Knockin' " became an international hit record. He didn't even have a band together in late 1970 and early '71 and never did a tour of America to promote the song then. It took him by complete surprise. It also proves once in a great while if you're doin' somethin' raw and real in rock 'n' roll and radio starts playin' it, young rock 'n' roll fans that are sick of the same old sappy sounds they usually are forced to listen to will jump on it and buy it every time. At least it worked in Dave Edmunds's case with "I Hear You Knockin'."

I bought Dave's follow-up record also, called "I'm Comin' Home," which debuted on the *Billboard* pop charts on May 1, 1971. It only reached #75 and only had a four-week ride on the charts, but Dave Edmunds had left his mark and name with me on those two 45s, and I'd be on the lookout from then on for anything by him.

There was a long gap of eight years before he'd wind up on the *Billboard* pop charts again. But Dave's chart numbers don't even begin to tell the story of his importance. In between those years, Dave recorded some good albums that were released here in America. In 1975, his album *Subtle as a Flying Mallet* was released by RCA Records, and it had some great old cover songs on it, true to the feel of modern rockabilly. One of which was a great version of "Leave My Woman Alone." After the one album on RCA Records, Dave Edmunds had four albums released on the Swan Song record label, which was distributed by the major label Atlantic Records. These albums all came out between 1976 and 1981. While the RCA album had failed to even dent the *Billboard* pop album charts, these four albums managed to creep into the lower end of those charts, and two of Dave's 45 single releases made it onto the *Billboard* pop single charts. While all four of these albums were loaded with great roots rock 'n' roll and solid rockabilly, Dave's first 45 to hit the *Billboard* pop singles charts was a song called "Girls Talk." It was a good solid rockin' tune from Dave's 1979 album titled *Repeat When Necessary,* but there were still better rockabilly songs on this album. But at least it did make it onto the charts. "Girls Talk" entered the *Billboard* pop singles charts on September 1, 1979, and reached #65, stayin' on the charts for a relatively short six weeks. But this song got an awful lot of airplay, especially on all the top college and progressive rock radio stations that were real popular at the time. This song also enabled Dave Edmunds to fast become a top concert draw in nightclubs, auditoriums, and college campuses across America.

Dave's regular backup band on his recordings during his years with Swan Song was known as Rockpile. In 1979, one of the members of this Rockpile backup band, Nick Lowe, got a solo artist contract with Columbia Records here in the U.S. At the same time Dave Edmunds was having his chart success on the *Billboard* pop charts in 1979, Nick Lowe was on his way to havin' the biggest 45 single chart hit of his career. Nick's first single, "Cruel to Be Kind," entered the *Billboard* pop charts on July 28, 1979, and by October 1979 had climbed all the way up to #12 and wound up having a long run of fifteen weeks on the *Billboard* pop charts. Nick Lowe's music stayed pretty true to roots rock 'n' roll and modern-day rockabilly music. Nick had a long stay with Columbia Records as a solo artist, at least through 1988. He had a half dozen or so album releases, plus quite a number of 45 single releases. Nick also had at least one album I know of in the early nineties. His only other 45 single *Billboard* chart hit came on November 30, 1985, when a song he'd written that Dave Edmunds had recorded in the late seventies and was a concert favorite of Dave Edmunds fans entered the *Billboard* pop singles charts. The song was called "I Knew the Bride (When She Used to Rock 'n' Roll)." Nick's version only reached #77, but it stayed on the *Billboard* pop charts until the first week of February 1986. It had a solid nine-week run on the charts. The song was produced by Huey Lewis of Huey Lewis & The News, who were real hot in rock 'n' roll music at that time.

Going back to 1979 and 1980, with both Dave Edmunds and Nick Lowe now becoming top concert draws in America and having worked together for a number of years, Dave Edmunds decided this band Rockpile, a name he'd always liked, should do what's always been considered a rockabilly album. So Dave and Nick Lowe, along with the other two members of Dave's backup band, recorded a solid twelve-song album called *Seconds of Pleasure,* and the group name was simply called Rockpile. This was one solid, tight roots rock 'n' roll and rockabilly band. They were definitely a supergroup at that time, and this was a powerful album. Dave Edmunds and Nick Lowe either took songs individually doin' the lead singin' or sang some songs together. Nick Lowe played bass, Dave Edmunds played guitar and piano, Billy Bremner played guitar and sang harmony and backup vocals, and Terry Williams was the drummer. A more solid all-around roots rock 'n' roll and rockabilly group couldn't be found in 1980. I saw it with my own eyes on November 30, 1980, when they played Washington, D.C., to an overflow crowd. The choice of songs they cut for this album were all great, also. Songs like "Teacher, Teacher," "If Sugar Was as Sweet as You," "Heart," "A Knife and a Fork," "When I Write the Book," "Now and Always," "You Ain't Nothin' But Fine," etc., were all solid as a rock if you wanted to hear the real sound of rock 'n' roll sung and played with only the basic instruments of rock 'n' roll and rockabilly music. No disco-soundin' synthesized crap was found anywhere on this album. It was also great when you first bought the first pressings of this 1980 LP, it came with a bonus of a four-song EP album of Dave Edmunds and Nick Lowe singing four Everly Brothers classic songs with the two of them only playin' their acoustic guitars and no other instruments.

Even though Rockpile did over a three-month-straight tour across the U.S. from November 1980 through February 1981, the first single off the album was the only one to make it onto the *Billboard* Hot 100 pop charts. The 45 single "Teacher, Teacher" reached #51 after it entered the *Billboard* pop charts on November 22, 1980, but remained on the charts for a fifteen-week run. The Rockpile album *Seconds of Pleasure* made it well into the *Billboard* Top 100 album charts, peaking out at #27. This was their only album as a total group under the name Rockpile. It was on the Columbia Records label, which Dave Edmunds signed on with in late 1981. His final album on the Swan Song label, called *Twangin'*, had been released during the spring of 1981. This would be the final Dave Edmunds album you'd find the other three members of Rockpile on. Nick Lowe would go on to concentrate on his solo career. He got married to Carlene Carter, who was June Carter Cash's oldest daughter from her first marriage, to the great country music legend Carl Smith. Carlene Carter recorded one album that Dave Edmunds sang a duet with her on in the early eighties on a song titled "Baby Ride Easy." A real good mid-tempo rockabilly-styled song. Terry Williams and Billy Bremner went on to do various other projects. These four guys parted ways as friends, though. Since that time, they've all gotten back together over the years on occasion and done various things in music together.

On Dave Edmunds's final *Twangin'* album for Swan Song, he only had one *Billboard* pop chart 45 single. That was when "Almost Saturday Night" (the former 1975 hit for John Fogerty) entered the charts on May 8, 1981, and reached a peak position of #54 while staying on those charts for eight weeks. For my taste in rockabilly music, with the exception of Dave Edmunds's first album on Swan Song, titled *Git It*, this was my favorite all-around album by Dave. My favorite songs on it were "Almost Saturday Night," "It's Been So Long," "Singin' the Blues," and "The Race Is On." The Stray Cats played and sang harmony with Dave Edmunds on "The Race Is On." They were virtually unknown at this time in the U.S. Those were and still are all favorite songs of mine. But there were three others that really knocked me out. One was called "(I'm Gonna Start) Living Again If It Kills Me." On this song, Dave Edmunds proves, where so many rockabilly bands of today can't, that he has his own unique roots style when he sings a great ballad song such as this one. The last track on side 2 of this album proves Dave Edmunds's love for primitive rockabilly music. It's a cover of the Elvis rockabilly-styled version of "Baby Let's Play House" that Dave recorded at his first Rockfield Studio in England back in 1968. He had the true sound on this tune. But my all-time favorite Dave Edmunds rockabilly tune that I've listened to over and over again during the past sixteen years or so was on this *Twangin'* album. It's pretty much a forgotten and little-known song by now. But it's rockabilly to the bone with me. It's called "I'm Only Human."

Probably the best all-around album that contained on the whole practically a full album of rockabilly music was his first album on Swan Song, recorded in late 1976 and released in 1977. The album was titled *Git It*, and there's not one bad cut on the whole thing. There's thirteen songs in all. Besides covering fifties rockabilly classics such as Gene Vincent's "Git It," Elvis's "My Baby Left Me," and Jerry Lee Lewis's "Let's Talk About It," Dave rocked original and hard on newer tunes, such as "I Knew the Bride (When She Used to Rock 'n' Roll)," "Back to School Days," "Here Comes the Weekend," and others. There's also an energetic rockabillyish version of the Hank Williams classic "Hey, Good Lookin'." All in all, it was his best album for rockabilly fans at the time who weren't purists and could accept a younger, newer artist singin' these songs. I certainly could.

When Dave signed with Columbia Records in late 1981 and recorded his first album of eleven songs, titled *D.E. 7th* (I guess because it was his seventh album up to this point in his career), this album seemed to really put him over the top with the younger college-age fans after its release in the late spring of 1982. Even though he didn't have any singles off it that made it onto the *Billboard* Hot 100 pop singles charts, it was a phenomenal artistic album. The album did manage to climb into the *Billboard* Top 100 albums charts, though. Also in 1982, Dave appeared as a musical and comedy acting guest on the popular "Second City" TV series.

During the summer of '83, Dave was ridin' high on the *Billboard* pop charts with a song produced by Jeff Lynne (from Electric Light Orchestra Band, or ELO, whichever you prefer), called "Slipping Away." It wasn't a rockabilly song, but I had the album it came off of, called *Information,* and that did have several good solid rockabilly numbers on it. "Slipping Away" was Dave's biggest chart hit in the U.S. since "I Hear You Knockin' " back in 1971. It climbed up to a peak position of #39 after it entered the *Billboard* pop charts on May 14, 1983, and stayed on those charts longer than any other 45 single here in the U.S. he ever had. A total of a fifteen-week ride. Dave's 1984 album *Riff Raff* also had several rockabillyish tracks on it, but there were no *Billboard* chart singles.

Dave's final *Billboard* chart single came from the *Porky's Revenge* movie soundtrack album, which he sang songs on and was the musical director for the film. The song was called "High School Nights." It entered the *Billboard* pop charts on April 20, 1985, and reached a peak position of #91, but was only on the charts for two weeks. By this time, Dave Edmunds was the most sought-after producer, arranger, musical director, etc. for movies, records, TV specials, etc. Dave had his own one-hour concert TV special on MTV in 1982. In 1983, Dave was heavily involved with the London comeback concert reunion of The Everly Brothers. He was the musical director in the credits when it became an HBO TV special. Dave then went on to produce their first two comeback albums in 1984 and 1986. In 1985, Dave was part of the HBO TV special that was a tribute to Carl Perkins. Also in 1985, he flew to Memphis to be part of the *Class of '55* album on Johnny Cash, Carl Perkins, Jerry Lee Lewis, and Roy Orbison that was recorded at the old Sun studios. Dave Edmunds couldn't help this project. He was only wanted because of his name in rockabilly circles at the time.

I can't say enough about Dave Edmunds as a producer. He's not only been at it for a long time, but he's also worked with some of the best there are; he first produced rockabilly music on Shakin' Stevens in the early seventies. If I only had one wish left in music before I die, it would be to have Dave Edmunds produce a roots rock 'n' roll/rockabilly album on me, even if it only sold two copies, one to my daughter and one to my sister. As a producer and all-around musician, that cat knows more about the real kind of music in the true rock 'n' roll vein than anyone I've heard in the last twenty-five years.

One of Dave's best rockabilly songs, "Stay with Me Tonight," was included on the *Light of Day* soundtrack album from the film that starred Michael J. Fox and Joan Jett. This was in 1986. In 1987, Dave was part of another supergroup band that backed up Roy Orbison for his HBO TV tribute special. These are only some of the things I can remember that this great artist who loves roots rock 'n' roll and rockabilly music so much found the time to do during most of the 1980s.

In 1987, Dave recorded what would be his final full solo album for Columbia Records. The album was called *I Hear You Rockin'*. It was a live album, but mostly a greatest hits or best-of and favorite concert songs Dave was known for by 1987. I was happy to see "Queen of Hearts" on this 1987 album, as country female artist Juice Newton had a #2 pop hit and #1 country hit on this song in 1981 that was produced in Nashville. Well, Dave had recorded it on his 1979 *Repeat When Necessary* album and rocked the song real good. The way it was meant to be done. It was always a huge concert favorite that he was known for. Out of the eleven songs on this great live album, there were only two he hadn't recorded before, and both of 'em were knockouts. Dave did such a hot rockin' version of the 1956 Elvis song "Paralyzed" he'd-a made Elvis proud. The other one was a cover of Dion's "The Wanderer," which a lot of people have covered since 1987, including Eddie Rabbitt, who did a pretty good job. But I'll take Dave Edmunds's version over all of 'em, including Dion's, 'cause Dave knew exactly how to rock this song better than anyone.

Dave Edmunds didn't slow up after 1987. He kept on doin' too many projects to go into. But it wouldn't be until 1990 that he released his next new album, titled *Closer to the Flame*. This album came out on Capitol Records, and even though he toured behind it, the album barely reached the bottom of the *Billboard* Top 200 album charts. Out of the twelve songs, there were only three solid rockabilly tunes on it, but there was a really great ballad called "Never Take the Place of You." So there was more than enough on there to satisfy me.

In 1993, Rhino Records released a double CD with a nice booklet that contained forty songs Dave Edmunds recorded between 1968 and 1990. This is a collection I'd recommend to any broad-minded rockabilly fan, 'cause Rhino made some great choices on the songs that are on this double CD.

Forgettin' to Remember to Forget

It was on a ninety-degree-plus day in July '82 when I took Pepper and Johnny Seaton down to a record shop in the Georgetown section of N.W. Washington, D.C., where Dave Edmunds was gonna do an album signing before his two live shows at The Bayou Club a few blocks away. His shows had sold out within a couple hours on the first day they'd been on sale, over a month prior to this day. He signed autographs at the shop from 3:00 to 5:00 that afternoon. We got down there early, about 2:30, I guess. There were only about a dozen or so fans in line in front of us then. But by 3:00, when we went in, there was a line goin' all the way down the block. I had missed out on gettin' tickets for his show, but all I really cared about was meetin' Dave, shakin' his hand, and lettin' him know I appreciated his brand of roots rock 'n' roll and rockabilly music. I'd brought his four Swan Song albums with me, plus his new *D.E. 7th* one for him to autograph.

I had one of Johnny Seaton's "Uptown" 45s with a picture sleeve I'd put out on my label and was gonna give him one if he seemed like an OK guy. Well, let me tell ya, he was more than an OK guy. He was one of the nicest, humblest, most sincere and laid-back cats I'd ever met during this entire rockabilly revival period. He was a star, and he didn't like the star treatment. I could tell that right off. We talked for a few minutes about his music and older artists I was connected to such as Charlie Feathers and others, and he seemed honestly real interested in that. He thanked me for the Seaton 45, and as I was leavin', after Pepper had snapped off a picture of me, him, and Seaton, Dave said to me, "Well, I'll see you at the show tonight, Billy, and after the first set, come on back to the dressing room and we'll chat some more then. I'll leave word for them to let you come back." I said, "Man, both your shows sold out so fast, Dave, I couldn't get tickets for either one of 'em, and we just drove down here for me to let you know I really dig your music and have for a long time." Dave then said, "Well, would you like to come to the shows, then?" I said, "Yeah, I'll be glad to pay for the tickets." Dave said, "Nonsense. I'll put your name at the door on my guest list. You won't have a problem gettin' in. I'll just leave word there's three in your party, and later we'll have time to talk awhile, after we've finished the night."

Sure enough, Dave left my name plus two guests on his list, and all three of us saw what was an unbelievable live performance. Evan Johns & The H-Bombs (who I knew real well at the time) were the opening band, and they did their usual solid set of good rock 'n' roll, blues, and rockabilly music. But when Dave Edmunds and his five-piece backup band hit that stage, me, Pepper, and Johnny Seaton couldn't believe our ears. Dave Edmunds is the only performer, rockabilly or otherwise, that I've ever seen in my whole life where every one of the songs he did sounded exactly like the records I had on him.

After the first set, I had no trouble goin' backstage to see Dave, as he had left my name with the person at the door. We both enjoyed talkin' music with each other. After Dave's second and final set, we talked even more, but there were a lot of people then who were comin' in to get his autograph and talk to him, so I told Dave I'd be in the next dressing room with the opening band, who I knew. Dave told me, "I'll see you before I leave." Well, I was in Evan Johns's dressing room, and it was now about 3:30 a.m., when Dave's road manager popped his head in the door and said, "Is there someone named Billy Poore in here?" Before I could say anything, somebody in the room said, "Yeah, he's right here." The road manager said, "Well, Dave would like to see him now, because he's gettin' ready to leave." Evan Johns liked to have choked on his Heineken beer bottle when he heard that. I got up from where I was at and followed the guy back to Dave's dressing room, where him and one other guy were standing, gettin' ready to leave. Dave told me how much he enjoyed talking to me and would like to stay in touch, so he gave me a card with his manager's address and phone number, and told me in a month or so, after he came off the road, to call his manager, and we'd get together again 'cause he was interested in some of the things I'd mentioned, and that I had a great knowledge of real rock 'n' roll music, so maybe we could become involved in something in the future. But I was heavily involved with Johnny Seaton's career then. Time moved on, things happened fast back then, and I never did make that call.

By 1990, Dave Edmunds had given so much solid, rockin' great music, he didn't have to do no more. It was time for him to kick back and relax if he so chose. He was happily married by this time and had a nice home in California, and if anybody in music deserved a break from the longtime fast, busy pace he'd been on, he did. But I guess he's always loved what he'd been doin' almost all his life, 'cause sure enough, he came out with a brand-new album in 1994 with eleven songs on it, titled *Plugged In*. Dave recorded this entire album at his home in Los Angeles, in his spare bedroom, between September 1993 and February 1994. It was released by Pyramid Records, but had national distribution by Rhino Records in California. Dave Edmunds produced and engineered the whole album, as well as playing all the instruments on it. Good for you, Dave. No one to argue with but yourself if you don't like something. I saw Dave on Conan O'Brien's "Late Night" national TV show, and I'm sure he toured some behind this album during the summer of 1994. On this album, once again Dave Edmunds laid down one hell of a hot, stone-hard rockin' rockabilly tune I love that I could also relate to. It was called "Standing at the Crossroads." There were also a couple other great tunes on there that were right down my rockabilly and roots rock 'n' roll alley. One was called "It Doesn't Really Matter," and the other was a mid-1960s instrumental written by Jerry Reed, called "The Claw." Plus there was a fantastic ballad called "Better Word for Love." So once more, Dave Edmunds proved he could put out top-notch modern-day rockabilly and rock 'n' roll. Dave has always had that music runnin' through his veins. There's a whole lot more people besides me who'll be there to buy it whenever he might decide to go for it just one more time, too!

The Blasters

That comes pretty close to covering all the artists and bands during the rockabilly revival period that charted 45 singles on the *Billboard* pop charts from 1977 on. I guess you could count Los Lobos, who during the late eighties had hits with "Come On Let's Go" and "La Bamba." They were huge hits, but their success was primarily due to the hit film based on the life of Ritchie Valens. You could also possibly count a Los Angeles-based more rock than rockabilly group called The Kingbees, who during the summer of 1980 had one song called "My Mistake" reach #81 on the *Billboard* pop charts. On their two albums for RSO Records in 1980 and 1981, they did do some decent versions of older rockabilly classics by Carl Perkins, Jerry Lee Lewis, and

Buddy Holly. They also did a good cover of the relatively unknown song Ray Smith had on Sun Records in the late fifties called "Right Behind You Baby." They sounded more rockabilly to me than Los Lobos did later.

One group that didn't have any *Billboard* pop chart singles but that had four or five successful albums that made it onto the *Billboard* albums charts between 1981 and 1986 were The Blasters. The Blasters called their music "American music" in 1981 when their first album was released on a major label. The label was Slash Records, which was distributed by Warner Brothers Records then, as all their albums on Slash during the 1980s were. Fans across America considered them rockabilly, though. Ronnie Weiser had first recorded The Blasters in 1979 and released their first album on his Rollin' Rock Records label in 1980. Their album on Rollin' Rock was pure great rockabilly in a primitive form all the way. Songs like "Marie, Marie" and "Crazy Baby" off that first Rollin' Rock album are great rockabilly tunes. Even their first album on Slash in 1981, which was more polished, had some top-notch rockabilly songs on it, such as "Stop the Clock," "I'm Shakin'," "So Long Baby Goodbye," and a new version of "Marie, Marie," which lead guitarist Dave Alvin wrote, and which became Shakin' Stevens's first Top 20 major hit song in England.

The Blasters remained a top concert and club act that drew a large audience of rockabilly fans between 1981 and 1987. When Ronnie Weiser put their first album out on Rollin' Rock Records, the group consisted of Phil Alvin on rhythm guitar and lead vocals, Dave Alvin (Phil's brother) on lead guitar, John Bozz on bass, and Bill Bateman on drums. When The Blasters were signed by Slash Records in Los Angeles, they added Gene Taylor to the group on piano, who stayed with the regular recording and touring group of Blasters until around 1986, and they also used legendary tenor sax man Lee Allen and baritone sax player Steve Berlin on their first three albums.

The Blasters' hottest period on the tour circuit was 1981 to 1985. They achieved a good deal of success during this period, with appearances in a couple of major movies, plus their albums sold well enough to at least hit the *Billboard* charts. Dave Alvin was always the primary songwriter. Dave either wrote or co-wrote twenty-four of thirty-three songs contained on their first three albums alone. Other than the songs I mentioned earlier, the other Blasters songs that have always been favorites of mine are "Red Rose," "Trouble Bound,"

"Little Honey," "Colored Lights," and especially one called "Help You Dream." I'd say that would be my personal favorite. I saw 'em live twice, the first time they came to Washington, D.C., when they played The Bayou Club in late 1981, and again in October 1982, up in Baltimore, at a club called Girard's. I got to know Dave Alvin a little bit around that time but haven't kept in touch with him since then. He stayed busy throughout the 1980s, and I've done the same.

By the end of the 1980s, The Blasters split up. During the 1990s, Dave Alvin has had several solo albums released on the Hightone Records label, as well as produced a great album, also on Hightone Records, by former 1950s Sun Records artist Sonny Burgess. Dave nailed a solid rockabilly sound on Burgess on this whole album. I have to admit I was never a real big fan of Sonny Burgess's Sun 45s. I think this Hightone Records album, titled *Tennessee Border,* by Sonny Burgess with Dave Alvin, is better than anything Burgess ever recorded in his whole career, and that also includes the few albums he recorded with the late-eighties and early-nineties band The Sun Rhythm Section. There ain't a bad song in the whole lot. Sonny had the fire in his vocals, and it's complemented by Dave Alvin's right-on tasteful rockabilly guitar pickin'. Dave couldn't-a got the overall sound any better, as far as I'm concerned.

Phil Alvin formed a new group of Blasters in late 1993, and Hightone Records, out of Oakland, California, released an album by Phil and his new group, which includes James Intveld on lead guitar, in 1994. So both Dave Alvin and his brother Phil continue to knock out old and new fans of roots rock 'n' roll and rockabilly with their live shows. The greatest songs by The Blasters can be found on a twenty-song CD Warner Brothers released in 1994.

Billy and Rocky Burnette

Everybody I've mentioned up to now in this chapter, with the exception of Dave Edmunds, basically got jump-started in rockabilly and roots rock 'n' roll music here in the U.S. because of Robert Gordon's success between 1977 and 1981. This also can include Billy Burnette, who was the son of Dorsey Burnette, and his cousin Rocky Burnette, who was Johnny Burnette's son. Billy was born May 8, 1953, and Rocky was born June 12, 1953. Both were born in Memphis.

Billy got his first recording contract with A&M Records in 1974 when he was twenty-one years old. Nothin' much happened with that, so Billy played guitar in his father Dorsey's country band from 1975 up until Dorsey passed away in August 1979. Dorsey was still havin' *Billboard* Top 100 country chart hits right up until his death. In 1979, Billy Burnette signed with Polydor Records and recorded an album that had one country-type song on it called "What's a Little Love Between Friends" that reached #76 in November 1979 on the *Billboard* Top 100 country charts, where it had a five-week run. But in 1980, Billy Burnette signed a big-money deal with Columbia Records to record several albums promoted as rockabilly. RCA Records had Robert Gordon doin' real well then, but they sure didn't pump the money into Robert the way Columbia Records did into Billy Burnette in hopes of puttin' him into the big-time *Billboard* Top 10 charts.

When Billy played The Bayou Club in Washington, D.C., in the fall of 1980, he had the nice shiny cat clothes, the look, he was a decent singer, a real good guitarist, but up there on that stage, he was tryin' to be "Mr. Cool," and the D.C. fans just didn't buy it. I mean, he sang and put across the old Johnny Burnette Trio songs such as "Honey Hush" with his fuzztone guitar sound all through it, but Billy lacked charisma and that rapport with an audience that's so important no matter what kind of music you're doin'. And it wasn't only the Washington, D.C., audience that didn't buy Billy Burnette's rockabilly music, it was the rest of the U.S. as well. Billy's first 45 single off his debut album for Columbia was called "Don't Say No." It entered the *Billboard* pop charts on November 1, 1980, reached a peak position of #68, and fell off the charts after only five weeks. The first album was the only one that hit the bottom end of the *Billboard* pop charts for a short four-week run at the same time, and that was pretty much it. Even though he toured for months on this first album, it failed badly, as did his other two albums for Columbia, along with the 45 single releases. When I met Billy Burnette on that night at The Bayou, he seemed like a pretty nice guy, maybe a little bit arrogant, but hey, he was ridin' high.

After his Columbia Records deal ran out, Billy Burnette went on to sign with Curb Records, where he recorded a couple albums and had several minor bottom-half *Billboard* country singles chart hits in 1985 and 1986. Nothin' worth mentioning to rockabilly fans. When he failed once more to make it in the country scene, he joined forces with Mick Fleetwood, who was one of the founders of the highly successful pop/rock/blues band Fleetwood Mac, who were huge between 1975 and 1982 on the *Billboard* charts. Mick Fleetwood was the original drummer of this superstar group, and after they all went their separate ways by the early eighties, he started his own band, in which Billy Burnette became their lead guitarist and part-time singer. Billy was with Mick Fleetwood's group for several years during the late eighties.

By 1992, Billy was able to land a one-album deal with Warner Brothers Records and charted once again one minor bottom-end *Billboard* country chart hit. I recently saw Billy Burnette in a low-budget film on HBO that was made in 1994. So I reckon he's still stayin' active in various forms of the entertainment business, but he just couldn't deliver the goods in rockabilly, and I don't believe it was totally in his heart.

That wasn't the case with Johnny Burnette's son, Rocky Burnette. Both times when I met Rocky, once in 1981 and then again in 1991, he appeared to have a much better knowledge of his father's, Johnny Burnette's, greatest songs and accomplishments in rockabilly music. It didn't seem to matter with his cousin Billy, but Rocky really seemed to cherish and hold in high regard the early rockabilly music of his father. I don't mean to sound like I'm puttin' Billy down, but from my impressions of both these young guys, Rocky seemed to be the warmer, more sincere, down-to-earth and honest one of the two of 'em.

Rocky Burnette did have one big *Billboard* pop Top 10 chart single hit. It wasn't really a rockabilly song, though some broadminded rockabilly fans may consider to put it into that category. Plus British rockabilly star Shakin' Stevens covered the song later in the 1980s. The song was called "Tired of Toein' the Line." It entered the *Billboard* pop charts on May 10, 1980. "Tired of Toein' the Line" climbed all the way up to #8 on the *Billboard* pop charts in August 1980 and had a long nineteen-week run on those charts. Rocky and this song were on EMI America Records out of Los Angeles at the time. The song came off Rocky Burnette's first album for EMI, titled *The Son of Rock 'n' Roll*. Rocky wrote all ten songs on the album. He had a couple more albums and a half dozen or so 45 singles, but he never had another national hit.

As the 1980s went on and over into the 1990s, Rocky Burnette has stayed extremely active in the rockabilly scene. Rocky's done projects, shows, and tours with legendary greats such as Paul Burlison, who was his father's original lead guitarist in the mid and late fifties in The Johnny Burnette Rock 'N Roll Trio. Rocky and Paul got

together and recorded an album of rockabilly tunes during the mid eighties with other original fifties musicians, as well as using younger new ones that were then in the rockabilly scene. Johnny Burnette would be awful proud that his son Rocky helped keep his original music alive some forty years later.

James Intveld

I bought James Intveld's first 1980 45 on his own Dog House Records label, called "My Heart Is Achin' for You" b/w "You're My Baby." After that, I'd try to get anything I could find on James, 'cause he was layin' down a style of rockabilly music I really liked a lot. By 1985, when one of my all-time latter-day rockabilly girls who I was managing at the time, by the name of LesLee "Bird" Anderson, moved from Baltimore to Los Angeles, I'd get to know James Intveld a lot better. LesLee got into the rockabilly scene out there, and by the mid eighties there was a real good one happenin'. LesLee knew I dug James Intveld's music, so she put the two of us together by phone, at least. James was just plain "cool." He looked exactly like a young rockabilly cat should be to me. Over the past ten years or so, James has worked hard in his own bands, other bands, done movie soundtrack work, both sang and acted in films, and done various recording projects of his own and for others. He's struggled for this music called roots rock 'n' roll, rockabilly, and hillbilly as much as any later day rockabilly artist I've ever met. I'm glad I can call this cat a friend, even though we've only been around each other on four occasions between 1991 and 1994.

The first movie he appeared in was in the early 1980s and it starred Judd Hirsch and was called *Roadhouse 66*. His actin' was easy, 'cause he played the part of a cat dressed and lookin' the way Elvis looked in his greatest rockabilly film, *Loving You*. James's band that backed him up in that film, which included his younger brother, the late Rick Intveld, is the same band that was killed in the plane crash with Ricky Nelson on December 31, 1985. James had put together the best true rockabilly band in all of California. It breaks my heart those cats had to go down in that plane crash. They were all so young and so full of life. But James rocked on in the L.A. rockabilly scene. I've never known a young cat that was in his twenties back then that not only had his head on straight but could also deliver rockabilly music better than most solo artists on the scene. I mean, James Intveld at a young age had the ball of wax to make it big, and he loved the music he was doin'. Most important, James knew how to conduct business in the right way, and he was one of the best all-around musicians you could find for solid roots rock 'n' roll and rockabilly music. I've never heard a bad word said against James, and if I did, I wouldn't believe it, 'cause I feel I know him well enough to know where his head's at.

Here's just a few of James Intveld's contributions to roots rock 'n' roll and rockabilly music. In 1986, James wrote several of the songs on Rosie Flores's major-label album which was released by Reprise Records in 1987. This album by Rosie was rockabilly oriented and promoted towards the country market because of Dwight Yoakam's recent huge success. Dwight's producer Pete Anderson produced the album. The only *Billboard* chart single Rosie had from it was written by James Intveld. The song was called "Crying Over You" and only reached the bottom end of the *Billboard* country charts, but up to that point, the only female artist that was occasionally puttin' anything close to rockabilly on those country charts was the gutsy and long-established wild chick Tanya Tucker. James Intveld played lead guitar on the album and toured in Rosie's band during 1987.

Also in 1987, James was heard singin' two Elvis songs in the film and soundtrack album of the major motion picture *Wild at Heart*. The two songs were fifties Elvis ballads, "Love Me Tender" and "Love Me." In the studio, James's backup musicians included James Burton, Elvis's lead guitarist from the 1970s, who had backed fifties rockabillys Bob Luman, Dale Hawkins, and Ricky Nelson back then on their recordings and live shows. Ronnie Tutt, Elvis's drummer from 1969 to 1977, was also on these songs, along with John Jorgenson and Herb Peterson on backup vocals.

James sang a hard-drivin', wild rockabilly tune called "Lookin' for a Backbeat" that he wrote and was also used in the pilot of the short-lived TV series titled "Private Eye" in 1987. James appeared in the two-hour pilot, and you saw him singin' this great tune in the show. He had some speakin'/actin' parts in the pilot and was also seen in several of the episodes in club scenes while this series lasted. Which wasn't long enough.

James and another Los Angeles-based rockabilly artist by the name of Ronnie Mack, who has a tremendous love and respect for Ricky Nelson's music, were good friends, and by the late 1980s, Ronnie Mack, who's made a number of real good rockabilly songs, such as "I Love Tracy Lords," which is my personal favorite when it came out on a 45 single, had a rockabilly "Barn Dance" live radio show each Tuesday night, where artists

such as James, LesLee "Bird" Anderson, Rosie Flores, Rose Maddox, Jackie Lee Cochran, and a lot of other older and newer California-based rockabillys performed semi-regularly each week. Ronnie Mack has certainly done his part to keep rockabilly goin' strong in Los Angeles over the past ten years or so, actually right up to the present.

James Intveld just kept pluggin' away in both recording studios and motion pictures through the rest of the 1980s. In 1990, film producer John Waters, who was born in Baltimore, planned to use James in his latest major motion picture about teenage America in the 1950s. James had the lead role sewed up in this 1990 film, *Cry Baby*, until John Waters decided at the last minute to use a young, basically unknown at the time actor by the name of Johnny Depp. But John Waters did use James on five songs that James had written to sing in the film and that would go on the soundtrack album that was released by MCA Records in 1990. Johnny Depp lip-sync'd to James Intveld's music and voice in the film, but James was given credit on the soundtrack. One of the songs got cut out of the film, but out of the eighteen songs on this soundtrack album and in the film, there were four songs by James Intveld. They were three rockabilly/rock 'n' roll songs and one doo-wop-soundin' tune. The song titles by James that were used were "King Cry Baby," "Doin' Time for Bein' Young," "High School Hellcats," and "Teardrops Are Falling." In 1991, James Intveld's different rockabilly arrangement on the song "Frankie and Johnny" was the title track for the remake of this major motion picture of the same title. The film starred movie superstars Al Pacino and Michelle Pfeiffer. So James has kept busy ever since '91, when I first got to see him perform at The Lincoln Center in New York City.

I saw him the next time out in Santa Barbara, California, when I was called up by Tony Balbinot of The Roadhouse Rockers, a California-based band who had a 45 release on Willie Lewis's great Denver-based Rock-A-Billy Records label. He called me up to ask if I'd come out to Santa Barbara to MC a benefit for the Santa Barbara Child Abuse Association with a long lineup of rockabilly artists. Besides all the great old and newer rockabilly artists on this show, my biggest highlights of this short four-day trip were gettin' to see LesLee "Bird" Anderson, who also worked hard to put on a second benefit at The Palomino Club in Los Angeles with all the rockabilly artists and bands, finally gettin' to meet Willie Lewis and his great wife Mary Lou, goin' out to meet and watch fifties rockabilly legend Jackie Lee Cochran perform at the Gaslight Club in Hollywood, and goin' to finally see Gene Vincent's star on the Rock Walk of Fame. James Intveld was the final highlight. These two benefits were held on Friday, February 7, and Sunday, February 9, 1992. Me and James were both glad to see each other again, but I was surprised to see James wasn't advertised on either benefit. I came to find out that it was because James was mainly there to play drums behind The Roadhouse Rockers. I thought at the time, "Man, here's the best rockabilly singer in this whole state, and the cat's back there playin' drums." But like LesLee "Bird" Anderson had been tellin' me for quite a few years by then, "That's just the way James is. He loves rockabilly music, and he's always happy to help anybody out when he can." What a refreshing cat to be around in this "git ahead of the next guy" crazy rockabilly world. I also did enjoy meetin' and watchin' perform other newer rockabilly acts I'd heard about, such as The Dave & Deke Combo and Big Sandy & His Fly-Rite Boys. Well, James

Forgettin' to Remember to Forget

*A*fter an offer from a Japanese record label, which I took, I decided after thirty years to go back in the studio and record five rockabilly tunes. Well, James Intveld was in Nashville, playin' guitar on a show Rosie Flores was doin', when I was goin' in to Erny Studios in a suburb outside Nashville called Whites Creek. James called me before I left the house and said he'd like to see me while he was in town, but his only free night was that night. So I told him to come on by the studio.

We'd laid down most, if not all, of the tracks and my main vocals by the time James got there, which was about 11:00 p.m. James brought Rosie Flores and Tammy Rogers, who's a really great fiddle player in Nashville and has worked with Randy Travis and others, with him that night. One of the songs I recorded, which I didn't particularly care for, though I'd written it, was called "A Whole Lotta Racket." I was usin' my buddy Laurence Beall's band, plus him, to back me up on this song I felt was stupid and had written as a joke. It was only at Laurence's insistence I recorded this song. I mean, I wanted to sing, but this was just a screamin'-on-key, wild, crazy song that I had arranged in an unusual way.

Anyway, James, Rosie, and Tammy walked in the studio, and Dave Erny, the owner, had what we done on this "Racket" song playin'. One of the first things out of James Intveld's mouth to me was, "Who's that singin'?" I told him it was this dumb rockabilly-type song I cut. James said, "You're kiddin', that's you singin'?" I said, "That's me screamin'." Then James said, "Yeah, but man, that's different." I said, "Don't tell me you like that." James just said, "I ain't never heard nothin' like it before, and sometimes that's a good sign." OK. I gave up. If the best pure, solid rockabilly singer in the 1990s liked it, I wasn't about to argue no more. I needed some backup (or call-back) vocals done on it, so all of us that were there overdubbed those. Rosie, Tammy, Pepper, Laurence Beall, Harry Fontana, James, Dave Erny, and myself all just had a good time layin' down those tracks.

I had some spare tape on my two-inch master reel, and I was more interested in recording a couple spontaneous, easy Elvis covers sung by James. So I picked two of my favorites that James knew well. Just James and Laurence Beall's acoustic guitar. James is a singer's singer, so that was all he needed. In two takes each, James gave me what I wanted just for my own listening pleasure. A solid version of the old Elvis Sun rockabilly tune called "You're a Heartbreaker" and the better side of Elvis's 1956 "Love Me Tender" 45, a song called "Any Way You Want Me." I was happier with those two songs than anything I'd done.

James asked me before he left that night if "A Whole Lotta Racket" was comin' out on a record label. I told him in Japan it was. James then said, "Well, after you get your mixes you want here, if you want to send me the master on that song and the other one you did tonight, I'll take 'em in the studio I work out of in Hollywood and put my own rhythm, lead guitar, and upright bass tracks on 'em, and I'm sure I know what you want, 'cause I know what you like, so I'll be glad to mix 'em for you." I told James, "Well, hell yeah. If you want to do that for me, I'll damn sure let you ride on with it, my man." Well, I sent 'em out to him, and James did a whale of a job of playin' and mixin', especially on the "Racket" tune. The Japanese loved it best out of the five choices I gave 'em, and even Willie Lewis out in Denver liked it so much he put it out as a 45 single here in the States. And let me tell you, by 1995, when Willie Lewis put something out on his Rock-A-Billy Records label, he had to really like it. So that just goes to prove what the hell do I know about the kind of rockabilly I believe I should do, anyway.

gave me a tape of a dozen songs that he'd cut that were unreleased, and still are to my knowledge, that he told me I was free and clear to release on my Renegade Records label if I wanted to. Me and James stayed in touch with each other quite a bit after those California benefit shows.

I saw James Intveld one time in 1994, when he came back here to Nashville to be the bass player in the band for the final movie the late young actor River Phoenix ever made. It was a major film called *This Thing Called Love.* A lot of this movie was shot right here in Nashville, about a strugglin' songwriter who was trying to be seen, heard, and get a break in country music during Songwriter Nights down at The Bluebird Cafe on Hillsboro Road.

I haven't spoken with James Intveld in awhile. But I know he's been keeping plenty busy. I've seen him in two recent motion pictures on HBO and Showtime cable TV. But the best surprise of all was when I went to Austin, Texas, in early 1996 for the South by Southwest Music Festival and the Spring Austin Record Fair & Convention. It was there I found a new, mostly all-original, twelve-song, limited-pressing album called *Introducing James Intveld,* plus an additional ten-song CD of the same name. These two pieces of top-notch rockabilly and pure hillbilly were released by the Bear Family Records label out of West Germany. They'd both come out only several months earlier in late 1995. This is all brand-new material, sung, mixed, engineered, produced, and with all instruments played by James Intveld himself. I bought these pieces off my friend Jürgen Koop. Jürgen is the U.S. distributor for all Bear Family records and products. He and his wife live in Austin. They're both good people. Jürgen told me James had been spending a lot of time over in Germany and other foreign countries over the past few months, and they loved James and his solid brand of rockabilly music over there. I'd known for the past couple years or so that James had been the lead guitarist for Phil Alvin's re-formed new Blasters band. But hey, I've always thought James Intveld would eventually become a big star one day. I'm still bettin' on it. It looks like maybe his time has finally really come, and it sure couldn't happen to a nicer still-young cat than James Intveld.

Ripsaw Records, Billy Hancock, and Tex Rubinowitz

As far as I was concerned then and even now, the most important record label that not only turned out rocka-billy 45 singles on a regular basis but also put out the best ones anywhere in the whole country between 1978 and 1981 during the rockabilly revival was Ripsaw Records, located in Easton, Pennsylvania, at that time. Although the two original partners in this small label only released seven records in less than a three-year period, all seven of those records should be in every rockabilly fan's collection today. The two original partners, Jonathan Strong and Jim Kirk, met at Haverford College, outside Philadelphia, in 1969, at a literary party for a mutual friend. They became good friends, as they shared the same musical interest, though Jonathan Strong lived in New York City and Jim lived in Easton, Pennsylvania, at the time. The two men formed Ripsaw Records in 1976 and released a 45 on a bluegrass group from the northeast sector of the U.S. that they liked, called Louie Setzer & The Appalachian Mountain Boys. Jonathan Strong was an attorney, and though he lived in New York City, he made trips to Washington, D.C., quite often on business. In 1977 he met Billy Hancock, who was workin' with Danny Gatton & The Fat Boys. Billy was the lead vocalist and bass player in the group. Strong was always a lover of all forms of roots rock 'n' roll and would always catch shows in various night spots in the D.C. area.

When Danny & The Fat Boys officially disbanded in 1977, Billy Hancock formed his own rockabilly band, called Billy Hancock & The Tennessee Rockets. Billy was one great vocalist, especially at gettin' a true feel for rockabilly music. His first band of Tennessee Rockets included Tex Rubinowitz as early as late 1977.

I have to say Billy Hancock did love rockabilly and all forms of roots rock 'n' roll, but by 1977, good ol' smilin' Billy sure did know his way around the music business. Every move he made, he made sure he'd come out on top of the deal. He was a shrewd cat you had to watch close if you were doin' business with him then (which I'm glad I wasn't). Jonathan Strong and Jim Kirk were, and I won't go into the details, 'cause it doesn't really matter because of the great music Billy recorded for their label, but ole Billy had Strong and Kirk runnin' in circles for awhile during 1977, from what Tex Rubinowitz has told me. Billy always seemed to have an answer for a lot of questionable things he was doin' in music at that time. What really does matter is that when Billy Hancock & The Tennessee Rockets recorded their first couple of songs during the summer of 1978 over at Bias Studios in Springfield, Virginia, which were released on Ripsaw Records in November 1978, Billy and his group nailed two of the best examples of pure authentic rockabilly music to be recorded in the Washington, D.C., area in at least twenty years. The two songs were "Rootie Tootie," which was written by Fred Rose and made famous by Hank Williams, and "I Can't Be Satisfied," an old blues tune written by Muddy Waters. Hancock was a tremendous arranger and put the old drivin', true-blue, authentic sound of mid-fifties rockabilly on 'em and mixed 'em in the great tradition of the mid-fifties original Sun sound of rockabilly music. He had the perfect voice for rockabilly of the true kind. He sure wailed on these cuts. The record not only did well in the Washington, D.C., to New York City areas, but also topped the independent rockabilly and rock 'n' roll charts in England and other countries in Europe where this sound of rockabilly was reachin' a really big cult audience, because promoters over there had started bringin' over the original Sun Records artists, such as Charlie Feathers, Warren Smith, Ray Smith, and others. This record received a lot of airplay on WHFS locally in D.C., as well as hundreds of college radio stations across the U.S. who were playin' more and more new rockabilly music because of the success Robert Gordon was havin' on the national scene.

I won't get into the sordid details, but Tex Rubinowitz and Billy Hancock parted ways in early 1979. Tex had his first 45 single released on Billy Hancock's Aladdin Records label a year after it was recorded, and he'd paid for it. But Billy didn't finally release it until the fall of 1978. By this time, Tex had no market for it, because when he recorded it, Tex had a group that did a little rockabilly, but primarily did old-styled hillbilly. When the record he paid for finally was released by Billy Hancock on Aladdin Records, Tex was fully entrenched in and becoming popular solely for his rockabilly music.

Ripsaw Records had Billy Hancock go back into Bias Studios and record another session of a number of songs for 'em in September 1978, even though they were yet to release "Rootie Tootie." By December 1978, Tex Rubinowitz decided to take it upon himself to go into Bias Studios and record five songs. Three rockabilly originals he'd written, plus two cover songs. By this time, Tex was really becoming popular on the local D.C. music scene. So, on December 16, 1978, Tex Rubinowitz went into Bias Studios and recorded "Bad Boy," "Red Cadillac and a Black Mustache," "Feelin' Right Tonight," "Hot Rod Man," and "Ain't It Wrong." The latter three Tex wrote. This session was produced by Tex, his late mother (who, way back in the 1930s, had been a

singer) Arthurea B. Rubinowitz, and Billy Hancock. Tex used Billy Hancock & The Tennesse Rockets to back him up.

Tex paid for these sessions and offered them to Ripsaw Records. After Billy Hancock's first 45 was released in late November 1978, Ripsaw next released a 45 on Tex. This time with a picture sleeve. From this time on, the rest of their 45 releases through 1982 would all have picture sleeves. "Rootie Tootie" and the 1976 bluegrass 45 had not. The two songs they chose to release for Tex's first 45 single were "Bad Boy" on the A side and "Feelin' Right Tonight" on the B side. According to Jonathan Strong of Ripsaw Records, this 45 was released in March 1979. Well, by this time, Tex had split from Billy Hancock & The Tennessee Rockets and formed his own band, which he decided to call Tex Rubinowitz & The Bad Boys. "Feelin' Right Tonight" by Tex Rubinowitz has been the only true authentic rockabilly song since the 1950s I've ever heard that not only had the pure, raw feel in the music but also had the words that were so important to me that described every single emotion I felt deep in my soul that was sayin', "Yeah, this is exactly what the hell true rockabilly is all about, always has been and always will be." All I had to hear was the fire Tex breathed when he sang the words to that song.

Tex went on and recorded and had released another eight more songs through 1985. He only had a total of ten songs released on records through that period, but he recorded over a dozen others in the studio that he didn't feel were up to his standards in rockabilly music to have released, but I can tell you, they were all great. Tex's best-known song the world over, and the biggest seller Ripsaw Records ever had, was on his second and only other release on the label. The song is called "Hot Rod Man," which he also wrote. Ripsaw released this record in October 1979, with a great rockin' rockabilly B side that Tex also wrote, called "Ain't It Wrong (When You Don't Do Right)." The song "Hot Rod Man" has been heard in major motion pictures and been licensed on various major and independent rockabilly compilation LPs and CDs. It still receives airplay on radio stations around the world to this day. The first record label to jump on "Hot Rod Man" was Silent Records in London. They released "Hot Rod Man" on a 45 single in the spring of 1980. A year later, in 1981, the B-Sharp Records label out of Montreal released a 12" EP album of all four of Tex Rubinowitz's songs that Ripsaw had previously released. Also, by the spring of 1981, the Big Beat Records label in Paris, which was owned by Jackie

Chalard, released a 10" mini-LP that contained all five songs, including "Red Cadillac and a Black Mustache" of Tex's on it. With the release of that five-song album on Big Beat, Tex did a tour of France over the summer of 1981 with fellow Ripsaw Records artist Billy Hancock, who also had ten songs released on his own Big Beat 10" LP at the same time in 1981. Don't get me wrong now, Billy Hancock had his own big success during this period between 1978 and 1981. It's just that by late 1979, Tex Rubinowitz & The Bad Boys were "the" rockabilly group that was leadin' the pack with Tex's brand of rockabilly music.

Billy Hancock's other three 45 singles for the Ripsaw label all deserve to be in every rockabilly fan's collection. "Boogie Disease" b/w "Knock Kneed Nellie" (1979), "Miss Jesse Lee" b/w "I'm Satisfied" (1980), and "Redskin Rock 'n' Roll" b/w "Lonely Blue Boy" (1980) are all some of the best examples of rockabilly music in its rawest and truest form that you'll want to hear. These eight songs (includin' "Rootie Tootie" b/w "I Can't Be Satisfied" from 1978), along with six others unreleased at that time, were all licensed to the well-distributed Solid Smoke Records label in California in 1981 to make for one great rockabilly album by Billy Hancock & The Tennessee Rockets.

During the summer of 1980, Tex took an unknown local female artist into Bias Studios and put his band of Bad Boys behind her, and he paid for and produced one of the first (if not the first) most scorchin' two-sided rockabilly 45 singles by a female artist you could hear at that time. The two songs were Tex's original song "Feelin' Right Tonight" and the Wanda Jackson 1950s classic "Fujiyama Mama." The artist who had a great voice on these two songs was a local girl by the name of Martha Hull. It was Martha Hull's only original great rockabilly 45 single, and it was released by Ripsaw Records in April 1981. Tex was the reason these two songs were so artistically great. Martha Hull had a great voice for rockabilly music, but it wasn't in her blood. This record was only a launchin' pad for her in the D.C. music scene, where she mainly concentrated on singin' early sixties female Shirelles and Angels type cover songs in her own group she called The Dynettes.

That Martha Hull 45 single was really the final release the two original partners of Ripsaw put out. Although there was one more that came as close as you could get to bein' released. That one was scheduled to be released in the fall of 1981. They had labels for both sides and a picture sleeve for it printed up. It was the two songs

Charlie Feathers had produced on Johnny Seaton when me and Pepper took him to Charlie's studio in Memphis during late July 1980. The single "Uptown" b/w "Git With It" remain unreleased to this day, as the two partners of Ripsaw Records dissolved their partnership, mainly because, as Jonathan Strong recently told me, "We still wanted to remain friends."

This was the end of Ripsaw Records' greatest artistic period and success. But by no means was it the end of Ripsaw Records. It was also not the end for either Tex Rubinowitz or Billy Hancock. The two partners came to a mutual agreement on the recordings they owned jointly, with Tex Rubinowitz becoming partners with Jim Kirk, and Billy Hancock staying on to record an album on the Ripsaw label. Jonathan Strong retained the name and logo of Ripsaw Records, and he went on to release a 45 single on a Detroit-based rockabilly group called Kid Tater & The Cheaters in 1982, and two later rockabilly albums. One was by Billy Hancock in 1985, titled *Wanted: True Rock 'n' Roll,* and the second was by a local Washington, D.C., artist I did some booking and producing for between 1987 and 1990, by the name of Bobby Smith. Bobby's 1987 Ripsaw rockabilly album was titled *Two Sides.* I should mention, when Jonathan took over the Ripsaw Records label in 1982, on the one 45 single release by Kid Tater & The Cheaters, that Donn Feleti of Relic Records in New York City was Jonathan's equal partner on that release. The only other release that Stong put out on Ripsaw Records was by a jump rhythm & blues group that was popular and playing the D.C. area a lot, called The Uptown Rhythm Kings. This was in 1990. It was a full album and also cassette release at the time on Ripsaw. By 1990, the heyday of authentic-soundin' original fifties-type rockabilly music had pretty much ended, at least in the D.C. area.

Besides Billy Hancock's great Ripsaw recordings, Big Beat Records in France released in 1983 an album of fifteen new songs by Billy that were produced by Washington, D.C., producer Spike Ostmann. This album holds up about as well as any of Billy's Ripsaw records. It's great rockabilly through and through. This is a rare album, at least here in the U.S., but if you can find it, you sure won't be disappointed. Every great rockabilly musician in D.C., just about, can be found somewhere on this album.

After this album, Billy Hancock went back to Ripsaw in 1985 and had I guess what was his last rockabilly album put out. Billy has continued to work pretty consistently in the D.C. music scene since then, plus continue to record all forms of roots rock 'n' roll. Billy is just a plain all-around lover of all kinds of music. I think there'll always be someplace you'll find Billy Hancock playin' around D.C., even in the year 2006, when he turns sixty years old. Billy just seems to keep on rockin'.

Tex Rubinowitz, on the other hand, hasn't done a live show since June 2, 1990, when he and his band performed at the final rockabilly festival I promoted shortly before I moved to Nashville. But in 1985, Tex finally released his one and only full-length album on a label called No Club Records that Tex and his partner Jim Kirk (formerly of Ripsaw Records) decided to put out. The album is titled simply *Tex Rubinowitz,* and it's a pretty hard album to find today, but if you do see it, grab it up, 'cause every single song on there is flat-out solid authentic rockabilly at its best. There are only nine songs on this 12" LP, but there's not a filler cut on the whole album. There's the four original songs that were released as two 45 singles on Ripsaw Records in 1979, "Feelin' Right Tonight," "Bad Boy," "Hot Rod Man," and "Ain't It Wrong," plus five songs Tex recorded between 1981 and 1984 with Eddie Angel on lead guitar. Eddie and Tex co-wrote one of these songs, called "No Club (Lone Wolf)," which Eddie Angel's early-1990s Nashville-based rockabilly band, The Planet Rockers, which featured Sonny George on vocals, re-recorded for a 45 single that came out on No Hit Records in England during the early nineties. Three of the other four songs were originals Tex wrote during the early eighties. They were "Rock 'n' Roll Ivy," "Missy Ann," and "No One Left to Turn To." The one other cut was a cover tune written by country songwriter Wayne Walker that Tex put a rockabilly arrangement on, called "Flood of Love." I'd like to say this sole album by Tex Rubinowitz could be called "Tex Rubinowitz's Rockabilly Best," but the truth remains that Tex has a whole lot more songs that are not only up to par with these, but some that are even better.

Tex believes in true-blue authentic rockabilly music as much as I do to this very day. He can put it across in the studio or live on the stage with total magic, 'cause he really cares about it. It was Elvis's early Sun recordings and then the Charlie Feathers records that turned Tex on and got rockabilly in his soul to where he developed his own style of true rockabilly with a real feel like nobody else that ever came out of the Washington, D.C., area, or practically anyplace else for that matter, that I ever heard. Tex is definitely a true artist in rockabilly music, and he touched and influenced so many rockabilly fans and musicians with his small output of recordings like

not many others have since 1977 when the so-called rockabilly revival began.

Tex has been one of my closest friends in this crazy music business, who's always been there for me. Jonathan Strong, Margie Coffy, and LesLee "Bird" Anderson are a few others. Good friends are hard to find these days. Tex actually had quit doin' live rockabilly shows by late 1988. His obligations to his family have always come first. By late 1988, his mother was in failing health and was in a nursing home, plus his father was up in age into his eighties by then, and his brother Ben had some terrible health problems that kept him in and out of the hospital on a regular basis. Since Tex's mom passed away in 1990, he's had to devote his time to taking care of his dad and his brother Ben, who has trouble gettin' around at times. But even though Tex had his personal problems at home, he still found time to perform at four big rockabilly festivals I promoted before I left Maryland between August 1989 and June 1990. Three of 'em were benefits for Charlie Feathers. Tex Rubinowitz is still in demand today to perform rockabilly music, and I know Tex has still got that "thang" better than most young or older rockabilly artists. That magical relationship that connected with his audience. Tex never did make it in the big time, but he was sure out there givin' his all for a lot of years for the sake of other people's enjoyment. If you never saw Tex do a live show between 1979 and 1990, you missed the best local rockabilly artist who ever got up on a stage in Washington, D.C., during those years.

Danny Gatton

Now this is, without a doubt, the most difficult part I have to write and tell you about in this entire book. This is the story of my business and personal relationship with the only musician I ever totally learned to have complete respect for his artistry plus learned to love as a real friend who never asked anything of me in this business, and I in turn did the same for him. His name is Danny Gatton. I know now Danny is referred to as the late Danny Gatton, which to this day still seems unbelievable to me. But here goes.

I had heard of Danny Gatton and his band Danny & The Fat Boys during the mid 1970s, when they were playin' the club scene in Washington, D.C. Danny formed this group in 1973. They performed all forms of roots rock 'n' roll, from jazz to blues, western swing to forties jump boogie woogie, as well as hillbilly and rockabilly music. I didn't actually meet Danny until sometime in 1979, when there was a Danny & The Fat Boys reunion at a local D.C. nightspot. Even though Danny & The Fat Boys played occasional live club shows in the Washington, D.C., area through at least 1981, the group parted ways officially by late 1977. I was friends with Billy Hancock, the lead vocalist and bass player with The Fat Boys, who was then goin' strong on the rockabilly scene. Billy had started his own independent record label in the early seventies, called Aladdin Records, in the Washington, D.C., area. Aladdin was the first to release the Danny & The Fat Boys 45 in 1975, and the group's only LP in 1976. When Billy introduced me to Danny in 1979, he seemed like a nice guy. But the Danny & The Fat Boys band just played way too many long instrumentals of blues and jazz for my taste back then. I do have to say, when I heard Danny's version of "Mystery Train" that night, it amazed me, as I felt his guitar work on it was far better than Scotty Moore's.

By 1977, Danny Gatton was already a huge guitar wizard of legendary status all over the Washington, D.C., area. After The Fat Boys, he went on to form his Redneck Jazz Band. Danny released his first album on his own NRG Records label, called *Redneck Jazz,* in 1978. He and his new band, which now included Evan Johns on vocals and bass, packed every nightclub they played.

I wouldn't see Danny Gatton play again until 1981. This time, though, he was playin' in D.C. with Robert Gordon, and Danny was tearin' up his guitar like nobody in the world could on rockabilly music that I loved. I had the album that Danny played on with Robert Gordon and liked it better than any other album Robert had ever done. I told Danny on that night that I felt out of the three guitarists Robert had used up to then, he was without a doubt the one that delivered the best feel on his guitar licks on this great rockabilly music. Danny shrugged my comments off and just smiled and said, "It's no big thing. It's fun to play, but it's easy. I'm here for the bread. I'd really rather be playin' my own music. But the dough's just too good to pass up." I asked Danny, "Would you be interested in doin' some studio work later on when you're in town, playin' rockabilly music?" Danny answered, "Sure, as long as you don't have some hot-shot producer tellin' me how to play it." I told him I'd be producing it, and I liked what I heard him do with Robert, so there wouldn't be any problems between us. Danny gave me his phone number and told me to call him.

I did call him a couple of times, and I told him about this artist by the name of Johnny Seaton who I believed

had a shot at makin' it, and he was comin' back from California to the D.C. area around Christmas 1981, and I wanted to try some rockabilly tunes on him, and I'd set that up later and let him pick the musicians he wanted to use who could play this stuff with the right feel to it. I told Danny I'd give him a free hand to do whatever he wanted, but I had certain styles of Scotty Moore's, Cliff Gallup's, and James Burton's I'd like him to bring into his playin', even if he stretched it farther than they had. Danny liked that idea and said, "Billy, I think we can work together real good. Why don't you set something up before this kid gets back, where me and you can go in the studio and just jam on some of this old stuff?" I said to Danny, "Well, man, I don't really sing. I used to twenty years ago, but I ain't about to try it at this late date." Danny said, "Aw, come on, I'll be home all next week and all I'm plannin' on doin' is workin' on this '32 Ford coupe I got, so set somethin' up and call me back." I told him OK.

I set up a four-hour session the next week, which was the last week of November 1981. Me and Pepper met Danny at the studio. He'd brought two guitars, a bass, and his amps and other doo-dads he had to get the sounds and effects he wanted. So, for a little over four hours, me and Danny and Pepper had a damn good relaxed time. No pressure. Just fun. I persuaded Danny to play for the first couple hours before he finally got me to sing, but all three of us had a great time. I told Danny when we were finished, that would be the last time he'd ever hear me sing. Danny just laughed and said, "There's a hell of a lot worse-soundin' ones on the radio than you, Billy." I paid Danny what we'd agreed on and told him I'd call him in a couple months when I had a session date for Seaton after he got back in town.

Now that's the first studio experience I'd ever had with Danny Gatton, and this guy was not only one great guitar picker, but also my kinda down-to-earth guy. Me and Pepper liked Danny right from that day on.

My first encounter with Johnny Seaton had been back in March 1978. He was a teenage Elvis imitator at the time, performing at the community center in Beltsville, Maryland. My friend Fred Jennings, who was the director of the community center, twisted my arm to come see this kid, so, reluctantly, I did. I was completely anti-jumpsuit Elvis imitators at the time, but what I saw up on that stage was an eighteen-year-old kid that maybe only had raw talent then but knew how to give his audience what they wanted. Plus I could see he had charisma and one hell of a good voice, although he reached too far at times. The main thing I knew back then was he was way too good to be wearin' a jumpsuit and singin' "Girl Happy." "My Way" and the silly movie songs were about all he knew at that time, 'cause he was so young and had only seen Elvis's sixties movies on TV.

A short time later, me and Pepper were invited over to this kid's house by his parents, after I'd had a couple conversations by phone with him and his mother, for dinner one evening. I liked this kid and his brother Al Jr., sister Loretta, mother Suzanne, and especially his dad, who was a hard-workin' union plumber at the time. After that night, I decided to use him for a couple "Tribute to Elvis" shows, which were really Charlie Feathers rockabilly shows. I went over and had him sign a contract for the two nights, as I had already done with Charlie, and the shows were a real big success.

This young guy had so much charisma and talent, it was unbelievable. Plus, we had good times together just partyin' between March 1978 and the fall of 1980, when he went to Hollywood, hopefully to make it big.

With everything Seaton had goin' for him throughout those years, I just couldn't understand why he hadn't made it by 1982. It was only in the fall of 1981, when he called me from California and told me he had to come back and was bein' (accordin' to him) forced to get married, settle down and get a real job, and get this music foolishness out of his head, that I stepped in and said, "Look, I'll put a record out on you." I told him I'd keep him goin', 'cause he was too damn talented not to have at least a real chance, but he'd have to sign a contract with me and do everything my way, and that we were gonna do rockabilly music from here on. Well, Johnny was more than happy to hear that and readily agreed.

When Johnny Seaton returned from California, the first thing he had to do was marry the girl he'd been goin' with since high school, as she was now seven months pregnant. He started workin' doin' side plumbing work with his father that January of '82, but much to the dismay of his new wife, he spent two to three nights a week over at my house pickin' out songs from my collection of about 18,000 records at the time that he was gonna record in the studio.

I took Johnny to meet Danny and gave him the date for the first session. Danny told me it was fine with him, and Evan Johns, who I knew at the time and was a popular act doin' some rockabilly songs of his own in his sets in D.C. clubs at the time, had told Danny for me to give

him a call, and he'd play both upright rockabilly slappin' bass, plus electric bass where needed on certain songs we wanted to do. So I called Evan and worked out the financial arrangements, which I'd already done with Danny. Danny liked Johnny a lot, right off the bat. Of course, me and Pepper did also, back in 1982.

Me and Pepper and Johnny met Danny Gatton and Evan Johns at the studio on February 23, 1982. Danny and Evan both knew the deal on this first Johnny Seaton session. No matter how long it took, we didn't come out of that studio until we got the four songs laid down and I was satisfied with the guitar, bass, and drum tracks. The drummer, John Britton, who also did a lot of the engineering on the session (and who was one terrific engineer), also knew this. The songs we recorded were Charlie Feathers's "Git With It," Buddy Holly's "I'm Gonna Set My Foot Right Down," Roy Orbison's "Uptown," and one I had written called "Don't Play With Me." I gave Johnny writer's credit on "Don't Play With Me" and other songs through 1987, because I knew major labels, where I was trying to place Seaton then, wanted to hear and sign artists that wrote their own material.

Well, you wouldn't think it would take fifteen hours to lay down these four tunes, especially with musicians that were total pros, but it really did, mainly because Danny Gatton was a total perfectionist (like no other I've ever known) when it came to layin' down the guitar parts he had in his genius mind on these, basically what most would consider relatively simple rockabilly tunes. Danny Gatton was not only one of the most special people I became close to in the music business, but Danny was also *the* most special all-around musician I ever knew, besides bein' the world's greatest guitar player. Every time Danny did a session for me, from the beginning until December 1988, although he was only gettin' one price, whether it was as low as $50 for the night or up to $200 for the night, Danny wanted every song he played on to be the complete best. Danny wanted it because he felt and loved the music so much. I've seen that gleam in his eye when he was really pleased with something he'd done for me on a song. That's what set Danny apart from all the other lesser and some inadequate guitar players I worked with. Don't get me wrong; there were many musicians who were great to work with, but there were just as many or more who were not. Danny Gatton, who like I said was the best of all, just happened to be the most special of all. That's why I always used him more than any other guitarist. Right up until the final time I was with Danny, this guy never raised his voice to me except when I was tellin' him about something he especially wanted to hear, and as usual my story was long and drawn out, and Danny would sometimes yell, "Damn it, Billy, will you get to the point?"

But anyway, everyone involved with that first long session was happy with it. Especially Johnny Seaton and me. So a couple days later, I went back in the studio and mixed the two songs I wanted to use for Johnny's first 45. They were the new version with Danny of "Uptown" b/w "Git With It." (As I mentioned earlier in this chapter, Charlie Feathers had produced these two songs on Johnny Seaton in July 1980 for a single on Ripsaw Records that was never released.) I had a good friend of mine at the time, who I hope reads this and contacts me, Jeff Allen, do a photo shoot at his house for the picture I used on the picture sleeve of what would be Seaton's first released 45 single. I put things in motion fast. By the first week of March 1982, I had the master mix sent to Sun Plastics in Newark, New Jersey, and I had Seaton's first 45 single out by May 1, 1982, on my Renegade Records label (which I named for the outlaw motorcycle gang I organized back in the sixties, which in turn I named after the rock 'n' roll/rockabilly instrumental group from the 1959 teen flick *The Ghost of Dragstrip Hollow*). All of March and April 1982 was spent at Timmie Norton's house, in his garage, rehearsing Johnny's first original music band. Those were two tough months, 'cause some of those early musicians just weren't up to par, and it was a slow process learnin' enough songs to put a set together. But by the time the 45 single came out on May 1, 1982, Johnny and the band had about a dozen songs that were good enough to perform. During May and June they played their first gigs and kept practicing.

June 1982 was a busy month, 'cause I had two recording sessions set up to finish an album I was plannin' on releasing by the end of 1982 on Seaton, called *Uptown*. One of the sessions I was once more using Danny Gatton and Evan Johns, along with John Britton on drums. This one was another marathon fifteen- or sixteen-hour session. We wound up gettin' four more great rockabilly tunes on this one also.

I needed or at least wanted to get four more songs so I'd have a completely solid twelve-song album. I had a final session booked for which I'd originally planned to use Danny Gatton and Evan Johns, but by then, there were a couple of the guys in the group grumblin' and whinin' to Johnny that they had put in almost three

months of hard work at rehearsals, and they felt it was owed to them by now for their dedication to him, that they should get to play on this last session, so they'd get their names on the upcoming album. Though I thought it was crybaby bullshit, which it was, and I lived to regret it, I let Seaton talk me into it. But I learned a real good lesson. From then on out for the next five and a half years, I was usin' Danny Gatton on whatever I was gonna pay for in the studio.

At the end of June I mixed all eleven songs for the album (we only managed to get three songs out of that session with the band, which lasted two days), including remixing the two we had out on 45. This was a difficult time, not only for Johnny, but for me also, because his older brother, Al Seaton Jr., had just been killed in a motorcycle accident. But when the album was all completely mixed, we had these eleven songs soundin' in the truest, rawest form of rockabilly that I loved so much. Sure, it was all done with the new current studio equipment, but with John Britton's help and players such as Danny Gatton and Evan Johns, it made for one powerful album at the time. Johnny Seaton never sounded better or more raw, clean, and honest in his sound, and from what many of his former rockabilly fans told me in the late eighties when Seaton moved away from rockabilly music and roots rock 'n' roll in general, he'd never sound this good again.

Between July 1982 and August 1987 I was able to achieve a lot for Johnny Seaton and had a lot of personal satisfaction from it. I got him into the DC-101 FM Battle of the Bands in the fall of 1982, and he won the $10,000 first prize. I licensed the *Uptown* album to Rockhouse Records in Holland in October 1983, which led to a six-show, eleven-day tour of Holland and England in early April 1984. I also sent this album to Rounder Records in late 1983, and I got him a one-album deal with them by early 1985. The album on Rounder came out in May 1986, but by that time Seaton was almost ready to go back to the Elvis imitator bit, 'cause there was a lot more money in it, and he was and probably still is the very best at it.

Danny Gatton believed so much in Seaton and his talent, he wound up doin', and bein' advertised as a special guest on, 183 live rockabilly shows Seaton did during that period. I got every one of 'em logged on the calendars I still have for this period. Danny also spent a total of thirty-nine days and nights in several D.C.-area studios, where I kept recording new tracks on Seaton, between February 23, 1982, and March 28, 1986. I wound up gettin' a total of ninety-seven songs with Danny Gatton on all guitars and also doin' a lot of great bass. These were all sessions specifically for new material for Johnny Seaton. This doesn't count other artists such as LesLee "Bird" Anderson (from November 1985 to January 1988), Robert Gordon (1983), and Todd Monroe (1988) that Danny did work for me in the studio on.

What ended Johnny and Danny's relationship was after I'd finally come to my senses and realized all the money I'd taken out of either mine or my wife's pockets by the end of 1986 by havin' to pay musicians a whole lot of extra money when we didn't make enough at live shows to go round had to come to a halt. So at the end of 1986, I told Johnny I'd still book certain shows and promote 'em to his fans with the flyer I continued to mail out through August 1987, to a mailing list of 200 fans of Seaton's that I'd collected by that time. I'd only do this if he wanted me to. He said of course he did. I said the two things I would not do any more were put together his set lists and pay the musicians at the end of each show like I'd done up to that time. Johnny told me, "That's no problem, I'll pay 'em." But he had trouble doin' so, and by early 1987, Danny refused to work with him anymore.

Me, even though my top priority was LesLee "Bird" Anderson and her career, I hung in there until, to be specific, October 18, 1989. Johnny was still under a personal management contract to me in writing until May 5, 1988. After March 1988, I didn't have to invest any more money into his career for "our" benefit, because by that time I'd put him over the top. I negotiated a deal and got him into the starring role of the biggest money-makin' road-touring show on the life of Elvis Presley, called *Elvis: An American Musical*. It toured for over sixteen straight months. This led to many other things, including the Andrew Lloyd Webber show *Joseph and the Amazing Technicolor Dreamcoat* on Broadway, which Seaton had second billing to Donny Osmond in.

But with all the frustrations I went through for so many years, devoting all my hard work and money to trying to make him an original music artist (which was a huge mistake I've never made again), I still have to say, "Thank you, Johnny Seaton." Thank you, for if it wasn't for you, I would have never become good friends with great real true artists such as Sleepy La Beef (who Johnny opened for several times), and especially thanks for allowing me the privilege of working with and producing the greatest real person in the music business. That person was Danny Gatton.

Forgettin' to Remember to Forget

*B*etween 1981 and 1987, I hired Danny Gatton a lot for either live shows or studio dates to back up or record with artists I was producing and managing at that time. The two main ones being Johnny Seaton and LesLee "Bird" Anderson. I don't think a week went by during that period that me and Danny weren't in touch at least by phone or rehearsing new material, which he hated, 'cause Danny could hear a song one to three times and he'd have his parts down and know what he wanted to do with the song, while the other musicians needed a whole lot more rehearsing.

By early 1985, me and Danny had become close friends, and I was down at his house in Accokeek, Maryland, and we took a break from rehearsing when the drummer, Dave Elliott, said to Danny, "Did you call Fogerty's people back yet?" Danny said, "Naw, I forgot. I got too busy tryin' to finish up this car." We were rehearsing out in Danny's garage where the old vintage cars he loved to restore were. So I said to Danny, "You gotta be talkin' about John Fogerty. What were you supposed to call him back about?" Danny just said casually, "Oh, Jan [Danny's wife] said Fogerty's people at Warner Brothers called me a couple weeks ago and wanted me to do this long tour with Fogerty in the spring and summer to promote his new album." I said, "John Fogerty wanted you to back him up and you didn't call back?" Danny said, "I got too many things to do around here. I can't be gone that long. It's no big deal. I guess I should-a called back. I just forgot." That was just Danny, though. He had been on the road and earned good money with Roger Miller, Robert Gordon, and others, but he was happier workin' on his old cars or playin' in the local bars around D.C.

After 1988, I didn't get to spend too much time with Danny until early 1990, when after I'd seen a couple rockabilly bands, Virginia & The Blue Dots and Go Cat Go, at The Bayou Club, I stopped in about one o'clock in the mornin' when he was ending his show at Club Soda, another D.C. club, that I had to pass by on my way home. Danny and his then band, called Funhouse, were finishin' up their last set when I got there. I hadn't seen Danny in almost a year by that time, and when he finished his set, I gave him the first three *Rockabilly Revue* magazines I had out at the time. Man, you'd-a thought I gave him the best vintage guitar magazine ever published, over his delight when he looked through 'em. Danny introduced me to Bill Kirtchen (who was sittin' in with Danny that night). Danny showed those magazines to Bill and started tellin' him how I knew more about rockabilly music than anybody. I told him it was all no big deal, I wasn't makin' any damn money. I remember Danny sayin', "Yeah, but all the stupid asshole writers that are don't know one-tenth of what you know. I'm gonna love readin' these." Well, before I left, Danny made me promise to send him any future issues of *Rockabilly Revue* that I'd write. I told him I'd put him on the list.

I saw Danny next when I went up to Maryland with Billy Lee Riley and his band of Little Green Men. They were both on the same bill as headliners, playing the annual Blue Bayou Outdoor Festival in Upper Marlboro, Maryland. This was in July 1991. I saw him at another big show in June 1992 in New York City, where he was playin' at the time, and finally, in the summer of 1993, Danny came to Nashville to The Ace of Clubs to play to a sold-out audience.

When I saw Danny in 1991 and 1992, he seemed real happy about the way things were goin' and that his first major album on Elektra Records, *88 Elmira Street,* had done well enough to make it up into the *Billboard* pop album charts. But Danny was a homebody and was definitely not into the star treatment trip, although today his guitar work is idolized by millions of fans and musicians around the world. When me and Pepper saw him in June 1993, Danny wasn't pleased at all about the music business. He'd just started out on a forty-date-plus tour to promote his second, brand-new album for Elektra Records, *Cruisin' Deuces.* He told us, "You know I'd rather be playin' down the road from where I live at the local Moose Lodge than be here, 'cause at least I know I'd be in my own bed tonight. I'm out here on the longest road tour I ever been on in my life because the

damn record company says that's what I have to do to sell records and make it big. Well, how in the hell you gonna sell records if they ain't got 'em in the stores yet? This tour's comin' out of my pocket. Not the record company's. I'll lose $20,000 before this thing's over next month."

Me and Pepper really felt bad for all the frustrations he was dealin' with on that long tour. But Danny cheered up when I gave him the latest *Rockabilly Revue* #8 I'd written. Danny said, "Man, I ain't gotten one of these from you in awhile." I said, "That's the first one I've done in about a year. I've been in the studio down here a lot, and I'm only doin' one every year or so now." Danny said, "I've read every one of all the other ones you sent me. Damn, I'm gonna love this, 'cause I got a whole month or so left on this bus. Your stories crack me up so much, I can't lay them down. Hell, they're the best bathroom readin' I've got at home, and I mean that as a compliment, too." Comin' from my pal Danny Gatton, that was the highest compliment he could pay me. I told Danny, though, "All I do, man, is write things the way they happened when I was there and just put 'em in blue-collar language that everybody can understand." Danny just said, "That's why this stuff is better than all the glossy shit on the newsstands, Billy. Keep it up." Well, Danny wanted me and Pepper to stay all night for the show, but I told him we'd just hang out until he went on. I told Danny I came there to visit with my buddy, not to marvel at what I'd seen him do hundreds of times before on his guitars. Danny understood exactly what I meant. He knew that by then I respected the hell out of his great guitar work but didn't idolize him for that.

A month later, in July 1993, Danny got me and Pepper into the NAMM (National Association of Music Merchants) convention in Nashville. These conventions are for music dealers from around the country. The big music companies, such as Fender guitars, which Danny was associated with as they had recently put out a signature guitar on him, other musical instrument companies, and others associated with this kind of thing all had booths set up there displaying their wares. Danny was in his environment. He was like a kid in a candy store takin' us from booth to booth and pickin' up the newest models of guitars, banjos, basses, etc, and demonstratin' the sounds comin' out of 'em. He was havin' a ball. We saw other musicians, too, and stars such as James Burton, Chet Atkins, and Ricky Scaggs there that day, among others. But Danny took me by the Hal Leonard booth (Hal Leonard published the printed music from Danny's album *88 Elmira Street*) three times before he finally found one of the two guys he was lookin' for. One was Chris Albano, and the other was Brad Smith. They were both in the place somewhere but hadn't been there the first two times we'd stopped by with Danny. On the third go-round, Chris Albano was there, so Danny introduced me to him, and he told Chris I knew more about rockabilly music than anybody in the world, and they needed a real book out on this music, 'cause there wasn't any, and I was the only guy who could write the real story of all of it, so for them to give me a book deal. Chris told Danny it sounded great, and bein' as it was comin' from him, they would be glad to do it. Danny told Chris to be sure to tell Brad what he'd said about me and this book and for him to be sure to do it. Chris assured him that he'd tell Brad, and he thought it was a great idea, and their company would for sure work out a book contract with me. That's pretty much the way it happened.

I saw Danny up in Wheaton, Maryland, in November 1993, where he was on a benefit show, with his two original Fat Boys, Billy Hancock and Dave Elliott, backing him up. The benefit was bein' held for the Darren Lee Spears family over at Tornado Alley in Wheaton. Darren was only twenty-eight years old when he was murdered. On this night in November 1993, my highlight, besides seein' old friends like Greg Milewski, who MC'd the show (and who tragically committed suicide in early 1994) and old rockabilly fans like Vince Habel, who had made the long trip from Columbia, Pennsylvania, was watchin' Danny Gatton play a whole set of rockabilly music with his Fat Boys. It was great for both Vernon Taylor and Danny Gatton when Vernon got up on stage and sang "Mystery Train" with Danny backin' him, to my and everyone else's delight. Tornado Alley was really packed for a Sunday night. I took a few pictures of Danny and his two Fat Boys, and I told Danny I'd be startin' on this humongous undertakin' of writing this book pretty soon, but he'd gotten me the deal, and I wanted him to write the foreword to the book. I told him I'd come back up some time during the summer of 1994 and have him give it to me on a cassette tape. Danny just told me, "No problem. Just call me ahead of time." So by the time I'd finished the introduction for this book, I called Danny and told him I'd be in the D.C. area around Labor Day weekend, 'cause I was involved in a rockabilly show up in Whippany, New Jersey, and that I'd like to come down to his house in Newberg, Maryland, right after Labor Day and record his foreword for this book. Danny said, "Fine, I'll be home that whole week.

I gotta put a motor in one of my old cars during the day, but my nights are free, so we'll do it then."

I spent six hours down at Danny's on the evening of September 8, 1994. Me and him and my friend Margie Coffy had a great time sittin' in his garage and talkin'. After I got more than I even needed for the foreword to this book, I just let the tape keep rollin' while we both talked about better times and days in music. What me and Danny both kept goin' back to was how great a city Washington, D.C., was to grow up in back in the 1950s, when rock 'n' roll and rockabilly music was all brand-new. The only aggravated state I saw Danny in that whole night was when he said in total disgust, "Look at D.C. now, Billy. What a shit hole mess it is now, with all the drug pushers, and then the biggest one of all, who they nailed on video tape, Marion Barry, doin' crack, gets re-elected mayor again." I told Danny, "It's not just D.C., Danny. It's everywhere. It's just the times we live in, man." I can swear to you right now, twenty-some days before Danny took his own life on October 4, 1994, and I've got ninety minutes on cassette to back it up, Danny Gatton was in a happy, good-natured state of mind and relaxed, like the same guy I always knew. Oh, he told me about some personal pressures he was under, but nothin' he couldn't handle. He assured me of that. He was relieved he was out from under his contract with Elektra Records, as now he was doin' a lot of things in music he really wanted to do, and he didn't have to be away from home as much.

What he brought up once more was that he'd like me to give him the master tape of a song I had him do with LesLee "Bird" Anderson, called "Runnin' Wild," that he cut with LesLee and that I produced at Glass Wing Studios in late 1987 and released as the title cut on her 1988 Renegade Records album. Danny said his mother Norma Gatton wanted to release an album of all the greatest unknown and rare songs he'd ever recorded, and he wanted that one on there, 'cause he felt it was one of his finest moments ever on the guitar parts. Well, when he asked me for this, as he'd done a couple times in the past, I finally gave in and told him I'd make him a deal he'd like. Danny said, "Oh, goodie, I like deals I like the most." We both started laughin' then. I said, "I know you've always wanted that track, and you feel you can mix it better than the mix I got, which everyone still seems to marvel at today, so here's what I'll do. You listened to a few of the older early sixties songs I recorded with The Trend-ells, and you heard the four new rockabilly ones I've recorded in the past year or so, and you said I should keep on singin' rockabilly songs, 'cause I sounded better than most of the ones around you've heard, so what I'll do, Danny, is cut that 'Runnin' Wild' out of my two-inch master tape from that album, and I'll hand it over to you lock, stock, and barrel, and it'll be yours forever, if you do something for me." Danny said, "Spit it out." I said, "I'm comin' back up here right after New Year's Day in early January '95 on business for a couple weeks, and if you get a studio and a drummer and a piano player and take care of any expenses there for one eight- to twelve-hour day and go into the studio and play guitar and bass, unless you want to get a bass player, too, for two original new rockabilly/rock 'n' roll-type songs and three cover tunes I can handle real well that are easy in the same vein, then I'll hand 'Runnin' Wild's' master over to you forever." Danny looked at me and said straight out, without hesitation, "You got yourself a deal. I got the perfect studio, and the musicians ain't no problem. Plus, we'll cut this stuff hot, live, and right like it should be. We'll have some real fun, and we'll show 'em what rockabilly should really sound like." I said, "We'll produce it together. I'll bring a roll or two of two-inch master, and you pick up any other costs, OK?" Danny chuckled, "There won't be any other costs. The studio that's perfect for this owes me, and the musicians'll play with me any time, 'cause they owe me, too. Hot damn, I can't wait to get my paws on 'Runnin' Wild.' "

Well, I ain't about to get into the dozen or so stories from some of Danny's so-called friends on why he took his life a little over three weeks later, but he sure didn't have nothin' like that in his mind on this great night. I had given him a brand-new issue of *Rockabilly Revue*, where I showed him a story in it on him I'd wrote, titled "Danny Gatton: He Ain't Changed a Lick." He liked that, of course, and when he saw a picture of him and his right-hand man Jay Montrose I'd used in it, I remember he said, "Jay'll like that a lot."

When I got the call on the afternoon of October 5, 1994, that Danny Gatton had taken his own life the night before, I was stunned for days. Like Pepper said then, "Something ain't right about that, 'cause Danny was always the sensible one out of all of us." Danny Gatton was the greatest guitar player ever in all styles of music. Nobody could touch him. Just ask Vince Gill (who was at Danny's funeral), or even Eddie Van Halen, who once walked off the stage instead of tryin' to match Danny Gatton lick for lick on the guitar. No guitarist alive could do it. Danny Gatton, as I've written, was real

important to rockabilly music. Ask Robert Gordon or some of his fans. But what counts the most is I still miss him, his boyish, mischievous smile, his friendship, and his great sense of humor. The Washington, D.C., music scene has sure got a big hole in it since Danny moved upstairs. But I don't miss his guitar playin'. What I miss most is my friend, Danny Gatton.

Young Guns

I'll just close out this chapter by running down the list of young artists and bands I remember who were labeled rockabilly between the late seventies and the late eighties.

Bands and artists that came out of the New York City scene included The Zantees in 1979. Two members of this group worked hard and started *Kicks* magazine in '79 and later, by the mid 1980s, had Norton Records goin' strong for 'em. Those two members are Billy Miller, the lead vocalist, and Miriam Linna, the drummer. Billy and Miriam got married in 1989, and by that time they had a new group they called The A-Bones. They're still rockin' on with a zillion projects goin' on constantly. Both their groups played the Washington, D.C., club scene from 1979 until at least up to the time I moved to Nashville in December 1990.

Black lead vocalist Buzz Wayne with his group Buzz & The Flyers played the D.C. club scene quite often during 1979 and 1980. This group had one great 7" EP out in 1980, and they were quite a real solid rockabilly group for my taste. Though Buzz & The Flyers didn't seem to stay around very long, they were a solid group that could lay down some real good rockabilly music during 1979 and 1980. Their original 45 EP was on Sing Sing Records back in 1980, but over a decade later now, there's a recent full fourteen-song CD out on probably just about everything they ever recorded in a studio back then.

Also popular in New York City was a group that was called rockabilly in 1980 when their first album came out on the major label Polydor Records. The group was called Blue Angel. They only made this one album at the time, and the lead singer of the group Blue Angel was a female singer by the name of Cyndi Lauper. This wasn't that bad of an album when I heard it at the time. The rest of the members of the group were all guys. I could see why music writers at that time were callin' the group and the album rockabilly. Of course, everybody should know the rest. Cyndi Lauper went on to record three albums as a solo artist between 1983 and 1986 for

Portrait Records in New York City that all wound up scoring big and at the very top of the *Billboard* pop album charts. Cyndi also racked up two #1 45 singles and five others that reached the *Billboard* Top 10 charts during this period. One single release from Cyndi's first Portrait album, which was considered and bordered on modern-day rockabilly music, and entered the *Billboard* 45 singles pop charts on July 21, 1984, was called "She Bop." This song stayed on the *Billboard* pop charts for a total of eighteen weeks, peaking out at #3 in October 1984.

Kristi Rose & The Midnight Walkers were a popular act that was considered rockabilly by many in the New York City club scene, where they were a popular act that toured up and down the East Coast from 1983 through most of the 1980s. I went out and saw the group in late 1984 at The 9:30 Club in Washington, D.C. Pepper and Johnny Seaton went with me. We went mainly because the Rounder Records people had told us to check 'em out, because they had just signed this group to their label at the same time they signed Seaton, and they considered 'em rockabilly and felt we should see 'em. Kristi Rose & The Midnight Walkers' album was released around the same time Johnny Seaton's Rounder Records album was. That was in the spring of 1986. I'll talk a little more about Kristi Rose in the next chapter.

There were other groups, such as The Rockats, with lead singer Levi Dexter, who came out of the New York City area and were signed by RCA Records in 1983, shortly after The Stray Cats hit it big across the U.S. But this group had virtually no success. The Rockats had the look, but that was about it.

I remember goin' to see a group that I believe was from Scotland, called The Shakin' Pyramids. I saw 'em down at The 9:30 Club in 1981. One of the songs they had out and did that night was called "Hellbent for Rockin'."

In Washington, D.C., you always had some band, either old or new, throughout the 1980s who were layin' down some solid rockabilly music almost any night of the week. There was just about everybody from Billy Hancock to The Atomics. Which covers the beginning of the decade to the end of it. Alan Veatch was (and still is) a lead vocalist who writes most of his own songs, who in the early eighties had a group called The Love Hounds, later changed it to The Vibrotto Brothers, and then when a good part of that band became Kelly (Willis) & The Fireballs, Alan's next group was called The Reluctant Playboys. He's got a group that's supposed to be doin' pretty well here in the 1990s, but I don't know what they're called. I'm sure they're probably doin' some form of rockabilly, though. Laurence Beall & The Sultans drew pretty well in the mid eighties playin' rockabilly music. Singer Bob E. Rock teamed up with guitarist Eddie Angel for awhile during the early 1980s in the D.C. area. The Dimensions were another band in the early 1980s that had both a 45 and an album out and called themselves rockabilly. During the early 1980s there was an all-female group called The Seductones who were around playin' clubs in D.C. and doin' rockabilly for a short while. Between 1984 and 1988, D.C. singer/songwriter Ace Smith also had a rockabilly band playin' the local club circuit. Ace had one 45 release at that time that I know of, on the old Carl Perkins classic "Lend Me Your Comb." By the late 1980s, Virginia (Veatch) & The Blue Dots were playin' quite a lot of female rockabilly stuff in the D.C. area. These are only the bands and artists I can think of off the top of my head in the D.C. area. But all of the 1980s was really a great time if you wanted to hear rockabilly music live in a D.C. club..

.Hard-Rockin' Mamas of the Present Day

Well, as far as hip-shakin' honeys doin' what I considered even remotely close to rockabilly music, there just wasn't any left after the early sixties, at least on the charts. It would take over a decade before I'd once again hear rockabilly-styled music by rockin' ladies. The first one I took notice of by the early seventies was Linda Ronstadt, who I covered in Chapter 9. But I always kept up with country music, and had since the very early fifties, 'cause if it was great, I loved it also.

Tanya Tucker

The first gutsy, gritty little hard-rockin' chick I seen come along in the early seventies who really had a voice for rockabilly and a wild attitude to go right along with it was one who's still as wild as ever today. She played the game in Nashville since she was thirteen years old, but damn if she didn't manage to break all the rules and still stay on top for right at twenty-five years now. The wild chick I'm talkin' about is Tanya Tucker. T 'n' T should stand for Tons of Trouble and loaded with dynamite, 'cause that's what she's laid down for a lot o' years now. Today, if you see Wynonna Judd on a Harley-Davidson in Nashville, she's posin' for pictures, but if you see Tanya on one, she'll be roarin' down the street, and you best get outta her way, 'cause she's always been a firecracker and don't seem to care whether Nashville likes it or not.

A whole lot of Tanya's music for the past years comes under that broad scale now considered rockabilly. It always has with me, anyway. Now, I'm not gonna go through her whole life story and every song she's made. I'm also not gonna get off on all her great wild escapades over the years, which I enjoyed readin' or hearin' the inside dope on from friends I've had in Nashville through the years. What I'm mainly gonna try to stay on is the rockabilly sound Tanya put across with fire in her records over the past two decades. Tanya had the strong voice for rockabilly music right from the beginning.

Her voice is as gravelly, gritty, and gutsy as Wanda Jackson's was in the late fifties on a rockabilly-style tune. The main difference is, the times have changed and the Nashville musical backup wasn't as raw and real as it was on Wanda's great records. But the vocal delivery was damn sure there on Tanya's seventies, eighties, and nineties records.

Today in *Billboard* country music female history, Tanya Tucker ranks as the #6 top female artist. Only Dolly Parton, Loretta Lynn, Tammy Wynette, Kitty Wells, and Reba McEntire rank ahead of Tanya through 1995, and she's liable to surpass a few of those before she's through, as she's still under forty years old now and still goin' strong. I never considered Tanya Tucker a child star, even though she was only thirteen years old when she had her first hit. Tanya came along with her first string of Top 10 and then #1 country hits at the perfect time, just when the outlaw country movement was kickin' into high gear in '73 and '74. If ever there was a female country rock outlaw, it had to be Tanya Tucker. From Tanya's first Top 10 hit in the summer of 1972, "Delta Dawn," which then reached #6 on the *Billboard* country charts and #72 on the pop charts, and a year later Helen Reddy took it to #1 on the *Billboard* pop charts and sold a million copies, right on through her 1995 hit "Find Out What's Happenin'," Tanya Tucker made no secret about how much she loved Elvis and his rockabilly/rock 'n' roll style. In fact, her 1995 hit was a Jerry Crutchfield song that Elvis had originally recorded on July 22, 1973, at the Stax Recording Studio and released on his album *Raised on Rock/For Ol' Times Sake* in October 1973. "Find Out What's Happenin' " was one of Elvis's best rockin' seventies songs (of course, buried on that 1973 album), but Tanya Tucker did Elvis and the song justice on her growlin', rockin' 1995 *Billboard* country chart hit.

I got into Tanya's music early on, 'cause this young chick had a voice for rockabilly and rock 'n' roll. Even at thirteen and fourteen years old, she was singin' adult, sexy hit songs, such as her early 1974 #1 *Billboard* country chart and pop crossover hit "Would You Lay with Me in a Field of Stone," which was written by the wildest and craziest of all outlaw country rockers, David Allen Coe.

Tanya was first on Columbia Records in Nashville from 1972 to 1975, when she had her first string of consistent big country hits. In 1975 she moved over to the MCA Records label, where her hits kept comin'. But it turned out to be a good change musically. The first couple years, from 1975 to '77, she turned out good Top 10 country hits. The best of which were the rockin' "Don't Believe My Heart Can Stand Another You" in early '76 and "It's a Cowboy Lovin' Night" in the spring of 1977. That kind of stuff is just what Tanya Tucker was all about,

especially at this late date when she was about ready to turn eighteen years old. But MCA Records was still ridin' with that nice little sweet country girl image, especially on #1 songs like "Here's Some Love" in the late summer of 1976.

By late 1977, Tanya Tucker evidently had had enough of how Nashville and country music had been portraying her, and I'm sure she was tired of some of the boring songs they had her sing up to that time. Although to me, anything I've ever heard by her since she started is still worth hearin', because of the emotion she puts into her vocals. But Tanya broke away from the whole Nashville country music system and their way of doin' things for a couple years. Tanya's father, Beau Tucker, was her personal manager, and they formed a company called Tanya Inc. and hit the trail to California, where she got a couple

Forgettin' to Remember to Forget

I got to see Tanya Tucker in February 1974, as "Would You Lay with Me in a Field of Stone" was startin' to climb up the charts, down at The Stardust Nightclub in Waldorf, Maryland. Tanya had just turned fifteen years old, and I had a couple of her albums and had bought all her 45s. I'd seen her on TV shows such as "Hee Haw" and others, and most of the time she was in dresses or those frilly country laced gowns and other garb like female country singers wore back then. I just liked her voice a lot, 'cause it sounded raunchy, so that's why I went.

She was already a big star in country music as well as havin' several crossover pop hits, so The Stardust was packed full. We were lucky to even get a table towards the back, but you could almost see from anywhere. I wasn't prepared for what I was about to see. When the lights went up and she hit the stage, the whole place came unglued when her openin' number was a tear-it-up, scorchin' fifties rock 'n' roll song, and she was wearin' a tough-lookin' two-piece leather pants-and-jacket outfit. You couldn't hear yourself talk, and she sent the whole place through the roof. Of course, she went on to do her big country hits, but for the most part, this raunchy little young chick rocked, moved, and scorched out some of the best rockin' tunes you'd ever want to hear. That whole audience loved it that night. One song I remember her doin' was the grittiest, wildest version I'd ever heard by a chick of "Heartbreak Hotel" (which she'd record four years later, when she left Nashville for Hollywood studios and musicians).

After I'd watched her stage moves, which reminded me of Elvis at his greatest, I had to ask her a couple questions after her show. I'll admit that I felt kind of stupid waitin' in a real long line of fans to ask a fifteen-year-old kid a couple questions, at my age. I was right at thirty years old by then. Everybody else in line was waitin' for an autograph, which I had to get but really didn't care about at this point in my life. When I got up to the door of her bus and it was finally my turn to get an autograph, I asked young Tanya, "How come you don't record some of that great rock 'n' roll you laid on us tonight? You were dynamite." Tanya said, "I love performin' that stuff. It really fires me up, and I'm gonna record it someday, but right now my producer in Nashville wants me to record what's been doin' real good on the charts for me, and they're pickin' all my songs, but I'm gonna cut loose on that soon, 'cause I've always loved it." Then Tanya's eyes lit up when I said, "Girl, the way you move on stage reminds me of Elvis at his best. You got it down right in your own style. You must like him a lot, huh?" Tanya quickly replied, "I don't just like him. He's the greatest. I love him. Since I was a little girl, I've idolized Elvis. I watched every movie and TV special I think he ever did, and I used to imitate all his moves. That's how I learned to move on stage was watchin' Elvis over and over. Nobody has ever been able to move like he did." I heard all I needed to hear. I was sold on Tanya Tucker from that night on.

producers out there, Jerry Goldstein and Mike Chapman, to produce her two next MCA Records albums in 1978 and 1979. Both these albums were recorded, mixed, and mastered at studios in Hollywood, Burbank, Van Nuys, and Glendale, California. Most musicians on these two albums were West Coast musicians, with the exception of certain ones Tanya knew who came in to play on 'em from her home state of Texas. Phil Everly even sang backup on one song. Both these albums allowed Tanya to record the songs she wanted to really do, probably for the first time. You can hear she had control of how she wanted to do her music and the kind she was best at doin'. Which was souped-up, updated rock 'n' roll. Not that everything on these two albums was great, but overall the first one, titled *TNT,* had five solid, hard-kickin' numbers that fit Tanya's rockin' side real well. Three of those songs were Tanya's versions of rockabilly and rock 'n' roll cover songs by Elvis, Buddy Holly, and Chuck Berry. Her versions of their songs "Heartbreak Hotel," "Not Fade Away," and "Brown-Eyed Handsome Man" are all rock solid. Two new originals on the first album that were also good were "If You Feel It" and the only real country or country/rock-type song, "Texas (When I Die)." It was co-written by old fifties rockabilly Sun artist Ed Bruce, and it was the only Top 5 *Billboard* country hit from the album during the late fall of 1978. The flip side of "Texas (When I Die)" was the Buddy Holly tune "Not Fade Away," which debuted on the *Billboard* pop charts on January 20, 1979, reaching a peak position of #70, and stayed on the charts for four weeks. That was Tanya's eighth song that had crossed over and made it onto the *Billboard* pop singles charts since 1972. That was about it on the pop charts from this *TNT* album. Tanya's follow-up song, though, "I'm the Singer, You're the Song," reached #18 in the late spring of 1979 on the *Billboard* country charts. *Billboard* still had their "Bubbling Under the Top 100 Songs" charts at the time, and the flip side of "I'm the Singer, You're the Song" did manage to reach #103 on those charts. It was an upbeat rock-type song, "Lover Goodbye." I've always noticed that on the back of this album, Tanya thanked the people at MCA Records for believing in this album and the next one that would come out later in 1979 that was also recorded, produced, mixed, etc. in California.

So the nineteen- and twenty-year-old Tanya Tucker really wanted to rock and proved she could hold her own with the best of 'em at the end of the 1970s, but the pop chart numbers didn't really come, so as 1980 came in, she'd wind up back in the studios of Nashville once more. But even though Tanya's second West Coast album failed to even make a dent on either the pop or country *Billboard* charts, the title track, "Tear Me Apart," is one of my all-time favorite rockabilly songs. To me in 1979, and now, it's more rockabilly than any female artist out there today still recording what they call rockabilly. Musically, "Tear Me Apart" rocks real good, and I don't know if Tanya's ever recorded another downright mean, spittin'-fire, fast-paced rocker as good as this one. That one song is worth the price you'll pay if you can find that album. Another one called "Better Late Than Never" is also a great, solid rockabilly tune. What makes these two songs great are Tanya's gravelly "I'm gonna kick your butt" vocals. She's got more of a natural ability on songs like these than any country female artist on the charts today. Fans want it, too. That's why I believe Tanya "Trouble" Tucker is still chartin' records today on the *Billboard* country charts while the others who started hittin' big in country around '72 when Tanya did, that are also female, can't buy a chart hit today in country music.

During the early eighties, Tanya got hooked up with Glen Campbell romantically. Right before things turned ugly with Glen, Tanya was back in the Top 10 on the *Billboard* country charts in the fall of 1980 and the early months of 1981 with two more big hit songs, "Pecos Promenade" and "Can I See You Tonight." In the fall of 1980 and the spring of 1981, MCA Records (Tanya's label) and Capitol Records (Glen Campbell's label) released a couple of weak, sappy duets by Tanya and Glen that were so bad they wound up way in the bottom half of the *Billboard* country charts and dropped off quickly after only four- and five-week stays. Tanya's final new album for the MCA label in 1981 produced three Top 100 *Billboard* country chart hits, but only one barely made it into the Top 40 on those charts.

In the late summer of 1982, Tanya Tucker moved over to the Arista Records label and cut an appropriately titled album called *Changes.* The first 45 single they released had the old Johnny Ray classic pop hit song "Cry" on the A side and a new song called "Feel Right" on the B side. On October 16, 1982, Tanya's version of "Cry" made its debut on the *Billboard* charts. The song only reached #77 and dropped off after only four weeks. Well, quite a few country disc jockeys around the country had begun playin' the B side of this record, 'cause it was great. When that happened, the B side, "Feel Right," debuted on the *Billboard* country charts on November 27, 1982, and you know what, "Feel Right" not only stayed on the *Billboard* country charts longer than any song she had since her first hit in 1972, which was up to a string of thirty by then, but it also remained on the *Billboard* country charts longer than any of the forty-seven songs that reached the #1 spot by the *Billboard* country charts during the year of 1982. "Feel Right" had a run of twenty-three weeks on those charts. It only reached a peak position of #10 during the early months of 1982 on the *Billboard* country charts, but the disc jockeys kept on playin' it, and it took a long time to die. Why? It had a rock-solid mid-tempo rockabilly feel to it (I produced "Feel Right" on Johnny Seaton in 1983) and the grittiest vocalist in Nashville singin' it.

After two more lower-end Top 40 ballad hits from her *Changes* album, Tanya took a couple years or so off. When she came back in late 1985, she signed a new record deal with Capitol Records. Tanya's legions of fans hadn't forgot her. Hell, she was still only twenty-six years old then, and Capitol Records promoted her well during her six-year stay with their label. She was hotter on the country charts than she'd ever been before. Just the first three years alone, from February 1986 to February 1989, Tanya rolled off nine consecutive Top 10 *Billboard* country hits, with four of 'em reachin' #1, three others reachin' #2, and one other one reachin' the #3 position on those charts. Not too many female artists during those three years (if any) can claim those chart numbers in country music. Country music was changin' a whole lot between 1986 and '89, with the more real traditional sound that was always its heart and soul becoming real popular once again. But all this helped Tanya Tucker and some others that would come later.

Tanya's #1 and Top 10 hit streak continued right on well into the early nineties and even up to the present day. In 1992 she switched over to Liberty Records. This was her best move yet. She had a new producer in Jerry Crutchfield, and in 1992 and 1993 alone, she was allowed to deliver a pretty consistent string of #1 and Top 5 songs that definitely come under the rockabilly banner. I'm speakin' of songs like "It's a Little Too Late," "Some Kind of Trouble," "If Your Heart Ain't Busy Tonight," and "Tell Me About It," which was the perfect gutsy rocker for her and the great Delbert McClinton to turn into a #4 chart duet song.

Tanya Tucker has just kept on truckin'. She blew a lot of minds on Music Row when she became pregnant and gave birth to her first child several years ago, a daughter she named Presley Tanita. Tanya was unwed and wouldn't reveal who the father of the child was. That created a stir among the old-timers who were still

around trying to keep the country image clean. But Tanya has too many fans and still sells too many records for 'em to stop her now.

In 1994 Tanya Tucker and Little Richard had one song they sang on a million-selling compilation album titled *Rhythm Country and Blues,* where the two of 'em sung the Eddie Cochran rockabilly classic hit from 1958 called "Somethin' Else." Tanya really rocked and tore this song up with her gritty vocal performance. It's a shame she didn't get the whole song, 'cause any more Little Richard has become a joke and a parody of his once-great fifties days as a great rock 'n' roller. But again, Tanya really turned it on in her untouchable rockin' style. If a doctor told me I only had six months to live, and the entire major music world came to me and said, "Billy, you choose whoever you want to do a duet with you on your final song and we'll do it," well, to their surprise I'd say, "Tanya Tucker." I could then meet the Good Lord knowin' I'd rocked with the best that's left.

But back to reality. Tanya became pregnant again in late 1995 and I believe married the guy who fathered her child. I wish her all the best, and the guy she married also. I just hope he realizes he's married to one wild Texas tornado, a chick that's like a wild bronco bull that nobody before him has been able to stay on and ride the full amount of time to date. I really do hope this cat's the right one for both of 'em, though. I've listened to Tanya's newest album, which came out in early 1997, over and over. It's called *Complicated.* It's on Capitol Records, and I'll be damned if it ain't got more rockin' songs than ever, the best bein' the Troy Seals-penned "You Don't Do It, You Just Think About It." One tough track, I tell ya that!

Tanya Tucker's always been one hell of a rocker who's recorded more rockabilly songs since the seventies than anybody out of the Nashville system, and she's done 'em all great in my book. Ya know, Tanya's just like that little pink battery-operated rabbit you always see in those commercials on TV. She's somehow been able to knock down all the obstacles in the Nashville country music regulated and controlled system and keep doin' things. Like that little pink rabbit, Tanya just keeps on goin' and goin' and goin'.

Becky Hobbs

While I'm on the female artists who've recorded and had hits doin' rockabilly music out of Nashville from the 1970s on, I gotta go next with a fireball of energy by the name of Becky Hobbs. Becky's never achieved the high-level stardom in rock 'n' roll, pop, and country music that Tanya Tucker has throughout the years, but she's left her high-powered impact on rockabilly music on major labels in Nashville during the eighties and nineties.

Becky Hobbs was born in Bartlesville, Oklahoma. When she was fourteen years old, she was performing with a $25 acoustic guitar her parents had given her. The following year, she moved over to an electric guitar and formed her own all-girl band. Becky attended Tulsa University from 1968 to 1971, and while attending classes by day, she joined and performed with another all-girl group called Surprise Package at nights and on weekends. Then Becky left her home state and moved to Baton Rouge, Louisiana, in 1971, where she played piano and sang in a band called Swamp Fox. Her next move was to Los Angeles in 1973, where she wrote songs that were recorded by pop singers of that period. Helen Reddy, Shirley Bassey, and Jane Olivor were only a few that recorded her songs during the early and mid seventies.

In 1976 and '77, Becky had two pop-oriented albums released on RCA Records' subsidiary label Tattoo Records. Kim Carnes was one of the backup singers on these two albums, and although one album has the old Buddy Holly song "Everyday" on it, they're both straight pop albums of that era. In 1978, Becky took an offer from Mercury Records to record country and country/pop music, which she took because, as she told me in 1989, "I grew up listenin' to country music and fifties and early sixties rock 'n' roll. That's where my roots have always been. My older sister left home when I was still a young teenager, and she left me all her old fifties Jerry Lee Lewis and Gene Vincent records. So that's where the rockin' side comes into the music I do today, 'cause I listened over and over to all their great records." The move to Mercury Records proved relatively successful. Between December 1978 and March 1981, Becky had six songs of hers reach the *Billboard* country charts between the #44 and #95 positions. Some of these tunes were really pretty doggone good. Especially the country rocker "Honky Tonk Saturday Night." But Becky knew that if she was gonna have a major hit song in country, she'd have to move to Nashville, so in 1982 she made that move and has been here ever since. Becky had made friends in Nashville while she was on Mercury and livin' in Los Angeles, so she was accepted into the Nashville music family not long after she arrived, and she had her original songs recorded by a lot of top country

artists during the early eighties. Becky was doin' both shows on the road, which were being booked by Dick Beacham, and also studio work. Her first big break came during the spring of 1983, when she recorded a real good cry-in-your-beer, tear-jerker duet with Moe Bandy called "Let's Get Over Them Together." Moe Bandy was still ridin' a hot streak of Top 10 country chart hits then as a solo artist, and also duet partner with Joe Stampley on all their "Moe & Joe" big hits. "Let's Get Over Them Together" by Moe Bandy and Becky Hobbs was released in the early summer of 1983, and by September 1983 reached a peak position of #10 on the *Billboard* country charts.

In the early months of 1984, Becky signed a short-lived record deal with Liberty Records and charted one 45 single called "Oklahoma Heart," which reached #46 on the *Billboard* country charts and had a run of ten weeks on those charts during the summer of 1984. But during that summer of 1984, Becky switched over to EMI America Records for a couple years. Becky had three *Billboard* country chart hits for EMI America between September 1984 and September 1985. This was when I first saw her on the "Nashville Now" show on TNN. What I liked about Becky Hobbs even from the first time I saw her on TV was her poundin' the keys of the piano she was playin' like a female Jerry Lee Lewis. This chick was rockin' like none of the other girl singers in Nashville in '84 and '85 (Tanya Tucker was off the charts during that period) on her Mercury Records first solo Top 40 *Billboard* country chart hit, "Wheels in Emotion," along with other Mercury hit songs such as "Hottest Ex in Texas" and "The Cat's Meow," plus she'd do great covers of rockin' fifties tunes like "Great Balls of Fire."

Although I saw her on TNN, I didn't hear her records on the three country radio stations out of Washington, D.C., and Baltimore until she had her biggest chart hits between 1988 and 1990. Becky was off the *Billboard* country charts in '86 and '87, but she was still on the road, tourin' an awful lot. She was also writing songs that were being recorded by artists such as Emmylou Harris, Conway Twitty, and others during that time. In fact, one song Becky co-wrote, called "I Want to Know You Before We Make Love," recorded by Conway Twitty, reached #2 on the *Billboard* country charts in October 1987. Although Conway would have nine more of his songs reach the *Billboard* country singles Top 10 charts into 1991, this #2 chart hit Becky co-wrote was the final time Conway would ever see this high of a *Billboard* chart number again in the ever-changing country music business that now wanted new sounds and youth at the top of their *Billboard* charts. Becky told me in 1989, the success of Conway's song that she'd co-written helped pay off her "Beckaroo" bus that she was tourin' in at that time.

It seemed like Becky Hobbs was about to break through big-time in 1988, when she was signed to a recording contract with MTM Records in Nashville. MTM Records was owned by top television comedy actress Mary Tyler Moore, although Moore played no active role in the running of this record label. MTM Records was only in existence for less than five years, but they had some huge successes (especially for an independently owned label during the mid to late eighties) with artists such as Judy Rodman and Holly Dunn by the time Becky Hobbs signed with the label at the beginning of 1988. The first song MTM released on Becky was a smash hit on the country charts. Randy Travis had brought the old traditional honky-tonk hillbilly sound back to the top of the country charts, and the song MTM released on Becky fit perfectly into this mold. The song was called "Jones on the Jukebox." Becky co-wrote the song with Don Goodwood (the guitar player in her band, The Heartthrobs) and the 1950s old rockabilly Sun artist Mack Vickery. The country music industry and record labels weren't doin' music videos as much at this time on about every release as they are today, but they shot a great one on this song. This song was a mid-tempo one that showcased Texas honky-tonk hillbilly music at its best. In the video, Becky was shown in an old Texas-type honky-tonk at the the bar with beer and whiskey on tap and cowboys around her drinkin' while she sang this great honky-tonk song. The drinkin' cowgirl-type image may have hurt the song at that time some, but Becky Hobbs was well liked by Ralph Emory and others in Nashville circles, and she toured and worked hard on the road promotin' this song and the others that would follow on her one and only MTM Records album, *All Keyed Up,* released in the late spring of 1988. "Jones on the Jukebox" made it up to #31 on the *Billboard* country charts during June 1988, after it had debuted on those charts on March 5, 1988. It stayed on the charts for a total of nineteen weeks, even after her next 45 single, "They Always Look Better When They're Leavin'," debuted on the *Billboard* country charts on July 9, 1988. This song made it up to #43 and had a ten-week run on the charts. Becky was all over TNN and touring around the country into the fall, but shortly after her third 45 single release debuted on the *Billboard* country charts on October 8, 1988, MTM Records closed its

doors in Nashville and got completely out of the country music business. Becky's final release, "Are There Any More Like You (Where You Came From)" did manage to reach #53 on the *Billboard* country charts in November 1988.

MTM Records closed its doors for good in early 1989. Whatever the reasons may have been, it's hard to believe that an independent label that put fifty-two songs by various artists on the *Billboard* country charts between early 1984 and late 1988 was losing a lot of money. A lot of those songs were big Top 10 hits during that period. All the artists on MTM who were still havin' hits were picked up by other major labels in Nashville by the spring and summer of 1989, but to be honest, they all lost some momentum as far as their top *Billboard* chart numbers were concerned. Judy Rodman never really regained her big Top 10 and 20 *Billboard* country successes; Holly Dunn did manage to hang in there with a few Top 10 hits for a couple years, but by 1990, country music had really changed, and there were loads of new both male and female artists bein' shoved out on the market at a record pace like never before.

Becky Hobbs's one MTM Records album, *All Keyed Up,* was picked up by RCA Records by the late spring of 1989 and re-released almost in its same form, cover and all. The only difference was RCA took one of the songs off the MTM album, "It's Because I Do," and added two new hot rockin' songs Becky had written. Both the MTM album and the RCA version of it a year later were bought by quite a few rockabilly fans I knew during '88 and '89 because of the title track. It's the most dynamic, hit-you-in-the-face, hard-drivin' rock 'n' roll/rockabilly song you could ever want to hear by a female artist recording in Nashville during the late eighties. Then, when you saw Becky rockin' out on "Nashville Now" on TV, she was a wild female version of Jerry Lee Lewis, poundin' the keys on her killer song. It's flat-out Jerry Lee Lewis rock 'n' roll when he was at his best. Becky fired the lyrics out at breakneck speed and just plain rocked harder than any new artist at that time.

There was no way either MTM or RCA would ever release a great true rockin' song like "All Keyed Up" as a single 45 and push it to country radio. It just plain rocked too damn hard in the right way, and Becky knew exactly how to wear herself out rockin' along with it. But the two new songs RCA had on their version of the *All Keyed Up* album in 1989 were released as 45 singles, and both of those songs were right in the rockabilly category. The first one they released was called "Do You

Feel the Same Way Too." Well, Becky Hobbs knew one thing for sure, and that was that the many fans she had from 1988 up to the present that came out to see her live shows at roadhouse honky-tonks, theaters, state fairs, etc. all loved to see her do one thing the most. That was to rock out on songs like "All Keyed Up." So when "Do You Feel the Same Way Too" was released during the summer of 1989 and a video was filmed, which was great, to go along with the promotion of it, the song at least made it up to #45 on the *Billboard* country charts. It's one of the best mid- to up-tempo modern original rockabilly tunes that you could want to hear. The video was totally rockabilly-oriented, also. The setting was in a fifties-type diner, and future Planet Rocker and solid rockabilly guitarist Eddie Angel can be seen sittin' in a diner booth jammin' along while Becky rocks her way through this great song, outfitted in a customized motorcycle jacket and other rockabilly garb. I was thinkin' as I watched her perform it on "Nashville Now" and in that video, maybe there's some hope left after all for rockabilly-type music in Nashville, but later in the nineties, though it keeps comin' back in dabs and flashes in country music right up to today, I'd find out that the country music industry would continue to treat it as that troublesome stepchild they wish would run away from home and never come back to their family again.

Becky's follow-up release to "Do You Feel the Same Way Too" in early 1990 failed to even make it onto the *Billboard* country charts at all. It was called "A Woman Needs," and it too also rocked, but Becky told me it really didn't stand a chance to begin with. Becky said Joe Galente, the head of RCA, which had been bought out by BMG by this time, really couldn't stand the traditional country music that was gainin' more ground than ever in early 1990, and that's why they were concentrating on the crossover pop sounds of K.T. Oslin and Restless Heart along with other new acts they were signing around 1989 and '90.

By the summer of 1990, Becky had her first 45 out on Curb Records, called "A Little Hunk o' Heaven." This was once again another good mid-tempo song with a rockabilly sound to it for the nineties. Becky had three or four more 45 releases on Curb Records through 1992. The best one came in the summer of 1991. I had been living and working out of the Nashville area for over six months by this time, and Becky returned a call I'd made to her to find out what was goin' on in her life and career, and at one point she told me about how her new 45 single came about. Becky said, "I usually write most

all of the songs I record [which I had known for quite awhile], but a young guy at Curb who was in charge of finding the right songs for the artists on their label called me up one day and said, 'Becky, I've found the perfect new song for you that we want you to record. You gotta hear this thing. It's perfect for your style, you'll love it. I don't know who's doin' it, but it's just a great new song we want you to cut.' So I told him I'd come down and give it a listen. Billy, when he put that song on, I started laughin' and told him I've loved that song since I was a kid in the early sixties, when it first came out. He was playin' me the original version of 'Talk Back Tremblin' Lips' by Ernie Ashworth. Ain't that a kick? This guy thought it was a new song." Well, Becky not only went on and did a great female up-tempo cover of this classic hillbilly song, but Curb Records also released a great video of her doin' the song, and Ernie Ashworth (the original 1963 #1 hit artist) was also included in this video.

Becky Hobbs was always on "Nashville Now" until it was taken off the air in the early fall of 1993. She went and stayed out on the road a lot well into 1995 doin' between 250 and 300 shows a year. She is known for her rockabilly brand of music as much as for her traditional country honky-tonk sound. At least some of the rockabilly cats in Europe and other parts of the world must consider her a rockabilly artist, because Becky's told me in the late eighties and early nineties when she goes to Europe and other parts of the world to perform, there's always a good number of rockabilly fans in motorcycle jackets and big pompadours that are in their twenties and thirties who always come out to her live shows over there.

The last album I know of that Becky's come out with was in the summer of 1994, called *The Boots I Came to Town In*, on the Intersound record label. Becky promoted and debuted this album at Fan Fair in Nashville in early June 1994, and then did a number of TNN shows and live shows on the road to promote it. It's a real good album. There's two real solid rockabilly songs on it. One, called "Mama's Green Eyes (and Daddy's Wild Hair)," is a scorchin', fast-paced, fiery rockabilly tune, and another, called "Gonna Rock You Baby," is a well-done mid-tempo rockabilly tune. Most of the rest of this album is classic country and just plain good hillbilly honky-tonk songs.

I spoke with Becky in August 1995, and she was takin' a break off a long tour she'd been on to write songs.

Becky Hobbs loves songwriting almost as much as performing. A song she had on *The Boots I Came to Town In* was recorded by Alabama and was on their *Greatest Hits, Volume 3* album, as well as becoming a Top 10 single for 'em in late 1994 on the *Billboard* country charts. The song was called "Angels Among Us."

Rockabilly fans today, mostly in other parts of the world, love Becky Hobbs's music for the same reasons I do. 'Cause it's original, she's got her own style, and whether it's solid rockabilly music or great honky-tonk, it's true-blue and real. Becky is definitely a rockabilly nineties chick!

Forgettin' to Remember to Forget

*B*ecky Hobbs's "Do You Feel the Same Way Too" video kept gettin' good airplay into the fall of 1989. It was in late October '89 that I decided to call down to Nashville and talk to Dick Beacham, who booked Becky, about her comin' up to do a show I was in the early stages of planning, at the Elks Lodge in Severna Park, Maryland. I had already done several fairly successful shows with Jack Scott and had such a hugely successful benefit show with an all-star lineup for Charlie Feathers that the Anne Arundel County Executive declared that day as "Rockabilly Music Day" in the county, so I was thinkin' about doin' one final "Second Annual Rockabilly Music Day" festival of stars sometime in early June 1990. I had another show with Janis Martin and Sleepy La Beef scheduled for February 1990, so I felt, as I was already thinkin' of movin' to the Nashville area by then, I'd put on one final extravaganza of rockabilly stars before I moved for good.

I liked what Marty Stuart was doin' a whole lot also at the time, so I was undecided on whether I'd have Marty or Becky Hobbs headline. I decided on Becky Hobbs, and I don't regret it one bit. I went over to the Zed Club, which was located in Alexandria, Virginia, the first time she played there in November 1989, and she put on one whale of a hot rockin' show. I met her after the show that night and asked her how she'd feel about headlining an all-rockabilly festival in early June, and she told me she'd love to. After talkin' to her for awhile on her bus, I went back home and called Dick Beacham in Nashville the next day, and we agreed on the price and a Saturday night date of June 2, 1990, and he sent the contracts, and that was that. It was up to me to do the rest, and as usual, it was tough, but I still got it done.

The Elks Lodge wasn't completely full that night, and I might-a done a little better if I had used Marty Stuart instead, 'cause "Hillbilly Rock" was a big hit by that time, plus male artists always seem to be an easier sell and a bigger draw, but everybody that I know who saw Becky's show was sure blown away by it, 'cause she and her band of Heartthrobs gave that whole crowd one professional firecracker rockin' show at the end of that night. I remember Don London, who co-wrote quite a number of songs with her, played lead guitar, and was really her right-hand man, was a nice guy.

Several of the bands on that show were real excited about playin' it and gettin' to showcase their new music to an audience who'd never heard of 'em before and was larger than any they'd played to up to that time. The two new rockabilly bands on that show were just that. New and young. High Noon from Austin, Texas, was doin' some of their first shows out of the Austin area, but nobody up in the Northeast had ever heard of 'em before this show, they didn't have any records at all out at that time, and were usually lucky to be playin' for thirty or forty people. They enjoyed doin' the show, and today High Noon is known in rockabilly circles all over the world. Darren Spears and Bill Hull from the band Go Cat Go always seemed to be eternally grateful to me after I decided to use them as the opening act for that show. They had only been doin' shows around the D.C. area for about six months, but Darren Spears, from the first time I saw him sing, I knew he had a voice better than any of the others in the D.C. rockabilly music scene that was most suited and had more pure feelin' in it for true rockabilly. Darren never gave up on it, while some of the other young acts I had on that show now wear cowboy hats and ride both sides of the fence, hopin' to get noticed.

I was certainly happy all the shows I put on were received well, but I was also now glad I didn't have the burden of coordinating between nine and seventeen acts on a rockabilly show bill. It was good for a lot of the artists and bands at the time, though. I can look back and watch and enjoy the shows better today, as I videotaped 'em all and wasn't able to enjoy 'em when they were goin' on, as there were too many worries with puttin' on big shows such as those.

Kelly Willis

I first saw and met Kelly Willis during the late spring of 1986. She was only sixteen years old then. The Twist & Shout Club, which was located inside the Bethesda, Maryland, American Legion in the hall where the live shows were held, was pretty much the hot new club in town where the popular local and, later on, bigger names from around the U.S. came to the D.C. area to perform their brand of roots rock 'n' roll, rockabilly, cajun, zydeco, rhythm & blues, and blues music. Once in a great while, even a real, tremendous, great old hill-billy honky-tonk legend could be found there, like Hank Thompson in 1988. For over five years, between 1986 and 1991, The Twist & Shout Club became the place that all local roots-type rock 'n' roll bands in the D.C. area most wanted to perform at.

The Twist & Shout was where Kelly Willis performed her first show with her band The Fireballs, when they opened for Tex Rubinowitz there in the spring of 1986. I was there that night, and I'd never seen Kelly before, although I knew the other three young rockabilly cats who were backing her up. All three, John Sherick, Jimmy Grey, and Mas Palermo, had been members of Alan Veatch's former rockabilly band The Vibrotto Brothers. Six months earlier, in the fall of 1985, I produced an eight-track recording session on The Vibrotto Brothers over at a basement studio in Gaithersburg, Maryland, but I really don't remember Kelly bein' present at that time. When Alan started a new band in 1986, called Pink & Black, these three guys that had left Alan's old band formed Kelly & The Fireballs. Kelly was the steady girlfriend of the drummer in the band, Mas Palermo.

On their first debut show when Kelly & The Fireballs opened for Tex Rubinowitz, I remember 'em doin' a real good show for bein' all young (real young) kids. I mean, Kelly was only sixteen then, and the three Fireballs were only between nineteen and twenty-three years old. Here it was 1986, and these four kids were knockin' out good versions of old fifties and early-sixties rockabilly classics such as Wanda Jackson's "Mean, Mean Man" and "Let's Have a Party" (her version), The Collins Kids' "Mercy" and "Rock Boppin' Baby," Gene Vincent's "Baby Blue" and "Unchained Melody" (his version), Elvis's "Ain't That Lovin' You Baby" and "Your Cheatin' Heart" (his version), Janis Martin's "Bang, Bang," Charlie Rich's "Lonely Weekends," and a whole lot of others. Kelly & The Fireballs had only one original song I remember 'em doin' that night. It was a song called "Mean Ol'

Moon" that lead guitarist John Sherick had written. But so what if they were doin' old fifties and early-sixties cover songs? It was still rockabilly, they did it good, no other young local groups were doin' the same material in the D.C. area at the time, and they were the perfect opening band for D.C.'s top rockabilly star, Tex Rubinowitz.

Well, Mark Gretchell, the owner of The Twist & Shout, evidently thought they were real good also. Mark booked Kelly & The Fireballs in his place a whole lot throughout the rest of the summer and into the fall of 1986. But always as a $50 opening act for other artists and bands. What I noticed the most from the first time I saw Kelly & The Fireballs was the strong, powerful, great voice of Kelly Willis. Even at sixteen years old, Kelly could sing anything. For a young girl who had never been on a real stage in front of several hundred people, her untrained voice could handle a scorchin' fast rockabilly version of "Mercy," but then she could turn right around and do a real slow ballad in the classic Gene Vincent style, like "Unchained Melody," which takes a strong voice to sing. I was hearin' Kelly reach and hold out notes on songs like that without her voice ever crackin' or goin' off-key. No other female singer in the D.C. music scene could do that, like Kelly Willis did at sixteen years old on about any song she'd choose (or at that time was chosen for her) to do.

Kelly Willis wore either basic, fifties-style cowgirl skirts, shirts, belts, and high heels, or fifties Marilyn Monroe-type dresses with a black motorcycle jacket during the year and a half she performed shows in the Washington, D.C., area. Her hair was always pulled straight tight back in a ponytail, and of course it was blond. She was just a quiet, sweet, very pretty young teenage girl in 1986 and '87. The three Fireballs dressed in the traditional fifties rockabilly style, wearin' black motorcycle jackets and boots, jeans, and black or pink shirts.

Lead guitarist John Sherick was actually the one at the start of the Kelly & The Fireballs group who was, or seemed to me to be, the leader and spokesman for the band when it came to takin' their bookings and demo tapes later in early '87. John had taken guitar lessons from Danny Gatton (like many other hopeful guitarists around D.C.) and during the early to late eighties became good friends with Tex Rubinowitz, who was John's rockabilly hero then. By this time, me and Tex were close personal friends, so I guess it was only natural for me and John Sherick to get around to his group, Kelly & The Fireballs. Besides The Twist & Shout, they were playin' in any little place or club that would take 'em. Plus they always played at private parties. This was all throughout the summer of 1986. Well, by the end of that summer, I was "down at The Twist & Shout" (to quote Mary Chapin Carpenter) one night, and John Sherick asked me if I could use their band for any openings for the artists I was booking. I told him, "Yeah, I'll see what I can do. I think y'all got a good young band that stands a decent chance at makin' it outside of D.C. sooner or later. I'll make some calls and get back to you."

What I wanted to do first was approach Mark Gretchell at The Twist & Shout Club on a show idea I had for doin' a double bill of "Rollabilly Music [which was my company] Presents a Night of Rockabilly Queens." Mark knew I'd be havin' an album out on LesLee, and he also knew how hard I worked on promotin' the artists I managed or booked (although Mark knew he had a certain amount of people who were comin' to his club most weekends, no matter who was performin', by this time), so we agreed on close to the deal I wanted at least. Friday nights always seemed to be the best-drawing nights at The Twist & Shout Club then, but Saturday nights weren't bad. Mark gave me the Saturday night of November 29, 1986. Up until that time, Mark had only used Kelly & The Fireballs as an opening act, but I knew they had a draw of their own, and I knew I could bring in LesLee's fans not only in D.C., but also up in Baltimore, where she was best known. I didn't care that Mark was only gonna agree to give me a $200 club guarantee versus 70 percent of the door, 'cause I knew I could pack that place, 'cause Kelly & The Fireballs had become a popular young act and were even outdrawing some of the more established acts that Mark was puttin' in his club at the time when he used Kelly to open for 'em for his usual $50 opening fee.

Well, this was a split bill, with each band doin' two forty-five-minute sets each between 9:30 p.m. and 2:00 a.m. Kelly & The Fireballs did the first and third sets, and LesLee did the second and fourth sets. The main thing different on this night was, I knew Kelly's group The Fireballs were more than capable to back up LesLee on her two sets, so I used them the whole night. What a night it turned out to be, too. Not only did me and LesLee both get along great with Kelly and the three Fireballs, and everybody had fun as well as pleasin' this packed-to-the-gills crowd that had come out to witness two top-notch, solid rockin' rockabilly girls do their thing, but

even me and Mark Gretchell were blown away by the money that was taken in at the door. The reason I know Mark Gretchell to be honest was that I got a copy of a receipt that I signed from Mark the night of November 29, 1986, for receiving $1,242, which was 70 percent of what was taken in on a $5 door admission on these two bands. So Mark had to take in around $1,800 or so at the door that night. Well, I knew there had to be well over 300 people in there that night, but there's always fifty or so on some nights that are musicians, local entertainers, etc. that are always allowed in and not charged. Then there's always the case where the person workin' the door for the owner always winds up makin' an extra $100 or $200 on good nights for themselves. I've caught 'em, fought 'em, and seen that happen quite a lot. But not on the night I proved Kelly & The Fireballs and LesLee could blow the house down playin' rockabilly music. I still got the live board tapes that Jimmy Barnett always made me, and at the end of this night, the crowd roared and roared when LesLee got Kelly back up on stage for one last song, which was one they both knew that rocked, called "Ain't That Lovin' You Baby." But nights like this one are special, and the exception to the rule. Money-wise and crowd-wise. I remember when I counted out $840 and handed it over to John Sherick that night, he almost passed out. That meant him, Mas Palermo, Jimmy Grey, and Kelly Willis would receive $210 apiece. John told me then that the whole band hadn't made over $200 for the whole group to split up till that night. Me and LesLee just split the other $400. That's why I quit takin' bookings and finally gave up on managing rockabilly artists as the 1990s came in. On a good night such as the Kelly/LesLee one, any other booking agent would only pay their artists a small fraction of the gross, to cover past losses. I never operated that way, because I knew bands and artists hardly ever made much money anyway.

John Sherick asked me after that night of November 29, 1986, if I'd manage the group, but I told him I just couldn't, 'cause I already had too many irons in the fire, but I did continue to book Kelly & The Fireballs on eleven more shows after that night, through June 1987. I had 'em open for Johnny Seaton and Danny Gatton on three nights, LesLee "Bird" Anderson on three nights, Bobby Smith on two nights, Billy Hancock on two nights, and Robert Gordon on one night, between December 1986 and June 1987. I never booked 'em in The Twist & Shout Club after November 29, 1986, as John Sherick was able to get those bookings on his own from then on, as well as the few regular smaller clubs in the area around D.C., Maryland, and northern Virginia they had already played at. Kelly Willis & The Fireballs primarily opened all my shows at the larger Washington, D.C., clubs, such as The Roxy Showplace, Bayou, East Side Club, and Club Soda during that seven- or eight-month period. All the rockabilly artists mentioned above already had one or more albums out or had one comin' out in the real near future. Kelly & The Fireballs didn't record anything in a real studio until January 1987, when I cut three songs on 'em plus used Kelly Willis and the other three members on four songs singing backup on the LesLee "Bird" Anderson thirteen-song album I finally released in July 1988. The three members of The Fireballs also played on two tracks on this album, which was called *Runnin' Wild*. Kelly and Mas Palermo did most of the backup singin' with Johnny Seaton, LesLee, and Billy Hancock on three different occasions between January and April 1987.

I was workin' and involved with Kelly and her young band so much in the early months of 1987, I wanted them to be the featured band on what's actually my official birthday (no time to explain that) on Saturday night, February 23, 1987. This was my final drunken birthday party, but after seventy-five to eighty D.C. and Baltimore rockabilly fans showed up at my house in Severna Park, Maryland, to see the likes of Kelly & The Fireballs, Billy Hancock, Johnny Seaton, and LesLee "Bird" Anderson sing sets of six to twelve songs each, this was what gave me the idea a year later in 1988 to start puttin' out full-production shows of numerous rockabilly acts, both national and local. That was a fun night, though. Other artists, such as Mike Riordan, The Bar Belles, Bruce Cornwell, and several others also sang. Tex Rubinowitz, Alan and Virginia Veatch, Jon Strong, Jimmy and Pat Cavanaugh, and almost everybody connected to the D.C. rockabilly music scene all showed up. Yeah, those were some really fun days. I'm glad I recorded and videotaped 'em to look back on now. But by the summer of 1987, Kelly Willis & The Fireballs were still playin' in the same ol' places in and around the D.C. area, still makin' the same little chunks of money, and they were one of the few bands (rockabilly or otherwise) up until that time that packed their bags and were smart enough to move to Austin, Texas. There at least you got somewhat of a shot at bein' noticed.

I felt I had to write all this about Kelly Willis's D.C.-area rockabilly days between the spring of 1986 and the fall of 1987, when Kelly & The Fireballs all moved to Austin.

The reason being is that since I got her first promotional press package on her first MCA Records album out of Nashville, there was not a thing said in it about her dues-payin' year and a half playin' the D.C.-area nightclubs when she was singin' her best raw rockabilly music ever. Now, I know for the past decade, Kelly's made her home in Austin, Texas, but from what I've read, what's been printed, and what most believe is that Kelly Willis and her great vocal ability is what it is because she's an Austin girl. Now, I love Austin, Texas, and if I was ever gonna move anywhere away from these west Tennessee hills, it would be to the Austin area. But the real truth on Kelly Willis is that she had that great vocal ability to sing any kind of music she so chose before she ever hit the Texas border. When she first got to Austin, Kelly & The Fireballs were still doin' the same brand of rockabilly music they'd been doin' for a full year and a half in D.C. nightclubs and dives. The only differences are she was singin' it now in a new set of nightclubs and dives where she had a decent chance at becoming discovered. Austin's one of the best roots rock 'n' roll and real country music towns in the U.S. Probably the best.

Austin claims Kelly now. But what happened to her when she signed on with a professional manager, by the name of Carlyne Majer, who went to get her a major record contract in Nashville with MCA Records? What happened was Kelly Willis was signed by her manager as a solo artist, and John Sherick and Jimmy Grey were discharged from her band and were back in Washington, D.C., by the fall of 1988. Mas Palermo was sure to be kept in Kelly's new backup band, now called Radio Ranch, because Mas had been Kelly's first and only boyfriend, who she was now engaged to be married to in the summer of 1989. Kelly's music changed as gradually her image also did, and between 1990 and 1993, Kelly went on to record three albums of well-polished music released and recorded in Nashville, as well as six music videos and seven 45s from these albums that were well promoted all over TNN and CMT (Country Music Television), but all of 'em failed to put Kelly up with the Reba McEntires, Lorrie Morgans, Trisha Yearwoods, and other top female performers doin' straight country music. By the time Kelly's third and final album, simply titled *Kelly Willis*, was released in June 1993, Mas Palermo (Kelly's husband) was now also out of the picture, and the two of them had parted ways. Those are the facts, my friends, about what happens a whole lot of times if you achieve even only a small degree of success in the real, big-time world of either country or pop music. Some of the biggest entertainers and artists ever in the world of music itself all eventually fell prey to these same pitfalls. Including the biggest and greatest of all, Elvis himself. When important people and major music corporations put up millions of dollars to hopefully make you a big star, you're gonna do what you're told. Then again, you have to do what you're told on your regular 9 to 5 job, or you'll be out there lookin' for another one.

I've always defended Kelly Willis and never blamed her in any way whatsoever for makin' the decisions she did, 'cause sometimes if you get a chance for a big-time major recording contract, and you blow it by doing what you feel is right, that chance may never come around again.

Kelly Willis is not a failure. Nashville just couldn't make her an assembly-line female country star, though they really tried. I saw Kelly and Mas Palermo both in Austin in March 1991. At that time, Mas was in a new band. When I spoke with Kelly in September 1995, she was signed to A&M Records out in Los Angeles. She was just beginning to pick songs to record for a new original pop/rock 'n' roll album. Pepper talked to her about the cat that she's had for so long. She's still the little nice girl to me and Pepper that she was ten years ago, but I know she's been hurt, and it's made her grow up a lot.

When I last saw Kelly on June 7, 1993, I mentioned those old rockabilly shows and recording sessions, birthday parties and such that she rocked and sang at for me back in '86 and '87. A sad look came over her face when she looked at me and said, "You know, Billy, I really miss those days, 'cause those shows were really fun." I could tell a lot had happened in her life by this time that I wasn't aware of, so I just grinned and tried to make a joke out of it by sayin', "You gotta be kiddin'. I was really headed for the poorhouse, and we were all starvin' to death back then." But Kelly said, "I know, but at least the music was fun." She meant rockabilly music! I knew that. That's what's always kept me goin'. On that night, she was on a double showcase with the country group The Mavericks, who are also on MCA Records. Some rockabilly fans are into what they do, and their music on a few songs does have rockabilly in it. Both The Mavericks and Kelly Willis were showcasing their new albums down at The Ace of Clubs, and the place was pretty crowded, but mostly with record label people or various recording artists such as Marty Stuart and Mark Collie, who I happened to see that night, and both are

MCA recording artists. It was good to see former Rockpile rockabilly band member Billy Bremner in Kelly's backup band that night, but neither Kelly nor Billy sounded right on the "new" song they were pushin' as Kelly's first single and video release from this album, titled "Heaven's Just a Sin Away," which had been a *Billboard* country chart-topper back in the fall of 1977. But all three of Kelly's Nashville country-oriented albums had at least one song that had a rockabilly feel to it, even though the sound kept gettin' slicker. I was glad me and Pepper went down and spent some time with Kelly after her show in the dressing room and out back of the club talking. In my book, Kelly's still that same sweet, sensitive young girl that hardly said a word (but could sing like a bird) ten years ago when we first met. I hope she goes on and shows Nashville that she can be marketed in the pop/rock world and become her own person and becomes a real success high up on the pop *Billboard* charts. I also believe Kelly's got a whole lotta love for singing rockabilly music, and whatever she does in the future (which, at age twenty-seven, there's a lot of left), rockabilly music'll be a part of it.

I'll just end my Kelly Willis story by saying at one point, Laurence Beall, who met me and Pepper at the show in June 1993, couldn't believe what Kelly Willis said back in the dressing room after Kelly excused herself and told us she'd be right back and continue our conversation, but she had to go out and up onto the stage to get her cup of orange juice that she'd forgotten up there. Laurence said, "That's crazy. I can't believe she's doin' that. She's the star or the attraction. She's got people or band members to do that kind of shit for her." I said to Laurence, "You don't know Kelly like I do, and she wouldn't think of it. Plus she wouldn't be the same Kelly Willis I've known if she did."

LesLee Anderson

Like Kelly Willis, LesLee Anderson went on to marry her first real boyfriend, in 1969 when she was only twenty years old. LesLee's husband's name was Roger Anderson, who LesLee had gone steady with since she was fourteen. Roger, who was only three years older than LesLee, was a roots rock 'n' roll, rhythm & blues, and blues musician who played his brand of this music in the tough bars in the blue collar city of Baltimore, Maryland, where both LesLee and Roger were born and grew up during the fifties and sixties. Roger passed on his passion and love for his early influences in rock 'n' roll, blues, and bluegrass music to LesLee. She loved all this music from an early age as much as she loved Roger. Roger was a blue collar man's man during the sixties and right up to his tragic, untimely death in April 1984.

When LesLee married Roger, his dream was to own a Baltimore bar or club where he could play, record, and put the kind of real rock 'n' roll music and the blue collar bands that did it in there so he could be absorbed by it twenty-four hours a day. Until 1976 Roger worked hard periodically on various blue collar jobs by day while he played his music at night. LesLee worked steady also. They saved the money they could and by 1976, Roger saw his dream come true when they went in together and bought the now defunct, but legendary, Marble Bar and Nightclub at 306 West Franklin St. in the inner city of downtown Baltimore.

The Marble Bar's reputation grew fast as the main place for roots rock 'n' roll and hard real blues, plus the incoming punk and new wave bands and artists knew it was the top place to play at in Baltimore. Roger and LesLee booked some big-name acts that were just startin' out during the late seventies and early eighties. Until LesLee finally let The Marble Bar go in 1985, a year after Roger's death.

I wouldn't meet LesLee or Roger Anderson until the summer of 1982, but we became good friends in a short time. LesLee was really down to earth, and I could tell from the first she really loved good rock 'n' roll music. Roger was totally dedicated to his Marble Bar because it allowed him to play all forms of real roots rock 'n' roll. But what I found out from LesLee after Roger passed on was, Roger was the drivin' force behind the talent LesLee had, and it was Roger that more or less made LesLee sing and perform. He knew she was good. Real good.

LesLee sold The Marble Bar and headed west to Los Angeles in June 1985. This was a great flourishing time for rockabilly and hillbilly out there during '85 and into '86. Dwight Yoakam was really gainin' momentum in places like The Palomino Club as well as numerous punk clubs he was appearing in. Without Roger, LesLee turned her full sights on the music he'd inspired in her. LesLee was excited about "Ronnie Mack's Weekly Barn Dance" shows at The Palomino Club, which she soon started playin', and just the whole scene in general. But me, Pepper, and Leslee always stayed close and didn't forget each other, and on one of her trips back to the Baltimore area to visit her parents and old friends during the Thanksgiving holidays in 1985, LesLee came

over to our house in Severna Park, Maryland, and she brought her guitar along. After listenin' to LesLee sing songs like Brenda Lee's "Sweet Nothin's" and Wanda Jackson's "Mean, Mean Man," I was a little shocked, to say the least. LesLee has always been just a close friend and was just LesLee from The Marble Bar up to that night. I knew she could sing all right, but I didn't know she had it in her vocals to come across in a real, true blue, gutsy way that drove with balls behind it. I was at that time still handling Johnny Seaton's affairs (I had booked him into The Marble Bar a total of twenty-three times between July 1982 and March 1985), but after a serious fallin' out we'd had, I was definitely in the mood for a fresh artist. I knew LesLee Anderson's character and felt she was the perfect one I could pick the songs for and do one great true rockabilly/rock 'n' roll album on. In 1989 and 1990 I invested my own money in recording on a D.C. rockabilly-style local artist by the name of Bobby Smith, who had one album out on Ripsaw Records in 1987, and I had plans to release an album on him. It never came out for various reasons at the time. As far as I know, Bobby Smith is still performing his brand of rockabilly, rock 'n' roll, and blues in D.C., and as far as I'm concerned, he's a good artist in the D.C. music scene that should be supported. I guess I was a little unsure with Bobby Smith during the last part of our relationship in the summer of 1990. With LesLee "Bird" Anderson, though, I had no reservations whatsoever in recording a full album plus in the D.C./Baltimore areas. I'd also taken on managing and booking her into clubs. I knew with the proper guidence LesLee and this future album could succeed.

LesLee went back to California after Christmas 1985, and she returned a month later, in late January 1986. Up to that time, LesLee didn't really have any professional studio experience, so first we went into an eight-track basement studio a friend of mine had and just loosely recorded about a half-dozen or so songs on a couple occasions with a couple of musicians LesLee knew from Baltimore, plus just her and Danny Gatton on one night. After several times in my buddy Richard Coon's basement studio, I felt LesLee was ready to go into a professional studio and let me get the top musicians anywhere in the area that all had the real feel for rockabilly and rock 'n' roll. By 1986 I already had nine years' experience producing six other artists. Glass Wing Studios was my favorite studio I ever worked out of (and remains so to this day). Primarily because of its owner, Richard Sales.

Now, LesLee's album would be only the third full album I'd produced that would actually see a full release on my label, Renegade Records, up to this point. Like everything else in the music business, especially all my studio work, I always strived for the latest project I was personally committed to, to surpass and be better than all previous work I had total control over. When I got into LesLee's album fully between April 1986 and October 1987, I remember I was obsessed with making this the best all-around real rock 'n' roll and rockabilly album by a solid, gutsy, raunchy female rocker that I'd heard do this music the way I wanted her to. I wanted to showcase the raw, but soft and sensual at times, total uniqueness of her solid vocal ability.

Where the problem lay on LesLee's album and it takin' so long to complete and finally be released was all because of me trying to get that total greatness out of everyone involved. Over the course of that year and a half, there were a lot of people involved in gettin' a total of twenty-six songs in more than a half-dozen styles of music. LesLee had to do more vocal takes (up to seventy on some songs) than any other artist before or since that I've produced. But the final outcome on the thirteen songs I chose to release on the album in July 1988 was all worth it. As were the six months I spent mixing those songs at Glass Wing Studio and over at East Coast Sound Lab studios in Baltimore, Maryland. Norman Nopluck, owner of the studio, was a huge help and inspiration in helping me get mixed ten of the twenty-six songs.

LesLee had spent at least half her time at our house in Severna Park, Maryland, and the other half in the L.A. music scene since we'd started on this album project in the spring of 1986. So during the two years of waitin' for her album to come out, I was bookin' LesLee on shows while she was back in Maryland. LesLee kept gettin' better all the time, even though some of the musicians I found to back her up really weren't up to par. I had her headline shows over Kelly Willis & The Fireballs, Bobby Smith, and others, as well as be the opening act for Johnny Seaton, Robert Gordon, Billy Hancock, etc. When I finally got the album out and both local and national reviews were 95 percent favorable, Leslee came back to the D.C. and Baltimore area and got more prestigious opening gigs, for the likes of Dwight Yoakam (thanks go to Seth Horowitz on that one), Jack Scott, Marty Stuart, etc. She also headlined a number of shows I bought for her on her own at that time. The album helped her gain some respect in L.A., also. I was glad to see that happen, because in the L.A. original music

scene, it's real tough to gain respect, 'cause out there most all the bands and artists really think they're the hottest thing goin'.

I titled LesLee's album *Runnin' Wild* for two reasons. One was because it was "runnin' wild" in so many different musical styles. Out of the thirteen songs, there were only six hard-core rockabilly numbers. The remaining seven were made up of Chuck Berry real rock 'n' roll, Texas blues, a fifties-style ballad tribute song from me to fifties British rocker Billy Fury, hillbilly, jazzed-up swing, a Les Paul pop tune (the title track), and a fun-filled rhythm & blues tune. The second reason I titled the album *Runnin' Wild* was because I had suggested the fifties Les Paul and Mary Ford tune "Runnin' Wild" to Danny Gatton. Danny got more excited than I'd ever seen him when we recorded this track. He told me at the time it was the most challenging song he'd ever attempted, 'cause I was givin' him the freedom to do the eleven guitar parts he wanted to lay down plus pull a lot of tricks out of his head to make this tune totally his. He played bass on it, also. He felt LesLee's vocal part was perfect and also felt it was one of his greatest pieces of work as a guitarist that the world would ever need to hear.

When LesLee performs in L.A. to this day, her most requested song is an original I wrote titled "Pink Slip," and that sure makes me feel like I'm right in believing in true rock 'n' roll and rockabilly and that it'll never die. To me, though, as well as Willie Lewis (owner of Rock-A-Billy Records), and many others who have a copy of this now-rare album, the most outstanding, in-your-face rockabilly song ever sung by a female artist (and best all-around on the album) is LesLee's version of a song Brenda Lee had out on Decca Records back in 1958, titled "Little Jonah." I always loved Brenda's version of this song since I bought it in late '58, and I never thought anyone could do it better than Brenda, but LesLee's rip-roarin' vocals proved it was possible. An added bonus was Danny Gatton's fiery, rockin' lap steel guitar work on it. I'm proud of that album. I always will be. It accomplished everything I had in mind to do at that time. LesLee also earned some respect that was justly deserved.

LesLee went back to L.A. in November 1988, and she continued to play consistently throughout the rockabilly and hillbilly music scene, winning fans and admirers along the way, until the summer of 1992. In 1989 and 1990, I brought LesLee back for several of the big festival shows I promoted while still living in Maryland. LesLee left L.A. in the summer of 1992, where she'd lived for seven years, and made a move to Pioneertown, California, which is a quiet, peaceful, desert western town about thirty miles from Palm Springs and 120 miles from L.A. She got out of the fast lane in L.A. and settled into a picturesque cowboy town that looks about as it did back in 1950 when Roy Rogers, Gene Autry, and Dick Curtis helped name the town they were there filming their TV series shows in. LesLee had been there prior to moving and had been offered a job singing at night and waitressing by day at the town's only nightspot, Pappy & Harriett's Pioneertown Palace. She's done that for five years, but also kept her name in the L.A. music scene, traveling back one to two times a month to play shows at The Palomino Club (before they closed down), The House of Blues, "Ronnie Mack's Weekly Barn Dance" at Jack's Sugar Shack, and various other venues that promote rockabilly and original roots music. So after seven years of being known as "L.A.'s Queen of Rockabilly" (Ronnie Mack gave her that title) and singin' rockabilly and hillbilly out in the desert at the Pioneertown Palace, even though she's got some really good friends both in Pioneertown and in L.A., LesLee's decided she needs a change both musically and spiritually. So there were only two music towns for her to choose from: Austin, Texas, and Nashville, Tennessee. After considering both options, she chose Nashville, because after visiting for two months in the late summer of 1996, LesLee said there was a real solid hillbilly, rockabilly, and blues music club scene in Nashville, where she'd have no trouble displaying her brand of rockabilly music, as well as showcasing her original songs. She's also got more real true-blue friends there. So in the early spring of 1997, LesLee made that move. In my opinion, it's the right choice for her and the rockabilly music she loves to sing and perform for appreciative fans. She'll win a lot of 'em over there. No doubt.

The only problem I have with LesLee (and it's always frustrated the hell out of me) is she's always been too much in awe of other (male and female) singers and performers' talents. It's a good quality to be humble and nice when people and fans you don't even know tell you you're the best live female chick they've ever seen doing rockabilly music. But LesLee seems to think these people are just bein' nice and, "Oh, ain't that sweet for them to say that." But it ain't just bullshit. It's true. She's worked hard over the past twelve years or so doin' her music and rockin' out on stage, and I ain't seen any other chick up on a stage anywhere (that at least ain't on a major

label) that can touch her live show when she's got the right, rehearsed band behind her. If you don't want to take my word for it, I've got it in print from a 1988 Washington, D.C., music newspaper in a quote from the late Danny Gatton where, when asked why he did so much work on LesLee's *Runnin' Wild* album, he replied, "'Cause LesLee was not only fun to work with in the studio, that girl can rock out better on stage than any damn woman I ever saw. She makes it all fun for everyone." Case closed!

Marti´ Brom

The final rockabilly honey I feel I have to give a good bit of space to is Marti´ Brom. Marti´ has been winning the *Music City Texas* magazine awards as Best Top Artist/Act and Female Vocalist not only in rockabilly but also in rock, and just about every other one she's been nominated for since 1993. In the past three years or so, she's gained popularity throughout Europe, Japan, Australia, and other foreign countries, as well as having offers thrust upon her to play there. Which, up to this writing, she's turned down. She has played sold-out shows as far away as New York City and done some touring with fifties Texas rockabilly artist Ronnie Dawson. But Marti´ rarely strays from the stages of those honky-tonks in Austin, Texas. To think all this commotion is now happening because I agreed to produce and release a 45 single record on her on my Renegade Records label that went on to become a jukebox cult classic in many parts of the world is kinda mind-boggling. Marti´ is still only in her early thirties, too. She's definitely still the best new kid on the block.

The only way I know how to tell you her short but successful story is to start at the beginning. Marti´ was born and raised in St. Louis, Missouri. That's where she met and married a guy named Bob Brom in 1990. Bob was a Captain in the Air Force and stationed in St. Louis at the time. During the summer of 1991, Bob was transferred by the Air Force to Austin, Texas. So Bob, Marti´, and their three-month-old daughter Ivy all packed up and moved to Austin then. Well, on the first weekend of October 1991, I was in Austin, set up and sellin' rockabilly records and memorabilia at the big fall Austin Record Show there. That's where Bob Brom ran into me. He'd read and liked the things I'd written in *Kicks* magazine, and he also knew in the past I'd produced Charlie Feathers, who was his biggest rockabilly hero. Bob gave me a six-song cassette on his wife, Marti´ Brom, that he told me had been recorded about six months earlier in a small studio when they were still living in St. Louis. Bob said they'd used the best fifties cover band in all of St. Louis. To say the least, I wasn't impressed by that, but the homemade snapshot on the cover of the cassette looked like she was at least a pretty damn hot-lookin' young chick. Bob said, "Please just give it a listen, Billy, and call me collect [that was somethin' new comin' from a stranger] after you get back to Nashville and tell me if you think she does rockabilly good enough to consider producing some songs on her in Nashville, and if you get a couple real good ones, maybe you'd also consider releasing a 45 on your Renegade Records label if I paid for everything." Well, there was certainly somethin' to be said for that. It was really a first for me, I can tell you that much. I said OK.

I reckon I was about 500 miles up the road the next day on the drive back home and had crossed over into Arkansas and was headin' towards Little Rock when I finally got bored and tired of playin' all the cassettes I had layin' all over the passenger seat of my van, when I spotted Marti´s tape. I first noticed all six songs were common cover rockabilly songs that had already been covered by newer rockabilly groups. These were all great songs that had been first recorded by Patsy Cline, The Collins Kids, Wanda Jackson, etc. But all I had was time to kill then, so I threw it on the tape deck, and I got to admit that Marti´s vocal work really took me aback! Right there on that strip of Interstate 30, I thought, "Hey, this chick really can sing. She's got one hell of a voice." Even that fifties band backin' her up wasn't all that bad. The band played all the six songs exactly the way they musta heard 'em on the original fifties records. But Marti´ had somethin' special in her voice on that demo. I felt if I got her in the really good studio I was workin' out of then that I could bring out some solid, gritty vocal tracks if I hand-picked a solid rockabilly band to back her up that could play the stuff I could choose in the real-feel way rockabilly should always be done. But after listening to that tape several more times in a row, Reality hit me, and I thought back on how things had soured with another artist I'd pinned my hopes on. So I calmed myself down about how good Marti´s vocals were and put it out of my mind and just drove on home.

For several days after I got back, I just let that tape lie around the house while I chilled out from the trip to Austin. Then one afternoon I told my wife how good this young girl's vocals were, but I was reluctant to get involved. Pepper said, "Put it on. Let me hear it." After she listened to it two times in a row, Pepper told me,

"Get on the phone with her husband and work the details out, or you'll regret it later." So I called Bob that night. On the phone, he was just like I remembered him from Austin. Excited as could be. I had a lot of work still to be done on a Christmas 45 release on Narvel Felts that had to be shipped to DJs around the world no later than November 1. I paid for distributors, consultants, etc. on this one, but even though I was up to my ears in work on it, I told Bob I'd start makin' a list of songs Marti´ should consider singin' whenever it was decided it would be the right time to fly her into Nashville for the session. Between early November 1991 and mid January 1992, me and Bob had numerous conversations, workin' out all the details, and I was makin' a list of musicians who I knew could be trusted to get the job done the right way in the studio on whatever number of hot rockin' songs I submitted for Marti´ to review and decide on doin'.

Marti´ only had one song she insisted on doin' that she sent to me. It was an original titled "Crazy Fever," written by Sean Mencher of the (at that time) Austin-based rockabilly trio band called High Noon. The song itself sounded OK to me, but this had to be one of the worst-soundin' basement or bedroom demos I've ever heard. Plus their arrangement on this song was also pretty bad. I knew a good arrangement had to be put on that one when Marti´ got here to rehearse with the two groups of musicians I was gathering for this project. So after I chose over sixty songs and sent Marti´ down three cassettes, she chose the seven or eight of them that she really wanted to do. Besides "Crazy Fever," the only others that were completely unknown were two original songs of mine that I had excellent (expensive, too!) demos on. So by early January 1992, Bob Brom had Marti´ booked on a flight that would arrive in Nashville on January 30. Me and Pepper picked her up at the airport and she stayed in a guest room at our house in Fairview the five days she was there. I believe Marti´ thought she was gonna do some sightseeing or somethin', but I had told Bob I wanted to work her with the two bands I'd picked to back her up, and practically all her time here was gonna be taken up with rehearsals or in the studio. Bob excitedly said, "Good! That's great. Work her. That's what I want you to do!"

Well, on January 31, we went to Laurence Beall's house in Nashville and rehearsed the five songs I wanted to get done on the following day. The rehearsal lasted from 5:00 p.m. to 11:30 p.m. The next day we all went into Burns Station Sound Studios in Burns, Tennessee. When you got a professional studio, solid musicians who all know exactly what and how you want 'em to play, an excellent engineer in Mike Dysenger, and a fantastic singer, as Martí Brom was even then, there's no way you can lose. And I didn't! I made sure I pushed the musicians (in a positive way) until I had all solid tracks laid down that I was completely happy with on the five songs along with Martí's scratch vocals. That took from 12:00 noon till 8:30 p.m. Then I pushed Martí for four more hours until we had her vocals on all five songs down that I was completely happy with. Don't get me wrong, everybody had fun. You can have fun, laugh and joke around, but you still got to get the job done and get it done real and right. Martí, me, and Pepper were all worn out by the time we got home, but I knew we had five great songs, no filler cuts, that I was proud of.

We got about seven hours sleep and were back up at Burns Station Sound at 11:30 a.m., this time with a different engineer and different musicians that included Bubba Feathers (Charlie's son). Between 12:00 noon and 8:00 p.m., all the tracks were laid down on a new batch of songs with Martí's scratch vocals. For anyone who may not know, scratch vocals are just one-time, runthrough, practice vocals for the musicians to get the all-around feel of the song. When the musicians left around

8:00 p.m., I put Martí through a grueling process of over four more hours to get the best final vocals I could get out of her on these five songs. Other producers might have settled for less, but I couldn't. Not on a girl that had a voice for almost any style of music, plus she had grit behind that voice. I knew she was in that vocal booth cussin' me and mad at me as much as any artist could get. But I got exactly what I wanted out of her. A couple days later, Martí flew back to Austin with a copy of the rough mixes of the ten songs we had gotten.

In late February and early March 1992, I went back to Burns Station Sound three times until I was happy with the mixes on the two songs, "Crazy Fever" and "Hiccups," Bob Brom wanted as Martí's first 45 single. Bob was really in a hurry to get Martí's first 45, so in July and August, I spent a lot of time gettin' it mastered, and I finally got it in full release on September 15, 1992. It made no sense to me, because even at this late date Martí still had not put a band together to do live shows, although she was gettin' up at various clubs and singin' with the group High Noon, who were probably at their peak in the Austin music scene at that time. Well, it took Martí another six months, until late February, until she actually found some barely adequate musicians to back her up on her first live opening show.

Forgettin' to Remember to Forget

Me, Martí, and Pepper have all laughed over the years about those two days and nights Martí spent in the studio. Pepper told me afterward that finally around 12:30 a.m., when she was completely done and I was satisfied, that Martí was starin' holes through me while I was gettin' Mike Dysenger to get me a good rough mix to take home. Pepper said Martí looked like she could-a killed me. Pepper told me she said to Martí then, "I'd give anything to know what you're thinkin' about him right now." Pepper said Martí just kept glarin' at me and replied, "I think your husband is totally out of his fuckin' mind." Pepper said she laughed and said to Martí, "You hang in there and just wait, 'cause down the road you'll wind up realizing why he put you through the last two nights the way he did when you hear the finished product he'll get after you've gone home."

Another thing that really blew Martí's mind back then was everybody that entered the studio—musicians, engineers, the studio owner, etc.—all smoked two or more packs of cigarettes a day, me and Pepper included. She said to me early on the second day, "Hardly any of the musicians in Austin smoke, and sometimes studios there won't allow it, from what I hear. I can't believe everybody here smokes." I told her, "Hey, Tennessee is known as the Tobacco State, and I don't know why you should be surprised, girl, 'cause this is real rock 'n' roll, rockabilly, and hillbilly music we're doin' here. Cigarettes and booze was what it was all built on. I don't know 'bout High Noon and other bands in Austin, but all of us are still doin' the real music, and livin' it too, like the ones that came before us. We ain't posin' for nobody." Martí just looked at me and said, "They'll never believe what I'm seein' back in Austin."

Even with barely adequate musicians, when Martí did a showcase at the spring 1993 South by Southwest Music Festival, she stood out above the rest. Bob sent me the rave reviews from the music writers at the *Austin Chronicle* and *Music City Texas* papers, and that gave me great satisfaction. (*Music City Texas*, by the way, is a great publication that I highly recommend, written, edited, and published by John Conquest.) From then on, she's been movin' right on up the ladder.

In the fall of 1994, Shaun Young and Kevin Smith put out a 45 on Martí on their label. Bob Brom sent me a copy of it and told me he was embarrassed by the way it was recorded and sounded. It was real poor. I wouldn't review it. It was recorded in a bedroom. But because of that first 45 I released, it still sold 1,000 copies, all in Europe and Japan, from what Bob told me. In 1995, Martí recorded ten songs that were broadcast live at the time at the radio station where they were being done. Martí's many fans both here in the U.S. and overseas wanted anything by her at this time, so Bob took it upon himself to release a ten-song cassette from that radio show early in 1995 on his own label, called Square Bird Records. This ten-song live cassette was much superior to the aforementioned 45 from 1994.

Later, towards the end of 1995, Martí went back in what sounded like a good Austin studio, and Bob told me that Monte Warden, formerly of the early-eighties rockabilly band The Wagoneers, produced nine new songs by her. Bob Brom finally got around to sendin' me a cassette of those nine songs after he was satisfied with 'em. Several of 'em are the best tunes I've heard Martí do since our 1992 session. At least they're all clean and well produced. A tad slick maybe, but Martí's vocals really come shining through. Bob had to admit to me I've still got a half-dozen or so songs from the 1992 session that are far superior that he'd like me to give him to put out. Now I just may put 'em out on a CD album, but after all the work I went through back then, the word "give" just don't cut it with me no more. Those recordings from 1992 are to me like Elvis's Sun recordings. Martí, like Elvis, was new and raw in the studio, with virtually no prior studio experience, and as the years pass by, in rare cases such as Elvis's and I believe Martí Brom's, those recordings will always be looked upon as best. You'll be able to decide for yourself one day. But Bob has decided to release eight of Martí's latest recordings on a package of four 45 vinyl singles.

In conclusion on Martí, if I never produce another new artist, I'll always know I had the best vocalist I could ever anticipate for my final one. I'm just happy that it was me who first got her started with her first record and it was my cigarette that lit the fire in her back in '92, 'cause now she's really smokin'.

Other Women

Just to conclude this chapter on the chicks that were or some that still are out there playin' and singin' rockabilly music in their own way, I'll just say I don't know and haven't even heard of all of 'em, past or present. I've only labored on tellin' you 'bout the ones that I believe are the best I've run into and witnessed or maybe at least heard a few songs on.

Some others worth noting include Rosie Flores, who I can't get too high on, though she did have one excellent album out back in 1987 on Reprise Records. The way I see it, Rosie just mainly wants a hit record. Don't matter whether it's rockabilly, country, pop, whatever, she'll take the deal if it's gonna make her a success. With me, it's always been if you don't believe in the music you're doin' and it ain't deep inside your soul, you shouldn't be doin' it. I'm not the only one who's got Rosie's number. After a couple of country albums failed to cause much attention on the Hightone Records label in the early nineties, she turned back and recorded an album titled *Rockabilly Filly* in 1995. I got dozens of phone calls and letters from rockabilly fans that know what real rockabilly music is, and they wound up buyin' it only because Rosie got Wanda Jackson and Janis Martin to record a track each on it. The response from all those who corresponded with me was one of disgust with it. I actually feel sorry for Rosie, because she seems desperate. In late 1995 and early '96, she got Wanda Jackson to tour with her, which got her on Ralph Emory's now-defunct morning show on TNN and got her in quite a number of original music clubs around the country, but it really didn't do anything for Rosie or her career. Everyone that I know who went to those shows around the country (me included, when they played Nashville) were there to see Wanda Jackson or line up to get her autograph and buy her pictures. After ridin' Wanda's coattails, later in 1996 she teamed up with Sun Records fifties legend Sonny Burgess, also with very little success for her. Recently I heard from Rosie that she signed a contract with Rounder Records to do three albums. Boy, I can't wait to see what happens when the dust settles. That label and Rosie deserve each other. I know both of 'em pretty well, and all hell's bound to break loose. They'll never make it to a third album together, I'll bet on that one.

A few others I'll at least mention that I felt had some good records out over the years are Little Tina & Flight 56 (1975, on Rockhouse Records in Holland), Martha Hull (1980, on Ripsaw Records, produced and paid for by Tex Rubinowitz), The Seductones (1982), Kristi Rose & The Midnight Walkers (1986, Rounder Records), Carlene Carter (1991), and Virginia & The Blue Dots (1993). Except for Carlene Carter, all of these girls have long since abandoned rockabilly music. Mostly 'cause they were ridin' the crest of the rockabilly revival from the late seventies into the mid to late eighties, or they had other music they preferred. I must say, though, Kristi Rose, who now lives in Nashville, still includes a rockabilly song or two in her sets to this day, and there is something to be said for that, 'cause I know Kristi well enough to know she only does songs that she really wants to do and believes in.

I'd have to say the best fairly new female rockabilly singer out of the Washington, D.C., area I've only heard a few songs by on one 45 and a compilation CD is Ruthie Noone, with her group The Wranglers. I know Ruthie's husband Mark fairly well from his new wave band The Slickee Boys, but I don't really know Ruthie all that well. What I do know is she does a real good rockabillyish cover of the old Johnny Cash classic from his Sun days, "Straight A's in Love," that I listen to quite a bit, and her 1996 45 single "Rockabilly Song #9" I also like. Ruthie & The Wranglers are real popular in the Washington, D.C., music scene currently, and they play a lot in and around there, as well as traveling and doing shows as far away as Atlanta. They've been to Nashville once that I know and played a club here, but I was out of town and missed 'em. They put out a new CD album I'm sure I'd like during the fall of '96, and I guess they'll get around to sendin' it to me one of these days. Mark and Ruthie are good people, and I'm just glad Ruthie is carryin' on the great tradition of laying down good solid rockabilly music in a place that's always been a hotbed for it. Good ol' Washington, D.C.

Country Comes Back to Rockabilly

op country music artists that recorded out of Nashville's main studios had been recording and covering rockabilly songs since Marty Robbins first covered "That's All Right, Mama" after Elvis's version on Sun Records in Memphis had broken out in a lot of regional markets in the South during the summer and fall of 1954. By the end of '54, Marty had his own version of the song out on Columbia Records that started gettin' airplay on country radio. Marty was probably the first. Between 1955 and 1958, during rockabilly music's hottest period, top country singers such as Webb Pierce, Faron Young, Don Gibson, Johnny Horton, George Jones, and of course Marty Robbins, and so many other established artists were forced to release records with a teenage or rockabilly sound that went on to sell well to country audiences. This new music that came out of Memphis had to be dealt with by the big record companies in Nashville. Nashville's biggest established stars from 1950 to 1955 were Eddie Arnold, Hank Snow, Carl Smith, and Hank Thompson. All had #1 records consistently throughout those years, but from 1956 through the end of the fifties, not one of those mentioned saw the top spot on the *Billboard* country charts. Only Marty Robbins, Ray Price, Jim Reeves, and Webb Pierce were able to reach #1 from '56 on. In the year of 1956 alone, Elvis Presley held down the #1 spot with five separate songs for 34 of the 52 weeks on the *Billboard* country charts. Elvis practically destroyed not only popular music the way adults and older people had grown to love it, but also did the same thing to country music for a few years. After Elvis, Nashville's old-timers also had to deal with the likes of Carl Perkins, Jerry Lee Lewis, and The Everly Brothers toppin' all their precious charts. So I can certainly understand why a lot of the established country music artists, such as especially Faron Young, held a whole lot of resentment, mainly at Elvis. But after 1958, Music City U.S.A. was able to go back to the kind of country music they understood and artists they had control of out of Nashville.

Music, whether it's country, pop, rock, jazz, blues, or whatever, always changes as the years pass, but it usually always comes back around, maybe in an updated, sometimes more hard-edged form, to where it once was. Young artists usually go back to the past even when they're writing their new music. Nowadays in country music, your older country artists who had all the big hits during the fifties, sixties, and seventies are all relegated to stages either in Branson, Missouri, or are seen on "The Grand Ole Opry." You see the forty-and-under-age artists on the *Billboard* country charts, as well as in CMT (Country Music Television) videos or on TNN cable TV videos and shows for today's young country music fans, who buy most of the records. Time changes everything. That's just a fact we have to live with.

Now, I've always loved country music. But only if it was what I considered real country. When I was a little kid, I loved cowboy singers like Gene Autry and Tex Ritter. Early 1950s Carl Smith and Ray Price records have always been among my favorites. Let's face it, if it sounds like Hank Williams, and they're singin' about drinkin', jukeboxes, and honky-tonk hardwood floors, that's my kind of country. The Waylon Jennings, Willie Nelson, David Allen Coe, outlaw country stuff ranks high up there with me, also. I ain't gonna name artists' names, 'cause I've told enough of the truth in this book to piss some artists off that believe their own press kits, but I just don't want to go to a show and see a country artist sing practically all teary, weepy, slow, boring ballads. That just don't git it with me.

The sixties were a great decade for country music, with such great artists as Buck Owens, George Jones, Merle Haggard, Johnny Cash, and others dominating the top of the charts. The seventies weren't all that bad, either. Merle Haggard, Loretta Lynn, Jerry Lee Lewis, Dolly Parton, Conway Twitty, and others were all on the radio. By the late seventies and early eighties, there were all forms of country music on the radio and high up into the charts. I just didn't go for the Kenny Rogers, Olivia Newton-John, Anne Murray stuff that they were constantly playin' on country radio stations then, 'cause it just sounded too pop for me. But there were still some of the all-time greats gettin' airplay, plus there were some real good new country artists from the late seventies through the early eighties, such as Joe Stampley, Gene Watson, Mel McDaniel, and John Conlee, that were right in the pocket of country music as far as I was concerned.

Johnny Cash and Narvel Felts

On country radio and the *Billboard* charts, there really wasn't much, if any, that came close to soundin' like rockabilly music to me, but from the late seventies on, right up to the present day, a whole lot of songs that have been what I've always considered an updated commercial sound of rockabilly music. Like I mentioned in the Chapter 13, Tanya Tucker was layin' down some solid updated rockabilly music in the late seventies and early eighties. Tanya just had that raw voice to put it across. She can still do it. Waylon Jennings was always reviving Buddy Holly and Elvis rockabilly classics, at least on his albums, in the late seventies and early eighties.

Johnny Cash, who had ridden a twenty-year hot streak of continuous Top 10 and #1 country *Billboard* chart records until 1975, when they slacked off somewhat, recorded a couple of the hottest-soundin' 45s with an old rockabilly edge to 'em in the late seventies. They both made it into the *Billboard* Top 40 country charts at the time. The best one of the two was called "After the Ball." This record debuted on the *Billboard* country charts on December 22, 1977, reached a peak position of #32, and rode those charts for twelve weeks. The second one was called "I Will Rock 'n' Roll with You." This song went on the *Billboard* country charts on January 13, 1979, made it up to a high position of #21, and stayed on the charts for thirteen weeks. Johnny Cash also made an album during the early eighties called *Rockabilly Blues* that had a few good tracks on it. Marty Stuart, who would later hit big on the country charts doin' his brand of rockabilly music, especially from 1989 on, was playing lead guitar for Johnny Cash all during this time, and Marty came across with some strong rockabilly lead guitar work on these Cash rockabilly-type songs.

Nashville in general kept a close eye on what was hittin' on the pop charts or creating excitement in new music, so I'm sure they were well aware of Robert Gordon, who

had kicked off a rockabilly revival by the fall of 1977, and who better than an original Sun artist like Johnny Cash to go back to his original style from the 1950s?

In the fall of 1981, Johnny Cash's daughter Roseanne Cash followed up her biggest-ever country and pop hit "Seven Year Ache" with one that everybody I knew at the time considered to be a rockabilly song. It was called "My Baby Thinks He's a Train." It reached #1 on the *Billboard* country charts on November 14, 1981, and had a sixteen-week run on those charts.

Narvel Felts was another one who was an original rockabilly artist from the 1950s. Narvel only had limited success but consistently stayed workin' in music through the 1960s and first half of the 1970s. He finally broke through with a forty-two-song streak of *Billboard* Top 100 chart hits between 1975 and 1987. Narvel's not only one great live stage act, but also probably the greatest high-singin' balladeer country music ever had. Narvel charted a lot of fifties and early sixties oldies R&B songs, but also had *Billboard* country chart hits with rockabilly versions of Chuck Berry's "Roll Over Beethoven" as late as 1982.

Steve Earle, Dwight Yoakam, and Eddie Rabbitt

It really wasn't until after the huge success The Stray Cats were havin' in 1982 and '83 on the *Billboard* pop charts that a major label out of Nashville decided to sign an artist by the name of Steve Earle and come out and call the music he was doin' rockabilly. Steve Earle moved from Texas to Nashville in 1974, where he played his music on the local club scene, wrote songs for other artists, recorded demos, worked at and managed music publishing companies, and so on. His break came when Lee Stoller, owner of LSI Records in Nashville, recorded a four-song 7" EP of original rockabilly songs Steve Earle had written and called the EP *Pink & Black*. This was in 1982. This record and Steve did well enough for Epic Records to sign him to a contract in 1983 and label his music rockabilly.

I bought all four Steve Earle singles Epic released between the fall of 1983 and the fall of 1984. One came out with a picture sleeve of Steve in an Elvis fifties-type legs-bent-and-spread stance. They seemed to promote the first few pretty good, but Steve wound up havin' only two minor *Billboard* country chart hits out of the four. One was "Nothin' but You," which debuted on the *Billboard* country charts on October 1, 1983, reached

#70, and only stayed on the charts for four weeks. This was a real good mid-tempo rockabilly tune, though, as was the B side of the 45, "Continental Trailways Blues." Steve's next two 45s didn't make it onto the *Billboard* country charts at all. I remember back then there was talk goin' around that Epic Records was planning to release an album on Steve Earle, but it never came out then. Steve's final 45 for the label was called "What'll You Do about Me." This song debuted on the *Billboard* country charts on December 8, 1984, reached #76, and stayed on the charts for six weeks.

Steve Earle did go on to greater success, and not with the normal Alabama group sound that was so hot in the mid eighties. Country music started to change and go back to a more old-style traditional sound in 1986, when Randy Travis came in with his first real big hit, "1982." Steve Earle and Dwight Yoakam both hit real big at that time, both with strings of hit singles as well as early big-sellin' albums that not only charted up at the top of the *Billboard* country charts, but also crossed over onto the *Billboard* pop charts. These three guys helped bring solo singers back at the time, and all three had different sounds in their music that rejuvenated music marketed towards the country field and went on to sell millions of records to pop music buyers as well.

Since 1986, both Randy Travis and Dwight Yoakam have continued to have consistent success on the *Billboard* country charts and in live concerts. Randy Travis's music was about as stone hard-core great country as you'd want to find, but Dwight Yoakam at first alienated the Nashville music old-timers, 'cause he wasn't part of their system in 1986, when he hit it big on the country charts with his first 45 single, "Honky Tonk Man." Dwight Yoakam created quite a bit of grumblin' in Nashville business circles at the time. Dwight was living in Los Angeles. His management company was there. He was being booked out of there. He was on Reprise Records out there, and he recorded all his music out there, which was basically old hillbilly-soundin' with a new modern beat that appealed to green- and purple-headed punk rockers in the original music clubs he'd been performin' in at the time. Original music and rock critics all started dubbin' Dwight Yoakam as the new Hank Williams in 1986, when he had that first hit single off his first Reprise Records album. The album went gold. It was called *Guitars, Cadillacs, Etc., Etc.,* while the single, "Honky Tonk Man," went into the *Billboard* Top 5 country charts. The album was in the *Billboard* pop Top 40 album charts.

Dwight was unusual because none of the money bein' made for his new country music was comin' into the main business base for country music. That bein' Nashville. As the years went on, this changed somewhat, though early on, even his original musicians and producer, Pete Anderson, were all on the West Coast. But country music fans, along with punk rockers, as well as rockabilly music fans, all embraced Dwight Yoakam's new and sometimes cuttin'-edge sound in his fresh country music. It was a great first album, and when he came to Washington, D.C., in August 1986, while he was ridin' high, Dwight's first show was at the alternative music club called The 9:30 Club. There was a lot of excitement about him at the time, and every local music writer and rockabilly fan was there on that night he played. I was managing and producing LesLee "Bird" Anderson at that time, and Seth Horowitz was good enough to book her as the opening act for that show. The show went great for LesLee and Dwight, who was goin' with and had Wynonna Judd with him at the time. I met and talked with Dwight quite a bit in the dressing room that night. He was a nice guy then, and he was still all right in March 1987, when me, Pepper, and LesLee spent some time with him in his dressing room at The Warner Theater, where he was on a split bill with Robert Gordon. Dwight's had a pretty good big-time ride since then, and at the time, country music sure needed him, 'cause in his music and live stage shows, he helped breathe some rocked-up sounds into what was becoming, for the most part, a standard, stale feeling in country music.

Steve Earle wasn't as fortunate back then. After a string of seven straight Top 10 or Top 40 *Billboard* country chart 45 singles for the MCA Records label in Nashville off his first two albums, he changed directions in his music and more or less turned away from Nashville. Steve's music bordered right on the edge of rockabilly with his Top 10 and Top 40 country hits such as "Guitar Town," "Sweet Little 66," and "Six Days on the Road," and all that appealed to a lot of rockabilly fans at the time. But by 1988, Steve dropped his rockabilly-soundin' band that he called The Dukes and went into doin' more progressive rock or abstract folk, I don't know what I'd call it, music. I know he ain't had a chart hit since. He had some personal problems during the late eighties and early nineties, but now I hear he's makin' somewhat of a comeback, workin' out of Nashville again.

Eddie Rabbitt, who'd gotten his first big break by Elvis recording his song "Kentucky Rain" in 1970, has always appealed to me, as I could hear some rockabilly sounds comin' out of his music. Eddie had a string of Top 10s and a whole lot of #1s on the *Billboard* country charts, as well as havin' some big Top 10 and Top 40 hits on the *Billboard* pop charts. Eddie had a long big-time run between 1974 and 1991. Eddie's two biggest songs that I consider right-on modern-day commercial rockabilly music were in the summer of 1984, when his song "B-B-Burnin' Up with Love" reached #3 on the *Billboard* country charts and had a long ride of eighteen weeks on the charts, and a year later, when he came back with another solid-sounding rockabilly tune called "Warning Sign." This song climbed up the *Billboard* country charts and peaked out at #4 during the late spring of 1985 and had another long ride of nineteen weeks on those charts. You could usually find rockabilly-type songs such as "Go to Sleep Big Bertha" and others buried on Eddie Rabbitt's mid-eighties albums. As late as the summer of 1988, Eddie had one of the better cover versions of the way-too-much-covered "The Wanderer." Eddie's version reached #1 then on the *Billboard* country charts and had an eighteen-week ride on 'em.

Dabblers

I'm just gonna mention some of the Nashville artists on major labels who at least dabbled in rockabilly music during the mid to late eighties. Nashville and their top country music artists have always recorded 1950s rockabilly songs. Sometimes when they shouldn't have. Two classic examples of when they should have left well enough alone are when in the late eighties they released "Don't Be Cruel" as a 45 single by The Judds, which by the way was rejected so badly by listeners at the time, it was the only song that broke their long string of *Billboard* country chart hits when it only made it into the Top 20 and then started droppin', and Alan Jackson's version of the Eddie Cochran classic rockabilly hit "Summertime Blues" in 1995. Even though that one went all the way to #1, man, it was terrible. Maybe not to Alan Jackson fans, but I just don't need to hear a nasal whinin' tone of voice on a classic song like that, and I like some of Alan Jackson's music.

Other artists, such as Rodney Crowell, had some rockabilly-type songs on a couple late-eighties albums. Mel McDaniel, who I've always liked and believe really does have a love for rockabilly music and fifties rock 'n' roll, recorded an album in 1989 for Capitol Records called *Rockabilly Boy*. The album and the 45s released from it basically went nowhere on the charts, and there were only two or three songs I liked a lot on it, but at least ol' Mel's heart was in the right place.

The Lonesome Strangers, a group from Los Angeles, landed a deal with the independent Hightone Records label out there. Hightone somehow got one big hit out of this group in 1989, when the old Johnny Horton song they did in a great rockabilly style, called "Goodbye Lonesome, Hello Baby Doll," made it all the way up to #32 on the *Billboard* country charts, for a fifteen-week ride. Those are real good numbers for a West Coast independent record label, I can tell you that.

Ricky Van Shelton had the hottest cover version I ever heard of the old Little Jimmy Dickens 1958 classic rockabilly tune "I Got a Hole in My Pocket." In 1988, Ricky's version of that tune reached the Top 5 of the *Billboard* country charts. I recommend it for a collector of solid rockabilly music. Ricky also recorded quite a few other tunes that I could hear a lot of rockabilly comin' from the sounds of those Nashville musicians on. Steve Buckingham was Ricky's producer on all those songs, and he has a good ear for rockabilly music done in the Nashville way.

Marty Stuart

I'm sure I'm leavin' out some other artists in country music that have had success with rockabilly music. Some of 'em I'm gonna leave over into the next chapter, as the ones I've got in mind are all still doin' rockabilly-type music in the nineties and didn't really start their careers until then. I'm closin' this chapter out with an artist whose roots were planted in bluegrass music, but his importance to commercial Nashville-styled rockabilly music is really more than any other rockabilly artist I can think of. That artist is Marty Stuart.

I got to know Marty a good bit between 1989 and 1991. Good enough at least to know even though he was then thoroughly embedded and accepted into the Nashville family, he truly cared for and loved the music he does. What I liked most about him was his total respect for hillbilly and rockabilly music of the past. I also liked him 'cause he was like I used to be. A bit of a "wild child." He liked to have a good time before, during, and after his shows.

Marty Stuart worked in Lester Flatt's bluegrass band for quite a while and went on to play lead guitar for Johnny Cash until 1985. In 1985, Marty signed with Columbia Records in Nashville and had a hit song called "Arlene," which was considered rockabilly by many fans at the time. The song made it up to #19 on the *Billboard* country charts in March 1986 and had a nice eighteen-week run on those charts. Marty had five more songs

Forgettin' to Remember to Forget

I got to know Marty Stuart pretty well at four shows his did in the D.C. area in 1989 and 1990. After May 1990, I wouldn't see him again until the first week of February 1991, about six weeks after I arrived in Nashville. One morning I heard on the radio that all Marty Stuart fans should go over to the Nashville Network studios at 10:00 a.m., because Marty and his band would be tapin' a TV show there, doin' songs from his new album on MCA Records that was the follow-up to *Hillbilly Rock*. I didn't have much to do that day, so I figured I'd go by and say hi to Marty and an old friend of mine, Dave Durocher, who used to be in Tex Rubinowitz's band but was now playing drums for Marty.

It was a cold, rainy day. I had to park about 200 yards away and walk in this nasty weather to the security guard and tell him why I was there. It was 9:50 by this time, and the security guard said I could wait inside his booth. There was only one other person in the booth waitin' to get into this show. It was a girl, or a woman, who looked to me to be in her early thirties. She was a big Marty Stuart fan, she told me, who followed him almost everywhere. She told me about how wonderful Marty was for the ten minutes we had to wait before we could walk over to where they were tapin' his show. When we got over there, we were told we had to wait outside the studio door, which was at least inside the building, until they let the audience in at 10:30. Well, at 10:05, the only audience I saw was me and this Marty Stuart groupie who I had to listen to for another twenty-five minutes. When she asked me how well I knew Marty and how many of his shows I'd seen, I told her I'd seen a few shows, liked him, and he knew who I was, and that was about it. When she asked me if I was in the music business, I said no.

By 10:30, there was still only me and this "girl," and I was wondering where the hell the audience was, 'cause the taping was supposed to start at 11:00. Well, at 11:05 (I kept lookin' at my watch), here comes a large tour group of senior citizens. It turns out they never even heard of Marty Stuart. They were supposed to be goin' to see the homes where the stars live. When this seventy-five-to-eighty-year-old lady said, "Daddy'll never forgive me if I don't show him a picture of Eddy Arnold's house," it was all I could do to keep from fallin' on the floor laughin'.

The doors finally opened at 11:25, and the Marty Stuart groupie said to me, "I'll hold you a good front seat next to me." I was thinkin', "Wonderful. This must be my lucky day." That girl practically ran up to the front-row seats. I don't know why, 'cause I didn't have any trouble walking well ahead of the senior citizens who were all following me. Finally, at 12:15, Marty's band was in place. When Dave Durocher first sat down behind the drums, he spotted me in the front row, so he waved to me and said, "Billy, I'll talk to you after the show." Well, the fan beside me wanted to know where I knew Dave from, but before I could answer, Marty came out on stage. Marty looked out and spotted me sittin' almost directly in front of the mike. Now, the last time I'd seen Marty up in Maryland, I joked that I was gonna move to the town of Murfreesboro, Tennessee, where he lived, buy a house there, and be an irritating neighbor of his. When he spotted me sittin' in the front row at this TV tapin', Marty came over and said, "Billy Poore, how ya doin? Did you buy that house in Murfreesboro yet?" I grinned and said, "Not yet, but I'm workin' my way out there. Right now, I'm on Murfreesboro Road." Marty grinned back and said, "I'll talk to you later on." Well, after that, this groupie just burned my ears off with stuff like, "I knew all the time by the way you look you were a songwriter or something. You work for Marty, dontcha, come on, I won't tell nobody, how come you know him so well? I need to talk to you after the show." And on and on until they finally started tapin', and Marty started singin', and that kept her jaws from flappin'.

After the show, Dave Durocher and I talked for a few minutes. Marty was signing autographs and havin' his picture taken with a couple of people, and this girl was right next to him the whole time, but I went over anyway and said hi to him. That groupie looked at me and said, "Now, don't you leave before we get to talk some more, ya hear?" Well, I went over and told Dave a quick so-long, and that I really had to split, 'cause as soon as Marty got outta there, that crazy groupie of his would be comin' after me. Dave laughed and said, "There's a side door over there you can slip out of." I said, "Thanks, man, and I'll see you next time." So I did make a clean getaway.

that made the *Billboard* Top 100 singles charts between 1986 and 1988 off the two albums he recorded for Columbia Records. They had an option for one other album if the first one did well enough. That's usually the case.

Marty then signed with MCA Records, and in 1989 they released an album on him titled *Hillbilly Rock*. I went out and bought this album when it first came out. The first 45 single they released off of it was a great version by Marty of Johnny Cash's first *Billboard* country hit on Sun Records, called "Cry, Cry, Cry." Marty did a great video on the song and dedicated it to Johnny Cash's late, great guitar player Luther Perkins. The song "Cry, Cry, Cry" went onto the *Billboard* country charts and made it into the lower end of the Top 40 songs. The album *Hillbilly Rock* was bein' bought by a good number of rockabilly fans in the D.C. area, and it was a solid mixture of rockabilly and honky-tonk hillbilly music.

Well, Marty's second 45 single off *Hillbilly Rock* didn't even reach the Top 40, and his third single didn't even do as well as the second one. About the time I saw Marty in Maryland in early 1990, the fourth and what was supposed to be the final song released from this album started to take off high up into the charts. The song was the title track from *Hillbilly Rock*. Marty told me that the people at MCA Records were only obligated to release one more 45 single off his *Hillbilly Rock* album and that was gonna be the end of his deal with the label, because he had failed to have one Top 10 country song from his first three 45 singles, so they didn't see any hope for him havin' one on the last one. Marty said to me, "The MCA people decided to release the song 'Hillbilly Rock' because they felt it was the worst and dumbest song on the whole album. So they'd be done with me after that. As it turned out, DJ's picked up on the song, and it really took off. Just goes to show the ones that choose the 45 releases that get pushed to country DJ's don't know what's gonna hit and what ain't." "Hillbilly Rock" got so big, they had to shoot a video and make up a dance for this song in 1990. The rest is history.

By the mid 1990s, broad-minded rockabilly fans around the world all supported Marty and his music for the respect he gave to rockabilly. I've got all Marty's albums and CD's in my collection, and this wild child has been layin' down and puttin' out some hot burn-me-down songs ever since. In Finland he was voted #1 rockabilly artist of 1991. Marty'll always be OK in my book. Outside of Tanya Tucker, I like him best out of the rest of the Nashville artists. He rocks.

Old and New Artists and Acts Still Carryin' On

*N*ow, before I get into listin' somewhere around 200 mostly new rockabilly artists and bands that are currently active and play the rockabilly club and festival circuits around the world, what I feel I have to do is give a lot of you fans, bands, and others that continue to write to me and tell me that you're thinkin' about startin' your own record label, promotin' shows, formin' a band, managing an artist or group 'cause they're just the greatest thing to ever come along in rockabilly music, etc., some true-to-the-bone honest advice with what you're gettin' yourself into. If you're between twenty-five and thirty-five years old, you're probably not gonna wanna read this, 'cause nobody can tell you anything like this, 'cause you love rockabilly music so much like I did when I was your age and still do. I wouldn't-a listened to anybody fifteen or twenty years ago, and I take responsibility for what I do, but just maybe somebody will gain something from what I'm about to say and not make some of the same mistakes I did. Also, I do not want anyone out there thinkin' I'm bitter about the losses me and my family sustained by one particular artist. I took many a beatin' from other artists, some of legendary status in rockabilly music, and I have no regrets. Only personal satisfaction and good memories.

First off, if you start your own record company because there's a band or an artist that you think is the greatest thing since sliced bread but is basically unknown and attracts only a handful of their friends out to their shows, but they know you're willing to put a record out on 'em, you make damn sure you sign 'em to a contract where whatever songs you're puttin' out, whether it's two songs on a 45 or fourteen or more on an album, that they have to turn over all ownership of these recordings to your label. That's only fair to both parties, 'cause you're gonna be the one who's payin' for these records or albums that are being pressed. Also, when you get these records, make the band members or artists pay you wholesale cost that you'd get from your distributors (if you're lucky) for the records they get from you to sell at their live shows. Get your money at the time they receive the records. That also is only fair. If that band or artist doesn't think so, you better remember if they were really that great, why would you have to put their record out? If they could get a better deal from someone else, they wouldn't need you to do it.

If you're a new band or artist just startin' out and doin' strictly rockabilly music, you're gonna have to play wherever you can for nothin' or next to nothin'. If you're a rockabilly band or artist who's been around four or five years and have a stack of press clippings two inches thick glorifyin' your accomplishments, just remember that all it is to club owners in the U.S. and around the world is nothin' more than paper. Don't overestimate your value, and try to find either a booking agent or manager that's for the most part honest (and there's a few out there) to negotiate your bookings for you. Booking agents and managers mainly only care about their percentage, and they earn it, 'cause they have to sell you and your music. They don't usually care that much about the music you love playin', only the amount of money they can earn from it. Also, don't ever think you're a better band or artist than other ones that you think may be doin' better than you, 'cause there's always someone out there that's better than you. Talent really don't mean a thing.

Finally, if you're gonna promote a rockabilly show or festival, and you're a diehard fan of a certain artist or band, you can bet that artist knows it and will ask for the highest amount of money he can get from you. You better have all the money in advance and make sure you have them sign a contract and live up to their end of it. Don't rely on every rockabilly fan that you know to show up at the show, 'cause that just don't happen. If you can't afford to lose that money, don't gamble it.

Washington, D.C.

Now for the fun part of it. I'm gonna be as brief as I can. With all the problems I had with my one primary very talented artist, Johnny Seaton, as I look back on it, the best thing that ever happened was when I finally got him to where he was making tons of money and could afford to dump me. Though I'll never forget it, and I didn't feel this way at the time, while Seaton was touring in that Elvis musical, I stayed right with the music I loved the best. Rockabilly music. I wasn't sidetracked much after that and was solidly producing all rockabilly, roots rock 'n' roll, and hardcore hillbilly music, and bookin' the bands I chose to that were doin' it best in D.C. at that time.

By the early months of 1988, though, I was gettin' pretty tired of the D.C. club scene and dealin' with club owners. I got completely out of booking any local bands in clubs. What I'd really get most of my enjoyment out of between 1988 and 1990 was going back to booking and promoting some of the greatest legendary acts in 1950s rockabilly and rock 'n' roll that either I'd never seen perform live and wanted to or some of which hadn't performed rockabilly here in the U.S. in almost thirty years. Each one of these rockabilly shows took four to five months of almost daily continuous work on mine and Pepper's part to promote. But it was worth it all. Not only to me, but to every person who ever attended any of 'em. My daughter Stacy was between fifteen and seventeen years old at that time, and at these shows she was a big help to me, too. I also became good friends with other rockabilly fans I had met in the prior couple years.

The first show I did at the Severna Park Elks Lodge in Severna Park, Maryland, when I brought Jack Scott to town, came about because of Pepper. She has always loved Charlie Feathers, Gene Vincent, Jo Ann Campbell, and other rockabilly artists, music I'd been playin' constantly for twenty years by then, and I'd occasionally play Jack Scott. I'd just gotten a double-album set on him from Europe in early 1988, and I was playin' that a lot at the time, and every once in a while, she'd hear a song and say, "I really like that. Who's singin' it?" I'd say, "Jack Scott." Well, after the answer was the same during the course of two straight days on about a half-dozen songs, Pepper popped up and said, "Now, I really like him a lot, so why can't you bring him to town for a live show?" I said, "Let me call Tex Rubinowitz and see if he's still got his phone number." Tex did, gave it to me, and that started the ball rollin'. A year later, when I got this

European album by Hayden Thompson that was on Charly Records in England, Pepper wanted me to bring him in for a show also, but I didn't have any idea of how to get ahold of him then.

But startin' with that Jack Scott show in July 1988 (Jack did six shows that first time), I just concentrated on the artists I most wanted to see that were basically only performing in Europe at the time, with the exception of Sleepy La Beef. Artists I booked, such as Jack Scott, Janis Martin, and Narvel Felts, from the fifties, who had all made great rockabilly records then, were only performing two or three times a year in Europe. Now, Narvel Felts has been on the country music circuit since the early seventies when he started havin' his Top 10 *Billboard* hits, but he was only primarily singin' to country audiences here in the U.S. Narvel was amazed at the Charlie Feathers benefit show he performed for me on August 12, 1989, that the almost entire audience was made up of rockabilly fans between eighteen and thirty years old, with their leather jackets, high hair, tattoos, etc., and they were all screamin' for him to sing rockabilly songs he'd recorded in the late fifties, such as "Foolish Thoughts," "Three Thousand Miles," "Cutie Baby," and others. He couldn't believe it. Narvel told this wild crowd that night just this: "This rockabilly thing has been happenin' for quite a while in Europe, where I play, but I didn't know it was happenin' here. I haven't sung these songs here in the U.S. or played to a crowd like this since the fifties. Thank you so much for remembering me and my rockabilly music." That whole audience of 500 fans screamed, whistled, and gave thunderous applause to what Narvel told 'em.

Every artist and band I had on the half-dozen shows I put on at the Severna Park Elks Lodge back then all gave top-notch performances. Except for Becky Hobbs, all the headliners I brought for these events were all 1950s original rockabilly artists that are known the world over today and are all still sellin' a lot of records. I was proud of the fact that I was able to give Vernon Taylor enough confidence that he was still great enough and good enough to hold his own to do his first rockabilly show, or any show for that matter, in over twenty-six years. I put a good band behind him and convinced him there was a whole new audience today waitin' to hear an original like him. Janis Martin was great when I called her to do a show in February 1990. Janis was just surprised that there were young kids right here in the U.S. that would still come out to see her perform her fifties rockabilly music. This was her first live show in the U.S. in thirty years. Jack Scott came back fourteen months after his first show for me to do a one-night, two-set show in September 1989. Sleepy La Beef, Narvel Felts, and Robert Gordon all gave first-class shows for me between 1988 and 1990. Vernon Taylor and Tex Rubinowitz performed at all of those shows in '89 and '90. But not only all the top legendary fifties rockabilly artists gave great shows, but also young local rockabilly bands like Go Cat Go, The Atomics, Virginia & The Blue Dots, Pink & Black, The Bobby Smith Band, and The Pick-Ups, along with out-of-state artists such as Todd Monroe and the Austin-based trio High Noon, all gave some of the best rockabilly performances you'd ever want to see.

I always had between six and seventeen acts on these live shows. The work was hard as nails. Rockabilly has

Forgettin' to Remember to Forget

The officials at the Severna Park Elks Lodge didn't seem to mind the first couple shows I put on there during the summer and fall of 1988, but they gave me some grief at the seventeen-act benefit for Charlie Feathers on August 12, 1989, which included performances by Charlie, Robert Gordon, Narvel Felts, Vernon Taylor, Tex Rubinowitz, Billy Hancock, Bubba Feathers, Todd Monroe, LesLee "Bird" Anderson, Bob E. Rock, Arizona Cool, The A-Bones, Pink & Black, Virginia & The Blue Dots, The Atomics, Victor McCullough, and The Pick-Ups.

While Billy Miller, the lead singer of The A-Bones, was singin' some wild song, one of the Grand Poo-Bahs, or whatever they're called, came up to me and said, "Mr. Poore, I'm a member of the board, and I'd like to let you know that we don't approve of the actions that are going on up there on our stage right now." I said, "What actions?" He replied, "Some of our members and their wives have noticed that person up there now singing his disgusting music has a hole in the crotch of his pants, and he's wearing no underwear, and we don't approve or allow that sort of thing." Well, there couldn't have been more than eight or ten Elks members in this whole place, including their wives, but I told this man, "Excuse me just a minute!" I milled my way through this sardine-packed crowd and got as close to Billy Miller as I could get to look. Sure enough, he did have a small- to medium-sized hole right in the crotch of his pants, and yes, he did not have any underwear on. There was none of his private parts hangin' out, but as he jumped around on stage, I did notice once, very quickly, inside his crotch, you'd get a flash of his private parts. Which I could have done without seein' on this or any other night.

So I weaved my way back to this old man, who was standin' with his arms folded across his chest, staring a hole through me. When I got to him, I said, "Now sir, I'd like you to listen to everything I have to say, and I do not mean it in any kind of disrespectful way towards your fine organization. True, that singer on stage does have a slight tear in his crotch, and also true, he is not wearing any underwear, but I do know that from where your group of members are seated, it would take either Superman's X-ray vision or high-powered binoculars to even see that hole or what's inside of it. Your group is seated almost to the back of the hall, near the bar, and there's no way, without walking all the way to the front, anyone would notice it, as no one else has complained about it." This man started to interrupt, and I said, "Hold on until you hear me out, please. Speakin' of the bar, your waitresses and bartenders can't come close to keepin' up with all the liquor that's bein' consumed in here tonight, that your organization is profiting from. I'm gettin' the most complaints about people not bein' able to get a drink. The Anne Arundel County Executive has declared August 12, 1989, this day, as 'Rockabilly Music Day' in this county, plus your Elks Lodge here has benefited from all the publicity that I've had to pay for plus work my tail off to get in every major newspaper from the *Washington Post* to the *Baltimore Sun*. My past shows have also given this Elks Lodge free publicity. You don't see any unruly people in here tonight. Finally, I'd like you to go back and tell whoever it is that don't approve of what they see on that stage tonight, I'll be glad to give them the money they paid to get in back to them, that happens to be going to that older artist who's unable to pay his hospital bills. Also, please remind the head of your organization that I have signed contracts by him to do four more live rockabilly festivals in here through June 1990, and I expect this Elks Lodge to live up to 'em." Well, he didn't say a word to me, but he walked back and evidently told 'em what I'd said. None of 'em asked for their money back, though, and all four of my future shows went on under their watchful eyes. I had way more problems out of those old fogies than I ever did out of any young tattooed, wild-lookin' girl or guy that was a hard-core modern-day rockabilly fan.

always been hard to sell. I'm talkin' about recent years by that statement. But I got a lot of personal gratification out of proving that I could put between 250 and 500 rockabilly fans in an Elks Lodge located in a section of Anne Arundel County, a mile from where I lived, with mostly yuppie neighbors all around the area. The local county newspapers didn't have a clue of what rockabilly music was, but they found out and covered these events and gave a great deal of press before and after the shows. I didn't see a review on a show Chubby Checker did at a local nightclub lounge in April 1990, so I felt I had to be doin' something real and right.

Besides these shows, from 1988 right up to the first week of November 1990, I could be found either in the studio with LesLee "Bird" Anderson, Tex Rubinowitz, Billy Hancock, Bobby Smith, Eva Cassidy, Todd Monroe, or Arizona Cool producing rockabilly or hillbilly songs on them, or out at a rockabilly-type show seein' Sleepy La Beef, The Sun Rhythm Section, Go Cat Go, Pink & Black (who later changed their name to The Reluctant Playboys), Bobby Smith, Danny Gatton, Virginia & The Blue Dots, and so on.

Nashville

I had been writin' a lot of songs that were country rock or downright hillbilly during the late eighties, after Dwight Yoakam hit it big, and I'd been sayin' to Pepper that I wouldn't mind moving down around Nashville and see what it was like there by this time. What really convinced me was on Father's Day weekend in mid June 1990, when me and my daughter Stacy drove down to Memphis to see Charlie Feathers. On the way back home, we stopped and spent the night in Nashville. Gerry Teifer, who was in the international licensing department at Acuff/Rose Publishing Company in Nashville, had called me a year earlier in 1989 on a song that Shakin' Stevens might want to record in England, and wanted some information on it. Gerry had found out from BMI that I was the writer of the song and had gotten my number and called me on it. I gave him all the information on the song, and then we went on to have a good conversation on music in general. Gerry told me then if I was ever in Nashville to stop in his office and visit with him. So that's what I did. I had this first demo of a Christmas song that me and Tex Rubinowitz had written during February 1990 on an idea I'd come up with. Well, I went and saw Gerry, and I mentioned this song, called "It's Not the Presents under My Tree (It's Your Presence Right Here Next to Me)," and that I had the first rough demo of it. Gerry wanted to hear it. So I gave it to him,

and he put it on his cassette deck and played this three-minute demo. When the song was over, I went on to say something, and he told me, "Hold on, I want to hear this again." Gerry rewound the tape and played it over. He told me, "That's without a doubt the best Christmas song I've heard in years. You need to move down here to Nashville." Well, I told him I'd been thinkin' about it, just 'cause I had a good number of country-type songs I'd like to push. Gerry Teifer was (and I'm sure still is, but now has since retired from Acuff/Rose and lives in Florida) one of the most decent, straightforward, honest people I got to know after I did move here. But I told him then that I was and always had been involved in rockabilly music, old and new, and still had a lot of things I wanted to complete in the D.C. area, and then I might just move somewhere close to Nashville.

I brought Gerry a copy of the final demo me and Tex did on the Christmas song, with Eva Cassidy singin' it once more. He'd requested it, and he thought it was great again and even better than the first one. I dropped this one off with him in August 1990, right after I'd left Memphis from bein' in the studio with Charlie Feathers when he recorded his Elektra Records album. I could relax a little now that Mission (almost) Impossible had been completed. When I got back to Maryland, I told Pepper I wanted to move to Nashville and for her to put the house up for sale. I had my mind made up. Not just because I had hopes of gettin' one of my songs in with a top artist or publisher, but also because I knew some other people like Eddie Angel who were playin' rockabilly music there, and I was pretty worn out with the Little League politics of the D.C. music scene. You always have to deal with politics in music, but at least if I had to be involved in it, I wanted to be in a place where somebody had a real chance of succeeding. Even Robert Gordon, who was from D.C., had to move to New York City to achieve a major-label record contract. Mary Chapin Carpenter is the only artist I've known that's ever gotten a deal out of the D.C. area and went on to superstar success.

So, after finishing up some recording projects with Bobby Smith and Arizona Cool that I was committed to, I left Pepper and Stacy back in Maryland right after Christmas 1990 and moved to Nashville. There were yuppies who were lookin' to get into our neighborhood, so I figured it wouldn't take her long to sell the house. It did take Pepper till April 1991, though. Eddie Angel told me before I got to Nashville that I could stay with him and Sonny George at their apartment till I found a place. So I stayed with Sonny and Eddie for over a month until I got a one-bedroom apartment in Hendersonville that suited me better because of all the stuff I brought with me. It was good that I stayed with Eddie and Sonny through that first month or so, as they had the best and hottest rockabilly band in all of Nashville during the early months of 1991. They called their band The Planet Rockers. During those early months of 1991, I saw The Planet Rockers do about a dozen hot, kickin', rockin' live shows. It was fun just to watch a solid rockabilly band in its early stages. The original members of the group were Sonny George on lead vocals and rhythm guitar, Eddie Angel on lead guitar and backup vocals, Mark Winchester on hot, slappin' upright bass and backup vocals, and Billy Swartz on drums. The Planet Rockers first formed, toured Europe and parts of the States that year, and started recording their first album that No Hit Records in England released in the summer of 1991. This tight four-piece rockabilly outfit only recorded two albums. The second one in 1992 for Sunjay Records in Sweden. This second album was a live album that was great, also. By 1993, Mark Winchester and Billy Swartz had left the group. But Sonny George and Eddie Angel carried The Planet Rockers on and continued to release 45s on various labels, such as No Hit, and Spinout Records here in Nashville. Today, Eddie and Sonny continue to do separate projects on their own and occasionally get back together as The Planet Rockers. Both of their first two Planet Rocker albums are still available through Spinout Records here in the U.S. and the original labels in Europe they were released on. I'd recommend both of 'em to rockabilly fans everywhere. One other note is that Mike Smyth, who owns Phonolux Records in Nashville, was a drivin' force in the early stages of The Planet Rockers and their first album.

During those first three or four months of 1991, I did spend some time during the weekdays having various Nashville publishers listen to my original songs, and Gerry Teifer over at Acuff/Rose was pushin' 'em for me there. But my heart wasn't really into this Clint Black Hat Pack that had taken over by this time in the major music scene, so I basically went back to what I loved most, and that was rockabilly music. During the time I was out meeting with top publishers and artists during those first months of 1991, I did become friends with a lot of really decent, nice, honest people. So I found out everybody in Nashville's real major music business wasn't all bad, like a lot of people seem to think. It's just that they have a certain system you have to work your way into and then go by their rules, and if you can do that, you got a good

shot at havin' somethin' really good happen for you. Two things with me, though, are that I didn't have the time, or at least I didn't want to take it to do a lot of politicking, which you really have to do, and I've never been any good at sellin' myself, songs I write, etc. I pass 'em out and leave it at that and always turn back to rockabilly.

High Noon

I've always been a collector, so I could always pay the bills by doin' conventions or workin' off my mailing list. I also kept my *Rockabilly Revue* goin' out on a steady basis through the rest of 1991, until I became really busy in the studio down here and started issuing more 45s on my Renegade Records label, along with workin' with Lucky & The Hot Dice. During late March 1991 I made my first trip to Austin, Texas. What a great time I had, too. I had only planned to go there for the Austin Record Convention, where I had a booth set up, but I wound up stayin' over a couple extra days to see a couple rockabilly bands and go to the best honky-tonk club I'd been to in quite a while. This little joint, called Henry's, had the rockabilly band High Noon get up and do some songs with the regular honky-tonk hillbilly band that played there, called Don Walser & The Pure Texas Band. Steel guitarist Jimmy Day was in Don Walser's band at that time. Jimmy had played with Elvis as early as 1954 on the "Louisiana Hayride" shows, as well as many dates throughout Texas in '54 and '55 while Elvis was still on Sun Records. Jimmy Day later went to Nashville and played steel guitar on so many great songs and hits, such as "More and More" by Webb Pierce, when country music meant real country.

I went out to see my old D.C. buddy Evan Johns & His H-Bombs on that first trip, but I really enjoyed the group High Noon a lot, and the music they were playin'. This was in the spring of 1991, and their first four-song vinyl EP was released on Willie Lewis's Rock-A-Billy Record company in Denver. I had booked High Noon on my final show in Maryland, only nine months prior, and they'd come a long way since then, and I was really glad to see 'em doin' so well as the top rockabilly band in Austin by that time. Since then, High Noon has traveled to England, Finland, and other parts of the world, playin' their young brand of rockabilly music. They've become one of Finland's favorite groups. In Finland, High Noon has had record releases on the Goofin' record label, owned by Pete Hakonen. In just a few short years, there's quite a bit of product out there on the High Noon rockabilly trio. There's at least four or five 45 single releases, a four-song EP, and three to four vinyl LPs. High Noon's members are Shaun Young on lead vocals and rhythm guitar, Sean Mencher on lead guitar and harmony and backup vocals, and Kevin Smith (Austin's #1 upright bass player) on standup, slappin' bass and backup vocals. Today, Sean Mencher, his wife and manager of High Noon, Leslie Frieda, and family have moved to Maine, while Shaun Young and Kevin Smith remain in Austin. Shawn and Kevin back up Marti´ Brom on most of her shows, and Shaun Young has recorded solo projects. The group High Noon as a whole has worked with fifties rockabilly artist Ronnie Dawson quite a lot the last couple years. But High Noon, the rockabilly trio, still performs together at the larger U.S. rockabilly festivals, as well as continuing to tour Europe and other parts of the world. They are a popular act among today's young rockabilly fans.

Ted Roddy

The guy who sings rockabilly music the way I love it today, who I'd never heard of until that first spring 1991 trip I made to Austin, is Ted Roddy. From the first time I saw Ted with his group The Talltops do their live show at The Continental Club, I thought to myself, that cat not only knows how to do rockabilly, honky-tonk hillbilly, and roots rock 'n' roll, but loves to perform it, also, and puts everything he's got into it. I was impressed. In the trips I've made to Austin since then, I've never gone there without finding out where Ted Roddy was playing, and no matter how tired I was, I'd drag my butt out to catch his show. Ted's definitely got the best male voice in all of Austin, out of any other singer I've heard down there singin' rockabilly music. In his bands, he always uses the best musicians that town's got. On my trip in March 1996, Ted had Lisa Pankrantz on drums. Now, I've heard and watched Lisa play drums behind Ronnie Dawson, The Planet Rockers, Ted Roddy, and others since 1992 or 1993, and without a doubt, she's not only the best female drummer on rockabilly, roots rock 'n' roll, and honky-tonk hillbilly, but she's also just plain out the best all-around drummer with the kind of feel this music calls for anywhere around.

Ted Roddy & The Talltops are still doin' the best rockabilly, roots rock 'n' roll, and honky-tonk hillbilly on a regular basis out of all of 'em I've seen in Austin. Ted Roddy has only released two CD albums that I know are still available. I'd recommend both of 'em. Though he's done other records, cassettes, etc. over the years, the two I'd recommend you to seek out include the one that came out on Johnny Sandberg's Sunjay Records label out

of Vargarda, Sweden, called *Rock 'n' Roll Honky Tonkin' with Ted & The Talltops*. This is one great seventeen-song CD album. Ted's got four original songs on there. He's a hell of a good rockabilly songwriter, but it's the spontaneous, honest, true feel that comes across in his great voice that grabs me. You wanna dance, you wanna rock to real 1950s rockabilly music, you sure won't have no trouble on Ted's original songs like "Where Can She Be," "Honky Tonk Hell," and "Cheatin' Jones." Plus Ted's covers of Conway Twitty's rockabilly B side to "It's Only Make Believe," called "I Vibrate," is the best I've ever heard. Other great old forgotten rockabilly songs he covers, like Big A. Downing's "Around the Corner" and Mel Tillis's "Honky Tonk Song," are just as good.

I believe Ted Roddy had an album or something out on Bruce Bromberg's Hightone Records out of Oakland, California, in the late eighties, but I've never been able to locate it. But in 1995, Bruce Bromberg produced a thirteen-song CD album, titled *Family Portrait*, of all-new Ted Roddy original songs for his label and released it that year. This one is definitely a must. This album is a great mixture of all forms of real rock 'n' roll. Hightone Records is pretty well distributed here in the U.S., so you should be able to find this one in any decent record store that carries good music. Now, this album has got more than enough nineties rockabilly to satisfy any fan. Ted's rockabilly songs, such as "The Settlin' Kind," "Give Me Back My Mind," and "I Was the One," are hard to best. The lead-off song, "Sparkling City," knocks me out, 'cause its a solid dancin', toe-tappin', feel-good rocker with a mixture of a cajun sound and rockabilly/rock 'n' roll. Every song is good on this whole album, but it's the soulful rockabillyish ballads with a blues feel that really get the job done for me. I mean, I can feel Ted Roddy pourin' his soul into these songs, such as "Seven Days," "Face the Night," and "Since I Lost You." Hey, now, don't think just 'cause I'm older now that I'm more into some of these bluesy rockabilly ballads. You young rockabilly fans out there better keep in mind that some of the heroes you dress like today and idolize, such as Gene Vincent and Eddie Cochran, did a whole lot of great rockabilly ballads. So, Ted Roddy's keepin' that tradition alive and doin' a whale of a job at it also.

Ted Roddy, like James Intveld, should definitely be a star on a major label. They both play and sing real music and already have large or good-sized followings of fans. They're both young, and if a major label would just give 'em a shot, maybe we could hear some real music on the radio once again that would stick around.

Darren Lee Spears and Go Cat Go

Now, I can't go into detail on every band and artist that's doin' rockabilly music today, but before I run down the list of as many as I can think of, I have to tell you of one great band that no longer is with us. That band was called Go Cat Go. The reason there's no more great Go Cat Go rockabilly music and no more Go Cat Go band is because the lead singer's great voice was silenced forever in September 1993. Darren Lee Spears was that lead singer. Darren was Go Cat Go. He was my personal favorite new young rockabilly singer, rhythm guitar player, and songwriter right from the first night I saw him perform and met him when Go Cat Go performed their first original nightclub show as the opening band for the popular rockabilly band Virginia & The Blue Dots at The Bayou Club in Washington, D.C., in January 1990.

Darren loved the old original sound of Sun Records and true fifties rockabilly. He was singin' new rockabilly songs with the real feel the fifties originals had thirty-five years before. The band also played it with the same true feel the music had back then. But it was Darren's voice that made this Go Cat Go group what it was, and that was special. A great rockabilly artist true to the old style just don't come around much anymore. I ain't heard one from any other young new group since Darren left us for a better place in September 1993.

Through 1990 and 1991, Go Cat Go garnered a solid following performing their real brand of rockabilly. They had their own six-song self-produced cassette out in 1990, which was great rockabilly. Then they went in the studio in 1991 and recorded their only actual 10" four-song vinyl mini-LP ever to come out during Darren's lifetime. Willie Lewis's Rock-A-Billy Records released it in December 1991. All four songs were great. It's a hard record to find now, 'cause Willie has his own way of doin' things, and after he presses so many copies of the records he releases, he won't press any more. But Willie did real well with this Go Cat Go record back then, especially in Europe, where they've always known the real thing when they hear it. The first song on side one was all I needed to hear. The song's a vibrant, blazin' rockabilly tune Darren wrote, called "Little Baby Doll." The other three songs, including one great rockabilly ballad, are all fabulous examples of how rockabilly music should always be done, especially if you're lucky enough to have the vocal feel and ability that Darren surely had.

Darren also was special in the respect that he didn't care if he became a major star or not. He just loved singin' rockabilly music in the same form and style it was first born in. I know he did. I got to know Darren too well to even remotely believe he was handin' me a line, as so many other rockabilly bands were doin' in 1990. I saw Go Cat Go at seven or eight of their shows in D.C. before I left for Nashville, not countin' the final show they did for me that summer. Darren was a twenty-five-year-old energetic kid who worked hard on his job to help his mom out in 1990. Rockabilly music was his greatest fun and release. Right up until a few months before he was killed in September 1993, Darren would either write or call me. When he called me, I never had to worry about keepin' my guard up 'cause somebody was wantin' or needin' me to do something for 'em or help in some way. Darren just wanted to tell me how good the band Go Cat Go was doin', see how me and Pepper were gettin' along, and then just plain out wanna talk about all the great rockabilly artists from the 1950s he loved so much. Darren bought all the reissue albums. Darren was a fan of rockabilly.

On June 1, 1992, I went down to the Douglas Corner club on 8th Avenue in Nashville, as Darren had called me a few weeks earlier, 'cause Go Cat Go was goin' out on the road between D.C. and Austin to play a half-dozen shows. Darren and the guys like Bill Hull in the band who had regular day jobs to support their families had arranged to take two weeks of their vacation time at the same time. That's just what it was, too. A vacation. They sure didn't make any money at all. These were just four young guys out on the road havin' the time of their life on what was their first real trip this far south in their adult life. I know they didn't make no money in Nashville at Douglas Corner, 'cause the only money the band got was from whoever paid the three bucks that came through the door. Between 9:30 p.m. and 12:30 a.m., Go Cat Go sang and played their asses off, doin' two sixty-minute sets of the best rockabilly music you'd want to hear anywhere. Eight people showed up during that time, so the whole band made $24. But those eight people and me and Pepper sure loved every minute of it, and Darren was just happy to be playin' the rockabilly music he loved so much.

I still have the last two-page letter Darren wrote and sent to me pinned to my bulletin board in my record room. It's postmarked August 15, 1993. Darren Lee Spears was murdered while he was dove hunting only a short distance from his home a month after he wrote me that final letter. Darren was shot, along with a buddy of his, in cold blood in the back by a black teenager who had a couple of his friends with him. His life was over and his voice silenced all because these three juveniles wanted Darren's and his friend's shotguns. That's all they took.

They held a benefit that Darren would have loved a couple months after his death, in November 1993, that Laurence Beall and I drove up for. This was to raise money for his mother and his wife. Darren had only been married for less than a year. He was only twenty-eight years old, and so full of life and love for rockabilly music, and then in a flash of fire he was gone. I sure miss him. Darren sent me a lot of live tapes of the band's shows. So those and the one four-song album are all I have left on one of the best young rockabilly kids I've ever known. I'll always think of Darren every Christmas, as during the Christmas season of 1993, Run Wild Records in Alexandria, Virginia, released an eighteen-song compilation CD album that had two Christmas songs on it Darren had written and recorded with just Bill Hull and one other musician, an upright bass player. This was just a little rockabilly trio Darren called The Juke Joint Jumpers. One of the songs that Darren wrote that's rockabilly all the way and sings with honest feel has a title that seems fitting with the way I miss Darren Spears as a great rockabilly kid with a lot of talent that I liked better than any I can think of. The title of Darren's song is "(It's Gonna be a) Blue, Blue Christmas (Without You)." Amen.

Original Artists Still Performin'

Now, I can't say everything I'd like to about the hundreds of rockabilly bands that continue to support what I do for the music we all love the most, but the least I can do is take this chapter out with mentioning all the names and states, areas, countries, etc., where they're out of. Most of these bands have records, CDs, or cassettes available. They are all still actively playing and performing rockabilly music, as far as I know. I'll start with the original artists that all had rockabilly record releases between 1954 and 1963 that are still touring out there somewhere in the world.

Sleepy La Beef: Sleepy still performs over 200 shows a year, more than any other 1950s rockabilly artist. Sleepy still rocks harder than any act out there, and he had another brand-new album come out on Rounder Records in 1996. Sleepy's known as the human jukebox, as he knows and performs live over 5,000 different songs. Don't miss this ol' cat when he comes to your town.

Ronnie Dawson: Ronnie does more than 150 live shows a year. Like Sleepy La Beef, Ronnie's live shows are solid rockabilly. But unlike Sleepy, Ronnie has only come to the attention of rockabilly fans here in the U.S. and overseas since the late 1980s. Sleepy La Beef has always been on the road since 1955. Ronnie has a 1996 album out on Crystal Clear Sound Records, out of Dallas. Ronnie does great rockin' live shows you shouldn't miss.

Narvel Felts: Narvel still performs more than 100 shows a year also, but mostly all of his live shows here in the U.S. are on the country music circuit that he's still best remembered for here in the States. Narvel will always include rockabilly music in his act upon request, but unlike Sleepy La Beef and Ronnie Dawson, who, when they tour across country, carry their own bands, Narvel Felts will always use whatever house band the club he's performin' in supplies. Don't let this stop you from goin' to see a Narvel Felts show, as he's one of the greatest singers you'll ever want to hear. He's a total professional and loved by rockabilly fans around the world today.

Sonny Burgess: Sonny was the main leader of the Sun Rhythm Section band, which was active up until a few years ago, until one of its members, the great Marcus Van Story, passed away. But that didn't stop Sonny, who still currently does tours of European countries, as well as playing the original nightclub circuit here in the U.S., doing more than 100 shows a year here in the U.S. alone.

Jack Scott: Jack probably still does over fifty shows a year. He performs in Europe two to three times a year and has been doin' so since 1977. But Jack also performs at various nightspots in and around the Detroit area, as well as doin' various shows in select spots in Canada.

Jackie Lee Cochran: Jackie toured Europe a dozen or more times between 1979 and 1990, but for over ten years now has been performing regularly four to five nights a week at a Los Angeles nightspot called the Gaslight Club. When I saw Jackie there in 1992, he was still performing his 1950s classic rockabilly songs and enjoying every minute of it.

Janis Martin: Janis tours Europe and other foreign countries two to three times a year. Her only performances here in the U.S. have been in 1990 in Maryland and some shows she did in California in 1994. She sounds as good as ever and still rocks hard on her great fifties rockabilly classic songs. Janis can be found singing with Rosie Flores on Rosie's 1995 album *Rockabilly Filly* on Hightone Records.

Wanda Jackson: Wanda can also be found on that Rosie Flores album, and Wanda did her first long cross-country tour of the U.S. with Rosie between November 1995 and January 1996 in support of that album. Wanda is still a top rockabilly attraction in Europe, where she's performed two to three times a year since the early 1980s. Wanda also does some U.S. shows on the country and gospel circuits.

Johnny Cash: There's only one Johnny Cash, and the classic Cash voice and sound is still out across the U.S. quite a lot each year. This true legend still performs his 1950s Sun Records songs in his shows today.

The Collins Kids: Larry Collins and his sister Lorrie hadn't performed a live show together in over thirty years until they performed all their 1950s classic rockabilly songs in England in the early nineties to an enthusiastic crowd of several thousand young and old rockabilly fans. The Collins Kids have since gone back to Europe twice and played several big shows in California and parts of the far Northwest. They are always backed by the great Dave & Deke Combo.

Billy Lee Riley: Billy Lee still puts on great live rockabilly shows. He started doin' rockabilly shows in Europe in 1979 through 1986, got out of music for awhile, but has since done occasional live shows, both in Europe and in various parts of the U.S., from 1990 up to the present. Billy Lee Riley rocks as hard as he ever did on all his old Sun Records rockabilly classics.

Vernon Taylor: Other than the four live shows Vernon did for me in Maryland in 1989 and '90, he hasn't performed any full rockabilly-type shows here in the U.S. He is starting to become in demand in Europe. Vernon performed his first-ever live concert in England at the Hemsby Festival in May 1995, and more shows are planned. Eagle Records in Germany has released a CD album of all previously unknown songs Vernon recorded at Sun Records in the 1950s. This album was released in the fall of 1995. During the spring of 1996, Vernon formed a new band and has started doin' live shows in the Maryland and Washington, D.C., areas.

Ray Campi: Ray's made a whole lot of tours all over Europe since 1979. He's extremely popular in Finland and still performs his upright slappin' bass rockabilly songs he recorded in the 1950s. Ray also does a lot of shows in the Los Angeles area, where he lives.

Matt Lucas: Matt did one tour of shows in Europe in the early nineties, but primarily performs in Florida, where he lives. He's one of the wildest rockabilly performers you'd ever want to see.

The Crickets: Buddy Holly's former 1950s original group still consists of Joe B. Mauldin, Jerry Allison, and Sonny Curtis. This great trio is more active and in demand than ever today. They perform a lot of shows in Europe, as well as here in the U.S., singin' both old Buddy Holly songs from the fifties and new rockabilly-type songs of today. The Crickets have a 1996 album with some of Nashville's top country rockers and old outlaws on it. The album is actually a tribute to Buddy Holly and his rockabilly music.

Hayden Thompson: Hayden has been makin' tours of Europe and other foreign countries since 1984. He still performs there two to three times a year, where he has many enthusiastic fans. He's only performed a handful of shows here in the U.S., but he resides in the Chicago area, which has a lot of young rockabilly bands that regularly perform his fifties songs. In 1990, the Sunjay label in Sweden released what I and many others consider to be Hayden's best all-around album, titled *The Time Is Now*. In 1994, the Go Cat Go label in Japan released his first CD album, *Feelin' Those Rockabilly Blues*, a twenty-five-song collection of all his best songs from between 1954 and 1970.

Johnny Powers: Johnny's been doin' two to three regular annual tours of Europe for about ten years. He recorded two new albums during the early nineties and does occasional shows here in the U.S., especially around the Detroit area, where he lives.

The Blue Caps: Paul Peek, Bubba Facenda, Dickie Harrell, Johnny Meeks, and other members of Gene Vincent's 1950s Blue Caps band, who in my opinion were the greatest all-time backup band in rockabilly or rock 'n' roll history, have consistently been brought back to Europe many times for shows since the early 1980s.

Jerry Merritt: Jerry resides in the far Northwest but still performs rockabilly shows both in Europe and in the Seattle, Washington, and Portland, Oregon, areas. Jerry was Gene Vincent's lead guitarist on a tour of Japan, played on many of his later Capitol Records releases in 1959 and '60, and wrote several good rockabilly songs Gene recorded during the early and mid 1960s.

Joe Clay: Nine songs by Joe appeared on the fantastic 1988 double album *Vintage RCA Rockabilly '56 – '59: Get Hot or Go Home* — more than by any other artist. Since then, this Louisiana native has performed from time to time around the U.S. and in Europe.

Gene Summers: Gene did quite a number of tours of Europe during the early and mid 1980s. Several albums of mostly 1950s through 1970s songs of Gene's were released in Europe during that period. Crystal Clear Sound Records released in 1997 the rockin'-est collection of thirty-two songs Gene Summers recorded between 1957 and 1977. Gene had a heart transplant not long ago, and he feels like a new man, so he's currently touring Europe and parts of the U.S. This cat's a great (and I mean great) rockabilly singer's singer. I'm sure gonna catch him the first chance I get.

Link Wray: Link's been living in Denmark for close to ten years now. In the late eighties and early nineties he was only tourin' and recordin' in Europe. In 1997 he's doin' his first shows of this decade back in the U.S.A.

The market here has been flooded with Link Wray albums in the past few years, and he's achieved total legendary status as he closes in on seventy years of age.

Dale Hawkins: Dale toured foreign countries on a number of occasions during the 1980s. He stopped for quite a few years, but then again in the early 1990s he reappeared, headlinin' big festivals over there. Now I hear he's also doin' shows in the U.S. here in the late nineties.

Jack Earls: Jack only had one record release, in 1956, but boy, what a great one it was. For the past twenty years, his one Sun 45 record of "Slow Down" has been held in high esteem in Europe. Here we are in the late nineties, and Jack is finally doin' shows over there.

Jerry Lee Lewis: Not much needs to be said here. Jerry Lee had his first new studio album in ten years released in 1996. He's steadily stayed out there now for over forty years. The Killer seems more subdued and calmer now, but I still believe he's as unpredictable as the weather.

Forgettin' to Remember to Forget

I first met Hayden Thompson in August 1991 at Lincoln Center in New York City, where he was one of the headliners on a seven-hour outdoor Rockabilly Extravaganza that included fellow Sun Records legends Billy Lee Riley, Sonny Burgess, Marcus Van Story, and others, as well as Rocky Burnette, Ronnie Dawson, James Intveld, Rosie Flores, Ray Campi, and more. Hayden's part of the show was great, as were all the others. But Hayden showed me something in his performance that some of the others seemed to lack. There were somewhere between 1,500 and 2,000 rockabilly fans in the audience on that hot afternoon and evening in mid August. For rockabilly here in the U.S., to watch artists mostly over the age of fifty perform, that's a big crowd.

Hayden was backed by Sonny Burgess and the rest of his Sun Rhythm Section band. He won the crowd over immediately with his relaxed, professional manner, and he rocked out. Everybody did a great job, but Hayden, like most involved, was there to have fun and give a great performance for that enthusiastic audience of all ages. He didn't show off or brag about the past, or band members he started off with who went on to become top rockabilly, rock 'n' roll, and country stars later on. He didn't wear authentic 1950s clothes like a couple others did. He was just himself, and he delivered where it counted. In his music. I spoke with both Hayden and his wife Georgia backstage, and what I found was a man who's just thoroughly happy and a little excited that people still remember and appreciate the music he gave to us all over thirty-five years ago. Me and Hayden have stayed in touch since that time, and I can tell ya he ain't got a jealous bone in his body.

In 1994, a poll was taken by Johnny Sandborg's Sunjay Records label on who were the Top 10 most popular of all American rockabilly artists and bands that were brought to Sweden for the annual Sunjay Music Festival over the past ten years since its beginning. A list of two dozen American bands and artists was sent out to all the many devoted fans who have continued to attend this event, held in July each year. It had been five years since Hayden had played this festival, but rockabilly fans have a good memory when they see the performers they love and idolize give a great live performance. This was what this poll was based on—the best performance given by an American artist over there. They voted Hayden's performance #1.

He's billed as The Living King of Rock 'n' Roll, and there's no argument there. He still does shows both in the U.S. and overseas.

Linda Gail Lewis: Linda Gail saw her first record released on Sun in 1963, as a duet with her older brother Jerry Lee. She did shows with Jerry Lee during the remainder of the sixties and into the seventies, as well as many shows on her own. She had numerous record releases during those years. In the late seventies she got out of music, but by the early nineties was back on the club circuit. When I saw her at a club in Memphis in 1991, she did a great rockabilly/rock 'n' roll-type show and looked better than ever. Linda Gail had a new album released in 1996 and has since done shows both here in the U.S. and in Europe. She's also the youngest of all the original artists I can think of that's still out there.

Ronnie Hawkins: Ronnie's been doin' tours of Europe since at least the early eighties and continues to do so. He also performs some shows here in the U.S. He's made his home in Canada for a lot of years, where he's become a popular attraction and has done many shows.

Scotty Moore: Scotty retired from live stage performin' well over twenty years ago. He's always been able to make a good livin' with his music business ventures in Nashville, where he resides. As the 1990s came in, with the encouragement of D.J. Fontana, The Jordanaires, and Ronnie McDowell, Scotty began performing with them on select Elvis-oriented tribute shows for the Elvis Presley estate. Since that time, he's toured Europe on some of the same package shows, as well as playing some larger venues here in the U.S.

Paul Burlison: The only survivin' member of the legendary Johnny Burnette Trio first came back and did shows here in the U.S., and a short time later in Europe, as part of the now-defunct Sun Rhythm Section, beginning in 1986. Paul hasn't stopped since. With a new 1997 album out, he continues to tour both here in the U.S. and abroad.

Johnny Hallyday: Johnny was France's top rockabilly and rock 'n' roll artist during the late fifties and early sixties. Today he still performs in France and other countries around the world. He comes to Las Vegas once a year for a series of shows that are always sold out. He's still one dynamic performer.

The Everly Brothers: Don and Phil still get together and do a select number of shows each year, both here in the U.S. as well as in Europe, although in recent years I haven't heard of The Everlys doin' too many shows abroad. They remain a top concert draw today any time they choose to go out and perform together.

Mac Curtis: Mac began doin' tours of Europe in the late seventies and has continued to do so ever since. I haven't heard of him performin' here in the U.S. in recent years.

Mike Berry: British rocker Mike Berry had the all-time best "Tribute to Buddy Holly" released in 1961 and scored a Top 10 hit all through Europe with it at that time. Mike had follow-ups that charted for him after that, and today he continues to perform at various rockabilly shows throughout Europe.

Tommy Sands: Tommy has lived and performed at night spots in Hawaii since the late sixties. Finally, in the early nineties, England and other foreign countries brought him over there for a series of shows. At this writing he still occasionally tours Europe, as well as performin' in Hawaii.

Buddy Knox: Buddy went over for the very first-ever big festival of rockabilly stars in England in 1977. Today he still performs at shows and festivals in various foreign countries, but other than oldies revival shows, I haven't seen him on the bill on the rockabilly club circuit here in the States.

Charlie Gracie: I don't know if Charlie does any shows here in the U.S., but he's been doin' tours overseas since at least the early eighties and continues to do so today.

Marty Wilde: Marty had a big chart hit in 1960, both here in the U.S. and in Europe, with his song "Bad Boy." Over the years and up to the present day, he's stayed actively involved with fifties rock 'n' roll and rockabilly shows in England, where he lives.

Larry Donn: Larry lives in Arkansas, and today he writes a fabulous column titled "Rockabilly Days" each month for *Now Dig This* magazine, which has been the longest-running and premier magazine of its kind for accurate information on true rock 'n' roll and rockabilly music in all of Europe (or anywhere, for that matter) since 1983. Larry Donn's one 45 record of "Honey Bun," on Vaden Records from 1959, is not only one of the final great examples of true, raw rockabilly, but also one of the rarest, most sought-after collectible records in the music's history. Larry also performs live shows throughout parts of Europe to this day, where he remains a popular attraction.

Billy Poore: I certainly have never considered myself an original artist. But since 1993, a number of stories, both overseas and in the U.S., have been written on me and placed me into that elite class because I happened to have a couple of 45 record releases in 1961 and '62 that are now considered rockabilly. Plus musicologists, historians, and self-proclaimed experts on obscure rockabilly artists such as the esteemed Dr. Howard A. DeWitt have all told me I take my early sixties records way too lightly. They tell me I am in this class (I don't feel this old). Well, if they say so (?), OK. So watch for me in 1998. I have a new CD album out, and being as I'm wanted again (but at least not on a Post Office wall), I'll be out there doin' shows across the U.S., rockin' again just as hard as I ever did.

I'm sure I'm leaving out a lot of original artists who made some rockabilly records back then, but to be honest, there's just too many to list, although they're all gettin' up in years now and some have passed on recently. Johnny Carroll passed away on February 18, 1995, Charlie Rich died suddenly on July 25, 1995, and Carl Perkins had a fatal stroke on January 19, 1998. All of the above performers and acts I've listed all still do great rockabilly music at their live shows, so I'd advise any fan of true rockabilly music to go out and see these performers if they come to your area. You may not have another chance to see these great artists do their brands of rockabilly music, though I wish all of 'em could stay out there forever.

Newer Artists

The rest of the artists and bands I'm gonna list now all had their first rockabilly record releases after 1963. In 1964, when The Beatles arrived, the golden era of rock 'n' roll and rockabilly was gone forever. While the majority of these bands and artists did not start releasing records until after the rockabilly revival of 1977, there were a few, mostly in foreign countries, that had rockabilly releases as early as the mid to late sixties. All the artists and bands listed below are still actively performing their brand of rockabilly music, to the best of my knowledge. Some have been doin' so for over twenty years, while others are new ones that have just come along in the past several years.

James Intveld—Los Angeles, CA

Ted Roddy—Austin, TX

LesLee "Bird" Anderson—Los Angeles, CA

Ronnie Mack—Los Angeles, CA

The Planet Rockers—Nashville, TN

High Noon—Austin, TX

Ruthie & The Wranglers—Takoma Park, MD

The Bobby Smith Band—Washington, DC

Big Sandy & His Fly-Rite Boys—Los Angeles, CA

Lucky Breaks—Huntsville, AL

The Three Blue Teardrops—Chicago, IL

The Moondogs—Chicago, IL

The Tailfins—Chicago, IL

Dave Alvin—Los Angeles, CA

Phil Alvin & The Blasters—Los Angeles, CA

The A-Bones—New York City, NY

James Richard Oliver—Blue Ridge, GA

The Reluctant Playboys—Washington, DC

Billy Hancock—Washington, DC

Marti´ Brom—Austin, TX

Herman The German—Austin, TX

Todd Monroe—Somerville, NJ

BR5-49—Nashville, TN

Billy Morokawa & The Blue Moon Boys—Tokyo, Japan

The Sandra Dee—Tokyo, Japan

The Bloomin' Brothers—Tokyo, Japan

Guy Bones—Tokyo, Japan

The Howlin' Cats—Tokyo, Japan

Rollin' Rocks—Tokyo, Japan

Chattanooga Choo Choo Boys—Tokyo, Japan

Santiago Tamura—Tokyo, Japan

Mutant Monster Beach Party—Tokyo, Japan

The Skinnys—Tokyo, Japan

Long Gone Daddy O's—Tokyo, Japan

Sunset Wranglers—Tokyo, Japan

Wildfire Willie & The Ramblers—Vargarda, Sweden

The Hal Peters Trio—Helsinki, Finland

Crazy Cavan & The Rhythm Rockers—London, England

Freddie Fingers Lee—London, England

Willie Lewis & The Stringpoppers—Denver, CO

Tony Maserati—Austin, TX

Sonny George—Nashville, TN

Eddie Angel—Nashville, TN

Kristi Rose—Nashville, TN

Rosie Flores—Los Angeles, CA

Jason D. Williams—Memphis, TN

Reverend Horton Heat—Memphis, TN

Tav Falco—Memphis, TN

Cub Koda—Chelsea, MI

The Dave & Deke Combo—Los Angeles, CA

The Steam Donkeys—Albany, NY

The Belmont Playboys—Charlotte, NC

The Dominos—Paris, France

The Ruffnecks—Reno, NV

Runnin' Wild—Rotterdam, Holland

The Forbidden Pigs—Phoenix, AZ

Colin Winski—Los Angeles, CA

The Lone Star Trio—Austin, TX

Ray Condo—Austin, TX

Marshall & The Shooting Stars—Austin, TX

The Stray Cats—Los Angeles, CA

The Rockats—Los Angeles, CA

Robert Gordon—New York City, NY

Going, Going, Gone—Washington, DC

Evan Johns—Austin, TX

Kelly Willis—Austin, TX

Marty Stuart—Nashville, TN

Frantic Flattops—Syracuse, NY

Roadhouse Rockers—Santa Barbara, CA

The Delta Angels—Little Rock, AR

Kathy Murray & The Kilowatts—Austin, TX

Dale Watson—Los Angeles, CA

Hillbilly Hellcats—Denver, CO

Little Roy Williamson—Denver, CO

Jumpin' Jupiter—Washington, DC

Bill Kirtchen & Rents Due—Washington, DC

The Flea Bops—Washington, DC

Slick Pelt—New York City, NY

Rocket-J—Newark, NJ

Mark Bristol—Duvall, WA (Mark also publishes *Blue Suede News,* one of the best independent magazines that supports all rockabilly music. I highly recommend it.)

Jack Smith & The Rockabilly Planet— West Greenwich, RI

Buck & The Black Cats—Burlington, VT

Jimmy Roy's 5 Star Hillbillies—Austin, TX

Blue Jean Blue—Austin, TX

Steven Ackles—Drobak, Norway

The Hyperions—Los Angeles, CA

Kidd Pharough—Denver, CO

Dave Phillips & The Blue Cats—London, England

Rocky Burnette—Reseda, CA

Hot Rod Lincoln—San Diego, CA

The Hooligans—Austin, TX

Dee Lannon—Los Angeles, CA

Mystery Train—Los Angeles, CA

Justin Curtis—Vancouver, BC

The Flapjacks—Portland, OR

The Starlight Trio—Portland, OR

Meline & The Delilahs—Seattle, WA

Thunder Road—Seattle, WA

The Sun Demons—San Diego, CA

Atomic Bombshell—San Diego, CA

Josie Creuzer—San Diego, CA

Pee Wee Thomas & The Safecrackers— San Francisco, CA

The Swing Rays—Indianapolis, IN

Wayne Hancock—Austin, TX

The Blue Moon Boys—Indianapolis, IN

The Bell Airs—Indianapolis, IN

The DuValls—Chicago, IL

The Cigar Store Indians—Chicago, IL

The Rover Boys—London, England

Dave Crimmen—Dale City, CA

The Swingin' Demons—Flint, MI

The Vibro Champs—Minneapolis, MN

The Ranch Girls & Ragtime Wranglers—Rotterdam, Holland

The Twilight Ramblers—Bethesda, MD

Rip Masters—Hollywood, CA

The Tennessee Boys—Portugal/Barcelona, Spain

Spo-Dee-O-Dee—Frankfurt, Germany

The Ricardos—London, England

The Go Getters—Helsinki, Finland

Harry Fontana—Helsinki, Finland

Victor McCullough—Port Stewart, Northern Ireland

The Amazing Royal Crowns—Providence, RI

Jump Cat Jump—London, England

Russell Scott & The Red Hots—Los Angeles, CA

The Rollin' Rocks—Yokohama, Japan

Shakin' Stevens—London, England

Mark Gamsjager & The Lustre Kings—Albany, NY

The Barnshakers—Vargarda, Sweden

King Kerosine—Glen Ridge, NJ

Darrel Higman—London, England

Ike & The Capers—Barcelona, Spain

The Hep Cats—Detroit, MI

The Bughouse Five—Vancouver, BC

Dave Edmunds—Los Angeles, CA

John Fogerty—Sherman Oaks, CA

Johnny & The Rocco's—London, England

The Class of '58—London, England

Matchbox—London, England

The Jets—London, England

The Corvettes—London, England

Good Rockin' Tonight—London, England

Ubangi Stomp—Amsterdam, Holland

Carl "Sonny" Leyland—Austin, TX

Buick '55—London, England

The Rimshots—Valley Stream, NJ

The Black Top Rockets—Denver, CO

etc.

The "etc." is for the hundreds more bands and performers that are currently performing yesterday or today's rockabilly music. Whoever I have left out, which I feel sure there are many, I have to apologize to, 'cause I know that all of you are all doing everything you can to keep this great music alive. Just be sure to keep the faith, as rockabilly music will survive because of y'all.

Rockabilly Music's Future and
Why It Continues to Appeal to the Young

Rockabilly music is the most real music I've ever heard, and I've learned to accept its eighties and nineties sound, and the way young people in their twenties perceive it today. When you say the word "rockabilly" to a true fan today, whether he or she is twenty years old or fifty-five years old, it's whatever they think it is, and whatever they want it to be. It could be only the music, the fifties cat clothes look, the fifties hillbilly string tie look, the bad-ass attitude, the newer high stiff sprayed hair look, the greasy hair, hell-bent for leather, tattoos, motorcycle jackets, switchblade knives, turned-up collars, and so on. Plain and simple. I've seen all these examples of what rockabilly fans think rockabilly means to them throughout the years. It has to start with the music of the fifties, Elvis, Gene Vincent, and Eddie Cochran, or Robert Gordon and The Stray Cats, or whoever. But it goes a lot deeper, with all forms of the style of dress the fans, who now emulate the bands, are into. I don't believe the fifties punk look is ever gonna die out, with the way young fans still dress today, but over the last several years, I've seen certain bands that are labeled rockabilly wearin' cowboy hats and old-style string tie cowboy suits. Then a lot of the music they're callin' rockabilly that they record and sing has steel guitars and fiddles in it. Now, I like some of it, but for me it just overall ain't rockabilly. Country singers wore cowboy hats in the 1950s. Rockabilly singers didn't. Now, when you git as old as me and Sleepy La Beef are, you can get away with wearin' cowboy hats and still bein' labeled a rockabilly.

The ultimate example of what rockabilly will always be for me as far as the attitude goes is in one five-to-seven-minute scene in the Elvis movie *Loving You* from 1957. In the sequence, Elvis's character, Deke Rivers, gets pushed over the edge by a rude, stone punk who wants him to sing a song for his girlfriend. The guy was a jerk about it, and this took place in a teenage cafe/diner where Elvis (Rivers) and a band member had come to eat. But Elvis (Rivers) sang "Mean Woman Blues." The

punk made a smart-ass comment to look like a big man around his girlfriend and other friends, a fight ensued, and Elvis kicked his ass. That's rockabilly to me. When you're pushed over the edge so far that it takes a jerk gettin' his ass kicked to rectify the situation at hand, it has to be done.

Rockabilly is also, and has always been over the years, rebellion. Today, I believe a lot of the new bands that are playin' rockabilly music and the fans who dress the way they do and wear tattoos and high hair are all rebelling against the whole damn political, plum pitiful major music industry and what they hear as so-called hits on the radio and shoved at 'em on MTV. So kids in their teens and twenties are turnin' to rockabilly music and its ever-changin' styles.

In 1994 alone, I got over a thousand pieces of mail from rockabilly fans under thirty-five years of age that live right here in forty-six different states in the U.S. Rockabilly music is sellin' and makin' money for a lot of independent record companies. Right here in the U.S., new ones such as Teen Rebel Records in Miami, Florida, have sent me CD albums on the likes of The Three Blue Teardrops and The Belmont Playboys. These are young newer 1990s-style rockabilly bands that perform and tour across the U.S. and in Europe. The bands sell their albums on the road, and the record company distributes to hundreds of select U.S. record stores right here in the U.S., as well as distributing them in the rest of the world. Crystal Clear Sound Records in Dallas is another great 1990s CD label doin' the same thing. And rockabilly has finally made the Internet in our new modern technology world. My point is, this music called rockabilly is not selling millions on each band or artist that does it, but it's sellin' tens of thousands on each one that gets good distribution. I stopped puttin' out records on my label, Renegade, in 1993, after eleven years of puttin' out over forty-five singles and eight albums. But I could always sell a thousand or so records, and I had no distribution because of my pay-before-you-order-the-records policy. What I'm tryin' to tell major record companies is this music will always sell. Sellin' 10,000 records I'm sure don't mean a thing to a major record label, but each little independent record label (and there are hundreds) that sells that amount of rockabilly music on their artists are all takin' money out of your pockets.

BR5-49

To be honest, I can't really see rockabilly music makin' a big comeback on the pop charts here in the U.S. the way it did in the late seventies with Robert Gordon, and again in the early eighties with The Stray Cats. The only way I can see it comin' back strong on the radio and at live shows on a national scale is through the Nashville country music side of it. I believe it'll happen that way. As far as the sound of the music is concerned, in 1994 Arista Records in Nashville released an album and initial 45 on a new group called The Tractors. The 45 they released was called "Baby Likes to Rock It." They had a video to go with it. This song was referred to by a lot of people as rockabilly. The song went Top 10. The album went multi-platinum and sold millions and also crossed over onto the *Billboard* pop charts. There were other rockabilly-soundin' songs on the album, such as the old Chuck Berry classic "Thirty Days." "Baby Likes to Rock It" was the biggest song off the album. The Tractors did great. There was only one problem. All the guys in the group were over fifty years old. In country, pop, rock, rap, whatever, if it's gonna go most of the time in a big time way, it has to appeal to the young audience. Even I know that. So you constantly are in need of young, good-lookin' singers and groups that are talented to make this appeal to the young audiences who are responsible for buying 90 percent of all new products on the charts today in pop and country music. I liked the Tractors album. But they ain't come back with a big hit since.

Now Arista Records has got a new group, and they're a young group. They call themselves BR5-49. The group plays a mixture of old-style 1950s hillbilly honky-tonk tunes, as well as 1950s rockabilly songs. BR5-49 consists of lead singers and guitarists Chuck Meade and Gary Bennett, drummer Shaw Wilson, upright bass player Jay McDowell, and, since sometime in 1995, fiddler, mandolinist, and steel guitar player Donnie Herron.

Marty Stuart was one of the top stars that would consistently stop in when BR5-49 played at Roberts Western Clothes Shop and Club in Nashville. Marty noticed this group's raw, real energetic talent from the very beginning. Later on, by the summer of 1995, other top artists like Mark Collie would come by just to sit in with BR5-49, and he'd have fun gettin' up on stage with 'em so he could play some real music. During the entire summer of 1995, you couldn't get in to see BR5-49. It was too crowded.

In August 1995, BR5-49's picture was on the cover of *Billboard* magazine. *Billboard* called them the hottest unsigned band in music. The group took their time deciding on who to sign with. Every major label in Nashville wanted to lock 'em into a big-time recording contract, videos, the whole works, 'cause BR5-49 was generating a lot of excitement with this "new" sound in country music. They finally decided to sign with Arista Records during the fall of 1995.

These cats have all gotta deal with a lotta pressure at a young age that this major label is gonna put on 'em to push the great music over the top and out and onto country mainstream radio. All of 'em are good-lookin'. They're all young. They're all a real good marketing product, and Arista is gonna put some big dough behind 'em to push 'em. I don't know what direction they're gonna push 'em in, though. Maybe more of the old hillbilly fifties sound of country music than the rockabilly. Whatever it is, you're still gonna hear 'em rock out live on their own original rockabilly tunes or the old ones from the fifties when they perform live.

I probably like Shaw's, Chuck's, and Jay's personalities the best. Don't take this wrong, now. They don't have an attitude problem, but they both have what I call rockabilly attitudes. They're not gonna blow this chance, and they know what Arista expects from 'em. But they're there because they love the pure real music they play and sing. These two cats don't want to quit playin' a Broadway honky-tonk like Roberts, even if they go on to sell a million records. They're still young, and from what I can see, a little stubborn about their music and the people and fans who were supportin' them before Arista ever heard of 'em. Time could prove me wrong, but I sure hope not. I'm hedgin' my bets that BR5-49 is not only gonna become the hottest new group in country music, but rockabilly music also, as time goes on, 'cause these young cats love to play, sing, and go wild on it.

Headin' for the Future

Whatever kind of rockabilly music your taste in the late 1990s craves for is sure to be found in some record store, honky-tonk, or festival somewhere right here in the U.S., and definitely in almost every country around the world. I got an invitation to attend Sleepy La Beef's sixtieth birthday party in July 1995 at the Ace of Clubs, so me and Pepper went down there. Sleepy La Beef is definitely still rockin' at sixty! He proved it that night. Friends, family, and fans of Sleepy's showed up from around the world. Sleepy's got the good fortune of still bein' in good health and can still hopefully keep rockin' till he's seventy, well into the next century. Sleepy's a real popular act in Spain right now. He's performed in probably more foreign countries than any other rockabilly artist ever. Charlie Feathers, on the other hand, probably won't do another show. Charlie turned sixty-five on June 12, 1997. In the past couple years, he's had triple bypass heart surgery and his heart's come close to givin' out several times. But if you stop in at his house and you

want to talk about rockabilly music, Charlie Feathers will liven up and feel twenty years younger, and you'll be privileged to hear him tell you what it was like when rockabilly was born, young and fun, before it all became a commercial commodity.

I'm more than satisfied about where I am in my rockabilly, roots rock 'n' roll, and honky-tonk hillbilly world. I've been blessed really, 'cause I not only got to see, meet, or get to know all my rockabilly heroes from the fifties, but I was also lucky enough to go in the studio with many of 'em as late as the early 1990s and get some of the best rockabilly songs from the likes of Charlie Feathers, Narvel Felts, Billy Lee Riley, and a few others. Since I've moved to Nashville, or at least ninety miles from it, I've also recorded and produced new young singers in rockabilly. Two of the best bein' Marti´ Brom

Forgettin' to Remember to Forget

In January 1994, I'd moved real deep in the Tennessee hills about ninety miles southwest of downtown Nashville, so I was only goin' in for shows or other business about once a week. Although I had known Jay McDowell since the summer of 1994, and he had joined BR5-49 in November or December of that year, I didn't get in to check them out until early February 1995. I was in town on some business, but later in the evening, me and Pepper met with our friend Barbara Nadine (Feliti), and the three of us went to Roberts Western Clothes Shop and Club on lower Broadway around 9:30 p.m., just when BR5-49 was startin' its first set, or so I thought. This band's first set turned out to be the only set they did when they played at Roberts. For a straight four hours and forty-five minutes, without one break, between 9:30 p.m. and 2:15 a.m., this four-piece group played some of the best, fresh, new mixture of old obscure rockabilly and hillbilly honky-tonk songs by the likes of Carl Perkins, Gene Vincent, Webb Pierce, Carl Smith, Elvis, Eddie Cochran, The Carlisles, Hank Williams, The Johnny Burnette Trio, Ray Price, Faron Young, Johnny Horton, Lefty Frizzell, and too many more to mention. This band was tight and knew how to perform this music in the high-energy way it had originally been done. They didn't repeat a song the whole night.

This was on a weeknight, either a Wednesday or Thursday. Other than the band and bartenders and a few others who worked at Roberts, there weren't more than twenty or so people in there watchin' BR5-49. You had no trouble finding a place to sit. For as long as BR5-49 stayed up there (which I couldn't believe) and kept poundin' this great old stuff out, I knew they were special. They were in there where you just walked in for free, and they had a tip jar at the front of the stage. Back then, the whole band was splittin' up $30 to $50 a night.

After that first night, me and Pepper went back again and seen this hot, rockin', tight four-piece outfit in March 1995. This time we took our daughter Stacy, who was down here visiting from Maryland. After these shows, I met and got to know Jay, Shaw, Chuck, and Gary pretty good. They were all just young cats havin' the time of their lives. In April '95, Jay and Shaw drove out to my house in the hills and bought old rockabilly and hillbilly records from me, and we all had a great visit one Saturday afternoon.

In late May 1995, I went back to Roberts again to see BR5-49 do another great long show. The big difference this time was even though it was on a weeknight once again, Roberts was really jam-packed. Me and Pepper got there about 11:30 and stayed until they got finished with their hot music. BR5-49 was gettin' better each time we'd see 'em. During June, July, and August 1995, BR5-49 just kept right on playin' Roberts, and the crowds kept gittin' bigger and bigger.

and James Intveld. I don't know what the future holds, but what I'm most grateful for is all the letters I receive from young fans around the world today who are as excited about rockabilly music now as I was in 1956 when I was only twelve years old. It's always the fans that count the most to me when it comes to rockabilly music, 'cause that's what I've always considered myself first and foremost. A rockabilly fan.

Sometimes I just sit and I think, man, how great it would be if I could go back to 1957, or even 1977, just for one twenty-four-hour day, and relive an Alan Freed show or even a Robert Gordon and Link Wray show. I can't turn that ol' clock back, but inside I'm just the same crazy cat I've always been when it comes to rockabilly music. The only difference is I don't have to get drunk no more to have fun. Fun for me today is climbin' in my old '64 Chevy pickup truck, then go roarin' out onto Interstate 40, headin' east into Nashville with my tape deck blastin' out a rockabilly tune like "Pretty Little Lights of Town" by The Le Roi Brothers, and then everything's OK once more. I don't need to wish I could go back in time now, 'cause before I know it, I'm down on Broadway at a club like Roberts, listenin' to a great band like BR5-49, and that's when I start once more thinkin', "Git Outta My Way, I'm Feelin' Right Tonight!"

Index